MOON

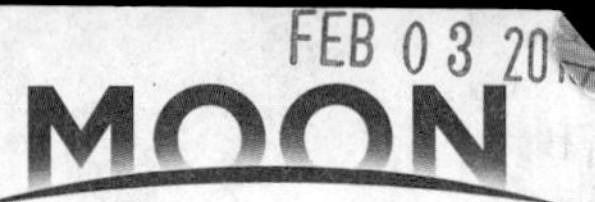

NEW ORLEANS

LAURA MARTONE

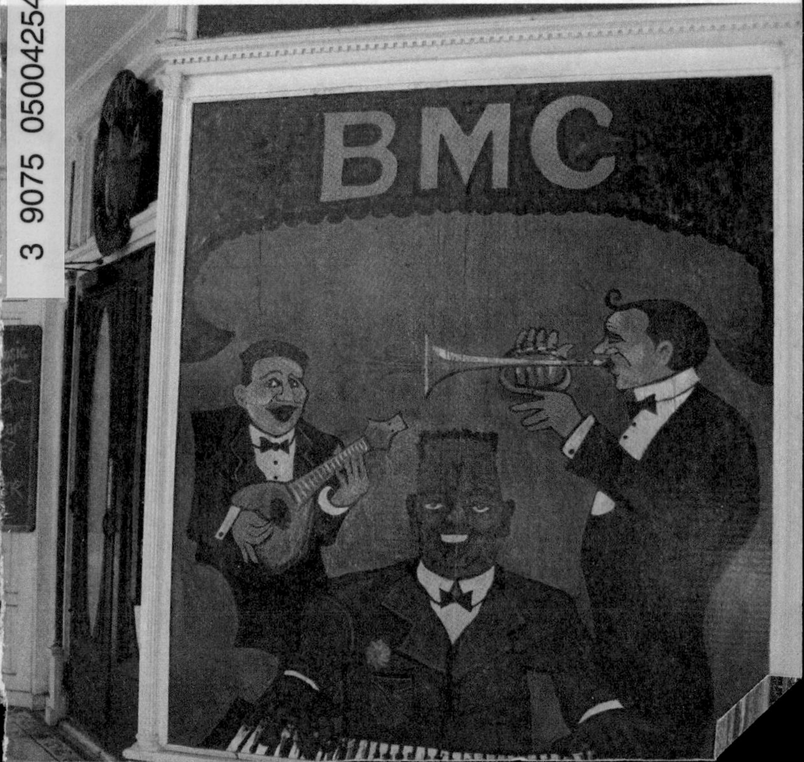

Contents

IMPERIAL
WOODPECKER
SNO-BALLS

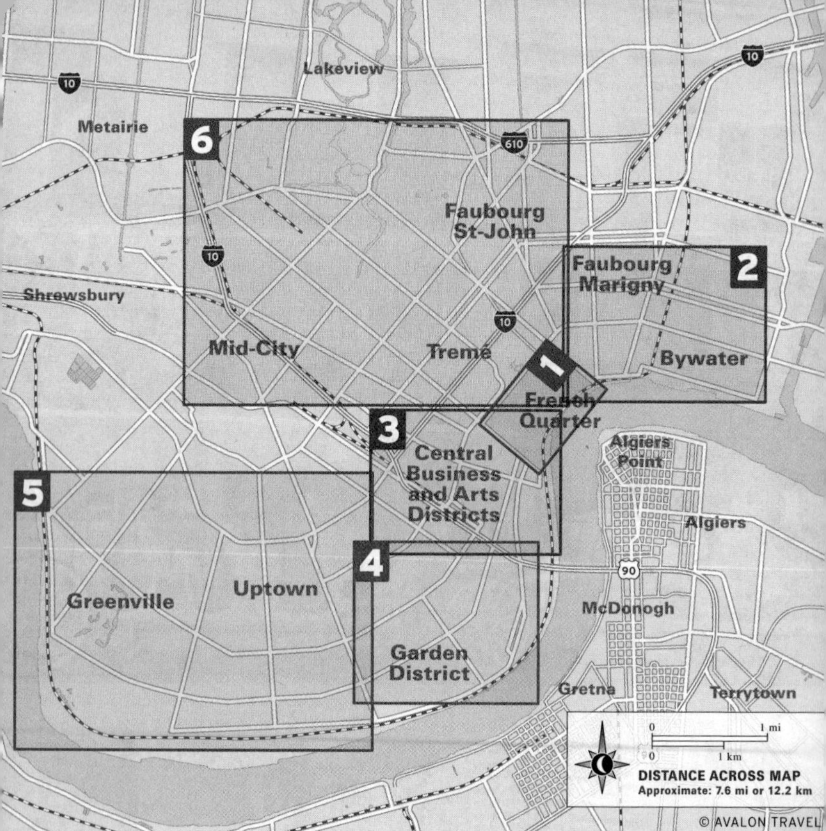
Lakeview
Metairie
6
Faubourg St-John
Faubourg Marigny
2
Bywater
Shrewsbury
Mid-City
Tremé
1
French Quarter
3
Central Business and Arts Districts
Algiers Point
Algiers
5
4
Greenville
Uptown
McDonogh
Garden District
Gretna
Terrytown
0
1 mi
0
1 km
DISTANCE ACROSS MAP
Approximate: 7.6 mi or 12.2 km
© AVALON TRAVEL

Maps

SIGHTS

1 VOODOO SPIRITUAL TEMPLE
14 NEW ORLEANS MUSICAL LEGENDS PARK
18 THE HERMANN-GRIMA HISTORIC HOUSE MUSEUM
48 THE HISTORIC NEW ORLEANS COLLECTION
87 THE CABILDO
89 ST. LOUIS CATHEDRAL
92 THE PRESBYTÈRE
97 MADAME JOHN'S LEGACY
103 THE BEAUREGARD-KEYES HOUSE AND GARDEN MUSEUM
104 THE GALLIER HISTORIC HOUSE MUSEUM
105 LALAURIE MANSION
116 THE NEW ORLEANS SCHOOL OF COOKING
118 JEAN LAFITTE NATIONAL HISTORICAL PARK AND PRESERVE
126 JACKSON SQUARE
127 PONTALBA BUILDINGS AND THE 1850 HOUSE
133 OLD URSULINE CONVENT
139 AUDUBON BUTTERFLY GARDEN AND INSECTARIUM
147 JACKSON BREWERY
151 NEW ORLEANS JAZZ NATIONAL HISTORICAL PARK
153 FRENCH MARKET
157 THE OLD U.S. MINT
158 AUDUBON AQUARIUM OF THE AMERICAS
159 WOLDENBERG RIVERFRONT PARK

RESTAURANTS

9 RALPH BRENNAN'S RED FISH GRILL
10 GALATOIRE'S RESTAURANT
11 GW FINS
12 ARNAUD'S
17 BAYONA
28 PORT OF CALL
29 DICKIE BRENNAN'S BOURBON HOUSE SEAFOOD
30 ACME OYSTER HOUSE
31 DICKIE BRENNAN'S STEAKHOUSE
32 FELIX'S RESTAURANT & OYSTER BAR
34 MR. B'S BISTRO
36 RESTAURANT R'EVOLUTION
41 OCEANA GRILL
42 BRENNAN'S
45 ANTOINE'S RESTAURANT
50 THE COURT OF TWO SISTERS
51 THE OLD COFFEEPOT RESTAURANT
54 YO MAMA'S BAR AND GRILL
65 CC'S COFFEE HOUSE
67 PALACE CAFÉ
74 RIB ROOM
81 TABLEAU
83 GUMBO SHOP
84 LA DIVINA GELATERIA
94 MURIEL'S JACKSON SQUARE
99 CAFÉ AMELIE
102 CROISSANT D'OR PATISSERIE
106 MONA LISA RESTAURANT
110 SEKISUI SAMURAI SUSHI
111 SOBOU
114 K-PAUL'S LOUISIANA KITCHEN
115 NOLA
121 JOHNNY'S PO-BOYS
122 CRESCENT CITY BREWHOUSE
125 CAFÉ MASPERO
128 TUJAGUE'S
131 IRENE'S CUISINE
135 COOP'S PLACE
137 ENVIE ESPRESSO BAR & CAFE
143 FELIPE'S TAQUERIA
149 CAFÉ DU MONDE

NIGHTLIFE

15 THE BOMBAY CLUB
19 BOURBON STREET BLUES COMPANY
22 CATS MEOW
23 GOOD FRIENDS BAR
25 BOURBON PUB & PARADE
26 THE CAFE LAFITTE IN EXILE
27 LAFITTE'S BLACKSMITH SHOP BAR
33 21ST AMENDMENT AT LA LOUISIANE
35 JEAN LAFITTE'S OLD ABSINTHE HOUSE
37 IRVIN MAYFIELD'S JAZZ PLAYHOUSE
46 THE DUNGEON
52 PAT O'BRIEN'S
53 PRESERVATION HALL
55 ORLEANS GRAPEVINE WINE BAR & BISTRO
58 OZ
66 GOLDEN LANTERN BAR
68 THE CAROUSEL BAR & LOUNGE
78 ONE EYED JACKS
108 HOUSE OF BLUES
113 THE KERRY IRISH PUB
119 NAPOLEON HOUSE
134 MOLLY'S AT THE MARKET
138 BALCONY MUSIC CLUB
155 PALM COURT JAZZ CAFE

ARTS AND CULTURE

6 MUSÉE CONTI WAX MUSEUM
13 GERMAINE CAZENAVE WELLS MARDI GRAS MUSEUM
43 MARTIN-LAWRENCE GALLERIES
62 NEW ORLEANS HISTORIC VOODOO MUSEUM
63 CRAIG TRACY'S FINE-ART BODYPAINTING GALLERY
70 A GALLERY FOR FINE PHOTOGRAPHY
71 MICHALOPOULOS GALLERY
76 KAKO GALLERY
80 JAMIE HAYES GALLERY
82 LE PETIT THÉÂTRE DU VIEUX CARRÉ
90 RODRIGUE STUDIO NEW ORLEANS
95 TANNER GALLERY
109 CALLAN FINE ART
120 NEW ORLEANS PHARMACY MUSEUM
152 DUTCH ALLEY ARTIST'S CO-OP

SPORTS AND ACTIVITIES

2 THE AMERICAN BICYCLE RENTAL COMPANY
88 FRIENDS OF THE CABILDO
148 ROYAL CARRIAGES
160 STEAMBOAT *NATCHEZ*

SHOPS

24 MARIE LAVEAU'S HOUSE OF VOODOO
39 KEIL'S ANTIQUES
40 VINTAGE 329
44 JAMES H. COHEN & SONS, INC.
47 FLEUR DE PARIS
49 TRASHY DIVA CLOTHING BOUTIQUE
56 ARCADIAN BOOKS & ART PRINTS
59 BOUTIQUE DU VAMPYRE
60 BOURBON FRENCH PARFUMS
72 BEVOLO GAS & ELECTRIC LIGHTS
73 BOTTOM OF THE CUP TEA ROOM
77 ROUX ROYALE
79 M.S. RAU ANTIQUES
85 FOREVER NEW ORLEANS
86 FAULKNER HOUSE BOOKS
91 MASKARADE
96 PAPIER PLUME
98 VOODOO AUTHENTICA
100 IDEA FACTORY
101 FIFI MAHONY'S
107 CRESCENT CITY BOOKS
117 CIGAR FACTORY NEW ORLEANS
123 NEW ORLEANS SILVERSMITHS
124 LUCULLUS
129 JAVA HOUSE IMPORTS
130 CENTRAL GROCERY
140 RHINO CONTEMPORARY CRAFTS CO.
141 THE SHOPS AT CANAL PLACE
142 DOLLZ & DAMES
145 SOUTHERN CANDYMAKERS
146 PEACHES RECORDS
150 EVANS CREOLE CANDY FACTORY
154 FRENCH MARKET
156 ARTIST'S MARKET & BEAD SHOP

HOTELS

3 THE RITZ-CARLTON NEW ORLEANS
4 COURTYARD NEW ORLEANS DOWNTOWN/IBERVILLE
5 CHATEAU LEMOYNE – FRENCH QUARTER
7 DAUPHINE ORLEANS HOTEL
8 AUDUBON COTTAGES
16 PRINCE CONTI HOTEL
20 THE OLIVIER HOUSE HOTEL
21 FOUR POINTS BY SHERATON FRENCH QUARTER
38 ROYAL SONESTA NEW ORLEANS
57 BOURBON ORLEANS HOTEL
61 BISCUIT PALACE GUEST HOUSE
64 THE CORNSTALK HOTEL
69 HOTEL MONTELEONE
75 OMNI ROYAL ORLEANS
93 PLACE D'ARMES HOTEL
112 W NEW ORLEANS – FRENCH QUARTER
132 HÔTEL PROVINCIAL
136 LE RICHELIEU IN THE FRENCH QUARTER
144 BIENVILLE HOUSE HOTEL

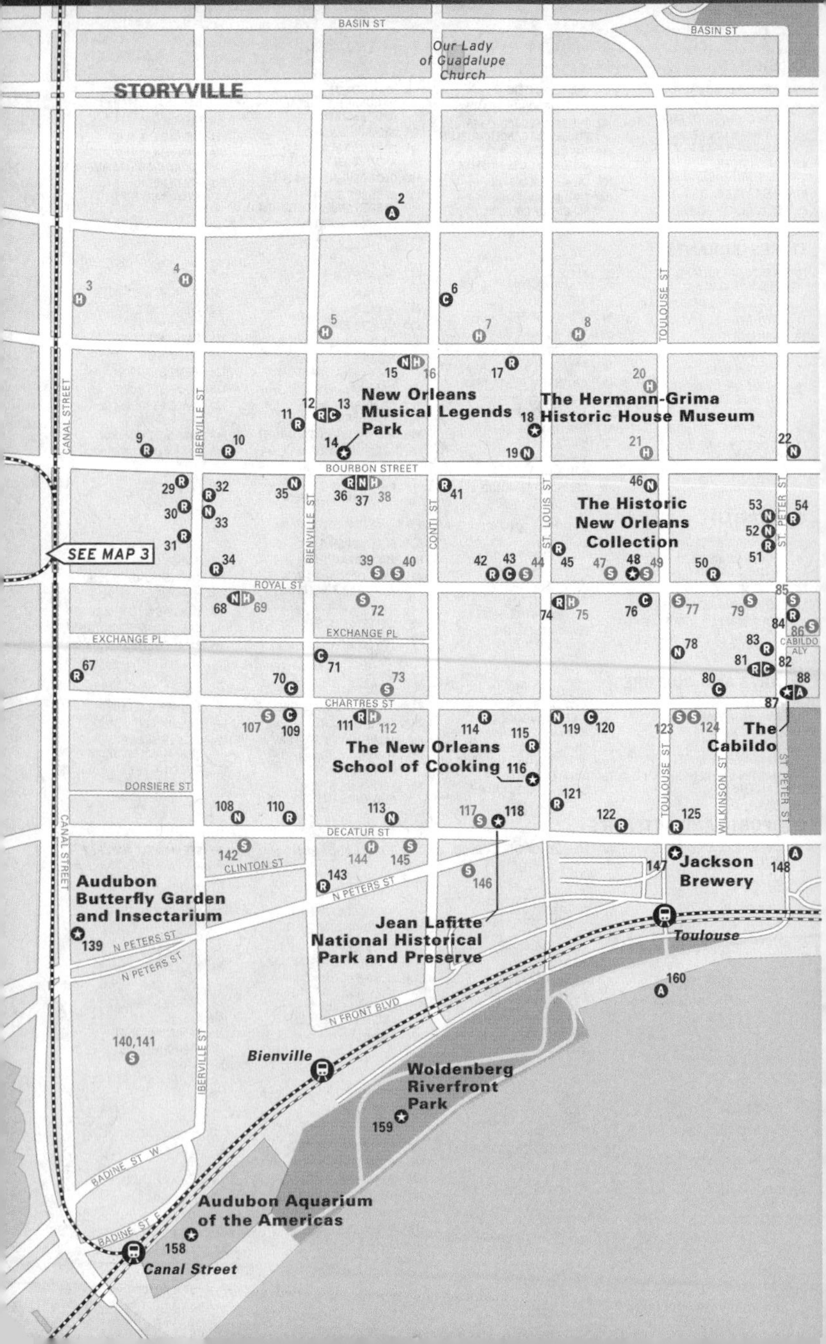

MAP 1

STORYVILLE
BASIN ST
Our Lady of Guadalupe Church
CANAL STREET
IBERVILLE ST
BIENVILLE ST
CONTI ST
ST LOUIS ST
TOULOUSE ST
ST PETER ST
WILKINSON ST
BOURBON STREET
ROYAL ST
EXCHANGE PL
CABILDO ALY
CHARTRES ST
DORSIERE ST
DECATUR ST
CLINTON ST
N PETERS ST
N FRONT BLVD
BADINE ST W
BADINE ST E
SEE MAP 3
New Orleans Musical Legends Park
The Hermann-Grima Historic House Museum
The Historic New Orleans Collection
The New Orleans School of Cooking
The Cabildo
Jackson Brewery
Audubon Butterfly Garden and Insectarium
Jean Lafitte National Historical Park and Preserve
Woldenberg Riverfront Park
Audubon Aquarium of the Americas
Toulouse
Bienville
Canal Street

2, 3, 4, 5, 6, 7, 8, 9, 10, 11, 12, 13, 14, 15, 16, 17, 18, 19, 20, 21, 22, 29, 30, 31, 32, 33, 34, 35, 36, 37, 38, 39, 40, 41, 42, 43, 44, 45, 46, 47, 48, 49, 50, 51, 52, 53, 54, 67, 68, 69, 70, 71, 72, 73, 74, 75, 76, 77, 78, 79, 80, 81, 82, 83, 84, 85, 86, 87, 88, 107, 108, 109, 110, 111, 112, 113, 114, 115, 116, 117, 118, 119, 120, 121, 122, 123, 124, 125, 139, 140,141, 142, 143, 144, 145, 146, 147, 148, 158, 159, 160

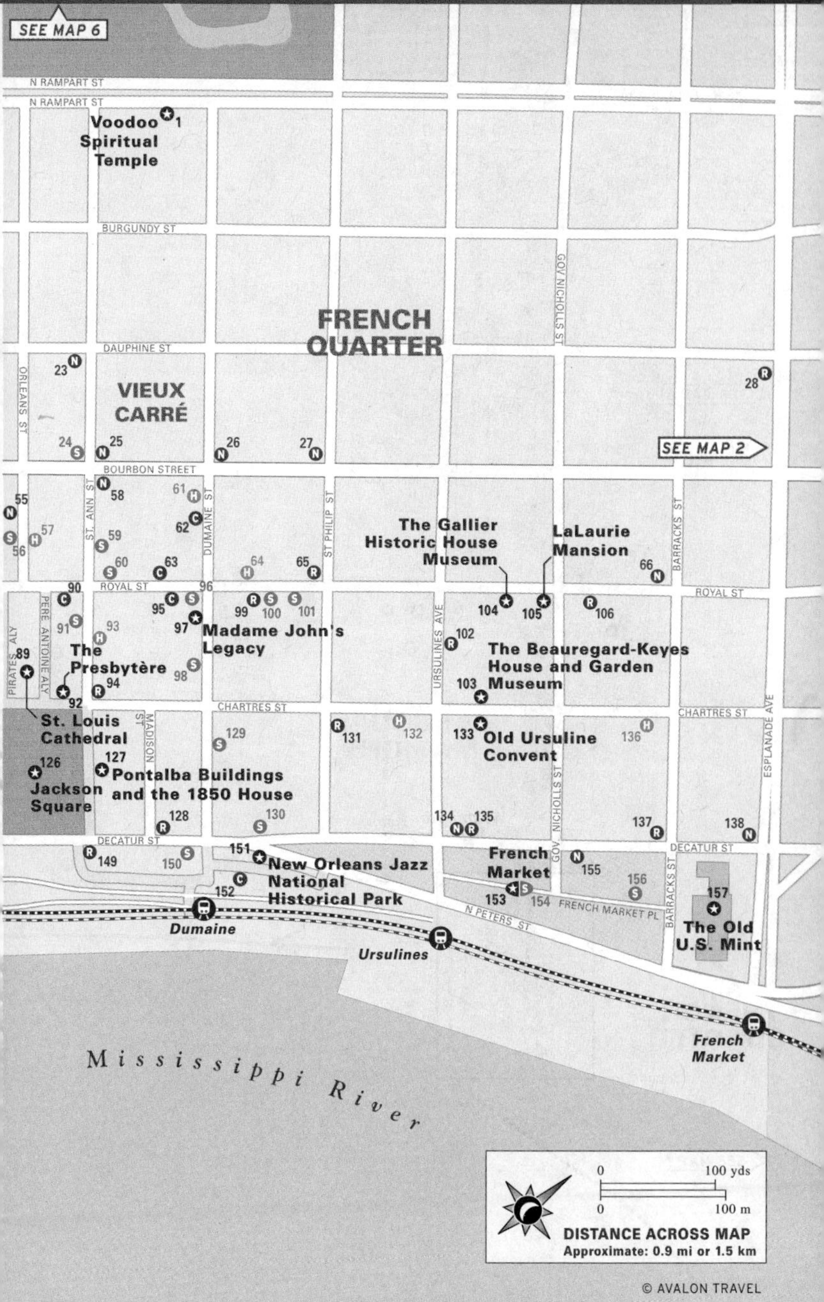

SEE MAP 6

N RAMPART ST

N RAMPART ST

Voodoo Spiritual Temple 1

BURGUNDY ST

FRENCH QUARTER

GOV NICHOLLS ST

DAUPHINE ST

ORLEANS ST

23 N

VIEUX CARRÉ

28 R

24 S

25 N

26 N

27 N

SEE MAP 2

BOURBON STREET

55 N

56 S

57 H

ST. ANN ST

58 N

59 S

60 S

61 H

62 C

63 C

DUMAINE ST

64 H

65 R

ST PHILIP ST

The Gallier Historic House Museum

LaLaurie Mansion

66 N

BARRACKS ST

90 C

ROYAL ST

96

ROYAL ST

95 C S

97 Madame John's Legacy

99 R

100 S

101 S

104

105

106 R

91 S

93 H

PIRATES ALY

PERE ANTOINE ALY

89 The Presbytère

92

94 R

98 S

URSULINES AVE

102 R

The Beauregard-Keyes House and Garden Museum

103

CHARTRES ST

CHARTRES ST

ESPLANADE AVE

St. Louis Cathedral

MADISON ST

129 S

131 R

132 H

133 Old Ursuline Convent

136 H

126 Jackson Square

127 Pontalba Buildings and the 1850 House

GOV NICHOLLS ST

128 R

130 S

134 N

135 R

137 R

138 N

DECATUR ST

DECATUR ST

149 R

150 S

151 New Orleans Jazz National Historical Park

152 C

French Market

153

154

155 N

156 S

FRENCH MARKET PL

N PETERS ST

BARRACKS ST

157 The Old U.S. Mint

Dumaine

Ursulines

French Market

Mississippi River

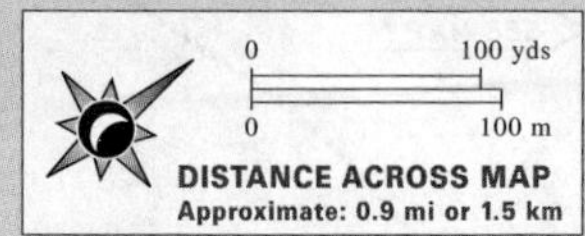

MAP 2

N JOHNSON ST
N PRIEUR ST
N ROMAN ST
N DERBIGNY ST
N CLAIBORNE AVE
N ROBERTSON ST
N VILLERE ST
URQUHART ST
MARAIS ST
ST. CLAUDE AVE
N RAMPART ST
BURGUNDY ST
DAUPHINE ST
ROYAL ST
DECATUR ST
N PETERS ST
ELYSIAN FIELDS AVE
PAUGER ST
TOURO ST
FRENCHMEN ST
MARIGNY ST
MANDEVILLE ST
SPAIN ST
ST. ROCH AVE
MUSIC ST
ARTS ST
FRANKLIN AVE
PAINTERS ST
PORT ST
ST. FERDINAND ST
PRESS ST
ARCHITECT ST
ALY
KERLEREC ST
BOURBON ST
BARRACKS ST
CHARTRES ST
ESPLANADE AVE

SEE MAP 6

FAUBOURG MARIGNY

FRENCH QUARTER

Washington Square Park

See Detail

The Old U.S. Mint

Mandeville Street Wharf

Esplanade Avenue Wharf

Gov. Nicholls Street Wharf

Mississippi River

SEE MAP 1

21 N
22 N
23 N
24 C
25 R
26 N
27 H
28 H
29 R
30 H
31 N
32 C
33 S
34 H
35 H
36 R
37 H
38 H
39 H
40 R
41 H
42 R
43 R
44 N
45 C
46 C
47 R

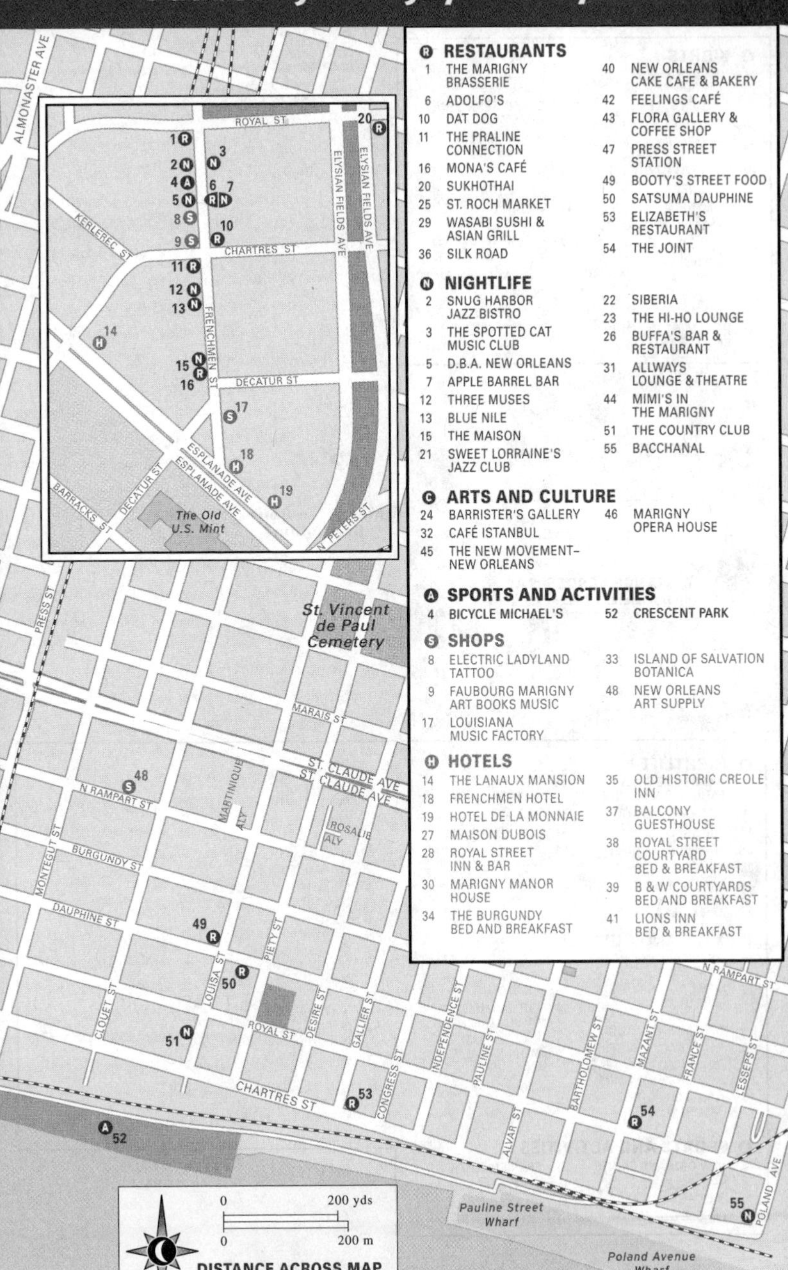
RESTAURANTS
1 THE MARIGNY BRASSERIE
6 ADOLFO'S
10 DAT DOG
11 THE PRALINE CONNECTION
16 MONA'S CAFÉ
20 SUKHOTHAI
25 ST. ROCH MARKET
29 WASABI SUSHI & ASIAN GRILL
36 SILK ROAD
40 NEW ORLEANS CAKE CAFE & BAKERY
42 FEELINGS CAFÉ
43 FLORA GALLERY & COFFEE SHOP
47 PRESS STREET STATION
49 BOOTY'S STREET FOOD
50 SATSUMA DAUPHINE
53 ELIZABETH'S RESTAURANT
54 THE JOINT
NIGHTLIFE
2 SNUG HARBOR JAZZ BISTRO
3 THE SPOTTED CAT MUSIC CLUB
5 D.B.A. NEW ORLEANS
7 APPLE BARREL BAR
12 THREE MUSES
13 BLUE NILE
15 THE MAISON
21 SWEET LORRAINE'S JAZZ CLUB
22 SIBERIA
23 THE HI-HO LOUNGE
26 BUFFA'S BAR & RESTAURANT
31 ALLWAYS LOUNGE & THEATRE
44 MIMI'S IN THE MARIGNY
51 THE COUNTRY CLUB
55 BACCHANAL
ARTS AND CULTURE
24 BARRISTER'S GALLERY
32 CAFÉ ISTANBUL
45 THE NEW MOVEMENT–NEW ORLEANS
46 MARIGNY OPERA HOUSE
SPORTS AND ACTIVITIES
4 BICYCLE MICHAEL'S
52 CRESCENT PARK
SHOPS
8 ELECTRIC LADYLAND TATTOO
9 FAUBOURG MARIGNY ART BOOKS MUSIC
17 LOUISIANA MUSIC FACTORY
33 ISLAND OF SALVATION BOTANICA
48 NEW ORLEANS ART SUPPLY
HOTELS
14 THE LANAUX MANSION
18 FRENCHMEN HOTEL
19 HOTEL DE LA MONNAIE
27 MAISON DUBOIS
28 ROYAL STREET INN & BAR
30 MARIGNY MANOR HOUSE
34 THE BURGUNDY BED AND BREAKFAST
35 OLD HISTORIC CREOLE INN
37 BALCONY GUESTHOUSE
38 ROYAL STREET COURTYARD BED & BREAKFAST
39 B & W COURTYARDS BED AND BREAKFAST
41 LIONS INN BED & BREAKFAST
ALMONASTER AVE
ROYAL ST
ELYSIAN FIELDS AVE
KERLEREC ST
CHARTRES ST
FRENCHMEN ST
DECATUR ST
ESPLANADE AVE
BARRACKS ST
N PETERS ST
The Old U.S. Mint
PRESS ST
St. Vincent de Paul Cemetery
MARAIS ST
ST. CLAUDE AVE
N RAMPART ST
MARTINIQUE ALY
ROSALIE ALY
BURGUNDY ST
MONTEGUT ST
DAUPHINE ST
LOUISA ST
PIETY ST
CLOUET ST
DESIRE ST
GALLIER ST
CONGRESS ST
INDEPENDENCE ST
PAULINE ST
ALVAR ST
BARTHOLOMEW ST
MAZANT ST
FRANCE ST
LESSEPS ST
POLAND AVE
Pauline Street Wharf
Poland Avenue Wharf
0 200 yds
0 200 m
DISTANCE ACROSS MAP
Approximate: 2 mi or 3.2 km

MAP 3

SIGHTS

2 MERCEDES-BENZ SUPERDOME
30 GALLIER HALL
37 ST. PATRICK'S CHURCH
56 LEE CIRCLE
57 THE NATIONAL WWII MUSEUM
63 BLAINE KERN'S MARDI GRAS WORLD
64 *SCRAP HOUSE*

RESTAURANTS

5 BORGNE
11 DOMENICA
20 RESTAURANT AUGUST
23 BESH STEAK
27 BON TON CAFE
28 MOTHER'S RESTAURANT
32 CAFÉ ADELAIDE
36 HERBSAINT BAR AND RESTAURANT
44 PÊCHE SEAFOOD GRILL
47 EMERIL'S NEW ORLEANS
48 TOMMY'S CUISINE
51 ROOT
58 THE AMERICAN SECTOR
59 COCHON
60 COCHON BUTCHER

NIGHTLIFE

1 HANDSOME WILLY'S PATIO BAR & LOUNGE
6 LITTLE GEM SALOON
12 THE SAZERAC BAR
21 POLO CLUB LOUNGE
38 W.I.N.O.
41 LUCY'S RETIRED SURFERS BAR & RESTAURANT
50 REPUBLIC NEW ORLEANS
52 MULATE'S
61 THE HOWLIN' WOLF
62 THE METROPOLITAN

ARTS AND CULTURE

35 AMERICAN ITALIAN MUSEUM
40 NEW ORLEANS SCHOOL OF GLASSWORKS & PRINTMAKING STUDIO
43 JEAN BRAGG GALLERY
45 LOUISIANA CHILDREN'S MUSEUM
46 SØREN CHRISTENSEN GALLERY
49 LEMIEUX GALLERIES
53 CONTEMPORARY ARTS CENTER
54 OGDEN MUSEUM OF SOUTHERN ART
55 CONFEDERATE MEMORIAL HALL MUSEUM

SPORTS AND ACTIVITIES

3 NEW ORLEANS SAINTS
4 NEW ORLEANS PELICANS
24 *CREOLE QUEEN*
25 SPANISH PLAZA
31 LAFAYETTE SQUARE
34 PIAZZA D'ITALIA

SHOPS

14 ADLER'S
15 RUBENSTEINS
16 MEYER THE HATTER
26 THE OUTLET COLLECTION AT RIVERWALK
39 AIDAN GILL FOR MEN

HOTELS

7 LE PAVILLON HOTEL
8 DRURY INN & SUITES–NEW ORLEANS
9 QUALITY INN & SUITES NEW ORLEANS
10 RENAISSANCE NEW ORLEANS PERE MARQUETTE HOTEL
13 THE ROOSEVELT NEW ORLEANS
17 INTERNATIONAL HOUSE NEW ORLEANS
18 OMNI ROYAL CRESCENT HOTEL
19 COUNTRY INN & SUITES BY CARLSON–NEW ORLEANS FRENCH QUARTER
22 WINDSOR COURT HOTEL
29 LE MÉRIDIEN NEW ORLEANS
33 LOEWS NEW ORLEANS HOTEL
42 RENAISSANCE NEW ORLEANS ARTS HOTEL
65 HAMPTON INN & SUITES NEW ORLEANS CONVENTION CENTER

SEE MAP 4

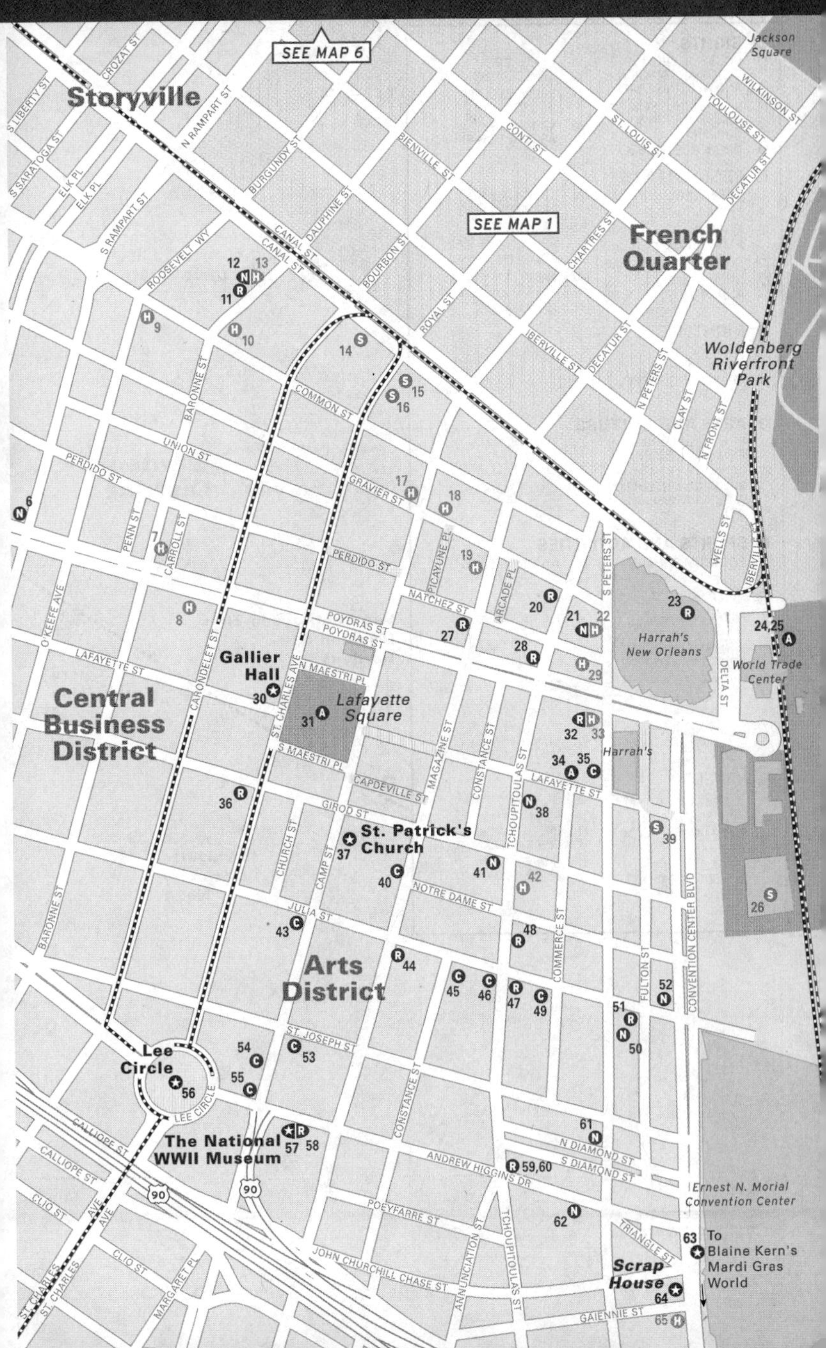
SEE MAP 6
SEE MAP 1
Storyville
French Quarter
Jackson Square
Woldenberg Riverfront Park
Harrah's New Orleans
World Trade Center
Harrah's
Gallier Hall
Lafayette Square
Central Business District
St. Patrick's Church
Arts District
Lee Circle
The National WWII Museum
Ernest N. Morial Convention Center
To Blaine Kern's Mardi Gras World
Scrap House
S LIBERTY ST
CROZAT ST
N RAMPART ST
S SARATOGA ST
ELK PL
S RAMPART ST
BURGUNDY ST
BIENVILLE ST
CONTI ST
ST. LOUIS ST
TOULOUSE ST
WILKINSON ST
DECATUR ST
CANAL ST
DAUPHINE ST
BOURBON ST
ROYAL ST
CHARTRES ST
IBERVILLE ST
N PETERS ST
CLAY ST
N FRONT ST
ROOSEVELT WY
BARONNE ST
COMMON ST
UNION ST
PERDIDO ST
GRAVIER ST
PENN ST
CARROLL ST
PICAYUNE PL
ARCADE PL
NATCHEZ ST
POYDRAS ST
S PETERS ST
WELLS ST
DELTA ST
O'KEEFE AVE
LAFAYETTE ST
CARONDELET ST
ST. CHARLES AVE
N MAESTRI PL
S MAESTRI PL
MAGAZINE ST
CONSTANCE ST
TCHOUPITOULAS ST
CAPDEVILLE ST
GIROD ST
CHURCH ST
CAMP ST
NOTRE DAME ST
JULIA ST
COMMERCE ST
FULTON ST
CONVENTION CENTER BLVD
ST. JOSEPH ST
LEE CIRCLE
CALLIOPE ST
CLIO ST
AVE
MARGARET PL
ANDREW HIGGINS DR
N DIAMOND ST
S DIAMOND ST
POEYFARRE ST
JOHN CHURCHILL CHASE ST
ANNUNCIATION ST
TRIANGLE ST
GAIENNIE ST
90

MAP 4

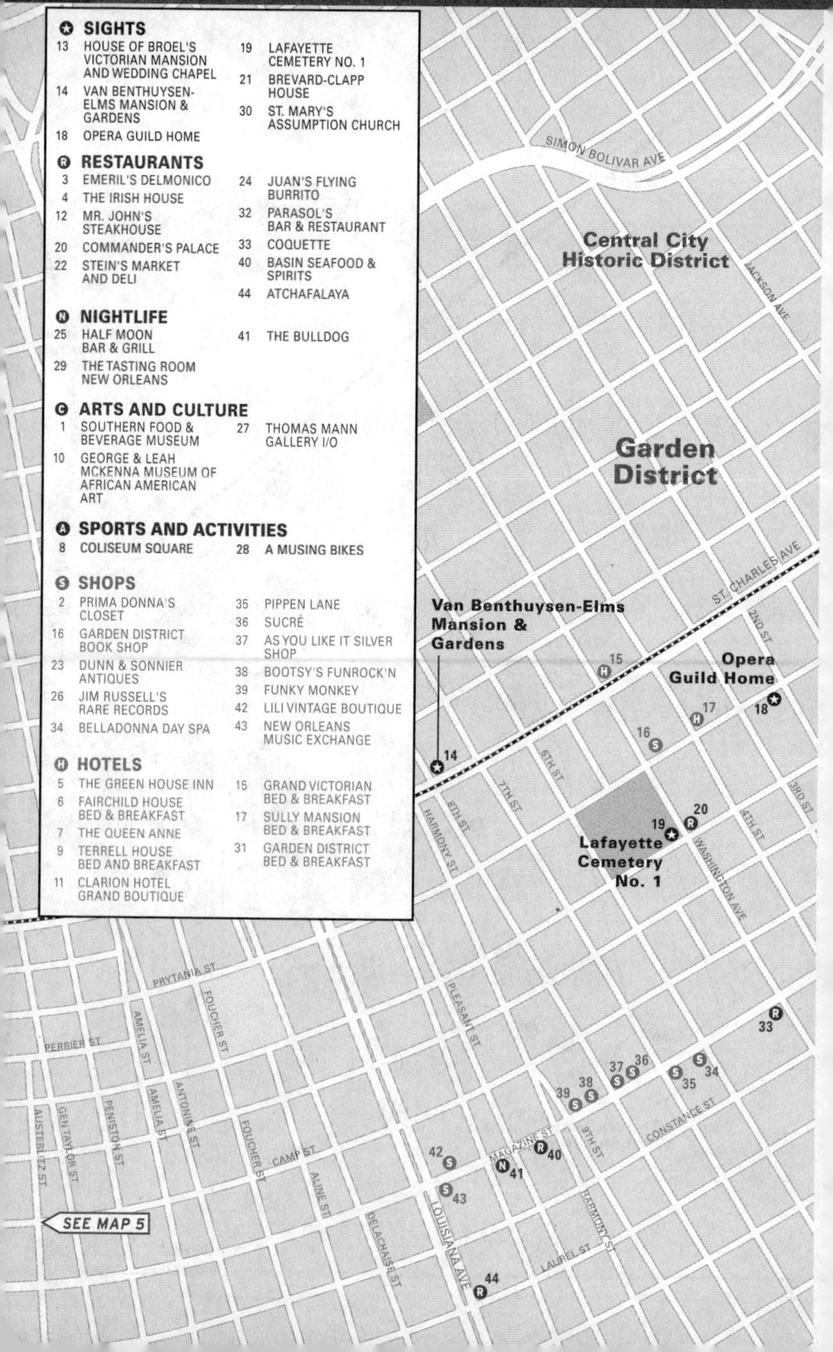

SIGHTS
- 13 HOUSE OF BROEL'S VICTORIAN MANSION AND WEDDING CHAPEL
- 14 VAN BENTHUYSEN-ELMS MANSION & GARDENS
- 18 OPERA GUILD HOME
- 19 LAFAYETTE CEMETERY NO. 1
- 21 BREVARD-CLAPP HOUSE
- 30 ST. MARY'S ASSUMPTION CHURCH

RESTAURANTS
- 3 EMERIL'S DELMONICO
- 4 THE IRISH HOUSE
- 12 MR. JOHN'S STEAKHOUSE
- 20 COMMANDER'S PALACE
- 22 STEIN'S MARKET AND DELI
- 24 JUAN'S FLYING BURRITO
- 32 PARASOL'S BAR & RESTAURANT
- 33 COQUETTE
- 40 BASIN SEAFOOD & SPIRITS
- 44 ATCHAFALAYA

NIGHTLIFE
- 25 HALF MOON BAR & GRILL
- 29 THE TASTING ROOM NEW ORLEANS
- 41 THE BULLDOG

ARTS AND CULTURE
- 1 SOUTHERN FOOD & BEVERAGE MUSEUM
- 10 GEORGE & LEAH MCKENNA MUSEUM OF AFRICAN AMERICAN ART
- 27 THOMAS MANN GALLERY I/O

SPORTS AND ACTIVITIES
- 8 COLISEUM SQUARE
- 28 A MUSING BIKES

SHOPS
- 2 PRIMA DONNA'S CLOSET
- 16 GARDEN DISTRICT BOOK SHOP
- 23 DUNN & SONNIER ANTIQUES
- 26 JIM RUSSELL'S RARE RECORDS
- 34 BELLADONNA DAY SPA
- 35 PIPPEN LANE
- 36 SUCRÉ
- 37 AS YOU LIKE IT SILVER SHOP
- 38 BOOTSY'S FUNROCK'N
- 39 FUNKY MONKEY
- 42 LILI VINTAGE BOUTIQUE
- 43 NEW ORLEANS MUSIC EXCHANGE

HOTELS
- 5 THE GREEN HOUSE INN
- 6 FAIRCHILD HOUSE BED & BREAKFAST
- 7 THE QUEEN ANNE
- 9 TERRELL HOUSE BED AND BREAKFAST
- 11 CLARION HOTEL GRAND BOUTIQUE
- 15 GRAND VICTORIAN BED & BREAKFAST
- 17 SULLY MANSION BED & BREAKFAST
- 31 GARDEN DISTRICT BED & BREAKFAST

SIMON BOLIVAR AVE
Central City Historic District
JACKSON AVE
Garden District
ST. CHARLES AVE
Van Benthuysen-Elms Mansion & Gardens
Opera Guild Home
Lafayette Cemetery No. 1
2ND ST
3RD ST
4TH ST
6TH ST
7TH ST
8TH ST
9TH ST
HARMONY ST
WASHINGTON AVE
PRYTANIA ST
PERRIER ST
AMELIA ST
FOUCHER ST
ANTONINE ST
PLEASANT ST
CONSTANCE ST
MAGAZINE ST
CAMP ST
ALINE ST
LOUISIANA AVE
DELACHAISE ST
LAUREL ST
AUSTERLITZ ST
GEN TAYLOR ST
PENISTON ST

SEE MAP 5

SEE MAP 3
S SARATOGA ST
S RAMPART ST
ORETHA C
HALEY BLVD
MARTIN LUTHER KING JR BLVD
TERPSICHORE ST
EUTERPE ST
POLYMNIA ST
FELICITY ST
BARONNE ST
CARONDELET ST
CLIO ST
ERATO ST
CALLIOPE ST
90
PRYTANIA ST
CAMP ST
MAGAZINE ST
CONSTANCE ST
ANNUNCIATION ST
Coliseum Square
EUTERPE ST
RACE ST
ST. MARY ST
COLISEUM ST
ST. ANDREW ST
JOSEPHINE ST
JACKSON AVENUE
SOPHIE WRIGHT PL
1ST ST
House of Broel's Victorian Mansion and Wedding Chapel
Brevard-Clapp House
St. Mary's Assumption Church
Lower Garden District
ROUSSEAU ST
0
500 yds
0
500 m
DISTANCE ACROSS MAP
Approximate: 2 mi or 3.2 km
© AVALON TRAVEL

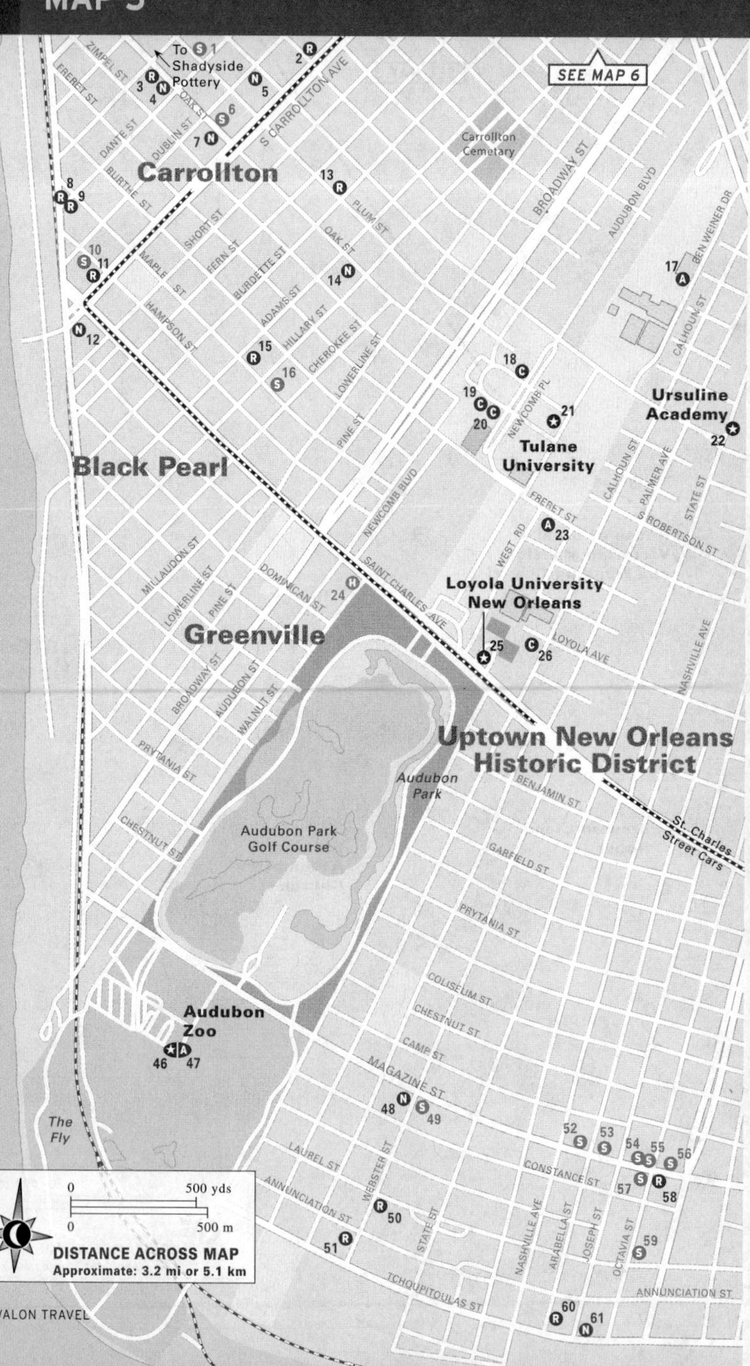
To 1 Shadyside Pottery
SEE MAP 6
Carrollton
Carrollton Cemetary
Black Pearl
Greenville
Tulane University
Ursuline Academy
Loyola University New Orleans
Uptown New Orleans Historic District
Audubon Park
Audubon Park Golf Course
Audubon Zoo
The Fly
St. Charles Street Cars
S CARROLLTON AVE
BROADWAY ST
AUDUBON BLVD
BEN WEINER DR
CALHOUN ST
NEWCOMB PL
NEWCOMB BLVD
FRERET ST
WEST RD
PALMER AVE
S ROBERTSON ST
STATE ST
SAINT CHARLES AVE
LOYOLA AVE
NASHVILLE AVE
DOMINICAN ST
MILLAUDON ST
LOWERLINE ST
PINE ST
AUDUBON ST
WALNUT ST
PRYTANIA ST
CHESTNUT ST
BENJAMIN ST
GARFIELD ST
COLISEUM ST
CAMP ST
MAGAZINE ST
CONSTANCE ST
LAUREL ST
ANNUNCIATION ST
WEBSTER ST
ARABELLA ST
JOSEPH ST
OCTAVIA ST
TCHOUPITOULAS ST
ZIMPEL ST
DANTE ST
DUBLIN ST
OAK ST
BURTHE ST
MAPLE ST
SHORT ST
FERN ST
BURDETTE ST
ADAMS ST
HILLARY ST
CHEROKEE ST
PLUM ST
HAMPSON ST
0 500 yds
0 500 m
DISTANCE ACROSS MAP
Approximate: 3.2 mi or 5.1 km

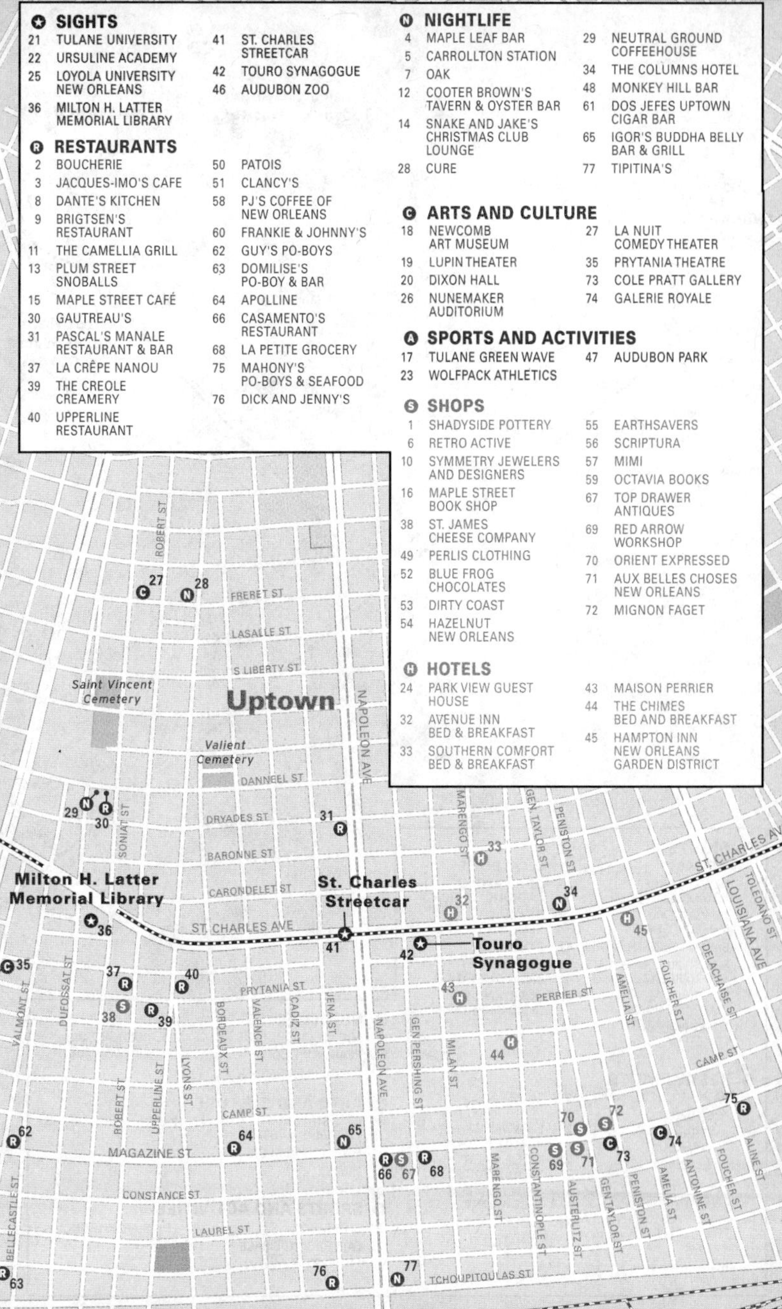
SIGHTS
21 TULANE UNIVERSITY
22 URSULINE ACADEMY
25 LOYOLA UNIVERSITY NEW ORLEANS
36 MILTON H. LATTER MEMORIAL LIBRARY
41 ST. CHARLES STREETCAR
42 TOURO SYNAGOGUE
46 AUDUBON ZOO
RESTAURANTS
2 BOUCHERIE
3 JACQUES-IMO'S CAFE
8 DANTE'S KITCHEN
9 BRIGTSEN'S RESTAURANT
11 THE CAMELLIA GRILL
13 PLUM STREET SNOBALLS
15 MAPLE STREET CAFÉ
30 GAUTREAU'S
31 PASCAL'S MANALE RESTAURANT & BAR
37 LA CRÊPE NANOU
39 THE CREOLE CREAMERY
40 UPPERLINE RESTAURANT
50 PATOIS
51 CLANCY'S
58 PJ'S COFFEE OF NEW ORLEANS
60 FRANKIE & JOHNNY'S
62 GUY'S PO-BOYS
63 DOMILISE'S PO-BOY & BAR
64 APOLLINE
66 CASAMENTO'S RESTAURANT
68 LA PETITE GROCERY
75 MAHONY'S PO-BOYS & SEAFOOD
76 DICK AND JENNY'S
NIGHTLIFE
4 MAPLE LEAF BAR
5 CARROLLTON STATION
7 OAK
12 COOTER BROWN'S TAVERN & OYSTER BAR
14 SNAKE AND JAKE'S CHRISTMAS CLUB LOUNGE
28 CURE
29 NEUTRAL GROUND COFFEEHOUSE
34 THE COLUMNS HOTEL
48 MONKEY HILL BAR
61 DOS JEFES UPTOWN CIGAR BAR
65 IGOR'S BUDDHA BELLY BAR & GRILL
77 TIPITINA'S
ARTS AND CULTURE
18 NEWCOMB ART MUSEUM
19 LUPIN THEATER
20 DIXON HALL
26 NUNEMAKER AUDITORIUM
27 LA NUIT COMEDY THEATER
35 PRYTANIA THEATRE
73 COLE PRATT GALLERY
74 GALERIE ROYALE
SPORTS AND ACTIVITIES
17 TULANE GREEN WAVE
23 WOLFPACK ATHLETICS
47 AUDUBON PARK
SHOPS
1 SHADYSIDE POTTERY
6 RETRO ACTIVE
10 SYMMETRY JEWELERS AND DESIGNERS
16 MAPLE STREET BOOK SHOP
38 ST. JAMES CHEESE COMPANY
49 PERLIS CLOTHING
52 BLUE FROG CHOCOLATES
53 DIRTY COAST
54 HAZELNUT NEW ORLEANS
55 EARTHSAVERS
56 SCRIPTURA
57 MIMI
59 OCTAVIA BOOKS
67 TOP DRAWER ANTIQUES
69 RED ARROW WORKSHOP
70 ORIENT EXPRESSED
71 AUX BELLES CHOSES NEW ORLEANS
72 MIGNON FAGET
HOTELS
24 PARK VIEW GUEST HOUSE
32 AVENUE INN BED & BREAKFAST
33 SOUTHERN COMFORT BED & BREAKFAST
43 MAISON PERRIER
44 THE CHIMES BED AND BREAKFAST
45 HAMPTON INN NEW ORLEANS GARDEN DISTRICT
Uptown
Saint Vincent Cemetery
Valient Cemetery
Milton H. Latter Memorial Library
St. Charles Streetcar
Touro Synagogue
ROBERT ST
FRERET ST
LASALLE ST
S LIBERTY ST
NAPOLEON AVE
DANNEEL ST
DRYADES ST
BARONNE ST
CARONDELET ST
ST. CHARLES AVE
SONIAT ST
MARENGO ST
GEN. TAYLOR ST
PENISTON ST
TOLEDANO ST
LOUISIANA AVE
PRYTANIA ST
PERRIER ST
VALMONT ST
DUFOSSAT ST
BORDEAUX ST
VALENCE ST
CADIZ ST
JENA ST
GEN PERSHING ST
MILAN ST
AMELIA ST
FOUCHER ST
DELACHAISE ST
CAMP ST
UPPERLINE ST
LYONS ST
MAGAZINE ST
CONSTANCE ST
LAUREL ST
BELLECASTLE ST
CONSTANTINOPLE ST
AUSTERLITZ ST
ANTONINE ST
ALINE ST
TCHOUPITOULAS ST

MAP 6

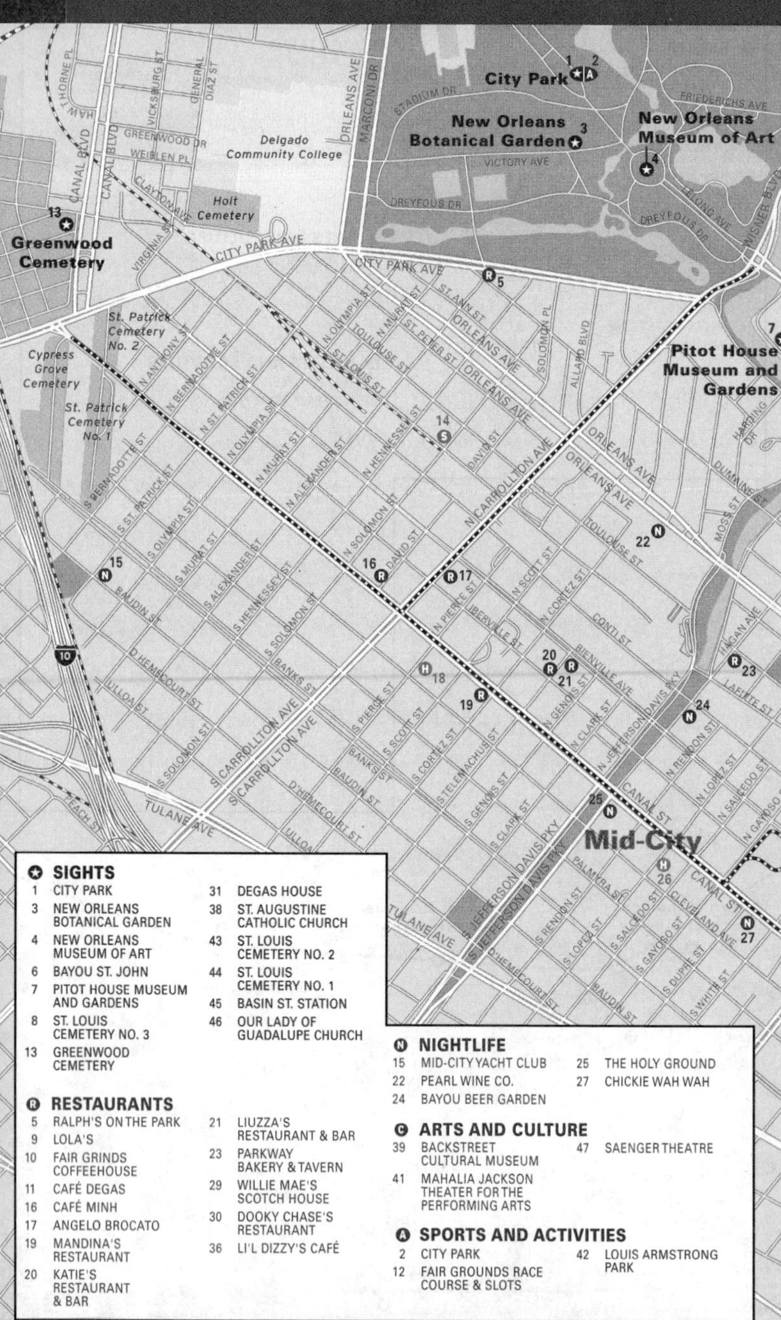
City Park
New Orleans Botanical Garden
New Orleans Museum of Art
Delgado Community College
Holt Cemetery
Greenwood Cemetery
St. Patrick Cemetery No. 2
Cypress Grove Cemetery
St. Patrick Cemetery No. 1
Pitot House Museum and Gardens
Mid-City
CITY PARK AVE
ORLEANS AVE
CANAL BLVD
CANAL ST
N CARROLLTON AVE
S CARROLLTON AVE
TULANE AVE
N JEFFERSON DAVIS PKY
S JEFFERSON DAVIS PKY
WISNER BLVD
MARCONI DR
STADIUM DR
VICTORY AVE
DREYFOUS DR
FRIEDERICHS AVE
LELONG AVE
BIENVILLE AVE
IBERVILLE ST
CONTI ST
TOULOUSE ST
LAFITTE ST
BAUDIN ST
D'HEMECOURT ST
ULLOA ST
BANKS ST
PALMYRA ST
CLEVELAND AVE
SIGHTS
1 CITY PARK
3 NEW ORLEANS BOTANICAL GARDEN
4 NEW ORLEANS MUSEUM OF ART
6 BAYOU ST. JOHN
7 PITOT HOUSE MUSEUM AND GARDENS
8 ST. LOUIS CEMETERY NO. 3
13 GREENWOOD CEMETERY
31 DEGAS HOUSE
38 ST. AUGUSTINE CATHOLIC CHURCH
43 ST. LOUIS CEMETERY NO. 2
44 ST. LOUIS CEMETERY NO. 1
45 BASIN ST. STATION
46 OUR LADY OF GUADALUPE CHURCH
RESTAURANTS
5 RALPH'S ON THE PARK
9 LOLA'S
10 FAIR GRINDS COFFEEHOUSE
11 CAFÉ DEGAS
16 CAFÉ MINH
17 ANGELO BROCATO
19 MANDINA'S RESTAURANT
20 KATIE'S RESTAURANT & BAR
21 LIUZZA'S RESTAURANT & BAR
23 PARKWAY BAKERY & TAVERN
29 WILLIE MAE'S SCOTCH HOUSE
30 DOOKY CHASE'S RESTAURANT
36 LI'L DIZZY'S CAFÉ
NIGHTLIFE
15 MID-CITY YACHT CLUB
22 PEARL WINE CO.
24 BAYOU BEER GARDEN
25 THE HOLY GROUND
27 CHICKIE WAH WAH
ARTS AND CULTURE
39 BACKSTREET CULTURAL MUSEUM
41 MAHALIA JACKSON THEATER FOR THE PERFORMING ARTS
47 SAENGER THEATRE
SPORTS AND ACTIVITIES
2 CITY PARK
12 FAIR GROUNDS RACE COURSE & SLOTS
42 LOUIS ARMSTRONG PARK

SHOPS
14 RICCA'S DEMOLISHING CORP.
28 F & F BOTANICA SPIRITUAL SUPPLY
HOTELS
18 1896 O'MALLEY HOUSE
26 INDIA HOUSE HOSTEL
32 DEGAS HOUSE
33 ASHTON'S BED & BREAKFAST
34 HH WHITNEY HOUSE
35 FIVE CONTINENTS BED AND BREAKFAST
37 MONROSE ROW BED & BREAKFAST
40 NEW ORLEANS GUESTHOUSE
500 yds
500 m
DISTANCE ACROSS MAP
Approximate: 3.2 mi or 5.1 km
Bayou St. John
St. Louis Cemetery No. 3
Fair Grounds Race Course & Slots
Faubourg St. John
Degas House
Tremé
Louis Armstrong Park
St. Augustine Catholic Church
St. Louis Cemetery No. 2
St. Louis Cemetery No. 1
Basin St. Station
Our Lady of Guadalupe Church
French Quarter
SEE MAP 1
SEE MAP 2
SEE MAP 3
DESAIX BLVD
PARKVIEW PL
BELFORT AVE
GENTILLY BLVD
ESPLANADE AVE
ORLEANS AVE
N BROAD ST
N CLAIBORNE AVE
N RAMPART ST
TULANE AVE
© AVALON TRAVEL

MAP 7

SIGHTS

12 METAIRIE CEMETERY
13 LONGUE VUE HOUSE & GARDENS
17 ALGIERS POINT HISTORIC DISTRICT
20 CHALMETTE BATTLEFIELD AND NATIONAL CEMETERY

RESTAURANTS

2 DRAGO'S SEAFOOD RESTAURANT
3 MORNING CALL COFFEE STAND
6 DEANIE'S SEAFOOD
8 MONDO
9 VEGA TAPAS CAFE
10 CAFÉ B
14 YE OLDE COLLEGE INN
19 ROCKY & CARLO'S RESTAURANT & BAR
21 TONY MANDINA'S RESTAURANT

NIGHTLIFE

15 ROCK 'N' BOWL

SPORTS AND ACTIVITIES

16 ROCK 'N' BOWL
22 CAJUN CRITTERS SWAMP TOUR
23 BARATARIA PRESERVE
24 JEAN LAFITTE SWAMP & AIRBOAT TOURS

SHOPS

4 LAKESIDE SHOPPING CENTER
5 MARTIN WINE CELLAR
11 HURWITZ MINTZ

HOTELS

1 COMFORT SUITES AIRPORT
7 ROSE MANOR BED & BREAKFAST INN
18 HOUSE OF THE RISING SUN BED AND BREAKFAST

0 1 mi
0 1 km
DISTANCE ACROSS MAP
Approximate: 17.2 mi or 27.7 km
Lake Pontchartrain
HAYNE BLVD
Seabrook
MORRISON RD
University of New Orleans
Spanish Fort
Pontchartrain Park
Gentilly
ROBERT E LEE BLVD
WEST END BLVD
CANAL BLVD
PARIS AVE
ELYSIAN FIELDS AVE
FRANKLIN AVE
FRANCE RD
JOURDAN RD
DOWNMAN RD
CHEF MENTEUR HWY
ALMONASTER AVE
Lakeview
HARRISON AVE
8
City Park
ST BERNARD AVE
Dillard University
ALVAR ST
Faubourg St. John
N MIRO ST
N GALVEZ ST
Saint Claude Heights
S CARROLLTON AVE
N BROAD ST
Mid-City
Tremé
Faubourg Marigny
FRANKLIN AVE
ESPLANADE AVE
39
N CLAIBORNE AVE
TULANE AVENUE
French Quarter
Bywater
ST CLAUDE AVE
Arabi
CANAL STREET
BELLEVILLE ST
PATTERSON DR
PELICAN AVE 17
18
VALLETTE ST
ANGELA ST
46
To 19
Rocky & Carlo's Restaurant & Bar
Algiers Point
N PETERS ST
Algiers Point Historic District
GEN. MEYER AVE
20
Algiers
Chalmette Battlefield and National Cemetery
Uptown
FRANKLIN AVE
WHITNEY AVE
90
SHIRLEY DR
WALL BLVD
Aurora Gardens
GEN DEGAULLE DR
Garden District
McDonogh
MACARTHUR BLVD
BEHRMAN HWY
DONNER DR
21
Gretna
Mississippi River
STEPHENS ST
STUMPF BLVD
Terrytown
4TH ST
HUEY P LONG AVE
GRETNA BLVD
WHITNEY AVE
WRIGHT AVE
LENNOX BLVD
Harvey
Marrero
PETERS RD
BARATARIA BLVD
90
MANHATTAN BLVD
TULLIS DR
TERRY PKY
23
45
To Barataria Preserve
and 24
Jean Lafitte Swamp & Airboat Tours
© AVALON TRAVEL

DISCOVER

New Orleans

New Orleans is a city that's hard to forget. Nestled between the brackish Lake Pontchartrain and the serpentine Mississippi River, it has been home to pirates and soldiers, plantation owners and voodoo queens. Today, their legacy is palpable in the city's Cajun-Creole cuisine and lively jazz, its Southern manners and dark history.

Those born and raised in New Orleans understand the city's relentless pull. Childhoods spent crabbing in Lake Pontchartrain, watching Mardi Gras parades, and munching on Plum Street sno-balls on sweltering summer days create memories that not only come alive but thrive long after families and homes are gone from the city. New encounters only enhance the life-long love affair. For curious outsiders who come to experience the Crescent City's exceptional cuisine, spirited music, and boisterous festivals, great adventures await.

New Orleans is no stranger to adversity—from devastating fires and historic battles to yellow fever epidemics and heartless hurricanes—but no matter what befalls this resilient town, it always rises from the ashes. The Big Easy will, for me, always feel like home. Once you experience its unique charms, laissez-faire attitude, and enduring spirit, you too will fall under its spell.

Clockwise from top left: a carriage ride through the French Quarter; Marie Laveau's House of Voodoo; cemetery monument; the St. Louis Cathedral as seen from Jackson Square.

Planning Your Trip

Where to Go

French Quarter

The undisputed heart of New Orleans, the French Quarter beckons with its wealth of **seafood restaurants, historical museums,** and varied street performers. Peruse the art galleries and antiques shops along **Royal Street,** stroll beside the **Mississippi River,** enjoy live music on **Bourbon Street,** or take a **carriage ride** through the fabled avenues. Iconic images like the **St. Louis Cathedral,** flickering gas lamps, and wrought-iron balconies make the Vieux Carré the city's most photographed neighborhood.

Faubourg Marigny and Bywater

Northeast of the French Quarter, the residential Faubourg Marigny and Bywater neighborhoods also lure their share of visitors. Sandwiched between Esplanade Avenue, the Mississippi River, and the Industrial Canal, this vast area is especially popular among local music lovers, who flock nightly to the **moody jazz clubs** and **low-key eateries** on Frenchmen Street.

Central Business and Arts Districts

Southwest of the French Quarter lies the Central Business District (CBD). Here, you'll encounter some of the city's **finest hotels,** plus diversions

wrought-iron balconies on Royal Street

like the prominent **Harrah's New Orleans casino.** The CBD also boasts the **Mercedes-Benz Superdome,** home to the New Orleans Saints football team. The adjacent Arts District, also known as the Warehouse District or Warehouse Arts District, contains numerous **art galleries,** the **Contemporary Arts Center, The National WWII Museum,** and **Lee Circle,** a roundabout featuring a statue of General Robert E. Lee.

Garden District

Technically part of the expansive Uptown area, the Garden District comprises several **historic mansions** and **art museums.** Although the neighborhood boundaries fluctuate, depending on whom you ask, most of the attractions, restaurants, inns, and stores worth noting lie along or within several blocks of **St. Charles Avenue,** between the Pontchartrain Expressway and Louisiana Avenue. Browse antiques shops and vintage clothing boutiques on funky **Magazine Street,** savor classic local cuisine at the award-winning **Commander's Palace,** and explore landmarks like **Lafayette Cemetery No. 1,** favored by filmmakers.

Uptown

The eclectic Uptown area is filled with as many rundown apartment buildings as well-landscaped estates. Shop for fashionable jewelry, clothing, and home furnishings along **Magazine Street,** ride the streetcars on oak-shaded **St. Charles Avenue,** explore popular bars and eateries in the **Riverbend neighborhood,** and stroll around the campus of the longstanding **Tulane University.** Uptown is also home to the famous **Audubon Zoo,** part of verdant **Audubon Park.**

the Audubon Zoo

the old state capitol of Louisiana in Baton Rouge

Tremé and Mid-City

Two areas flooded by Hurricane Katrina, the Tremé and Mid-City have slowly rebounded since that devastating storm. Situated northwest of Rampart Street, the Tremé has nurtured many local musicians over the years and now entices tourists with places like **Louis Armstrong Park** and **St. Louis Cemetery No. 1,** site of Marie Laveau's celebrated tomb. Farther north, Mid-City features several popular attractions, including **City Park,** the **New Orleans Museum of Art,** and the **Fair Grounds Race Course,** home to the annual **New Orleans Jazz & Heritage Festival.**

Greater New Orleans

Stretching from Lake Pontchartrain to the western bank of the Mississippi River, Greater New Orleans encompasses several unique neighborhoods and attractions. **Metairie** offers shopping centers and restaurants, while the **West Bank** invites hikers, anglers, and canoeists to explore **Barataria Preserve.** Not far from Mid-City, music lovers flock to **Rock 'n' Bowl,** a popular bowling alley and concert hall. Near Old Metairie, **Longue Vue House & Gardens** features a Classical Revival-style manor house that's one of the city's most impressive attractions.

Excursions from New Orleans

Southern Louisiana offers a slew of diversions. On the **Northshore,** you can tour a brewery, visit assorted state parks and animal attractions, and enjoy biking, fishing, and other outdoor activities. Explore antebellum plantation homes, from haunted Myrtles to photogenic Oak Alley, along the **Great River Road.** Head northwest to **Baton Rouge,** the state capital, where you can explore several museums and landmarks, including the present and former state capitol buildings. In **Cajun Country,** take a swamp tour, learn about Acadian culture, and stroll through well-preserved historic districts.

When to Go

While you can get a taste of New Orleans in a long weekend, try to allow yourself at least a week (or longer) to fully experience the city. Although New Orleans is a year-round destination, **summer** is the least crowded time to visit, except during major events like the **Essence Festival** and **Southern Decadence.** Temperatures are fairly high June-September, with an average high of about 91°F, when hurricane season is at its peak. While **fall** is more comfortable, **winter** and **spring** constitute the high season here. Annual events, such as **Mardi Gras,** the **French Quarter Festival,** and the **New Orleans Jazz & Heritage Festival,** lure the bulk of out-of-towners during these months. Those interested in visiting for Mardi Gras should note that the date shifts every season (February 9 in 2016, February 28 in 2017, February 13 in 2018, March 5 in 2019, and February 25 in 2020). Lodging rates are inflated in high season, as well as during major events and holiday weekends, and advance reservations may be necessary.

springtime magnolias at Longue Vue House & Gardens

The Best of New Orleans

The following three-day tour is an all-too-brief sampling of the best cultural and recreational attractions that New Orleans has to offer. If possible, try to visit the city during one of its signature events, such as Mardi Gras, the French Quarter Festival, the New Orleans Jazz & Heritage Festival, Southern Decadence, or Halloween.

Day 1

Start your day in the French Quarter with some warm café au lait and sugar-covered beignets at the world-famous **Café Du Monde,** part of the historic **French Market,** a collection of eateries, gift stores, and praline shops.

After breakfast, stroll through picturesque **Jackson Square** and tour the stunning structures that surround this well-landscaped park and promenade. Besides the majestic **St. Louis Cathedral,** you'll see curious historical exhibits inside the **Cabildo** and the **Presbytère** and glimpse period Creole furnishings inside the **1850 House,** part of the lovely **Pontalba Buildings.**

Stroll past the quaint boutiques and verdant balconies of Chartres Street, stop by the **Beauregard-Keyes House and Garden Museum,** then cross the street for a self-guided tour of the **Old Ursuline Convent.** Afterward, walk over to Royal Street for a guided stroll through the **Gallier Historic House Museum.** A few blocks away, you'll spot the **Old U.S. Mint,** a

Café Du Monde, part of the French Market

magnificent, red-brick edifice that now houses a state-of-the-art concert space and an engaging museum about the city's musical heritage.

At night, don your finest attire for a quintessential French Creole dinner at **Galatoire's Restaurant** on Bourbon Street. Afterward, walk to the world-famous **Preservation Hall** for a short jazz concert. End your evening at the candlelit **Lafitte's Blacksmith Shop Bar** for a late-night drink.

Day 2

Take a walk along the Mississippi riverfront and explore the varied marine exhibits inside the **Audubon Aquarium of the Americas.** Then check out the fascinating, if sometimes creepy, displays at the nearby **Audubon Butterfly Garden and Insectarium.**

Next, enjoy a river cruise aboard the ***Creole Queen,*** an authentic paddlewheeler. As an alternative, head through the CBD to **The National WWII Museum,** where you can watch an immersive documentary and experience a variety of exhibits pertaining to the Allied victory in the Second World War.

In the afternoon, catch a **Canal Street streetcar** ride to verdant **City Park,** a beloved 1,300-acre sanctuary. Rent bikes, ride a classic carousel, or stroll through the **New Orleans Botanical Garden** and **New Orleans Museum of Art.** Afterward, enjoy a sumptuous meal of contemporary Creole cuisine at **Ralph's on the Park.**

At night, have a drink in the courtyard of **Pat O'Brien's** in the French Quarter, known for its flaming fountain. Listen to live music or watch a burlesque show at **One Eyed Jacks.**

If you're still wide awake, head to **Bourbon Pub & Parade,** a 24-hour gay

a Canal Street streetcar

Top Five Attractions for Kids

an elephant at Audubon Zoo

Despite its reputation as a debauchery-laden party town, New Orleans is quite family-friendly. If you've traveled here with your children, make time for these top five diversions:

Audubon Aquarium of the Americas: Watch playful penguins and sea otters, touch sting rays, feed colorful parakeets, and walk amid all manner of marine creatures, from gigantic sharks to albino alligators (page 65).

Audubon Butterfly Garden and Insectarium: After observing a wide array of creepy-crawlies like subterranean termites, pesky mosquitoes, speedy cockroaches, and kaleidoscopic butterflies, little ones can sample bug-enhanced dishes in the on-site kitchen (page 65).

Blaine Kern's Mardi Gras World: Take a tour here for a fascinating behind-the-scenes look at the art of designing and constructing vibrant floats and sculptures for the Carnival season (page 85).

Audubon Zoo: Venture upriver to this zoo, where children can pet goats and sheep, watch sea lion and elephant shows, scamper up Monkey Hill, and view alligator feedings (page 94).

City Park: In addition to riding rented bikes, horses, and paddleboats, kids relish the chance to explore a fairytale-themed playground, take a spin on an antique carousel, and board a miniature train that tours much of City Park (pages 99 and 230).

nightclub that features variety shows, drag queen competitions, comedy showcases, burlesque performances, and late-night dancing.

Day 3

Board the **St. Charles streetcar** and head to the **Garden District,** where you can relax in verdant **Coliseum Square,** visit **Lafayette Cemetery No. 1,** and stroll amid historic homes, such as the **Brevard-Clapp House,** where novelist Anne Rice once lived. Take time to explore the antiques shops, art galleries, and varied boutiques along funky **Magazine Street.**

Hop back on the streetcar and head west to lush **Audubon Park** to play golf or tennis, go horseback riding, or gaze at the orangutans and elephants at **Audubon Zoo.**

Take the streetcar or a cab back to **Commander's Palace** and splurge on a modern Creole dinner at this classic New Orleans-style restaurant. Afterward, catch some live rock, funk, jazz, and blues music at well-loved Uptown joints like **Tipitina's** or the **Maple Leaf Bar,** or venture to **Rock 'n' Bowl** for a concert and a round of bowling.

A Romantic Getaway

History, luxury, and revelry converge in this sensual city, a popular place for romantic getaways. Accommodations range from intimate guesthouses in the Faubourg Marigny and Mid-City to elegant B&Bs in the Garden District to historic hotels in the French Quarter, and though all promise a romantic weekend, staying in the Quarter will ensure the most atmospheric experience.

Friday

Check into your hotel and have lunch at **Muriel's Jackson Square,** a stunning, supposedly haunted Creole restaurant not far from the **St. Louis Cathedral.** Stroll northeast to Frenchmen Street, where you can rent bikes from **Bicycle Michael's,** then take a self-guided tour of the Faubourg Marigny and French Quarter.

Either return your bikes when you're done or keep them for the weekend, then head to **The Historic New Orleans Collection** and tour the historical structures and exhibits that this engaging complex comprises. Afterward, mosey amid the antiques shops, art galleries, bookstores, and clothing boutiques along **Royal and Chartres Streets.**

Once the sun goes down, have a romantic dinner at the Marigny's **Feelings Café,** which features an intimate courtyard and live piano music, or the Quarter's **Mona Lisa Restaurant,** a cozy restaurant serving classic Italian cuisine. After dinner, enjoy some live jazz and a midnight burlesque show at **Irvin Mayfield's Jazz Playhouse.**

Saturday

Pick up a few pastries from the **Croissant d'or Patisserie,** then take a stroll along the riverside **Moonwalk** and have a morning picnic at **Woldenberg Riverfront Park,** a 16-acre green space dotted with sculptures. Afterward, take a breezy riverboat cruise on the **Steamboat *Natchez,*** a nostalgic paddlewheeler famous for its peppy calliope.

Enjoy a late lunch at the **Palace Café,** then walk two blocks to the magnificent **Hotel Monteleone,** where you and your sweetheart can relish an intimate couples massage at **Spa Aria.** Unwind even further with a drink at **The Carousel Bar & Lounge,** the hotel's on-site watering hole, where literary legends once mingled.

Mosey back to your hotel, then venture down Royal Street for a romantic dinner in the dimly lit courtyard at **Café Amelie.** After dinner, take a private carriage ride through the French Quarter via **Royal Carriages.**

Sunday

After checking out of your hotel, stroll to **The Court of Two Sisters** for a lively jazz brunch. Following brunch, take a music tour via **Historic New Orleans Tours,** which guides participants on a walking tour of sites like **St. Louis Cemetery No. 1,** the **Basin St. Station,** and **Louis Armstrong Park.** After the tour, head to **La Divina Gelateria** for a cup of artisanal gelato, then take one last stroll around the photogenic French Quarter.

the Steamboat *Natchez*

Haunted New Orleans

Given its voodoo lore and Catholic traditions, the spooky marshes and swamps that surround it, and a checkered past rife with piracy, slavery, and murder, the Crescent City is seemingly fertile ground for the spirit world. Here are just some of its spookiest destinations:

Antoine's Restaurant: Some diners claim that this 1840 eatery is still overseen by proprietor Antoine Alciatore, whose tuxedo-clad spirit has been known to appear in various dining rooms (page 117).

The Beauregard-Keyes House: At General Beauregard's former home, visitors have allegedly heard the screams and moans of dying soldiers from the Battle of Shiloh (page 67).

The Columns Hotel: Overnight guests have witnessed the spirits of a well-dressed gentleman in various bedrooms, a "woman in white" in the garden, and a young girl wandering the third floor of this Uptown hotel (page 196).

Hotel Monteleone: This historic landmark is supposedly home to more than a dozen entities, not the least of which is a 10-year-old boy who plays hide-and-seek with other young spirits (page 282).

Hôtel Provincial: At this French Quarter hotel, guests have seen and heard the spirits of wounded soldiers, allegedly treated at this site during the Civil War (page 282).

LaLaurie Mansion: In 1834, neighbors discovered several tortured, starving slaves chained in the attic of this ornate house. Since then, passersby have claimed to hear moans and screams emanating from the premises. Though closed to the public, it's routinely included on ghost tours in the French Quarter (page 76).

Muriel's Jackson Square: This upscale restaurant is supposedly haunted by Pierre Antoine Lepardi Jourdan, the building's former owner, who committed suicide upstairs after losing his dream house in a poker game (page 121).

The Columns Hotel

The Myrtles Plantation: Guests of this St. Francisville plantation, considered one of America's most haunted homes, have often photographed strange apparitions, heard inexplicable noises at night, and found their belongings have been mysteriously misplaced, presumably by the young ghosts that still dwell here (page 317).

Oak Alley Plantation: Visitors have seen ghosts, felt inexplicable caresses, and heard the mysterious clip-clops of an invisible horse-drawn carriage at this famous Vacherie plantation (page 318).

St. Louis Cathedral: Some have heard the tenor voice of Père Dagobert, an 18th-century priest who insisted on the proper burial of six French rebel leaders who had been killed by the Spanish and left outside in the heat and rain (page 82).

St. Louis Cemetery No. 1: According to local legend, you can request a favor of the spirit of Marie Laveau, the so-called "Voodoo Queen of New Orleans," by visiting this Tremé cemetery, leaving an offering before her supposed resting place, and knocking on her crypt three times (page 107).

Classic Cuisine

Foodies will fare well in New Orleans, where the most popular dishes derive from Cajun, Creole, and Southern recipes. In addition to the items below, New Orleans is also known for its **oysters** (page 119) and fabulous **desserts** (page 157).

Beignet

A beignet (ben-YAY) consists of fried doughnut batter sprinkled with powdered sugar. This pastry was popularized by **Café Du Monde** (page 125) in the French Market, where it's served with café au lait (KAFF-ay oh LAY) made from coffee (usually with chicory) and steamed milk.

Gumbo

A thick filé soup begun with a roux (ROO; a slowly cooked mixture of butter or water and flour); filled with ingredients like chicken, andouille, okra, and shrimp; and usually served with rice. Two perennial favorites are the French-Creole seafood gumbo served at **Galatoire's Restaurant** (page 119) and the rich, hearty version found at **Dooky Chase's Restaurant** (page 162).

Po-Boy

The quintessential New Orleans sandwich, made on French bread with fillings like roast beef or fried shrimp. Be sure to order it "dressed" (with lettuce, tomato, mayo, etc.). Though lots of restaurants make delicious po-boys, many locals prefer **Mahony's Po-Boys & Seafood** (page 155) in the Uptown area or **Parkway Bakery & Tavern** (page 162) in Mid-City.

Oysters are a local specialty.

Jambalaya

Jambalaya (juhm-buh-LAHY-uh) is a Cajun or Creole rice dish containing tomatoes, spices, and meats such as chicken, andouille, and seafood. Try **Mother's Restaurant** (page 144) for a traditional, mildly spicy version, or head upriver to **Jacques-Imo's Cafe** (page 154), a Riverbend eatery that prepares classic dishes with a twist.

Muffuletta

A round, oversized sandwich with ham, salami, mortadella, provolone, and olive salad. Tasty versions of the muffuletta (muff-uh-LET-uh) are available at **Central Grocery** (page 249), **Café Maspero** (page 132), and **Cochon Butcher** (page 145).

Shrimp Rémoulade

Shrimp rémoulade (rey-moo-LAHD) consists of boiled shrimp on a bed of lettuce—or, even better, fried green tomatoes—covered with a spicy, mustard-based sauce. Try this tasty appetizer at **The Marigny Brasserie** (page 139) or the **Upperline Restaurant** (page 155).

Shrimp Creole

A stew-like sauce served over rice. The long ingredient list may include butter, green peppers, tomatoes, TABASCO and Worcestershire sauces, cayenne, parsley, and, of course, peeled shrimp. **Mother's Restaurant** (page 144) in the CBD offers a tasty mild version.

Crawfish Étouffée

A dark, buttery roux of crawfish and seasoned vegetables, usually poured over rice. Shrimp étouffée (ay-too-FAY) is a popular alternative. In the

Hard-to-resist beignets are offered 24 hours daily at Café Du Monde.

CBD, **Mother's Restaurant** (page 144) offers a classic, though mild version, while the **Bon Ton Cafe** (page 142) serves some of the best in the city.

Turtle Soup

A stew-like concoction that begins with a roux, followed by ingredients like butter, garlic, tomatoes, lemon juice, Worcestershire sauce, hard-boiled eggs, cayenne, parsley, and, of course, cubed turtle meat. Many locals savor turtle soup (with dry sherry) at **Commander's Palace** (page 150) and **Café Adelaide** (page 142).

Blackened Redfish

Redfish coated with spicy seasonings and flash-fried in a cast-iron pan. **K-Paul's Louisiana Kitchen** (page 120) popularized this Cajun dish. Due to its popularity, and the resulting decline in the local redfish population, alternatives like blackened black drum are common.

Red Beans and Rice

A traditional New Orleans dish consisting of kidney beans and spicy gravy, often served with ham hocks, tasso, or andouille. For a classic version, especially on Mondays (the city's traditional day for washing laundry and eating beans), many locals head to **The Praline Connection** (page 135) in the Marigny or **Willie Mae's Scotch House** (page 163) in the Tremé.

Grillades and Grits

Grillades (gree-YAHDZ) are diced meat marinated in vinegar to produce a rich gravy. **Elizabeth's Restaurant** (page 135) prepares an excellent version during its weekend brunch.

an Italian-style muffuletta at Café Maspero

Festivals and Events

Look for ★ to find recommended festivals.

Highlights

★ **Rowdiest Celebration:** Countless tourists venture to New Orleans every winter for **Mardi Gras,** a pre-Lenten season marked by colorful parades, spirited balls and parties, and, yes, crowds of drunken, bead-catching revelers (page 38).

★ **Best Free Music Event:** Now considered Louisiana's largest free music event, the **French Quarter Festival** brings together an array of regional jazz, gospel, funk, zydeco, classical, bluegrass, folk, rock, and blues acts (page 42).

★ **Biggest Fest for Music Lovers:** The famous **New Orleans Jazz & Heritage Festival** lures visitors to Mid-City's Fair Grounds Race Course in late April and early May for two long weekends of live musical performances, ranging from local jazz, blues, and zydeco talent to major rock 'n' roll headliners (page 45).

★ **Best Chance to Tour Private Homes:** For roughly eight decades, the **New Orleans Spring Fiesta** has highlighted the city's unique history and charm with tours of nearly two dozen private homes, gardens, and courtyards (page 49).

★ **Finest Way to Hobnob with Writers:** Typically held in late March or early April, the weeklong **Tennessee Williams/ New Orleans Literary Festival** celebrates the city's most famous playwright with poetry readings, theatrical performances, and the climactic Stanley and Stella Shouting Contest (page 51).

★ **Best Summertime Music Fest:** In late July or early August, New Orleans honors the legacy of musician Louis "Satchmo" Armstrong with **Satchmo SummerFest,** a three-day event that features live music by brass, swing, early jazz, and contemporary jazz bands (page 53).

★ **Largest Gay Street Fair:** Bold participants and eager onlookers flood the bars, streets, and gay-friendly venues in the French Quarter and the Faubourg Marigny every Labor Day weekend for **Southern Decadence,** celebrating the city's gay culture with everything from drag shows to beefcake contests (page 53).

★ **Tastiest Way to Spend a Sunday:** The one-day **Oak Street Po-Boy Festival** attracts an impressive horde of hungry mouths to Uptown's Riverbend neighborhood in late November. Sample a cornucopia of local cuisine, from Creole turducken tacos to cochon de lait po-boys (page 57).

★ **Most Family-Friendly Event:** From late November through the end of December, City Park comes alive for **Celebration in the Oaks,** a marvelous holiday light show. Kids especially enjoy the illuminated Storyland and Carousel Gardens and the animated *Cajun Night Before Christmas* tableau (page 58).

★ **Best View of Mardi Gras Indians:** Begun in New Orleans as an Italian American holiday, **St. Joseph's Day** (March 19) is honored with elaborate, multihued altars throughout the city. It's typically preceded or followed by **Super Sunday,** when the Mardi Gras Indians, an African American troupe of Carnival revelers, host a vibrant parade (page 61).

With a reputation for revelry, the Big Easy offers a cornucopia of festivals worth planning a trip around, especially in fall, winter, and spring.

In fact, in a town where locals need little reason to celebrate, well-known events like Mardi Gras and the New Orleans Jazz & Heritage Festival are just the tip of the iceberg. Like the outstanding French Quarter Festival, most events revolve around food and music. Similar, if smaller, events include Satchmo SummerFest (late July or early Aug.), the Crescent City Blues and BBQ Festival (mid-Oct.), and the Voodoo Music + Arts Experience (around Halloween). If you happen to be in town during June or September, you can enjoy several different free festivals in the French Market, Louis Armstrong Park, and City Park that focus on quintessential local delights, such as seafood, Creole tomatoes, and Cajun and zydeco music. Other summertime events worth braving the heat and humidity range from July's weeklong Tales of the Cocktail to Labor Day weekend's Southern Decadence, a Mardi Gras-like event honoring the gay lifestyle.

Considering that New Orleans has long inspired writers, artists, and performers of all kinds, it only makes sense that the city would also nurture events like the Tennessee Williams/New Orleans Literary Festival (late Mar.) and the New Orleans Burlesque Festival (mid-Sept.). Architecture lovers might also appreciate the New Orleans Spring Fiesta (late Mar.), an event that allows you to explore a variety of private homes and gardens in historic neighborhoods like the French Quarter and the Garden District.

New Orleans also has its share of holiday-related events. Besides Mardi Gras and St. Joseph's Day, both of which are favored by Catholics and Mardi Gras Indians alike, you'll discover plenty of Christmas revelry during the

Previous: Mardi Gras Indian on Super Sunday; New Orleans Jazz & Heritage Festival.

month of December, when the St. Louis Cathedral offers free jazz concerts, restaurants offer special *réveillon* menus, and the trees and structures of City Park are illuminated during Celebration in the Oaks. No matter when you choose to visit, be aware that, during popular events—especially Mardi Gras and Jazz Fest—the city can fill up quickly, so it's wise to book your trip well ahead. (Or avoid the city during these times if you're not a fan of crowds.)

Top Festivals

★ MARDI GRAS

Few festivals exemplify the joyous spirit of New Orleans more than **Mardi Gras** (MAHR-dee grah), a French term meaning "Fat Tuesday." If you're a fan of colorful, exciting festivals, there's no better time to visit New Orleans than during Mardi Gras season, which usually falls in February or early March and lasts 2-3 weeks prior to Lent (from Epiphany to Ash Wednesday). Festivities include everything from colorful street masks and costumes to gala balls and events. But Mardi Gras's most famous events are the free public parades sponsored by krewes and featuring colorful floats, marching bands, motorcycle squads, dancers, entertainers, and, sometimes, a royal court (the king, queen, maids, and dukes of a krewe). Participants often toss beaded necklaces, stuffed animals, commemorative doubloons, and other trinkets to spectators lining the route. For most krewes, each year brings a new theme, usually with a historical, mythical, or topical bent. Some of the most worthwhile parades include the krewes of Endymion, Bacchus, Orpheus, Zulu, and Rex. Dog lovers might appreciate the Mystic Krewe of Barkus in the French Quarter, while sci-fi and fantasy fans look forward to the Intergalactic Krewe of Chewbacchus.

VARIOUS LOCATIONS: www.mardigrasday.com; hours vary; free

Planning Checklist

Know when to go. Carnival season technically begins on January 6 (known as Twelfth Night, or the Feast of the Epiphany), but Mardi Gras Day itself shifts every season (February 9 in 2016, February 28 in 2017, February 13 in 2018, March 5 in 2019, and February 25 in 2020). Mardi Gras parades usually start about two weeks prior to Fat Tuesday, but most revelers venture to New Orleans for the weekend preceding the climactic day—from the Friday before Fat Tuesday through midnight on Mardi Gras.

Book a bed. Make reservations at least three months in advance. Note, too, that many hotels require a minimum stay of three nights (if not more) during Mardi Gras weekend, and costly special-event rates may apply. Although you'll find cheaper hotels in suburbs like Metairie and Kenner (near the airport), staying there will require renting a pricey car and enduring long commutes to reach the main festivities. You'll save time by

Mardi Gras Lingo

traditional Mardi Gras doubloons, king cake, and beads

- **Ball:** a masquerade or lively extravaganza that usually occurs at the end of a parade, includes the presentation of krewe royalty, and offers entertainment for krewe members, their guests, and, sometimes, the paying public
- **Boeuf gras** (BUFF grah): the fatted bull or ox, the ancient symbol of the final meat eaten before the Lenten season of fasting, used as a symbol of the Carnival season and, more specifically, the Krewe of Rex
- **Captain:** the leader of each Carnival krewe
- **Den:** a warehouse where floats are constructed and stored
- **Doubloon:** large coins made from aluminum, plastic, or other materials and stamped with the insignia and theme of a Mardi Gras krewe
- **Favor:** a souvenir, given by krewe members to friends attending the ball and usually bearing the krewe's name, insignia, and year of issue
- **Flambeaux** (FLAM-bohz): naphtha-fueled torches, once carried by white-robed black men as the only source of nighttime parade illumination, still used in many nighttime parades but without the racially charged outfits
- **Invitation:** a printed, nontransferable request for attendance at a Carnival ball, used in lieu of the more casual term "ticket"
- **King cake:** an iced or sugared coffee cake, often shaped like an extra-large ring, served during the Mardi Gras season, and containing a small plastic baby, the finder of which, according to tradition, must purchase the next king cake or throw the next party
- **Krewe:** private Carnival organization
- **Lundi Gras** (LUN-dee grah): the day before Mardi Gras, also known as Fat Monday
- **Mardi Gras Indians:** groups of local black men who, led by separate Big Chiefs, chant, dance, and compete with one another in ceremonial processions along ever-changing routes through residential neighborhoods on Mardi Gras Day, all while wearing handmade beaded and feathered costumes as a tribute to American Indians, who often assisted escaping slaves
- **Masker:** a masked krewe member, usually riding on a horse or float during a parade
- **Throw:** an inexpensive trinket, such as an aluminum doubloon or plastic medallion necklace, tossed by costumed, often masked krewe members

staying in a more convenient neighborhood, such as the French Quarter, where much of the revelry takes place. For a good night's sleep, consider staying in the CBD or Faubourg Marigny, both of which lie within walking distance of the Quarter. As an alternative, you can stay in some of the quieter inns throughout the Garden District, Uptown, and Mid-City, most of which are accessible via the streetcar lines.

Use social media. Utilize Facebook, Twitter, and other social networks for last-minute hotel deals, ride-sharing possibilities, and other ways to save time and money during peak travel weeks. You can view the status updates of organizations like the New Orleans CVB, which routinely posts information about upcoming events.

Beware of scams. During Mardi Gras, many residents rent out rooms and cottages. While you may find a good deal this way, make arrangements as early as possible and be aware of unscrupulous landlords.

Pick your neighborhood. If you seek debauchery, the French Quarter will not let you down. However, celebrations elsewhere in the city—notably in Uptown along the St. Charles Avenue parade route or in Metairie along Veterans Memorial Boulevard—are much more family-oriented and tend to be dominated by locals, or at least Louisianians.

Strategize your transportation. During Mardi Gras, the French Quarter is closed to non-essential vehicular traffic. (Emergency vehicles and residents with proper ID are still allowed passage.) Hailing a cab can be difficult, so many visitors prefer getting around town via bus, streetcar, or foot. Some even opt to rent a bicycle (or bring their own); just don't forget to wear a helmet.

Prepare for mayhem. The French Quarter might be the rowdiest neighborhood, but the less wholesome aspects of Mardi Gras, such as public nudity, drunkenness, suffocating crowds, and opportunistic crime, can occur anywhere. To be safe, travel in groups, arrange regular meeting spots with friends, avoid quiet streets at night, conceal money and valuables, and exercise caution at all times. Even the parades can be dangerous: you may be shoved or stepped on by those seeking beads and trinkets tossed from the floats. Float riders in the major parades, like Endymion and Bacchus, tend to hurl such items with unnecessary force, so look out.

Stake out seats. If you want to be close to the floats, it's often necessary to arrive at parade routes several hours early. For major parades, such as Endymion on the Saturday evening prior to Mardi Gras, many people set up blankets, chairs, and ladders the day before. (Be advised that it's actually illegal to leave such marked areas unattended.) While it's best to choose a spot near a public restroom, be sure to purchase something at the bar or restaurant in question before using its facilities. Consider bringing snacks, beverages, and portable chairs. Finally, given the influx of out-of-towners, it's also advisable to make restaurant reservations or opt to dine at odd meal times.

Wear a costume. New Orleanians plan their Mardi Gras costumes well in advance, and, especially on Mardi Gras Day itself, you'll see plenty of

Above: a dog at the Mystic Krewe of Barkus parade. Below: a colorful Mardi Gras float.

Laissez les Bon Temps Rouler!

Only a few official **Mardi Gras parades** run through the French Quarter, including the raunchy Krewe du Vieux, the wine-themed Krewe of Cork, and the dog-filled Krewe of Barkus. Most of the other parades in and around the city (including Uptown, Mid-City, Metairie, and communities on the Westbank and along the Northshore) are surprisingly family-friendly. Some have special throws, such as the hand-decorated shoes offered by the Krewe of Muses, which usually rolls on the Thursday before Mardi Gras weekend. Parade routes are listed in *The Times-Picayune* and online (www.nola.com, www.mardigras.com, www.mardigrasday.com, www.mardigrasneworleans.com). Here are the major parades:

Endymion

First presented in 1967, the Krewe of Endymion (www.endymion.org) is the city's largest parade, a "super-krewe" that features enormous floats, magnificent court costumes, and celebrity grand marshals.

When: 4:30pm on the Saturday prior to Mardi Gras.

Where: The parade starts near City Park and travels down Canal Street and St. Charles Avenue, culminating with its "Extravaganza" in the Mercedes-Benz Superdome.

Bacchus

Established in 1968 and presented the following year, the Krewe of Bacchus (www.kreweofbacchus.org) is a "super-krewe" that features incredible floats and celebrity kings, from Danny Kaye to Will Ferrell. Signature floats include the Bacchasaurus, Bacchagator, and Baby Kong.

When: 5pm on the Sunday prior to Mardi Gras.

Where: From Napoleon Avenue and Tchoupitoulas Street, it rolls through Uptown on Napoleon Avenue, along St. Charles Avenue, and down Canal Street, ending at the Ernest N. Morial Convention Center.

costumed revelers dressed as everything from pop culture icons to political statements. Do as the locals do and wear a costume (or at least purchase a mask, available in shops throughout the Quarter). Remember to prepare for the possibility of cold, rainy weather, which is common in February and March.

Eat king cake. King cake, essentially a large cinnamon roll-style cake, is the season's most famous treat. Grab a slice at a local coffeehouse or pick up an entire cake at places like Rouses Market, Gambino's Bakery, Haydel's Bakery, Maurice French Pastries, and the seasonal Manny Randazzo King Cakes.

★ FRENCH QUARTER FESTIVAL

Begun in 1984 to support local musicians, the four-day French Quarter Fest, which typically occurs in early or mid-April, has since evolved into Louisiana's largest free music event. The roughly 20 outdoor stages—from The Old U.S. Mint to Jackson Square to Woldenberg Riverfront Park—host

Orpheus

Co-founded in 1993 by Harry Connick Jr. and presented in 1994, the Krewe of Orpheus (www.kreweoforpheus.com) is the largest of the newer parades and has featured a slew of celebrity monarchs, from Stevie Wonder to Anne Rice.

When: 6pm on Lundi Gras.

Where: From the corner of Napoleon Avenue and Tchoupitoulas Street, it rolls through Uptown on Napoleon Avenue, then along St. Charles Avenue, down Canal and Tchoupitoulas Streets, to the Orpheuscapade, a black-tie event at the convention center.

Zulu

Officially begun in 1909, the Zulu Social Aid & Pleasure Club (www.kreweofzulu.com) presents one of the season's most anticipated parades, during which spectators vie for painted coconuts, the krewe's signature throw. Zulu also hosts the Lundi Gras Festival, a free music event on the day before Fat Tuesday.

When: 8am on Mardi Gras.

Where: From the corner of Jackson and South Claiborne Avenues in Uptown, it travels along Jackson Avenue, continues north on St. Charles Avenue, follows Canal and Basin Streets, and ends at Orleans Avenue and Broad Street in the Faubourg Tremé.

Rex

Since 1872, the king of the Krewe of Rex (www.rexorganization.com) has reigned as the king of Mardi Gras. The parade features majestic floats, masked riders, and, naturally, a royal court. Mardi Gras officially ends with the Rex Ball at the Sheraton New Orleans Hotel on Canal Street.

When: 10am on Mardi Gras.

Where: The parade travels down Napoleon Avenue from the intersection with South Claiborne Avenue in Uptown, then along St. Charles Avenue and down Canal Street toward the Mississippi River.

local and regional jazz, gospel, funk, zydeco, classical, bluegrass, folk, and blues acts, so you likely won't see mega-stars like Sting here (unless he's one of the attendees). Besides live music, you'll also find plenty of food for sale, including jambalaya, boiled crawfish, and sno-balls.

FRENCH QUARTER: Various locations, 504/522-5730 or 800/673-5725, http://fqfi.org/frenchquarterfest; hours vary; free, though food and beverage costs apply

Planning Checklist

Reserve a room. Advance hotel reservations are highly recommended, and you can expect minimum-stay requirements (and higher rates) for most accommodations. Keep an eye out for last-minute deals on social media networks, and beware of too-good-to-be-true situations with unlicensed inns and room rentals. While you'll save money by staying in the suburbs, you'll likely lose time in trying to commute to the French Quarter (where the entirety of French Quarter Fest takes place), especially since it usually has limited parking. Save time by either staying in the French Quarter or

Above: the Krewe of Zulu on Mardi Gras Day. Below: the Krewe of Orpheus on Lundi Gras.

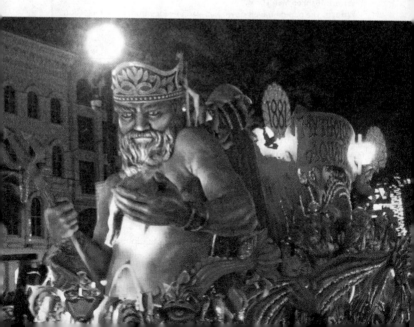

finding a place in the nearby Faubourg Marigny or near the streetcar lines in the CBD, the Garden District, Uptown, and Mid-City.

Peruse the schedule. The music schedule for the four-day event is usually posted online well in advance of the festival weekend. There's also a free mobile app available, so if you fancy a certain band, you can plan your festival itinerary ahead of time.

Prepare for any weather. Springtime in New Orleans can be blazing hot one day and cool and rainy the next. Anticipate all conditions, and pack sunscreen, a hat and sunglasses, and maybe even a small umbrella. Storms sometimes cancel or delay musical performances, so be prepared for that as well.

Plan your transport. You can easily find a cab at the airport, but once in town, hailing a cab can be difficult. Unless you're staying in the French Quarter, you may have to rely on buses, streetcars, bikes, or your own two feet to reach the various stages.

Claim your spot. Crowds assemble early each day, especially for perennial favorites like the Rebirth Brass Band or highly anticipated headliners, who usually play in the late afternoon and early evening. If being close to a particular stage matters to you, stake your claim in the morning, preferably before the first musical act begins. I recommend wandering among the various stages, from one end of the Quarter to the other, listening to a variety of music. You might, after all, discover a new favorite singer or band.

Sample the cuisine. Selling food and beverages through assorted vendors—most of whom represent area bars and restaurants—is one way that French Quarter Fest has remained a free event. Bringing your own supplies isn't even allowed in fenced areas like Jackson Square and The Old U.S. Mint, and you'll get more out of the festival experience if you sample some of the goodies on offer, from po-boys and boiled crawfish to Plum Street sno-balls. Be advised, though: food costs can add up quickly. In general, vendors set up in Jackson Square, near The Old U.S. Mint, and throughout Woldenberg Riverfront Park.

★ NEW ORLEANS JAZZ & HERITAGE FESTIVAL

Established in 1970, this musical extravaganza, which takes place at Mid-City's Fair Grounds Race Course, has grown to be nearly as popular as Mardi Gras. Held on two long weekends in late April and early May, this event, also known as Jazz Fest, features music workshops, artisanal and culinary demonstrations, Native American powwow performances, arts-and-crafts vendors, an unbelievable array of food stalls, and numerous stages that buzz with jazz, blues, zydeco, rock, gospel, and folk musicians. Among the top acts who have performed at Jazz Fest are Fats Domino, Etta James, and various members of the Marsalis and Neville clans.

The **New Orleans Jazz & Heritage Foundation** (1205 N. Rampart St., 504/558-6100 or 888/652-8751, www.jazzandheritage.org), the organization

Above: the French Quarter Festival. **Below:** the New Orleans Jazz & Heritage Festival.

behind this popular festival, also sponsors smaller food-and-music events, all of which are free to attend—though, as with Jazz Fest, food and beverage costs always apply. Two of these events occur in the Tremé's Louis Armstrong Park: the **Congo Square New World Rhythms Festival** (late Mar.) and the **Louisiana Cajun-Zydeco Festival** (early June). The other two take place in the CBD's Lafayette Square: the **Crescent City Blues and BBQ Festival** (mid-Oct.) and the **Tremé Creole Gumbo Festival** (mid-Nov.).

TREMÉ AND MID-CITY: Fair Grounds Race Course & Slots, 1751 Gentilly Blvd., 504/410-4100, www.nojazzfest.com; hours vary; $58-70 adult, $5 child 2-10, free under 2, food and beverage costs also apply

Planning Checklist

Pick a weekend. Unless you can afford a 10-day trip to New Orleans, you'll probably need to choose one of the two festival weekends: the first, which usually spans the last Friday-Sunday in April, or the second, which typically covers the first Thursday-Sunday in May. The complete, seven-day music schedule is usually posted online ahead of time, or you can access the free mobile app. Of course, by the time the detailed schedules are uploaded, it might be too late to book a room, so keep an eye out for information regarding headliners, which is usually leaked to the public well in advance of the finalized schedule.

Consider a pass. If you plan to stay for an entire weekend, consider purchasing one of the limited passes. The **Krewe of Jazz Fest VIP Pass** ($600-700 per weekend) enables you to watch all the action at the Acura Stage from an exclusive area, with pedestrian re-entry privileges and access to upscale restroom facilities, a private beverage concession area, and, if available, reserved parking. The **Grand Marshal VIP Pass** ($975-1,125 per weekend) offers everything that the Krewe of Jazz pass includes as well as exclusive, upfront access to the other two main stages, the Gentilly Stage and the Congo Square Stage. The **Big Chief VIP Experience** ($1,200-1,400 per weekend) includes everything that the other two passes offer, plus access to a private, air-conditioned VIP Hospitality Lounge and private viewing areas near the Jazz and Blues Tents.

Secure your hotel. Advance hotel reservations are highly recommended. You can expect minimum-stay requirements, special-event rates, and last-minute deals, but be aware of potential scams. While concerts and other activities occur throughout New Orleans during Jazz Fest, the main event takes place at the Fair Grounds Race Course, meaning you might prefer staying in Mid-City. Otherwise, you can easily use public transportation from inns and hotels in the Marigny, Quarter, CBD, Garden District, and other Uptown neighborhoods.

Plan for heat or rain. It's usually hot and humid during Jazz Fest, but rain is always an unpredictable factor, and given the ever-present dirt and hay, the Fair Grounds can quickly become muddy. Pack sunscreen, sunglasses, a hat, a small umbrella, a poncho, a towel, and clothes that you don't mind getting soiled.

Stake your claim. Crowds assemble early each day, especially for perennial favorites and major headliners, who usually play in the late afternoon and early evening. If seeing a certain band matters to you, claim your spot in the morning, preferably before the first musical act begins.

Taste the food. Outside food and beverages are not allowed, so take advantage of the regional cuisine, water, soda, alcohol, strawberry lemonade, and other beverages for sale throughout the festival grounds. You'll encounter a slew of delicious (if pricey) dishes, from meat pies and turkey legs to jambalaya and crawfish bread.

Don't forget souvenirs. Beyond music, exhibits, and demonstrations, Jazz Fest features three separate arts-and-crafts areas—the Congo Square African Marketplace, the Louisiana Marketplace, and Heritage Square (contemporary crafts)—plus various souvenir tents, selling commemorative posters, T-shirts, and the like. Bring enough money to purchase a few souvenirs, ranging from colorful hats to glass jewelry to Acadian furniture. While many of these items are relatively affordable, some are far from cheap.

Spring

While the French Quarter Fest (early or mid-Apr.) and Jazz Fest (late Apr. and early May) are the biggest springtime events, the city offers several other opportunities for celebration in this season.

CRESCENT CITY CLASSIC

Since 1979, the Crescent City Classic (now known as the Allstate Sugar Bowl Crescent City Classic), one of the nation's largest 10K road races, has been held in New Orleans every March or April, usually on the Saturday of Easter weekend. Roughly 20,000 people from around the globe participate. From its start at the Mercedes-Benz Superdome, the course runs through the French Quarter, then heads up Esplanade Avenue to culminate in City Park. A rollicking post-race festival, a celebration of local music and cuisine, is free for participants; all other attendees must pay a fee ($10 pp). The pre-race, two-day health and fitness expo is free.

VARIOUS LOCATIONS: Mercedes-Benz Superdome to City Park, 504/861-8686, www.ccc10k.com; free to watch, $30-50 to enter race

LOUISIANA CRAWFISH FESTIVAL

If you're a "mudbug" lover, do yourself a favor and head to Chalmette in late March for the Louisiana Crawfish Festival. Since 1975, this popular, family-friendly event has celebrated crawfish season with live music, arts and crafts, amusement games and rides, and, of course, regional cuisine. Besides shrimp and alligator dishes, sno-balls and king cakes, and classic all-American options, the samplings encompass almost every crawfish-related meal imaginable, including crawfish étouffée over fried green tomatoes.

GREATER NEW ORLEANS: Frederick J. Sigur Civic Center, 8245 W. Judge Perez Dr., Chalmette, 504/278-1506, http://louisianacrawfishfestival.com; hours and costs vary

MID-CITY BAYOU BOOGALOO

For roughly a decade, the MotherShip Foundation has presented this free, spirited celebration of local culture alongside the sunny western bank of Bayou St. John, between Dumaine and Lafitte Streets. Typically occurring in mid-May, this three-day event presents a slew of live music, which, in the past, has included local performers like Anders Osborne, Washboard Chaz, and the Rebirth Brass Band. As with other Big Easy festivals, you can expect an assortment of arts and crafts for sale, from stained glass to handcrafted jewelry, as well as a cornucopia of food vendors, from The Praline Connection to Ralph's on the Park.

TREMÉ AND MID-CITY: 500 N. Jefferson Davis Pkwy., http://thebayouboogaloo.com; hours vary; free, though food and craft costs apply

NEW ORLEANS GREEK FESTIVAL

Alongside Bayou St. John, and within a quick drive of both Lake Pontchartrain and City Park, stands the impressive Holy Trinity Cathedral, which has hosted this lively, well-attended festival every Memorial Day weekend since the mid-1970s. Like any self-respecting Hellenic bash, this one presents live Greek music, Greek-style dancing, and, naturally, traditional Greek cuisine, from souvlaki to baklava. The festival also features a playground, a 5K race, and tours of the cathedral.

GREATER NEW ORLEANS: Holy Trinity Greek Orthodox Cathedral, 1200 Robert E. Lee Blvd., 504/282-0259, www.greekfestnola.com; $7 pp, free under 12, food costs also apply

★ NEW ORLEANS SPRING FIESTA

Typically held in late March, the Spring Fiesta grants you the unique opportunity to step inside nearly two dozen private homes, gardens, and courtyards in the French Quarter, Garden District, and Uptown neighborhoods—an unparalleled experience that is completely worth the seemingly steep cost. For eight decades, this one-of-a-kind event has honored the city's unique history and charm by offering such eye-opening tours, plus a delightful parade of horse-drawn carriages and the presentation of the Spring Fiesta Queen and her court at Jackson Square.

VARIOUS LOCATIONS: 504/581-1367 or 800/550-8450, www.springfiesta.com; $25-30 pp for home tours, $15-20 pp for walking tours

NEW ORLEANS WINE & FOOD EXPERIENCE

Late May is the perfect time for foodies and wine connoisseurs to visit the Big Easy, as that's typically when you'll encounter the four-day New Orleans Wine & Food Experience (NOWFE). For more than two decades,

Above: Jackson Square, a frequent stop on the New Orleans Spring Fiesta walking tour.
Below: A participant in the Stanley & Stella Shouting Contest at the Tennessee Williams/New Orleans Literary Festival.

this mouthwatering event has benefited local nonprofit organizations while showcasing hundreds of national and international wines from more than 100 wineries, including the Northshore's Pontchartrain Vineyards, along with food from about 75 of the city's top restaurants, from Antoine's to the Oceana Grill. Featuring various dinners, tastings, and seminars, the NOWFE also celebrates local celebrity chefs like John Besh and Susan Spicer.

VARIOUS LOCATIONS: 504/934-1474, www.nowfe.com; hours and costs vary

★ TENNESSEE WILLIAMS/NEW ORLEANS LITERARY FESTIVAL

Devotees of the city's most famous literary luminary rush to the Big Easy in late March or early April to attend the Tennessee Williams/New Orleans Literary Festival. For three decades, this event has celebrated the playwright who gave us such iconographic works as *A Streetcar Named Desire* and *The Glass Menagerie*. The five-day gathering is replete with writing classes helmed by experts, celebrity interviews, panel discussions, stagings of Williams's plays, fiction and poetry readings, and the endlessly entertaining Stanley and Stella Shouting Contest. Speakers, instructors, and attendees have included George Plimpton, Dorothy Allison, and Piper Laurie.

FRENCH QUARTER: Various locations, 504/581-1144 or 800/990-3378, www.tennesseewilliams.net; hours and costs vary

Summer

Summer events, such as the rowdy Southern Decadence bash around Labor Day, are held when tourism slows and often appeal more to locals.

CREOLE TOMATO FESTIVAL

The French Market District is home to the Creole Tomato Festival, which has celebrated one of the state's most popular fruits for roughly three decades. During the free, two-day event, which usually takes place during the second weekend of June, you'll encounter live concerts, cooking demonstrations, culinary discussions, eating contests, tempting food booths, and children's activities. You can also purchase fresh produce, including Creole tomatoes, at the on-site farmers market.

FRENCH QUARTER: French Market and The Old U.S. Mint, 504/522-2621, www.frenchmarket.org; free, though food costs apply

ESSENCE FESTIVAL

In early July, visitors typically descend upon New Orleans for the annual Essence Festival, a four-day celebration of African American music and culture. Besides DJ parties at the Sugar Mill, the main events of this much-anticipated festival consist of concerts and comedy shows at the

Mercedes-Benz Superdome and empowerment presentations at the Ernest N. Morial Convention Center. Recent headliners have included Usher, Mary J. Blige, and Erykah Badu.

CENTRAL BUSINESS AND ARTS DISTRICTS: Various locations, www.essence.com/festival; hours and costs vary

GO 4TH ON THE RIVER

At about the same time as the Essence Festival, Go 4th on the River beckons locals and tourists to celebrate not only America's independence but also the New Orleans riverfront. Besides promoting attractions alongside the Mississippi River, such as the Jax Brewery and Audubon Aquarium of the Americas, this all-day extravaganza features live music at Washington Artillery Park and Spanish Plaza, cruises on two vintage paddlewheel riverboats, and one of the largest fireworks displays in the country.

VARIOUS LOCATIONS: www.go4thontheriver.com; hours vary; free, though some activity fees apply

LOUISIANA CAJUN-ZYDECO FESTIVAL

Besides the world-famous Jazz Fest, the New Orleans Jazz & Heritage Foundation also presents the Louisiana Cajun-Zydeco Festival, a free, two-day music event that typically occurs during the first weekend of June. Featuring live music from some of Louisiana's best Cajun and zydeco performers, such as Dwayne Dopsie and the Zydeco Hellraisers, this celebration also offers regional cuisine, kid-friendly diversions, and a sizable arts-and-crafts fair.

TREMÉ AND MID-CITY: Louis Armstrong Park, 504/558-6100, www.jazzandheritage.org/cajun-zydeco; free, though food costs apply

LOUISIANA SEAFOOD FESTIVAL

During the first weekend of September, foodies flock to the Louisiana Seafood Festival, where you can sample charbroiled oysters, blackened alligator tacos, fried shrimp po-boys, and other regional delicacies. This free, three-day event also features live music, cooking demonstrations, book signings, a beer garden, a kids' tent, and an arts-and-crafts market.

TREMÉ AND MID-CITY: City Park, 504/957-7241, http://louisianaseafoodfestival.com; free, though food costs apply

NEW ORLEANS BURLESQUE FESTIVAL

In a city known as the birthplace of jazz, where a legal red-light district once thrived, and which once had the largest concentration of burlesque clubs in the country, it's no surprise that burlesque shows are once again popular. In mid-September, an entire four-day event dedicated to this sexy, glamorous, and comedic art descends upon the city. Founded in 2009, the annual New Orleans Burlesque Festival features parties and performances in various locations, plus the main event: a competition in which the world's finest burlesque dancers vie for the Queen of Burlesque title. Indeed, a sight worth seeing.

VARIOUS LOCATIONS: 504/975-7425, http://neworleansburlesquefest.com; hours and costs vary

★ SATCHMO SUMMERFEST

New Orleans celebrates the legacy of one of its most famous sons in early August with Satchmo SummerFest, a popular, three-day event that's organized by the same folks behind the equally popular French Quarter Festival. This festival, which mainly takes place on the well-manicured grounds of The Old U.S. Mint, includes live music by brass, swing, and early jazz bands, plus free dance lessons and an assortment of local cuisine. At other locations throughout the Quarter, you can experience seminars and exhibits about Louis "Satchmo" Armstrong and his era. During the festival, make time for the special jazz Mass at the St. Augustine Church, followed by a traditional second-line parade.

FRENCH QUARTER: The Old U.S. Mint, 400 Esplanade Ave., 504/522-5730 or 800/673-5725, http://fqfi.org/satchmosummerfest; $5 adult, free under 13, plus food and seminar costs apply

★ SOUTHERN DECADENCE

Every Labor Day weekend, the French Quarter and the Faubourg Marigny are flooded with eager participants and onlookers of Southern Decadence, an annual Mardi Gras-like festival that's been celebrating the city's gay lifestyle, music, and culture since 1972. Held at various gay-friendly venues, from Rawhide 2010 to Bourbon Pub & Parade, the six-day event includes dance and pool parties, beefcake contests, singles' mixers, drag shows, and a leather-gear block party. It's one of the wildest and most popular gay-and-lesbian celebrations in the country.

VARIOUS LOCATIONS: www.southerndecadence.com; hours and costs vary

TALES OF THE COCKTAIL

Given that the Big Easy is known as a late-night party town, it's only apt that it would be home to the annual Tales of the Cocktail. Started in 2003 and usually occurring in mid- or late July, this five-day event lures a slew of mixologists, authors, bartenders, chefs, and cocktail enthusiasts with its impressive lineup of seminars, dinners, competitions, and tasting rooms. Activities take place in a variety of locations, from the French Quarter's historic Hotel Monteleone to the Harrah's casino in the CBD.

VARIOUS LOCATIONS: 504/948-0511, http://talesofthecocktail.com; hours and costs vary

Halloween in the Crescent City

Randy Jackson of Zebra performs at the New Orleans Vampire Ball.

New Orleans is a wildly popular place for All Hallows' Eve. People venture here to visit the many voodoo shops and cemeteries, take a haunted walking tour of the French Quarter, and mingle with hordes of costumed revelers along Bourbon and Frenchmen Streets. Locals and visitors alike flock to seasonal attractions like **The Mortuary Haunted House** (www.themortuary.net), set inside a former mortuary that's supposedly haunted.

Many horror aficionados also appreciate the city's longtime vampire connection. The principal setting for Anne Rice's famous novel *Interview with the Vampire,* New Orleans is home to two annual vampire balls: the **New Orleans Vampire Ball,** sponsored by Anne Rice's Vampire Lestat Fan Club (www.arvlfc.com), and the **Endless Night Vampire Ball** (www.endlessnight.com). Vampire tours, which are available through **Haunted History Tours** (www.hauntedhistorytours.com) and **Bloody Mary's New Orleans Tours** (www.bloodymarystours.com), are also popular.

For less bloodthirsty revelry, purchase a ticket to the **New Orleans Witches' Ball,** hosted by the **New Orleans Black Hat Society** (www.nobhs.org), or take a walking ghost tour through **Historic New Orleans Tours** (www.tourneworleans.com) or **Spirit Tours New Orleans** (www.neworleanstours.net).

In a town known for gay-friendly bashes like Southern Decadence, it's no surprise that there's also a gay-friendly Halloween celebration. Simply known as **Halloween in New Orleans** (www.gayhalloween.com), this weekend-long bash has evolved from a small gathering in 1984 into one of the biggest gay-and-lesbian parties in the country. If you're looking for well-dressed drag queens, this is definitely the time to visit the Big Easy.

New Orleans also hosts family-friendly events like Audubon Zoo's **Boo at the Zoo** (www.auduboninstitute.org/boo-zoo), which usually occurs during the last two weekends of October and features trick-or-treat fun, a ghost train, and a haunted house. On Halloween itself, Molly's at the Market presents **Jim Monaghan's Halloween Parade** (www.mollysatthemarket.net/halloween), a spirited procession through the French Quarter. Since 2007, however, the **Krewe of Boo!** (www.kreweofboo.com) has been the city's official Halloween parade, typically entailing a downtown procession of colorful, mildly scary floats created by Kern Studios.

New Orleans is predominantly Catholic, which means that **All Saints' Day** (Nov. 1) and **All Souls' Day** (Nov. 2) are fairly important holidays—a time when many residents make a point of visiting their loved ones at cemeteries. Simultaneously, lots of locals celebrate the Mexican holiday of **Día de los Muertos** by dressing in black, painting skulls on their faces, and congregating in front of the St. Louis Cathedral—truly a sight to behold.

CRESCENT CITY BLUES AND BBQ FESTIVAL

The Crescent City Blues and BBQ Festival brings together two of my favorite things: Southern-style soul and blues music and delicious, finger-lickin' barbecue. Head to the CBD's picturesque Lafayette Square for this three-day, mid-October event, where you can savor a pulled-pork sandwich while grooving to the likes of Tab Benoit, Marcia Ball, and Kenny Wayne Shepherd. This often crowded event features two stages, roughly a dozen food vendors, a regional crafts fair, an Abita-sponsored sports bar, secured bike parking, and, in nearby Gallier Hall, an oral history stage that presents live, free-to-attend interviews of participating musicians.

CENTRAL BUSINESS AND ARTS DISTRICTS: Lafayette Square, 540 St. Charles Ave., 504/558-6100, www.jazzandheritage.org/blues-fest; free, though food costs apply

GRETNA HERITAGE FESTIVAL

In early October, thousands of revelers cross the Mississippi for Gretna's Heritage Festival, a three-day event presenting live performances by local and international jazz, country, rock, blues, soul, Latino, and Cajun musicians on six different stages. Previous performers have included Cowboy Mouth, the Iguanas, and Amanda Shaw & the Cute Guys. In addition to events at the downtown German Heritage Center, this family-friendly festival features a German beer garden, an Italian village, carnival-style rides and games, and a multiethnic food court. Tickets are usually cheaper online; if you plan to stay the whole weekend, consider purchasing the $47.50 weekend pass or the $350 VIP Package.

GREATER NEW ORLEANS: Downtown Gretna, 504/361-7748, www.gretnafest.com; $20-25 pp, free under 13

NEW ORLEANS FILM FESTIVAL

Established in 1989, the nonprofit New Orleans Film Society (NOFS) presents several annual events favored by local cinephiles. In early March, NOFS hosts the free **New Orleans International Children's Film Festival** at the Main Branch of the New Orleans Public Library. At Uptown's Prytania Theatre, meanwhile, NOFS presents **filmOrama,** a weeklong, late May showcase of foreign, local, and independent films—including recent flicks like *13 Assassins, Hobo with a Shotgun,* and *Grey Gardens*—as well as the **French Film Festival** in early August. The pinnacle of NOFS programming is the New Orleans Film Festival (NOFF), a popular mid-October event that has honored independent cinema for more than two decades. In fact, one of NOFF's earliest winners was *Hated* (1994), a well-received documentary by first-time director Todd Phillips, who has since directed such comedic hits as *Old School* (2003) and *The Hangover* (2009). The weeklong event

Above: the Crescent City Blues and BBQ Festival. **Below:** a shrimp rémoulade and fried green tomato po-boy at the Oak Street Po-Boy Festival.

usually takes place in multiple venues throughout the city, including the Prytania and the CAC.

VARIOUS LOCATIONS: 504/309-6633, www.neworleansfilmsociety.org; hours and costs vary

NEW ORLEANS FRINGE FESTIVAL

Boasting more than 80 fresh, weird, wild, and cutting-edge performances in venues all around the city, Fringe Fest does much to entertain and educate a wide array of theater lovers over the course of a couple of weeks in November. With a motto that promises "fearless performers" and "fearless audiences," it's no wonder that New Orleanians, especially young, artistic types, eagerly anticipate this festival every year.

VARIOUS LOCATIONS: www.nofringe.org; hours and costs vary

★ OAK STREET PO-BOY FESTIVAL

Though relatively new on the Big Easy's foodie scene, the Oak Street Po-Boy Festival has quickly become a much-anticipated event every fall. For one day in late November, residents and out-of-towners converge at the intersection of Oak Street and South Carrollton Avenue in Uptown's Riverbend area for this mouthwatering event. Besides listening to a slew of live music, attendees can peruse arts and crafts, learn about the history of the po-boy, and, of course, sample a variety of local cuisine from more than 40 restaurants. You'll have the chance to taste an assortment of po-boys, including a shrimp rémoulade po-boy, which is especially tasty if served with fried green tomatoes.

UPTOWN: Oak St. and S. Carrollton Ave., www.poboyfest.com; free, though food costs apply

VOODOO MUSIC + ARTS EXPERIENCE

Halloween weekend is usually a busy time of year in New Orleans. Besides vampire balls and impromptu parades, the city has long been host to the three-day Voodoo Music + Arts Experience, a boisterous City Park event that features art installations as well as live musical performances. Past performers have dramatically ranged from Soundgarden and Snoop Dogg to Beausoleil and Dr. John. Tickets are offered as general admission ($125 per weekend) or Loa VIP ($350 per weekend), the latter of which includes express entrance onto the festival grounds, free massages and hot shaves, food and drink specials, full bar services, and exclusive access to the Loa Lounge, air-conditioned restrooms, and reserved viewing areas, among other amenities. Though tickets might be available on-site, be prepared for sold-out crowds. For ticketing questions, contact **Elevate** (877/569-7767).

TREMÉ AND MID-CITY: City Park, 1 Palm Dr., http://worshipthemusic.com; $125-350 pp for weekend, child under 10 free

WORDS & MUSIC, A LITERARY FEAST IN NEW ORLEANS

New Orleans has inspired many well-known American writers, including William Faulkner (1897-1962), who, while occupying a building in Pirate's Alley, wrote his first novel, *Soldiers' Pay* (1926). Today, the Pirate's Alley Faulkner Society, founded in 1990 and based in the novelist's old haunt, now known as the Faulkner House, celebrates this Nobel Laureate with this multi-arts festival, which usually occurs in October or November. Normally based at the Hotel Monteleone, the Words & Music festival features writing seminars and workshops, book signings and readings, live concerts and performances, agent and editor consultations, cocktail parties, literary discussions, and, of course, writing competitions. In conjunction with the festival, the Faulkner Society also produces *The Double Dealer,* an annual literary journal established in 1993 as an homage to the original *Double Dealer,* which existed in the 1920s and featured the early work of William Faulkner, Ernest Hemingway, and Sherwood Anderson.

FRENCH QUARTER: Hotel Monteleone, 214 Royal St., http://wordsandmusic.org; hours and costs vary

Winter

In addition to Mardi Gras, which typically occurs in February or early March, the Big Easy boasts several other wintertime events that are worth planning a trip around.

ALLSTATE SUGAR BOWL

The Mercedes-Benz Superdome is the site of one of the most beloved college football games, the Allstate Sugar Bowl. Typically, it's played in early January between two of the nation's top collegiate teams. In addition to the Sugar Bowl, there's usually an Allstate Fan Fest, a free music event that takes place in the parking lot beside Jax Brewery; past performers have included Blues Traveler, the Gin Blossoms, and Trombone Shorty. It's nearly impossible to find a hotel room in New Orleans when this event comes to town, so plan well ahead if you wish to attend.

CENTRAL BUSINESS AND ARTS DISTRICTS: Mercedes-Benz Superdome, 1500 Sugar Bowl Dr., 504/828-2440, www.allstatesugarbowl.org; hours and costs vary

★ CELEBRATION IN THE OAKS

From late November through early January, City Park comes alive for Celebration in the Oaks, a fabulous holiday light show that draws more than 165,000 visitors annually. Sights include a lighted tableau inspired by the beloved children's tale *Cajun Night Before Christmas,* a 20-foot-tall poinsettia Christmas tree in the botanical garden, and the fancifully illumined Storyland and Carousel Gardens. You can drive through the park, walk the two-mile route, or see it via a quaint train ride ($5 pp). This magical trip through the largest live-oak forest in the world is not to be missed

Christmas New Orleans Style

Christmastime is simply huge in New Orleans, celebrated with great fanfare as befits a city that loves to have fun and clings dearly to long-held traditions. Known as "Christmas New Orleans Style," our celebration entails a variety of events and activities throughout the month of December. Besides City Park's dazzling **Celebration in the Oaks,** there are jazz, gospel, and choral concerts held at **St. Louis Cathedral** and a variety of clubs, including **Preservation Hall. Jackson Square** plays host to public Christmas caroling, usually a free event that occurs on the Sunday prior to Christmas. Historic buildings throughout the French Quarter and Garden District, not to mention plantations along the Great River Road, are gussied up with Christmas lights and decorations. Revelers can enjoy a variety of seasonal walking tours, including the **Candlelight Tour of Historic Homes and Landmarks,** held in mid-December and often including such attractions as the Beauregard-Keyes House, the Old Ursuline Convent, the 1850 House, the Gallier Historic House, and The Historic New Orleans Collection.

Beyond the moderate weather, Hanukkah celebrations, and New Year's Eve fireworks extravaganza, December is also an excellent time for foodies. After all, this is the season of ***réveillon,*** an ancient Creole and Catholic celebratory feast dating to the 1830s. Although it was originally held on Christmas Eve and New Year's Eve, *réveillon* now happens throughout the month of December and is celebrated by everyone, regardless of religious affiliation.

Still, for many people, the most special *réveillon* dinners are held on Christmas Eve or New Year's Eve. The Christmas meal, typically the more restrained of the two eves, was traditionally held after midnight Mass at St. Louis Cathedral. Families would return home and spend time together sharing a fairly austere meal of egg dishes, sweetbreads, and a rum cake. The New Year's Eve feast consists of elaborate desserts, plenty of whiskey and wine, and lots of laughing, singing, and dancing.

a home gussied up for the holidays

Dozens of restaurants in New Orleans offer special *réveillon* menus in December. These are prix-fixe menus, usually four or five courses, and many establishments offer *réveillon* on Christmas Eve, Christmas Day, New Year's Eve, and New Year's Day, although you should reserve well ahead for these dates. Favorite venues for this celebration include **Galatoire's Restaurant, Antoine's Restaurant, Commander's Palace, Tujague's, Rib Room, Muriel's Jackson Square,** and the **Gumbo Shop.**

At traditional Tujague's, the choices are limited and the menu straightforward: shrimp rémoulade, a soup of the day, boiled beef brisket with tomato-horseradish sauce, a handful of entrée choices such as braised lamb shanks in a Creole stew, bread pudding, and chicory-laced coffee. More cutting-edge places around town have fancier and more unusual offerings.

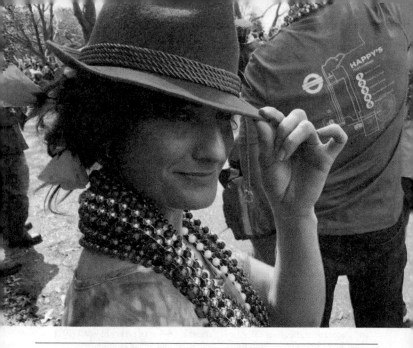

Above: a visitor enjoying the St. Patrick's Day Parade. **Below:** Mardi Gras Indians typically emerge on Super Sunday.

during the holidays. Be sure to take advantage of the live music and inexpensive refreshments as well.

TREMÉ AND MID-CITY: City Park, 1 Palm Dr., http://neworleanscitypark.com/celebration-in-the-oaks; $8 pp, free under 3

SOUL FEST

In early March, the Audubon Zoo hosts the family-friendly Soul Fest, a terrific excuse to visit this historic zoological park (especially if the weather is mild and more appealing to the animals). Happily, the two-day festival is included with the zoo's daily general admission cost, so you won't pay any extra for the event. Soul Fest celebrates the state's African American culture and heritage with handmade arts and crafts, authentic soul food, and live jazz, gospel, and rhythm and blues.

UPTOWN: Audubon Zoo, 6500 Magazine St., 504/861-2537 or 800/774-7394, www.audubonistitute.org; Mon.-Fri. 10am-5pm, Sat.-Sun. 10am-6pm; $19 adult, $15 senior 65 and over, $14 child 2-12, free under 2

★ ST. JOSEPH'S DAY

Introduced to New Orleans during the 19th century by its many Sicilian immigrants, St. Joseph's Day is still celebrated with great ardor in the city's Italian American community. The observance of this feast on March 19 traces back to the Middle Ages, when people built altars to St. Joseph, who they believed had answered their prayers and delivered them from famine. Modern participants continue to celebrate by constructing elaborate and riotously colorful altars in their homes and churches. Besides a public parade in the French Quarter, smaller celebrations take place in private homes; signs welcome friends and strangers alike to view family altars and enjoy cakes and breads. Oddly enough, the Italian holiday has also become significant for the city's Mardi Gras Indians, an African American troupe of Carnival revelers who usually host a vibrant parade on **Super Sunday,** the Sunday preceding or following St. Joseph's Day.

VARIOUS LOCATIONS: www.mardigrasneworleans.com/supersunday.html; hours vary; free

ST. PATRICK'S DAY PARADE

New Orleans has a large contingent of Irish Americans. St. Patrick's Day is a significant holiday here, and Irish establishments throughout the city—including The Kerry Irish Pub in the French Quarter—hold lively parties on St. Paddy's Day (traditionally Mar. 17). Molly's at the Market hosts its own music-filled St. Patrick's Day Parade within a week of the actual holiday, but the city's biggest annual parade by far usually rolls down Magazine Street and St. Charles Avenue, with large Mardi Gras-style floats, oodles of marchers, and plenty of green beads and doubloons. No matter which parade you choose to attend, wear something green or risk many a stranger's pinch!

VARIOUS LOCATIONS: hours vary; free

Sights

With a fascinating history that involves pirates and prostitutes, soldiers and slave owners, voodoo queens and vampire lore, New Orleans has lured curious outsiders for decades.

Families come for kid-friendly places like the Audubon Aquarium of the Americas, Blaine Kern's Mardi Gras World, and the Audubon Zoo. Art lovers flock to the Degas House and the New Orleans Museum of Art, and outdoor enthusiasts appreciate oases like City Park. But it's history buffs who are particularly enamored with the Big Easy.Besides engrossing exhibits at The National WWII Museum, the Crescent City—and especially the French Quarter—boasts an array of historic structures. The city's original neighborhood was laid out in 1722 and suffered various fires and regime shifts before becoming the well-favored heart of New Orleans that it is today. Most visitors venture to Jackson Square, the bustling sanctuary on Decatur Street, bounded by classic wrought-iron fencing and surrounded by several noteworthy buildings. Not far from here, the charming Hermann-Grima Historic House Museum awaits, as does the magnificent Old U.S. Mint and the assorted structures known as The Historic New Orleans Collection.

History buffs also find plenty to love beyond the Quarter, from the distinctive homes of the Faubourg Marigny and Garden District to the crumbling cemeteries in the Tremé and Mid-City neighborhoods. In a city defined—for both good and bad—by water, many natives enjoy simply wandering through Woldenberg Riverfront Park alongside the Mississippi River.

Naturally, you might think about the negative aspects of water at such times—namely, the damage and floods of Hurricane Katrina. While that destruction is still evident in places like Lakeview, Mid-City, the Ninth Ward, and New Orleans East, New Orleans has experienced a renaissance since 2005, and this fast-growing city is now brimming with refurbished attractions, brand-new establishments, and re-energized residents.

Previous: a picturesque lagoon in the sculpture garden at the New Orleans Museum of Art; Jackson Square.

Look for ★ to find recommended sights.

Highlights

★ **Best Place to Take the Kids:** Overlooking the Mississippi River, the spectacular **Audubon Aquarium of the Americas** delights youngsters as much as adults. It presents fascinating exhibits about aquatic habitats around the world, from the Amazonian rain forest to the Gulf of Mexico (page 65).

★ **Finest Glimpse of History:** Situated on Royal Street, **The Historic New Orleans Collection** encompasses several notable structures, from a Creole cottage to the Greek Revival-style Merieult House (page 71).

★ **Most Iconic Landmark:** The historic heart and soul of the French Quarter—and, by extension, New Orleans—is verdant **Jackson Square.** It's a scenic spot for a picnic, and the perfect place to get your bearings before exploring the Big Easy (page 72).

★ **Tastiest Spot for Culinary Enthusiasts:** If you're interested in learning how to prepare gumbo, shrimp Creole, and other local staples, head to **The New Orleans School of Cooking** in the French Quarter (page 78).

★ **Most Colorful Attraction:** At the world-renowned **Blaine Kern's Mardi Gras World,** you can stroll amid kaleidoscopic floats, observe the artists at work, and learn about the history of the Carnival season (page 85).

★ **Most Patriotic Locale:** No matter your perspective on the necessity of war, you'll find it hard not to be impressed by **The National WWII Museum,** where you can watch an immersive documentary about America's "greatest generation," have an old-fashioned dining experience in the Stage Door Canteen, and peruse a wealth of exhibits (page 87).

★ **Best Place for Animal Lovers:** Visit the **Audubon Zoo,** where you can watch elephant and sea lion shows, observe the antics of primates and jaguars, and experience a Louisiana swamp (page 94).

★ **Most Enchanting Stroll:** A 1,300-acre swath of greenery, **City Park** is an excellent place for walking across picturesque bridges, amid moss-covered oak trees, and through the park's New Orleans Botanical Garden (page 99).

★ **Best Sculpture Collection:** In addition to showcasing a marvelous array of French, American, African, and Japanese artwork, the **New Orleans Museum of Art** features a picturesque five-acre sculpture garden with winding paths, pedestrian bridges, and scenic lagoons (page 104).

★ **Best Attraction Off the Beaten Path:** Not far from the city's border with Metairie lies the area's most underrated historic site, the **Longue Vue House & Gardens,** a lush oasis featuring a Classical Revival-style mansion that once belonged to local community pillars Edgar and Edith Stern (page 112).

Despite the round-the-clock presence of bicycles and cars, the French Quarter is a pedestrian-friendly neighborhood with a deliciously contradictory nature. At once marked by traditional European architecture, lush Caribbean-style courtyards, high-end art galleries, Bohemian shops, traditional jazz clubs, and rowdy karaoke bars, this eclectic historic district appeals to tourists and residents alike. Simply walking amid the old-fashioned gas lamps constitutes a sight in itself—albeit a tantalizing, multisensory one. While strolling along the cracked, ankle-spraining sidewalks, enjoy the varied street musicians, the clip-clop of passing carriages, and an air often scented with the mingled perfume of sweet olive trees, chicory-laced coffee, boiled seafood, and, yes, mule manure.

★ AUDUBON AQUARIUM OF THE AMERICAS

Established in 1990 by the Audubon Nature Institute—the same folks who operate the historic Audubon Zoo—the Audubon Aquarium of the Americas is one of the most popular tourist destinations in downtown New Orleans. Situated at the southern end of 16-acre Woldenberg Riverfront Park, alongside the Mississippi River, this contemporary glass-and-brick building houses several intriguing exhibits, most notably the 400,000-gallon Gulf of Mexico habitat, which features a variety of sharks, stingrays, and other saltwater creatures amid the barnacled pilings of an offshore oil rig replica. Kids especially favor this family-friendly attraction, where they can touch cownose rays, climb above an Amazonian rain forest, and, via an underwater glass tunnel, stroll through the moray eels and tropical fish of a Caribbean coral reef.

Visitors to this exceptional, two-story aquarium will observe a wide array of aquatic and amphibious creatures—not to mention Spots, the unusual white alligator who lives in the Mississippi River gallery. There are also two gift shops on the premises. Adjacent to the aquarium is the **Entergy IMAX Theatre** (504/581-4629; daily 10am-5pm; $10.50 adult, $9.50 senior 65 and over, $8 child 2-12, free under 2), which typically showcases vibrant 3D nature documentaries. Typically, the last ticket is sold an hour before closing. Discounted self-parking is available whether you have your ticket validated at the aquarium or the IMAX theater, and it's possible to save money by purchasing a combo ticket for both attractions ($29 adult, $23 senior 65 and over and child 2-12, free under 2). Note that the aquarium is closed most Mondays in fall, winter, and spring.

MAP 1: 1 Canal St., 504/565-3033 or 800/774-7394, www.auduboninstitute.org; daily 10am-5pm; $24 adult, $19 senior 65 and over, $18 child 2-12, free under 2

AUDUBON BUTTERFLY GARDEN AND INSECTARIUM

Part of the stately U.S. Custom House, a 30,000-square-foot intimidating gray structure that occupies an entire block, is home to the Audubon Butterfly Garden and Insectarium, which contains the largest freestanding

Big Easy Bargains

Admission fees in New Orleans can add up quickly, but money-saving tricks do exist, particularly in the form of combination packages. If you're planning to visit the **Audubon Zoo, Audubon Butterfly Garden and Insectarium, Audubon Aquarium of the Americas,** and **Entergy IMAX Theatre,** consider the **Audubon Experience Package** (www.audubоninstitute.org; $42 adult, $30 senior 65 and over and child 2-12), which can save you $22-28 per person. The package (valid for 30 consecutive days) includes one visit to each facility. The ultimate combination ticket is the five-day **New Orleans Power Pass** (www.visiticket.com, $136 adult, $98 child), which provides access to nearly 30 tours, attractions, and other diversions throughout the Crescent City and beyond, from **Blaine Kern's Mardi Gras World** to the **Oak Alley Plantation.**

Not far from the Aquarium and the Insectarium, pedestrians can enjoy an inexpensive trip across the Mississippi River via the **Algiers Point/Canal Street Ferry** (http://nolaferries.com; $2 adult, $1 senior 65 and over, free under 3), which transports you between the foot of Canal Street and historic Algiers Point. A cheap ride on the **St. Charles Streetcar** (www.norta.com; $1.25 adult and child, $0.40 senior 65 and over, free under 3) will show you some of the gorgeous mansions, not to mention two historic universities, that line this verdant Uptown thoroughfare.

In the French Quarter, the **Louisiana State Museum** (www.louisianastatemuseum.org) operates several historic properties, including the **Old U.S. Mint** and **Madame John's Legacy** (both free), as well as the **Cabildo,** the **Presbytère,** and the **1850 House** (all of which surround Jackson Square, charge nominal $2-6 admission fees, and offer free entry to children under 13). Additionally, you'll receive a 20 percent discount if you purchase tickets for two or more of the Jackson Square museums. Combined admission to the **Hermann-Grima Historic House Museum** (www.hgghh.org) and the **Gallier Historic House Museum** ($25 adult, $20 senior, student, child, and military personnel) saves you up to $5 per person.

At **The National WWII Museum** (www.nationalww2museum.org) in the city's Arts District, admission isn't cheap ($23 adult, $20 senior 65 and over,

collection of insects in the United States—about 900,000 species in all. Visitors have the opportunity to touch all kinds of creatures, although many others (like the despised cockroaches) are presented through clever displays from a safe distance. Even the museum's Tiny Termite Café has an insect-themed appearance—and the glass-topped tables are actually terrariums, so you might find yourself eating directly over a live tarantula. The museum's bug-cooking demonstration "café," Bug Appétit, illustrates how people around the world routinely snack on insects as an excellent source of protein. Less harrowing for squeamish visitors is the massive butterfly room set within a Japanese-style garden. The Audubon Butterfly Garden and Insectarium is closed most Mondays in fall, winter, and spring.

MAP 1: 423 Canal St., 504/524-2847 or 800/774-7394, www.auduboninstitute.org; daily 10am-5pm; $17 adult, $14 senior 65 and over, $12 child 2-12, free under 2

$14 student and military personnel), but given the museum's size and comprehensive nature, you might wish to return the following day, which you can happily do for an additional $6 per person.

Consider a combo package that covers the Audubon Butterfly Garden and Insectarium.

Naturally, New Orleans has plenty of free attractions as well. It costs nothing to visit the various local units of **Jean Lafitte National Historical Park and Preserve** (www.nps.gov/jela), which includes the **French Quarter Visitor Center** on Decatur Street and the **Chalmette Battlefield** east of the city. The city's two largest urban parks—Uptown's **Audubon Park** and Mid-City's **City Park**—are also free to explore. Within City Park, the **New Orleans Museum of Art** (www.noma.org) offers free admission for Louisiana residents every Wednesday, and the adjacent **Sydney and Walda Besthoff Sculpture Garden** is always free to the public.

Remember, too, that New Orleans itself is a bargain-friendly sight. It's absolutely free to stroll the streets of the **French Quarter,** absorbing all the historic architecture, hidden gardens, and sheer vibrancy of the city's oldest neighborhood. Although some of the historic sites charge entrance fees, other attractions—such as **Jackson Square,** the **St. Louis Cathedral,** the **French Market,** the **New Orleans Musical Legends Park,** and the art-filled windows along **Royal Street**—cost nothing. An enjoyable walk along the riverfront, from the **Moonwalk** to **Woldenberg Riverfront Park** is also delightfully free. Naturally, it's also free to explore the city's public plazas and historic churches, not to mention some of its legendary cemeteries.

THE BEAUREGARD-KEYES HOUSE AND GARDEN MUSEUM

Opposite the Old Ursuline Convent stands the Beauregard-Keyes House, one of relatively few raised cottages in the French Quarter; the entrance and main floor are one level above the street. After the Civil War, the handsome mansion, which was finished in 1826, became the home of the Confederate general P. G. T. Beauregard. Over the years that followed, the house had a number of owners, and by the mid-1920s, it was nearly slated for demolition before a group of women, aware that Beauregard had lived here after the Civil War, began a campaign to save it. In 1944, novelist Frances Parkinson Keyes (pronounced "KIZE") took possession of the house and hired a firm to restore it. She lived here until 1969 and wrote several of her 50-odd books here. Today, her extensive collections of antique dolls, fans, and folk costumes are on display, and some of her books are available in the on-site gift shop.

One of the lead attractions is the formal garden, laid out by the wife of Switzerland's consul to New Orleans, who owned the house in the 1830s. From beyond the outer wall, you can see the parterre garden through brick "windows" fashioned with iron grills. A stroll through this lovely space is included in any of the guided, 45-minute house tours, which depart every hour on the hour. Roses, daylilies, crape myrtle, azaleas, sweet olive trees, irises, magnolia trees, and evergreen shrubs blend and bloom in one of the Quarter's loveliest gardens.

MAP 1: 1113 Chartres St., 504/523-7257, www.bkhouse.org; Mon.-Sat. 10am-3pm; $10 adult, $9 senior and student, $4 child 6-12, free under 6 and military

THE CABILDO

On the upriver side of the St. Louis Cathedral stands the Cabildo, the building in which the formal transfer of Louisiana to the United States took place after the Louisiana Purchase. The Spanish first constructed the Cabildo as their seat of government in the 1770s, but it and its replacement were destroyed during both major city fires in the late 18th century. The current structure, made of brick and stucco and built in the Spanish style with Moorish influences, was erected in 1794, serving again as home to the Spanish administrative body, after which it became the Maison de Ville (Town Hall) during the very brief time the French reclaimed New Orleans. It served as the Louisiana Supreme Court headquarters for much of the 19th and early 20th centuries, and it was actually the site where the landmark *Plessy v. Ferguson* decision (which legalized segregation) originated in 1892. Many prominent visitors have been officially received in the Cabildo, from the Marquis de Lafayette to Mark Twain. The building looks more French than Spanish today, because the original flat-tile roof was replaced with a Second Empire mansard roof in the late 1840s.

Part of the Louisiana State Museum since 1908, the Cabildo contains a fascinating exhibit tracing the history of Louisiana through the past two centuries, beginning with the region's Native Americans and ending with Reconstruction. Each section uses maps, photographs, drawings, historical documents, and narrative signs to describe the period and theme. The museum is closed on state holidays.

MAP 1: 701 Chartres St., 504/568-6968 or 800/568-6968, www.louisianastatemuseum.org; Tues.-Sun. 10am-4:30pm; $6 adult, $5 senior, student, and military, free under 13

FRENCH MARKET

One of the city's most famous attractions, the French Market is a picturesque, multi-block collection of shops, eateries, and stalls that's part of the slightly larger French Market District. Legend has it that this site stood as a Choctaw trading post long before the Spanish established an early market here in 1791. Parts of the current structure date to 1813. Originally, the stalls contained only a meat market, but subsequent structures were added all along North Peters Street throughout the 19th century, housing markets of fresh produce, flowers, and spices. Coffee stands were opened at opposite ends of the stalls, and one remains to this day—the delightful **Café Du Monde** (www.cafedumonde.com).

The **farmers market,** a covered, open-air market building, is fun for any gourmand. Besides a few other eateries, which often host live music, the market also contains retail and crafts shops, which sell everything from local artwork to Latin American hammocks. A small shaded seating area, **Latrobe Waterworks Park,** is a peaceful spot to munch on the edibles you might have purchased. In addition, the French Market District encompasses **Washington Artillery Park,** a **Joan of Arc statue,** the art-filled **Dutch Alley,** and the **New Orleans Jazz National Historical Park Visitor Center.** Beyond these sites, you might also enjoy visiting the French Market during annual events like the Creole Tomato Festival in early June.

MAP 1: Decatur St. and N. Peters St. btwn. St. Peter St. and Barracks St., 504/522-2621, www.frenchmarket.org; hours vary depending on the business; free, though dining and shopping costs apply

THE GALLIER HISTORIC HOUSE MUSEUM

On the riverside of Royal Street stands the Gallier House, part of a museum that also includes the Hermann-Grima House on St. Louis Street. The former home of famed New Orleans architect James Gallier Jr., who designed the house in 1857, it's filled with exquisite furnishings from the 19th century, plus elaborate faux marble and faux bois (wood painted very carefully to resemble a more precious type of wood). Considered one of the more accurately restored landmarks in New Orleans, the two-story stucco facade is noted for its ornate balustrade balcony and slender, finely crafted columns. The 45-minute guided tour, which is available on the hour, includes a look at the Victorian home, the on-site carriageway, the carefully restored slave quarters, and a finely maintained garden, which sparkles with fountains and slate walks. Note that the last tour of the day starts an hour before closing time.

MAP 1: 1132 Royal St., 504/525-5661, www.hgghh.org; Mon.-Tues. and Thurs.-Fri. 10am-3pm, Wed. by appt., Sat. noon-3pm; $15 adult, $12 senior, military, student, and child

THE HERMANN-GRIMA HISTORIC HOUSE MUSEUM

Just off rowdy Bourbon Street, you'll encounter one of the Quarter's best house-museums: the Hermann-Grima House, a steep-roofed Federal-style mansion built in 1831 and resembling the sort of home you'd more often see in Savannah or other old cities of British origin. One unusual feature is the Quarter's only horse stable, adjacent to the charming courtyard garden. The house, which is run by the same folks who operate the Gallier House on Royal Street, offers informative, on-the-hour tours that reveal the customary lifestyle enjoyed by prosperous Creole families between 1830 and 1860. Note that the last tour of the day starts an hour before closing time.

For an even greater understanding of dining and entertaining traditions

Above: the Audubon Aquarium of the Americas. **Below:** the French Market's Latrobe Waterworks Park.

Romeo Spikes and Haint Blue Paint

New Orleans boasts a medley of architectural styles, ranging from Creole cottages in the French Quarter to Greek Revival-style plantation homes in the Garden District. As the city's oldest neighborhood, the Vieux Carré (French Quarter) boasts the lion's share of photogenic elements, including the upper-level galleries, wrought-iron railings, and hidden courtyards ironically influenced by the city's Spanish era. You'll also spot structures anachronistically known as **slave quarters,** smaller, often two-story houses situated behind street-facing mansions. You may also notice protective spikes, broken glass pieces, and other deterrents atop gates and fences. Particularly ominous are the **Romeo spikes** at the top of ground-floor gallery polls; relics of 19th-century New Orleans, these cast-iron protrusions were installed to prevent male suitors from making nighttime visits to young women. Throughout the city, you'll encounter curiosities like **haint blue** paint on the underside of porch ceilings, meant to repel evil spirits, or **shotgun houses,** one-level structures in which all rooms are positioned consecutively and interconnected by doors in lieu of a hallway.

menacing Romeo spikes

in 19th-century New Orleans, opt for an **open-hearth demonstration** (most Thursdays Oct.-May) in the restored, open-hearth kitchen (the only functional one left in the French Quarter, a holdover from the home's antebellum days). These demonstrations enable you to watch the museum's culinary experts as they prepare seasonal dishes by utilizing traditional techniques of 19th-century New Orleans. Afterward, be sure to stop by **The Exchange Shop** (in the former carriage house), which offers books as well as jewelry, ceramics, textiles, photographs, and paintings from female artists based in Louisiana and along the Gulf Coast.

MAP 1: 820 St. Louis St., 504/525-5661, www.hgghh.org; Mon.-Tues. and Thurs.-Fri. 10am-3pm, Wed. by appt., Sat. noon-3pm; $15 adult, $12 senior, military, student, and child

★ THE HISTORIC NEW ORLEANS COLLECTION

Amid the art galleries of Royal Street lies one of the city's most underrated attractions, The Historic New Orleans Collection (THNOC). Established in 1966 by avid collectors General L. Kemper Williams and his wife, Leila, this complex includes the Greek Revival-style **Merieult House.** Built in 1792, the house now contains the **Williams Gallery,** featuring rotating history exhibits, and the **Louisiana History Galleries,** 13 chambers that each explore a specific period of the state's history (from the French colonial years to the 20th century) by using authentic maps, books, furniture, and artwork.

From the courtyard, you'll notice a few other buildings, such as the Spanish colonial-style **Counting House** and the three-story **Maisonette,** which now contain administrative offices. One exception is the **Williams Residence,** an 1880s Italianate townhouse that the museum founders occupied until 1963. Docent-led tours (Tues.-Sat. 10am, 11am, 2pm, and 3pm, Sun. 11am, 2pm, and 3pm) enable you to view this room-by-room survey of how an upscale early 20th-century home would have been furnished, including several antiques, various watercolors, and vintage maps of New Orleans. You can also join a guided architectural tour of the buildings and courtyards that comprise the Royal Street complex. Note that the collection is closed on major holidays.

This impressive complex of interconnected buildings also includes three structures on Toulouse Street: a former banking house, a Creole cottage, and the two-story **Louis Adam House,** where Tennessee Williams once boarded. While here, you should also make time for the impressive museum shop in the Merieult House, where you'll find everything from local novels and history books to vintage maps and iconic jewelry. In addition, THNOC oversees the **Williams Research Center** (410 Chartres St., 504/598-7171; Tues.-Sat. 9:30am-4:30pm; free), a Beaux Arts-style brick structure containing an extensive library of roughly 35,000 documents and manuscripts, plus more than 300,000 photographs, drawings, prints, and paintings about the history of New Orleans.

MAP 1: 533 Royal St., 504/523-4662, www.hnoc.org; Tues.-Sat. 9:30am-4:30pm, Sun. 10:30am-4:30pm; free, though tours cost $5 pp

JACKSON BREWERY

On the riverside of Decatur, not far from Jackson Square, stands the regal Jackson Brewery building, once the largest independent brewery in the South. German architect Dietrich Einsiedel designed the fanciful structure, with its imposing central tower, in 1891. The brewery closed in the 1970s, and the four-story building, with expansive views of the river, has since been restored as **The Shops at Jax Brewery,** a collection of varied bars, restaurants, and shops, mainly selling clothing, jewelry, and artwork.

MAP 1: 600 Decatur St., 504/566-7245, http://jacksonbrewery.com; daily 10am-7pm; free, though dining and shopping costs apply

★ JACKSON SQUARE

Jackson Square was named in honor of the seventh U.S. president, Andrew Jackson, who led the United States to victory during the Battle of New Orleans. A 14-foot-tall bronze statue of Jackson serves as the square's centerpiece and ranks among the city's favorite photo ops.

Filled with trees, benches, and grassy areas, Jackson Square is a wonderful place to sit and read a newspaper, eat a muffuletta from one of the nearby cafés, and absorb the oldest section of New Orleans. (Note that no dogs or bikes are permitted; littering, soliciting, and feeding the birds are also illegal.) More often than not, you'll spy mimes, musicians, and other entertainers along the promenades that fringe Jackson Square, sometimes even after the park has closed at night. Horse-drawn carriages usually line the gated park alongside Decatur Street, awaiting tourists for guided excursions through the Quarter.

This picturesque green space is surrounded by several historic buildings, including the gorgeous **St. Louis Cathedral,** as well as the **Cabildo** and the **Presbytère.** Along the northeastern and southwestern sides of the square lie the lower and upper **Pontalba Buildings,** the oldest apartment buildings in the country. Here, you'll find the historic **1850 House** and, on the lower levels, several eateries and worthwhile shops, including food lovers' emporiums like Creole Delicacies and an outpost of the TABASCO Country Store.

MAP 1: Decatur St. and Chartres St. btwn. St. Peter St. and St. Ann St., 504/658-3200, www.experienceneworleans.com/jackson-square.html; daily 8am-7pm in summer, daily 8am-6pm in winter; free

JEAN LAFITTE NATIONAL HISTORICAL PARK AND PRESERVE

A couple of blocks upriver from Jackson Square is the main office of Jean Lafitte National Historical Park and Preserve, established in 1978 to preserve natural and historical resources and properties throughout the Mississippi River Valley. The park actually has six distinct units: this one, the **French Quarter Visitor Center;** two others in metro New Orleans (**Chalmette Battlefield and National Cemetery,** just east of the city, as well as **Barataria Preserve** on the West Bank); and three in Cajun Country (in Thibodaux, Lafayette, and Eunice) that deal in Cajun culture. Although the visitor center presents a film and several exhibits on various historical and cultural aspects of New Orleans, Louisiana, and the Mississippi River Delta, its best feature is its one-hour ranger-led walking tour along the riverfront, given at 9:30am Tuesday-Saturday. These free tours are limited to 25 people and can fill up quickly; availability is first come, first served. The center is closed on federal holidays as well as Mardi Gras Day.

On a small grassy island along Decatur Street, across from the park's visitor center, note the dignified statue of the man who first plotted New Orleans at the site of the present-day French Quarter, Jean Baptiste Le Moyne, Sieur de Bienville, brother of the explorer Pierre Le Moyne, Sieur d'Iberville. Jean Baptiste's decision in 1699 to establish a fortification on this miserable swampy spot raised the skepticism of many, but, of course, New Orleans has become one of the world's most charming (yet swampiest and, at times, hottest) cities.

MAP 1: 419 Decatur St., 504/589-2636 or 504/589-3882, www.nps.gov/jela; Tues.-Sat. 9am-4:30pm; free, though donations are accepted

An Architectural Driving Tour

For free, self-guided excursions of the city's most notable architectural areas, stop by the **Preservation Resource Center of New Orleans** (PRCNO, 923 Tchoupitoulas St., 504/581-7032, www.prcno.org; Mon.-Fri. 9am-5pm), where you can procure 20 different brochures, each of which features a background history, detailed map, and suggested walking tour of a particular neighborhood. You can also access and download these brochures by visiting the PRCNO website. For a fun cursory education of local architecture, take the following drive through this relatively compact city:

Tremé and Mid-City

Start in Mid-City at the **Pitot House** (1440 Moss St.), a Creole colonial country home beside Bayou St. John. Named for James Pitot, the first "American" mayor of New Orleans and the fourth owner of the house, the two-story plantation house was supposedly constructed in the 1790s by Don Bartólome Bosque, a Spanish colonial official. Curiously, the house was moved several blocks from its original site in the 1960s to prevent its demolition.

From here, head south on Esplanade Avenue for about a mile to the **Degas House** (2306 Esplanade Ave.). Built in 1852, during the original development of the Esplanade Ridge neighborhood, the restored home is the only former residence of famed French Impressionist Edgar Degas that's open to the public. The artist lived here briefly from 1872 to 1873. During his stay, he painted at least 22 works of art, including *A Cotton Office in New Orleans* (1873), which became the first Impressionist painting ever purchased by a museum.

French Quarter

Continue down Esplanade toward the French Quarter and turn southwest onto Decatur Street. Just past the famous Café Du Monde, you'll see **Jackson Square** (700 block of Decatur St.), a lovely park surrounded by several historic buildings, including the **Cabildo,** the **Presbytère,** and the **St. Louis Cathedral,** three side-by-side structures built in the Spanish style in the 1790s. Along the southwestern and northeastern edges of the park lie the lower and upper **Pontalba Buildings,** gorgeous, multi-tiered structures commissioned by Baroness Micaela Almonester de Pontalba in the mid-1850s and now considered the oldest apartment buildings in America.

Drive two blocks to St. Louis Street, turn right and head to Bourbon, where you'll turn right again and continue toward Governor Nicholls. At the corner of Governor Nicholls and Royal stand two local landmarks: the **LaLaurie Mansion** (1140 Royal St.), an imposing gray structure built in the 1830s and now believed to be one of the city's most haunted houses, and the **Gallier House** (1132 Royal St.), the former home of famed New Orleans architect James Gallier Jr., who designed the Victorian-style house in 1857. Today, the Gallier House is considered one of the most accurately restored landmarks in New Orleans, completed with an ornate balustrade balcony, slender columns, rear slave quarters, and a well-maintained garden. Curiously, Gallier's father, James Gallier Sr., was also a laudable architect, who, between 1845 and 1853, constructed the CBD's Gallier Hall (545 St. Charles Ave.), a white, Greek Revival-style building that served as the New Orleans City Hall from the mid-19th through mid-20th centuries.

From the Gallier House, head two blocks down Royal, turn left onto St. Phillip Street, then left onto Chartres Street, where you'll soon spot the expansive **Old Ursuline Convent** (1100 Chartres St.), constructed in 1745 and, as one of the few structures to have survived the Quarter's 18th-century fires, now considered the oldest existing building in the Mississippi River Valley. Across the street, take note of the **Beauregard-Keyes House** (1113 Chartres St.), one of relatively few raised cottages in the French Quarter. Completed in 1826, this gorgeous mansion became the post-Civil War home of the Confederate general P. G. T. Beauregard. Novelist Frances Parkinson Keyes lived here from 1944 to 1969, during which she wrote several of her most famous novels.

Central Business and Arts Districts

From this picturesque block, hop back onto Decatur, continue southwest to the CBD, and follow Magazine Street into the Arts District, where, near Lee Circle, stands **Confederate Memorial Hall** (929 Camp St.). Designed by Thomas O. Sully, one of the city's most distinguished architects, and opened in 1891, this Romanesque structure is the state's oldest continuously operating museum, dedicated to Southern military history and heritage.

Garden District

Take Magazine into the Garden District and veer onto Constance Street, where you'll encounter two regal churches: **St. Mary's Assumption Church** (2030 Constance St.) and **St. Alphonsus Church** (2025 Constance St.). Constructed between 1858 and 1866, St. Mary's is a massive, German Baroque Revival-style structure with an incredibly intricate facade, several arched stained-glass windows, and an interior distinguished by ornate columns, a vaulted ceiling, and a hand-carved altar reportedly imported from Munich. It was built for the German Catholic immigrants who arrived in this French-speaking area in the early 1840s. Nearby St. Alphonsus served the neighborhood's Irish parishioners.

You can't leave this area without heading to St. Charles Avenue, the oak-lined boulevard that features a number of memorable edifices, from the Garden District's Victorian-inspired **House of Broel** (2220 St. Charles Ave.) and Italianate-style **Van Benthuysen-Elms Mansion** (3029 St. Charles Ave.), both of which were erected in the mid- to late 19th century, to Uptown's **Tulane University** (6823 St. Charles Ave.), the campus that boasts a variety of architectural styles, including Romanesque, Italian Renaissance, and mid-century modern.

Greater New Orleans

To gaze at more beautiful buildings, take Broadway and Pine Streets to Washington Avenue, and head northwest toward the border between Orleans and Jefferson Parishes. That's where you'll find one of the city's least-visited hideaways, the **Longue Vue House & Gardens** (7 Bamboo Rd.), a lush eight-acre estate that once belonged to local community pillars Edgar and Edith Stern. Designed and built between 1939 and 1942 by architects William and Geoffrey Platt and landscape architect Ellen Biddle Shipman, the tranquil property was meant to be one organic whole, seamlessly uniting the Classical Revival-style manor house and its various ponds and gardens.

LALAURIE MANSION

This curious gray house is worth mentioning if only because of its dark history. Routinely included on the walking ghost tours offered in the French Quarter, this notoriously haunted mansion was once owned by the twice-widowed Madame Delphine Macarty de Lopez Blanque and her third husband, Dr. Louis LaLaurie. After moving into this home in 1832, the couple soon became the toast of the town, dazzling their peers with lavish parties. According to legend, when a fire broke out in the mansion in 1834, the neighbors made a horrifying discovery: several tortured, starving slaves chained in the attic. Apparently, the neighbors were further enraged to learn that some of Delphine's slaves had died under mysterious circumstances. To evade punishment, Delphine and her family fled to Europe, where she supposedly died several years later. Over the ensuing decades, the building has served as headquarters of the Union Army, a gambling house, and the home of Nicolas Cage. Through all of its incarnations, however, the LaLaurie Mansion has often been the source of ghostly tales.

MAP 1: 1140 Royal St.; closed to the public

MADAME JOHN'S LEGACY

Considered a fine example of a Louisiana French colonial-style (or Creole) home from the late 18th century, Madame John's Legacy was built to replace a home lost in the Great Fire of 1788. It survived the next, smaller fire of 1794 and is today one of just a few remaining pre-1800s buildings in the Quarter. The historic complex, which fronts Dumaine Street, comprises three buildings: a main house, a two-story *garçonniere,* and a kitchen with a cook's living quarters. Designated a National Historic Landmark and now part of the Louisiana State Museum, the home currently houses "The Palm, the Pine and the Cypress: Newcomb Pottery of New Orleans," an exhibit that features more than 50 glazed ceramics pieces, plus archival photographs that document the history of this much-loved local pottery. Note that the museum is closed on state holidays.

MAP 1: 632 Dumaine St., 504/568-6968 or 800/568-6968, www.louisianastatemuseum.org; Tues.-Sun. 10am-4:30pm; free

NEW ORLEANS JAZZ NATIONAL HISTORICAL PARK

While the official headquarters (419 Decatur St.; Tues.-Sat. 9am-4:30pm) of New Orleans Jazz National Historical Park are technically located at the same address as those of Jean Lafitte National Historical Park and Preserve, the visitor center is actually situated in the French Market District. Here, you can participate in weekly ranger-led programs, from lectures to musical demonstrations, that explore the origin, development, and evolution of New Orleans-style jazz. You can pick up brochures featuring an 11-stop tour of historic jazz sites in the Crescent City as well as the **Jazz Walk of Fame** in Algiers Point, a line of old-fashioned lampposts that highlight several jazz greats, from Louis Armstrong to Louis Prima. Self-guided audio tours are also available through the website or by phoning 504/613-4062.

Clockwise from top left: the visitor center for the New Orleans Jazz National Historical Park; the LaLaurie Mansion; mule-drawn carriages at Jackson Square.

Moreover, the park oversees jazz-related exhibits at the **Old U.S. Mint** as well as special events at **Perseverance Hall,** a historic building in Louis Armstrong Park (701 N. Rampart St., 504/658-3200) that was once the oldest Masonic Lodge in Louisiana and later a multiuse event venue where African American jazz musicians would perform for black and white audiences. Note that the visitor center, headquarters, and Mint building are all closed on certain holidays.

MAP 1: 916 N. Peters St., 504/589-4841 or 877/520-0677, www.nps.gov/jazz; Tues.-Sat. 9am-5pm; free

NEW ORLEANS MUSICAL LEGENDS PARK

While strolling down Bourbon, note the small New Orleans Musical Legends Park, which was established in 1999 and now contains several bronze statues honoring some of the city's most legendary performers, including jazz clarinetist Pete Fountain, trumpet greats Al Hirt and Louis Prima, and singers Allen Toussaint and Irma Thomas. Additional statues, busts, and plaques will be added through the years as notable jazz musicians are inducted. Besides the statues, the park includes a lovely fountain, several tables and chairs, and a few food stalls, selling surprisingly tasty fare, from gumbo to beignets. So, grab some food, find a seat, and listen to live jazz music (daily 10am-close), courtesy of Steamboat Willie and other musicians. Don't forget to bring along the family pet; leashed dogs are welcome in the park.

MAP 1: 311 Bourbon St., 504/888-7608, www.neworleansmusicallegends.com; Sun.-Thurs. 8am-10pm, Fri.-Sat. 8am-midnight; free, though food costs apply

★ THE NEW ORLEANS SCHOOL OF COOKING

While most people visit New Orleans to taste its one-of-a-kind food, it's also possible to learn how to create such wonderful cuisine. Since 1980, The New Orleans School of Cooking, situated in a renovated, 19th-century molasses warehouse, has invited local Cajun and Creole chefs to teach residents and visitors alike the basics of Louisiana-style cooking, sharing history and tall tales along the way. The popular **demonstration lunch classes** (Mon.-Sat. 10am-12:30pm and 2pm-4pm, Sun. 10am-12:30pm; $28-32.50) include generous samplings of the demonstrated menu items, plus recipes, coffee, iced tea, and Abita beer. Three-hour, hands-on **cooking classes** (Tues. and Fri. 6pm-9pm, Sun. 10am-1pm and 4pm-7pm; $139 pp) are also available, provided you are 18 or older. Besides beverages and the prepared meal, you'll receive a souvenir apron and related recipes. Depending on the class, dishes may include jambalaya, crawfish etouffée, or shrimp and artichoke soup. Non-chefs can peruse the on-site **Louisiana General Store,** which offers a plethora of Cajun and Creole products, from cookbooks and cookware to spices and gift baskets.

MAP 1: 524 St. Louis St., 504/525-2665 or 800/237-4841, www.neworleansschoolofcooking.com; Mon.-Sat. 9am-6pm, Sun. 9am-4pm, though class times vary; cost varies depending on the class

OLD URSULINE CONVENT

King Louis XV of France established the Old Ursuline Convent in 1745 to house the Ursuline nuns who first came to New Orleans in the late 1720s, making them the first nuns to establish a permanent foothold in what is today the United States. This convent was their second home, completed in 1753 and now believed to be the oldest extant building in the Mississippi River Valley; they moved to Dauphine Street in 1824, and then to their present Uptown home, at 2635 State Street, in 1912. In those early decades, the convent housed everyone from French orphans and wounded British soldiers to exiled Acadians and the city's destitute masses. During the early 1800s, the nuns conducted a school for the education of daughters of wealthy Louisiana plantation owners. Today, the Ursuline Academy still functions at its State Street locale as the country's oldest continuously operated school for women.

The convent on Chartres Street is part of a large ecclesiastic complex called the Archbishop Antoine Blanc Memorial, owned by the Catholic Archdiocese of New Orleans. The entire complex—which includes the adjacent gardens, the attached **St. Mary's Church,** and several related outbuildings—is named for the first archbishop of New Orleans, Antoine Blanc. Today, the complex and the St. Louis Cathedral in Jackson Square form the Catholic Cultural Heritage Center of the Archdiocese of New Orleans.

The **Old Ursuline Convent Museum,** which encompasses the exhibits on the first floor of the main convent building, is open for self-guided tours. Simply purchase a ticket in the gift shop (1112 Chartres St.), and then, at your own pace, explore the convent exhibits, the rear garden, and the adjacent church. The last admission occurs at 3:15pm on weekdays, 2:15pm on Saturdays. During the low season (June-Sept.), the exhibits are scaled back, and the admission price is $5 for adults.

MAP 1: 1100 Chartres St., 504/529-3040, www.stlouiscathedral.org/convent-museum; Mon.-Fri. 10am-4pm, Sat. 9am-3pm; $10 adult, $9 senior, $8 student, free under 8

THE OLD U.S. MINT

Fashioned with a granite facade and made of stucco and Mississippi River mud brick, the Old U.S. Mint was constructed in 1835 at the behest of U.S. president Andrew Jackson. This is the only building in the country to have functioned as both a U.S. and a Confederate mint. It also housed Confederate troops for a time during the Civil War. With the Union occupation, the mint was shut down until Reconstruction, at which time it resumed service.

In 1909, the mint was decommissioned, and in 1981, it was added to the state museum system. Today, it's home to the **Louisiana Historical Center,** an archive open to the public and containing priceless collections of colonial-era maps and manuscripts. The site is also home to **Music at the Mint** (http://musicatthemint.org), which features a variety of music-related artifacts, such as posters, sheet music, and memorabilia, from Sidney Bechet's soprano sax to Fats Domino's piano. A living museum, the Mint

Clockwise from top left: pedestrians strolling past The Presbytère; The New Orleans School of Cooking; the Old Ursuline Convent.

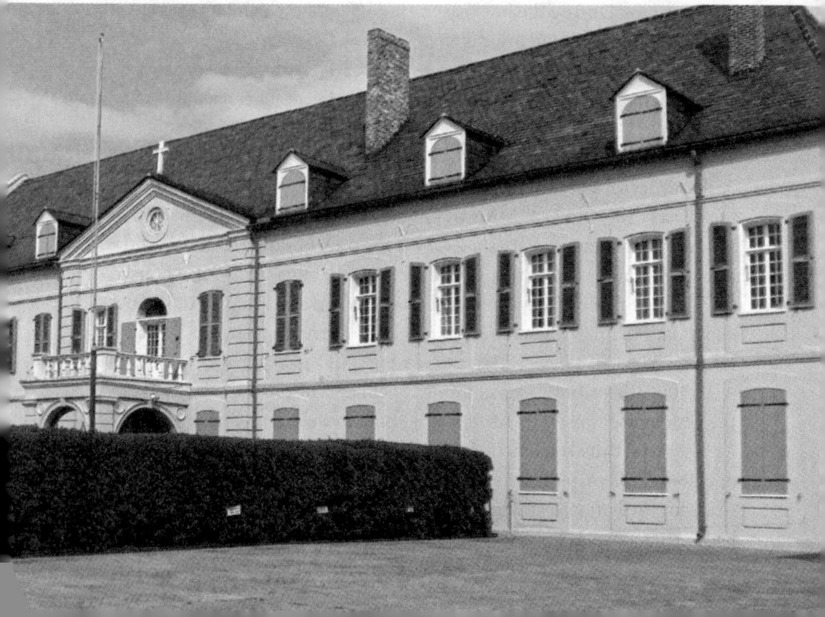

also houses historic musical recordings, showcases live performances, and presents on-site interviews of performing musicians. There's also a large tribute to Louis Armstrong, as well as three colorful murals depicting New Orleans's fabled Storyville red-light district, one of the city's cultivators of jazz. A small display is dedicated to the building's architect, William Strickland, who trained under famous Greek Revival architect Benjamin Latrobe and who also designed the Tennessee State Capitol, as well as the mints in Charlotte and Philadelphia. Note that it's closed on state holidays.

MAP 1: 400 Esplanade Ave., 504/568-6993 or 800/568-6868, www.louisianastatemuseum.org; Tues.-Sun. 10am-4:30pm; free

PONTALBA BUILDINGS AND THE 1850 HOUSE

The Pontalba Apartments were commissioned by Baroness Micaela Almonester de Pontalba in 1849 (the lower building, on St. Ann) and 1851 (the upper building, on St. Peter). She had inherited the land from her father, Don Andres Almonester, the man who had financed the Cabildo, the Presbytère, and St. Louis Cathedral after the devastating fire of 1788.

Each row of buildings contained 16 separate houses on the upper levels and a series of shops on the lower levels. After the Civil War, Jackson Square and its environs began to deteriorate and the Pontalba Apartments functioned as rather unfashionable tenements. In 1921, William Ratcliffe Irby bought the Lower Pontalba Building and willed the property to the Louisiana State Museum. The grand old townhouses were subdivided into smaller apartments.

The 1850 House was restored in 1955 by the museum to serve as an example of a fine New Orleans townhouse of the 1850s. Most of the interior furnishings were donated to the museum but are authentic to the exact period. Today, the 1850 House is a small but popular museum, which also has an excellent book and gift shop. The actual apartment occupies the two floors above the shop. Visitors can stand at edges of the doorways and peer into the rooms, gaining a sense of an 1850s row house owned by a family of somewhat considerable means. Plaques on the third floor detail the lives of the home's inhabitants from 1850 to 1861. The museum is closed on state holidays.

MAP 1: 523 St. Ann St., 504/524-9118, www.louisianastatemuseum.org; Tues.-Sun. 10am-4:30pm; $3 adult, $2 senior, military, and student, free under 13

THE PRESBYTÈRE

Built in 1797 as a home for the priests of the St. Louis Cathedral, and standing just on the downriver side of it, the two-story Presbytère on Jackson Square bears a structural resemblance to the Cabildo. It was never used for its intended purpose, as its financier, Don Andres Almonester (a Spaniard of considerable means who also funded the Cabildo and St. Louis Cathedral), died before it was completed. The new U.S. government eventually completed it and used it to house the Louisiana state courts during the 19th century.

In 1911, it became part of the Louisiana State Museum, and today, it houses a colorful permanent exhibit on the history of Mardi Gras traditions both in the city and the state. Videos, audiotapes, and a wide array of artifacts detail how Louisianians have celebrated Carnival through the years and how this event has grown to become one of the most popular festivals in the world. You'll also encounter "Living with Hurricanes: Katrina and Beyond," a heartbreaking yet inspiring exhibit that utilizes photographs, eyewitness accounts, artifacts, and multimedia displays to explore the history and science of hurricanes. In particular, you'll learn more about the loss and destruction caused by Hurricanes Katrina and Rita in 2005, as well as the service, solidarity, and resilience demonstrated by residents and others in their aftermath. The Presbytère is closed on state holidays.

MAP 1: 751 Chartres St., 504/568-6968 or 800/568-6968, www.louisianastatemuseum.org; Tues.-Sun. 10am-4:30pm; $6 adult, $5 senior, military, and student, free under 13

ST. LOUIS CATHEDRAL

The lakeside end of Jackson Square is dominated by the St. Louis Cathedral, one of the most magnificent cathedrals in the United States. The current building was constructed in 1794 in the Spanish style, with two round spires rising from the facade, and then virtually rebuilt and remodeled in 1849. Simpler churches have stood on this site since the 1720s, not long after the arrival of the French explorer Jean Baptiste Le Moyne, Sieur de Bienville, who established New Orleans as a permanent settlement in 1718. During the 1849 remodel, huge steeples were added to the two symmetrical round towers, and the building has received additional restorations over the years. The cathedral was designated a minor basilica in 1964 by Pope Paul VI. Mass is held every day, and the gift shop (daily 9am-6pm) offers an assortment of religious and spiritual items. Visitors are welcome to take a guided tour of the property; as an alternative, simply wander inside and explore the gorgeous architecture, including kaleidoscopic stained-glass windows, on your own. For a $1 donation, you can even pick up a self-guided brochure near the front entrance. Keep in mind that this is an actual church, so be respectful of those who have come for prayer and quiet reflection. Also, if you're in town during December, consider attending one of the free jazz concerts on offer here.

MAP 1: 615 Père Antoine Alley, 504/525-9585, www.stlouiscathedral.org; daily 7:30am-4pm; free, though donations are accepted

VOODOO SPIRITUAL TEMPLE

Operated by Priestess Miriam, this center of voodoo worship and healing offers voodoo consultations, rituals, and workshops, as well as city tours. An on-site gift shop, meanwhile, sells handcrafted voodoo dolls, gris-gris and mojo bags, aroma oils, and books and CDs related to voodoo. The Voodoo Spiritual Temple is a frequent stop on other city tours, like the walking tour hosted by the New Orleans Historic Voodoo Museum; while on such tours, you'll typically be able to experience the temple's impressive altar room, filled with spiritual altars of all kinds. Be respectful; these altars constitute a strictly "look but don't touch" attraction. The hours of the temple are flexible, so don't be surprised to find the front door locked at random times.

MAP 1: 828 N. Rampart St., 504/522-9627, www.voodoospiritualtemple.org; Mon.-Sat. 10:30am-6pm, Sun. noon-2pm; free, though donations are accepted

WOLDENBERG RIVERFRONT PARK

Named for philanthropist Malcolm Woldenberg (1896-1982), lovely Woldenberg Riverfront Park is a 16-acre green space and redbrick promenade that extends along the riverfront from the aquarium to Jackson Brewery. It's along this stretch that the site of New Orleans was established in 1718. Crape myrtle and magnolia trees shade the numerous park benches, affording romantic views of the Mississippi River. One of the original quays, **Toulouse Street Wharf,** is home to the palatial excursion riverboat, the **Steamboat *Natchez.*** Fringing the park is the **Moonwalk,** a wooden boardwalk that stretches along the riverfront, between St. Philip and St. Peter Streets. Musicians, tourists, and homeless individuals are all drawn to this scenic spot; it's often a little sketchy at night.

Within Woldenberg Riverfront Park (which serves as one of the main sites for the French Quarter Festival and other annual events) are several significant sculptures. The stunning, 20-foot-tall ***Monument to the Immigrant*** statue, by noted New Orleans artist Franco Alessandrini, commemorates New Orleans's role as one of the nation's most prolific immigrant ports throughout the 19th century. It's fashioned from white Carrara marble. Other sculptures include Robert Schoen's bizarre ***Old Man River,*** an 18-foot tribute to the Mississippi River, and John Scott's ***Ocean Song,*** a series of eight slender, 10-foot-tall, stainless-steel pyramids, topped by a grid of rings. My favorite is the mesmerizing ***New Orleans Holocaust Memorial*** (www.holocaustmemorial.us), created by Israeli artist Yaacov Agam, dedicated in 2003, and featuring nine colorful panels, which meld to form different images depending on where you're standing.

MAP 1: Mississippi River btwn. Canal St. and St. Peter St.; daily 24 hours; free

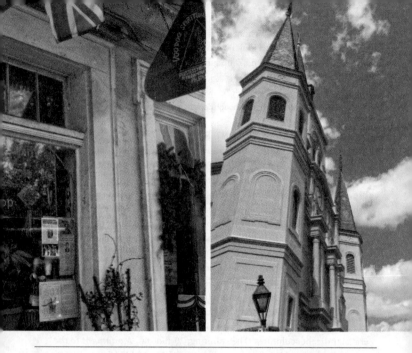

Clockwise from top left: the Voodoo Spiritual Temple; the St. Louis Cathedral; the *New Orleans Holocaust Memorial* by Yaacov Agam overlooking the Mississippi River.

Central Business and Arts Districts

Map 3

★ BLAINE KERN'S MARDI GRAS WORLD

The top reason that families venture to the Port of New Orleans is to visit Blaine Kern's Mardi Gras World, the public face of world-renowned Kern Studios, which, since 1947, has been the largest builder of Carnival sculptures and parade floats in the country. Formerly situated in Algiers, Mardi Gras World is now across the river on the East Bank, between the Central Business District (CBD) and the Garden District, where visitors can take a guided tour of the facility. The one-hour tour includes a stroll amid kaleidoscopic floats, the observation of working artists and artisans, and a video about the history of the city's Mardi Gras celebration. Though Mardi Gras may take place over a relatively short period late each winter, this place hums with activity every day of the year (with the exception of Easter Day, Thanksgiving Day, Christmas Day, and, perhaps understandably, Mardi Gras Day). Note that the last tour begins at 4:30pm, and a complimentary shuttle is available for visitors in the CBD and French Quarter.

MAP 3: 1380 Port of New Orleans Pl., 504/361-7821, www.mardigrasworld.com; daily 9:30am-5:30pm; $20 adult, $16 senior 65 and over and college student, $13 child 2-11, free under 2

GALLIER HALL

Gallier Hall, a hulking, white, Greek Revival-style building, was named for its architect, James Gallier Sr., who designed and erected the structure between 1845 and 1853. Boasting massive Ionic columns, the stunning, three-story marble structure served as the New Orleans City Hall from the mid-19th through mid-20th centuries. Today, it's used as a special-events facility and reception hall; it's also the spot where the city mayor greets the royal courts of Mardi Gras krewes like Zulu and Rex. Several important people have been laid in state here, including Confederate President Jefferson Davis, Confederate General P. G. T. Beauregard, and R&B musician Ernie K-Doe. Guided tours are available by appointment.

MAP 3: 545 St. Charles Ave., 504/658-3627, www.nola.gov/gallier-hall; Mon.-Fri. 9am-5pm; free

LEE CIRCLE

Lee Circle is the hub for a small arts and museum district that has evolved on the streets just downriver from here since the mid-1990s. This is the one regal traffic circle in downtown New Orleans, and it imparts a slightly formal, urban air—a hint of Paris or London. Rising high over the traffic circle, which is a stop on the St. Charles streetcar line, stands a magnificent bronze statue of Robert E. Lee, the Confederate Civil War general; it sits atop a graceful marble column, the entire memorial rising 60 feet over

Mister Mardi Gras

the original Mardi Gras World in Algiers

For many years, families have flocked to **Blaine Kern's Mardi Gras World** (www.mardigrasworld.com). This vibrant attraction offers visitors a behind-the-scenes glimpse at the magic of Mardi Gras, one of the city's oldest traditions. Here, you'll see a variety of colorful floats and get the chance to watch the artists and artisans of **Kern Studios** (www.kernstudios.com) hard at work.

As the names indicate, the heart and soul behind Blaine Kern's Mardi Gras World (also known simply as Mardi Gras World) and Kern Studios is Blaine Kern Sr. himself—the man known as Mister Mardi Gras. Born in 1927, Blaine grew up on the West Bank of the Mississippi River. His early interest in the arts was inspired by his proximity to New Orleans as well as the vocation of his father, Roy, a sign painter who survived the Depression by painting names on the bows of freighters.

When Blaine's mother was hospitalized, he offset the family's medical bills by painting a mural in the hospital—a mural that captured the attention of a surgeon who was also the captain of a Mardi Gras krewe. Blaine began designing floats soon afterward and was eventually hired to fashion a complete parade. In 1947, he established Blaine Kern Artists (which eventually evolved into Kern Studios) in Algiers and, over time, became the Big Easy's leading parade creator, working with Rex, Zulu, Bacchus, and all the legendary krewes.

Following his travels to Italy, where he was impressed by the extravagant animation and prop concepts that distinguished the European style of float building, Blaine began to embrace the monumental scale and lavish ornamentation that mark contemporary Mardi Gras parades. Today, Kern Studios produces floats and props for more than 40 New Orleans parades, including Endymion and Orpheus, as well as pageants throughout the world. Kern props and sculptures also enhance themed environments in Walt Disney World, Universal Studios, and Japan's Toho Park.

the circle. Depending on which direction you're coming from, it serves as a gateway to the Garden District or the CBD.

MAP 3: St. Charles Ave. and Howard Ave.; daily 24 hours; free

MERCEDES-BENZ SUPERDOME

This massive, 52-acre structure is home to NFL's New Orleans Saints, college football's Allstate Sugar Bowl, as well as major concerts and some of the city's most popular annual events. The city commissioned construction of the dome in 1966; however, construction didn't begin until 1971, finishing four years later. The gargantuan arena is the largest domed stadium in the world, holding more than 76,000 fans for football. The roof alone covers about 13 acres and rises to a height of about 273 feet (nearly as tall as a 30-story building).

In the immediate wake of Hurricane Katrina, the Superdome became infamous for its role as an evacuation center. The roof and interior were completely refurbished in 2006, in time for the Superdome to host the Saints' 2006-2007 season opener—which the Saints won handily over the Atlanta Falcons, with a crowd of more than 70,000 "Who Dats" cheering. In 2011, the Superdome underwent an $85 million renovation that completely modernized the facility, adding three elevators, more than 3,000 new seats, extra restrooms, and other amenities.

MAP 3: 1500 Sugar Bowl Dr., 504/587-3822 or 800/756-7074, www.superdome.com; hours vary depending on the event; cost varies depending on the event

★ THE NATIONAL WWII MUSEUM

One of the nation's most exalted historians, the late Stephen Ambrose, founded The National WWII Museum in the early 1990s. Ambrose, a professor at the University of New Orleans, lived in New Orleans until his death in 2002. He is best known for such riveting World War II histories as *Band of Brothers, The Wild Blue, D-Day, Citizen Soldiers,* and *The Victors.*

The museum opened to the public on June 6, 2000, the 56th anniversary of the amphibious World War II invasion. This is the only museum in the United States dedicated to this event, which involved more than a million Americans. The Andrew Higgins factory, which now houses the museum, built ships during World War II, including some of the very vehicles that transported infantrymen to Normandy.

A museum visit can be an all-day (or multiday) affair; after all, it might take that long to absorb the enormous collection of exhibits documenting the Allied victory in World War II, not to mention exploring "Final Mission: The USS Tang Submarine Experience" (Sun.-Thurs. 9:35am-4:35pm, Fri.-Sat. 9:35am-5:35pm, $5 pp), which allows visitors to relive the last epic battle of the most successful submarine in World War II, or watching the immersive 4-D, Tom Hanks-narrated documentary *Beyond All Boundaries* (Sun.-Thurs. 10am-4pm, Fri.-Sat. 10am-5pm, $5 pp) in the relatively new 250-seat **Solomon Victory Theater.** If you have time, consider a meal at the on-site restaurant, **The American Sector** (daily 11am-9pm),

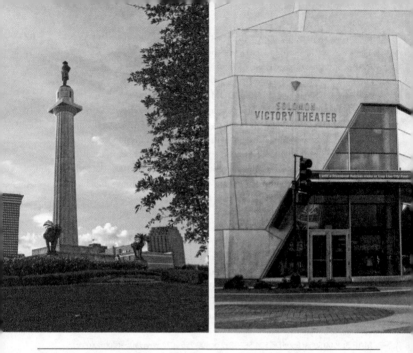

Clockwise from top left: the monument at Lee Circle; the Solomon Victory Theater at The National WWII Museum; Blaine Kern's Mardi Gras World.

or an old-fashioned dinner theater experience in the **Stage Door Canteen** (hours vary depending on performance).

MAP 3: 945 Magazine St., 504/528-1944, www.nationalww2museum.org; daily 9am-5pm; $23 adult, $20 senior 65 and over, $14 military, college student, and child 5-17, free under 5

SCRAP HOUSE

As you drive past the enormous Ernest N. Morial Convention Center, keep an eye out for the colorful sculpture that's simply known as *Scrap House*. Completed by artist Sally Heller in 2008 and fashioned from ordinary materials and recycled elements (wood, wallpaper, oil drums, and solar lights), this outdoor installation resembles a denuded tree that's cradling a ramshackle house. Not surprisingly, this powerful yet whimsical piece is meant to serve as a monument to Mother Nature's unpredictable powers, inspired as Heller was by the remnants of houses and other cultural debris left in the wake of Hurricane Katrina in 2005.

MAP 3: Convention Center Blvd. and John Churchill Chase St., www.sallyheller.com; daily 24 hours; free

ST. PATRICK'S CHURCH

Not far from Lafayette Square and Gallier Hall, St. Patrick's Church was the first place of worship built in the city's American Sector. The sector was so named because it's where 19th-century Americans built their homes and businesses in order to distinguish their lifestyles from those of the Creoles residing in the French Quarter, New Orleans's original settlement. Blessed by Bishop Antoine Blanc in 1838 and completed by 1840, St. Patrick's Church is one of the few structures left in a district once filled with magnificent mansions and high-end mercantile stores. When the parish was first established in 1833, the area was known as the Faubourg St. Mary; the church itself developed from a need for the Americans, many of whom were Irish, to worship in a structure as noteworthy as the French Quarter's St. Louis Cathedral.

In the early 1850s, it was this stunning church where Bishop Antoine Blanc received the pallium as the first Archbishop of New Orleans. Though severely damaged by a hurricane in 1915, the church has since been renovated several times. Today, this national historic landmark is celebrated not only for its historic significance but also for its lavishly ornate interior, high vaulted ceilings, majestic paintings, and fine stained-glass windows.

MAP 3: 724 Camp St., 504/525-4413, http://oldstpatricks.org; hours vary daily; free, though donations are accepted

BREVARD-CLAPP HOUSE

Long celebrated as a haven for writers, New Orleans has inspired several famous American authors, not the least of which is Anne Rice, whose best-selling novel *Interview with a Vampire* (1976) put her on the literary map. Born in New Orleans on October 4, 1941, she lived in the Big Easy for the first 16 years of her life. Returning in 1978, she eventually moved into the Brevard-Clapp House, a stately Greek Revival and Italianate mansion in the Garden District. Built in 1857 by James Calrow and Charles Pride, this stunning structure was first home to a wealthy merchant named Albert Hamilton Brevard and was later acquired by Reverend Emory Clapp.

Rice called the Brevard-Clapp House home from 1989 to 2004. During that time, it served as the inspiration for Mayfair Manor, the fictional home of Rice's Mayfair Witches. Rice, who became a fixture in the neighborhood, also bought and restored St. Elizabeth's Orphanage at 1314 Napoleon Avenue, a massive former boarding house and girls' orphanage built in 1865. Though Rice has since sold the orphanage and relocated to California, she will always be considered one of the city's finest literary assets.

MAP 4: 1239 1st St.; closed to the public

HOUSE OF BROEL'S VICTORIAN MANSION AND WEDDING CHAPEL

Near the corner of St. Charles and Jackson Avenues, you'll come to one small but noteworthy attraction, especially if you favor miniatures. Originally built in 1850 by George Washington Squires, the House of Broel was converted by William Renaud, three decades later, into the immense three-story mansion that exists today. With its original woodwork, black marble fireplaces, and ornate chandeliers, the house is a remarkable example of Victorian architecture and interior design, which certainly justifies its popularity among wedding parties and other celebrants. The tour, which accepts walk-ins, not only highlights the living quarters and furnishings of an exceptional Garden District residence, but also offers a look at the numerous dolls, miniatures, dollhouses, antiques, and other collectibles that fill the rooms on the lower and upper floors.

MAP 4: 2220 St. Charles Ave., 504/522-2220 or 800/827-4325, www.houseofbroel.com; Mon.-Fri. 11am-3pm; $10 adult, $5 child

LAFAYETTE CEMETERY NO. 1

Established in 1833, Lafayette Cemetery No. 1 is one of only a few "cities of the dead" in New Orleans that are relatively safe to explore, at least during the day. Bordered by Prytania Street, Washington Avenue, Coliseum Street, and 6th Street in the Garden District, the cemetery is especially popular with fans of Anne Rice's *The Vampire Chronicles* trilogy and was featured in the movie *Interview with the Vampire* (1994). The Lafayette Cemetery was once part of a plantation owned by the Livaudais family. As a cemetery, it has always been nonsegregated and nondenominational; you'll see the tombs of American merchants, African families, and German, Irish, Italian, English, Scottish, and Dutch immigrants, not to mention several Union and Confederate soldiers.

If visiting alone, note that the office is at 1427 6th Street. Taking a properly vetted, guided tour is preferable, especially for history buffs. Tours are offered by various companies, most notably **Save Our Cemeteries** (SOC, 501 Basin St., #3C, 504/525-3377, www.saveourcemeteries.org; $15 adult, free under 12), a nonprofit organization that preserves the city's burial grounds. The one-hour walks occur daily 10:30am, which means that it's still possible to experience the cemetery on Sunday, when it's normally closed to the public. Whether you come alone or with a group, please be respectful; this is an active cemetery that still welcomes mourners. Note that it's closed on certain holidays.

MAP 4: 1400 Washington Ave., www.lafayettecemetery.org; Mon.-Fri. 7am-2:30pm, Sat. 7am-noon; free

OPERA GUILD HOME

Built in 1859, this eye-catching, Greek Revival-style mansion became the home of the Women's Guild of New Orleans Opera Association in 1965. It's particularly noted for its small octagonal tower, though the color scheme—all white with dark-green shutters—plus the manicured lawn and wrought-iron fencing all make for a lovely photograph. Furnished with 18th- and 19th-century European and American furniture, artwork, and collectibles, this well-appointed Garden District home is the frequent site of wedding ceremonies and receptions. Public tours are available on Monday, from early September to late May.

MAP 4: 2504 Prytania St., 504/899-1945, http://operaguildhome.org; Mon. 10am-4pm; $15 pp

ST. MARY'S ASSUMPTION CHURCH

Despite suffering damage during Hurricane Katrina, the regal St. Mary's Assumption Church is still gorgeous. Constructed between 1858 and 1866, this massive, German Baroque Revival-style structure boasts an incredibly intricate facade, with several stunning, arched stained-glass windows. The interior is equally impressive, with a high, vaulted ceiling, ornate columns, and a hand-carved altar reportedly imported from Munich.

Prior to the American Civil War, the Garden District and the Irish Channel composed a separate town called Lafayette. In the early 1840s, when numerous German and Irish immigrants, many of whom were Catholic, arrived in this French-speaking area, Bishop Antoine Blanc asked a German-speaking Redemptorist priest, Father Peter Czackert, to minister to them. Initially, he rented a dance hall for services; eventually, a frame church, the first St. Mary's Assumption, was constructed on Josephine Street, becoming the state's first Catholic Church for Germans.

Above: the Van Benthuysen-Elms Mansion & Gardens. **Below:** the entrance to Lafayette Cemetery No. 1.

By the late 1850s, the Redemptorists had built three permanent churches: St. Alphonsus, serving the Irish parishioners; St. Mary's Assumption, which replaced the frame church and served the German parishioners; and the Romanesque Notre Dame de Bon Secours, intended for the French-speaking Catholics but ultimately damaged by a 1918 hurricane and demolished in 1925.

Today, you can attend Mass at St. Mary's or simply listen to the wonderful bells. At nearby **St. Alphonsus Church** (2025 Constance St., 504/524-8116, www.stalphonsusneworleans.org; Tues., Thurs., and Sat. 10am-2pm), you can appreciate historical art, ornate architecture, and a display about the city's Irish Catholic experience.

Make time for the nearby **Seelos Welcome Center and National Shrine of Francis Xavier Seelos** (919 Josephine St., 504/525-2495, www.seelos.org; Mon.-Fri. 9am-3pm, Sat. 10am-3:30pm, free), a museum dedicated to the heroic, ever-cheerful Redemptorist priest who came to New Orleans during the dreaded yellow fever epidemic, ministered tirelessly at St. Mary's, and ultimately succumbed to the fever in 1867. Besides featuring a self-guided tour of the exhibits, the museum presents a short informational film and houses a small gift shop.

MAP 4: 2030 Constance St., 504/522-6748, http://stalphonsusno.com; hours vary daily; free, though donations are accepted

VAN BENTHUYSEN-ELMS MANSION & GARDENS

Amid the many elegant buildings along St. Charles Avenue stands this grand, Italianate-style mansion, which was built in 1869 for Watson Van Benthuysen II, a New Yorker who moved to New Orleans in the 1840s. During the American Civil War, Van Benthuysen (who was a relative of President Jefferson Davis by marriage) became an officer in the Confederate Army. Nicknamed the "Yankee in Gray," he earned prominence in New Orleans as a wine and tobacco merchant as well as president of a streetcar company. Van Benthuysen died in his home in 1901; three decades later, the mansion served as the German Consulate until the commencement of World War II. In 1952, the home was purchased by John Elms Sr., who at the time was the owner of the largest coin-operated amusement company in the South. Following his death in 1968, his relatives began hosting private functions here—a practice continued today by the third generation of the Elms family. The picturesque home is filled with antique furnishings, gold sconces, and ornamental cornices and is the site of weddings, corporate parties, and other social occasions; it's also available for private group tours.

MAP 4: 3029 St. Charles Ave., 504/895-9200, www.elmsmansion.com; by appt.; free

★ AUDUBON ZOO

Below Magazine Street lies 58-acre Audubon Zoo, a significant part of the larger Audubon Park. Established in 1914, it now contains historic buildings, notable sculptures, and nearly 2,000 animals from around the world. This relatively small zoo is a wonderful place to stroll, watch the animals' antics (especially in mild weather), and explore verdant gardens rife with nearly every species of flora known to Louisiana.

The award-winning **Louisiana Swamp** exhibit is the next best thing to taking a swamp tour and even better in one respect: You're guaranteed to see marsh wildlife up close and personal. The swamp exhibit is an actual recreation of a Depression-era Cajun swamp settlement, complete with old bayou shacks and a trapper's cottage. Besides learning about alligators, red foxes, and other critters, you'll see Spanish moss, cypress knees, and other flora common in the swamp. It's hard to leave this part of the zoo—the albino alligators never cease to amaze and the ever-frisky river otters are endlessly amusing.

Another highlight of the zoo is the **Jaguar Jungle** exhibit, which recreates a Mayan rain forest and houses two dignified yet powerful jaguars, along with toucans, spider monkeys, and sloths. The display features realistic reproductions of the stone carvings at famous Chichén Itzá and Copán archaeological sites.

Kids especially love to pet free-roaming goats and sheep in the spacious **Watoto Walk,** navigate the 44-foot-high **Kamba Kourse** ($15 pp), and ride the **carousel** ($2 pp), which features 60 figures of endangered species. Daily **animal feedings** are a big draw, especially involving the giraffes and gators.

If you're taking the St. Charles streetcar, disembark at the Audubon Park stop for both the park and the zoo. If you're coming by car, the zoo has plenty of free parking, though the lot and nearby grassy areas can fill up quickly during annual events like Soul Fest or Boo at the Zoo. Note that during the fall, winter, and spring, the Audubon Zoo has shorter operating hours and is closed most Mondays.

MAP 5: 6500 Magazine St., 504/861-2537 or 800/774-7394, www.auduboninstitute.org; Mon.-Fri. 10am-5pm, Sat.-Sun. 10am-6pm; $19 adult, $15 senior 65 and over, $14 child 2-12, free under 2

LOYOLA UNIVERSITY NEW ORLEANS

Opposite verdant Audubon Park stands Loyola University, Tulane University's most prominent neighbor. Established by the Jesuit order in 1904 as Loyola College, the school had been a long time in coming. The Jesuits were among the earliest settlers of New Orleans; a Jesuit chaplain even accompanied Pierre Le Moyne, Sieur d'Iberville, on his second expedition to the region. Credited with introducing the sugarcane crop to Louisiana, the Jesuits were sadly banned from the French colonies in 1763.

After the Jesuit order was restored, however, the Bishop of New Orleans beseeched the French Jesuits to establish a Jesuit college here.

In 1849, despite concerns about the city's yellow fever epidemic, Jesuit priests opened the College of the Immaculate Conception at Baronne and Common Streets in what is now the CBD. Though the college became a beloved institution, local Catholic leaders still longed for a school in a less-congested area. Following the 1884 World's Industrial and Cotton Centennial Exposition in Audubon Park, it became clear that the nearby Foucher Plantation—which was owned by Paul Foucher, the son-in-law of Etienne De Boré, New Orleans's first mayor—would be an ideal location for a school. By 1904, Loyola College had opened, along with a Catholic college-prep academy; in 1911, the Jesuit schools in New Orleans were reorganized, and all college-prep students were sent to the College of the Immaculate Conception, paving the way for Loyola to become a full-fledged private university in 1912. Over the years, it grew and expanded, eventually becoming one of the most well-respected universities in the South, open to all faiths and currently nurturing roughly 5,000 students annually. Today, visitors are free to wander amid the school's stately redbrick buildings, built in the Tudor Gothic style; it's also not a bad place to catch concerts and sporting events.

MAP 5: 6363 St. Charles Ave., 504/865-3240 or 800/456-9652, www.loyno.edu; hours vary daily; free

MILTON H. LATTER MEMORIAL LIBRARY

Besides being a delightful place to relax for a while, the art-filled Milton H. Latter Memorial Library is a much-loved architectural landmark. Built in 1907, this enormous, Italianate-Beaux Arts mansion was home to a variety of curious residents, including Marguerite Clark, an American stage and silent film star known for *The Prince and the Pauper* and *Uncle Tom's Cabin*. Following Clark's death, the gorgeous Uptown mansion was purchased by the Latter family, who bequeathed it to the city in 1948. Intended to commemorate the Latters' son, who had died in World War II, the stunning structure became a branch of the New Orleans Public Library and has beckoned both bibliophiles and architectural aficionados ever since.

MAP 5: 5120 St. Charles Ave., 504/596-2625, www.neworleanspubliclibrary.org; Mon. and Wed. 9am-8pm, Tues. and Thurs. 9am-6pm, Sat. 10am-5pm, Sun. noon-5pm; free

ST. CHARLES STREETCAR

No one should leave New Orleans without taking a ride on one of the city's famous, oft-photographed streetcars. While there are presently five separate lines—the St. Charles, the Loyola-UPT, the Canal-Cemeteries, the Canal-City Park/Museum, and the Riverfront—the most famous by far and most beloved by residents and tourists alike is the St. Charles line, which dates back to 1835 and has been featured in numerous films over the years, including *Runaway Jury* (2003) and *The Skeleton Key* (2005). Because of the line's presence on the National Register of Historic Places, the olive-green

Clockwise from top left: a streetcar on St. Charles Avenue; Loyola University; an orangutan in the Audubon Zoo.

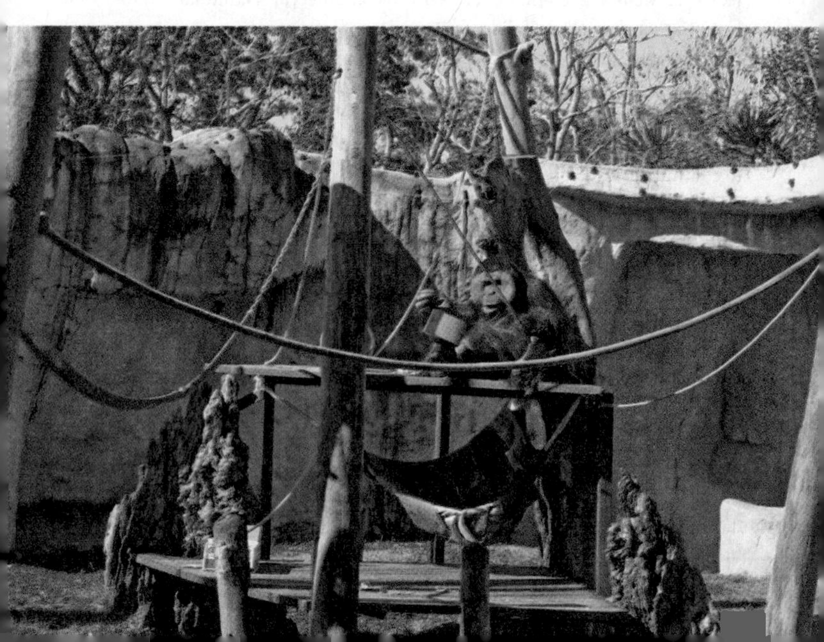

Perley Thomas streetcars currently in use must be preserved as they looked in 1923, which makes for a historical riding experience. Complete with old-fashioned wooden seats, the St. Charles streetcar takes passengers from Canal Street, at the lower edge of the CBD; past the historic homes, restaurants, and attractions of oak-shaded St. Charles Avenue, including the Garden District, Loyola and Tulane Universities, and Audubon Park; to the restaurants, boutiques, and residential areas of South Carrollton Avenue. The line terminates at South Claiborne Avenue, a transfer point for the city's bus lines. A one-way ride on the St. Charles line, which runs 24 hours daily, lasts about 45 minutes and is well worth the time.

MAP 5: Canal St. and Carondelet St. to S. Carrollton Ave. and S. Claiborne Ave., 504/248-3900, www.norta.com; hours vary daily; $1.25 one-way

TOURO SYNAGOGUE

With a domed sanctuary, stunning stained-glass windows, and a tremendous organ, Touro Synagogue is one of the city's most impressive religious edifices. Its history stretches back to 1828, when Congregation Gates of Mercy was founded on North Rampart Street, becoming the first synagogue outside of America's original 13 colonies. Years later, the congregation adopted the name Touro Synagogue in honor of their benefactor, a Jewish merchant-philanthropist named Judah Touro who spent much of his life in New Orleans. Besides being a benefactor of Jewish, Catholic, and Protestant charities, he also served in the War of 1812 and founded Touro Infirmary, which still exists today.

Touro Synagogue joined the Reform movement in 1891, and the current sanctuary, designed by local architect Emile Weil, was dedicated on New Year's Day of 1909. Visitors are welcome to venture inside, particularly for events like the Jazz Fest Shabbat—a worship service that combines Judaism and jazz. Free and open to the public, this popular Friday evening Sabbath service usually occurs during the first weekend of the New Orleans Jazz & Heritage Festival and has featured some of the city's most famous jazz musicians, including Allen Toussaint, Irma Thomas, and Marcia Ball.

MAP 5: 4238 St. Charles Ave., 504/895-4843, www.tourosynagogue.com; hours vary daily; free, though donations are accepted

TULANE UNIVERSITY

Whether you drive or hop aboard the historic streetcar, you're sure to spot Tulane University on the lakeside of St. Charles Avenue, adjacent to Loyola University. This private nonsectarian research university began as the Medical College of Louisiana in 1834, the South's second-oldest medical school; the need for it partially arose from the city's constant struggles to contain deadly yellow fever epidemics. In 1847, it became the University of Louisiana, a public institution, but an enormous bequest by wealthy New Orleanian Paul Tulane allowed the university to be reorganized as a private university in 1884 and ultimately expand into a much more comprehensive facility; it was renamed Tulane in honor of this financial gift, which totaled more than $1 million in land, cash, and securities. In 1886, the women-only H. Sophie Newcomb Memorial College was established as part of the university; eight years later, the entire school moved to its present campus on St. Charles Avenue.

Over the ensuing decades, Tulane became one of the top schools in the South. In 2005, Hurricane Katrina resulted in the merging of Newcomb College with Tulane. Today, the university has approximately 13,500 students, and the 110-acre Uptown campus encompasses more than 80 buildings. The older edifices stand along or near St. Charles and include several Romanesque structures of considerable architectural acclaim. A pretty campus for a stroll, it's also popular for its yearly schedule of affordable concerts and plays, including those offered during the **New Orleans Shakespeare Festival at Tulane** every summer.

MAP 5: 6823 St. Charles Ave., 504/865-5000, http://tulane.edu; hours vary daily; free

URSULINE ACADEMY

Established in 1727 by a dozen Ursuline nuns from France and part of the Sisters of the Order of Saint Ursula, the Ursuline Academy is distinctive for two reasons: It's the country's oldest continuously operating school for girls *and* the oldest Catholic school in the United States. Although the academy's first permanent location was the Old Ursuline Convent in the French Quarter, it relocated, without interruption, to Dauphine Street in 1824, before finally settling at its current spot near Loyola University in 1912. In the 1920s, a gilded statue was erected in the chapel here; the ***National Shrine of Our Lady of Prompt Succor*** (2701 State St., www.shrineofourladyofpromptsuccor.com), which was consecrated in 1928, commemorates the miraculous military victory of the Battle of New Orleans that took place during the War of 1812. In 1976, the shrine was declared a national historic landmark. Every year on January 8, Our Lady and her infant are honored by the Archbishop of New Orleans during a splendid High Mass.

MAP 5: 2635 State St., 504/861-9150, www.ursulineneworleans.org; hours vary daily; free

Tremé and Mid-City

Map 6

BASIN ST. STATION

The massive building situated at Basin and St. Louis Streets looks as though two buildings have merged into one—the first made of red brick and the second a more modern canary yellow. Despite its incongruous appearance, Basin St. Station serves as a pseudo-gateway to the historic Faubourg Tremé neighborhood. Situated next to St. Louis Cemetery No. 1, which is famous as Marie Laveau's supposed resting place, the former New Orleans Terminal Company/Southern Railway Freight Office Building has been newly renovated and ultimately transformed into a cultural center. Built in 1904 in the neoclassical style, the original building has been retained as the facade of the now partially new structure. The first level is the one intended for visitors. Here, you'll find a staffed visitor and information center, a walking tour kiosk, educational exhibits, a coffee shop, and a gift shop—not a bad place to start before beginning your neighborhood wanderings.

MAP 6: 501 Basin St., 504/293-2600, www.basinststation.com; daily 9am-5pm; free

BAYOU ST. JOHN

Bayou St. John runs along the eastern side of Wisner Boulevard, from Lafitte Avenue to Lake Pontchartrain. At one time it was a lot longer than it is today. In fact, a portage once linked this bayou to the Mississippi River, making it particularly attractive to early French explorers, traders, and trappers. In 1701, the French established a small fort at the lake end of the bayou to protect this important route. Originally called Fort St. Jean, it would eventually be known as Old Spanish Fort by many native New Orleanians. Despite the bayou's smaller stature, this link to the Mississippi was partially the reason that the French established New Orleans where they did—at the river end of the portage route, where the French Quarter sits today. Dredged to accommodate larger vessels, Bayou St. John supposedly became the site of Marie Laveau's voodoo rituals in the 19th century; by the early 20th century, commercial use of this once-important waterway had declined. Until the 1930s, houseboats were allowed on the bayou. Today it's simply a picturesque, slow-moving body of water, lined by greenery and frequented by sunbathers, anglers, and privacy-seeking residents of Mid-City. It's also the site of various annual events, such as the Mid-City Bayou Boogaloo in mid-May and the New Orleans Greek Festival in late May.

MAP 6: Wisner Blvd., btwn. Lafitte Ave. and Lake Pontchartrain

★ CITY PARK

Situated near the Lakeview and Mid-City neighborhoods, City Park is bordered by Robert E. Lee Boulevard, Marconi Drive, City Park Avenue, and Wisner Boulevard. Considerably larger than New York City's Central Park, this 1,300-acre spread sits on what was once a swampy oak forest. It still contains the nation's largest collection of mature live oaks, some believed to date to the 1400s or earlier. Stop by the **Timken Center,** housed in a 1913 Spanish Mission-style building, for sandwiches, ice cream, and refreshments before exploring the park.

City Park encompasses several worthwhile attractions. The **New Orleans Botanical Garden** is filled with a variety of thematic gardens, making it a wonderful place for a relaxing stroll. Another tranquil locale is the **Sydney and Walda Besthoff Sculpture Garden,** a free outdoor extension of the New Orleans Museum of Art. It's just as pleasant to meander through the rest of City Park, where you'll find various old-fashioned stone bridges and oodles of moss-covered oak trees.

Children are especially fond of the **Carousel Gardens Amusement Park** (Mar.-May and early Aug.-mid-Nov. Sat.-Sun. 11am-6pm, June-early Aug. Tues.-Thurs. 10am-5pm, Fri. 10am-10pm, Sat. 11am-10pm, Sun. 11am-6pm, late Nov.-early Jan. Sun.-Thurs. 6pm-10pm, Fri.-Sat. 6pm-11pm; $4 pp entry, $4 per ride or $18 for unlimited rides), which features numerous rides and a mini train that tours the park. The historic carousel was established here in 1906 and eventually listed on the National Register of Historic Places; it's now considered the last antique wooden carousel in Louisiana.

Another kid-friendly spot is the year-round **Storyland** (Tues.-Fri. 10am-5pm, Sat.-Sun. 10am-6pm; $4 pp). The property features 25 larger-than-life sculptures, each based on a different fairy tale, from Captain Hook's pirate ship to the Three Little Pigs. Paid admission to Storyland, the New Orleans Botanical Garden, or the Carousel Gardens Amusement Park allows you access to all three. Admission prices only apply to those 36 inches in height or taller; children shorter than that are entitled to free entry as well as free amusement park rides, if accompanied by a paid adult (and if tall enough for the rides with minimum height requirements).

Families might also appreciate the park's newest attraction, **City Putt** (Sun. and Tues.-Thurs. 10am-10pm, Fri.-Sat. 10am-midnight; $8 adult, $6 child 4-12, free under 4), which encompasses two 18-hole courses.

MAP 6: 1 Palm Dr., 504/482-4888, http://neworleanscitypark.com; hours vary seasonally; free, though activity fees apply

DEGAS HOUSE

Constructed in 1852, the expertly restored Degas House is the only former residence of famed French Impressionist Edgar Degas that's open to the public. The artist, whose mother and grandmother were born in New Orleans, lived here from 1872 to 1873 while visiting relatives. During his stay, he painted at least 22 works of art, including *A Cotton Office in New Orleans* (1873), which became the first Impressionist painting ever purchased by a museum. The Edgar Degas House Creole Impressionist Tour (daily 10:30am and 1:45pm; $29 adult, $26 senior and student) is usually conducted by Degas's great-grandnieces. During the tour, which usually lasts 2 hours and 15 minutes, you'll enjoy a narrated walk through the house (which is also a well-regarded B&B), view the documentary *Degas in New Orleans: A Creole Sojourn,* and take a guided stroll around the neighborhood, exploring locales mentioned in the artist's letters from New Orleans. For $50 per person, you can opt for the early tour plus a Creole breakfast (9am-10am); reservations are required.

If you have artistic inclination, consider joining the **Painting with Passion** class (various days at 6:30pm; $40 pp). Typically featuring a Degas-inspired creation or an iconic New Orleans image, these sessions usually include an hour of socializing, followed by a painting lesson. Reservations are required and include paint, brushes, canvases, hors d'oeuvres, and an adult beverage. Wear comfortable clothes—anything that paint and/or wine won't ruin. There's a dedicated parking lot nearby, though if it fills up, street parking may still be available.

MAP 6: 2306 Esplanade Ave., 504/821-5009, www.degashouse.com; tour times and prices vary

Above: the Basin St. Station. **Below:** Storyland at City Park.

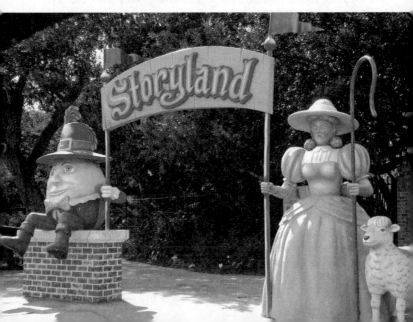

GREENWOOD CEMETERY

At the convergence of Canal Street, City Park Avenue, and Canal Boulevard, you'll encounter several old aboveground graveyards. If you only have time for one, venture inside Greenwood Cemetery, the 150-acre "city of the dead" just east of I-10. Established by the Firemen's Charitable & Benevolent Association in 1852, Greenwood helped to relieve the overcrowding (due to a major yellow fever epidemic) at nearby **Cypress Grove Cemetery** (120 Park Ave., 504/482-8983, www.greenwoodnola.com, daily 8:30am-4:30pm, free), which had been established in 1838 as the first cemetery to honor New Orleans's volunteer firemen and their families.

Today, Greenwood is notable for several reasons. It's the site of New Orleans's first Civil War memorial, dedicated in April 1874. The **Confederate Monument** is a masonry mausoleum topped with a marble pedestal, on which stands the statue of a Confederate infantryman. Designed by architect Benjamin M. Harrod and carved in Italy, the statue features, at its base, integral busts of Robert E. Lee, Stonewall Jackson, and other Confederate generals. The memorial marks the mass grave of 600 Confederate soldiers, whose remains were gathered by the Ladies Benevolent Association of Louisiana.

Other impressive landmarks here include the six-foot-high **Firemen's Monument,** an Italian marble statue erected in 1887 to honor the 50th anniversary of the Firemen's Charitable & Benevolent Association, and the marble tomb of **Lodge No. 30 of the Benevolent and Protective Order of Elks,** which was erected in 1912 by Albert Weiblen and is guarded by a majestic bronze elk. Several tombs are dedicated to fraternal organizations, such as the **Police Mutual Benevolent Association,** and to key New Orleanians, such as **John Fitzpatrick,** a 19th-century mayor of New Orleans, and **John Kennedy Toole,** the Pulitzer Prize-winning author of *A Confederacy of Dunces*.

MAP 6: 5200 Canal Blvd., 504/482-8983, www.greenwoodnola.com; daily 8am-4:30pm; free

NEW ORLEANS BOTANICAL GARDEN

The 12-acre New Orleans Botanical Garden opened in 1936 as the City Park Rose Garden, the Big Easy's first public classical garden. A project of the Works Progress Administration (WPA), it brought together the unique visions of landscape designer William Wiedorn, building architect Richard Koch, and artist Enrique Alférez.

Rechristened the New Orleans Botanical Garden in the early 1980s, this lovingly tended sanctuary now contains more than 2,000 types of plants, including azaleas, camellias, and palm trees, all set within thematic gardens. Unfortunately, Hurricane Katrina damaged some of the trees, flooded the outer gardens, and destroyed electricity-dependent greenhouse plants like the orchids and bromeliads, but thanks to donors and dedicated volunteers, the botanical garden reopened in March of 2006 and has flourished ever since.

Storyville

One block west of the French Quarter along Basin Street, which parallels Rampart, lies a still-dicey neighborhood that has been infamous for well over a century. Once known as Storyville, it was, from 1897 until 1917, the only officially sanctioned and legal red-light district in the country.

Over the course of nearly two centuries, prostitution thrived all over New Orleans, a city that had more than its share of sailors, traders, and laborers seeking intimate company during long spells away from home. For years, city politicos debated the best way to deal with this social fact of life, figuring that if they couldn't root out prostitutes and bordellos, they might as well sanction them—and tax them. It was city alderman Sidney Story who, in 1897, came up with the bright idea to create a legal red-light district, a neighborhood that was obviously named after him.

By all accounts, the system worked wonderfully well. Potential customers could peruse a directory, the *Blue Book,* containing names of brothels and prostitutes, along with prices, the various services available, and photos of many of the women. The city's illegitimate music movement, jazz, flourished in the city's legitimate sex district, as many bordellos hired jazz musicians (including Jelly Roll Morton and King Oliver) to entertain the patrons. At its peak, the neighborhood licensed 750 ladies of the evening, and prostitution continued to be a successful business in Storyville well into the 1960s, more than four decades after the red-light district was made illegal again.

To get a sense of the neighborhood's history, watch the Louis Malle-directed movie *Pretty Baby,* released in 1978. For more information, read *Storyville, New Orleans: Being an Authentic, Illustrated Account of the Notorious Red Light District,* by Al Rose, published in 1978.

Special attractions here include the colorful **Butterfly Walk** and **Hummingbird Garden;** the tranquil **Yakumo Nihon Teien Japanese Garden;** the **Historic New Orleans Train Garden,** a fascinating, Paul Busse-designed layout that represents the city of New Orleans in the early 19th century; and the **Conservatory of the Two Sisters,** a gorgeous, glass-domed building erected in the 1930s and situated beside a lovely, rose-flanked lily pond. Amateur botanists may also appreciate the **Plano Demonstration Garden,** while history buffs should stroll through the **Original WPA Formal Garden** and the **Stove House,** which, as the garden's original greenhouse, now nurtures a cactus collection.

The garden's entrance is located near the **Pavilion of the Two Sisters** on Victory Avenue. Though the Historic New Orleans Train Garden is open during regular hours, the train only operates on the weekends (Sat.-Sun. 10am-4:30pm; $6 adult, $3 child 5-12, free under 5) and during special events, such as City Park's Celebration in the Oaks. Free parking is available in the nearby parking lot, but pets, bikes, and skates aren't permitted.

MAP 6: 1 Palm Dr., City Park, 504/483-9386, http://neworleanscitypark.com/botanical-garden; Tues.-Sun. 10am-4:30pm; $4 pp

★ NEW ORLEANS MUSEUM OF ART

The vast holdings of the fabulous New Orleans Museum of Art (NOMA) total about 40,000 objects that span a variety of cultures and eras—from pre-Columbian, Native American, and Mayan artwork to French Impressionist paintings. The city's oldest fine arts institution is justly known for its excellent rotating exhibits, including everything from creative bookmarks to the 19th-century mass production of British decorative arts. The museum is also an architectural marvel, an imposing Beaux Arts-style building that dates to 1911. A cleverly appended modern addition was completed in 1971 and renovated in the 1990s.

The permanent collection is as eclectic as it is extensive. A few rooms are decorated with period 18th- and 19th-century American furnishings and decorative arts, as well as a survey of European and American artists. Included are several paintings by Degas; priceless Easter eggs and other decorative items created by Peter Carl Fabergé; photographs by Ansel Adams, Diane Arbus, and Walker Evans; and works by Monet, Picasso, Chagall, Cassatt, and O'Keeffe. One wing contains the impressive Decorative Arts Department, a fascinating array of glasswork and ceramics, mostly of the 19th and 20th centuries. You'll also find African and Asiatic works in a network of smaller galleries, plus an eclectic gift shop and a contemporary cafe.

The **Sydney and Walda Besthoff Sculpture Garden** (Mon.-Fri. 10am-6pm, Sat.-Sun. 10am-5pm) is an outdoor attraction that's free to visit. Peppered with magnolias, pines, and ancient, Spanish moss-draped live oaks, this peaceful, five-acre spread encompasses lagoons, pedestrian bridges, and more than 60 impressive sculptures. Noted works include sculptures by Pierre Auguste Renoir, Ida Kohlmeyer, and Claes Oldenburg. A free cell-phone tour is available.

NOMA offers ample free parking, but you can also reach the museum by bike, bus, or the Canal streetcar line. Each Wednesday, the museum is free to Louisiana residents, but note that the last admittance to the museum occurs 45 minutes before closing. The sculpture garden is barred to newcomers 30 minutes prior to closing. As with many attractions in New Orleans, both the museum and the garden are closed on Mardi Gras Day.

MAP 6: 1 Collins C. Diboll Circle, City Park, 504/658-4100, www.noma.org; Tues.-Thurs. 10am-6pm, Fri. 10am-9pm, Sat.-Sun. 11am-5pm; $10 adult, $8 senior and college student, $6 child 7-17, free under 7

OUR LADY OF GUADALUPE CHURCH

Situated along the southeastern edge of the historic Tremé neighborhood, this stunning church has been serving local Catholics since 1826. In fact, it's the oldest surviving church building in New Orleans and was originally erected as a burial church for victims of yellow fever. Over the decades, it has served Confederate veterans, Italian immigrants, and Spanish-speaking citizens. Although it was temporarily abandoned on three occasions—during the Civil War, in the early 1870s, and again in 1915, likely due to its proximity to the infamous Storyville district—it returned to service each time. Today, Our Lady of Guadalupe Church is the official chapel of the New Orleans Police and Fire Departments. The church, which also serves as the International Shrine of St. Jude, is just a short stroll from Louis Armstrong Park and St. Louis Cemetery No. 1, and is often a stop on the lengthy voodoo tour offered by the New Orleans Historic Voodoo Museum. **MAP 6:** 411 N. Rampart St., 504/525-1551, www.judeshrine.com; hours vary daily; free, though donations are accepted

PITOT HOUSE MUSEUM AND GARDENS

Alongside the eastern bank of Mid-City's peaceful Bayou St. John is one of the few surviving Creole colonial plantations in the South. The Pitot House Museum, which overlooks the slow-moving bayou, is named for an early occupant, James Pitot, the first mayor of New Orleans after it was incorporated, who lived in the house from 1810 to 1819. At one time or another, lawyers, nuns, and other interesting New Orleanians have dwelled in this lovely home.

In the 1960s, the Louisiana Landmarks Society carefully restored the Pitot House to its appearance in the early 1800s, filling it with American antiques that date from the first half of the 19th century. Because it had been moved 300 feet down Moss Street, it was impossible to research the original gardens surrounding the home. The current gardens include plants commonly used from the late 1700s to the early 1840s—such as roses, herbs, and okra, as well as grapefruit, sweet olive, and magnolia trees. Besides serving as the headquarters for the Louisiana Landmarks Society, the museum sheds light on the lifestyle of those who once lived alongside the bayou. The Pitot House Museum is fairly close to St. Louis Cemetery No. 3, City Park, and the New Orleans Museum of Art. To reach it, take the Canal streetcar; drivers must rely on street parking. It's closed on major holidays. **MAP 6:** 1440 Moss St., 504/482-0312, www.pitothouse.org; Wed.-Sat. 10am-3pm; $10 adult, $7 senior, student, and child, free under 6

ST. AUGUSTINE CATHOLIC CHURCH

Built on a former plantation estate and dedicated in 1842, the St. Augustine Catholic Church is the country's oldest African American Catholic parish. This is not surprising, perhaps, given its location in the Faubourg Tremé, the oldest African American neighborhood in the United States. Prior to the American Civil War, the church welcomed both free black citizens and enslaved individuals as worshippers. Even today, the congregation promotes and celebrates freedom from sin and oppression. Curiously, one of the church's former parishioners was Homer Plessy, the American plaintiff in the landmark U.S. Supreme Court case of *Plessy v. Ferguson*, which ultimately confirmed the "separate but equal" rule (that segregation was legal as long as both blacks and whites had equal facilities). In 2008, Mitch Landrieu (then the state's lieutenant governor) designated the church as one of several historic sites on Louisiana's **African American Heritage Trail** (www.astorylikenoother.com), which includes St. Louis Cemetery

Clockwise from top left: Our Lady of Guadalupe Church; the entrance to St. Louis Cemetery No. 1; Greenwood Cemetery.

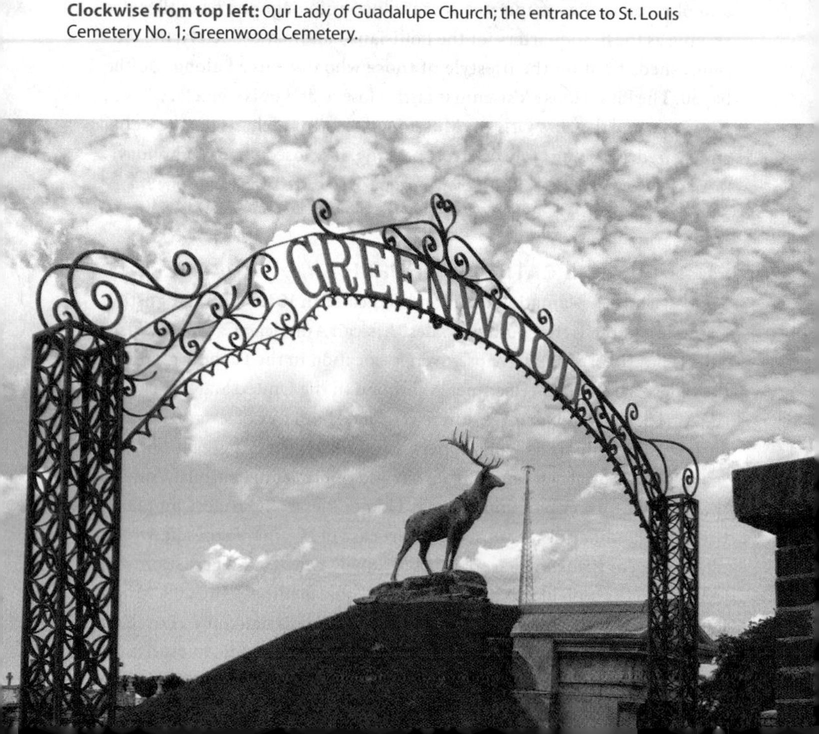

No. 1, the French Market, Congo Square, the Laura Plantation, and other attractions in southeastern Louisiana.

Tours of the historic church are arranged through the rectory and include its vibrant stained-glass windows as well as an impactful Tomb of the Unknown Slave. You can also visit during the Sunday morning Mass (10am), which can be an inspirational experience for believers and nonbelievers alike. Note that St. Augustine's is situated two blocks from Louis Armstrong Park in a rather sketchy area, so it's best not to come alone.

MAP 6: 1210 Gov. Nicholls St., 504/525-5934, www.staugustinecatholicchurch-neworleans.org; hours vary daily; free, though donations are accepted

ST. LOUIS CEMETERY NO. 1

Arguably the oldest and most famous of New Orleans's "cities of the dead," St. Louis Cemetery No. 1 was established in 1789, following the Great Fire of 1788, and set outside what was then the city border. Since New Orleans sits below sea level and has a high water table, bodies were buried aboveground, as earlier attempts to bury the dead underground had resulted in caskets floating to the surface during floods.

Bordered by Basin, Conti, Tremé, and St. Louis Streets, the cemetery currently contains more than 700 tombs and has interred thousands of people. Most of these aboveground structures are owned by families and designed to hold multiple sets of remains. Though constructed of brick, the elaborate tombs are often covered in concrete or stucco; some of the oldest ones are little more than crumbled ruins and piles of brick dust. One curious element is the segregated Protestant section near the rear of the predominantly Catholic cemetery.

Famous residents here include Homer Plessy (of *Plessy v. Ferguson* fame) and the much-loved voodoo priestess **Marie Laveau,** whose supposed tomb is a frequent stop on daily tours. Movie star Nicolas Cage has staked his own perpetual claim in this crowded cemetery; just look for the incongruous white pyramid that many locals consider an eyesore.

As of March 2015, the Archdiocese of New Orleans requires all tourists (those unrelated to the deceased) to enter the premises with a licensed tour guide. While several organizations offer guided tours, one of the most well-respected is **Save Our Cemeteries** (504/525-3377, www.saveourcemeteries.org; Mon.-Sat. 10am, 11:30am, and 1pm, Sun. 10am; $20 adult, free under 12), which leads hour-long excursions through the cemetery. Tours depart from the lobby of the nearby Basin Street Station.

MAP 6: Basin St. and St. Louis St., 504/482-5065; Mon.-Sat. 9am-3pm, Sun. 9am-noon; free, though tour fees apply

ST. LOUIS CEMETERY NO. 2

Driving through New Orleans via I-10, you'll notice several aboveground cemeteries, including St. Louis Cemetery No. 2, situated directly below the interstate in the historic Tremé neighborhood. Bordered by North Robertson Street, Iberville Street, North Claiborne Avenue, and St. Louis

Marie Laveau: Voodoo Queen

Voodoo experienced its heyday in New Orleans in the 19th century, but while most voodoo paraphernalia available in the French Quarter today is bought by tourists, there's no question that some people still take the practice very seriously. Unfortunately, misconceptions about voodoo abound and are often encouraged by its depiction in popular culture. Voodoo is based on the worship of spirits, called Loa, and a belief system that emphasizes spirituality, compassion, and treating others well. Although there's nothing inherently negative about voodoo, its practice does allow its followers to perform rites intended to bring calamity upon their enemies. These traditions, such as burning black candles or piercing miniature effigies with pins, are the most familiar among outsiders.

The origins of voodoo as a religious practice are unclear. Voodoo rituals are based on a variety of African religious traditions, which were brought to the United States by West African slaves. In 18th-century New Orleans, where slaves were kept by French and Spanish residents, voodoo began to incorporate some of the beliefs and rituals of Catholicism as well.

Marie Laveau (circa 1794-1881) is the historical figure most connected with southern Louisiana's rich voodoo tradition. A beautiful woman of French, African, and Native American extraction, she was New Orleans's high priestess of voodoo from roughly 1830 onward. She had numerous children, and at least one daughter continued to practice for many years after her mother's death, fueling rumors that the original Marie Laveau lived into the early 20th century. Her supposed grave in **St. Louis Cemetery No. 1,** on Basin Street, is still a site of pilgrimage for voodoo practitioners.

Laveau combined the understanding ear of a psychologist with the showmanship of a preacher to become one of the city's most vaunted spiritual figures. As a young woman, she practiced as a hair stylist in New Orleans, a position that afforded her the opportunity to work inside some of the city's most prominent homes. As she soaked up the gossip of the day, she also dispensed both practical and spiritual advice to her clients, no doubt sprinkling her words with healthy doses of voodoo mysticism and lore. Word of Laveau's talents as a voodoo priestess spread rapidly, and soon she was staging ceremonies in the small yard of her St. Ann Street home. Her most notorious ceremony, held annually in a swamp cabin along Bayou St. John on June 23 (St. John's Eve, the night before the Feast Day of St. John the Baptist), became the stuff of legend.

Laveau was the most famous priestess to captivate New Orleans's residents, but she wasn't the last. Throughout the centuries, a number of women and even some men have carried on the tradition of the voodoo priestess. According to legend, believers can invoke her powers by marking her tomb with three X's (a gris-gris, or charm), scratching the ground three times with their feet, knocking three times on the grave, and leaving a small offering before making a wish. In addition, many people in New Orleans continue to celebrate St. John's Eve and believe that, on this night, the spirit of the Voodoo Queen makes herself known.

Street, this curious "city of the dead" was established in 1823 as the city's fourth cemetery. Encompassing three city blocks, it's actually three times the size of the more famous St. Louis Cemetery No. 1. At the time that it was established, the city was being ravaged by numerous fatal diseases, including smallpox, yellow fever, and the bubonic plague. Residents wanted the much-needed cemetery to be placed as far from the French Quarter as possible, if only to keep away the evil spirits that were supposedly being spread by the diseased. City planners obliged.

Eventually, St. Louis Cemetery No. 2 became the permanent resting place of several significant people, including Dominique You, a lieutenant in the Gulf's largest pirate operation, and Jacques Phillipe Villere, Louisiana's first native-born governor. Despite the graveyard's historical significance, few official tours come here. **Save Our Cemeteries** (504/525-3377, www.saveourcemeteries.org; $20 adult, free under 12), a nonprofit that was established to protect St. Louis Cemetery No. 2 from being demolished, offers three 90-minute tours each month: at 10am on the second Monday, the fourth Sunday, and the fourth Monday. Reservations are required. If you visit on your own, come with a group, as it's not located in the safest area.

MAP 6: N. Robertson St. and St. Louis St., 504/482-5065; Mon.-Sat. 9am-3pm, Sun. 9am-noon; free

ST. LOUIS CEMETERY NO. 3

Following the huge yellow fever outbreak of 1853, New Orleans required yet another cemetery. Established in 1854 as Bayou Cemetery, this graveyard was built on an old leper colony, a governor-sanctioned place of exile nicknamed "Leper's Land." Located on Esplanade Avenue between Lada Court and Moss Street, St. Louis Cemetery No. 3 is actually one of the city's safer cemeteries for daytime exploration—even without an official tour. Just stop by the small office near the entrance gate to pick up a map before meandering through this narrow "city of the dead," which abuts the Fair Grounds Race Course in places and lies only a short stroll away from Bayou St. John and City Park. Here, you'll see several society tombs, such as those of the Dante Lodge of Masons, the United Slavonian Benevolent Association, and the Hellenic Orthodox community. As is true for all cemeteries and even most parks in New Orleans, you should not enter after dark; it's also wise to explore with a friend or two.

MAP 6: 3421 Esplanade Ave., 504/482-5065; Mon.-Sat. 8am-4:30pm, Sun. 8am-4pm; free

Above: the New Orleans Museum of Art. **Below:** Longue Vue House & Gardens.

ALGIERS POINT HISTORIC DISTRICT

Known as Algiers Point, this residential West Bank neighborhood is filled with a vast cache of notable, if generally modest, residences from the early 18th to the mid-20th centuries, including French colonial-style plantation houses, Creole cottages, Haitian shotguns, Greek Revival-style mansions, Victorian structures, and British craftsman-style homes. New Orleans's second-oldest neighborhood, Algiers Point features a handful of pleasant parks, a few B&Bs, several pubs and eateries, and a smattering of shops.

Although it's easy to reach, this neighborhood has always felt and continues to feel distinct from the rest of the city, owing to that mile-wide boundary line, also known as the Mississippi River, that separates it from the French Quarter and the CBD. From the foot of Canal Street, catch the **Algiers Point/Canal Street Ferry** (504/376-8180, http://nolaferries.com or www.friendsoftheferry.org; Mon.-Fri. 6am-10pm, Sat. 10:45am-8:15pm, Sun. 10:45am-6:15pm; $2 adult, $1 senior, free under 3), which has been sending people back and forth across the river since 1827. The trip usually takes about five minutes each way, with the ferry leaving each side every 30 minutes, and although cars aren't welcome, you're allowed to bring pets, bikes, and scooters onboard. Note that the final return trips from Algiers Point occur at 9:30pm Monday-Friday, 7:45pm Saturday, and 5:45pm Sunday.

MAP 7: Newton St. and Atlantic Ave. to Mississippi River, Algiers, www.algierspoint.org

CHALMETTE BATTLEFIELD AND NATIONAL CEMETERY

The Chalmette Battlefield commemorates the victory by Andrew Jackson and his troops during the Battle of New Orleans in 1815—a victory that represented the triumph of American democracy over European aristocracy. Sandwiched between St. Bernard Highway and the Mississippi River, the battlefield lies six miles southeast of downtown New Orleans; it's the only one of the six sites within Jean Lafitte National Historical Park and Preserve that touches on Louisiana's military history.

Your first stop should be the visitor center, which features maps, period weapons, and interactive exhibits about the War of 1812, the Battle of New Orleans, and the far-reaching effect of the American victory. Afterward, follow the 1.5-mile tour road, where you'll encounter interpretive placards at six pull-offs, plus the **Malus-Beauregard House** and the Chalmette National Cemetery, which was actually commissioned in 1864 as a graveyard for Union soldiers felled during the Civil War. You can also visit the graves of four men who fought in the War of 1812. Near the visitor center, you'll notice a 100-foot-tall obelisk towering over the battlefield; known as the **Chalmette Monument,** it was commissioned in 1840 shortly after former president Jackson returned to the scene of the battle to mark its 25th anniversary.

Free talks are given at 2:45pm Tuesday-Saturday, and the park hosts an annual Battle of New Orleans celebration every January. Although many visitors arrive here by private vehicle, you can also board the ***Creole Queen,*** which makes a daily trip from the French Quarter. The visitor center is closed on most holidays.

MAP 7: 8606 W. St. Bernard Hwy., Chalmette, 504/281-0510, www.nps.gov/jela; Tues.-Sat. 9am-4pm; free

★ LONGUE VUE HOUSE & GARDENS

One of the city's most impressive attractions is often overlooked by visitors simply because it's slightly off the beaten path. Situated near the border between New Orleans and Old Metairie, the Longue Vue House & Gardens is a lush, exotic, eight-acre estate that once belonged to local community pillars Edgar and Edith Stern and their children. Designed and constructed between 1939 and 1942 by architects William and Geoffrey Platt and landscape architect Ellen Biddle Shipman, the tranquil property was intended to be one organic whole, uniting the house and gardens seamlessly. Ultimately, the designers did just that.

Today, this serene place represents one of the last Country Place Era homes built in America. It comprises a period-furnished Classical Revival-style manor house, several outbuildings, 14 spectacularly landscaped garden areas, and 22 ponds and fountains. Such large residential properties had their heyday between 1880 and 1940, when designers worked closely with their clients to create extravagant, European-influenced gardens. Guided house tours are offered every hour on the hour (the last one at 4pm). On such tours, you'll not only see well-appointed chambers like the dining room, library, ladies' reception room, and master bedroom, but also modern art exhibits and displays about the creation of Longue Vue. For a slightly lower fee ($7 adult, $4 student and child, free under 3), you can opt to skip the house tour and simply explore the gardens, but I wouldn't recommend missing the opportunity to see as much as you can. Note that Longue Vue is closed on several major holidays.

MAP 7: 7 Bamboo Rd., 504/488-5488, www.longuevue.com; Mon.-Sat. 10am-5pm, Sun. 1pm-5pm; $12 adult, $10 senior, $8 student 11-17, $5 child 3-10, free under 3 and active military

METAIRIE CEMETERY

Where I-10 passes over City Park Avenue, just east of the suburb of Metairie, you'll spot several historic cemeteries, including the confusingly named Metairie Cemetery. After all, it's actually located in New Orleans, not far from the now-infamous 17th Street Canal, which busted open in the aftermath of Hurricane Katrina. Bordered by Fairway Drive, Metairie Road, and I-10, this property once contained a popular racetrack, which was originally built in 1838. Unfortunately, the Civil War and Reconstruction era took their toll, and in May of 1872, the faltering racetrack was converted into a cemetery. Listed on the National Register of Historic Places in 1991, this scenic, aboveground cemetery is filled with a variety of magnificent family tombs, private mausoleums, and elaborate memorials. Some of these serve as the final resting places of notable individuals, including nine Louisiana governors, seven New Orleans mayors, General P. G. T. Beauregard and two other Confederate generals, jazz singer Louis Prima, and silent movie star Marguerite Clark. Unlike other cemeteries in New Orleans, this one is relatively safe to visit, though you should always be respectful of the mourners around you.

MAP 7: 5100 Pontchartrain Blvd., 504/486-6331, www.lakelawnmetairie.com; daily 7:30am-5:30pm; free

Restaurants

PRICE KEY

$ Entrées less than $15
$$ Entrées $15–30
$$$ Entrées more than $30

New Orleans may be known for its beautiful architecture and seemingly never-ending nightlife, but it's the food that beckons most visitors.

The city's world-renowned reputation for culinary excellence is well-deserved. This is the place that shaped famous chefs Paul Prudhomme, Emeril Lagasse, and John Besh—all of whom embraced the Big Easy's Cajun and Creole roots, not to mention its abundance of fresh seafood.

While New Orleans certainly has its share of upscale, dinner-only restaurants celebrated for their impeccable service, creative fusion cuisine, ever-changing menus, and reliance on fresh, seasonal ingredients, it also boasts a wide array of old-time neighborhood haunts. Historic joints, such as Café Maspero in the French Quarter and Mandina's Restaurant in Mid-City, are often known for classic local staples like roast beef po-boys, gumbo, and crawfish étouffée. Thus, New Orleans caters as much to gourmands as it does to budget-conscious travelers just looking for a tasty meal between stops.

New Orleans's restaurants can fill up quickly, especially on the weekends, around holidays like Christmas and Mardi Gras, and during special events, such as Jazz Fest. At such times, reservations are highly recommended; for places where reservations aren't accepted, such as Mona Lisa Restaurant in the Quarter, it's best to dine on the weekdays when it's generally less crowded. Depending on the restaurant and neighborhood, you'll often avoid crowds and save money by visiting at lunchtime. And despite New Orleans's laid-back vibe, not all of the city's restaurants are suitable for children. In the French Quarter, Faubourg Marigny, Garden District, and Riverbend, for instance, several eateries are more appropriate for couples in the mood for romance.

Previous: Palace Café; Gumbo Shop.

Look for ★ to find recommended restaurants.

Highlights

★ **Finest Classic Creole Cuisine:** One of the few restaurants in Louisiana where men are still expected to wear jackets, **Galatoire's Restaurant** is the quintessential old-school New Orleans tradition, serving superb Creole fare from time-tested recipes (page 119).

★ **Heftiest Late-Night Burgers:** Though locals disagree over the city's best burger joint, many revelers head to **Yo Mama's Bar and Grill** to satisfy their late-night burger cravings. The burgers are always well prepared, with toppings that range from blue cheese to peanut butter (page 125).

★ **Most Romantic Courtyard:** Established in 1979, **Feelings Café** now occupies much of the D'Aunoy Plantation in the Faubourg Marigny. Lovers can enjoy an intimate, eclectic dinner in the lush brick courtyard (page 139).

★ **Tastiest Sandwiches:** There's considerable debate about this category in New Orleans, but many folks concur that the cozy **Cochon Butcher** produces heavenly sandwiches, from Cubanos and muffulettas to several other meat-filled delights (page 145).

★ **Best See-and-Be-Seen Restaurant:** The domain of talented and much-adored chef John Besh, **Restaurant August** pulls in a stylish crowd of movers and shakers, who delight in the restaurant's superbly crafted contemporary cuisine (page 148).

★ **Finest Special-Occasion Restaurant:** Whether you're celebrating a wedding anniversary, treating your mom on Mother's Day, or simply hoping to enjoy one of the best meals that New Orleans has to offer, book a table at the legendary **Commander's Palace** in the Garden District (page 150).

★ **Quirkiest Place for Great Cooking:** Long waits are not uncommon at funky **Jacques-Imo's Cafe** in the Riverbend area of Uptown, known for innovative Creole and Cajun food, huge portions, and sassy service (page 154).

★ **Yummiest Desserts:** For more than a century, **Angelo Brocato** has doled out delicious homemade ice cream and Italian pastries from its quaint Mid-City storefront space (page 163).

★ **Best Brunch Venue:** Part of the fun of brunching at **Ralph's on the Park** is sampling the creative and beautifully presented nouvelle Creole cuisine, but the other benefit is exploring adjacent City Park after your meal (page 164).

★ **Best Dining Option in the Burbs:** Situated in a nondescript section of Metairie, **Drago's Seafood Restaurant** has earned a cult following for its delicious charbroiled oysters and other fresh Cajun and Creole seafood dishes (page 170).

CAJUN AND CREOLE

ANTOINE'S RESTAURANT $$$

One of the true granddaddies of old-fashioned French-Creole cooking, Antoine's opened in 1840 and has since served everyone from President Coolidge to Judy Garland. Several well-known dishes, from oysters Rockefeller to eggs Sardou, were invented at this elegant restaurant, and the solicitous waitstaff will happily explain the endless menu of culinary options, all available à la carte. Deciding what to eat, though, is only half the challenge; you'll also have to choose from one of 14 dining rooms, including the Mardi Gras-themed Rex Room. Before dinner, have a cocktail in the on-site **Hermes Bar,** and during the day, enjoy a treat at **Antoine's Annex** (513 Royal St.), a small coffeehouse offering gelato and pastries.

MAP 1: 713 St. Louis St., 504/581-4422, www.antoines.com; Mon.-Sat. 11:30am-2pm and 5:30pm-9pm, Sun. 11am-2pm

ARNAUD'S $$$

The active corner of Bourbon and Bienville might seem an unlikely place for a fine-dining establishment, but Arnaud's is still a terrific spot to sample traditional Creole cuisine and enjoy friendly, attentive service. Established by Arnaud Cazenave, a French wine salesman, in 1918, Arnaud's serves favorites like baked oysters, seafood gumbo, and speckled trout amandine. Dine in the elegant main dining room or the smaller jazz bistro. Before dinner, have a cocktail in **French 75,** the on-site bar that was once a gentlemen-only area, and check out the stunning costumes at the **Germaine Cazenave Wells Mardi Gras Museum** (free). For a more casual meal, head next door to Arnaud's other eatery, **Remoulade** (309 Bourbon St., 504/523-0377, www.remoulade.com; daily 11:30am-11pm).

MAP 1: 813 Bienville St., 504/523-5433, www.arnaudsrestaurant.com; Sun.-Thurs. 6pm-10pm, Fri.-Sat. 6pm-10:30pm

BRENNAN'S $$$

It's hard to bypass Brennan's, the legendary pink eatery that initiated the Brennan clan's rise as the Crescent City's first family of the restaurant business. Opened in 1946 by Owen Edward Brennan and recently renovated by Ralph Brennan, the restaurant encompasses several dining areas, plus a lush courtyard. While the atmosphere can be loud, and visiting celebrities tend to get better service than regular folks, the food is definitely worth sampling. Two of the dishes invented on-site include eggs Hussarde, which combines poached eggs with Canadian bacon, hollandaise, and Marchand de Vin sauce, and bananas Foster, bananas sautéed in butter, brown sugar, cinnamon, and banana liqueur, then flamed in rum and served over vanilla ice cream.

MAP 1: 417 Royal St., 504/525-9711, www.brennansneworleans.com; Tues.-Sat. 8am-2pm and 6pm-10pm, Sun. 8am-2pm

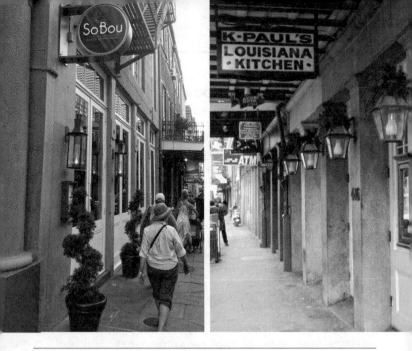

Clockwise from top left: SoBou; K-Paul's Louisiana Kitchen; Galatoire's Restaurant.

The City is Your Oyster

While in town, oyster-lovers should sample some versions of the shellfish for which New Orleans is known:

- **Oysters Bienville:** Oysters that have been baked in their shells, along with shrimp, mushrooms, green onions, herbs, and seasonings in a white wine sauce. Since the dish was invented at **Arnaud's** (page 117), you should sample it there first.
- **Oysters Rockefeller:** Baked oysters on the half-shell, topped with bread crumbs, butter, and a green sauce made of puréed herbs (such as parsley). **Antoine's Restaurant** (page 117), where it was invented, serves some of the city's finest (and keeps the recipe a closely guarded secret).
- **Oyster Artichoke Soup:** Created by the late local chef Warren LeRuth, oyster artichoke soup is my favorite New Orleans dish on a cold winter's day. Besides oysters and artichoke hearts, it's normally made with butter, green onions, celery, garlic, flour, chicken stock, cream, sherry, and various seasonings. Try one of the best versions at **Mandina's Restaurant** (page 165) in Mid-City.

COOP'S PLACE $$

The owner of Coop's sought to create a space that's equally bar and restaurant, and indeed this underrated hangout on raffish Decatur Street succeeds on both counts. Since 1983, this popular local joint has offered the convivial spirit of a neighborhood pub, complete with a pool table in the rear, as well as New Orleans-style cuisine that's consistently high caliber. Dark wooden tables and exposed brick walls give the place a warm feel, as does the welcoming staff. Reservations are not accepted, and, thanks to the presence of video poker machines, guests must be 21 and older.

MAP 1: 1109 Decatur St., 504/525-9053, www.coopsplace.net; daily 11am-close

THE COURT OF TWO SISTERS $$$

The French Quarter boasts several historic restaurants, including the Court of Two Sisters, established in 1880 by two Creole sisters, Emma and Bertha Camors; it is now run by the Fein brothers. Though the old-fashioned interior can be an elegant yet casual spot for a romantic dinner, the real appeal is the lush, spacious courtyard, particularly during the daily jazz brunch buffet, which features a live jazz trio and an array of hot and cold dishes, including made-to-order omelets, turtle soup, and shrimp rémoulade.

MAP 1: 613 Royal St., 504/522-7261, www.courtoftwosisters.com; daily 9am-3pm and 5:30pm-10pm

★ GALATOIRE'S RESTAURANT $$$

Among those few remaining New Orleans restaurants where men must wear a jacket in the evening (and all day Sunday)—and no patron may stroll in wearing shorts—is Galatoire's, which opened in 1905 and has been run by the Galatoire family ever since. While rowdy Bourbon Street might seem an unlikely place for such an elegant restaurant, Galatoire's actually lures many loyal patrons, and true regulars have been coming here for generations, often taking their seat at the same table. Almost as much fun as dining here is watching the local politicos hobnob and broker deals, especially on Friday afternoons. The enormous French-Creole menu includes everything from lavish high-end dishes, such as filet béarnaise, to affordable chicken and seafood entrées. Sweet potato cheesecake and banana bread pudding stand out among the rich desserts. Though the lower dining room maintains a "no reservations" policy, you can reserve a seat in the recently remodeled upstairs area.

MAP 1: 209 Bourbon St., 504/525-2021, www.galatoires.com; Tues.-Sat. 11:30am-10pm, Sun. noon-10pm

GUMBO SHOP $$

Given its location near Jackson Square, the Gumbo Shop can be a fairly touristy place, which, unfortunately, doesn't always live up to the hype. Granted, many of the dishes are worth sampling, from shrimp Creole to crawfish étouffé. The seafood okra and chicken andouille gumbos, however, could be better: Though the thick broths are tasty, the gumbos are often skimpy with the ingredients, such as shrimp. Still, the complete Creole dinners are a steal, offering you the choice of an appetizer, vegetable, entrée, and dessert for around $25; the Creole creamed spinach and warm bread pudding are particularly good options.

MAP 1: 630 St. Peter St., 504/525-1486, www.gumboshop.com; Sun.-Thurs. 11am-10pm, Fri.-Sat. 11am-11pm

K-PAUL'S LOUISIANA KITCHEN $$$

It's probably not fair to describe K-Paul's Louisiana Kitchen as traditional, since much of the food at Paul Prudhomme's famous restaurant is quite innovative. The celebrity chef was largely responsible for popularizing Cajun cooking outside Louisiana, and this is still an excellent, though pricey, place to sample such fare. Situated within an 1834 building with a cozy courtyard, K-Paul's (named after Paul and his wife, K) has an open kitchen on both the first and second floors, allowing diners the chance to watch their dishes being prepared.

MAP 1: 416 Chartres St., 504/596-2530 or 877/553-3401, www.kpauls.com; Mon. 5:30pm-10pm, Tues.-Sat. 11am-2pm and 5:30pm-10pm

MR. B'S BISTRO $$$

Opposite the imposing Hotel Monteleone, Mr. B's Bistro is a popular place for business lunches, and given its fashionable bar, attentive service, and classy decor, it's easy to understand why. It also doesn't hurt that this bustling eatery—operated by Cindy Brennan, of the famous Brennan clan—serves some truly delicious Creole cuisine. Though the ever-changing menu depends on seasonal ingredients, you can expect classic dishes like gumbo ya-ya, barbecue shrimp, and pasta jambalaya. Save some money by opting for weekday cocktail specials and two-course luncheons. Mr. B's also offers a wonderful jazz brunch on Sunday, and there's usually live piano music during dinner, 7pm-10pm. Reservations are accepted but not required, and the dress code is upscale casual.

MAP 1: 201 Royal St., 504/523-2078, www.mrbsbistro.com; Mon.-Sat. 11:30am-9pm, Sun. 10:30am-9pm

MURIEL'S JACKSON SQUARE $$$

Despite the name, Muriel's isn't actually on Jackson Square, but given its corner location at St. Ann and Chartres Streets, it definitely offers a picturesque view of this historic plaza. One of the more elegant restaurants in the Quarter, Muriel's appeals to a wide array of diners. The menu boasts delicious contemporary Creole cuisine, such as mirlitons filled with shrimp and andouille, a Gulf seafood stew, and vanilla bean crème brûlée. In addition to offering two-course lunch specials and three-course prix fixe dinners, Muriel's features a pre-theater menu available on the evening of any local theater performance. Curiously, Muriel's is one of the few supposedly haunted establishments that seems to relish its past residents.

MAP 1: 801 Chartres St., 504/568-1885, www.muriels.com; Mon.-Fri. 11:30am-2:30pm and 5:30pm-10pm, Sat. 11:30am-2:30pm and 5pm-10pm, Sun. 11am-2pm and 5pm-10pm

THE OLD COFFEEPOT RESTAURANT $$

If you don't mind sassy service, make a beeline for the Old Coffeepot, which was established in 1894 and now features one of the best breakfasts in the Quarter. Some of my favorite morning dishes include Callas cakes, essentially spiced, deep-fried rice balls dusted with powdered sugar and served with creamy grits and maple syrup; eggs Sardou, which consists of poached eggs, creamed spinach, and artichoke bottoms; and the Rockefeller omelet, combining creamed spinach, oysters, and cheese. Lunch and dinner, featuring Cajun and Creole dishes, are also available.

MAP 1: 714 St. Peter St., 504/524-3500, www.theoldcoffeepot.com; Sun.-Mon. and Thurs. 8am-10pm, Tues.-Wed. 8am-2:30pm, Fri.-Sat. 8am-11pm

PALACE CAFÉ $$$

The Palace Café ranks among the most cosmopolitan of the several outstanding Brennan family restaurants in New Orleans. True, it can seem touristy, but don't let that dissuade you—the kitchen consistently prepares some of the city's best and most exciting local fare, and the staff is highly personable and efficient. Signature dishes include andouille-crusted fish, an oyster pan roast, and a crabmeat cheesecake baked in a pecan crust.

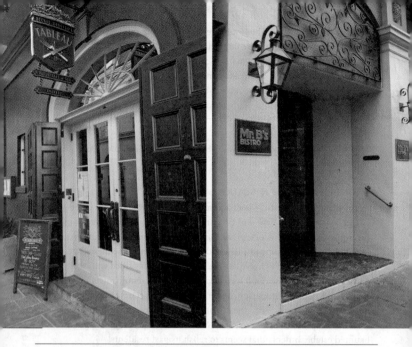

Clockwise from top left: Tableau; Mr. B's Bistro; Muriel's Jackson Square.

Every dish is tasty and presented with great flourish. Housed within the historic Werlein's building, this classy restaurant also serves a particularly enjoyable Sunday jazz brunch.

MAP 1: 605 Canal St., 504/523-1661, www.palacecafe.com; Mon.-Sat. 11:30am-2:30pm and 5:30pm-close, Sun. 10:30am-2:30pm and 5:30pm-close

RESTAURANT R'EVOLUTION $$$

Nestled inside the posh Royal Sonesta New Orleans since opening in June 2012, Restaurant R'evolution is the brainchild of award-winning chefs John Folse and Rick Tramonto. The menu consists of varied, re-imagined versions of classic Cajun and Creole cuisine, ranging from Creole Louisiana snapping turtle soup with deviled quail eggs to crawfish-stuffed redfish Napoleon with artichoke and oyster stew. The Sunday jazz brunch (10:30am-2pm), which brings together local favorites crab beignets, eggs Sardou, and strawberry pain perdu. At the very least, grab a drink in the on-site **Bar R'evolution** (Mon.-Sat. 5pm-close, Sun. 10:30am-close).

MAP 1: 777 Bienville St., 504/553-2277, www.revolutionnola.com; Mon.-Sat. 5:30pm-close, Sun. 10:30am-2pm and 5pm-close

SOBOU $$$

Described as a modern Creole saloon, SoBou (short for "south of Bourbon") was created inside the W New Orleans—French Quarter by the culinary experts behind Café Adelaide and Commander's Palace. The menus, which feature signature cocktails and classy Louisiana street food, change throughout the day. You might have Louisiana strawberry pancakes for breakfast, sweet potato beignets for lunch, and, for dinner, egg and duck bacon on brioche with a foie gras ice cream float. Besides the main dining room—which is stylishly illuminated by shelves of glowing bottles that often entice passersby—SoBou offers an on-site bar (daily 11:30am-close), a beer garden, and semi-private dining areas, plus limited complimentary parking via the hotel.

MAP 1: 310 Chartres St., 504/552-4095, www.sobounola.com; daily 7am-10pm

TABLEAU $$$

Situated inside the same historic building that houses Le Petit Théâtre du Vieux Carré, Dickie Brennan's latest offering has earned rave reviews for its French Creole cuisine. Classic dishes include shrimp rémoulade, Creole courtbouillon, and praline monkey bread pudding. Given its grand staircase, elegant decor, and modern, open kitchen, Tableau is a fine addition to the New Orleans dining scene. The dress code is upscale casual, and as with most Brennan-helmed establishments, reservations are recommended, especially on Le Petit's performance nights, when pre-theater menus are available. If possible, schedule your meal during the Sunday brass brunch (10am-2:30pm) or live music Thursday-Saturday.

MAP 1: 616 St. Peter St., 504/934-3463, www.tableaufrenchquarter.com; Mon.-Thurs. 11:30am-10pm, Fri.-Sat. 11:30am-11pm, Sun. 10am-10pm

TUJAGUE'S $$$

Tujague's is an atmospheric corner tavern that's been around since 1856, making it the second-oldest continuously operated restaurant in New Orleans. It sits opposite the French Market and serves much of the local Louisiana produce and seafood sold there. The six-course Creole menu varies little from what diners might have eaten more than a century ago: beef brisket in Creole sauce, shrimp rémoulade, soup du jour, and a choice of entrée, dessert, and beverage. In addition to the usual cocktails and wines, Tujague's serves its own microbrewed beer. Drinking here has quite a legacy—the cypress-wood bar is original, shipped from France the year that the restaurant opened, and it's played host to everyone from President Truman to Harrison Ford.

MAP 1: 823 Decatur St., 504/525-8676, www.tujaguesrestaurant.com; Mon.-Fri. 5pm-10pm, Sat.-Sun. 11am-3pm and 5pm-10pm

AMERICAN

DICKIE BRENNAN'S STEAKHOUSE $$$

Red-meat lovers swear by the hefty cuts served at Dickie Brennan's Steakhouse, which is known for its oyster-topped filet served with creamed spinach and roasted potatoes. Garlic-crusted redfish, blackened prime rib, and the grilled rib eye enhanced with Abita beer-flavored barbecue shrimp are also big draws, not to mention classic desserts like pecan pie, Creole cheesecake, and bananas Foster bread pudding. Though a clubby, upscale space, the restaurant has a relaxed mood, and presentable casual attire is customary.

MAP 1: 716 Iberville St., 504/522-2467, www.dickiebrennanssteakhouse.com; Sat.-Thurs. 5:30pm-10pm, Fri. 11:30am-2:30pm and 5:30pm-10pm

JOHNNY'S PO-BOYS $

Johnny's Po-Boys opened in 1950 as an unprepossessing, family-owned eatery with tables sheathed in red-checkered cloths and surrounded by bentwood chairs. Though it's only open until the afternoon, Johnny's fills up daily for breakfast and lunch. Not surprisingly, it's best known for its namesake sandwiches, but you can also order omelets, seafood platters, and ice cream treats. Classic po-boys include boudin, shrimp, and the Judge Bosetta (stuffed with ground beef, Italian and hot sausage, and Swiss cheese).

MAP 1: 511 St. Louis St., 504/524-8129, http://johnnyspoboys.com; daily 8am-4:30pm

PORT OF CALL $$

This dark and divey corner tavern is so popular for its hefty burgers—made with freshly ground beef and piled high with mushrooms or melted cheddar—that there's often a line outside the door. Besides burgers, the simple menu also features traditional comfort foods like steaks, salads, and loaded baked potatoes. The nautical decor and strong cocktails make Port of Call a worthy stop.

MAP 1: 838 Esplanade Ave., 504/523-0120, www.portofcallnola.com; Sun.-Thurs. 11am-midnight, Fri.-Sat. 11am-1am

RIB ROOM $$$

Situated in the elegant Omni Royal Orleans, the historic Rib Room is one of the city's best steak houses. The dining room is unabashedly retro, with its soaring ceilings, comfortable leather chairs, and huge arched windows overlooking Royal Street. The staff is deft and fun-loving—many employees have been here for several decades. Though nouvelle foodies may scoff, frequent patrons favor this hip dining venue for its delicious, sometimes innovative, dishes, ranging from well-prepared prime rib and seared tuna medallions to local favorites like crab cakes, Creole gumbo, and turtle soup. Rib Room offers a delectable Sunday jazz brunch.

MAP 1: Omni Royal Orleans, 621 St. Louis St., 504/529-7046, http://ribroomneworleans.com; Mon.-Thurs. 6:30am-10:30am, 11:30am-2pm, and 6pm-9:30pm, Fri. 6:30am-10:30am, 11:30am-2:30pm, and 6pm-10pm, Sat. 6:30am-10:30am, 11:30am-2pm, and 6pm-10pm, Sun. 6:30am-10:30am, 11:30am-2:30pm, and 6pm-9:30pm

★ YO MAMA'S BAR AND GRILL $$

Not far from Bourbon Street, this late-night hole-in-the-wall lures plenty of repeat customers. While some locals dispute this fact, Yo Mama's is one of the city's best burger joints, offering a variety of toppings, from peanut butter to blue cheese. Unfortunately, the place is often understaffed, and the three booths and curving bar don't accommodate many patrons. But you'll typically find a spot during the off-hours—and if not, the well-stocked jukebox and 89 tequila varieties will keep you busy while you wait.

MAP 1: 727 St. Peter St., 504/522-1125, www.yo-mamas.com; Mon.-Fri. 11am-close, Sat.-Sun. 10am-close

ASIAN

SEKISUI SAMURAI SUSHI $$

Though New Orleans isn't known for sushi, Sekisui Samurai isn't a bad option if you're craving edamame, sashimi, and miso soup. Situated between the House of Blues and the Kerry Irish Pub, this cozy, often tranquil eatery offers a slew of freshly prepared *nigiri* and sushi rolls, plus tuna *tataki*, seafood udon, and shrimp tempura.

MAP 1: 239 Decatur St., 504/525-9595, www.samuraineworleans.com; Sun.-Thurs. 11:30am-10pm, Fri.-Sat. 11:30am-10:30pm

COFFEE AND DESSERTS

CAFÉ DU MONDE $

Beginning as a humble coffee stand to serve the customers and employees of the produce stalls in the French Market in 1862, Café Du Monde has grown into one of the most legendary food operations in the country. Part of its mystique and popularity is due to its round-the-clock hours (except for Christmas) and its small menu, conveniently plastered on the napkin dispensers. The mainstays are beignets and dark-roasted coffee laced with chicory and traditionally served *au lait*. The mostly open-air

Round-the-Clock Eats

For night owls, the Big Easy really delivers. In addition to bars, pubs, and live music venues that stay open until the wee hours, you'll find a slew of 24-hour eateries, ideal for late-night or early-morning cravings.

Perhaps the most well known of these round-the-clock joints is **Café Du Monde,** which, except for a brief time around Christmas (6pm on Dec. 24 to 6am on Dec. 26), is open 24 hours daily. The spacious, open-air patio, with its green-and-white striped awning, old-fashioned ceiling fans, and bustling uniformed servers, has been depicted in countless magazines, television shows, and movies, including 2003's *Runaway Jury.* A simple menu, pasted on each table's napkin dispenser, features a limited selection of items (such as beignets, milk, coffee, and hot chocolate) that have changed little over the years. This charming place lures a wide assortment of patrons, from local families and Midwest tourists to post-prom couples and on-duty police officers.

If you have a yen for more than dessert in the French Quarter, head to the **Clover Grill** (900 Bourbon St., 504/598-1010, www.clovergrill.com), a cozy diner where seating is often hard to snag and sassy waiters serve up hamburgers, sandwiches, and omelets.

A couple blocks down Bourbon, the **Quartermaster** (1100 Bourbon St., 504/529-1416, www.quartermasterdeli.net) offers only a few seats alongside the front window, but plenty of culinary options at the deli counter in the rear of this often crowded, albeit dingy, store. After a night of tireless bar-hopping, the Quartermaster, also known as The Nellie Deli, is a popular place to stock up on junk food in addition to jambalaya, stuffed potatoes, and roast beef po-boys. Be aware, the employees here are rife with attitude.

Just a block east on nearby Royal, in the shadow of the supposedly haunted LaLaurie Mansion, stands another longtime, 24-hour market and deli. Popular with the late-night crowd, especially post-shift bartenders and servers, **Verti Marte** (1201 Royal St., 504/525-4767) prepares a slew of options, from omelets to BBQ and seafood entrées to scrumptious desserts.

Patrons 21 years old and over might prefer the **Déjà Vu Bar & Grill** (400 Dauphine St., 504/523-1931, www.dejavunola.com), where you'll find a wide

café has dozens of small marble tables beneath the green-and-white awning, the sides of which can be unfurled on chilly days, though you can also sit inside the small, fully enclosed dining area. Servers clad in white shirts with black bow ties and white-paper hats whisk about gracefully, delivering plates of beignets at almost breakneck speed. While no visit to New Orleans is complete without experiencing this original location, you may notice other branches throughout the city, including those in the Riverwalk (500 Port of New Orleans, Ste. 27) and Lakeside malls (3301 Veterans Blvd., Ste. 104).

MAP 1: 800 Decatur St., 504/525-4544 or 800/772-2927, www.cafedumonde.com; daily 24 hours

CC'S COFFEE HOUSE $

The Quarter has a branch of one of the city's most famous coffeehouse chains, CC's, at the corner of Royal and Dumaine Streets, just opposite

Quartermaster on Bourbon Street

selection of beers, cocktails, and tasty vittles—from burgers and po-boys to seafood platters and breakfast specialties. If you're staying in the French Quarter and would rather not leave your apartment or hotel room, note that the Quartermaster, Verti Marte, and Déjà Vu offer free delivery for all phone-in food orders.

If you find yourself near Frenchmen Street in the wee hours, you can always head to **Buffa's Bar & Restaurant** (1001 Esplanade Ave.), a 24-hour bar and music club that lies on the border between the French Quarter and the Faubourg Marigny. It also happens to serve some terrific American, Cajun, and Creole grub, such as shrimp Creole omelets, redfish po-boys, and bratwurst jambalaya, any time of the day.

the neighborhood's only elementary school. It's a cozy spot, meaning that seating is limited, but it's also warmly lit and charmingly furnished, with several cushy armchairs. Besides tasty coffee drinks and delectable cookies, muffins, and scones, this café provides free wireless Internet access. Numerous other CC's coffeehouses can be found throughout New Orleans and southern Louisiana, from Metairie to Lafayette.

MAP 1: 941 Royal St., 504/581-6996, www.ccscoffee.com; Mon.-Fri. 6am-9pm, Sat.-Sun. 7am-9pm

CROISSANT D'OR PATISSERIE $

A source of delightful pastries, from napoleons to dark chocolate mousse, the Croissant d'or is a classic French bakery that also serves delicious sandwiches, fresh salads, and yummy breakfasts. Situated in the Lower Quarter, not far from the Old Ursuline Convent, this spacious café—with plenty of tables, local artwork, and a simply furnished courtyard—makes a nice break from exploring the neighborhood's rich architecture. Be prepared for long lines, especially in the morning.

MAP 1: 617 Ursulines Ave., 504/524-4663, www.croissantdornola.com; Wed.-Mon. 6am-3pm

ENVIE ESPRESSO BAR & CAFE $

A wonderful place to while away an afternoon, hang out with friends, and watch curious passersby, EnVie brews a strong coffee and serves plenty of interesting teas and pastries. This local favorite prepares decent salads and sandwiches, not to mention excellent breakfasts, including a prosciutto and asparagus omelet. Patrons will find lots of seating, free wireless Internet access, and open French doors that make this corner café even airier.

MAP 1: 1241 Decatur St., 504/524-3689; Sun.-Thurs. 7am-midnight, Fri.-Sat. 7am-1am

LA DIVINA GELATERIA $

In the alley behind the Cabildo sits a delightful café with limited outdoor seating, heavenly panini, and plenty of artisanal gelato. Though the gelato flavors change often, standards include dark chocolate and pineapple mint sorbetto. Some of the best flavors take advantage of local ingredients, such as bourbon pecan, sweet potato, and bananas Foster. For sandwiches, try the Muffalino, a reinvented New Orleans classic featuring mortadella, Italian ham, provolone cheese, and homemade olive salad. You'll find two other locations of La Divina in southern Louisiana: one on Loyola's Uptown campus (501 Pine St.) and another in Baton Rouge (3535 Perkins Rd., Ste. 360 Acadian Village).

MAP 1: 621 St. Peter St., 504/302-2692, http://ladivinagelateria.com; Mon.-Wed. 11am-10pm, Thurs. 8:30am-10pm, Fri.-Sat. 8:30am-11pm, Sun. 8:30am-10pm

ECLECTIC

BAYONA $$$

A highly regarded restaurant on a quiet stretch of Dauphine, Bayona fuses traditions, recipes, and ingredients from a handful of cultures, namely American, French, Italian, Mediterranean, Asian, and North African. Award-winning chef Susan Spicer dreams up such imaginative combos as peppered lamb loin with goat cheese-zinfandel sauce. Desserts are no mere afterthought, and there's a commendable wine list. The setting—an 18th-century Creole cottage filled with trompe l'oeil murals of the Mediterranean countryside, plus a lush courtyard—is the quintessence of romance, though the odd interior acoustics can make it rather loud on certain nights.

MAP 1: 430 Dauphine St., 504/525-4455, www.bayona.com; Mon.-Tues. 6pm-9:30pm, Wed.-Thurs. 11:30am-1:30pm and 6pm-9:30pm, Fri.-Sat. 5:30pm-10pm

CAFÉ AMELIE $$

Opposite the oft-photographed Cornstalk Hotel, you'll encounter the enticing Café Amelie, a cute, warmly furnished spot that sits beyond a lush, intimate courtyard, which is favored for anniversaries and other romantic

Above: EnVie Espresso Bar & Cafe. **Below:** the original Café Du Monde, part of the French Market.

occasions. Locals and tourists alike often pause before the simple, ever-changing menu that's posted daily by the wrought-iron gates. The menu, while eclectic, definitely embraces Louisiana-style cuisine, including such classics as chicken and andouille gumbo, citrus-drizzled crab cakes, and jumbo shrimp and grits with corn maque choux.

MAP 1: 912 Royal St., 504/412-8965, www.cafeamelie.com; Sun. and Wed.-Thurs. 11am-3pm and 5pm-9pm, Fri.-Sat. 11am-3pm and 5pm-10pm

CRESCENT CITY BREWHOUSE $$

Though some locals consider the Crescent City Brewhouse—which occupies the first two floors of a white-brick building on Decatur—a tourist magnet, I find that, as brewpubs go, it serves surprisingly decent and varied food. Offerings include baked brie, shucked oysters, and seafood cheesecake. Many diners come to sample the various microbrews, which are prepared Bavarian-style, with simple, natural ingredients. The light Weiss beer is a house favorite. This inviting space lures passersby with its exposed brick walls, shiny brewing equipment, and live music. If possible, opt for balcony or courtyard dining.

MAP 1: 527 Decatur St., 504/522-0571 or 888/819-9330, www.crescentcitybrewhouse.com; Sun.-Thurs. 11:30am-10pm, Fri.-Sat. 11:30am-11pm

NOLA $$$

Though most people have heard about NOLA—Emeril Lagasse's restaurant in the French Quarter—not everyone loves it. However, NOLA delivers great cooking and a lively dining experience that very nearly lives up to the hype. The menu changes often, but favorites include garlic-crusted drum, a stuffed chicken wings appetizer with homemade hoisin dipping sauce, and fried green tomatoes with shrimp rémoulade. There's also a selection of excellent desserts, such as king cake bread pudding with Creole cream cheese ice cream. It can be hard to get a table, so book ahead and expect a wait even when you show up on time for your reservation.

MAP 1: 534 St. Louis St., 504/522-6652, http://emerils.com; Tues.-Wed. 6pm-10pm, Thurs.-Mon. 11:30am-2pm and 6pm-10pm

ITALIAN

IRENE'S CUISINE $$$

In the quieter Lower Quarter, at the corner of Chartres and St. Philip Streets, stands a nondescript building that looks more like a warehouse than a fine-dining establishment. Nevertheless, the well-favored Irene's Cuisine is popular among gourmands, especially for romantic dinners and special occasions. The service is attentive, and the Italian and French cuisine is often quite tasty, with highlights like bruschetta, soft-shell crab pasta, and crème brûlée. Given the restaurant's popularity, reservations are definitely recommended; be prepared for the crowded nature of the restaurant and surprise charges on soda refills.

MAP 1: 539 St. Philip St., 504/529-8811; Mon.-Sat. 5:30pm-10pm

Above: the Crescent City Brewhouse. **Below:** Café Amelie's picturesque courtyard.

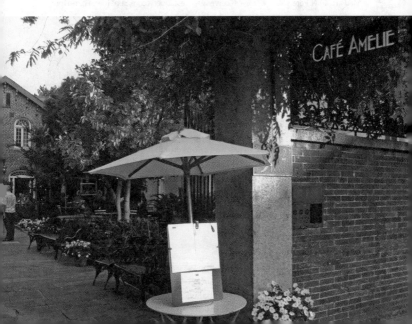

MONA LISA RESTAURANT $$

If you appreciate well-prepared Italian cuisine and would rather avoid the crazier end of the French Quarter, head to the more residential part of Royal Street, where you'll find a local favorite, the Mona Lisa Restaurant. As ideal for romantic dinners as it is for family outings, this cozy eatery has at least three things going for it: friendly service; affordable yet delicious food; and warm, homey decor, including ceiling fans, red-and-white checkered tablecloths, and walls that are covered with assorted *Mona Lisa* renditions, from copies of the classic da Vinci painting to a Picasso-style version. Recommended menu items include the Mediterranean pizza, chicken parmesan, and Mardi Gras pasta, which features shrimp and sausage with linguini and a creamy red sauce.

MAP 1: 1212 Royal St., 504/522-6746; Mon.-Thurs. 5pm-10pm, Fri.-Sun. 11am-10pm

MEXICAN

FELIPE'S TAQUERIA $

A favorite late-night haunt for inexpensive and tasty tacos, burritos, and tamales is Felipe's Taqueria. Opened in 2004, the space itself is attractive and inviting, with high ceilings, solid wood tables, and a separate bar area, where the television is always tuned to sporting events. The menu is fairly simple, and all dishes are made right in front of you, which explains why everything, from the super burrito to the chicken flauta, tastes so fresh. Be sure to order the Felipe's Special, an appetizer consisting of corn chips, salsa, guacamole, and queso dip. There are also locations in Uptown (6215 S. Miro St.) and Mid-City (411-1 N. Carrolton Ave.).

MAP 1: 301 N. Peters St., 504/267-4406, www.felipestaqueria.com; Sun.-Tues. 11am-11pm, Wed. 11am-1am, Thurs. 11am-11pm, Fri.-Sat. 11am-2am

SEAFOOD

ACME OYSTER HOUSE $$

Since 1910, the Acme Oyster House has been a reliable option for fresh bivalves. Decked out with red-checkered tablecloths and packed with tourists, this casual place is crazy at times, but for some, it's worth braving the frenzy for tasty soft-shell crab po-boys, shrimp platters, and a first-rate oyster Rockefeller bisque. While it might not be oyster nirvana, as some people claim, Acme's rich history and convenient location make it a decent choice. There are additional Acme Oyster Houses in Harrah's casino (8 Canal St.), Metairie (3000 Veterans Blvd.), Covington (1202 N. Hwy. 190), and Baton Rouge (3535 Perkins Rd.).

MAP 1: 724 Iberville St., 504/522-5973, www.acmeoyster.com; Sun.-Thurs. 11am-10pm, Fri.-Sat. 11am-11pm

CAFÉ MASPERO $

For more than four decades, Café Maspero has been one of the Quarter's most popular eateries. Ideal for budget-conscious travelers, it features several local staples, including jambalaya, muffulettas, and fried seafood platters. Despite the reasonable prices, portions are usually gigantic, and while there are occasional lulls, this spacious, admittedly dingy joint is typically hopping with full tables, bustling servers, and long lines of tourists and locals. The oft-open French doors invite refreshing breezes from the Mississippi River.

MAP 1: 601 Decatur St., 504/523-6250, www.cafemaspero.com; Sun.-Thurs. 11am-10pm, Fri.-Sat. 11am-11pm

DICKIE BRENNAN'S BOURBON HOUSE SEAFOOD $$$

Across the street from Ralph Brennan's Red Fish Grill, you'll encounter Dickie Brennan's Bourbon House Seafood, an often-crowded seafood eatery. Besides the enormous raw oysters, other favorite dishes include the grilled alligator, seafood gumbo, and shrimp po-boy. Aptly, this popular restaurant also houses an incredible assortment of bourbon; in fact, it's the official home of the New Orleans Bourbon Society. With its large glass windows, it offers entertaining views of the madness along Bourbon Street, but service can be slow, and the wait for a table can be long.

MAP 1: 144 Bourbon St., 504/522-0111, www.bourbonhouse.com; Sun.-Thurs. 6:30am-10pm, Fri.-Sat. 6:30am-11pm

FELIX'S RESTAURANT & OYSTER BAR $$

Just off crazy Bourbon Street, Felix's Restaurant & Oyster Bar has been serving local seafood fanatics since the early 1900s. Though known for its oysters on the half shell, this super-casual joint prepares all of New Orleans's seafood favorites well, including the shrimp rémoulade, blackened alligator, and oysters Bienville. Unfortunately, the service can be spotty.

MAP 1: 739 Iberville St., 504/522-4440, www.felixs.com; Mon.-Thurs. 10am-11pm, Fri.-Sun. 10am-1am

GW FINS $$$

Although many local dishes are offered at GW Fins, their kitchen serves fresh fish from all over the world, ranging from Canadian salmon to New Zealand John Dory. The setting, a converted warehouse with lofty ceilings, warm wood, and cushy booths, is contemporary and upbeat—seemingly more suitable for the CBD than the French Quarter. Worthy specialties include wood-grilled pompano, New Bedford sea scallops, and parmesan-crusted lemon sole. There's nothing overly convoluted or cutesy about the cooking—just fresh fish with modern ingredients, presented with flair—and the wine list is equally impressive. Reservations are recommended, and the dress code is business casual.

MAP 1: 808 Bienville St., 504/581-3467, www.gwfins.com; daily 5pm-10pm

OCEANA GRILL $$

The multilevel Oceana Grill encompasses numerous, colorfully decorated rooms, plus a courtyard. It's not far from bustling Bourbon Street. This

Clockwise from top left: the Mona Lisa Restaurant; Café Maspero; the Oceana Grill.

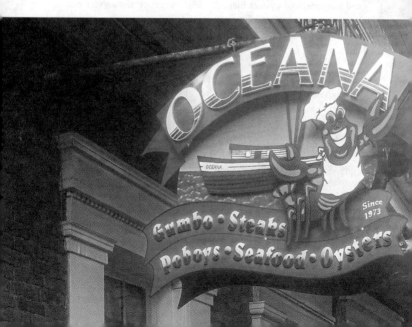

late-night, family-owned joint offers friendly service and specialty cocktails, not to mention dishes like crabmeat cakes, Cajun jambalaya pasta, and chocolate Kahlua mousse. My favorite item is the platter of raw oysters, which are usually large, clean, and perfectly chilled.

MAP 1: 739 Conti St., 504/525-6002, www.oceanagrill.com; daily 8am-1am

RALPH BRENNAN'S RED FISH GRILL $$$

Ralph Brennan's Red Fish Grill on exuberant Bourbon Street is worth seeking out. Opened in 1996, the restaurant, just a block from Canal, helped to revive a block that once felt a bit dark and ominous at night. The cavernous main dining room reverberates with piped-in rock music, and huge redfish mobiles dangle overhead. The noisy, festive ambience makes it fun for singles, friends, and anybody hoping to experience Bourbon's nightlife. To one side lies a spacious oyster bar with huge oyster half-shell sculptures; you can order from the main menu in here, too. The barbecued oysters are a great starter, served with a tangy blue-cheese dipping sauce, and the kitchen also turns out an amazingly decadent chocolate bread pudding. Few dishes, though, beat the hickory-grilled redfish topped with jumbo lump crabmeat.

MAP 1: 115 Bourbon St., 504/598-1200, www.redfishgrill.com; Sun.-Thurs. 11am-10pm, Fri.-Sat. 11am-3pm and 5pm-11pm

Faubourg Marigny and Bywater

Map 2

CAJUN AND CREOLE

ELIZABETH'S RESTAURANT $$

Situated within a modest white-frame house by the levee, along the southern edge of the Bywater, easygoing Elizabeth's serves exceptional breakfast and lunch, though it does require a lengthy journey from the Quarter. Elizabeth's is operated by chef Bryon Peck, who maintains the beloved eatery's commitment to imaginative meals and friendly service. One popular choice is the salmon and brie grilled cheese on rye, topped with fried eggs and hash or grits, but be sure to order a side of praline-flavored bacon. Lunch favorites include smoked turkey sandwiches, fried shrimp po-boys, and fried green tomatoes with shrimp rémoulade.

MAP 2: 601 Gallier St., 504/944-9272, www.elizabeths-restaurant.com; Tues.-Sat. 8am-2:30pm and 6pm-10pm, Sun. 8am-2:30pm

THE PRALINE CONNECTION $$

For a sublime blend of soul and Creole cooking, drop by The Praline Connection. Since it opened in 1990, it's been famous for both its crawfish étouffée and its bread pudding with praline sauce. In two simple dining rooms, the staff, clad in natty white shirts, black bow ties, and black fedoras, move about efficiently with hot platters of jambalaya, red beans and rice, and fried okra. Local beers and wines are sold here, and you can pick up the ingredients and seasonings to prepare your own versions of these foods back home.

MAP 2: 542 Frenchmen St., 504/943-3934, www.pralineconnection.com; Mon.-Sat. 11am-10pm, Sun. 11am-9pm

AMERICAN

DAT DOG $

This enormous, garishly colored eatery recently appeared in the heart of the Marigny triangle. The latest outpost of the local Dat Dog chain offers a variety of tasty hot dogs and sausages, from Polish kielbasas to Louisiana-style sausages made from crawfish or alligator meat. My favorite is the very filling Guinness dog, which pairs well with the slightly sweet bun and toppings like mustard, bacon, and onion. Various condiments, fries, shakes, and cocktails round out the menu, but it's the dogs that draw the crowds, especially those with a case of the late-night munchies. A friendly, casual joint, Dat Dog has indoor and outdoor seating. You'll find two other Dat Dog restaurants in the Uptown area (5030 Rue Freret St. and 3336 Magazine St.).

MAP 2: 601 Frenchmen St., 504/309-3362, http://datdognola.com; Sun.-Wed. 11am-midnight, Thurs. 11am-1am, Fri.-Sat. 11am-3am

THE JOINT $

New Orleans might not be known for its barbecue, but that doesn't stop local meat lovers from heading to The Joint, a super-casual dive on the eastern end of the Bywater celebrated throughout the city for its "carnivore cuisine." Featured on Guy Fieri's popular Food Network show *Diners, Drive-ins, and Dives,* this down-home, often crowded place offers delicious pork spareribs, beef brisket plates, and Cajun sausage. Even the sides are stellar, so save room for the macaroni and cheese, baked beans, and cole slaw. If you're really hungry, you won't go wrong with the desserts either, particularly the peanut butter pie.

MAP 2: 701 Mazant St., 504/949-3232, www.alwayssmokin.com; Mon.-Sat. 11:30am-9pm

SATSUMA DAUPHINE $

Plenty of locals swear by this spacious, art-filled Bywater eatery despite its slow service and hipster crowd. In addition to standard coffeehouse fare, such as espresso drinks and lemon-blueberry muffins, Satsuma Cafe has a wide array of delectable, often healthy breakfast, lunch, and dinner options, such as the tofu and black bean scramble, toasted pear and brie melt, and shrimp ceviche. The freshly squeezed juices are worth sampling, especially the Popeye, which consists of spinach, lemon, kale, and apple. Some of the soups, sandwiches, and muffins are vegan.

MAP 2: 3218 Dauphine St., 504/304-5962, www.satsumacafe.com; Sun.-Tues. 7am-5pm, Wed.-Sat. 7am-5pm and 6:30pm-10pm

Above: Dat Dog. **Below:** The Praline Connection.

ASIAN

SUKHOTHAI $$

For some of the best Thai food in the city, drop by SukhoThai, a relatively quiet eatery nestled in the Faubourg Marigny. Here, the friendly service and local artwork help to create a hip yet informal vibe, and the menu is quite extensive, offering tasty soups, vegetarian dishes, and seafood specialties, including the glass noodle shrimp bake. In case you get hungry while antiques shopping, there's also a **SukhoThai** (4519 Magazine St., 504/373-6471; Tues.-Fri. 11:30am-2:30pm and 5:30pm-10pm, Sat.-Sun. 11:30am-10pm) in the Uptown area.

MAP 2: 2200 Royal St., 504/948-9309, www.sukhothai-nola.com; Tues.-Fri. 11:30am-2:30pm and 5:30pm-10pm, Sat.-Sun. 11:30am-10pm

WASABI SUSHI & ASIAN GRILL $$

Near the edge of the Faubourg Marigny, just a few blocks up Frenchmen Street from the main cluster of bars and restaurants, sits this dark, cozy space, at once a mellow neighborhood bar and a stellar Japanese restaurant. Besides excellent sushi and sashimi, Wasabi serves delightful dishes like crab asparagus soup, squid salad, and wasabi honey shrimp, plus daily specials. If you're in Lakeview, be sure to stop by Wasabi's West End location (8550 Pontchartrain Blvd.).

MAP 2: 900 Frenchmen St., 504/943-9433, www.wasabinola.com; Mon.-Thurs. 11:30am-2:30pm and 5pm-10pm, Fri.-Sat. 11:30am-2:30pm and 5pm-11pm, Sun. 5pm-10pm

COFFEE AND DESSERTS

FLORA GALLERY & COFFEE SHOP $

Occupying a busy corner about four blocks east of Washington Square Park, the Flora Gallery & Coffee Shop is a funky little place with sidewalk seating, worn-in furnishings, big portions of coffee elixirs, and home-style cooking. While it's not a bad place to read a book, peruse groovy art, or chat with eccentric locals, it's admittedly not for everyone—particularly at night. After all, it's not far from the somewhat sketchy border between the Marigny and Bywater.

MAP 2: 2600 Royal St., 504/947-8358; daily 6:30am-midnight

NEW ORLEANS CAKE CAFE & BAKERY $

To satisfy your sweet tooth, venture to this homey café in the Faubourg Marigny that prepares to-die-for treats, such as red velvet cake with cream cheese frosting, plus specialty cupcakes flavored with champagne, mimosa, and chocolate mousse. This well-regarded neighborhood eatery also serves delicious breakfast and lunch items, including spinach and goat cheese omelets, shrimp and grits, and roasted vegetable sandwiches. The service is friendly and easygoing, and the crowd is a comfortable mix of students, retirees, artists, and hipsters. Be prepared for long lines, especially during the weekend brunch.

MAP 2: 2440 Chartres St., 504/943-0010, www.nolacakes.com; daily 7am-3pm

ECLECTIC

BOOTY'S STREET FOOD $

Nestled deep within the funky Bywater neighborhood lies this laid-back, ultra-creative eatery. Inspired by the global explorations of owner and travel journalist Nick Vivion, Booty's Street Food celebrates the world's diverse cuisine with an assortment of easy-to-eat dishes, which, depending on the day, might include a Thai chicken salad, Vietnamese catfish tacos, and a zesty Cubano. Besides the affordable vittles, this airy café provides plenty of pastries, craft cocktails, homemade ice cream, and speedy WiFi access. Meal times vary, with brunch on the weekend (9am-3pm), lunch on weekdays (10am-3pm), and dinner and dessert daily.

MAP 2: 800 Louisa St., 504/266-2887, http://bootysnola.com; Sun.-Thurs. 9am-11pm, Fri.-Sat. 9am-midnight

★ FEELINGS CAFÉ $$

One of the city's definitive gay restaurants, Feelings Café is set on a quiet street in a charmingly decrepit-looking old building several blocks past Frenchmen Street, roughly a 10-minute walk from the Quarter's edge. Though known best for its Sunday brunch, it serves first-rate Creole and continental fare at every meal. Specialties include blue cheese steak, Gulf fish Florentine, and seafood-baked eggplant—essentially, a slice of fried eggplant, topped with a combination of dirty rice, shrimp, crabmeat, and crawfish and covered with a rich hollandaise. Peanut butter pie is the trademark dessert. The setting is a shabby-chic dining room with local artwork for sale, along with a shady courtyard and a piano bar. It's a real locals' favorite, worth venturing a bit off the beaten path, especially if you're looking for a little privacy.

MAP 2: 2600 Chartres St., 504/945-2222, www.feelingscafe.com; Thurs.-Sat. 6pm-close, Sun. 11am-2pm and 6pm-close

THE MARIGNY BRASSERIE $$

Located in the same block as Frenchmen Street's most famous music clubs, the Marigny Brasserie is a slick, modern space whose kitchen puts a unique spin on Louisiana, Southern, Italian, French, and Mexican ingredients and recipes. The BBQ shrimp with rosemary grits reflects the kitchen's simple approach to contemporary food. Besides tasty salads, tacos, and sandwiches, classic New Orleans dishes are available, including fried green tomatoes and shrimp rémoulade. The stylish bar is a pleasant place to sip creative cocktails and listen to live music before heading to one of the nearby clubs.

MAP 2: 640 Frenchmen St., 504/945-4472, www.marignybrasserie.com; Sun.-Thurs. 11:30am-10pm, Fri.-Sat. 11:30am-11pm

PRESS STREET STATION $

Not long ago, the **New Orleans Center for Creative Arts** (NOCCA, 2800 Chartres St., 504/940-2850, www.nocca.com) added culinary arts to its

Above: Booty's Street Food. **Below:** Feelings Café.

impressive list of instructional offerings. So, it's little surprise that the NOCCA Institute also assisted in opening Press Street Station, whose menu features dishes from NOCCA's culinary students. Helmed by chef Jonathan Schmidt, Press Street offers a medley of breakfast, lunch, and dinner dishes, which are all served all day. You can sample an assortment of treats, from boudin-stuffed mirlitons to shrimp tamales. Profits from the restaurant support financial aid for NOCCA students and guest artists.

MAP 2: 5 Press St., 504/249-5622, http://pressstreetstation.com; Tues.-Thurs. 10am-9pm, Fri. 10am-10pm, Sat. 9am-10pm, Sun. 9am-3pm

ST. ROCH MARKET $

Perched on the edge of the St. Roch neighborhood, sandwiched between the Faubourg Tremé and the Faubourg Marigny, stands this cavernous, high-ceilinged edifice, a refurbished gathering place for foodies and families alike. With its white, minimalist decor, plentiful indoor and outdoor seating, and assorted stalls, offering everything from cold-pressed juices and savory crepes to raw oysters and Korean-Creole dishes like the "Japchalaya," it's a welcome addition to the local food scene. It's also a decent place to pick up coffee, pastries, specialty meats, fresh produce, and wine.

MAP 2: 2381 St. Claude Ave., 504/609-3813, www.strochmarket.com; daily 9am-11pm

INDIAN

SILK ROAD $$

Set inside a strikingly restored historic building in the heart of the Faubourg Marigny, Silk Road is a full-service restaurant offering both highly praised Indian fare as well as classic New Orleans dishes. On any given day, you might sample BBQ shrimp and grits for breakfast, Louisiana crawfish egg-rolls and masala shrimp wraps for lunch, and samosas, chicken and andouille gumbo, and lamb vindaloo for dinner. If you really love it here, you can even spend the night, as the family-owned **Balcony Guesthouse** (504/810-8667, www.balconyguesthouse.com) is located upstairs.

MAP 2: 2483 Royal St., 504/944-6666, www.silkroadnola.com; Tues.-Sat. 7:30am-10pm, Sun. 7:30am-3pm

ITALIAN

ADOLFO'S $$

Large portions of traditional Italian and Creole fare are heaped onto the plates at Adolfo's, a longtime neighborhood standby that's especially strong on seafood dishes, such as oysters Pernod and the "ocean sauce," which features shrimp, crawfish, and crab. Granted, it's a small hole-in-the-wall, where the service can be slow, reservations are typically not accepted, and no credit cards are allowed, but it's a good choice for dining before heading to one of Frenchmen's nearby music clubs. Downstairs, the **Apple Barrel Bar** (609 Frenchmen St., 504/949-9399; Sun.-Thurs. 1pm-3am, Fri.-Sat. 1pm-5am) is a dark and cozy spot to nurse a cocktail before or after dinner.

MAP 2: 611 Frenchmen St., 504/948-3800; daily 5:30pm-10:30pm

MEDITERRANEAN

MONA'S CAFÉ $$

In addition to offering a richly stocked Lebanese and Greek grocery, Mona's Café serves inexpensive Middle Eastern food, including appetizers like falafel, imported olives, and spinach pie. The extensive menu boasts savory entrées, such as chicken kabobs, gyros, and grape-leaf platters. The only drawback is the easily distracted waitstaff. Be sure to stop by Mona's other locations in Uptown (4126 Magazine St.) and Mid-City (3901 Banks St.).

MAP 2: 504 Frenchmen St., 504/949-4115, http://monascafeanddeli.com; Mon.-Thurs. 11am-10pm, Fri.-Sat. 11am-11pm, Sun. noon-9pm

Central Business and Arts Districts

Map 3

CAJUN AND CREOLE

BON TON CAFE $$$

Housed within a historic building erected in the 1840s and featuring brick walls, wrought-iron chandeliers, and red-checkered tablecloths, the nostalgic, amiable Bon Ton Cafe has been serving well-favored Cajun cuisine since 1953. Dishes like the turtle soup, seafood gumbo, and bread pudding with whiskey sauce are popular among the regulars. Given the challenging street-parking situation, arriving by foot, cab, or streetcar is recommended.

MAP 3: 401 Magazine St., 504/524-3386, www.thebontoncafe.com; Mon.-Fri. 11am-2pm and 5pm-9pm

CAFÉ ADELAIDE $$$

Set inside the glamorous Loews New Orleans Hotel, Café Adelaide is a highly touted, relative newcomer from the Brennan family, offering delicious food for breakfast, lunch, and dinner. Start the day with honeycomb waffles, and try a corn-fried oyster salad for lunch. At dinner, you might begin with the shrimp and tasso corn dogs, then consider notable main dishes like shrimp courtbouillon, jumbo seared sea scallops with beluga lentils, and filet mignon with garlic-roasted artichokes. Lighter fare, as well as a long list of colorful cocktails, is available in the trendy **Swizzle Stick Bar.**

MAP 3: Loews New Orleans Hotel, 300 Poydras St., 504/595-3305, www.cafeadelaide.com; Mon.-Thurs. 7am-10am, 11:30am-2pm, and 6pm-9pm; Fri. 7am-10am, 11:30am-2:30pm, and 6pm-9:30pm; Sat. 7am-12:30pm and 6pm-9:30pm; Sun. 7am-12:30pm and 6pm-9pm

COCHON $$

Noted chef Donald Link, of Herbsaint Bar and Restaurant, runs Cochon, a rustic, renovated warehouse space that opened in April 2006 in the Arts District. It serves a stellar blend of Cajun and contemporary American

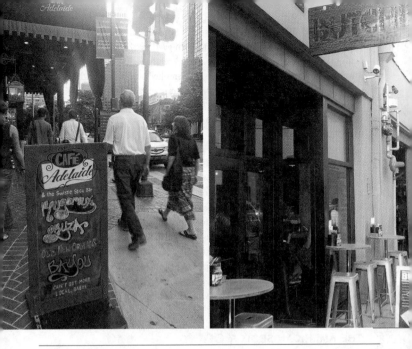

Clockwise from top left: Café Adelaide; Cochon Butcher; The American Sector.

victuals, specializing in small, tapas-style portions, such as baked oyster and kale dressing, fried alligator with chili garlic aioli, and fried boudin with pickled peppers. Highlighted entrées include rabbit and dumplings, smoked ham hocks with bitter greens, and smoked beef brisket with horseradish potato salad. Save room for the hummingbird cake, made with pecans, pineapples, bananas, and a cream cheese frosting.

MAP 3: 930 Tchoupitoulas St., 504/588-2123, www.cochonrestaurant.com; Mon.-Thurs. 11am-10pm, Fri.-Sat. 11am-11pm

MOTHER'S RESTAURANT $$

The celeb photos lining the walls of Mother's attest to its longstanding popularity. Opened in 1938, this glorified cafeteria with brash lighting, Formica tables, and chatty servers draws a mix of downtown office workers, hungry tourists, and local politicos. The most famous dishes are the roast beef and baked ham po-boys, but you'll also find delicious jambalaya, seafood gumbo, and crawfish étouffée. It opens earlier than most CBD restaurants—a handy fact if you happen to be returning to your hotel with hunger pangs after a night of barhopping.

MAP 3: 401 Poydras St., 504/523-9656, www.mothersrestaurant.net; daily 7am-10pm

AMERICAN

THE AMERICAN SECTOR $$

Named in honor of the CBD's former moniker, the American Sector is a wonderful addition to The National WWII Museum. With decor that resembles an old-fashioned airport, this delightful eatery features creative versions of American staples, such as mini-cheeseburgers with bacon-onion marmalade, heirloom tomato soup with grilled ham and cheese, and bananas Foster shakes. The portions are generous. Try a vintage cocktail, such as the Last Waltz, which blends vodka, strawberries, mint, ginger, and champagne. Parking is free for patrons after 3pm.

MAP 3: The National WWII Museum, 945 Magazine St., 504/528-1940, www.nationalww2museum.org/american-sector; Sun.-Thurs. 11am-9pm, Fri.-Sat. 11am-11pm

BESH STEAK $$$

The popular local chef John Besh struck gold with Besh Steak at Harrah's, a lavish restaurant that keeps gamers happy and gives the big spenders something to blow their cash on. Opened in 2003, this is a loud, fancy place, with brown leather seats, bold canvases of George Rodrigue's iconic "Blue Dog," and other contemporary touches. A Louisiana spin on a traditional steak house, Besh Steak offers large portions and tasty entrées, such as the New York strip steak (aged 30 days) with blue-cheese butter and Abita Amber-battered onion rings.

MAP 3: Harrah's New Orleans, 8 Canal St., 504/533-6111, www.harrahsneworleans.com; daily 5pm-close

★ COCHON BUTCHER $

Situated just around the corner from the well-respected Cochon, the aptly named Cochon Butcher offers some of the city's most delectable sandwiches. Its small but eclectic menu ranges from classics like pastrami and sauerkraut on rye, to local twists like the Cajun pork dog on a pretzel bun, to more exotic fare such as the Moroccan spiced lamb with cucumbers, tzatziki, and chili oil on flatbread. The muffuletta and the Cubano are highly recommended. Given the eatery's proximity to the convention center, it's a popular spot at lunchtime. Bear in mind that it's very cozy, with limited outdoor seating, so you might have to take your sandwich "to go."

MAP 3: 930 Tchoupitoulas St., 504/588-7675, www.cochonbutcher.com; Mon.-Thurs. 10am-10pm, Fri.-Sat. 10am-11pm, Sun. 10am-4pm

ECLECTIC

EMERIL'S NEW ORLEANS $$$

If you can reserve a table here, go for it—Emeril didn't become famous for no reason. He's an excellent cook with a great kitchen staff, and the food here is more complex and imaginative than at NOLA, his French Quarter restaurant. The bigger and louder of Emeril Lagasse's acclaimed restaurants, Emeril's takes its hits from critics who complain about haughty service and high prices, but this is the domain of one of the world's most famous chefs, and it's always packed. The menu changes often, though you might be lucky enough to sample dishes like the innovative "mac 'n' cheese"—essentially, sautéed Gulf shrimp with *trofie* pasta, vermouth cream, *guanciale,* and brioche crumbs. Desserts might include classics like Black Forest Doberge with cherry compote or Dutch apple tart with maple ice cream. The space is airy, high-ceilinged, and dramatic, the quintessence of Arts District chic.

MAP 3: 800 Tchoupitoulas St., 504/528-9393, www.emerils.com; Mon.-Fri. 11:30am-2pm and 6pm-10pm, Sat.-Sun. 6pm-10pm

ROOT $$$

Since opening in November 2011, Root has been praised by all manner of publications, including *Bon Appétit.* Helmed by executive chef and co-owner Phillip L. Lopez, Root offers an incredibly varied menu, not to mention an extensive wine, beer, and cocktail list. Whether you come for lunch or dinner, expect to share an assortment of house-made charcuterie and sausages with your dining mates and sample creatively presented dishes like smoked scallops, grilled cobia, and "sweet tea" country-fried chicken wings. Naturally, the menu changes often, the decor (including exposed wooden rafters and vivid green chairs with branch-like designs) is modern and fresh, and reservations are recommended.

MAP 3: 200 Julia St., 504/252-9480, http://rootnola.com; Mon.-Thurs. 11am-2pm and 5pm-11pm, Fri. 11am-2pm and 5pm-2am, Sat. 5pm-2am, Sun. 5pm-11pm

Famous Big Easy Chefs

The most well-known dynasty on the Crescent City's restaurant scene is undoubtedly the Brennan clan, members of which own and operate several restaurants throughout New Orleans. In the French Quarter, you can sample a scrumptious breakfast of eggs Hussarde and finish with bananas Foster at **Brennan's,** established in 1946. Opt for dinner at **Dickie Brennan's Steakhouse,** known for its well-prepared steaks and exceptional desserts. For fresh seafood, dine at **Ralph Brennan's Red Fish Grill** or **Dickie Brennan's Bourbon House Seafood,** situated opposite each other. While in the Quarter, you can also savor New Orleans-style cuisine at **Palace Café,** a Sunday jazz brunch at **Mr. B's Bistro,** and a pre-theater meal at the new **Tableau.**

Beyond the Quarter, you'll encounter creative Creole cuisine at Brennan-owned restaurants like **Café Adelaide** in the CBD, **Commander's Palace** in the Garden District, and **Ralph's on the Park** in Mid-City. You'll even find evidence of the Brennan family in the suburb of Metairie, where **Café B** specializes in New American cuisine and **Heritage Grill** (111 Veterans Memorial Blvd.) features creative Cajun and Southern-style dishes.

Brennan isn't the only big name in New Orleans. Given the city's longtime reputation for marvelous cuisine, it seems only natural that the Big Easy would boast several famous chefs. For a taste of such culinary expertise, consider visiting one of their well-respected restaurants.

Chef John Besh

Raised in southern Louisiana, John Besh (www.chefjohnbesh.com) is dedicated to the culinary bounty and traditions of his native homeland. Today, he celebrates his roots in eight acclaimed restaurants, six of which lie within walking distance of one another in the CBD. These include **Besh Steak,** a modern steakhouse in Harrah's New Orleans; **Restaurant August,** a contemporary French restaurant; **Lüke** (333 St. Charles Ave.), an homage to Franco-German brasseries of old; **Domenica,** an inviting Italian eatery in the Roosevelt New Orleans; **Borgne,** a seafood restaurant in the renovated Hyatt Regency New Orleans; and the relatively new **Johnny Sánchez New Orleans** (930 Poydras St.), a lively taqueria. If you're headed Uptown, you'll also find **Pizza Domenica** (4933 Magazine St.), a casual spinoff of Domenica. Besh even has a restaurant outside the city on the bucolic Northshore. Nestled amid verdant grounds, **La Provence** (25020 U.S. 190, Lacombe) is a country-style French restaurant offering dinner and Sunday brunch.

Chef Emeril Lagasse

While Emeril Lagasse (www.emerils.com) grew up in Massachusetts, polished his culinary skills in France, and worked in fine restaurants throughout New York, Boston, and Philadelphia, he definitely has an affinity for New Orleans. Lured to the Big Easy by Dick and Ella Brennan, Lagasse became a celebrity at the legendary Commander's Palace, where he served as the executive chef for more than seven years. In 1990, he established **Emeril's New Orleans,** a fine Louisiana-style restaurant in the Arts District. In 1992, he opened **NOLA,** a French Quarter eatery that offers creative seafood dishes and other innovative cuisine. Six years later, he established **Emeril's Delmonico,** featuring modern Creole cuisine in the historic Garden District. Though Lagasse is also the chef-proprietor of eateries in Las Vegas, Orlando, and Bethlehem, Pennsylvania, his

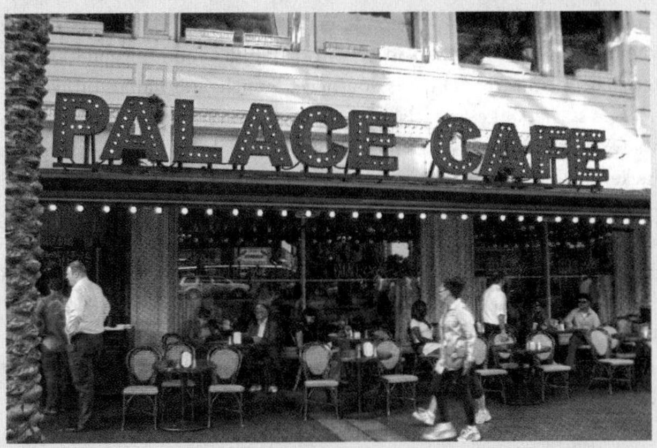

Palace Café is owned and operated by members of the Brennan family.

passion for Louisiana's cuisine makes it impossible to avoid at least one of his New Orleans-based restaurants during your visit.

Chef Donald Link

Inspired by his grandparents' cooking styles, Louisiana native Donald Link (www.donaldlink.com) infuses his local restaurants with his Cajun and Southern roots. Such winners include the **Herbsaint Bar and Restaurant,** which features French-inspired Southern cuisine; **Cochon,** a rustic eatery serving traditional Cajun dishes; **Cochon Butcher,** where popular sandwiches include the muffuletta and the Cubano; and the newest offering, **Pêche Seafood Grill.** All four are located in the Arts District.

Chef Paul Prudhomme

Born and raised in Louisiana, Paul Prudhomme (www.chefpaul.com), the youngest of 13 children, developed a passion for cooking at his mother's side and, as an adult, learned how to blend his native cuisine with other cultural influences. The results of such innovation are evident at his distinctive restaurant, **K-Paul's Louisiana Kitchen,** which Prudhomme and his wife, K, opened in a historic French Quarter building in 1979. Today, the ever-changing menu includes such classic dishes as crawfish étouffée and blackened Louisiana drum.

Chef Susan Spicer

In 1979, Susan Spicer began her cooking career in New Orleans as an apprentice to Chef Daniel Bonnot at the award-winning Louis XVI Restaurant. Following extensive travels and several stints in local hotel eateries, Spicer established her own restaurant in 1990. Housed in a 200-year-old cottage in the French Quarter, **Bayona** presents an eclectic, ever-evolving menu that embraces a variety of cuisines, including American, French, Italian, Mediterranean, Asian, and North African. In 2000, she and three partners opened Herbsaint, which she's since sold to Donald Link. Most recently, Spicer opened **Mondo,** a casual, family-style restaurant in Lakeview, where she's lived for the past two decades.

FRENCH

HERBSAINT BAR AND RESTAURANT $$$

A boisterous power-lunch bistro that's also a hit with the dinner crowd, trendy Herbsaint sits along a nondescript stretch of St. Charles, its setting brightened by tall windows, soft-yellow walls, and a youthful, good-looking staff. The menu, which blends Southern, French, and Italian influences, includes starters like mussels, beef short ribs, and shrimp and grits with tasso and okra. Main courses range from the fish du jour to grilled organic chicken with turnip mashed potatoes and roasted mushrooms. The wine selection is terrific, though you can also try a variety of cool cocktails.

MAP 3: 701 St. Charles Ave., 504/524-4114, www.herbsaint.com; Mon.-Fri. 11:30am-10pm, Sat. 5:30pm-10pm

★ RESTAURANT AUGUST $$$

Restaurant August is presided over by talented and charismatic chef John Besh, the Louisiana born-and-bred kitchen wizard who helms several acclaimed eateries in New Orleans. He opened this Arts District restaurant in 2001, inside a handsome 19th-century French-Creole building, and it's been tough to get a table here ever since. Besh presents uncomplicated yet richly nuanced contemporary French fare, with healthy doses of both local and Mediterranean ingredients. As with Emeril's CBD locale, the menu here is ever-evolving, though you'll often find appetizers like foie gras and gnocchi. Main courses might include a prime filet of beef with porcini and oxtail marmalade or fried soft-shell crab amandine with a warm crab and haricots verts salad. Though it might prove difficult, try to save room for the goat-milk cheesecake with almonds, honey ice cream, and balsamic caramel.

MAP 3: 301 Tchoupitoulas St., 504/299-9777, www.restaurantaugust.com; Mon.-Fri. 11am-2pm and 5:30pm-10pm, Sat.-Sun. 5:30pm-10pm

ITALIAN

DOMENICA $$

Located inside the longstanding, extensively renovated Roosevelt hotel, chef John Besh's Domenica is a warm yet contemporary space that features rustic Italian fare. Popular dishes include the fried eggplant panini, redfish with celery root purée, and spiced apple cake with buttermilk gelato. If possible, come for happy hour (daily 3pm-6pm), when all pizzas, beers, well cocktails, and wines by the glass are offered at half price. Domenica boasts an amiable, knowledgeable staff and a classy ambience, punctuated by the high ceilings, unusual chandeliers, and dark wooden tables. For a more casual experience, stop by **Pizza Domenica** (4933 Magazine St.), chef Alon Shaya's Uptown spinoff, which offers wood-fired pizzas as well as traditional Italian appetizers.

MAP 3: The Roosevelt New Orleans, 123 Baronne St., 504/648-6020, www.domenicarestaurant.com; daily 11am-11pm

TOMMY'S CUISINE $$$

Tommy's Cuisine is a reliable pick for creative, Creole-inspired Italian fare. Housed within a charming space in the Arts District, the warmly lit dining room—with its paneled walls, mirrors, and old-fashioned sconces—creates an appealing scene. Menu items include mussels marinara, oysters Tommy (baked in the shell with Romano cheese, pancetta, and roasted red pepper), or chicken roasted with white wine, olive oil, and rosemary-garlic jus. If you have room, try the pecan praline bread pudding with a bananas Foster sauce and vanilla ice cream—a glorious combination of the city's greatest desserts.

MAP 3: 746 Tchoupitoulas St., 504/581-1103, www.tommysneworleans.com; Sun.-Thurs. 5:30pm-10pm, Fri.-Sat. 5:30pm-11pm

SEAFOOD

BORGNE $$

Borgne is one of the newest of John Besh's varied restaurants in the CBD. Located on the ground floor of the Hyatt Regency New Orleans, the casual yet stylish eatery features local artwork, a lengthy concrete bar, and large columns of Louisiana oyster shells that anchor the spacious dining area. Helmed by chef Brian Landry and named in honor of nearby Lake Borgne, the restaurant focuses on coastal Louisiana cuisine, such as raw oysters, seared yellowfin tuna salad, and seafood paella. Weekday Southern-style lunch specials ($10 pp) include red beans and rice on Monday and fried chicken on Thursday, and there are always several sinful desserts on offer, from dark chocolate pâté to Ponchatoula strawberry shortcake.

MAP 3: Hyatt Regency New Orleans, 601 Loyola Ave., 504/613-3860, www.borgnerestaurant.com; Sun.-Thurs. 11am-10pm, Fri.-Sat. 11am-11pm

PÊCHE SEAFOOD GRILL $$

Like Borgne, the Pêche Seafood Grill is a relative new kid on the block—focused on regional seafood and owned by a local culinary star. In this case, it's Donald Link, the man behind other CBD favorites (Cochon, Cochon Butcher, and Herbsaint Bar and Restaurant). Save for the elegant bar area, Pêche exudes a chic rustic vibe, and the menu includes entrées as well as small plates and raw bar items. So, whether you come for lunch or dinner, you'll likely relish dishes like the seafood salad, curried shrimp bisque, and smothered catfish. Wine, beer, specialty cocktails, non-seafood dishes, and scrumptious desserts are also available, and reservations are recommended, especially on the weekend.

MAP 3: 800 Magazine St., 504/522-1744, www.pecherestaurant.com; Mon.-Thurs. 11am-10pm, Fri.-Sat. 11am-11pm

CAJUN AND CREOLE

ATCHAFALAYA $$

Down in the Irish Channel, off the beaten tourist path, lies this hidden gem, a neighborhood bistro with a very loyal following. The aptly named Atchafalaya, a lengthy, multihued building occupying the corner of Laurel Street and Louisiana Avenue, features high ceilings, natural lighting, excellent service, and contemporary Creole cuisine. Highlights on the menu include affordable classics like eggs Atchafalaya, which combines poached eggs with fried green tomatoes, jumbo lump crabmeat, and hollandaise; Gulf shrimp with bacon, smoked tomatoes, and a crispy grit cake; and a Louisiana crab salad that features mixed greens, hearts of palm, and green curry vinaigrette. The veggie-packed Bloody Marys are also popular. Unless you stop by during lunchtime on a weekday, expect this place to be packed with locals.

MAP 4: 901 Louisiana Ave., 504/891-9626, www.atchafalayarestaurant.com; Mon. 5:30pm-10pm, Tues.-Sat. 11am-2:30pm and 5:30pm-10pm, Sun. 10am-2:30pm and 5:30pm-9pm

★ COMMANDER'S PALACE $$$

If you must put one place at the top of your restaurants list, make it Commander's Palace, which was established in 1880 and became part of the famed Brennan family empire in 1974. Nestled within a blue-and-white Victorian mansion in the Garden District, this local landmark is a terrific place to try turtle soup, griddle-seared Gulf fish, and bread pudding soufflé—especially if you're uninitiated to such famous New Orleans dishes. Lunch isn't too expensive, especially if you opt for the wonderful three-course Creole luncheon (about $35). At dinner, consider the pecan-crusted Gulf fish, truffled Creole cream cheese gnocchi, and grilled filet mignon served with Yukon gold potato purée, caramelized onions, roasted mushrooms, and tasso *marchands de vin.* The weekend jazz brunches are the stuff of legend, and advance reservations are usually a must for any meal.

MAP 4: 1403 Washington Ave., 504/899-8221, www.commanderspalace.com; Mon.-Fri. 11:30am-2pm and 6:30pm-10pm, Sat. 11:30am-1pm and 6:30pm-10pm, Sun. 10:30am-1:30pm and 6:30pm-10pm

EMERIL'S DELMONICO $$$

Situated along the St. Charles streetcar line in the Lower Garden District, Emeril's Delmonico is a worthy nighttime spot for fans of steak, seafood, Cajun dishes, and Creole cuisine. Originally established in 1895, this legendary restaurant was reopened in 1998 by chef Emeril Lagasse. Today, with its stylish, upscale interior, Delmonico offers such classics as barbecue shrimp with a baked grit cake, dry-aged New York strip steaks and rib eyes, and pan-fried drum with fingerling potato lyonnaise and bacon-stewed

Clockwise from top left: Restaurant August; Emeril's New Orleans; Commander's Palace; Juan's Flying Burrito.

green beans. Besides the weekday happy hour (5pm-7pm) at the on-site cocktail bar, the complimentary valet parking is another big plus, as is the live music on offer Thursday-Saturday.

MAP 4: 1300 St. Charles Ave., 504/525-4937, www.emerils.com; Sun.-Thurs. 6pm-9pm, Fri.-Sat. 6pm-10pm

AMERICAN

MR. JOHN'S STEAKHOUSE $$$

Conveniently located on the St. Charles streetcar line, this classy shrine to carnivores is one of the most highly recommended steak houses in the city. Besides showcasing simply seasoned steaks, from filet mignon to a two-person porterhouse, the menu features lobster tails with roasted new potatoes and haricots verts, crabmeat ravioli with aged Asiago cheese cream sauce, and baby veal sautéed in white wine, capers, lemon, and butter. Even the salads, sides, and appetizers are delicious; try the seared yellowfin tuna, escargot in puff pastry, or fried green tomatoes with jumbo lump crabmeat. Be prepared to pay a premium for such quality.

MAP 4: 2111 St. Charles Ave., 504/679-7697, www.mrjohnssteakhouse.com; Tues.-Thurs. 5:30pm-9:30pm, Fri. 11:30am-2pm and 5:30pm-9:30pm, Sat. 5:30pm-9:30pm

PARASOL'S BAR & RESTAURANT $

For inexpensive, overstuffed sandwiches, head to the Irish Channel, where Parasol's Bar & Restaurant has been serving residents of the Garden District and beyond since 1952. A magnet for locals and tourists—especially around St. Patrick's Day—this friendly neighborhood hangout offers a wide array of delicious po-boys, with classic fillings like roast beef, fried shrimp and oysters, and meatballs. Parasol's also serves gumbo, fried seafood baskets, and specialty sandwiches, like the smoked sausage deluxe, which includes cheddar, onions, and Creole mustard.

MAP 4: 2533 Constance St., 504/302-1543, www.parasolsbarandrestaurant.com; Sun.-Thurs. 11am-9pm, Fri.-Sat. 11am-10pm

ECLECTIC

COQUETTE $$$

A lovely, two-story structure houses Coquette, an intimate space that resembles a romantic French bistro and presents eclectic, contemporary American cuisine. Although the simple menu changes daily, dependent on seasonal ingredients and the chef's whim, past highlights include roasted Gulf oysters with bacon, Swiss chard, and Herbsaint liqueur; collard green ravioli with duck confit, orange, and bacon; and a pork loin with foie gras, cabbage, and apple marmalade. The three-course lunch ($30) is a more affordable way to sample the kitchen's delectable creations, like the charred octopus, steak tartine, and butterscotch pudding.

MAP 4: 2800 Magazine St., 504/265-0421, www.coquette-nola.com; Sun.-Tues. 5:30pm-10pm, Wed.-Sat. 11:30am-3pm and 5:30pm-10pm

ITALIAN

STEIN'S MARKET AND DELI $

Amid the quaint stores and antiques shops along offbeat Magazine Street, you'll encounter Stein's Market and Deli, a casual, often crowded joint featuring communal tables, deli-style sandwiches, a terrific beer selection, and a slew of specialty goods, from balsamic vinegars to loose-leaf teas. Try the smoked salmon and cream cheese bagel for breakfast, the classic Reuben for lunch, and the homemade cookies and brownies anytime. There's quite a variety of breads, meats, cheeses, and sides available. The deli's spacious parking lot is also a plus, as are the picnic tables out front—a great spot for people-watching.

MAP 4: 2207 Magazine St., 504/527-0771, www.steinsdeli.net; Tues.-Fri. 7am-7pm, Sat.-Sun. 9am-5pm

IRISH

THE IRISH HOUSE $

Locals favor the extensive beer and whiskey selection at the Irish House, a lively spot in the Lower Garden District. Owned by chef Matt Murphy, this two-story, mahogany-trimmed gastropub offers upscale pub fare and classic Irish dishes, such as a corned beef and cabbage sandwich, bangers and mash, and Guinness chocolate trifle. Like many local watering holes, the Irish House features a weekday happy hour (3pm-6pm), and the bar menu is available daily 3pm-close. You'll hear live Celtic music almost every night.

MAP 4: 1432 St. Charles Ave., 504/595-6755, www.theirishhouseneworleans.com; Mon.-Fri. 11am-10pm, Sat.-Sun. 9am-10pm

MEXICAN

JUAN'S FLYING BURRITO $

Youthful and raffish Juan's Flying Burrito has wooden booths, an artsy staff, and an eclectic crowd. Art covers the brick walls, and loud music fills this joint, one of the best quick bites along the lower stretch of Magazine. The fare is a mod take on Tex-Mex, with such filling fare as pork 'n' slaw tacos, bacon and blue cheese quesadillas, and the Veggie Punk burrito, stuffed with potatoes, jalapeños, and pinto beans. You'll also find a nice range of beers and margaritas. There is a second location in Mid-City (4724 S. Carrollton Ave.), which is a little less funky but has a dedicated parking lot.

MAP 4: 2018 Magazine St., 504/569-0000, www.juansflyingburrito.com; Sun.-Thurs. 11am-10pm, Fri.-Sat. 11am-11pm

SEAFOOD

BASIN SEAFOOD & SPIRITS $$

Owned by pals Edgar Caro and Antonio Mata, Basin Seafood & Spirits serves modern versions of Louisiana classics, such as crab and crawfish beignets, fried oyster po-boys, and BBQ shrimp and grits. Besides the indoor dining area, Basin offers a lush rear courtyard as well as sidewalk seating along bustling Magazine Street, ideal for people-watching. Many locals come here for the weekday happy hour (3pm-7pm), especially on Monday when $0.50 raw oysters are available 3pm-10pm.

MAP 4: 3222 Magazine St., 504/302-7391, www.basinseafoodnola.com; Mon.-Sat. 11:30am-10pm, Sun. 11:30am-9pm

Uptown

Map 5

CAJUN AND CREOLE

BRIGTSEN'S RESTAURANT $$$

One of the first eateries to lure tourists to the Riverbend area, Brigtsen's occupies a lovely Victorian cottage with a warm, homey dining room, enhanced by soft lighting and lovely wallpaper. The restaurant is perhaps most famous for its amazingly delicious and ever-changing seafood platter (around $34), which might include grilled drum fish with shrimp and jalapeño lime sauce, baked oyster Rockefeller, and a sea scallop with Asiago cheese grits. Other commendable dishes include oyster-artichoke gratin with lemon-parmesan sauce, roast duck with cornbread dressing and tart dried cherry sauce, and pecan pie with caramel sauce.

MAP 5: 723 Dante St., 504/861-7610, www.brigtsens.com; Tues.-Sat. 5:30pm-10pm

DICK AND JENNY'S $$$

Dick and Jenny's keeps regulars happy with its neighborhood feel, outgoing staff, and reasonably priced contemporary city fare. Abita Amber-braised lamb belly grillades with thyme-goat cheese grits is a dazzling main dish, and don't miss the shrimp ravigote served atop fried green tomatoes. There's often a pretty long wait for a table, though reservations are now accepted.

MAP 5: 4501 Tchoupitoulas St., 504/894-9880, www.dickandjennys.com; Mon. 5:30pm-10pm, Tues.-Thurs. 11am-2pm and 5:30pm-10pm, Fri. 11am-2pm and 5:30pm-10:30pm, Sat. 5:30pm-10:30pm

★ JACQUES-IMO'S CAFE $$

Situated on bustling Oak Street, funky Jacques-Imo's Cafe presents a mix of eclectic contemporary dishes and New Orleans standbys. I can't rave enough about the charismatic staff and the ever-changing list of specials, which has, at times, featured smothered rabbit with roasted-pepper grits and country-fried venison chop with wild mushrooms. The fried mirlitons with oysters and rich oyster-tasso hollandaise are also commendable, as is the shrimp and alligator sausage cheesecake. Every meal comes with delicious butter-topped cornbread muffins, salad, and sides, such as mashed sweet potatoes and smothered cabbage. Finish off your meal with energy-pumping coffee-bean crème brûlée. Reservations are available for large groups, and the place fills up quickly, so expect a wait on most nights. You can always pass the time at the charming bar. To reach the loud, rambling dining room, you have to walk through the oft-crowded bar and bustling kitchen, where you can take a peek at the dishes being prepared.

MAP 5: 8324 Oak St., 504/861-0886, www.jacquesimoscafe.com; Mon.-Thurs. 5:30pm-10pm, Fri.-Sat. 5:30pm-10:30pm

MAHONY'S PO-BOYS & SEAFOOD $$

While shopping along Magazine Street, do yourself a favor and head to Mahony's Po-Boys & Seafood for one of its signature sandwiches. Favorites include the root beer-glazed ham and cheese, cochon with Creole slaw, and the Peacemaker, which consists of fried oysters, bacon, and cheddar. You'll also find classics like overstuffed fried shrimp po-boys and muffulettas, plus salads, scrumptious desserts, and a full bar. No wonder Guy Fieri included Mahony's on his cross-country tour of America's "diners, drive-ins, and dives" for his Food Network show.

MAP 5: 3454 Magazine St., 504/899-3374, www.mahonyspoboys.com; Mon.-Sat. 11am-10pm

UPPERLINE RESTAURANT $$$

One of the city's most convivial restaurants, Upperline is run by colorful owner JoAnn Clevenger, who loves to chat with patrons about her wonderful art and photography collection, which fills the restaurant's eclectically furnished dining rooms. Executive chef Ken Smith prepares Creole food with inventive twists and global spins, like slow-roasted duckling with garlic port or ginger peach sauce, or spicy shrimp with jalapeño cornbread and aioli. A fine way to enjoy a meal is to order the three-course dinner ($40), which might include fried green tomatoes with shrimp rémoulade, Louisiana grillades with cheese grits, and warm honey-pecan bread pudding with toffee sauce.

MAP 5: 1413 Upperline St., 504/891-9822, www.upperline.com; Wed.-Sun. 5:30pm-close

AMERICAN

BOUCHERIE $$

Uptown boasts several unique restaurants, including Boucherie, a quaint, romantic eatery that offers friendly service, a classy ambience, and upscale, Southern-style cuisine at affordable prices. Both tapas and large plates are available, featuring items like blackened shrimp and grit cakes with bacon vinaigrette; duck confit po-boys with roasted garlic, bread-and-butter pickles, and Creole tomatoes; and smoked beef brisket with garlicky parmesan fries. Unfortunately, the small size of the restaurant means that it can get a bit claustrophobic.

MAP 5: 1506 S. Carrollton Ave., 504/862-5514, www.boucherie-nola.com; Tues.-Sat. 11am-3pm and 5:30pm-9:30pm

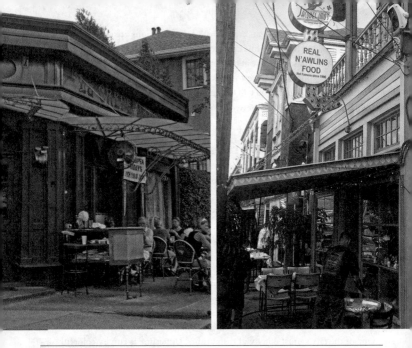

Clockwise from top left: La Crêpe Nanou; Jacques-Imo's Cafe; The Creole Creamery.

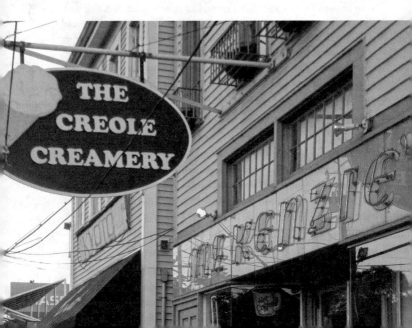

Sweet Treats

Beignets aren't the only dessert worth sampling in New Orleans. Below are some of the city's quintessential treats and where to try them:

- **Bananas Foster:** A rich dessert consisting of bananas, butter, brown sugar, cinnamon, and rum, invented by Paul Blangé at **Brennan's** (page 117) in 1951. It's often prepared as a flambé in a tableside performance, then promptly served over vanilla ice cream.
- **Bread pudding:** A traditional dessert made from soaked French bread and often served with rum or whiskey sauce. For the classic version, head to the CBD's **Bon Ton Cafe** (page 142). For something more unusual, try the Krispy Kreme bread pudding at Uptown's **Boucherie** (page 155).
- **Calas** (KAH-luhs): Creole rice fritters usually covered with cane syrup or powdered sugar. Similar to beignets, they're a popular breakfast dish at **The Old Coffeepot Restaurant** (page 121) in the French Quarter, though you'll see them as "callas cakes" on the menu.

THE CAMELLIA GRILL $

A longtime stalwart for delicious comfort food, the famous Camellia Grill is a down-home restaurant that specializes in burgers, onion rings, and other greasy-spoon favorites. Breakfast is enjoyable in this funky old white house in the Riverbend section of Uptown. There's also a long list of pies, cakes, and ice-cream treats. The low prices are ideal, but expect limited seating, long waits, and surly waitstaff.

MAP 5: 626 S. Carrollton Ave., 504/309-2679, Sun.-Thurs. 8am-midnight, Fri.-Sat. 8am-2am

DOMILISE'S PO-BOY & BAR $$

About 10 blocks west of the intersection of Napoleon Avenue and Tchoupitoulas Street—the starting point for Mardi Gras parades like Bacchus and Orpheus—lies a weathered building that belies the yummy eatery inside. A popular, oft-crowded stop for local foodies, the no-frills Domilise's Po-Boy & Bar offers an assortment of po-boys, with fillings like roast beef and Swiss cheese, hot smoked sausage, and fried shrimp. Though rather pricey, these enormous po-boys are worth every penny, and given its location, this isn't a bad lunchtime or early dinner option for Tulane students, Magazine Street shoppers, and those exploring nearby Audubon Park.

MAP 5: 5240 Annunciation St., 504/899-9126; Mon.-Wed. and Fri.-Sat. 10:30am-7pm

GUY'S PO-BOYS $

A lovable dive on a quiet Uptown street corner, Guy's Po-Boys offers daily-changing sandwich specials, to-die-for po-boys (with fillings like shrimp, roast beef, and alligator sausage), and other comfort chow. The bare-bones decor and friendly staff add to the down-home experience. It doesn't hurt either that the prices are low. This is a cash-only joint, and the service sometimes crawls.

MAP 5: 5259 Magazine St., 504/891-5025; Mon.-Sat. 11am-4pm

COFFEE AND DESSERTS

THE CREOLE CREAMERY $

For traditional ice cream, sherbet, or sorbet, check out the Creole Creamery, a handsome retro-hip Uptown ice cream parlor that serves such tantalizing flavors as lavender-pecan chocolate, mint julep, and key lime pie. These guys are constantly dreaming up new and often deliciously bizarre flavors—there are so many, in fact, that they rotate often, enabling you to try something new each time you visit. There's a second Creole Creamery in Lakeview (6260 Vicksburg St.).

MAP 5: 4924 Prytania St., 504/894-8680, www.creolecreamery.com; Sun.-Thurs. noon-10pm, Fri.-Sat. noon-11pm

PJ'S COFFEE OF NEW ORLEANS $

Though you'll find numerous branches of this popular local coffeehouse chain throughout New Orleans and southeastern Louisiana, my favorite spot is this Uptown location. It's an ideal pit stop during a shopping trip along Magazine Street. Founded in 1984, this is the original shop, where, in addition to enjoying locally roasted coffee and freshly baked pastries, you may appreciate the colorful patrons, relaxing courtyard, and free wireless Internet access. The operating hours are slightly shorter during the summer months.

MAP 5: 5432 Magazine St., 504/895-2202, www.pjscoffee.com; Mon.-Fri. 6am-9pm, Sat.-Sun. 7am-9pm

PLUM STREET SNOBALLS $

Plum Street Snoballs has been a Crescent City tradition since 1945. Typically served in cardboard containers (the kind you might store leftover fried rice in), these somewhat pricey but oh-so-tasty sno-balls boast such flavors as cherry, ice coffee cream, and sugar-free pink lemonade. Besides the seasonal stand on Burdette, Plum Street also sells sno-balls at annual events, such as the French Quarter Festival and Jazz Fest.

MAP 5: 1300 Burdette St., 504/866-7996 or 504/256-3298, www.plumstreetsnoball.com; Mid-Mar.-Oct. Sun.-Fri. 2pm-8pm, Sat. noon-8pm

ECLECTIC

APOLLINE $$$

Gourmands often trek to quaint Apolline, an elegant yet laid-back dinnertime spot known for its attentive service, quiet atmosphere, and diverse cuisine. Favorite appetizers include the homemade boudin with Dijon mustard, baked Louisiana oysters with leek confit, and sautéed sweetbreads with stone-ground grits, while main dishes range from grilled diver scallops to the grilled pork porterhouse. Save room for the goat cheese mousse, which includes honey pâté de fruit, lavender crème anglaise, and pistachio powder.

Like many Uptown eateries, Apolline is located in a former bungalow; the simple setting, including white linen tablecloths, flickering candles, and mirrors and ceiling recesses that seemingly enlarge the space, makes this restaurant ideal for a romantic dinner. Outdoor seating is available.

MAP 5: 4729 Magazine St., 504/894-8869, www.apollinerestaurant.com; Tues.-Sat. 5:30pm-10:30pm

DANTE'S KITCHEN $$$

On a quiet street in Uptown's Riverbend neighborhood stands an adorable, canary-yellow bungalow, which houses one of the neighborhood's most popular restaurants. Featuring multiple rooms, each of which is uniquely decorated with colorful walls and abstract artwork, Dante's Kitchen accommodates numerous diners while providing an intimate dining experience. Dinnertime options range from small plates, such as the slow-smoked pork belly with cannellini beans, parsley sauce, and a pork cracklin' salad, to entrées like the pan-roasted Gulf fish with red grape and oxtail marmalade, herb coconut rice, and smoked salt. The weekend brunch might include such favorites as bread pudding French toast, accompanied by a seasonal fruit sauce, and grilled shrimp, served with grits and an andouille red-eye gravy. Though reservations are recommended for dinner, they're not accepted for brunch.

MAP 5: 736 Dante St., 504/861-3121, www.danteskitchen.com; Mon. and Wed.-Fri. 6pm-close, Sat.-Sun. 10:30am-2pm and 6pm-close

GAUTREAU'S $$$

After exploring Uptown attractions, indulge in a fancy meal at Gautreau's, a uniquely elegant restaurant only a few blocks north of the St. Charles streetcar line. Situated in what appears to be an old house, this small, extremely popular restaurant features high ceilings, drape-like walls, and a knowledgeable, accommodating staff. Given the noise level at times, Gautreau's is probably more suitable for small groups of friends than romantic dinners. The menu is constantly evolving, and most of the dishes are creative and memorable. Favorite dishes have included duck confit with German potato salad and mustard crème fraiche, sautéed halibut with preserved lemon yogurt and fried artichokes, and caramelized banana split. Reservations are highly recommended.

MAP 5: 1728 Soniat St., 504/899-7397, www.gautreausrestaurant.com; Mon.-Sat. 6pm-10pm

FRENCH

LA CRÊPE NANOU $$

For a hint of Europe, head two blocks south of the St. Charles streetcar line, where you'll find La Crêpe Nanou, a red, 1950s-style French bistro known for its intimate ambience, gracious service, and unpretentious wine list, all of which make it ideal for romantic dinners and special occasions. The old-fashioned cuisine is equally winning. Dinnertime highlights include French onion soup, seafood au gratin, and, of course, the crepes, with fillings like smoked salmon, ratatouille, and crawfish with lobster sauce. The salads and dessert crepes are also worth sampling. Depending on the weather, consider sitting outside.

MAP 5: 1410 Robert St., 504/899-2670; Sun.-Thurs. 6pm-10pm, Fri. 11am-3pm and 6pm-11pm, Sat. 6pm-11pm

LA PETITE GROCERY $$$

Situated in a historic, lovingly restored building on bustling Magazine, La Petite Grocery is at once elegant and casual. Helmed by executive chef Justin Devillier, who worked here for six years before purchasing it in 2010, this award-winning restaurant specializes in French, Southern, Cajun, and Creole cuisine. The menu might include such favorites as blue crab beignets, turtle Bolognese, and Gulf shrimp and grits. Be sure to pair your meal with a glass of wine or signature cocktail, and save room for dessert, which might range from butterscoth pudding to a bittersweet chocolate torte. Conveniently, La Petite Grocery isn't far from the St. Charles streetcar line and it also offers limited parking in a nearby lot.

MAP 5: 4238 Magazine St., 504/891-3377, www.lapetitegrocery.com; Tues.-Thurs. 11:30am-2:30pm and 5:30pm-9:30pm, Fri.-Sat. 11:30am-2:30pm and 5:30pm-10:30pm, Sun. 10:30am-2:30pm and 5:30pm-9:30pm

PATOIS $$$

Owned by three New Orleans natives and fellow Jesuit High School graduates—chef Aaron Burgau and brothers Leon and Pierre Touzet—Patois occupies an airy, carefully restored building not far from Audubon Zoo and the Magazine Street shopping district. Though the dishes here are eclectic and ever-evolving, the menu primarily consists of French, New American, and Cajun cuisine, ranging from frog legs and potato gnocchi to almond-crusted Gulf fish and boudin-stuffed fried chicken. Besides Sunday brunch, Patois serves numerous wines, several specialty cocktails, and assorted desserts, such as the refreshing lemon tart with mint, burnt meringue, and toasted almonds.

MAP 5: 6078 Laurel St., 504/895-9441, http://patoisnola.com; Wed.-Thurs. 5:30pm-10pm, Fri. 11:30am-2pm and 5:30pm-10:30pm, Sat. 5:30pm-10:30pm, Sun. 10:30am-2pm

ITALIAN

PASCAL'S MANALE RESTAURANT & BAR $$

Pascal's Manale Restaurant & Bar is a casual neighborhood joint that captures the New Orleans of old. Founded in 1913 and usually filled with colorful locals, this friendly, family-run eatery offers both classic Italian and Creole cuisine, plus a lively, cash-only oyster bar. Popular dishes include barbecue shrimp, freshly shucked oysters, and pasta with crabmeat. Be prepared for inconsistent service and a long wait, even if you reserved a table.

MAP 5: 1838 Napoleon Ave., 504/895-4877, www.neworleansrestaurants.com/pascalsmanale; Mon.-Fri. 11:30am-2pm and 5pm-close, Sat. 5pm-close

MEDITERRANEAN

MAPLE STREET CAFÉ $$

Make the trek way Uptown to the Maple Street Café, a dapper neighborhood restaurant opened in 1995 and now serving first-rate contemporary versions of continental and Mediterranean cooking. A bountiful Greek salad or oyster amandine makes a delightful starter, while a pepper-crusted duck breast drizzled with a fig sauce is typical of the main dishes, which change often. Housed within a small cottage amid quaint boutiques and other eateries, the narrow two-tier dining room has a tile floor and cream-colored walls. Seating is also available in a small courtyard.

MAP 5: 7623 Maple St., 504/314-9003, www.maplestreetcafenola.com; Mon.-Thurs. 11am-2:30pm and 5pm-9:30pm, Fri.-Sat. 11am-10pm, Sun. noon-9pm

SEAFOOD

CASAMENTO'S RESTAURANT $$

New Orleans abounds in classic seafood joints, the kind of friendly, family-owned restaurants that have been serving large portions of fried shrimp and oysters to eager locals for decades. Casamento's is definitely one such place. Established in 1919 by Joe Casamento, this cozy, mosaic-tiled restaurant serves a slew of seafood dishes, such as oyster stew, fried seafood platters, and sandwiches filled with trout, catfish, or soft-shell crab. Like many landmark eateries in the Big Easy, Casamento's has lured its share of celebrities over the years, from Robert Duvall to Peyton Manning. It's closed June-August.

MAP 5: 4330 Magazine St., 504/895-9761, www.casamentosrestaurant.com; Tues.-Wed. 11am-2pm, Thurs.-Sat. 11am-2pm and 5:30pm-9pm

CLANCY'S $$$

Uptown has become such a great dining destination that Clancy's, which had been a discreet locals' hangout for many years, has almost come to feel a tad touristy. No matter the increasing crowds, the staff works hard to accommodate everyone and make both regulars and newcomers feel right at home. The loosely Creole-meets-Italian menu changes often but usually has a few reliable standbys, such as fried oysters with brie, seared sea scallops in a basil-walnut pesto sauce, and filet mignon with stilton and a red-wine demi-glace. There are several dining areas in this rambling building: the quietest and most romantic is upstairs; the more convivial and social is in the front room adjacent to the bar.

MAP 5: 6100 Annunciation St., 504/895-1111, www.clancysneworleans.com; Mon.-Wed. 5:30pm-10:30pm, Thurs.-Fri. 11:30am-2pm and 5:30pm-10:30pm, Sat. 5:30pm-10:30pm

FRANKIE & JOHNNY'S $$

Frankie & Johnny's is one of my favorite neighborhood eateries. Situated in a residential area, this no-frills dive offers several New Orleans-style dishes, such as red beans and rice, boudin balls, and muffulettas. Seafood, though, is the specialty. Beyond fried shrimp, oyster, and catfish platters and po-boys, many patrons come for whatever boiled seafood is in season. Don't be surprised to see celebrities here; I once witnessed John Goodman happily munching on boiled crawfish.

MAP 5: 321 Arabella St., 504/899-9146, www.frankyandjohnnys.com; Sun.-Thurs. 11am-9pm, Fri.-Sat. 11am-10pm

Tremé and Mid-City

Map 6

CAJUN AND CREOLE

DOOKY CHASE'S RESTAURANT $$

Established in 1941, Dooky Chase's is one of New Orleans's most famous restaurants. This unassuming place is definitely worth a stop, if only for the classy ambience and rich history. Indeed, many locals swear by its Creole and Southern dishes, especially the okra gumbo, fried chicken, and peach cobbler, which are all part of the lunchtime buffet. Walk-ins and reservations are both welcome. Unfortunately, the food is pricey, and the servers, while friendly, often seem harried.

MAP 6: 2301 Orleans Ave., 504/821-0535; Tues.-Thurs. 11am-3pm, Fri. 11am-3pm and 5pm-9pm

LI'L DIZZY'S CAFÉ $$

Situated in the Faubourg Tremé, about five blocks from the French Quarter, Li'l Dizzy's Café is not much to look at. Nevertheless, this nondescript corner restaurant has long been a favorite among locals. The friendly staff and down-home surroundings make you feel as though you're dining in someone's house, and the homestyle Creole and Southern cuisine is well worth the price. Highlights on the lunch buffet include fried catfish, macaroni and cheese, and red beans and rice.

MAP 6: 1500 Esplanade Ave., 504/569-8997, www.lildizzyscafe.com; Mon.-Sat. 10am-3pm, Sun. 10am-2pm

AMERICAN

PARKWAY BAKERY & TAVERN $

Founded in 1911 near Bayou St. John and closed for nearly four months following Hurricane Katrina, the Parkway Bakery & Tavern is a terrific place to dine after exploring City Park. Despite the name, this popular eatery is mainly known for its delicious, well-stuffed po-boys, with fillings like pastrami, fried catfish, and alligator sausage. Many patrons rave about the potato salad, sweet potato fries, and "surf & turf" po-boy, a winning combination of hot roast beef, fried shrimp, and gravy. Beyond the food, the Parkway has a friendly staff and nostalgic atmosphere—the walls, after all, are filled with old photographs and local memorabilia.

MAP 6: 538 Hagan Ave., 504/482-3047, www.parkwaypoorboys.com; Wed.-Mon. 11am-10pm

WILLIE MAE'S SCOTCH HOUSE $

Between the historic Tremé and Esplanade Ridge neighborhoods, you'll encounter Willie Mae's Scotch House, a legendary, old-school joint primarily known for its fried chicken, which is both crispy and juicy. The flavorful red beans and rice, cornbread, and lemonade are well regarded, but no matter what you order, you can bet that it won't break the bank. The staff is friendly and attentive. Given the sketchy neighborhood, I'd highly recommend arriving by car or cab.

MAP 6: 2401 St. Ann St., 504/822-9503; Mon.-Sat. 11am-5pm

ASIAN

CAFÉ MINH $$

Café Minh occupies an old-fashioned house on a residential block, only a few steps from the Canal Street streetcar line. The restaurant boasts a fusion of Vietnamese, French, and Creole cuisines. Favorite dishes include the Asian pear salad, Creole tomato and crabmeat napoleon with wasabi vinaigrette, and colorful peach and blueberry cobbler, but the menu changes often. The interior is elegant, more so than the homey exterior might indicate; the seating, however, is limited, so try to dine here during off-hours.

MAP 6: 4139 Canal St., 504/482-6266, www.cafeminh.com; Mon.-Thurs. 11:30am-2:30pm and 5pm-9pm, Fri. 11:30am-2:30pm and 5pm-10pm, Sat. 5pm-10pm

COFFEE AND DESSERTS

★ ANGELO BROCATO $

After a day of exploring City Park, head southwest on Carrollton, toward Canal Street, and take a snack-break detour at Angelo Brocato, an old-world bakery and ice cream parlor that's famous not only known for its superb Italian pastries, such as the classic cannoli, but for tantalizing house-made ice cream, Italian ice, and gelato in all kinds of tempting flavors, such as spumoni, chestnut, and amaretto. The most popular treat is the lemon ice, a simple yet expertly blended concoction of water, granulated sugar, and fresh lemons. This beloved Mid-City eatery celebrated its 100th anniversary in 2005, only to be smacked hard by the wrath of Katrina. The storm caused the place to close for nearly a year, but the rebuilt Angelo Brocato reopened, much to the relief of sweet-toothed devotees.

MAP 6: 214 N. Carrollton Ave., 504/486-1465, www.angelobrocatoicecream.com; Tues.-Thurs. 10am-10pm, Fri.-Sat. 10am-10:30pm, Sun. 10am-9pm

FAIR GRINDS COFFEEHOUSE $

A cheerful neighborhood coffeehouse just off Esplanade Avenue and only two blocks from the historic Fair Grounds Race Course, the amusingly named Fair Grinds serves all the usual hot and iced coffee drinks, plus fresh-squeezed juices and a variety of muffins, quiches, and empanadas. Filled with racetrack collectibles and framed photographs, the homey space is well suited for reading or working on your laptop.

MAP 6: 3133 Ponce de Leon St., 504/913-9072, www.fairgrinds.com; daily 6:30am-10pm

ECLECTIC

★ RALPH'S ON THE PARK $$$

Located within steps of leafy City Park, the aptly named Ralph's on the Park is one of only two Brennan family-helmed dining operations in Mid-City, and it's absolutely worth the trip. First off, it's far from the madding crowds of the Quarter and CBD, making for a relaxed, convivial dining experience. It's also set inside a lovely historic building that was constructed in 1860 as a coffeehouse and concession stand for the nearby park. Then there's the elegant, innovative food, such as flaky mushroom tarts, blue crab beignets, and rib-eye-wrapped scallops with foie gras, cauliflower purée, and port wine beef sauce. It's also one of the best brunch options in town, offering tasty dishes like turtle soup, crawfish Benedict, and Gulf shrimp and grits.

MAP 6: 900 City Park Ave., 504/488-1000, www.ralphsonthepark.com; Mon. 5:30pm-9pm, Tues.-Thurs. 11:30am-2pm and 5:30pm-9pm, Fri. 11:30am-2pm and 5:30pm-9:30pm, Sat. 5:30pm-9:30pm, Sun. 11am-2pm and 5:30pm-9pm

FRENCH

CAFÉ DEGAS $$

Nestled amid foliage on tree-lined Esplanade Avenue, the cozy Café Degas serves such superb French cuisine as French onion soup, salade niçoise, and Dijon-crusted rack of Australian lamb with ratatouille, haricots verts, and smoked Vidalia onions. There's nothing overly trendy or complicated about Degas. The cooking is authentic and reminiscent of a true French bistro fare. The ambience is winning, too—it's the ideal spot for a romantic dinner. In warm weather, you can enjoy a meal on the lush garden patio, which is the perfect place to end an afternoon of exploring Mid-City.

MAP 6: 3127 Esplanade Ave., 504/945-5635, www.cafedegas.com; Wed.-Sat. 11am-3pm and 6pm-10pm, Sun. 10:30am-3pm and 6pm-9:30pm

ITALIAN

LIUZZA'S RESTAURANT & BAR $

Situated about two blocks from the Canal Street streetcar line, this downhome bar and restaurant has been a Mid-City landmark since 1947. The menu features classic Cajun, Creole, and seafood dishes, though it excels with Italian items like stuffed artichokes, lasagna, and the Frenchuletta, essentially a muffuletta on French bread. Two of my favorite pasta dishes are the crawfish Telemachus, which features a crawfish cream sauce, and eggplant St. John, which includes eggplant medallions in a shrimp and artichoke sauce. After a visit to the Fair Grounds Race Course, consider stopping by **Liuzza's by the Track** (1518 N. Lopez St.), an equally popular joint among Mid-City denizens.

MAP 6: 3636 Bienville Ave., 504/482-9120, www.liuzzas.com; Mon.-Sat. 11am-10pm

MEDITERRANEAN

LOLA'S $$

Part of the bumper crop of fine restaurants along the historic Esplanade Ridge, Lola's, which opened in 1994, is a casual, small-scale operation whose owners have focused on food above all else. Indeed, the Spanish- and Mediterranean-inspired cooking stands up to any in the city: Consider the fresh ceviche, refreshingly chilled gazpacho, and fragrantly seasoned paella heaped with shrimp, calamari, and mussels. Reservations are not accepted. Also, while there's a limited selection of beer, wine, and homemade sangria, you're welcome to bring your own alcohol for a $5-per-bottle corkage fee.

MAP 6: 3312 Esplanade Ave., 504/488-6946, www.lolasneworleans.com; Sun.-Thurs. 5:30pm-9:30pm, Fri.-Sat. 5:30pm-10pm

SEAFOOD

KATIE'S RESTAURANT & BAR $$

This well-loved neighborhood eatery is known for its friendly staff, easy-going atmosphere, and delicious food. Though the menu features both Italian and New Orleans-style cuisine, the specialty is seafood, such as crawfish beignets, over-stuffed crab cakes, and fried green tomato and shrimp rémoulade po-boys. Multiple diners may choose to share the Barge, an entire French bread loaf stuffed with fried shrimp, oysters, and/or catfish, which can serve up to four people. Opened in 1984, the family-owned Katie's Restaurant enjoyed many years of success, until Hurricane Katrina's devastation forced its closure. After a 4.5-year renovation, Katie's is once again a favorite spot for Mid-City denizens and other New Orleans foodies.

MAP 6: 3701 Iberville St., 504/488-6582, www.katiesinmidcity.com; Mon. 11am-3pm, Tues.-Thurs. 11am-9pm, Fri.-Sat. 11am-10pm, Sun. 9am-3pm

MANDINA'S RESTAURANT $$

If you're seeking a classic New Orleans-style restaurant—where the dress code is casual and the menu features local Creole and Italian staples like oyster-artichoke soup, stuffed bell peppers, and bread pudding—look no farther than Mandina's. Established as an Italian grocery store in 1898, the family-owned Mandina's eventually became a full-service restaurant in 1932. Since then, this multi-room restaurant has been a popular local hangout, particularly for cops, attorneys, and politicians at lunchtime. Reservations aren't accepted, but it's rarely difficult to find a table, and while the parking lot is rather small, there's usually ample street parking. It's also conveniently located on the Canal Street streetcar line. The only drawback is that the servers, many of whom have been here awhile, aren't as friendly and attentive as one might like.

MAP 6: 3800 Canal St., 504/482-9179, www.mandinasrestaurant.com; Mon.-Thurs. 11am-9:30pm, Fri.-Sat. 11am-10pm, Sun. noon-9pm

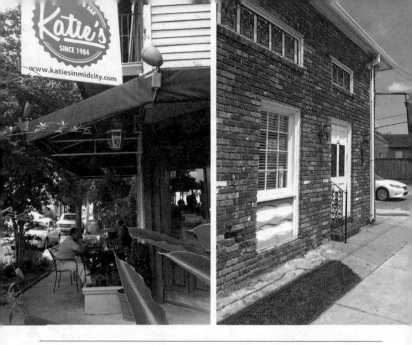

Clockwise from top left: Katie's Restaurant & Bar; Dooky Chase's Restaurant; Angelo Brocato.

CAJUN AND CREOLE

ROCKY & CARLO'S RESTAURANT & BAR $$

After visiting the Chalmette Battlefield, be sure to stop by Rocky & Carlo's Restaurant & Bar, a quintessential New Orleans eatery in the town of Chalmette. This beloved cafeteria is not particularly fancy or award-winning, but it's always consistent, boasting a family-friendly vibe and enormous portions of Southern and Italian staples, such as barbecue ribs, jambalaya, and veal parmesan. Muffulettas and macaroni and cheese are just a couple of the other popular items.

MAP 7: 613 W. St. Bernard Hwy., Chalmette, 504/279-8323; Tues.-Thurs. 11am-8pm, Fri.-Sat. 11am-8:30pm

COFFEE AND DESSERTS

MORNING CALL COFFEE STAND $

Morning Call serves a short menu that includes specialties like beignets and piping-hot café au lait. Originally established on Decatur Street in 1870, Morning Call moved to its present Metairie spot in 1974. The interior is quite elegant: long mirrored marble counters line one side of the room; the other contains small wooden tables. Servers in white paper caps skirt about the room, delivering coffee and doughnuts. Next door is **Lakeside News** (3323 Severn Ave., 504/889-1425; daily 4:30am-10pm), a good place to pick up newspapers and magazines, and a second Morning Call is located in City Park (56 Dreyfous Dr.).

MAP 7: 3325 Severn Ave., Metairie, 504/885-4068, www.morningcallcoffeestand.com; daily 24 hours

ECLECTIC

CAFÉ B $$$

Local restaurateur Ralph Brennan has expanded his empire to Metairie Road, a winding thoroughfare punctuated by curious shops and eateries. Happily, the location of Café B, a casual bistro with simple decor and a cheery ambience, makes it an ideal dining choice for visitors to the nearby Longue Vue House & Gardens. Helmed by chef Chris Montero, the menu features New Orleans-style dishes and gourmet twists on old American favorites, ideal for lunch, dinner, or Sunday brunch. Highlights include shrimp beignets, oyster-artichoke soup, and chicken pot pie.

MAP 7: 2700 Metairie Rd., Metairie, 504/934-4700, www.cafeb.com; Mon.-Thurs. 11:30am-2pm and 5pm-9pm, Fri. 11:30am-2pm and 5pm-10pm, Sat. 5pm-10pm, Sun. 10am-2pm

MONDO $$

In June 2010, Susan Spicer, the well-regarded chef behind the French Quarter's romantic Bayona, opened an easygoing, unpretentious neighborhood place in Lakeview, one of the areas hit hardest by Hurricane Katrina. Since then, this delightful spot has become a favorite among Mid-City and Lakeview residents who appreciate the easily accessible parking and creative cuisine. Aptly named Mondo, this bright, modern-looking eatery features flavors from around the world. Though the menu changes often, you'll typically find eclectic dishes like Thai shrimp and pork meatballs, Chinese braised duck leg, and pear and gorgonzola pizza. The Sunday brunch is equally varied. Reservations are only available for large groups.

MAP 7: 900 Harrison Ave., 504/224-2633, www.mondoneworleans.com; Mon.-Thurs. 11:30am-2:30pm and 5:30pm-10pm, Fri. 11:30am-2:30pm and 5:30pm-10:30pm, Sat. 5:30pm-10:30pm, Sun. 11am-2pm

VEGA TAPAS CAFE $$

One of a handful of Southshore suburban restaurants that actually merit making a special trip from downtown, the Vega Tapas Cafe is the classiest of several eateries in an Old Metairie strip mall. Peach walls and high ceilings create an elegant but informal ambience for sampling innovative tapas, most with a vaguely Mediterranean spin. Favorite dishes have included the jumbo lump crabmeat and baby arugula salad with crumbled feta, crispy shallots, and a blood orange vinaigrette; an eggplant napoleon layered with sun-dried tomatoes, fresh mozzarella, and basil pesto; and pan-roasted veal sweetbreads and mushrooms with crispy serrano and sherry butter.

MAP 7: 2051 Metairie Rd., Metairie, 504/836-2007, www.vegatapascafe.com; Mon.-Sat. 5:30pm-close

ITALIAN

TONY MANDINA'S RESTAURANT $$

One of the West Bank's best restaurants is the family-owned Tony Mandina's, a good bet for Italian cooking. Specializing in southern Italian cuisine, the menu strays from the traditional with a handful of exceptional, locally influenced seafood dishes. Come for the classic lasagna, chicken parmesan, and eggplant Dominic Jude, which features battered eggplant medallions layered with shrimp and crabmeat and topped with a creamy shrimp Alfredo sauce. On the weekend, you'll be treated to live piano music while you dine.

MAP 7: 1915 Pratt St., Gretna, 504/362-2010, www.tonymandinas.com; Tues.-Thurs. 11am-2pm, Fri. 11am-2pm and 5pm-9pm, Sat. 5pm-9pm

SEAFOOD

DEANIE'S SEAFOOD $$

Deanie's Seafood is a small, casual eatery in Metairie's Bucktown—a former fishing village on the western side of the 17th Street Canal, which so famously flooded Lakeview after Hurricane Katrina. Established in 1961 as the neighborhood's first seafood market, Deanie's is often crowded with locals, who come for seafood and okra gumbo, fried artichoke hearts, and, for mudbug lovers, the crawfish quartet, which features crawfish balls,

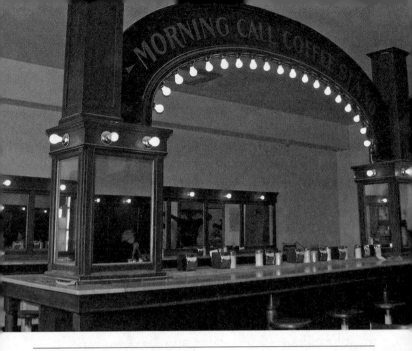

Above: Morning Call Coffee Stand. **Below:** Café B.

fried crawfish tails, crawfish au gratin, and crawfish étouffée. Even the complimentary spicy red potatoes that precede the meal are worth tasting. Although many prefer this comfortable, family-friendly spot in Bucktown, there's also a more modern-looking Deanie's in the French Quarter (841 Iberville St.).

MAP 7: 1713 Lake Ave., Metairie, 504/831-4141, www.deanies.com; Tues.-Sun. 11am-10pm

★ DRAGO'S SEAFOOD RESTAURANT $$$

Try to make a reservation a few days in advance for Drago's, a riotously popular restaurant with limited seating and parking. As the name indicates, the emphasis is on seafood, much of it prepared with a Louisiana slant. The lobster dishes are particularly noteworthy; try the lobster Marco, a whole lobster stuffed with fresh sautéed shrimp and mushrooms in a light cream sauce over angel hair pasta. Apart from the usual local seafood options, such as raw oysters and fried shrimp platters, you'll find delicious choices like the blackened duck breast over linguini with oysters and cream sauce. You can sit at the bar, which affords a clear view of the grill-cooked charbroiling oysters, or dine in one of the noisy but festive dining rooms. With the high volume of business, the waitstaff often seems harried. If you'd rather not trek out to Metairie, there's also a Drago's inside the CBD's Hilton New Orleans Riverside (2 Poydras St.).

MAP 7: 3232 N. Arnoult Rd., Metairie, 504/888-9254, www.dragosrestaurant.com; Mon.-Sat. 11am-9pm

YE OLDE COLLEGE INN $$

Part of a complex that now includes the Rock 'n' Bowl—a wonderful place to spend an evening bowling with the family and listening to live music—Ye Olde College Inn has been a New Orleans landmark since 1933. Expect friendly service, a nostalgic vibe, an eclectic crowd of families and sports fans, and well-prepared classics like turkey and andouille gumbo, fresh Gulf fish with lump crabmeat, and, for dessert, a fried bread pudding po-boy. Keep a lookout for the daily specials.

MAP 7: 3000 S. Carrollton Ave., 504/866-3683, www.collegeinn1933.com; Tues.-Sat. 4pm-11pm

When Orleans was the
of the Province
siana.
1762 — 1803
This street bore the

Nightlife

Look for ★ to find recommended nightlife.

Highlights

★ **Most Historic Bar:** Locals, tourists, and celebrities converge at **Lafitte's Blacksmith Shop Bar,** a small, moody, often noisy tavern housed within one of the oldest buildings in the French Quarter (page 175).

★ **Most Memorable Courtyard Cocktails: Pat O'Brien's** spacious courtyard—with a flaming fountain as its unique centerpiece—is a wonderful place to enjoy classic hurricanes and other cocktails in the humid night air (page 178).

★ **Best Gay Bar:** Situated on a busy Bourbon Street corner, the **Bourbon Pub & Parade** is the top game in town for the gay and lesbian crowd, featuring cocktails on the ground floor and dancing upstairs (page 179).

★ **Most Inviting Neighborhood Haunt:** Locals favor **The Kerry Irish Pub,** a small yet welcoming French Quarter bar known for its laid-back bartenders, assortment of imported beers, and nightly live music, ranging from Irish to country to classic rock (page 180).

★ **Most Historic Jazz Venue:** Opened in 1961, the intimate, world-renowned **Preservation Hall** presents wonderful old-time jazz concerts within its inviting vintage confines. Line up early (page 181).

★ **Best Jazz in the Marigny:** Though the Faubourg Marigny is a hotbed of live music, **The Spotted Cat Music Club** is your best bet for an assortment of jazz, from old-time tunes to modern improvisation. Often cramped inside, the dark bar on Frenchmen Street still provides limited space for dancing (page 186).

★ **Most Refined Hotel Bar:** If you're looking for an elegant watering hole where patrons prefer cognac and caviar, don your finest duds and head to the **Polo Club Lounge,** a longtime fixture inside the glamorous Windsor Court Hotel (page 189).

★ **Best Wine Bar:** Though New Orleans offers several worthwhile wine bars, the CBD's **W.I.N.O.** distinguishes itself with its varied wine selection and its informative wine-tasting classes (page 190).

★ **Best All-Around Music Club:** If you have the chance to watch live music at just one club, venture away from the French Quarter and stop by **Tipitina's,** a long-running locals' favorite that draws top zydeco, jazz, blues, and Cajun talents (page 195).

★ **Most Unusual Spot for Zydeco:** Situated between Uptown and Mid-City, the ever-popular **Rock 'n' Bowl** allows couples, families, and music lovers the chance to knock down some pins amid live zydeco, blues, jazz, and swamp pop performances (page 199).

New Orleans is famous for its nightlife. The entire city boasts a cornucopia of funky watering holes, festive gay bars, stylish hotel lounges, and legendary tourist magnets—like Pat O'Brien's, famous for its knock-me-under-the-table hurricanes.

The Big Easy's reputation as a party town is well deserved, and the pulse of that party is often found on Bourbon Street in the French Quarter. Unabashed strip clubs, karaoke bars, daiquiri shops, pulsating dance spaces, and a few well-respected jazz venues line the colorful strip. But it can also be a loud, sometimes obnoxious, often smelly thoroughfare that can become frighteningly crowded at certain times of the year (such as Mardi Gras and Halloween). Truly a drunken scene most nights, Bourbon is not for everyone, but it's worth a look—at least once—if only to experience the fervor with which this city indulges in music, alcohol, and socializing.

Thankfully, relishing a night out can involve a wide array of activities, and it's the boisterous music scene that truly distinguishes New Orleans. This is one of the world's premier destinations for jazz, blues, rock, soul, zydeco, and Cajun music. The city's live music venues are equally varied, ranging from friendly neighborhood bars like The Kerry Irish Pub to capacious music halls like Tipitina's. Locals tend to favor Frenchmen Street in the Faubourg Marigny, home to several longstanding joints that mainly cater to jazz, blues, and rock fans, though even that strip has gotten more crowded in recent years, compelling residents to shift toward bars and clubs along St. Claude Avenue. Beyond music, visitors might also appreciate the resurgence of burlesque that's

---

Previous: a historic street sign in the French Quarter; Bourbon Street in the evening.

taken place throughout the city—in joints like the AllWays Lounge & Theatre in the Marigny and One Eyed Jacks in the Quarter. Given the prevalence of 24-hour bars and restaurants, New Orleans is a wonderful place for night owls.

SAFETY IN THE BIG EASY

The city's unabashed revelry can be deceptively disarming. This is a town with drive-through daiquiri shops, where you can walk down Bourbon with enormous "go-cups" of beer, and where residents tend to be a very friendly bunch. Unfortunately, though, this is still a relatively dangerous city, where inebriated tourists have been known to wander off the beaten path, misplace their hotel, and encounter aggressive muggers. The best advice is to travel in groups, have fun in moderation, and make sure that someone is sober enough to find a safe path back to your hotel.

If partying on Bourbon Street, note that, while it's closed to automobile traffic at night, you should still be careful at each intersection, where vehicles are allowed to cross. Bear in mind, too, that many bars are cash-only, and restrooms are typically reserved for paying customers; in fact, on busy nights like New Year's Eve, many no-cover music venues will charge a nominal fee.

French Quarter

Map 1

BARS AND LOUNGES

THE BOMBAY CLUB

While this elegant restaurant, decorated in the style of an exclusive British gentlemen's club, offers sumptuous contemporary Creole cuisine, many patrons come for its reputation as a fashionable martini bar. Indeed, it's well known for its leather-bound, velvet-lined cocktail menu, featuring designer martinis, such as the James Bond-influenced Vesper or the Sweet Heat Margarita. On most weekends, you'll be treated to live jazz. As with many upscale establishments in New Orleans, casual attire is permitted, though jackets are preferred for men.

MAP 1: 830 Conti St., 504/577-2237, www.bombayclubneworleans.com; Sun.-Fri. 4pm-10pm, Sat. 5pm-midnight

THE CAROUSEL BAR & LOUNGE

Even if you're not staying at the legendary Hotel Monteleone, you can still enjoy a libation in the colorful Carousel Bar on the first floor. The prime attraction—the rather kitschy, 1940s-style, 25-seat bar—is festooned with bright lights and garish decorations, but the real treat is that, as its name implies, the bar almost imperceptibly revolves around the center of the room. Stop by to savor the old-world ambience, watch passersby on Royal

Street, listen to live music in the adjacent lounge, and drink in the literary company of Tennessee Williams and Truman Capote.

MAP 1: Hotel Monteleone, 214 Royal St., 504/523-3341, http://hotelmonteleone.com; daily 11am-close

JEAN LAFITTE'S OLD ABSINTHE HOUSE

Contained within a building that dates back to the early 1800s, the Old Absinthe House is especially popular among lawyers and other professionals. Furnished with antique chandeliers, a copper-topped bar, and the paraphernalia of famous football legends, this cozy tavern is an ideal spot to sip malt scotches and fancy concoctions like the Ramos Gin Fizz or Absinthe House Frappe. With friendly, well-trained bartenders, it can definitely get crowded at night, but this historic place is well worth a stop even if it's only a quick one.

MAP 1: 240 Bourbon St., 504/524-0113 or 504/523-3181, www.ruebourbon.com/oldabsinthehouse; daily 9am-3am

★ LAFITTE'S BLACKSMITH SHOP BAR

According to legend, pirate Jean Lafitte operated this spot as a blacksmith shop to serve as a front for other, less legitimate enterprises. Built before the city's devastating 18th-century fires, Lafitte's is one of the few original French-style buildings left in the Quarter. A bar since the 1940s, when Tennessee Williams frequented it, this cozy, candlelit place is now one of the city's most popular hangouts. Tourists, locals, and celebrities alike flock here to listen to live piano music, commune with the on-site ghost, and watch the eccentric passersby.

MAP 1: 941 Bourbon St., 504/593-9761, www.lafittesblacksmithshop.com; daily 10am-3am

MOLLY'S AT THE MARKET

If you find yourself wandering down Decatur in the wee hours, you'll discover relatively deserted sidewalks and many closed-up establishments, save for places like the 24-hour Café Du Monde and Molly's—a boisterous dive bar that's often the savior of night owls. Founded in 1973, this often-loud hangout has a loyal local following. Patrons appreciate the fun-loving ambience, embrace the ongoing food and drink specials, such as $1 tacos on Tuesdays and Thursdays, and flock here for special events like the annual Halloween and St. Patrick's Day parades.

MAP 1: 1107 Decatur St., 504/525-5169, www.mollysatthemarket.net; daily 10am-6am

NAPOLEON HOUSE

After strolling around Jackson Square, head a couple of blocks down Chartres to another fabled locale, the Napoleon House, which Mayor Nicholas Girod once proffered as a refuge for Napoleon during his exile. Built in 1797 and owned by the Impastato family since 1914, this

Jean Lafitte: Pirate or Privateer?

Piracy and its slightly more acceptable cousin, privateering, have been part of southern Louisiana lore since the region's settlement. In the 16th century, thieves in the Gulf of Mexico began targeting Spanish galleons loaded with silver and gold and headed for Spain's colonies in the New World. During times of war, European nations legitimized piracy, authorizing the crews of these renegade vessels to seize the ships of opposing nations. Louisana's shoreline was punctuated with hundreds of hidden coves, perfect havens for pirates. During the 19th century, the most infamous of these spots was Barataria Bay, which lies about 40 miles south of New Orleans at the north-central tip of the Gulf of Mexico, about 500 miles north of Mexico's Yucatán Peninsula, 650 miles northwest of Cuba, 450 miles west of Florida, and 450 miles east of Texas. Strategically, no location offered better access to so many lucrative colonial shipping routes.

In this bay, the infamous Baratarians established a colony for illicit deeds. Pirate ships returned here with their bounties, which included precious metals, rum, and African slaves, and then auctioned them to visitors from New Orleans. Sometimes, they hauled their goods directly to New Orleans, where they found a vast and eager market. They were led during the height of their success by Jean Lafitte and his brother Pierre.

Authorities in New Orleans turned a blind eye to Lafitte's operations, unwilling to shut off the stream of valuable goods into the city. It wasn't until Lafitte's disregard for the law became too flagrant that Governor William Claiborne finally ordered his arrest.

In 1814, a fleet of American military ships descended upon the Baratarians' headquarters, seizing eight schooners, about 40 houses, nearly 100 men, and countless spoils. Jean Lafitte had heard of the impending attack before its onset and successfully hid from authorities before making his escape.

The War of 1812 was now in full swing, and late in 1814, the British launched plans to attack New Orleans. Lafitte's exploits had become legendary, and the British approached Lafitte with an offer of $30,000 and a captainship in the British Navy if he would join their attack on the Americans. They figured that he'd jump at the opportunity to exact revenge against U.S. authorities.

Lafitte declined (likely because he believed he stood to gain more by aligning himself with the U.S. government) and tipped off Governor Claiborne about the impending British attack. He then volunteered his own considerable militia and fleet to defend New Orleans against the British—if Claiborne would agree to drop all charges against Jean and Pierre Lafitte and their fellow Baratarians.

Claiborne relayed the offer to General Andrew Jackson, who had arrived to lead the defense of New Orleans against the British. Jackson accepted without hesitation. In January 1815, during the Battle of New Orleans, Jean Lafitte and his cohorts performed admirably, greatly assisting American forces in turning back the British attack. Claiborne and Jackson kept their word, and U.S. authorities left the Baratarians alone from that point forward.

The final fate of the Lafitte brothers is unrecorded. Several years later, they moved their operations to Galveston Bay in Texas, but few additional details can be confirmed. In 1819, the U.S. Congress declared piracy a crime punishable by death, and the government began pursuing and prosecuting pirates more vigorously. Such circumstances may have curtailed the Lafittes' operations, but no matter what became of the dashing buccaneer, his legacy lives on.

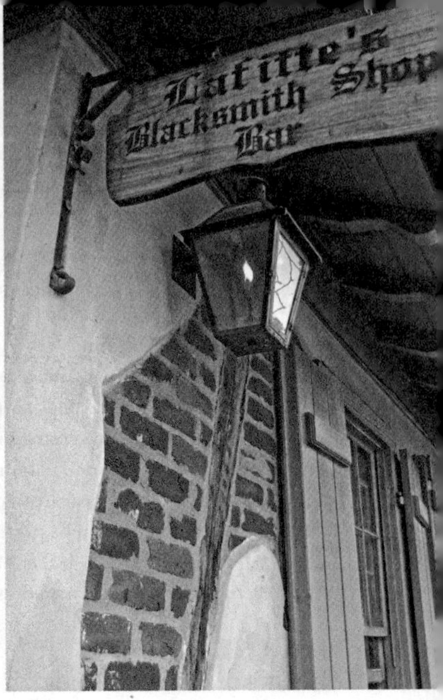

Clockwise from top left: The Dungeon; Lafitte's Blacksmith Shop Bar; Pat O'Brien's.

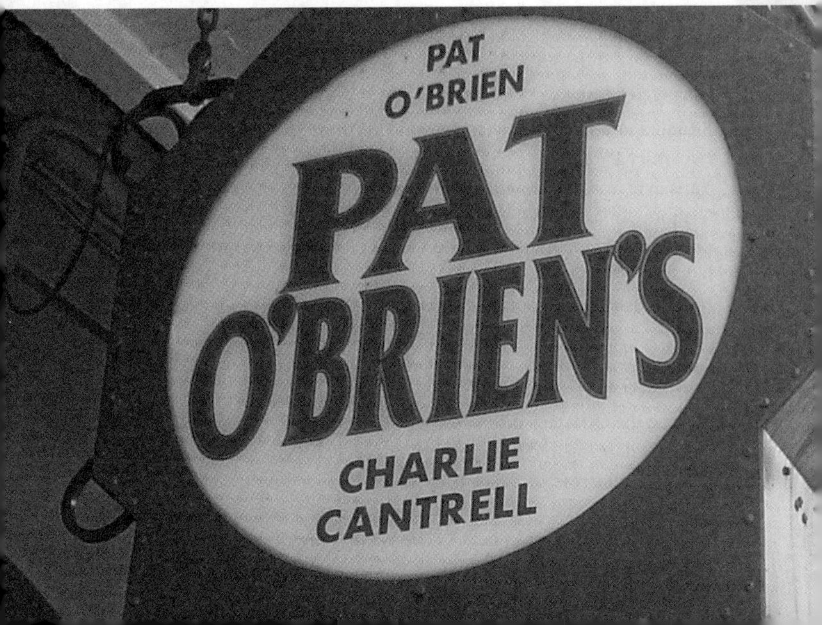

world-famous landmark is a terrific place to park your feet, especially if you favor classical music and a casual atmosphere. Even the food is worth a stop; the menu features Italian and New Orleans-style cuisine, from bruschetta and spumoni to boudin and jambalaya. Food is typically served until 5:30pm on Monday, 10pm Tuesday-Thursday, and 11pm Friday-Saturday.

MAP 1: 500 Chartres St., 504/524-9752, www.napoleonhouse.com; Mon.-Sat. 11am-close

★ PAT O'BRIEN'S

Even if you shy away from pricey tourist traps, you should experience the world-famous Pat O'Brien's at least once. Here, you'll find several unique spaces, including the crowded main bar, the lively piano bar (where the show begins at 6pm Mon.-Thurs. and 2pm Fri.-Sun.), the courtyard restaurant (624 Bourbon St.; daily 11am-close), the intimate Bourbon Bar, and the spacious patio, which features a rather cool flaming fountain. The hurricanes and mint juleps can be particularly strong, so sip slowly.

MAP 1: 718 St. Peter St., 504/525-4823 or 800/597-4823, www.patobriens.com; Mon.-Thurs. noon-close, Fri.-Sun. 10am-close

DANCE CLUBS

BOURBON STREET BLUES COMPANY

Despite the name, the Bourbon Street Blues Company is essentially a dance club, where twentysomething revelers groove to a cover band or DJ. Expect a three-for-one happy hour every day, from opening until 9pm, and feel free to venture upstairs, where the balcony is ideal for people-watching. The hours here are never constant; sometimes, the doors won't open until 2pm, while at other times, the place is hoppin' for 24 hours straight.

MAP 1: 441 Bourbon St., 504/566-1507; hours vary daily; no cover, save for special events

CATS MEOW

Situated at a rather busy corner on Bourbon Street, this ever-popular, two-story karaoke bar has a loyal following. Celebrities like "Weird Al" Yankovic and Tori Spelling have stopped by to entertain the masses. Visitors can dance to live and DJ-mixed swing, classic rock, disco, dance, pop, and hip-hop music, or opt for a bit of people-watching on the upper balcony.

MAP 1: 701 Bourbon St., 504/523-2788 or 504/523-2951, www.catskaraoke.com; Mon.-Thurs. 4pm-3am, Fri.-Sun. 2pm-4am; no cover, save for special events

THE DUNGEON

Among the Quarter's more energetic haunts, the Dungeon is a preferred place for dancing into the wee hours. Accessible via a pseudo-creepy outer gate and a narrow alleyway, the club features a typically crowded dance floor, plus three unique bar areas, decorated with fake skulls and human-size cages. House drinks include the Witch's Brew, the Dungeon's answer to Pat O'Brien's traditional hurricane. Adjacent to the gateway is a front bar that the staff jokingly refers to as the "daycare dungeon"—mainly because it's open earlier (daily 6pm-close).

MAP 1: 738 Toulouse St., 504/523-5530; Tues.-Sun. 10:30pm-close; no cover, save for special events

ONE EYED JACKS

Perhaps my favorite place to dance in the Quarter, One Eyed Jacks is a spacious, bordello-style venue, with red walls, curious paintings, and moody lighting. Beyond the intimate front bar, revelers will encounter a large showroom, which features a horseshoe-shaped bar, limited seating, an ample stage, and oodles of room for dancing. While live concerts are common here, regulars also come for thematic events, like 1980s-style dance parties, burlesque shows, and vaudeville nights, which often include comedy sketches, old-fashioned jazz performances, acrobatics, and sexy dance routines.

MAP 1: 615 Toulouse St., 504/569-8361, www.oneeyedjacks.net; hours vary depending on the event; cover varies

GAY AND LESBIAN VENUES

★ BOURBON PUB & PARADE

One of the most popular gay dance clubs sits at the often-rowdy corner of Bourbon and St. Ann. The Bourbon Pub & Parade has a typically packed video bar on the ground level, a slick dance floor upstairs, and a long wraparound balcony on the second floor—a favorite perch from which to gaze at the throngs of revelers on Bourbon Street. Music lovers can expect to see plenty of retro music videos downstairs, while everything from drag and burlesque shows to hot guy contests to karaoke nights is happening upstairs.

MAP 1: 801 Bourbon St., 504/529-2107, www.bourbonpub.com; daily 24 hours; cover varies

THE CAFE LAFITTE IN EXILE

Cafe Lafitte in Exile has been serving the local gay community for roughly as long as any bar in town. It draws a thirty- to fiftysomething crowd. You can watch music videos in the downstairs bar and observe curious passersby from the upstairs balcony, which can be particularly eye-opening during uninhibited, skin-baring events like Mardi Gras and Southern Decadence.

MAP 1: 901 Bourbon St., 504/522-8397, www.lafittes.com; daily 24 hours; no cover

GOLDEN LANTERN BAR

If you prefer a relaxed, off-Bourbon watering hole that's inviting to gay and heterosexual patrons alike, head to the Golden Lantern, a small, dark locals' bar on a quiet, residential stretch of Royal that serves one of the best Bloody Marys in the city.

MAP 1: 1239 Royal St., 504/529-2860; daily 24 hours; no cover

GOOD FRIENDS BAR

The mellow, longstanding Good Friends Bar isn't too loud or flashy. It's just a casual, pet-friendly neighborhood watering hole, where you'll find a pool table, affordable beer and cocktails, a slightly fancier upstairs area, and attentive bartenders. Saints fans come here, as do low-key locals, and no matter your sexual orientation, you're welcome to join in the karaoke fun every Tuesday night (9pm-midnight).

MAP 1: 740 Dauphine St., 504/566-7191, www.goodfriendsbar.com; Mon.-Thurs. 1pm-5am, Fri.-Sun. 24 hours; no cover

OZ

Oz often seems to be far less crowded than other venues in the Quarter. Nevertheless, many locals consider it one of the city's top gay dance clubs, especially during special events like Mardi Gras and New Year's Eve. Situated opposite Bourbon Pub & Parade, Oz provides plenty of room for dancing on the ground floor and more lounge-like spaces upstairs.

MAP 1: 800 Bourbon St., 504/593-9491, www.ozneworleans.com; daily 24 hours; cover varies

LIVE MUSIC

Blues and Rock

HOUSE OF BLUES

Part of the famous chain, this predictably popular tourist haunt has been enticing legions of music fans since its 1994 opening. Home to a large folk art collection, the funky, colorful concert venue features two music halls, which can accommodate about 370 and 840 guests, respectively. Various performers play here, from major rock bands to local jazz and blues musicians, and the on-site restaurant serves New Orleans favorites like shrimp po-boys and key lime pie. Especially popular is Sunday's Gospel Brunch, which combines world-class performances with a Southern-style buffet.

MAP 1: 225 Decatur St., 504/310-4999, www.houseofblues.com/neworleans; daily 11:30am-close; cover varies

Country and Folk

★ THE KERRY IRISH PUB

At this cozy neighborhood hangout, diehard regulars and curious out-of-towners converge for imported beers, friendly conversation, and live music nightly. In addition to Irish, most of the performers play country, folk, and classic rock selections. Situated beside a firehouse in a rather touristy part of the Quarter, the Kerry features, besides the small stage, a projection set-up and two televisions ideal for Saints' game-viewing, several tables and chairs, mounted photographs of past musicians, and a small space that, despite the brick floors, allows for dancing. Some patrons may also appreciate the pool table, laid-back but efficient bartenders, and entertaining graffiti in the women's restroom. The hours here are flexible; Saints' games and special events might inspire an earlier opening, while a well-attended concert can keep the doors open until well past 2am.

MAP 1: 331 Decatur St., 504/527-5954; Mon.-Fri. 1pm-close, Sat.-Sun. noon-close; no cover, though a one-drink minimum applies

Jazz

BALCONY MUSIC CLUB

No matter the evening, it's difficult to cross the corner of Decatur Street and Esplanade Avenue without catching some of the fantastic tunes coming from the usually open doors of the funky Balcony Music Club (known colloquially as the BMC). Though you're most likely to hear brass, jazz, or funk, anything is possible. If you're still in the mood for fun after this place closes, just hop across Esplanade to **Igor's Check Point Charlie** (501 Esplanade Ave., 504/281-4847), a lively 24-hour bar, grill, music club, game room, and self-service laundromat.

MAP 1: 1331 Decatur St., 504/301-5912; daily 5pm-4am; cover varies

IRVIN MAYFIELD'S JAZZ PLAYHOUSE

Situated on the ground floor of the elegant Royal Sonesta hotel, in the heart of Bourbon Street's revelry, this stylish club welcomes jazz aficionados and curious tourists every night of the week. Although the musicians rotate nightly, you're always guaranteed to hear some stellar performers. On Friday night, be sure to stick around until midnight, when you'll be able to experience a classy burlesque show. Given the cozy space, zero cover charge, and no-reservation policy, the room fills up quickly, so get here early.

MAP 1: Royal Sonesta New Orleans, 300 Bourbon St., 504/553-2299 or 504/586-0300, www.irvinmayfield.com; Sat.-Tues. 8pm-close, Wed.-Thurs. 5pm-close, Fri. 6pm-close; no cover

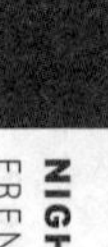

PALM COURT JAZZ CAFE

One of the Big Easy's most famous and delightful live jazz venues is the Palm Court Jazz Cafe, situated in a handsome, 19th-century building near the historic French Market. Besides Southern-style ceiling fans and an elegant mahogany bar, the restaurant features exposed-brick walls lined with photos of jazz greats, plus a kitchen producing tasty Creole fare. Because seating is arranged at tables over dinner, reservations are a must.

MAP 1: 1204 Decatur St., 504/525-0200, www.palmcourtjazzcafe.com; Wed.-Sun. 7pm-close; no cover

★ PRESERVATION HALL

Since 1961, Preservation Hall has been one of the city's top places to hear true New Orleans jazz. The band and the venue were formed expressly to keep the legacy of the city's distinctive style of jazz music alive for generations to come, and top musicians continue to perform in the surprisingly intimate concert hall. Housed within a weathered, 1750s-era house, it's a charming, laid-back place, with vintage wooden benches, folding chairs, and a good bit of standing room. After the all-too-brief concert (usually less than an hour), feel free to stroll along the carriageway, to the landscaped courtyard for a breath of fresh air. Be sure to get here early, as the line forms quickly for these nightly concerts (8pm, 9pm, and 10pm). If you'd rather skip the line altogether, consider the limited "Big Shot" seating option ($35-50 pp).

MAP 1: 726 St. Peter St., 504/522-2841, www.preservationhall.com; daily 8pm-11pm; $15-20 pp

21ST AMENDMENT AT LA LOUISIANE

One of the newest jazz joints in the French Quarter, 21st Amendment at La Louisiane honors America's Prohibition era of the 1920s, when both the mafia and speakeasies thrived. Decorated with black-and-white images of the country's most notorious mobsters, including Capone himself, this cozy bar occupies part of a 19th-century building that was owned by local mobsters Diamond Jim Moran and Carlos Marcello from the 1950s to the 1980s. Today, you can savor a delicious cocktail, made from homemade syrups and infused spirits, while listening to live old-time jazz and blues music, which is offered nearly every afternoon and evening.

MAP 1: 725 Iberville St., 504/378-7330, www.21stamendmentlalouisiane.com; Mon.-Wed. 2pm-11pm, Thurs. 2pm-midnight, Fri.-Sat. noon-2am, Sun. 11am-11pm

WINE BARS

ORLEANS GRAPEVINE WINE BAR & BISTRO

The intimate Orleans Grapevine is one of the rare reasonably priced yet sophisticated bars in the French Quarter. Set inside a restored 1809 building, it's a classy yet casual bistro located in the oft-overlooked block between the peaceful rear garden of the St. Louis Cathedral and the craziness of Bourbon Street. Besides featuring an extensive list of 450 bottled wines and 75 varietals by the glass, the Grapevine turns out an elegant and tasty menu, including revolving delicacies like baked brie and stuffed flounder. Expect meal service Sunday-Thursday 5pm-10:30pm and Friday-Saturday 5pm-11:30pm.

MAP 1: 720 Orleans St., 504/523-1930, www.orleansgrapevine.com; daily 4pm-close

Faubourg Marigny and Bywater

Map 2

BARS AND LOUNGES

MIMI'S IN THE MARIGNY

Nestled within a quiet residential part of the Faubourg Marigny, Mimi's has long been a popular hot spot, particularly among locals. Downstairs, you'll find a neighborhood bar with couches, stools, and a pool table, while the upstairs space is often a live music venue, with a decent amount of room for

Above: Preservation Hall. **Below:** the Bourbon Street Blues Company.

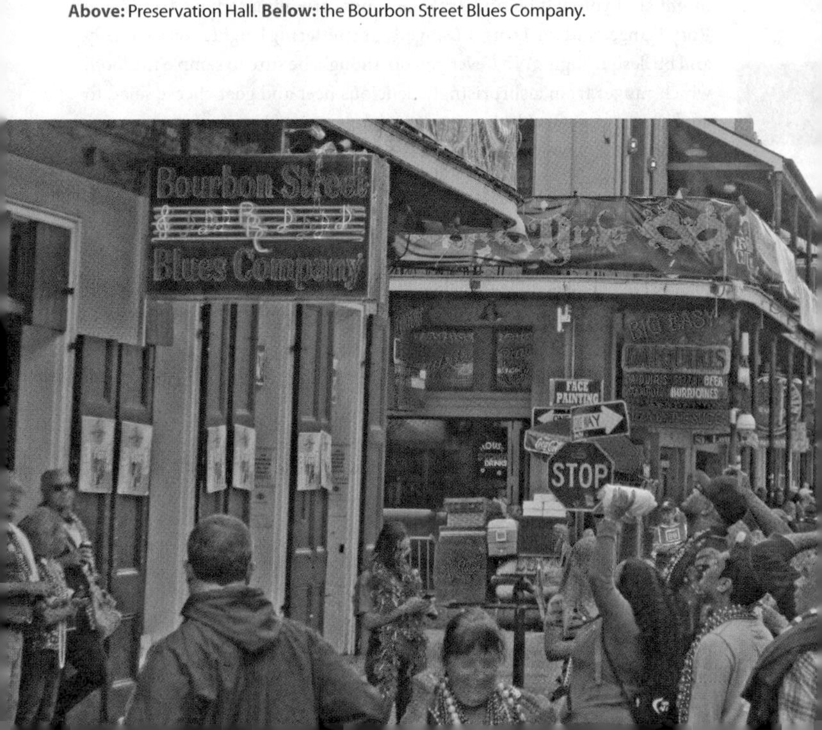

dancing. At times, you can expect concerts and DJ-helmed dance parties, not to mention dance lessons. Try the tasty tapas on offer, from almond-stuffed dates to beef empanadas; the kitchen is typically open Sunday-Thursday 6pm-2am and Friday-Saturday 6pm-4am.

MAP 2: 2601 Royal St., 504/872-9868, http://mimismarigny.com; Sun.-Thurs. 3pm-4am, Fri.-Sat. 3pm-5am; no cover

DANCE CLUBS

THE MAISON

One of the more spacious venues in the Marigny, this multilevel bar, restaurant, and live music venue consists of three separate areas: a front dining and music room; a rear lounge and stage; and the upper Penthouse bar, which comprises a separate stage, a comfortable lounge, and plenty of room for dancing. The Maison is home to concerts and DJ-helmed dance parties, featuring jazz, funk, soul, Latin dance music, and even swing dance lessons.

MAP 2: 508 Frenchmen St., 504/371-5543, www.maisonfrenchman.com; Sun.-Thurs. 5pm-close, Fri.-Sat. 4pm-close; no cover, save for special events

SIBERIA

As with many nighttime venues in New Orleans, Siberia defies categorization. Depending on the night it can be an eclectic live music venue, a DJ-spinning dance club, or a Slavic restaurant. At any given time, you might find yourself belting karaoke songs, grooving to local bands like Rory Danger and the Danger Dangers, or sputtering laughter on a comedy and burlesque night. Whatever you do, though, be sure to sample the food, which ranges from a surprisingly delicious beet and goat cheese salad to apple and asparagus blinis to traditional pierogi and kielbasa.

MAP 2: 2227 St. Claude Ave., 504/265-8855, www.siberianola.com; daily 4pm-close; cover varies

GAY AND LESBIAN VENUES

ALLWAYS LOUNGE & THEATRE

Definitely not for the faint-hearted, the rowdy AllWays Lounge & Theatre welcomes everybody, though it has a predominantly gay and lesbian following. Nudity, wacky sexual acts, and strange musical performances are common in the lounge. The theater features ever-changing productions, including bizarre concerts and counterculture musicals like *The Rocky Horror Show*. Shows generally start at 10pm.

MAP 2: 2240 St. Claude Ave., 504/218-5778, www.theallwayslounge.com; daily 6pm-close; cover varies

THE COUNTRY CLUB

Although this magnificent Bywater mansion isn't technically a gay bar, it definitely embraces an "anything goes" vibe, with its clothing-optional pool, sauna, Jacuzzi, and on-site massage and spa services. You can sip cocktails in the indoor or outdoor bars, enjoy creative cuisine in the restaurant (Sun.-Thurs. 10am-9pm, Fri.-Sat. 10am-10pm), or watch movies, music videos, and sporting events on the 25-foot screen. If the crowd is really hoppin,' the joint might not close until 2am or later. Expect to pay $8-15 to access the rear area, where you'll find the pool.

MAP 2: 634 Louisa St., 504/945-0742, www.thecountryclubneworleans.com; daily 10am-1am; no cover

LIVE MUSIC

Blues and Rock

APPLE BARREL BAR

Just steps from The Spotted Cat Music Club, in the heart of the Marigny's lively music scene, this intimate, somewhat dingy bar lures an ever-revolving crowd of blues and jazz lovers nightly. Hip yet happily low-keyed, this is an ideal spot for sipping cocktails before heading out to the noisier music clubs along Frenchmen—though, be advised, it can still get pretty loud in here, depending on who's playing.

MAP 2: 609 Frenchmen St., 504/949-9399; Sun.-Thurs. 1pm-3am, Fri.-Sat. 1pm-5am; no cover, though a one-drink minimum applies

BLUE NILE

A Faubourg Marigny mainstay and a frequent sight on HBO's now-canceled *Treme,* the spacious Blue Nile presents a broad mix of cool music, from blues and jazz to reggae and garage rock. Frequent acts include the Honey Island Swamp Band and local fave Kermit Ruffins and the BBQ Swingers. Typically, there are two shows each night, with the first starting around 7 or 8pm and the second kicking off at 10 or 11pm. With its plush lounge seating and tile floors, it's a funky yet elegant place to socialize early in the evening.

MAP 2: 532 Frenchmen St., 504/948-2583, http://bluenilelive.com; Sun.-Thurs. 7pm-2am, Fri.-Sat. 6pm-4am; cover varies

D.B.A. NEW ORLEANS

Located in a building from the late 19th century, this dimly lit, hipster-infested hangout in the Faubourg Marigny is a good place to meet locals, hear live rock and blues bands, and, on occasion, catch performances from the likes of Jimmy Buffett and Stevie Wonder. The drink selection encompasses about a zillion beers (including plenty of imported options), plus many types of whiskey and tequila, and the crowd is young and laid-back but with a touch of style.

MAP 2: 618 Frenchmen St., 504/942-3731, www.dbaneworleans.com; Mon.-Thurs. 5pm-close, Fri.-Sun. 4pm-close; cover varies

Country and Folk

THE HI-HO LOUNGE

While the Hi-Ho might not be in the safest part of town, it's nevertheless a wonderful spot for music lovers and those itchin' to dance. On at least three, if not five, nights a week, you might hear folk, bluegrass, country, funk, punk, or even hip-hop. Besides offering food at times—such as $2 red beans and rice on Monday, Korean cuisine on Tuesday, and barbecue on Thursday—this low-key, cash-only dive bar hosts special events.

MAP 2: 2239 St. Claude Ave., 504/945-4446, http://hiholounge.net; daily 5pm-2am; cover varies

Jazz

BUFFA'S BAR & RESTAURANT

Situated between the French Quarter and the Faubourg Marigny since 1939, Buffa's feels like a well-kept secret, despite its obvious location on Esplanade. A popular neighborhood hangout, Buffa's offers a variety of vittles and libations all day and night. The real treat is the back room (Mon.-Tues. 6pm-close, Wed.-Sat. 11am-close, Sun. 10am-close), where patrons can listen to traditional jazz musicians. One of my favorite regular bands is the Royal Rounders, whose eclectic, often chuckle-worthy shows might feature, in addition to jazz, everything from blues to pop to R&B.

MAP 2: 1001 Esplanade Ave., 504/949-0038, www.buffasbar.com; daily 24 hours; no cover

SNUG HARBOR JAZZ BISTRO

At the aptly named Snug Harbor Jazz Bistro, a cozy, classy, contemporary spot in the Faubourg Marigny, you can sip cocktails in the downstairs bar or relish tasty regional cuisine in the adjacent dining room, before heading upstairs to catch some of the city's top jazz acts. Occupying a renovated, 19th-century storefront on Frenchmen, Snug Harbor has been showcasing top musicians, from Ellis Marsalis to Charmaine Neville, as well as nurturing young talent for more than three decades.

MAP 2: 626 Frenchmen St., 504/949-0696, www.snugjazz.com; Sun.-Thurs. 5pm-midnight, Fri.-Sat. 5pm-1am; $15-35 pp

★ THE SPOTTED CAT MUSIC CLUB

Practically across the street from Snug Harbor lies the Spotted Cat, a less famous, cash-only jazz club that qualifies as one of the coolest little music finds in the city. Often featured on HBO's former *Treme* series, this happily cramped, dark, and sweaty dance hall offers a long happy hour, a nice selection of designer martinis, and terrific live bands. Although you'll occasionally hear rock, blues, bluegrass, salsa, and other dance-worthy musical styles, modern and traditional jazz are definitely the mainstays here. Local favorite Meschiya Lake and the Little Big Horns, known for their old-time jazz performances, often pack in the crowds and inspire old-fashioned dancing among the regulars.

MAP 2: 623 Frenchmen St., www.spottedcatmusicclub.com; Mon.-Fri. 4pm-2am, Sat.-Sun. 2pm-2am; no cover, though a one-drink minimum applies

SWEET LORRAINE'S JAZZ CLUB

On a historic street along the sketchy edge of the Faubourg Marigny, you'll find Sweet Lorraine's, a definite local favorite for live jazz. While you listen to the ever-changing performers, be sure to sample Southern-style dishes like blackened catfish, cornbread-stuffed chicken breasts, and pecan pie with praline sauce. The club also features a selective wine and martini menu.

MAP 2: 1931 St. Claude Ave., 504/945-9654; Tues.-Sat. 5pm-close, Sun. 7pm-close; cover varies

THREE MUSES

Featuring a snug dining area, a small bar, and an even smaller stage, Three Muses is a terrific place to sample eclectic tapas-style dishes like Moroccan eggplant bruschetta, Gulf fish tacos, and cardamom panna cotta while listening to some of the finest blues, jazz, and swing musicians in town. Though reservations are necessary on the weekends, be prepared to relinquish your table after 90 minutes. Seemingly a harsh policy, it's actually quite reasonable given the enormous popularity of this cozy joint.

MAP 2: 536 Frenchmen St., 504/252-4801, www.3musesnola.com; Wed.-Mon. 5pm-close; no cover

WINE BARS

BACCHANAL

Often spotted in HBO's acclaimed show *Treme,* Bacchanal is at once a wine bar and retail shop, a New York-style deli, an international bistro, and, when weather allows it in the exposed courtyard, a live music venue. This local favorite offers an ever-changing, culinary experience that you must embrace firsthand to understand. "Get your wine and cheese up front, get your food and music out back," explains one patron. "Help yourself, have fun, get funky, this ain't no Galatoire's!" Remember, the kitchen usually closes around 11pm.

MAP 2: 600 Poland Ave., 504/948-9111, www.bacchanalwine.com; daily 11am-midnight

Central Business and Arts Districts

Map 3

BARS AND LOUNGES

HANDSOME WILLY'S PATIO BAR & LOUNGE

You have to admire the perseverance of the folks who run Handsome Willy's—a rockin' music club and bar that opened on the site of a former brothel in 2005, was virtually destroyed by Hurricane Katrina and yet managed to reopen only a few months later. The club has developed a loyal

Hey, Big Spenders!

While it's not exactly Las Vegas—and the Louisiana cities of Shreveport and Lake Charles are considerably more popular as gambling hubs—the Greater New Orleans area does boast three major gaming facilities.

The mother ship for gamblers here, **Harrah's New Orleans** (228 Poydras St., 504/533-6000 or 800/427-7247, www.harrahsneworleans.com or www.caesars.com/harrahs-new-orleans), opened in the late 1990s under a cloud of controversy. It's one of the largest gaming facilities in the South, a massive property with more than 1,700 slot machines and 100 gaming tables, plus a full-service hotel. It has several excellent restaurants, including the vaunted Besh Steak, the casual Grand Isle Seafood Restaurant, a Gordon Biersch brewpub, a pretty good buffet, and an outlet of local chain Acme Oyster House.

The metro area's second big gaming hall is the **Treasure Chest Casino** (5050 Williams Blvd., Kenner, 504/443-8000 or 800/298-0711, www.treasurechest.com), which is actually an ornate floating casino docked on Lake Pontchartrain, not far from the Louis Armstrong New Orleans International Airport. Here, you'll find live entertainment, various table games, a buffet restaurant, and a casual café.

If that's not enough, head across the Mississippi River to the West Bank, where **Boomtown New Orleans** (4132 Peters Rd., Harvey, 504/366-7711 or 800/366-7711, www.boomtownneworleans.com) offers more than 30 table games and 1,400 slot machines, plus a comfortable hotel. You can choose from four dining venues: a scrumptious buffet, an express café, the intimate Pier 4, and the aptly named Asia, featuring Chinese and Vietnamese specialties.

following for booking great bands, from funk to hip-hop. Its proximity to the Superdome and Smoothie King Center also makes it popular among sports fans. Besides offering weekday happy hours (2pm-6pm), Willy's serves free food on Friday (5pm-9pm) and opens on Sunday during the Saints' home games.

MAP 3: 218 S. Robertson St., 504/525-0377, www.handsomewillys.com; Mon.-Wed. 2pm-midnight, Thurs. 1pm-3am, Fri. noon-4am, Sat. 6pm-3am

LUCY'S RETIRED SURFERS BAR & RESTAURANT

Nestled within the Arts District, Lucy's Retired Surfers Bar feels like a frat-sorority party on most evenings, especially on weekends. It's known as one of the city's more popular meat markets, and it's also a great place to slurp down a few margaritas. You can enjoy a delicious brunch on Saturday and Sunday mornings—the perfect cure for a hangover. The shrimp and grits happens to be one of the tastiest versions in the city. Interestingly, there's also a Lucy's up the river in Baton Rouge (151 3rd St.).

MAP 3: 701 Tchoupitoulas St., 504/523-8995, www.lucysretiredsurfers.com; Mon.-Fri. 11am-close, Sat.-Sun. 10am-close

★ POLO CLUB LOUNGE

The elegant Windsor Court Hotel is home to the Polo Club Lounge, a classy space furnished with equestrian oil paintings, historical memorabilia, and leather furniture, all of which recall the ambience of a private British club. Adjacent to the Grill Room, this second-floor lounge presents live nightly jazz in addition to hard-to-find wines, champagnes, and specialty liquors, and a menu that includes caviar and truffle fries.

MAP 3: Windsor Court Hotel, 300 Gravier St., 504/522-1992 or 504/523-6000, www.grillroomneworleans.com or www.windsorcourthotel.com; Mon.-Thurs. 11:30am-midnight, Fri.-Sat. 11:30am-1am, Sun. 11am-midnight

THE SAZERAC BAR

The Sazerac Bar, located at the CBD's grand Roosevelt New Orleans, is perhaps the most famous hotel lounge in the city. Named for the noted cocktail—a concoction of rye whiskey, Pernod, sugar, lemon oil, and the local Peychaud's bitters—the bar was once a favored haunt of Governor Huey P. Long, the infamous "Kingfish" of Louisiana.

MAP 3: The Roosevelt New Orleans, 130 Roosevelt Way, 504/648-1200, www.therooseveltneworleans.com; daily 11am-close

DANCE CLUBS

THE METROPOLITAN

One block from the Ernest N. Morial Convention Center, you'll encounter this massive, two-story, Los Angeles-style nightclub, which, at more than 36,000 square feet in size, is often the premier choice for major events, from tailgate parties to fashion shows. This enormous warehouse-turned-club contains two main rooms, equipped with smoke machines, strobe lights, and video screens and featuring DJ-spun hip-hop, rock, house, techno, and other popular formats. In addition to a slew of bartender stations and VIP sections, the Metropolitan offers valet parking and VIP table service. Given this upscale vibe, expect pricey drinks and high cover charges.

MAP 3: 310 Andrew Higgins Dr., 504/568-1702, www.themetropolitannightclub.com; hours vary depending on the event; cover varies

LIVE MUSIC

Blues and Rock

THE HOWLIN' WOLF

For the most part, you'll catch top blues and funk acts at the Howlin' Wolf, a cavernous nightclub in the Arts District, not far from the city's convention center. This is indeed one of the Big Easy's largest and most prominent live music venues, which has been known to host rock, alternative, pop, and R&B bands, too. Over the years, some of the more famous performers have included Allison Krauss, Harry Connick Jr., and the Foo Fighters.

MAP 3: 907 S. Peters St., 504/522-9653, www.howlin-wolf.com; daily 5pm-2am; cover varies

REPUBLIC NEW ORLEANS

Situated in the downtown Arts District, Republic New Orleans occupies a cavernous, historic space that was once a coffee warehouse and a set for Oliver Stone's film *JFK*. Now, this upscale music club and special-events facility is often the site of concerts, parties, and fashion shows.

MAP 3: 828 S. Peters St., 504/528-8282, www.republicnola.com; hours vary depending on the show; cover varies

Cajun and Zydeco

MULATE'S

Mulate's features live bands, plenty of dancing space, and a menu filled with Louisiana favorites. Located in the Arts District, this down-home Cajun restaurant and dance hall occupies a large building. The music is far superior to the food. In fact, you can expect live entertainment nightly (Sun.-Thurs. 7pm-10pm, Fri.-Sat. 7pm-10:30pm).

MAP 3: 201 Julia St., 504/522-1492 or 800/854-9149, www.mulates.com; Sun.-Thurs. 11am-10pm, Fri.-Sat. 11am-11pm; no cover

Jazz

LITTLE GEM SALOON

The Little Gem Saloon is part bar, part restaurant, and part live music venue. While many patrons come for the tasty Cajun and soul food, which ranges from crawfish cheesecake to fried chicken, plenty of others flock here for the live music, whether during the weekday happy hour (5pm-7pm), on a weekend night, or during the Sunday jazz brunch. Regular performers include local favorites like the New Orleans Swinging Gypsies, The Messy Cookers Jazz Band, and Kermit Ruffins and the BBQ Swingers. Given the popularity of this venue, you must reserve a table to guarantee seating.

MAP 3: 445 S. Rampart St., 504/267-4863, www.littlegemsaloon.com; Tues.-Thurs. 11am-2pm and 5pm-10pm, Fri. 11am-2pm and 5pm-11pm, Sat. 5pm-11pm, Sun. 10am-2pm; cover varies

WINE BARS

★ W.I.N.O.

Situated in the CBD, the cleverly abbreviated Wine Institute of New Orleans is more than just a wine bar and retail shop. In addition to sampling a variety of wines in the front area of this modern-looking emporium, wine connoisseurs can take informative and enjoyable classes in the rear, from an introduction to wine class ($35 pp) to food and wine pairings ($40 pp). Reservations are usually necessary, though walk-ins are welcome.

MAP 3: 610 Tchoupitoulas St., 504/324-8000, www.winoschool.com; Mon.-Thurs. 11am-10pm, Fri. 11am-1am, Sat. noon-1am, Sun. 2pm-10pm

BARS AND LOUNGES

THE BULLDOG

The Bulldog is often a late-night haven for college students, especially those from nearby Tulane and Loyola. But well-past-college-age locals favor this casual, dog-friendly watering hole, too. Both the tasty burgers and eclectic beer selection, which includes 50 draft varieties and 100 more in bottles, are definite lures. The courtyard, though often crowded, provides excellent people-watching opportunities along Magazine Street.

MAP 4: 3236 Magazine St., 504/891-1516, http://bulldog.draftfreak.com; Mon.-Fri. 11:30am-close, Sat.-Sun. 11am-close

HALF MOON BAR & GRILL

Memorably featured in films as diverse as *Ray* (2004) and *The Skeleton Key* (2005), Half Moon has been a fixture in New Orleans for more than seven decades. In general, you'll find a gaggle of locals at this friendly joint, which isn't far from Coliseum Square in the funky Lower Garden District. A decent place to hang out with friends, unwind after antiques shopping, watch a Saints or Pelicans game, or play pool, darts, air hockey, or Skee-Ball, Half Moon also serves up half-pound burgers and chicken sandwiches from 5pm until the wee hours.

MAP 4: 1125 St. Mary St., 504/593-0011, http://halfmoongrillnola.com; daily 5pm-2am

WINE BARS

THE TASTING ROOM NEW ORLEANS

With its exposed brick walls and moody ambience, The Tasting Room is a cozy, inviting lounge for wine lovers, particularly small groups of friends and couples with a mind for romance. In addition to offering their signature flights, which usually consist of three well-paired wines, this exceptional wine bar prepares complimentary, tapas-style dishes, which, depending on the night, might include truffle fries, red eye mussels, and crème brûlée.

MAP 4: 1906 Magazine St., 504/581-3880, www.ttrneworleans.com; Tues.-Sun. 3pm-11pm

BARS AND LOUNGES

CARROLLTON STATION

Located in the Riverbend area of Uptown and named after a nearby streetcar barn, the rustic Carrollton Station is a classic neighborhood bar. It's a well-favored locals' hangout, where you can sample more than 50 reasonably priced beers, relax with friends in the backyard patio, watch your favorite spectator sport, and listen to live local music on the weekend. Video poker machines, darts and ping-pong, wireless Internet access, and weekly events, such as stand-up comedy on Wednesday (9pm) and pub trivia on Thursday (6:30pm), are also big draws.

MAP 5: 8140 Willow St., 504/865-9190, www.carrolltonstation.com; Mon.-Sat. 3pm-close, Sun. noon-close

COOTER BROWN'S TAVERN & OYSTER BAR

Situated in Uptown's Riverbend neighborhood, not far from the Mississippi River, this casual sports bar is a favorite among nearby residents and college students alike. Established in 1977 and filled with caricatures of dead, beer-drinking celebrities, this lovable watering hole features pool tables and video poker machines, numerous televisions for diehard sports fans, more than 400 bottled brands of domestic and imported beers (and roughly 40 draft selections), plus to-die-for raw oysters, boiled seafood, and enormous po-boys. As a bonus, Cooter Brown's lies within walking distance of the St. Charles streetcar line, so there's no excuse to drink and drive.

MAP 5: 509 S. Carrollton Ave., 504/866-9104, www.cooterbrowns.com; Mon.-Sat. 11am-2am, Sun. 11am-1am

CURE

With its weathered brick interior walls, funky chandeliers, and stylishly lit liquor display, Cure simultaneously evokes the vibe of a quintessential New Orleans bar and a swanky, Los Angeles cocktail lounge. Besides signature concoctions like the Generation Adrift—which combines tequila, orange and lemon juice, peach liqueur, and old-fashioned bitters—this stylish Uptown hot spot also offers delectable tapas dishes, such as pear salad and spicy Jamaican meat pie.

MAP 5: 4905 Freret St., 504/302-2357, http://curenola.com; Sun.-Thurs. 5pm-midnight, Fri.-Sat. 5pm-2am

IGOR'S BUDDHA BELLY BAR & GRILL

This funky dive bar lures a variety of slackers, artists, and students, particularly from Tulane and Loyola. One of the better late-night options on Magazine, it occupies an odd space that includes both a dining area and

College Haunts

It might be common knowledge that Louisiana State University (LSU) in Baton Rouge has more of a "party school" reputation than the collegiate institutions of New Orleans, but the Big Easy isn't a bad place to spend your college years. It's also a pretty cheap town to enjoy late-night libations. Bourbon Street alone has its share of bargains, including inexpensive beers at the **Rat's Hole** (410 Bourbon St., 504/568-9338) and **Huge Ass Beers** at the Steak Pit (609 Bourbon St., 504/525-3406, www.hugeassbeers.com), where you can purchase enormous, relatively cheap souvenir cups filled with your beer of choice. Depending on the time of day, hawkers carrying signs for happy-hour drink specials are also a common sight.

Though you'll find plenty of college-aged youths in live music venues throughout the city, from the Marigny's **d.b.a. New Orleans** to Uptown's **Maple Leaf Bar** to various meat-market dance spaces in the French Quarter, you're most likely to spot them in local hangouts close to the adjacent campuses of Tulane University and Loyola University New Orleans on St. Charles Avenue. Popular spots include **The Boot Bar & Grill** (1039 Broadway St.), which sits next to Tulane and offers all manner of drink specials, and **Cooter Brown's Tavern & Oyster Bar,** a Riverbend sports bar that features numerous televisions, more than 400 brands of domestic and imported beers, plus to-die-for raw oysters and boiled seafood. Though a bit of a hike from the universities on St. Charles, the stretch of Magazine Street between Jefferson and Jackson Avenues also has its share of student-friendly joints, including **The Bulldog,** a late-night watering hole with decent grub and a diverse beer selection; **Igor's Buddha Belly Bar & Grill,** another late-night spot where you can enjoy delicious burgers while doing your laundry; and **Le Bon Temps Roule** (4801 Magazine St.), which, as the name's meaning ("the good time rolls") implies, is a loud dive bar with live music, a decent jukebox, and room for dancing.

There's one thing to remember if you're a student in New Orleans: While the drinking age is officially 21 and over, some establishments welcome patrons 18 and over, which means, even if you can't drink, you'll still be able to listen to live music and mingle with your friends.

a self-service laundry. The half-pound burgers are seriously good, and on Monday, Igor's has been known to serve free red beans and rice.

MAP 5: 4437 Magazine St., 504/891-6105; daily 11am-3am

MONKEY HILL BAR

Located three blocks east of Audubon Zoo, this inviting yet stylish bar was no doubt named after Monkey Hill, a slope in the zoo's African Savanna section that many a local child has gleefully rolled down. In the fun-filled spirit of its namesake, this watering hole has become an adult's playground, offering a sizable drink selection, relaxing couches, pool and shuffleboard tables, and a 120-inch, high-definition screen, ideal for watching sports. Monkey Hill opens earlier on Sunday during football season.

MAP 5: 6100 Magazine St., 504/899-4800; daily 5pm-close

Above: Tipitina's. **Below:** the Snug Harbor Jazz Bistro.

SNAKE AND JAKE'S CHRISTMAS CLUB LOUNGE

Open every day of the year—including Christmas—Snake and Jake's is indeed one of the Crescent City's most legendary dive bars. Routinely voted a favorite among locals, this neighborhood joint is cozy, friendly, and open into the wee hours. Happy-hour specials are offered 7pm-10pm nightly. Be sure to keep a lookout for Jake, the bar's cute feline mascot; just be aware of the occasional mood swing.

MAP 5: 7612 Oak St., 504/861-2802, www.snakeandjakes.com; daily 7pm-close

LIVE MUSIC

Blues and Rock

MAPLE LEAF BAR

One of Uptown's most popular live music venues, the Maple Leaf Bar serves up some of the best blues, jazz, funk, rock, and zydeco in the city. Established in 1974 and now one of the Big Easy's longest-running music clubs, the Maple Leaf has played host to music students from Tulane, local legends like the Radiators, and surprise headliners such as Bonnie Raitt. Fashion shows, poetry readings, and other non-musical events aren't uncommon either.

MAP 5: 8316 Oak St., 504/866-9359, www.mapleleafbar.com; daily 3pm-3am; cover varies

★ TIPITINA'S

For catching rock (both hard-edged and down-home), jazz, zydeco, Cajun, and blues, there may be no club in the city more acclaimed or more festive than Tipitina's, a longstanding venue in the heart of Uptown. Purists may tell you that Tip's has lost its edge and no longer presents the best—or at least most distinctive—local acts, but anybody looking for an introduction to the city's eclectic music scene should head here. Entertainment varies greatly, but no matter what's playing, you can probably dance to it.

MAP 5: 501 Napoleon Ave., 504/895-8477, www.tipitinas.com; hours vary depending on the show; cover varies

Country and Folk

NEUTRAL GROUND COFFEEHOUSE

This funky coffeehouse and live music venue has long been a favorite haunt for many New Orleanians. Though this cozy, quirky joint typically offers coffee, tea, and pastries, refreshments aren't the specialty here. The real draw is the live entertainment, which, depending on the night, might entail a poetry slam, a folk concert, or something else altogether. Quiet reading, conversation, and board games are popular diversions, too.

MAP 5: 5110 Danneel St., 504/891-3381, www.neutralgroundcoffeehouse.com; Sun.-Thurs. 7pm-midnight, Fri.-Sat. 7pm-1am; no cover

Jazz

THE COLUMNS HOTEL

This stately plantation-style mansion, erected in 1883, is typically hard to miss while gazing out the window of a St. Charles Avenue streetcar. On every night save for Sunday, the hotel presents exceptional New Orleans jazz, Brazilian samba, and other live entertainment in its romantic Victorian Lounge. Offering an extensive menu of beer, wine, mint juleps, tapas dishes, and other cocktails and bistro fare, the space has hosted an array of celebrities over the years, from John Goodman to Clint Eastwood.

MAP 5: 3811 St. Charles Ave., 504/899-9308 or 800/445-9308, www.thecolumns.com; Sun.-Thurs. 10:30am-midnight, Fri.-Sat. 10:30am-2am; no cover

DOS JEFES UPTOWN CIGAR BAR

Not far from the river, the laid-back Dos Jefes Uptown Cigar Bar draws locals and college students alike for live jazz and folk music. As the name implies, patrons can also take advantage of the on-site humidor, which is filled with an assortment of premium cigars. The bar offers a daily happy hour (5pm-7pm), which features $2 long necks, $3 wines, and $4 mojitos and martinis.

MAP 5: 5535 Tchoupitoulas St., 504/891-8500, http://dosjefes.com; daily 5pm-close; no cover

WINE BARS

OAK

Nestled within Uptown's Riverbend area, near the happenin' corner of Oak Street and Carrollton Avenue, this cosmopolitan yet comfortable wine bar features hundreds of hand-selected wines, as well as numerous beers and signature cocktails. While sampling the varietals, you can also partake of various small plates, such as duck confit and Gulf shrimp tacos. Food is typically served until 11pm on weekdays and midnight on weekends. You'll be treated to live jazz, folk, or R&B music Wednesday-Saturday. The kitchen usually closes at 11pm on weekdays and midnight on weekends.

MAP 5: 8118 Oak St., 504/302-1485, www.oaknola.com; Tues.-Sat. 5pm-close

BARS AND LOUNGES

BAYOU BEER GARDEN

The Bayou Beer Garden appeals mainly to locals, but given its laid-back ambiance, tasty wraps and sandwiches, and wide selection of local, domestic, and imported beers, from Abita to Guinness, it's not a bad spot for visitors to unwind, too. Besides comfy patio seating, patrons appreciate the friendly bartenders, Tuesday night trivia games, free wireless Internet access, and a chance to watch all manner of local and regional sporting events with their pals.

MAP 6: 326 N. Jefferson Davis Pkwy., 504/302-9357, http://bayoubeergarden.com; daily 11am-2am

THE HOLY GROUND

Conveniently situated beside the Canal streetcar line, at the intersection of Canal Street and Jefferson Davis Parkway, The Holy Ground is a spacious, dimly lit, stupendously popular neighborhood bar and Irish pub. The vibe is casual, the drinks are fairly cheap, the on-site sandwiches satisfy any post-booze cravings, and given the presence of New Orleans characters (and often their frisky canines), people-watching opportunities abound. Besides a fully stocked bar and accommodating bartenders, The Holy Ground offers pool tables, dartboards, a jukebox, and televised sporting events, particularly soccer matches and Saints games.

MAP 6: 3340 Canal St., 504/821-6828; hours vary daily

MID-CITY YACHT CLUB

Housed within a two-story building in a Mid-City residential neighborhood, this casual, super-friendly watering hole isn't a bad place to relax after exploring nearby City Park or the area's historic cemeteries. Definitely a favorite among local football, baseball, and other sports fans, the Yacht Club has eight high-definition televisions and an enormous projection screen, so you'll be able to watch several games at once. Other amenities include a well-stocked jukebox, a decent beer and flavored vodka selection, free wireless Internet access, air-conditioning that's especially welcome during baseball season, and free hot dogs, meatballs, and other vittles on game days.

MAP 6: 440 S. St. Patrick St., 504/483-2517, www.midcityyachtclub.com; Mon.-Thurs. 11am-2am, Fri. 11am-4am, Sat. 10:30am-4am, Sun. 10:30am-2am

LIVE MUSIC

Jazz

CHICKIE WAH WAH

One of the city's most offbeat live music venues is the cozy, aptly named Chickie Wah Wah. On most evenings, you'll be treated to some of the best local musicians, like the Pfister Sisters, old-time singer Meschiya Lake,

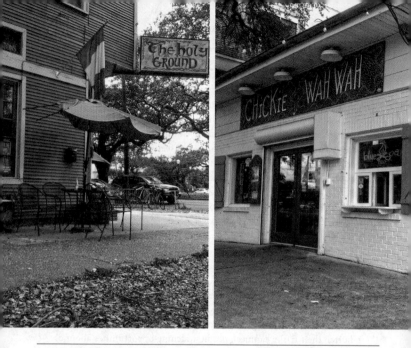

Clockwise from top left: The Holy Ground; Chickie Wah Wah; Rock 'n' Bowl.

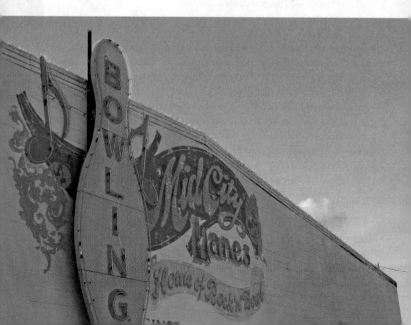

and stellar piano player Tom McDermott. While listening, you can enjoy pulled pork sandwiches and beef brisket plates from the on-site **Blue Oak BBQ** (504/822-2583, www.blueoakbbq.com; Mon.-Fri. 4pm-11pm, Sat. 6pm-11pm, Sun. 6pm-10pm). Besides a convenient rear parking lot, this popular club offers an on-site ATM, free wireless Internet access, and a weekday happy hour (5:30pm-7:30pm).

MAP 6: 2828 Canal St., 844/244-2543, www.chickiewahwah.com; Mon.-Fri. 4pm-midnight, Sat.-Sun. hours vary; cover varies

WINE BARS

PEARL WINE CO.

Located inside the imposing American Can Building, Pearl Wine Co. houses a full-service cocktail and wine bar plus an impressively stocked wine, beer, and liquor store. You'll discover special offerings almost every day, such as "Mani & Martini Monday" (6pm-9pm), when $20 will get you a drink and a manicure. On Saturdays, meanwhile, you can enjoy happy hour specials 4pm-7pm and live jazz beginning at 8pm. Beer and wine are served at all times, while cocktails begin flowing around 4pm each day. Plenty of free parking is available in the adjacent lot.

MAP 6: 3700 Orleans Ave., 504/483-6314, http://pearlwineco.com; Mon.-Sat. noon-midnight, Sun. noon-8pm

Greater New Orleans

Map 7

LIVE MUSIC

Cajun and Zydeco

★ ROCK 'N' BOWL

Rock 'n' Bowl is a music (and bowling) institution, luring couples and families alike. An offbeat place to catch live bands of all types, it's especially known for zydeco, jazz, blues, and swing, but anything is possible here, including performances by regional favorites like Tab Benoit and Amanda Shaw. Savvy locals often show up early for a few rounds of bowling, which, if you time it right, could enable you to catch the concert without paying a cover charge.

MAP 7: 3000 S. Carrollton Ave., 504/861-1700, www.rocknbowl.com; Mon.-Thurs. 11:30am-midnight, Fri.-Sat. 11:30am-2am, Sun. hours vary; cover varies

Arts and Culture

SOUTHERN FOOD & BEVERAGE

A longtime haven for artists, writers, and musicians, New Orleans has a rich, multicultural tradition in the arts.

The city is home to numerous outstanding galleries, with particularly strong concentrations along Royal and Chartres Streets in the French Quarter, around Julia Street in the Arts District, and along funky Magazine Street in Uptown. The Big Easy also nurtures several impressive museums, most of which focus on locally significant topics, from voodoo and the Mardi Gras Indians to African American art and Southern cuisine. Not far from The National WWII Museum in the Arts District, for instance, you'll find several worthwhile attractions, including the Ogden Museum of Southern Art and the adjacent Confederate Memorial Hall Museum.

Just opposite these two repositories stands the hard-to-miss Contemporary Arts Center (CAC), a multifaceted, vividly painted edifice that houses an art gallery as well as several performing arts spaces. Despite the fact that the performing arts aren't as pervasive in New Orleans as in other cities, there is a variety of other worthy venues, such as the longstanding Le Petit Théâtre du Vieux Carré near Jackson Square, the refurbished Mahalia Jackson Theater of the Performing Arts in Louis Armstrong Park, and several cutting-edge performance halls in the Faubourg Marigny, from Café Istanbul to the Marigny Opera House. And in recent years, New Orleans has become a popular place for filmmakers and TV producers, offering residents and tourists alike the chance to observe a variety of star-studded shoots, mainly in the French Quarter.

Previous: a carriage tour passing the Confederate Memorial Hall Museum; the Southern Food & Beverage Museum.

Look for ★ to find recommended arts and culture.

Highlights

★ **Most Tantalizing Gallery:** Amid the varied art galleries on Royal Street, you'll spot **Craig Tracy's Fine-Art Bodypainting Gallery,** a showcase of the artist's eye-popping paintings. Each entails crafting a backdrop, painting and arranging live models, and photographing the entire scene (page 203).

★ **Most Engrossing Cemetery Tour:** Besides displaying artifacts and information related to the legends, mysteries, and traditions of the voodoo faith, the **New Orleans Historic Voodoo Museum** offers lengthy walking excursions into St. Louis Cemetery No. 1 and its environs (page 206).

★ **Most Historic Community Theater:** One of America's oldest community theaters, **Le Petit Théâtre du Vieux Carré** houses both a highly regarded Louisiana Creole restaurant and a comfortable place for patrons to watch a wide range of dramas, comedies, and musicals (page 208).

★ **Most Interactive Art Gallery:** Although many visitors come to the **New Orleans School of GlassWorks & Printmaking Studio** to watch skilled artisans at work, another main draw is the chance to take one of several engaging classes, from a paper marbling course to a stained glass-making workshop (page 210).

★ **Best Downtown Spot for Art Lovers:** Experience one of the country's largest collections of Southern artwork at the **Ogden Museum of Southern Art,** including the paintings of celebrated Louisiana folk artist Clementine Hunter (page 211).

★ **Most Diverse Arts Haven:** Given its varied film screenings, theatrical performances, concerts, dance presentations, and visual art exhibitions, the **Contemporary Arts Center** serves as an ideal stop for art lovers of all kinds (page 211).

★ **Best Attraction for Foodies:** The **Southern Food & Beverage Museum** explores and celebrates all the cultures and food producers who have shaped the American South's unique culinary heritage (page 213).

★ **Finest Shrine to Mardi Gras Indians:** Not far from Louis Armstrong Park, the **Backstreet Cultural Museum** presents one of the world's largest collections related to African American masking and processional traditions, such as jazz funerals, social aid and pleasure clubs—and Mardi Gras Indians (page 218).

★ **Best Live Performance Venue:** Named for the beloved New Orleans-born gospel singer, the restored **Mahalia Jackson Theater for the Performing Arts** lures cultural enthusiasts to Louis Armstrong Park with live concerts, operas, musicals, comedy shows, and dance performances (page 218).

GALLERIES

CALLAN FINE ART

Fine art lovers should head to the aptly named Callan Fine Art, which focuses on European paintings from 1830 to 1950. You'll find representative works from the Academic, Pastoral, Neoclassic, Impressionist, and Post-Impressionist movements, with the artwork of French Barbizon painters a particular specialty. Curiously, local musician Tony Green displays quite a few of his own drawings and paintings here, most of which capture the vibrancy of jazz musicians, Mardi Gras, and the French Quarter.

MAP 1: 240 Chartres St., 504/524-0025, www.callanfineart.com; Mon. and Wed.-Sat. 10am-5pm, also by appt.

★ CRAIG TRACY'S FINE-ART BODYPAINTING GALLERY

This eye-catching space presents the innovative creations of Craig Tracy, an internationally known artist who paints landscapes, storms, animal prints, and other patterns on naked human bodies, then photographs his living creations. Gorgeous and mesmerizing, his artwork typically requires intense concentration to discern the human form. At the gallery, you can often speak to the artist himself and watch videos that document his fascinating process.

MAP 1: 827 Royal St., 504/592-9886, http://craigtracy.com; daily 10am-6pm

DUTCH ALLEY ARTIST'S CO-OP

As you stroll through the historic French Market, be sure to visit the Dutch Alley Artist's Co-op, founded in 2003 by artist Ric Rolston. Operated by the two dozen artists whose work is on display, the gallery features a wide array of creations, from John Fitzgerald's prints to Kimberly Parker's seafood collages to Linda Sampson's beaded accessories and mourning jewelry.

MAP 1: 912 N. Peters St., 504/412-9220, www.dutchalleyartistsco-op.com; daily 10am-6pm

A GALLERY FOR FINE PHOTOGRAPHY

Although New Orleans boasts several art galleries that focus exclusively on photography, you'll probably find the largest assortment at the aptly named Gallery for Fine Photography. Established in 1973, this prestigious emporium features the work of such titans as Ansel Adams, Walker Evans, and Diane Arbus, plus the visionary creations of newer artists. Be prepared for hefty price tags.

MAP 1: 241 Chartres St., 504/568-1313, www.agallery.com; Tues.-Wed. by appt., Thurs.-Mon. 10:30am-5:30pm

JAMIE HAYES GALLERY

In the shadow of the St. Louis Cathedral, this gallery features the whimsical, multicolored paintings, dolls, and jewelry of color-blind artist Jamie Hayes, who, though born in Indiana and raised in Austria, has long considered New Orleans his true home. Many New Orleanians favor his unique perspective of the city, which celebrates in a wacky, childlike way the unique music, traditions, and festive spirit of this one-of-a-kind place. If you're in Uptown's Riverbend neighborhood, head to Jamie's other gallery (8314 Oak St.).

MAP 1: 617 Chartres St., 504/596-2344, www.jamiehayes.com; daily 9am-7pm

KAKO GALLERY

If you favor offbeat contemporary art from local artists and artisans, then the Kako Gallery might be right up your alley. You'll find unique sculptures, paintings, and jewelry from artists like Don Picou, who frequently paints muted scenes of bayous and swamps, and Stan Fontaine and Diane Millsap, two visionaries whose kaleidoscopic paintings feature the city's most famous landmarks and neighborhoods, from the St. Louis Cathedral to Pirate's Alley.

MAP 1: 536 Royal St., 504/565-5445, www.kakogallery.com; daily 10am-6pm

MARTIN-LAWRENCE GALLERIES

World-famous Martin-Lawrence Galleries has locations throughout the United States. It's no surprise then that New Orleans, a city favored among art lovers, would boast its own branch on venerable Royal Street. Founded in 1975, Martin-Lawrence Galleries specializes in sculptures, original paintings, and limited edition graphics by such astounding artists as Pablo Picasso, Marc Chagall, and Andy Warhol.

MAP 1: 433 Royal St., 504/299-9055, www.martinlawrence.com; daily 10am-6pm

MICHALOPOULOS GALLERY

Owned by one of the most respected artists in Louisiana, the eponymous Michalopoulos Gallery carries dozens of James Michalopoulos's vibrant, architectural renderings, with their trademark skewed angles and impressionistic brushwork. Many of his works feature Creole houses or classic French Quarter townhouses. Sharon Stone, Bruce Willis, and Bonnie Raitt are among his most notable collectors, and the New Orleans Jazz & Heritage Festival and Foundation often commissions him to create the official Jazz Fest poster. His actual studio is situated in the nearby Marigny (527 Elysian Fields Ave.).

MAP 1: 617 Bienville St., 504/558-0505, www.michalopoulos.com; Mon.-Wed. 10am-6pm, Thurs.-Sat. 10am-7pm, Sun. 11am-6pm

RODRIGUE STUDIO NEW ORLEANS

Although the famous Cajun "Blue Dog" artist George Rodrigue passed away in 2013, you can still visit his studio on Royal Street, situated in a warmly lighted space not far from the St. Louis Cathedral. Here, you can buy everything from inexpensive gifts to original oil paintings, depicting the "Blue Dog" amid swamps, cemeteries, and other picturesque places. The inspiration for these works was twofold: a Cajun legend about the *loup-garou* (werewolf) and the owner's terrier, Tiffany, who had died several years before.

MAP 1: 730 Royal St., 504/581-4244, https://georgerodrigue.com; Mon.-Sat. 10am-6pm, Sun. noon-5pm

TANNER GALLERY

Enticing to many a passerby, Tanner's storefront features his spellbinding, often eerie paintings of stark forests shrouded in fog, illumined by sunshine or starlight, or enhanced by otherworldly hues. The scenes resembling photo negatives are especially haunting. You can purchase canvas and paper reproductions or, if you're lucky, the original paintings, but the prices here aren't cheap. Even if you can't afford one of his paintings, you can still peer through the window of the adjacent **Tanner Open Studio** (832 Royal St.), where the artist may be working on his latest creation.

MAP 1: 830 Royal St., 504/524-8266, www.hauntingart.com; Thurs.-Mon. 10am-7pm

Resources for Culture Seekers

If you're interested in Louisiana's unique culture, one of the most useful resources is the **Louisiana Department of Culture, Recreation, and Tourism** (www.crt.state.la.us), a state agency that oversees state museums, cultural districts, and tourism in general. For more specific information about the Big Easy's arts scene—including architecture, visual arts, theater, dance, music, film, literature, and culinary arts—consult the **Arts Council New Orleans** (www.artsneworleans.org). You'll also find up-to-date gallery listings through the websites for the **New Orleans Arts District** (NOAD, www.neworleansartsdistrict.com) and the **Magazine Street Merchants Association** (www.magazinestreet.com); the periodical ***ART + DESIGN New Orleans*** (www.artdesignmag.com) is also a helpful resource.

Music lovers especially favor the publication ***OffBeat Magazine*** (www.offbeat.com), an excellent resource for learning about Louisiana's music scene, recordings by local artists, and upcoming live performances; foodies also appreciate the magazine's dining recommendations. The alternative weekly ***Gambit*** (www.bestofneworleans.com) offers comprehensive music listings, as well as information about local bars and restaurants, film screenings, shopping, and the arts. Another great way to enjoy local music while visiting New Orleans is via the radio; many locals swear by **WWOZ** (90.7 FM, www.wwoz.org), which typically plays jazz, blues, and R&B, plus healthy doses of swing, Cajun and zydeco, country and bluegrass, and gospel.

When all else fails, you can always consult the **New Orleans Convention & Visitors Bureau** (www.neworleanscvb.com), which provides plenty of information about the city's architecture, cultural attractions, entertainment, and arts scenes.

MUSEUMS

GERMAINE CAZENAVE WELLS MARDI GRAS MUSEUM

Those curious about the glamour of Carnival should head to the Germaine Cazenave Wells Mardi Gras Museum at the fabled restaurant Arnaud's. The museum, named for the daughter of restaurant founder Count Arnaud, opened in 1983 as a tribute to Ms. Wells—the former queen of more than 22 Mardi Gras balls (1937-1968). On hand are several of Wells's elaborate ball costumes, intricate masks, lavish jewelry, and vintage photographs.

MAP 1: 813 Bienville St., 504/523-5433, www.arnaudsrestaurant.com/mardi-gras-museum; Mon.-Sat. 6pm-close, Sun. 10am-2:30pm and 6pm-close; free

MUSÉE CONTI WAX MUSEUM

Though this musty museum, which opened in 1964, has long showed its age, visitors can learn much about the history of New Orleans from its costumed wax figures and detailed tableaux. You'll spy Napoleon Bonaparte during the Louisiana Purchase, Andrew Jackson amid the Battle of New Orleans, plus the pirate Jean Lafitte, voodoo queen Marie Laveau, and musician Louis Armstrong. Children especially enjoy the Chamber of Horrors, which features gruesome scenes involving Dracula, Frankenstein's monster, and the Phantom of the Opera. Self-guided tours usually take an hour, and helpful programs are available in French, German, Spanish, Italian, and Japanese.

MAP 1: 917 Conti St., 504/525-2605, www.neworleanswaxmuseum.com; Mon. and Fri.-Sat. 10am-4pm; $8 adult, $7.25 senior, $7 child 4-17, free under 4

★ NEW ORLEANS HISTORIC VOODOO MUSEUM

Established in 1972, this small, somewhat cramped museum offers a decent, respectful overview of a practice still shrouded in mystery yet taken very seriously by its practitioners. Displays include a variety of masks, ritual art, and artifacts from Africa and Haiti, where the city's distinctive brand of voodoo practice originated. The exhibits, though ominous, aren't gory in nature, so kids often find them appealing. The focus here is on Marie Laveau, the anointed voodoo priestess who lived in New Orleans from the 1790s until her death in 1881. Though you can arrange private consultations and healing seminars with museum staff, the true highlight is the historian-led walking tour ($19 adult, $10 child under 12), which includes a stroll through St. Louis Cemetery No. 1 (supposed site of Marie Laveau's tomb), an encounter with a contemporary voodoo priestess, and plenty of engrossing stories about voodoo, zombies, jazz funerals, Mardi Gras Indians, and other curious aspects of the city's colorful history.

MAP 1: 724 Dumaine St., 504/680-0128; daily 10am-6pm; $7 adult, $5.50 senior and college student, $4.50 high school student, $3.50 child under 12

NEW ORLEANS PHARMACY MUSEUM

This museum occupies a genuine apothecary shop from the 1820s. Original shop owner Louis J. Dufilho Jr. was the first licensed pharmacist in the

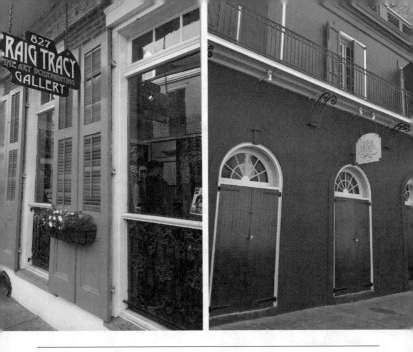

Clockwise from top left: Craig Tracy's Fine-Art Bodypainting Gallery; Le Petit Théâtre du Vieux Carré; the New Orleans Historic Voodoo Museum.

nation, having earned his certification in 1816. Displays show what a period pharmacy looked like, including rows of 1850s-style hand-carved mahogany cabinets filled with everything from established drugs to gris-gris voodoo potions; exhibits tell the story of Louisiana's development in medicine and health care. Interesting features include an assortment of bloodletting equipment, a medicinal herb garden in the courtyard, and an 1855 Italian marble soda fountain. Guided tours are offered Tuesday-Friday at 1pm.

MAP 1: 514 Chartres St., 504/565-8027, www.pharmacymuseum.org; Tues.-Sat. 10am-4pm; $5 adult, $4 senior and student, free under 6

PERFORMING ARTS

★ LE PETIT THÉÂTRE DU VIEUX CARRÉ

Founded in 1916 and relocated to its current spot near Jackson Square in 1922, Le Petit Théâtre du Vieux Carré is one of America's oldest community theaters. Following an extensive renovation, Le Petit houses both a highly regarded Louisiana Creole restaurant (Dickie Brennan's latest, Tableau) and a comfortable place for patrons to watch a wide range of dramas, comedies, musicals, and intimate concerts. Recent productions have included *Hair, Merrily We Roll Along, Death of a Salesman,* and musical performances by local legends Marcia Ball and Terence Blanchard.

MAP 1: 616 St. Peter St., 504/522-2081, www.lepetittheatre.com; hours and costs vary depending on show

Faubourg Marigny and Bywater

Map 2

GALLERIES

BARRISTER'S GALLERY

This curious gallery is located at the edge of the Faubourg Marigny, a funky neighborhood that seems to suit the variety of Asian, African, Haitian, and Oceanic folk and outsider art available at Barrister's. Its primary focus is on monthly contemporary exhibits that have an eclectic, unorthodox bent. Unfortunately, the gallery's location isn't the safest place in the city.

MAP 2: 2331 St. Claude Ave., 504/710-4506, www.barristersgallery.com; Tues.-Sat. 11am-5pm

PERFORMING ARTS

CAFÉ ISTANBUL

Occupying a 3,800-square-foot performance hall in the rear of the 55,000-square-foot New Orleans Healing Center, Café Istanbul does a lot to foster local performance art. In addition to presenting live concerts, dance and theatrical performances, and comedy shows, Café Istanbul offers poetry readings, film screenings, and an upper gallery dedicated to visual arts, particularly the paintings and photography of local artists.

MAP 2: 2372 St. Claude Ave., 504/975-0286, http://cafeistanbulnola.com; hours and ticket prices vary depending on show

MARIGNY OPERA HOUSE

The imposing structure that now houses the Marigny Opera House once served as the Holy Trinity Catholic Church, which was founded in 1847 for German Catholics, built in 1853 by architect Theodore Giraud, and known for its excellent music. Perhaps it's fitting then that the Marigny Opera House considers itself a nondenominational, neighborhood "church of the arts." Home to the Marigny Opera Ballet, a professional contemporary ballet company founded in 2014, the Opera House hosts various musical concerts, spotlighting everything from classical to jazz, as well as other cultural events.

MAP 2: 725 St. Ferdinand St., 504/948-9998, www.marignyoperahouse.org; hours and ticket prices vary depending on show

THE NEW MOVEMENT–NEW ORLEANS

Founded in Austin, Texas, The New Movement (TNM) is ostensibly an improv comedy school that also presents comedic performances, some of which are free to the public (or at least nominally priced). TNM offers several events each week, including student-run showcases, comedy competitions, veteran-led improv shows, and performances at other venues, such as The Howlin' Wolf (907 S. Peters St.) in the Arts District and The Hi-Ho Lounge (2239 St. Claude Ave.), seven blocks from TNM.

MAP 2: 2706 St. Claude Ave., 512/788-2669, http://newmovementtheater.com; hours and ticket prices vary depending on show

Central Business and Arts Districts

Map 3

GALLERIES

JEAN BRAGG GALLERY

A longtime fixture on the New Orleans arts scene, Jean Bragg opened her first antiques shop here in 1979. Since 2005, the Jean Bragg Gallery has been located in the Arts District, where it presents a fine collection of late 19th and 20th-century crafts and paintings from Louisiana artists, including Newcomb College and Gulf Coast Shearwater pottery.

MAP 3: 600 Julia St., 504/895-7375, www.jeanbragg.com; Mon.-Sat. 10am-5pm

LEMIEUX GALLERIES

In the city's Arts District, posh New York-style galleries seem to prevail, so LeMieux offers an intriguing change of pace. LeMieux provides a wide assortment of visionary, contemporary artwork, including Wozniak's infrared photographs, Theresa Honeywell's knitted piec

John Donovan's small yet impactful sculptures, which invariably make political statements about America's military history.

MAP 3: 332 Julia St., 504/522-5988, www.lemieuxgalleries.com; Mon.-Sat. 10am-6pm and by appt.

★ NEW ORLEANS SCHOOL OF GLASSWORKS & PRINTMAKING STUDIO

At the 25,000-square-foot New Orleans School of GlassWorks & Printmaking Studio, you can observe highly skilled glassblowing, torch-working, printmaking, metalworking, and stained-glass artisans in action. Besides browsing their wares, you can also learn how to create your own glasswork, jewelry, and paper arts by taking one of the studio's exceptional classes, which range from two-hour courses on paper marbling to six-week workshops about Venetian glassblowing.

MAP 3: 727 Magazine St., 504/529-7279, www.neworleansglassworks.com; Mon.-Sat. 10am-5pm

SØREN CHRISTENSEN GALLERY

With its high ceilings, lofty windows, white brick walls, and uncluttered displays, the spacious Søren Christensen Gallery resembles the kind of place you might find in New York City. I've often relished a stroll through this elegant gallery, where art lovers will find contemporary paintings, sculptures, and photography by nationally and internationally recognized artists.

MAP 3: 400 Julia St., 504/569-9501, www.sorengallery.com; Tues.-Fri. 10am-5:30pm, Sat. 11am-5pm, and by appt.

MUSEUMS

AMERICAN ITALIAN MUSEUM

Inside the American Italian Cultural Center, you'll find the American Italian Museum, which, via family histories, vintage photographs, and other memorabilia, chronicles the history and cultural influence of American Italians in southeastern Louisiana. Visitors who often associate New Orleans with the French, Spanish, and Caribbean cultures may find the Italian contributions to the city's cuisine, music, festivals, and demographics especially curious. The center supports a comprehensive research library, containing numerous oral histories, immigration records, books, and photographs, located in the East Bank Regional Library (4747 W. Napoleon Ave., Metairie).

MAP 3: 537 S. Peters St., 504/522-7294, www.americanitalianmuseum.com; Tues.-Fri. 10am-4pm; $8 adult, $5 senior, free under 12

CONFEDERATE MEMORIAL HALL MUSEUM

The Confederate Memorial Hall Museum commemorates the military history and heritage of the American South. Alternately known as Louisiana's Civil War Museum at Confederate Memorial Hall, it holds the country's

second-largest collection of Confederate memorabilia, including uniforms, battle flags, and more than 500 tintypes, daguerreotypes, and other vintage photographic images, plus the personal items of General Robert E. Lee and General P. G. T. Beauregard. Designed by Thomas O. Sully, one of the city's most distinguished architects, and opened in 1891, this Romanesque structure is the state's oldest continuously operating museum.

MAP 3: 929 Camp St., 504/523-4522, http://confederatemuseum.com; Tues.-Sat. 10am-4pm; $8 adult, $5 child 7-14, free under 7

LOUISIANA CHILDREN'S MUSEUM

The Louisiana Children's Museum is an enormous, touch-friendly cache of interactive exhibits, many of which re-create grown-up activities on a small scale. Kids can shop in a grocery store, pilot a tugboat on the Mississippi River, and play house inside a Cajun cottage. While most of these exhibits target toddlers and adolescents, older children appreciate scientific displays like the electrifying plasma balls. Visitors under 16 years old must be accompanied by an adult, and the museum is closed on major holidays and on Mondays in the fall, winter, and spring (when the museum closes a half-hour earlier than during the summer).

MAP 3: 420 Julia St., 504/523-1357, http://lcm.org; Mon.-Sat. 9:30am-5pm, Sun. noon-5pm; $8.50 pp, free under 1

★ OGDEN MUSEUM OF SOUTHERN ART

Not far from Lee Circle and adjacent to the Confederate Memorial Hall Museum, you'll find it hard to miss the Ogden Museum of Southern Art, which contains one of the country's largest collections of artwork related to the American South. This impressive complex comprises the contemporary, five-story Stephen Goldring Hall, the restored Howard Memorial Library, and the Clementine Hunter Education Wing, named for the famous Louisiana folk artist who grew up on a cotton plantation in Cloutierville and produced about 4,000 works during her storied career. The artwork here includes all mediums and spans the 18th to 21st centuries, representing artists from 15 Southern states as well as Washington, D.C. The last admission to the museum is at 4:45pm each day, save for on Thursday evenings, when the museum reopens for "Ogden After Hours," presenting live music 6pm-8pm. Louisiana residents are entitled to free admission to the museum every Thursday, and docent-led tours are available at 2pm on the first and third Saturdays of each month.

MAP 3: 925 Camp St., 504/539-9650, www.ogdenmuseum.org; Wed.-Mon. 10am-5pm; $12.50 adult, $10 senior 65 and over, student, teacher, and military, $6.25 child 5-17, free under 5

PERFORMING ARTS

★ CONTEMPORARY ARTS CENTER

Within walking distance of Lee Circle, the Contemporary Arts Center (CAC) is a multipurpose venue that houses an innovative art gallery as well

Clockwise from top left: the Confederate Memorial Hall Museum; the Søren Christensen Gallery; the New Orleans School of GlassWorks & Printmaking Studio.

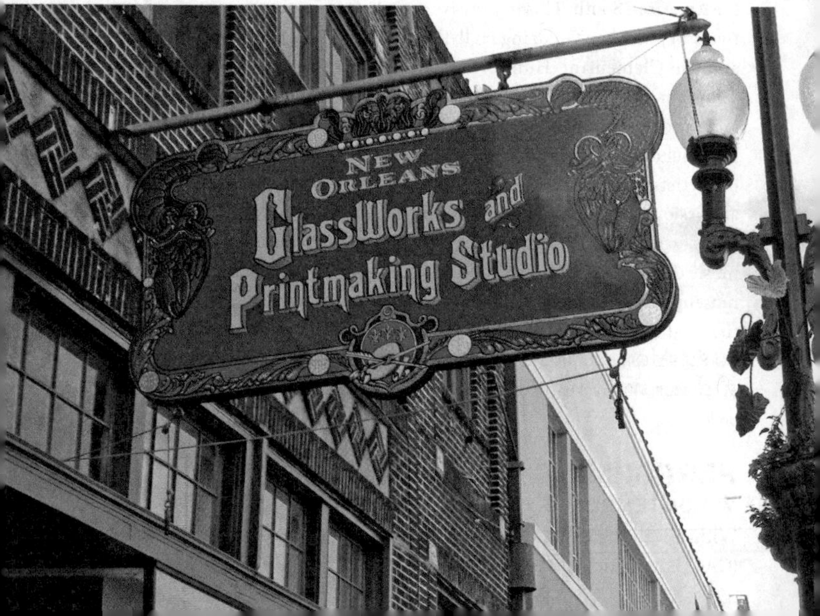

as performing arts spaces. In addition to staging lectures, performances, and concerts, the CAC often serves as a main location for the New Orleans Film Festival and other annual events. Stop by the on-site café (Mon.-Fri. 10am-5pm, Sat.-Sun. 11am-5pm) for refreshments. Louisiana residents can enjoy the gallery for free on Sundays.

MAP 3: 900 Camp St., 504/528-3800 or 504/528-3805, http://cacno.org; art gallery Wed.-Mon. 11am-5pm; event hours vary; $10 adult, $8 senior and college student, free under 18, ticket prices vary for shows and events

Garden District

Map 4

GALLERIES

THOMAS MANN GALLERY I/O

Thomas Mann, a nationally recognized artist who specializes in jewelry and home accessories, sells his work in galleries throughout the country. His flagship store, the Thomas Mann Gallery I/O, has been in New Orleans since 1988. Here, you'll find the largest collection of Mann's techno-romantic and one-of-a-kind jewelry in addition to whimsical contemporary art, glassware, stemware, jewelry, and gifts made by Mann and other designers. If you're curious about the meaning behind "I/O" in the gallery's name, it stands for "Insight-Full Objects," engaging art that's often decorative, sometimes functional, and typically a medley of American craft, European design, and fine art traditions.

MAP 4: 1812 Magazine St., 504/581-2113 or 800/875-2113, www.thomasmann.com; Mon.-Sat. 11am-5pm

MUSEUMS

GEORGE & LEAH McKENNA MUSEUM OF AFRICAN AMERICAN ART

Named after the parents of museum founder Dr. Dwight McKenna, this African American art museum endeavors to collect, interpret, and preserve African Diasporan fine art, whether fashioned by emerging artists or renowned masters like Henry Ossawa Tanner and Clementine Hunter. The museum also features temporary exhibits, and with advance notice, docent-led tours ($10 adult, $7 senior and student) are available for groups of 5-30 people. Similar art is available for purchase at **Stella Jones Gallery** (201 St. Charles Ave., 504/568-9050, www.stellajonesgallery.com) in the CBD.

MAP 4: 2003 Carondelet St., 504/586-7432, www.themckennamuseum.com; Tues.-Wed. by appt., Thurs.-Sat. 11am-4pm; $7 adult, $5 senior and student, $3 child 5-12, free under 5

★ SOUTHERN FOOD & BEVERAGE MUSEUM

In a city that is celebrated around the world for its cuisine, it's surprising that the Southern Food & Beverage Museum (SoFaB) has only been open since 2008. The museum features both the **Museum of the American**

Cocktail as well as **Purloo,** an on-site restaurant that highlights the cuisine of various Southern states. Dedicated to the discovery and appreciation of the food, drinks, and related culture of the American South, the museum's temporary and permanent exhibits explore an assortment of tasty topics, including Southern barbecue and liquor, Gulf Coast seafood, and praline vendors. A visit will surely stimulate your appetite for the Big Easy's varied culinary offerings, if not those throughout the South.

MAP 4: 1504 Oretha Castle Haley Blvd., 504/569-0405, http://southernfood.org; Thurs.-Mon. 11am-5:30pm; $10 adult, $5 senior over 60 and student, free under 12 (with paying adult)

Uptown

Map 5

CINEMA

PRYTANIA THEATRE

This old-fashioned movie house shows Hollywood blockbusters, classic films, and midnight movies on its massive single screen. It's also a principal venue for the annual **New Orleans Film Festival** (504/309-6633, www.neworleansfilmsociety.org) in the fall. Parking is sometimes hard to find in the residential neighborhood that surrounds the theater, but the matinee price ($5.75 pp) is a bargain.

MAP 5: 5339 Prytania St., 504/891-2787, http://prytaniatheatreneworleans.com; hours vary daily depending on the show; $11.50 adult, $10.50 college student, $9.50 senior over 62 and child under 12

CONCERT VENUES

DIXON HALL

Erected in 1929 and named after the first and only president of Newcomb College, this Italian Renaissance-style building houses music classrooms, practice and listening rooms, and a 1,000-seat auditorium that usually features jazz and classical music concerts, plus musical theater performances—most of which are free.

MAP 5: Tulane University, near Newcomb Pl. and Freret St., 504/862-3214 or 504/865-5269, www.tulane.edu; hours and ticket prices vary depending on the show

NUNEMAKER AUDITORIUM

At Loyola University, something interesting is often happening at the Nunemaker Auditorium, a 400-seat lecture and concert hall where students of the school's College of Music and Fine Arts present recitals, solo and ensemble performances, and live opera. Next to the Monroe building, the Communications/Music Complex also houses the 600-seat **Louis J. Roussel Performance Hall** (504/865-2074, http://cmfa.loyno.edu) on the second floor. There, you can enjoy free concerts of the university's chamber orchestra, symphony orchestra, jazz band, and concert band.

MAP 5: Loyola University, Monroe Science Complex, Calhoun St. and Marquette Pl., 3rd Fl., 504/865-2074, www.loyno.edu; hours and ticket prices vary depending on the show

GALLERIES

COLE PRATT GALLERY

Pay a visit to the Cole Pratt Gallery, which features the paintings of more than 40 contemporary Southern artists. Founded in 1993 by the late Cole Pratt, the gallery is now operated by owner and longtime director Erika Olinger, who continues Pratt's legacy of supporting imaginative artists like Phil Sandusky, Robert Lansden, and Karen Stastny.

MAP 5: 3800 Magazine St., 504/891-6789, www.coleprattgallery.com; Tues.-Sat. 10am-5pm

GALERIE ROYALE

Established in 1988, this elegant fine art gallery sits in the heart of Uptown's Magazine Arts District. Here, you'll find the contemporary artwork of local painters and sculptors: Adrian Wong Shue's pensive portraits; Mike Klung's otherworldly landscapes; and Joseph Derr's whimsical wooden sculptures, which have captured everything from elegant divas to dancing couples to an old-time jazz band.

MAP 5: 3648 Magazine St., 504/894-1588, www.galerieroyale.net; Tues. and Thurs.-Fri. 11am-3pm, Wed. by appt., Sat. 11am-6pm

The King of Oak Street

King of Oak Street (www.kingofoakstreet.com) is an intriguing, feature-length documentary about Randy Leo Frechette, a New Orleans-based performance painter affectionately known as "Frenchy" (www.frenchylive.com). Filmed by George Hamilton and Andrew Scott between 2005 and 2008, *Oak Street* offers an engaging look at this eccentric artist, who, though born in Boston, has a deep affinity for the Crescent City, his adopted home. During the course of filming, Hamilton and Scott were able to capture Frenchy as he interacted with creative colleagues and friends, dealt with the aftermath of Hurricane Katrina's devastation, helped displaced artists and musicians with on-the-road benefits, and, ultimately, pursued his art.

Once named the "King of Oak Street" as part of the city's annual Mid-Summer Mardi Gras, this beloved local celebrity is primarily known for his vibrant, energetic paintings of musicians and athletes, from Dr. John and Trombone Shorty to Drew Brees and Marcus Colston. In particular, Frenchy tends to paint his subjects while they're in action, whether playing their instruments or catching footballs in the end zone. That's why he's often spotted at New Orleans Saints games, annual festivals like the New Orleans Jazz & Heritage Festival, and live music venues all around town, painting with unabashed fervor on the sidelines. If you're curious about his one-of-a-kind creations, be sure to stop by his two **Frenchy Galleries,** located in the French Quarter (610 Toulouse St., 504/581-3522) and Uptown's cool Riverbend area (8319 Oak St., 504/861-7595).

MUSEUMS

NEWCOMB ART MUSEUM

Opened in 1887, the Newcomb College Art School was once at the forefront of the American Arts and Crafts Movement, earning international fame for its unique pottery and for producing talented graduates like modernist Ida Kohlmeyer and fine jewelry creator Mignon Faget. Unfortunately, Hurricane Katrina forced the school's closure, but you can still see some amazing creations at the Newcomb Art Museum, which contains more than 400 examples of pottery, metalwork, embroidery, and bound books produced at Newcomb College from the late 19th through the early 20th centuries. Situated on Tulane University's campus, the museum's exhibits and programs are free to the public.

MAP 5: Tulane University, Woldenberg Art Center, near Newcomb Pl. and Drill Field Rd., 504/865-5328, www.newcombartmuseum.tulane.edu; Tues.-Fri. 10am-5pm, Sat.-Sun. 10am-4pm

PERFORMING ARTS

LA NUIT COMEDY THEATER

Nestled within an Uptown residential neighborhood, this delightful, well-loved club presents several different shows, including open-mic, stand-up routines (Fri. and Sat. 11pm; free), and ComedySportz matches (Sat. 8pm; $10 adult, $8 child). Besides offering improv comedy and sketch comedy-writing classes, La Nuit is home to the annual **New Orleans Comedy and Arts Festival (NOCAF),** which usually takes place during the Mardi Gras season.

MAP 5: 5039 Freret St., 504/231-7011, www.lanuittheater.com; hours and ticket prices vary depending on the show

LUPIN THEATER

Situated on Tulane University's Uptown campus, the Lupin Theater hosts most of the theatrical productions and dance performances presented by Tulane's Department of Theatre and Dance. Although the lineup changes with each school year, shows typically range from Greek comedies and Shakespearean plays to ballet and modern dance performances by the Newcomb Dance Company. Lupin is also home to the annual **New Orleans Shakespeare Festival at Tulane** (http://neworleansshakespeare.org), which usually features three plays, including at least one of Shakespeare's seminal works, during the summer months.

MAP 5: Tulane University, Dixon Performing Arts Center, near Newcomb Pl. and Freret St., 504/865-5105 or 504/865-5106, www.tulane.edu; hours and ticket prices vary depending on the show

Above: the Mahalia Jackson Theater for the Performing Arts. **Below:** the Backstreet Cultural Museum.

MUSEUMS

★ BACKSTREET CULTURAL MUSEUM

If you're a fan of HBO's acclaimed show *Treme* or simply curious about the Big Easy's vibrant African American culture, you're in for a treat. Not far from Louis Armstrong Park—the original site of Congo Square—lies the fascinating Backstreet Cultural Museum. The museum contains the world's most comprehensive collection of costumes, films, and photographs from jazz funerals and pleasure clubs, plus Carnival-related groups like the Mardi Gras Indians, Baby Dolls, and Skull and Bone Gang. Beyond the permanent exhibits, the museum presents public performances of traditional music and dance.

MAP 6: 1116 Henriette Delille St., 504/522-4806, www.backstreetmuseum.org; Tues.-Sat. 10am-5pm; $8 pp

PERFORMING ARTS

★ MAHALIA JACKSON THEATER FOR THE PERFORMING ARTS

Located within Louis Armstrong Park, the Mahalia Jackson Theater is a popular venue for live concerts, operas, musicals, comedy shows, dance performances, and festival events, especially since its complete restoration following Hurricane Katrina. Named for New Orleans-born gospel singer Mahalia Jackson, the theater hosts regular performances by the **New Orleans Opera Association** (504/529-2278 or 504/529-3000, www.neworleansopera.org), the **Louisiana Philharmonic Orchestra** (504/523-6530, www.lpomusic.com), and the **New Orleans Ballet Association** (504/522-0996, www.nobadance.com), which books some of the world's most important ballet companies.

A Roving Rep

Founded in 1986 by playwright and scholar Dr. Rosary O'Neill, the award-winning **Southern Rep Theatre** (504/523-9857, www.southernrep.com) produces an eclectic mix of Broadway and off-Broadway selections, classic plays, and world premieres. Every year, Southern Rep presents roughly half a dozen productions, at least one of which has been written by a New Orleans-based writer or noted Southern playwright, such as Lillian Hellman or Lorraine Hasberry. Recent shows include Tennessee Williams's *Suddenly Last Summer,* the Pulitzer Prize-nominated *Detroit,* and a live, ongoing soap opera called *Debauchery!* Southern Rep holds its performances at various venues throughout the city. Tickets are available online, at the theater, or by calling the **box office** (504/522-6545, Tues.-Sat. 2pm-5pm); hours and ticket prices vary depending on the show.

Parking is located inside the gated park, accessible via the Orleans Avenue entrance. This can be an unsafe part of town, especially at night, so avoid coming to the theater alone, and be aware of your environs at all times.

MAP 6: 1419 Basin St., 504/287-0350, www.mahaliajacksontheater.com; hours and ticket prices vary depending on the show

SAENGER THEATRE

Designed by Emile Weil and built by Julian Saenger in 1927, the Saenger Theatre cost a record $2.5 million to complete. With its ornate arches, columns, and moldings, Greek and Roman statues, and a domed ceiling that resembled a starry night sky, it exuded the ambience of a 15th-century Italian courtyard and soon became one of the South's grandest movie palaces. Sadly, Hurricane Katrina damaged the magnificent structure, but with much community support, the Saenger underwent a $53-million restoration and reopened in September 2013. Today, patrons can attend concerts, comedic performances, and Broadway shows at this state-of-the-art performing arts venue.

MAP 6: 1111 Canal St., 504/525-1052, www.saengernola.com; hours and ticket prices vary depending on the show

Sports and Activities

Given the compact nature of New Orleans, many outdoors-lovers are surprised by the prevalence of bike shops, verdant parks, restful plazas, and public golf courses, including those in Uptown's Audubon Park and Mid-City's City Park.

For sports lovers, New Orleans nurtures two major teams—the New Orleans Saints and the New Orleans Pelicans—plus a Minor League baseball team, a historic horse-racing track, and a variety of spectator sports through Tulane University, Loyola University New Orleans, and the University of New Orleans (UNO). Indeed, although most travelers venture to New Orleans for its vibrant festivals, scrumptious cuisine, and spirited music scene, some visitors actually come here for year-round recreational pursuits.

Perhaps not surprisingly, live music enhances most of the Crescent City's recreational diversions. Concerts and festivals frequently take place in City Park, Lafayette Square, and other area parks, and even bowlers can enjoy live zydeco, jazz, blues, swing, and other types of music at the spacious Rock 'n' Bowl, one of my favorite places to catch regional luminaries like Tab Benoit, Amanda Shaw, and Kermit Ruffins.

But perhaps the most popular way to appreciate this vibrant city is via guided tour. Luckily, you'll find an assortment of memorable options, including citywide biking excursions, romantic carriage rides, and intimate boat trips through the surrounding marshes and swamps. You can even take a breezy jaunt down the Mississippi River via two authentic paddlewheelers: the Steamboat *Natchez* and the *Creole Queen*. Most visitors opt

---

Previous: the Steamboat *Natchez* rolling down the Mississippi River; a horse race at the Fair Grounds Race Course & Slots.

Look for ★ to find recommended activities.

Highlights

★ **Most Romantic Tour of the French Quarter:** From Jackson Square, couples can embark upon a mule-drawn carriage excursion of the Vieux Carré through **Royal Carriages.** Relish the historic architecture, curious characters, and romantic vibe of one of the country's most atmospheric neighborhoods (page 223).

★ **Breeziest Trip down the Mighty Mississippi:** Whether you opt for a daytime or evening cruise aboard the authentic **Steamboat *Natchez*,** you'll be treated to live jazz, Creole refreshments, and marvelous views of the river (page 224).

★ **Most Liberated Way to Explore the City:** To experience New Orleans at your own pace, rent a bicycle from **Bicycle Michael's,** a full-service store and repair shop in the Faubourg Marigny. Take your time exploring the French Quarter, City Park, the Lake Pontchartrain shoreline, and other key areas in this relatively compact city (page 224).

★ **Best Spot to Enjoy Free Concerts:** A relaxing oasis amid the city's bustling CBD, **Lafayette Square** hosts a variety of free music events throughout the year, including YLC Wednesday at the Square in the spring and summer, and the Crescent City Blues and BBQ Festival in mid-October (page 226).

★ **Most Scenic Excursion to a Battlefield:** The ***Creole Queen*** paddlewheeler hosts a historical river cruise that features a self-guided tour of the Chalmette Battlefield, site of the Battle of New Orleans in 1815 (page 227).

★ **Best All-Around Park:** Extending from St. Charles Avenue to the Mississippi River, historic **Audubon Park** offers a slew of recreational opportunities, including swimming, golf, playgrounds, tennis, bird-watching, and horseback-riding (page 229).

★ **Finest Site to Catch the Races:** In addition to being the home of the New Orleans Jazz & Heritage Festival, Mid-City's **Fair Grounds Race Course & Slots** happens to be the third-oldest thoroughbred-racing course in the nation. Watch seasonal horse, ostrich, and zebra races, and enjoy a year-round, off-track-betting parlor (page 230).

★ **Largest Adult Playground:** With its tennis center, golf course, dog park, boat and bike rentals, horseback-riding facility, biking routes, fishing-worthy lagoons, and oodles of picnicking spots and sports fields, as well as two stadiums, Mid-City's 1,300-acre **City Park** is truly a paradise for outdoor enthusiasts (page 230).

★ **Most Promising Place for Bird-Watching:** The 23,000-acre **Barataria Preserve** encompasses bayous, swamps, marshes, forests, and roughly nine miles of hiking trails, all ideal for viewing more than 300 bird species (page 234).

★ **Most Eclectic Tour Company:** At once authentic and eclectic, **Historic New Orleans Tours** leads narrated strolls that focus on everything from French Quarter history and voodoo culture to literary luminaries and legendary hauntings. Swamp and plantation tours are also available (page 237).

for at least one of the innumerable walking and driving tours available, such as cemetery excursions, van rides through various neighborhoods, and narrated French Quarter strolls that focus on everything from cocktails and cuisine to ghosts and vampires.

French Quarter

Map 1

BIKING

THE AMERICAN BICYCLE RENTAL COMPANY

Despite potholes, narrow streets, and steady traffic, New Orleans lures its share of biking enthusiasts, particularly in the Quarter, the Marigny, and City Park. It helps that the city has relatively flat terrain and an increasing number of bike-friendly roadways. To tour the Big Easy at your own pace, head to this helpful shop, which rents cruisers by the hour or by periods of 4, 8, or 24 hours. Each rental includes a lock, helmet, basket, and cycling map, plus lights for nighttime riding. You can also book an excursion with the on-site **Free Wheelin' Bike Tours** (504/522-4368, www.neworleansbiketour.com; $35-49).

MAP 1: 325 Burgundy St., 504/324-8257, www.bikerentalneworleans.com; daily 9am-5pm; $10 hourly, $40 daily

GUIDED AND WALKING TOURS

FRIENDS OF THE CABILDO

For an intimate tour of the French Quarter, take one of the two-hour, narrated strolls led by the nonprofit Friends of the Cabildo. Conducted by licensed guides, these well-respected tours highlight the history, folklore, and architecture of one of the country's oldest neighborhoods, known alternately as the Vieux Carré. Tours depart from the **1850 House Museum Store** (523 St. Ann St., 504/524-9118; Tues.-Sun. 10am-4:30pm) and are offered Tuesday-Sunday 10:30am and 1:30pm. All proceeds benefit the Friends of the Cabildo, a volunteer group that supports the Louisiana State Museum, which oversees such historic properties as The Cabildo and The Presbytère.

MAP 1: 701 Chartres St., 504/523-3939, www.friendsofthecabildo.org; Mon.-Fri. 9:30am-4:30pm; $20 adult, $15 senior, student, and active military

★ ROYAL CARRIAGES

While strolling along Decatur Street in front of Jackson Square, you'll surely notice the mule-drawn carriages waiting beside the sidewalk. Whether you're a tourist or not, do yourself a favor and join one of these narrated carriage excursions at least once. Whether you opt for a romantic ride in one of the smaller carriages or join one of the larger groups, you'll remember this unique tour of the Vieux Carré. After all, there's nothing quite like clip-clopping along these historic streets, relishing the historic architecture and curious characters through the eyes of a local guide.

MAP 1: Jackson Square, 700 Decatur St., 504/943-8820, www.neworleanscarriages.com; daily 8:30am-midnight; cost varies

RIVERBOAT TOURS

★ STEAMBOAT *NATCHEZ*

Launched by the **New Orleans Steamboat Company** (504/586-8777 or 800/365-2628) in 1975, the Steamboat *Natchez* is an authentic, steam-powered sternwheeler modeled after the *Virginia* and the *Hudson,* two sternwheelers of old. The *Natchez* offers two-hour **harbor cruises** (Mon.-Sat. 11:30am and 2:30pm; $29.50 adult, $12.25 child 6-12, free under 6), departing from the foot of Toulouse Street, just behind the Jax Brewery. While on board, you can visit the steam engine room, listen to live narration about the history of the port, enjoy a concert of the onboard, 32-note steam calliope, and opt for a Creole lunch ($11.50 adult, $8 child under 13). Alternatively, you can board a **dinner jazz cruise** (daily 7pm; with dinner $77 adult, $34 child 6-12, $14 child under 6; without dinner $46 adult, $21.50 child 6-12, free under 6), which features decent buffet-style dining, live jazz by the Dukes of Dixieland, and gorgeous views of the city. Although sightseeing on the deck is a highlight of any *Natchez* excursion, climate-controlled indoor seating is always available (and especially welcome on hot or rainy days). Be sure to make reservations, especially for the dinner cruise, and arrive a half hour before boarding time.

MAP 1: Toulouse St. Wharf, 504/569-1401 or 800/233-2628, www.steamboatnatchez.com; hours and cost vary

Faubourg Marigny and Bywater

Map 2

BIKING

★ BICYCLE MICHAEL'S

Amid the live music clubs of Frenchmen Street stands this laid-back, full-service bike store, which handles sales, provides rentals, and even offers repair services. Choose among city hybrids, mountain bikes, off-road bikes, and tandems. Then, depending on how long you keep the rental (from a half day to a full, seven-day week), you can explore the Faubourg Marigny, the nearby French Quarter, City Park, the Lake Pontchartrain shoreline, and other key areas in this relatively compact city. Although locks, biking advice, and local tips are free, there are nominal costs for helmets ($5 daily), baskets ($5), and maps ($6-8).

MAP 2: 622 Frenchmen St., 504/945-9505, www.bicyclemichaels.com; Mon.-Tues. and Thurs.-Sat. 10am-7pm, Sun. 10am-5pm; $35-110 daily, $140-320 weekly

Clockwise from top left: the Steamboat *Natchez;* a carriage waiting for riders in the French Quarter; biking in the French Quarter.

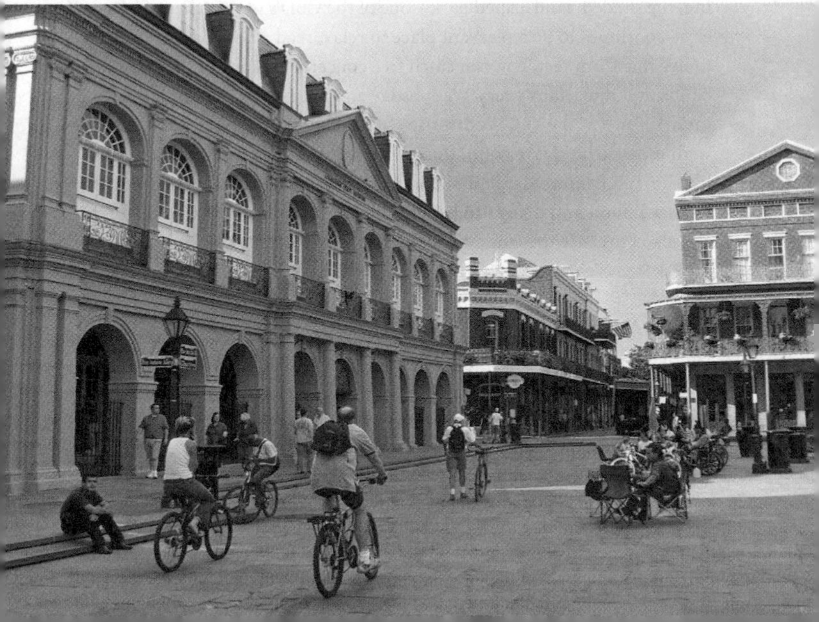

PARKS AND PLAZAS

CRESCENT PARK

Since Crescent Park, an edgy Bywater sanctuary, opened in February 2014, the 1.4-mile-long, 20-acre strip has lured countless recreationists. Besides scenic views of the downtown New Orleans skyline, the Mississippi River, and Algiers Point, you'll find picnic areas, a fenced dog run, and a network of paths suitable for walking, jogging, and biking. A parking lot is situated near Piety and Chartres Streets, where you'll also spot the Piety Street Bridge, a rusted steel arch that safely delivers pedestrians over the active riverfront railroad tracks. Certain activities, such as cooking, swimming, and littering, are not allowed, as are skateboards, motorcycles, and bottles.

MAP 2: Mississippi riverfront btwn. Elysian Fields Ave. and Mazant St., 504/658-3200, www.nola.gov; daily 8am-6pm; free

Central Business and Arts Districts

Map 3

PARKS AND PLAZAS

★ LAFAYETTE SQUARE

South of Poydras Street lies the attractive Lafayette Square, which was laid out in the late 18th century as the American Quarter's version of the Place d'Armes (now Jackson Square). Bound by St. Charles Avenue, Camp Street, and North and South Maestri Places, it is named in honor of the Marquis de Lafayette, who visited the city in 1825. With its ample park-bench seating, the shaded, landscaped park—one of the CBD's few patches of greenery—continues to be a pleasant place to relax, read a newspaper, or listen to live music. In fact, you can catch free concerts by some of the city's top bands and musicians every Wednesday at 5pm, from late March to mid-June. Known as the **YLC Wednesday at the Square** (504/585-1500, http://wednesdayatthesquare.com), this 12-week concert series has featured the likes of Tab Benoit, Marcia Ball, and The Iguanas. Local bars and restaurants sell food and drinks to benefit the Young Leadership Council. You can also purchase the work of local artisans in the Artist Village.

MAP 3: St. Charles Ave. and Lafayette St., www.lafayette-square.org; daily 24 hours; free

PIAZZA D'ITALIA

Not far from the American Italian Cultural Center, you'll encounter the picturesque Piazza d'Italia, which is dedicated to the city's Italian American community and its indelible influence on New Orleans. Designed in 1978 by the renowned, postmodernist architect Charles Moore and partially restored in 2004, the plaza serves as a gathering place for residents, a relaxing spot for a lunch break, and site of St. Joseph's Day celebrations.

MAP 3: Lafayette St. and Commerce St.; daily 24 hours; free

SPANISH PLAZA

Between the Audubon Aquarium of the Americas and The Outlet Collection at Riverwalk, this pleasant square is an ideal spot to gaze at the bustling Mississippi. The square was rededicated by Spain in 1976 to commemorate its influence on the Crescent City's history and to serve as an ongoing promise of fraternity. As a symbolic reminder, the seals of Spanish provinces encircle the central fountain. Spanish Plaza is a common gathering place for residents and tourists alike, as well as the site of free public concerts throughout the year.

MAP 3: 1 Poydras St.; daily 24 hours; free

RIVERBOAT TOURS

★ *CREOLE QUEEN*

For a memorable excursion along the Mississippi River, board the majestic *Creole Queen*, an authentic paddlewheeler that, with its Victorian-style furniture and wrought-iron deck railings, harkens back to those of the mid-1800s. Operated by New Orleans Paddlewheels, Inc., the *Creole Queen* leaves at 2pm daily from The Outlet Collection at Riverwalk for an engaging, 2.5-hour **cruise** ($28 adult, $13 child 6-12, free under 6) that travels past the French Quarter to the site of the 1815 Battle of New Orleans; guests can disembark here to tour the Chalmette Battlefield before reboarding for the return trip. On certain days, you can also opt for a three-hour **dinner jazz cruise** (daily 6:30pm; with dinner $77 adult, $34 child 6-12, $12 child 3-5; without dinner $44 adult, $20 child 6-12, free under 6), which includes a scenic river cruise, a Creole buffet, and live jazz music. It's strongly recommended to make reservations and arrive a half hour before boarding time.

MAP 3: 1 Poydras St., 504/529-4567 or 800/445-4109, www.creolequeen.com; hours and cost vary

SPECTATOR SPORTS

Basketball

NEW ORLEANS PELICANS

Adjacent to the Mercedes-Benz Superdome, the **Smoothie King Center** (504/587-3822, ww.smoothiekingcenter.com) is the official home of the New Orleans Pelicans, the NBA basketball team that moved from Charlotte to New Orleans in 2002 and was, until recently, known as the New Orleans Hornets. Before that, New Orleans had gone many years without an NBA team. Open since 1999, the 18,000-seat Smoothie King Center is also a popular concert and performing arts venue, which has hosted the likes of Katy Perry, Def Leppard, and Cirque de Soleil.

MAP 3: Smoothie King Center, 1501 Dave Dixon Dr., 504/525-4667, www.nba.com/pelicans; hours and costs vary

Who Dat!

Fans proudly represent the Who Dat Nation.

If you're ever in town during the NFL football season, you'll probably notice "Who Dat" flags and banners hanging from many porches and balconies, and you might even hear someone shout "Who Dat!" at no one in particular. If you're wondering about the origins of such a funny-sounding call of solidarity, just know that you've arrived in the heart of the **Who Dat Nation** (www.whodatnation.com), a popular term used to describe the entire community of fiercely loyal Saints' fans.

Once a common dialogue exchange between performers and spectators at minstrel shows and vaudeville acts in southern Louisiana, the "Who Dat" chant was eventually adopted by the **New Orleans Saints** in the 1980s. Part of a longer chant—"Who dat say dey gonna beat dem Saints?"—that is often heard at Saints' games, "Who Dat" has now become a rallying cry of team support for New Orleanians everywhere. Not surprisingly, the cry resounded through the French Quarter when the Saints won their first Super Bowl in 2010.

Football

NEW ORLEANS SAINTS

The National Football League's Super Bowl has been held in the **Mercedes-Benz Superdome** (504/587-3822, www.superdome.com) several times since 1978. Built in 1975, the iconic 73,000-seat Superdome is a popular event and performance venue as well as the home stadium of the NFL's New Orleans Saints, the seemingly jinxed team that finally won its first Super Bowl in 2010, a win that the Katrina-ravaged city desperately needed. The Saints' unusual name derives from both the popular jazz anthem "When the Saints Go Marching In" and the fact that this predominantly Catholic city was awarded the NFL franchise on November 1, 1966 (All Saints' Day).

MAP 3: Mercedes-Benz Superdome, 1500 Sugar Bowl Dr., 504/731-1700, www.neworleanssaints.com; hours and cost varies

Garden District

Map 4

BIKING

A MUSING BIKES

Based in the Lower Garden District, this friendly shop has been offering bike rentals since it opened in 2011. Options include a 1-speed beach cruiser and a 21-speed hybrid. Some bikes include baskets, but every rental comes with a U-lock, a helmet, and safety lights. Bike and bike parts sales as well as repairs and maintenance are available.

MAP 4: 1818 Magazine St., 504/208-9779, www.amusingbikes.com; daily 10am-5:30pm; $8-11 hourly, $30-45 daily, $110-145 weekly

PARKS AND PLAZAS

COLISEUM SQUARE

Bordered by Coliseum, Race, and Camp Streets, this oddly shaped park offers residents in the Lower Garden District a lush, peaceful place to read, picnic, or walk a dog. Filled with shady oak trees, inviting benches, and well-manicured lawns, the park is punctuated by a lovely fountain, an ideal, if popular, spot to hang out with friends and neighbors. Unfortunately, there are no public bathrooms here.

MAP 4: Coliseum St. and Race St., www.coliseumsquare.org; daily 24 hours; free

Uptown

Map 5

PARKS AND PLAZAS

★ AUDUBON PARK

One of New Orleanians' favorite places for strolling is verdant Audubon Park, a 340-acre property that occupies the former estate of Etienne de Boré, the city's fist mayor, and extends from St. Charles Avenue to the Mississippi River. Besides encompassing Audubon Zoo, this beloved park features a pleasant lagoon, moss-draped live oak trees, and lush lawns with picnic areas. Named after ornithologist John James Audubon, who once lived in southern Louisiana, Audubon Park offers a slew of athletic facilities, including tennis courts and soccer fields, three playgrounds, a golf course, a swimming pool, and a paved 1.8-mile path ideal for walking, jogging, and in-line skating. You can take horseback-riding lessons at **Cascade Stables** or view a variety of egrets, herons, and cormorants on **Ochsner Island,** which sits within the park's lagoon and is more commonly known as Bird Island.

MAP 5: 6500 Magazine St., 504/861-2537, www.auduboninstitute.org; daily 5am-10pm; free

SPECTATOR SPORTS

Basketball

WOLFPACK ATHLETICS

Adjacent to Tulane's campus along verdant St. Charles Avenue, Loyola University offers a variety of spectator sports, including a men's basketball team that dates back to 1945 and a much newer women's basketball team. Both teams hold their home games at The Den, a facility on the fifth floor of the university's massive sports complex.

MAP 5: Loyola Recreational Sports Complex, Freret St. and Engineering Rd., 5th Fl., 504/864-7225, www.wolfpack.loyno.edu; hours vary; $6 adult, $3 senior and child

Football

TULANE GREEN WAVE

Until recently, the Mercedes-Benz Superdome hosted the home games of the Tulane Green Wave, Tulane University's football team, which was established in 1893. In the fall of 2014, however, the team moved to an on-campus, 30,000-seat stadium known as Benson Field at Yulman Stadium. Though especially known for its football team, Tulane is also a major force in men's baseball and women's basketball.

MAP 5: Benson Field at Yulman Stadium, 333 Ben Weiner Dr., 504/861-9283, www.tulanegreenwave.com; hours and cost vary

Tremé and Mid-City

Map 6

HORSE RACING

★ FAIR GROUNDS RACE COURSE & SLOTS

Mid-City's Fair Grounds Race Course & Slots is the third-oldest thoroughbred-racing course in the nation, offering live racing from Thanksgiving through March. An off-track-betting parlor is open year-round, so you can always wager on events elsewhere in the country. Key events at the track include the Louisiana Derby and the Fair Grounds Oaks; it's also the longtime home of the annual **New Orleans Jazz & Heritage Festival** (www.nojazzfest.com). Besides concession stands and two "grab-and-go" eateries, the Fair Grounds offers a fancy Clubhouse dining room, which has a strict dress code and is only open on live racing days.

MAP 6: 1751 Gentilly Blvd., 504/944-5515 or 504/948-1111, www.fairgroundsracecourse.com; daily 9am-midnight; $10 pp for clubhouse, $0-5 pp for grandstand

PARKS AND PLAZAS

★ CITY PARK

Encompassing 1,300 acres of lawns, lagoons, and moss-covered oak trees, City Park has long been a preferred spot for rest and recreation, especially for the nearby communities of Mid-City, Lakeview, and Gentilly. Families

Above: Audubon Park. **Below:** exploring the waterways in City Park.

Congo Square

a festival in Congo Square

Between the aftermath of Hurricane Katrina and the popularity of HBO's acclaimed series *Treme*, a national spotlight has been cast on the Faubourg Tremé, the country's oldest African American neighborhood and an area celebrated for its musical contributions. Within the Tremé lies Louis Armstrong Park, named after one of the city's most famous musicians and featuring an open space historically known as Congo Square. It was here during the French and Spanish colonial era of the 1700s that slaves gathered on Sunday to sing, dance, and play music together.

Following the Louisiana Purchase, these weekly gatherings grew in size and influence, luring visitors from around the country as well as African and Creole slaves. Residents gathered to observe African-style dancing, marveling at the hundreds of costumed women and half-dressed men that moved to the rhythms of varied musical instruments, from African drums to European violins to American-style banjos.

As harsh American slavery practices usurped the more lenient French colonial style, the gatherings declined, stopping well before the American Civil War. By the late 1800s, the square once again became a famous musical venue, featuring a series of Creole brass band concerts, and was renamed Beauregard Square in honor of Confederate General P. G. T. Beauregard. In the 1920s, part of the Tremé community behind Beauregard Square was displaced to make way for the Municipal Auditorium, which opened in 1930. In the 1960s, a controversial urban renewal project commandeered even more land, which eventually became Louis Armstrong Park.

In 1970, the city held the first New Orleans Jazz & Heritage Festival at Beauregard Square. Attendees witnessed performances by luminaries like Mahalia Jackson, Duke Ellington, and the Preservation Hall Jazz Band. The annual festival's growth ultimately forced a move to its present location in Mid-City, but Beauregard Square has continued to be a significant gathering place in the community, playing host to music festivals, brass band parades, drum circles, and protest marches. The legacy of this historic space has influenced numerous generations of New Orleans musicians, including Johnny Wiggs, Donald Harrison, and Wynton Marsalis, all of whom have written African-themed jazz music inspired by the former slave gatherings at Congo Square. Fittingly, the New Orleans City Council officially voted in 2011 to restore the traditional Congo Square moniker to this legendary part of the Tremé.

are drawn here to feed the ducks, stroll across picturesque bridges, and ride bikes along the winding roads. Outdoor enthusiasts can take advantage of the on-site golf course; eight miles of lagoons ideal for fishing, canoeing, and pedal-boating; boat rentals ($15-30 hourly) and bike rentals ($8-35 hourly, $40-50 daily); a tennis center (504/483-9383; $12-15 hourly); and the 13-acre **Equest Farm** (504/483-9398, www.equestfarm.com), which offers horseback-riding lessons. The park has two stadiums: the renovated **Pan American Stadium,** home to the New Orleans Jesters soccer team (www.nolajesters.com), and the **Tad Gormley Stadium,** often a concert venue.

If you've brought along your dog, be sure to take advantage of **NOLA City Bark** (504/483-9377; Wed.-Mon. 5:30am-9pm, Tues. 1pm-9pm), a 4.6-acre, off-leash dog park, featuring an event lawn, a walking trail, on-site restrooms, and separate play areas for small and large dogs. Purchase a permit online or at the City Park Administration Building (Mon.-Fri. 8am-5pm). Depending on the length of your visit to New Orleans, you can opt for either a 3-day pass ($10) or a 14-day pass ($15). All dogs must be neutered, have current vaccinations, and adhere to dog park rules. For safety reasons, children under the age of eight are not permitted inside the dog park.

MAP 6: 1 Palm Dr., 504/482-4888, www.neworleanscitypark.com; 24 hours daily, facility hours vary seasonally; free, though activity fees apply

LOUIS ARMSTRONG PARK

Though created by two controversial "land grabs" of the Faubourg Tremé (one in the 1920s and another in the 1960s), Louis Armstrong Park is currently one of the lovelier urban parks in New Orleans. Unfortunately, it's also one of the more dangerous ones, so it's best not to wander through this gated park alone. Named after the famous New Orleans-born jazz trumpeter and singer, Louis Armstrong Park comprises pleasant lagoons and grassy areas, historic **Congo Square,** which is designated by a historical marker, and the renovated **Mahalia Jackson Theater for the Performing Arts** (1419 Basin St., 504/287-0350, www.mahaliajacksontheater.com).

MAP 6: 701 N. Rampart St., 504/658-3200; daily sunrise-sunset; free

Greater New Orleans **Map 7**

BOWLING

ROCK 'N' BOWL

While the Rock 'n' Bowl is one of the city's most popular live music venues—and certainly one of my favorite places to catch local acts like Kermit Ruffins, Amanda Shaw, and Tab Benoit—it's still primarily a family-friendly bowling alley. There's a maximum capacity of six bowlers per lane and, given how busy this joint can get, it's advisable to call ahead for lane availability. There's a limited menu, with basic vittles like cheeseburgers, hot dogs, and chicken wings.

MAP 7: 3000 S. Carrollton Ave., 504/861-1700, www.rocknbowl.com; Mon.-Thurs. 11:30am-midnight, Fri.-Sat. 11:30am-2am, Sun. hours vary; $24 hourly per lane, $1 shoe rental

PARKS AND PLAZAS

★ BARATARIA PRESERVE

The 23,000-acre Barataria Preserve, a unit of Jean Lafitte National Historical Park and Preserve, is a popular bird-watching spot among locals and visitors. Situated on the West Bank of the Mississippi River, this enormous preserve comprises bayous, swamps, marshes, forests, and roughly nine miles of hiking trails (where pets, even leashed ones, aren't allowed). Don't miss the **Bayou Coquille Trail,** a half-mile, pavement-and-boardwalk path that's known for myriad sightings of snakes, alligators, nutrias, and some of the more than 300 bird species that dwell here. At the **visitor center** (Wed.-Sun. 9:30am-4:30pm), you'll spot exhibits that highlight how the Mississippi River created Louisiana's wetlands, the national significance of this region, and the relationship between the land and its people. In the bookstore, you'll find music, field guides, and children's books. Free guided wetlands walks are available Wednesday-Sunday at 10am, and varied ranger talks occur at 2pm on the same days. The park, which is only closed on Mardi Gras Day, is also favored among canoeists, kayakers, boaters, and licensed anglers.

MAP 7: 6588 Barataria Blvd., Marrero, 504/689-3690, www.nps.gov/jela; daily 9am-5pm; free

SWAMP TOURS

CAJUN CRITTERS SWAMP TOUR

Based on the West Bank, the Cajun Critters Swamp Tour provides informative, two-hour excursions through the area's bayous, marshes, and swamps. While aboard the wheelchair-accessible *Swamp Queen,* you might be lucky enough to spy pelicans, egrets, otters, rabbits, armadillos, and, of course, alligators. From spring to fall, Cajun Critters also offers a 3:30pm tour. Prices are higher ($42 adult, $30 child 4-12) if you need transportation to the launch site.

MAP 7: 363 Louisiana St., Westwego, 504/347-0962 or 800/575-5578, www.cajunswamptour.com; daily 9:30am and 1:30pm; $24 adult, $15 child 4-12, free under 4

JEAN LAFITTE SWAMP & AIRBOAT TOURS

From the West Bank town of Marrero, you can embark on an educational trip into the wildlife-rich bayous and swamps of southeastern Louisiana. Jean Lafitte Swamp & Airboat Tours features knowledgeable Cajun guides and a two-hour tour aboard a roomy swamp boat (daily 10am and 2pm; $29 adult, $12 child 3-12) or a speedy airboat (daily 9:45am and 2pm; $65-85 pp). You're bound to see snakes, egrets, and alligators amid the moss-draped cypress trees. Children under age eight aren't permitted on the airboats, and prices are higher if you require transportation to the launch site. Additional trip times may be available.

MAP 7: 6601 Leo Kerner Lafitte Pkwy., Marrero, 504/689-4186, www.jeanlafitteswamptour.com; hours and cost vary

Various Locations

BIKING

BIG EASY BIKE TOURS

While biking can be a great way to explore New Orleans, not everyone is eager to do it alone. If you'd prefer a guided excursion, consider Big Easy Bike Tours, which offers three separate routes. Although all of these narrated, customizable tours begin in the historic French Quarter, passing such landmarks as Jackson Square and the French Market, they each head in a different direction: into the American Sector and Garden District, up the Creole-influenced Esplanade Avenue, or on a 20-mile course that includes places like the Tremé, City Park, and Lake Pontchartrain.

VARIOUS LOCATIONS: 504/377-0973, www.bigeasybiketours.com; daily 8am-11am, 1:30pm-4:30pm, and 5pm-8pm; $49 pp

CONFEDERACY OF CRUISERS

More intimate than a bus excursion yet faster than a walking tour, guided bike trips can be an excellent way to experience this laid-back city, and if you'd prefer to see less-traveled neighborhoods, then Confederacy of Cruisers is the ideal operator. Using comfortable, easy-to-ride cruising bikes, these slow-paced, three-hour, customizable tours cover areas like the Faubourg Marigny, Faubourg Tremé, and Bywater—places not seen by most tourists. Along the way, you'll learn about the unique history, architecture, and culture of New Orleans.

VARIOUS LOCATIONS: 504/400-5468, http://confederacyofcruisers.com; hours vary daily; $49 pp

JOY RIDE BIKE RENTALS

Perhaps the most convenient way to procure a bike is through the aptly named Joy Ride Bike Rentals, a delivery rental service that caters to both residents and out-of-towners. No matter where you're staying, the Joy Ride staff will bring a bike to you and pick it up the following day (reservations are required). All rentals are one-speed, cruiser-style bikes, though various sizes are available. Every rider must have a valid ID or credit card, wear a helmet at all times, and lock up the bike whenever it's not in use.

VARIOUS LOCATIONS: 504/982-1617, www.joyridebikerentals.com; hours vary; $35 daily, $160 weekly

Recreational Resources

Beyond its unique culture, southern Louisiana also offers a wealth of outdoor diversions, such as canoeing, kayaking, rafting, boating, fishing, hunting, hiking, biking, golfing, and bird-watching. For information on boating safety, fishing seasons, and hunting regulations, contact the **Louisiana Department of Wildlife & Fisheries** (http://wlf.louisiana.gov). You can also consult **Mike Lane's RodnReel.com** (www.rodnreel.com) for extensive recreational information, including fish and game statistics, maps and charts, and suggested fishing charters and hunting guides. For advice on canoeing and kayaking around New Orleans, consider joining the **Bayou Haystackers Paddling Club** (www.bayouhaystackers.com), or at the very least, consult the website for suggested paddling areas, local canoe/kayak rentals, and guided excursions.

Besides information about state museums and cultural districts, the website for the **Louisiana Department of Culture, Recreation, & Tourism** (www.crt.state.la.us) provides the lowdown on each of the dozen golf courses that constitute Louisiana's Audubon Golf Trail, plus details about Louisiana's 22 state parks, 19 state historic sites, and one state preservation area. The website even offers a helpful interactive map; simply click on the park in question, and you'll learn about the property's history, location and hours, and facilities.

For those interested in bird-watching, you can't go wrong with the **Orleans Audubon Society** (www.jjaudubon.net), the southeastern Louisiana chapter of the National Audubon Society. The organization's website contains a full Southeast Louisiana Bird Finding Guide, with detailed descriptions of 11 key bird-watching areas in and around New Orleans, including City Park.

Another helpful group for outdoor enthusiasts is the **New Orleans Bicycle Club** (www.neworleansbicycleclub.org), which, though geared toward racing, lists a number of good biking routes and bike shops on its website. The state-run website **Bike Louisiana** (www.bikelouisiana.com) offers detailed itineraries for biking throughout the state, from off-road routes to leisurely rides, as well as road rules and events.

Naturally, you can always consult the **New Orleans Convention & Visitors Bureau** (www.neworleanscvb.com), which provides plenty of information about the city's parks, sports, tours, and cruises.

GUIDED AND WALKING TOURS

HAUNTED HISTORY TOURS

To hear a few spooky tales, consider one of the entertaining excursions offered by Haunted History Tours, one of the city's oldest walking-tour companies. Options departing from Reverend Zombie's House of Voodoo (723 St. Peter St.) include a stroll through St. Louis Cemetery No. 1 and several French Quarter tours focused on ghosts, voodoo, scandals, or neighborhood history. You can also join ghost-related or historical tours through the Garden District, all of which begin in Lafayette Cemetery No. 1, as well as a vampire tour that departs from the St. Louis Cathedral. Reservations are typically required for all tours.

VARIOUS LOCATIONS: 504/861-2727, www.hauntedhistorytours.com; hours vary; $25 adult, $18 senior, student, and military, $14 child 6-11

★ HISTORIC NEW ORLEANS TOURS

As you might have guessed, photogenic New Orleans boasts a slew of guided tour companies. One of the most authentic is Historic New Orleans Tours; walking tours focus on French Quarter history, voodoo culture, the city's jazz scene, the Garden District, and legendary hauntings. On the two-hour Garden District Tour, guides explain the history of the city's American Sector, point out notable buildings (including the former homes of Anne Rice and Peyton Manning), and discuss their colorful heritage; you'll also get the chance to explore the aboveground tombs within Lafayette Cemetery No. 1, which has made notable appearances in such films as *Interview with the Vampire* (1994) and *Double Jeopardy* (1999). This well-respected company also offers swamp and plantation tours, plus van excursions through the city's varied neighborhoods.

VARIOUS LOCATIONS: 504/947-2120, www.tourneworleans.com; hours vary; $20 adult, $15 senior 62 and over and student, $7 child 6-12, free under 6

LE MONDE CRÉOLE TOURS

If you're curious about the Creole culture that helped to shape New Orleans, then take one of the guided strolls offered by Le Monde Créole Tours. Inspired by the memoirs of Laura Locul (1861-1963), a Creole woman and plantation mistress in Vacherie, these excursions offer glimpses into private courtyards and shed some light on positive and negative aspects of the city, including the ubiquitous slave quarters, Creole classism, and the ill-fated effects that the American Civil War, jazz era, and changing society ultimately had on the Creoles. The tour begins at one of the Quarter's several Forever New Orleans shops (622 Royal St.), and reservations are required.

VARIOUS LOCATIONS: 504/568-1801, www.mondecreole.com; daily 10:30am; $25 adult, $20 student and child 10-18, free under 10

NEW ORLEANS CULINARY HISTORY TOURS

For an in-depth understanding of the city's incredible, often diet-busting cuisine—including the differences between Creole and Cajun traditions—take an immersive, three-hour tasting tour of the French Quarter (daily 2pm; $46 pp). Through the locally operated New Orleans Culinary History Tours, you'll have the chance to visit some of the neighborhood's oldest restaurants, such as Antoine's and Tujague's. You can also opt for a two-hour cocktail tour (daily 4pm; $60 pp). Tickets for the tasting or cocktail tour can be purchased through **Zerve** (877/278-8240, www.zerve.com).

VARIOUS LOCATIONS: 504/427-9595, http://noculinarytours.com; hours and cost vary

SPIRIT TOURS NEW ORLEANS

To honor New Orleans's reputation as one of America's most haunted cities, join one of the walking tours led by Spirit Tours New Orleans, which focuses on local ghosts, cemeteries, voodoo legends, and vampire lore. The Cemetery & Voodoo tour, which leaves at various times throughout the week from Little Vic's Cafe (719 Toulouse St.), includes a visit to St. Louis Cemetery No. 1. The Ghost Tour, which typically departs from Toulouse Royale Gifts (601 Royal St.) at 8:15pm every night, explores the city's tragic history, from disease to piracy to slavery. You can also opt for a guided stroll through the Garden District at 10am Thursday-Saturday.

VARIOUS LOCATIONS: 504/314-0806, www.neworleanstours.net; hours vary; $25 adult, $12 child 6-12, free under 6

Shops

Look for ★ to find recommended shops.

Highlights

★ **Finest Antiques Shop:** If you've ever longed to decorate your home in the fashion of those regal mansions that line the streets of the Garden District, you need to browse the elegant pieces at **Keil's Antiques,** a Royal Street shop especially known for its shimmering chandeliers (page 242).

★ **Best Shop for a Nostalgic Makeover:** On a bustling stretch of Royal Street, you'll encounter the **Trashy Diva Clothing Boutique,** which offers vintage dresses, corsets, shoes, and accessories (page 246).

★ **Sweetest Emporium:** With two stores in the French Quarter, **Southern Candymakers** lures many a passerby with its wide assortment of pralines, chocolate alligators, and other local confections (page 250).

★ **Best Place to Lift a Curse:** For spell kits, voodoo dolls, tarot cards, and other talismans, head to **Marie Laveau's House of Voodoo,** an often crowded Bourbon Street shop that offers private spiritual readings (page 252).

★ **Most Historic Shopping District:** Encompassing several blocks from Jackson Square to Barracks Street, the architecturally pleasing **French Market** houses a variety of emporiums, including a flea market, a farmers market, art galleries, and a crafts bazaar (page 252).

★ **Best Music Source:** You'll find a wide array of local and regional blues, jazz, zydeco, and Cajun tunes at the **Louisiana Music Factory,** which also stocks an assortment of relevant books, DVDs, and T-shirts (page 254).

★ **Best Haven for Retail Therapy:** If you need to unwind after a long day of indulging in the city's hospitality, head to the **Belladonna Day Spa,** a favorite among locals for its array of massages, facials, manicures, and pedicures (page 264).

★ **Friendliest Place for Book Lovers:** For a wide array of local books, many signed by authors, venture to **Octavia Books,** an Uptown bookstore popular for its weekly events, from author signings to book club meetings (page 267).

★ **Finest Jewelry Shop:** An esteemed local chain, **Mignon Faget** carries stunning jewelry, much of it designed with traditional Louisiana icons. Browse fleur-de-lis cuff links, oyster earrings, redfish pins, and sno-ball pendants (page 269).

★ **Biggest Architectural Treasure Trove:** When old New Orleans homes are torn down, **Ricca's Demolishing Corp.** salvages and sells the beautiful architectural remnants. You might find mahogany doors, wrought-iron gates, and vintage hardware (page 270).

In New Orleans, shopping opportunities embrace the most popular aspects of the city's heritage—its cuisine, music, art, literature, and historical preservation.

The French Quarter is rife with praline shops, and visitors rarely leave without strolling through the varied food stalls of the historic French Market. Music and book lovers will find numerous stores that offer the best in everything from local jazz to Faulkner novels. Art and antiques hounds can browse the emporiums along Royal and Chartres Streets, which carry some of the most lavish and expensive furnishings in the South, while the Garden District stretch of Magazine Street is considered a less pricey yet still ample source of art, antiques, jewelry, and vintage clothing.

On any given day, shopping in the Big Easy can involve perusing rare first editions, pricking voodoo dolls, decking yourself out in artisan jewelry or Mardi Gras masks, spicing up your wardrobe with old-fashioned corsets and feather boas, or bringing a little bit of the city's culture back home in the form of handblown glass, antique ironwork, or Cajun and Creole seasonings. Though you'll find plenty of national chain stores here, much of what you see is unique to this region. The most interesting shops and boutiques lie in the French Quarter, Arts District, and Uptown neighborhoods.

Remember that New Orleans is an easygoing town, where a flexible sense of time seems to be the norm. When it comes to shopping, that means that posted hours aren't always strictly enforced. Hours can also change from season to season; in the summer, when the weather is fairly unbearable and tourism slows, shops tend to close a bit earlier. On the positive side, window-shopping in this eclectic city can be a wonderful way to pass the afternoon.

Previous: a young trumpet player in front of a French Quarter shop; Mardi Gras dolls for sale.

SHOPPING DISTRICTS

French Quarter

Known for upscale antiques and first-rate art galleries, **Royal Street** is the most exclusive address for shopping in the French Quarter, though parallel **Chartres Street** has similarly high-end emporiums. In the **Lower Quarter,** from Jackson Square to Esplanade Avenue, you'll find funkier, more youthful boutiques, such as mod clothiers and edgy galleries. **Decatur Street,** meanwhile, is a good place to find cheesy T-shirts, TABASCO sauce, crawfish-embroidered items, souvenir "go-cups," as well as gifts, toys, and novelties that emphasize the off-color humor and irreverent aspects of this festive town. Decatur is also sandwiched by two shopping malls: the **French Market,** which contains retail shops, food stalls, and a flea market, and **The Shops at Canal Place,** a more upscale offering beside Canal Street.

Garden District and Uptown

Magazine Street, which follows the curve of the Mississippi River for about six miles from the CBD to Audubon Park, offers an astonishing variety of shops and boutiques. Sassy secondhand clothiers, colorful oyster bars, jamming music clubs, convivial java joints, and historic homes line the way, but it's the lower stretch of Magazine—from about Canal Street to Jackson Avenue—that possesses the city's most fascinating antiques district. While you'll spot a few chain stores, the neighborhood maintains its independent, offbeat vibe. Uptown also boasts the **Riverbend** area, which features several curious shops around the intersection of St. Charles and Carrollton Avenues.

French Quarter

Map 1

ANTIQUES AND VINTAGE

JAMES H. COHEN & SONS, INC.

Established in 1898, James H. Cohen & Sons is the oldest and largest coin store in the city. Known for its vast, rather expensive, selection of ancient coins, Western-style rifles and revolvers, and other authentic artifacts, from poker chips to iron shackles, it's understandably a popular place to browse.

MAP 1: 437 Royal St., 504/522-3305 or 800/535-1853, http://shop.cohenantiques.com; Mon.-Sat. 9:30am-5:30pm

★ KEIL'S ANTIQUES

Since 1899, when it was established by Hermina Keil, Keil's Antiques has been specializing in 18th- and 19th-century antiques from France and England. The inventory includes everything from marble mantels to magnificent crystal chandeliers to garnet chokers. The Keil family operates two other well-respected stores in the Quarter, **Moss Antiques** (411 Royal St.)

and **Royal Antiques** (309 Royal St.), but Keil's has perhaps the most enticing window displays, especially at Christmastime.

MAP 1: 325 Royal St., 504/522-4552, www.keilsantiques.com; Mon.-Sat. 9am-5pm

LUCULLUS

Occupying a 19th-century building near Jackson Square, this charming shop appeals to gourmet cooks, wine connoisseurs, and avid entertainers—not surprising given that it's run by Patrick Dunne, author of *The Epicurean Collector: Exploring the World of Culinary Antiques.* You'll find a wide assortment of culinary treasures, including bronze mortars, English basaltware teapots, and Italian lace tablecloths. The store also offers decorative items like candlesticks, chandeliers, and framed still lifes.

MAP 1: 610 Chartres St., 504/528-9620, http://lucullusantiques.com; Mon.-Fri. 9am-5pm, Sat. 9:30am-5pm

M.S. RAU ANTIQUES

A family-owned, French Quarter landmark since Max Rau opened its doors in 1912, M.S. Rau Antiques is indeed one of the oldest antiques shops in New Orleans. Today, the 30,000-square-foot showroom houses a stupendous collection of 19th-century paintings and sculptures, exquisite clocks and music boxes, and striking bedroom and dining sets. If you're looking for a special piece of jewelry, you might find it here as well; precious items range from Colombian emerald rings to Cartier diamond necklaces to bangle bracelets courtesy of Tiffany & Co.

MAP 1: 630 Royal St., 888/711-8084, www.rauantiques.com; Mon.-Sat. 9am-5:15pm

VINTAGE 329

Here, you might find signed Hemingway novels, an autographed Aerosmith guitar, or an oversized golf ball bearing the signatures of Rodney Dangerfield, Bill Murray, Chevy Chase, Ted Knight, and Michael O'Keefe—the principal cast members of *Caddyshack.* In addition to signed first editions, music memorabilia, and vintage movie posters, you'll spy old maps, swords, and sports-related items, including football helmets signed by entire NFL teams. Vintage 329 is truly an oasis for history buffs, especially those with deep pockets.

MAP 1: 329 Royal St., 504/525-2262, www.vintage329.com; daily 10am-6pm

ARTS AND CRAFTS

ARTIST'S MARKET & BEAD SHOP

Literally across the street from the historic French Market, this somewhat cluttered store is filled with paintings, photographs, pottery, textiles, woodwork, and hand-blown glass from more than 75 local and regional artists and artisans, plus curious gifts and decorative items, such as snow globes and red velvet Carnival masks. Beading enthusiasts will find a large selection of glass and sterling silver beads, semiprecious stones, and beading

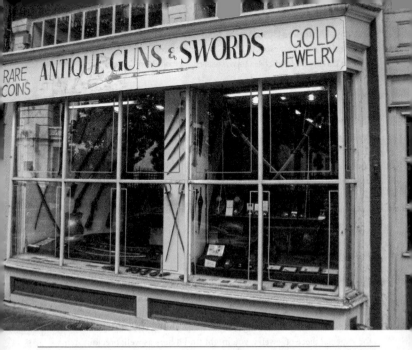

Above: James H. Cohen & Sons, Inc., a mecca for gun and coin collectors. **Below:** Carnival masks at Maskarade.

tools. Newbies can even take a jewelry-making class. The shop has two entrances; the second one is at 1228 Decatur Street.

MAP 1: 85 French Market Pl., 504/561-0046, www.artistsmarketnola.com; Mon.-Fri. 10am-5pm, Sat.-Sun. 10am-6pm

MASKARADE

A half block from Jackson Square, this charming shop presents a wide assortment of masks, crafted by artists from New Orleans and elsewhere around the country. You'll spy feathery Carnival masks, golden Venetian-style masks, and black leather masks, as well as masks that resemble creatures like ladybugs, leopards, and dragons. If, despite such a selection, you don't spot what you like, an artist can customize a mask for you—just in time for Mardi Gras, Halloween, or any other occasion.

MAP 1: 630 St. Ann St., 504/568-1018, www.themaskstore.com; daily 10am-5pm

RHINO CONTEMPORARY CRAFTS CO.

The mission of RHINO Contemporary Crafts Co. is to promote and sell the handcrafted ceramics, jewelry, furniture, accessories, and decorative arts of local talents. RHINO stands for Right Here in New Orleans, and, indeed, that's where all the goods were created. So, be sure to stop by before attending a show at the nearby cinema, located on the third floor of Canal Place.

MAP 1: The Shops at Canal Place, 333 Canal St., 2nd Fl., 504/523-7945, www.rhinocrafts.com; Mon.-Sat. 10am-7pm, Sun. noon-6pm

BOOKS AND MUSIC

ARCADIAN BOOKS & ART PRINTS

Situated on the relatively quiet block behind the St. Louis Cathedral, Arcadian is the quintessential, well-used bookstore, filled with cramped, musty pathways and stacks upon stacks of new and secondhand volumes, some stretching close to the high ceiling. Owned and operated by one of the friendliest, most helpful, and most knowledgeable proprietors in the French Quarter, this shop particularly appeals to locals and visitors in search of French books as well as titles related to New Orleans and Louisiana. Vintage postcards and art prints are also available.

MAP 1: 714 Orleans St., 504/523-4138; Mon.-Sat. 10am-7pm, Sun. 10am-5pm

CRESCENT CITY BOOKS

This French Quarter bookstore contains two floors of out-of-print and antiquarian titles, plus antique maps and prints. Open since 1992, it's always been an exceptional source for local history and literature, scholarly books, and hard-to-find titles on philosophy, ancient history, and literary criticism—a real book lover's bookstore.

MAP 1: 230 Chartres St., 504/524-4997 or 800/546-4013, www.crescentcitybooks.com; Mon.-Sat. 10am-8pm, Sun. 10am-5pm

FAULKNER HOUSE BOOKS

Hidden in the alley between the Cabildo and the St. Louis Cathedral, this small bookstore occupies the same space that novelist William Faulkner inhabited in 1925, when he first arrived in New Orleans as a young poet. It was here, in fact, that he wrote *Soldiers' Pay.* Operated by a knowledgeable staff, frequented by writers and collectors alike, and only closed on Mardi Gras Day, this charming place sells new and used books, including rare first editions, titles about Southern Americana, and literature by Faulkner, Tennessee Williams, and Walker Percy.

MAP 1: 624 Pirate's Alley, 504/524-2940; daily 10am-5:30pm

PEACHES RECORDS

A few doors down from the local Hard Rock Cafe, you'll encounter this spacious music store, which features a slew of local tunes, from traditional jazz standards by Louis Armstrong and Jelly Roll Morton to modern funk by the Meters and the Neville Brothers—plus blues, rap, and zydeco. Ernie K-Doe, Rockin' Dopsie, and the Dukes of Dixieland are just some of the local performers represented. Beyond music, there's a small selection of local books, such as travel guides, historical nonfiction, and Cajun children's tales.

MAP 1: 408 N. Peters St., 504/282-3322, www.peachesrecordsneworleans.com; Mon.-Sat. 10am-8pm, Sun. 11am-7pm

CLOTHING AND SHOES

DOLLZ & DAMES

Although the local Trashy Diva chain seems to have cornered the vintage-inspired clothing market for women, you can never have too many places to buy retro dresses, shoes, and accessories reminiscent of the early- to mid-20th century. Boasting two carefully decorated store windows that entice customers with their bold patterns, curvy bodices, and flared skirts, this shop has quickly become a welcome find for women of all shapes and sizes.

MAP 1: 216 Decatur St., 504/522-5472, www.dollzanddames.com; daily noon-6pm

FLEUR DE PARIS

The striking window displays of this elegant boutique always tempt me to linger for just a moment. Beyond the lovely, Parisian-style facade, this classic, well-renowned millinery, which opened in 1980, specializes in customized hats for various occasions, whether an afternoon tea or a Mardi Gras gala. Additionally, you'll find elegant evening gowns, antique jewelry, and, not surprisingly, classy lingerie.

MAP 1: 523 Royal St., 504/525-1899 or 800/229-1899, www.fleurdeparis.net; daily 10am-6pm

★ TRASHY DIVA CLOTHING BOUTIQUE

Not far from historic Jackson Square, Trashy Diva Clothing Boutique specializes in vintage-style dresses that suit a wide array of female shapes and sizes. Be sure to stop by the sister stores, which offer more dresses (2048 Magazine St.) as well as corsets and lingerie (712 Royal St. and 2044 Magazine St.) and old-fashioned shoes (2050 Magazine St.)—all of which can make for a killer retro look, though not a bargain purchase.

MAP 1: 537 Royal St., 504/522-4233, www.trashydiva.com; Sun.-Fri. 11am-7pm, Sat. 10am-7pm

FURNITURE AND HOME DECOR

BEVOLO GAS & ELECTRIC LIGHTS

While strolling through the French Quarter, it's hard to miss the old-fashioned gas and electric lights posted along the sidewalks, hanging beneath the galleries, and mounted beside many doorways. If you're eager to possess this atmospheric aspect of New Orleans, then be sure to stop by Bevolo. Open since 1945, this spacious showroom features an eye-pleasing variety of copper light fixtures. Bevolo has an extensive collection of antiques and reproduction pieces, including alabaster mirrors, sugar kettles, and iron chandeliers. Handmade Christmas ornaments and copper office accessories are also available. Bevolo has a second, smaller location (521 Conti St.).

MAP 1: 318 Royal St., 504/522-9485, www.bevolo.com; Mon.-Wed. 9am-5:30pm, Thurs.-Sat. 9am-7pm, Sun. 10am-4pm

JAVA HOUSE IMPORTS

This small, ever-fascinating store presents an intriguing collection of imported wares. The walls are covered with elongated African masks, the shelves are teeming with misshapen wooden bowls and Buddha figurines, and you'll see a wide array of colorful tunics from foreign lands. If you're looking for statues of Hindu deities, kites shaped as dragons, and intricately carved faces that might frighten small children at night, then Java House Imports is definitely the place for you.

MAP 1: 523 Dumaine St., 504/581-1288, www.javahouseimports.com; daily 10am-9pm

GIFTS AND SOUVENIRS

CIGAR FACTORY NEW ORLEANS

If you need a late-night cigarette fix, you can always stop by Mary Jane's Emporium in the 1200 block of Decatur, but for something more distinctive, venture to the Cigar Factory, where you can actually watch cigars being rolled. Besides various tables for enjoying a smoking break, cigar lovers will appreciate the wide selection, walk-in humidor, and knowledgeable staff. There are two smaller Cigar Factory branches (206 Bourbon St. and 925 Decatur St.).

MAP 1: 415 Decatur St., 504/568-1003 or 800/550-0775, www.cigarfactoryneworleans.com; Sun.-Thurs. 10am-10pm, Fri.-Sat. 10am-11pm

FOREVER NEW ORLEANS

Located on the first floor of one of the most photographed buildings in the entire French Quarter, this gift shop gets quite a lot of foot traffic. It doesn't hurt that it's halfway between Jackson Square and Bourbon Street. I've been

Above: the stunning window display of Fleur de Paris. **Below:** Vintage 329.

lured inside by the plethora of fleur-de-lis souvenirs, from jewelry sets to stationery to glassware. The inventory seems to change often, so it's easy to find a new trinket that you never noticed before. Not surprisingly, Forever New Orleans is especially popular with tourists, so much so that there are now four other locations in the French Quarter (301 Royal St., 606 Royal St., 622 Royal St., and 407 Decatur St.).

MAP 1: 700 Royal St., 504/586-3536; daily 9am-10pm

IDEA FACTORY

Owned by a sometimes-surly local named Ken Ford, the Idea Factory is one of my favorite shops in New Orleans. This cozy place contains a treasure-trove of handcrafted wooden objects, including clocks, mechanical toys, and chessboards. This fascinating place sells marvelous gifts, from gorgeous clipboards and odd-looking back massagers to curious puzzle boxes and ingenious cooking utensils.

MAP 1: 924 Royal St., 800/524-4332, www.ideafactoryneworleans.com; Mon. and Wed.-Sat. 10am-6pm, Sun. 10am-5pm

PAPIER PLUME

As the name indicates, this small, elegant corner shop offers a plethora of high-end writing supplies and utensils, neatly arranged throughout the well-lit space. Amid the stylish pens, dipping feather quills, brass seals and wax sticks, and leather-bound journals, you might find something to appeal to that special writer in your life.

MAP 1: 842 Royal St., 504/988-7265, www.papierplume.com; daily 10am-6pm

ROUX ROYALE

Unlike most tourist-focused shops, Roux Royale has a definitive purpose: to celebrate the unique cuisine of New Orleans. From colorful aprons and fleur-de-lis glassware to fabulous local cookbooks and TABASCO products, you'll find almost everything you need to bring the taste of the Big Easy home with you—even boxed pralines. If you can't find the right cookbook here, head around the corner to the **Kitchen Witch** (631 Toulouse St.), a bookstore that specializes in rare secondhand cookbooks, including those that pertain to Cajun, Creole, and Louisiana cuisine.

MAP 1: 600 Royal St., 504/565-5272 or 855/344-7700, http://shoprouxroyale.com; daily 9am-10pm

GOURMET TREATS

CENTRAL GROCERY

For specialty food items, there's no place quite like the Central Grocery on bustling Decatur. Famous for its oversized muffulettas—and the orderly, strictly enforced line that's required to purchase them—this often-crowded grocery stocks all manner of gourmet goodies and seasonings, from olive salad to Italian cookies to Zatarain's crawfish boil.

MAP 1: 923 Decatur St., 504/523-1620; Tues.-Sat. 9am-5pm

EVANS CREOLE CANDY FACTORY

Not surprisingly, the French Market boasts more than one praline vendor. A few doors down from **Aunt Sally's Creole Pralines** (810 Decatur St., 800/642-7257, www.auntsallys.com; daily 8am-7pm), you'll encounter one of the city's oldest such stores. For more than a century, Evans Creole Candy Factory has been crafting delicious pralines. Still today, you can watch the candy-makers working on a fresh batch of pralines through the big windows of this shop, which is also an excellent source for hand-dipped chocolates, dark-chocolate turtles (Creole pecans topped with caramel and dipped in chocolate), and chocolate-covered maraschino cherries.

MAP 1: 848 Decatur St., 800/637-6675, http://evanscreolecandy.com; Mon.-Thurs. 10am-6pm, Fri.-Sun. 10am-7pm

★ SOUTHERN CANDYMAKERS

Southern Candymakers stands out among the French Quarter's longstanding praline shops. A couple blocks from Canal Street, this is a full retail shop with pralines, toffees, nut clusters, chocolate alligators, marzipan, peanut brittle, and fudge. If you find yourself closer to Esplanade, stop by the Quarter's other location in the historic French Market (1010 Decatur St., 504/525-6170).

MAP 1: 334 Decatur St., 504/523-5544, www.southerncandymakers.com; daily 10am-7pm

HEALTH AND BEAUTY

BOURBON FRENCH PARFUMS

For more than 160 years, this aromatic perfumery has been creating custom-blended fragrances. Schedule a one-hour private sitting with a specialist who will analyze your body chemistry, assess your personality, and record your preferred scents. Once your "secret" formula is created, you can order an entire set of toiletries, including perfume, lotion, and foaming bath gel. If you lack the time or patience, you can just as easily choose from the perfumes, musk oils, and voodoo potions available on-site. Also on display are elegant perfume bottles, decorated with everything from frogs to fleurs-de-lis.

MAP 1: 805 Royal St., 504/522-4480, www.neworleansperfume.com; daily 10am-5pm

JEWELRY AND ACCESSORIES

FIFI MAHONY'S

Whether you have a Halloween parade, Mardi Gras party, or special occasion in your future, outrageous Fifi Mahony's is your one-stop salon and makeup counter if you're hoping to make a bold statement. Pop in and browse the wigs that come in every color of the rainbow, Tony and Tina cosmetics, and offbeat handbags.

MAP 1: 934 Royal St., 504/525-4343, www.fifimahonys.com; Mon.-Fri. noon-6pm, Sat. 11am-7pm, Sun. noon-6pm

NEW ORLEANS SILVERSMITHS

A French Quarter fixture since 1938, New Orleans Silversmiths specializes in modern gold jewelry, estate jewelry, and antique silver holloware. You'll also find decanters, candlesticks and candelabra, and handcrafted, sterling silver animal figurines. For a taste of New Orleans, the shop even offers café au lait sets as well as fleur-de-lis jewelry and cuff links.

MAP 1: 600 Chartres St., 504/522-8333 or 800/219-8333, http://nolasilver.com; Mon.-Sat. 10am-5pm, Sun. 11am-4pm

OCCULT AND VOODOO

BOTTOM OF THE CUP TEA ROOM

Besides offering more than 100 varieties of fine tea, this cozy shop has been giving authentic psychic readings since 1929. In fact, the name of the store is derived from its early days, when the resident psychic would read

Voodoo vs. Hoodoo

Given the Big Easy's historical ties to the voodoo religion, it surely comes as no surprise that the city is still home to several voodoo practitioners. So, whether you're seriously interested in the faith or just curious about this often misunderstood aspect of New Orleans's culture, you'll find several voodoo-related shops in town, most of which provide everything from gris-gris bags to potion oils to handmade African crafts, not to mention rituals and readings. In the French Quarter, such emporiums include **Voodoo Authentica, Reverend Zombie's House of Voodoo,** and **Marie Laveau's House of Voodoo.**

If you've seen *The Skeleton Key* (2005), you might be aware that some southern Louisianians also practice hoodoo. So, what, you might wonder, is the difference between voodoo and hoodoo? Well, depending on who you ask, that can be a rather complicated question.

The voodoo of New Orleans is similar to that of Haiti, Cuba, and other Caribbean islands, where the ancient West African religion of Vodoun has been heavily influenced by Catholicism. Hoodoo, by contrast, is not a religion, but a folk magic that blends the practices of various cultures, from African and Native American traditions to European grimoires. Often referring to magic spells, potions, and charms that include conjuration, witchcraft, rootwork, and Biblical recitation, hoodoo supposedly enables people to access supernatural forces in order to improve aspects of their daily lives, including love, luck, health, wealth, and employment. Naturally, some people also use hoodoo for more nefarious reasons, such as revenge on those who have "crossed" them. No matter what your intentions, though, as with other magico-religious traditions, hoodoo often involves the utilization of herbs, roots, minerals, animal bones, candles, bodily fluids, and an individual's possessions.

In truth, many modern-day voodoo followers integrate hoodoo folk magic into the practice of their religion. For more information about both traditions, consult Jim Haskins's *Voodoo & Hoodoo: Their Tradition and Craft as Revealed by Actual Practitioners* (New York: Original Publications, 1978), Stephanie Rose Bird's *Sticks, Stones, Roots & Bones: Hoodoo, Mojo & Conjuring with Herbs* (St. Paul: Llewellyn Publications, 2004), and Denise Alvarado's *The Voodoo Hoodoo Spellbook* (San Francisco: Red Wheel/Weiser, LLC, 2011).

the tea leaves left at the bottom of a customer's cup. This is also a good spot for tarot cards and metaphysical gifts like crystals, amulets, and wands.

MAP 1: 327 Chartres St., 800/729-7148, www.bottomofthecup.com; daily 10am-6pm

BOUTIQUE DU VAMPYRE

In a city obsessed with vampire lore and Anne Rice's legacy, it's hard to believe that there aren't more vampire shops. The only one that comes to mind is Boutique du Vampyre, one of my favorite browsing haunts. In this cozy spot between Bourbon and Royal Streets, you'll find plenty of vampire accouterments, from sexy capes and old-fashioned hats to customizable fangs and temporary bite tattoos. The proprietors, Marita and Steve, stock candles, books, soap, tarot cards, wine-related paraphernalia, and Gothic jewelry.

MAP 1: 709 1/2 St. Ann St., 504/561-8267, www.feelthebite.com; daily 10am-9pm

★ MARIE LAVEAU'S HOUSE OF VOODOO

Amid the inebriated tourists on Bourbon Street lies a small, often crowded space filled with incense, voodoo literature, symbolic pendants and figurines, locally crafted voodoo dolls, and souvenir posters and T-shirts. Opposite the register, you'll spy a cluttered, hands-off voodoo altar, while in the rear room, you can experience private tarot-card readings (daily noon-close). The folks behind Marie Laveau's also operate **Reverend Zombie's House of Voodoo** (723 St. Peter St., 504/486-6366), which offers many of the same items and services, plus a wide array of cigars. Photos aren't allowed in either store.

MAP 1: 739 Bourbon St., 504/581-3751, http://voodooneworleans.com; Sun.-Thurs. 10am-11:30pm, Fri.-Sat. 10am-1:30am

VOODOO AUTHENTICA

Owned and operated by voodoo practitioners since 1996, Voodoo Authentica carries the typical French Quarter voodoo shop items: incense, potions, gris-gris bags, ritual kits, handmade voodoo dolls, Haitian crafts, helpful books and DVDs, and unusual jewelry, such as necklaces made of alligator claws and teeth. Besides offering spiritual consultations, this unique cultural center presents **Voodoofest,** a free annual festival that occurs on Halloween and celebrates the voodoo religion's influence on New Orleans traditions through educational presentations, book signings, and an ancestral healing ritual.

MAP 1: 612 Dumaine St., 504/522-2111, www.voodooshop.com; daily 11am-7pm

SHOPPING CENTERS AND MALLS

★ FRENCH MARKET

Not far from Jackson Square lies the French Market, a picturesque, multi-block collection of shops, eateries, and stalls that partially date to 1813. Besides **Café Du Monde** (800 Decatur St., 504/525-4544 or 800/772-2927, www.cafedumonde.com) and other eateries, the market houses retail shops

Farmers Markets

the farmers market in the French Market

Farmers markets have been a part of life in New Orleans since the French and Spanish governments ruled the city in the 18th century, and they remain just as vibrant to this day. In fact, the recently renovated farmers market in the historic **French Market** is perhaps the most famous place in the city to procure gourmet edibles. Here, you'll find pralines and baked goods, fresh seafood and produce, Cajun spices and cooking kits, plus an array of freshly prepared foods, from gumbo and boudin to smoothies and sno-balls.

If you love browsing market-fresh food, also consider the **Crescent City Farmers Market** (504/861-4488, www.crescentcityfarmersmarket.org), held four times a week at different locations around town and featuring a phenomenal roster of vendors and chefs. Throughout the year, you'll spy pastries, Creole cream cheese, tamales, alligator sausage, Cornish hens, and fresh-cut flowers. Depending on the month, you might also see fresh shrimp, soft-shell crabs, kumquats, and figs. It's held in the Uptown area on Tuesday (200 Broadway St.; 9am-1pm), in the French Market on Wednesday (1235 N. Peters St.; 2pm-6pm), in Mid-City on Thursday (3700 Orleans Ave.; 3pm-7pm), and in the Arts District on Saturday (700 Magazine St.; 8am-noon). Vendors only accept cash and market tokens, a special currency that comes in $1 and $5 increments, never expires, and can be purchased in the Welcome Tent via credit card.

that sell everything from toys, souvenirs, and candies to African oils, Latin American hammocks, and local artwork. One of the highlights here is the open-air pavilion at the eastern end. It features a small **farmers market** offering bottled hot sauce, Cajun spices, homemade pralines, fresh seafood and produce, sandwiches, sno-balls, and other local vittles, plus a collection of locally made arts and crafts. There's also a daily **flea market,** which presents a wide array of jewelry, dresses, cookbooks, and African masks. Though it's rather crowded on the weekends, nothing here costs much.
MAP 1: Decatur St. and N. Peters St. btwn. St. Peter St. and Barracks St., 504/522-2621, www.frenchmarket.org; hours vary depending on the business; free, though dining and shopping costs apply

THE SHOPS AT CANAL PLACE

Situated along the southwestern edge of the French Quarter, this massive building is the fanciest full-scale mall in the immediate downtown area, with branches of such acclaimed emporia as Saks Fifth Avenue, Brooks Brothers, and Anthropologie. Other fine shops include Jeantherapy, known for upscale denim; local jeweler Mignon Faget; and Wehmeiers, purveyor of alligator boots and ostrich handbags. There's also a small food court, a Westin hotel that features amazing river views, and a movie theater that serves gourmet meals along with independent films and blockbusters.

MAP 1: 333 Canal St., 504/522-9200, www.theshopsatcanalplace.com; Mon.-Sat. 10am-7pm, Sun. noon-6pm

Faubourg Marigny and Bywater

Map 2

ARTS AND CRAFTS

NEW ORLEANS ART SUPPLY

Artists in need of supplies will surely find what they're looking for in the Bywater at this well-regarded store, part of the New Orleans Conservation Guild. In addition to art books and magazines, you'll find a sizable selection of high-quality supplies for glassblowers, printmakers, painters, ceramic artisans, and sketch artists.

MAP 2: 3041 N. Rampart St., 504/949-1525, http://nolabarkmarket.com; Mon.-Fri. 9am-7pm, Sat. 9am-5pm, Sun. 10am-5pm

BOOKS AND MUSIC

FAUBOURG MARIGNY ART BOOKS MUSIC

Located at the corner of Chartres and Frenchmen Streets in the heart of the Marigny's famous music scene, this cramped, no-frills secondhand bookshop is often still open when the bands are starting to play. Somehow fitting with its authentic environs, this eclectic store is rife with curious choices, including New Orleans cookbooks, local short-story collections, and vintage gay porn.

MAP 2: 600 Frenchmen St., 504/947-3700, www.fabonfrenchmen.com; daily noon-10pm

★ LOUISIANA MUSIC FACTORY

The Louisiana Music Factory is located in the Marigny, not far from the famous music clubs of Frenchmen Street. This noted music shop offers a great selection of local and regional blues, jazz, funk, R&B, gospel, Cajun and zydeco, reggae, swamp pop, rock, and hip-hop. This is an especially great place if you're looking for Mardi Gras music, performers of which range from brass bands to Mardi Gras Indians to the Neville Brothers. You'll find CDs, vinyl records, books, and T-shirts. This popular store also does a brisk mail-order business.

MAP 2: 421 Frenchmen St., 504/586-1094, www.louisianamusicfactory.com; Sun.-Thurs. 11am-8pm, Fri.-Sat. 11am-10pm

Above: the French Market. **Below:** Faubourg Marigny Art Books Music.

Quintessential Albums

New Orleans has long been a hotbed for jazz, blues, soul, funk, and zydeco, producing world-famous musicians. I highly recommend the following albums to music lovers, especially those new to New Orleans culture:

- ***Best of the Bayou Blues*** (2006): Born in Baton Rouge and raised in nearby Houma, **Tab Benoit** is known for his unique brand of blues, which is tinged with rock, country, and Cajun sounds. Although this Grammy-winning singer, songwriter, and guitarist has released more than a dozen albums since the early 1990s, perhaps the best primer for newbies is this compilation, which features popular songs such as "Voodoo on the Bayou" and "Nice and Warm" as well as classics like Hank Williams's "Jambalaya."
- ***Funkify Your Life*** (1995): **The Meters,** an American funk band based in New Orleans, performed and recorded their own music from 1969 to 1977. Together, the five principal members produced eight albums, many songs of which constitute this two-disc compilation. While The Meters didn't achieve the mainstream success of artists like Harry Connick Jr., you may still recognize some of their songs, including "Hey Pocky A-Way" and "They All Ask'd for You."
- ***Goin' Back to New Orleans*** (1992): Born in 1940, the world-renowned singer, songwriter, pianist, and guitarist known as **Dr. John** was raised in New Orleans—a fact that permeates his one-of-a-kind style, which combines blues, jazz, pop, zydeco, and rock 'n' roll. Filled with the kind of streetside music (also called "barrelhouse," "gut bucket," and "funky butt") that you might hear during a parade, at a voodoo ceremony, or in a gospel-style church, this album includes such classics as "Basin Street Blues" and "Good Night, Irene."
- ***Live on Planet Earth*** (1994): Known as New Orleans's "first family of funk," the **Neville Brothers** are internationally celebrated for their unique brand of bluesy funk and soul. Consisting of four brothers—Art, Aaron, Cyril, and Charles—as well as background musicians, the Neville Brothers have performed all over the world. This live album features crowd-pleasers like "Shake Your Tambourine" and "Congo Square."
- ***Louisiana Spice*** (1995): Produced by Rounder Records, this two-disc collection features such well-respected performers as **Marcia Ball, James Booker, Irma Thomas, Beausoleil, Zachary Richard,** and **Buckwheat Zydeco,** making this an excellent primer for those unfamiliar with the music of southern Louisiana.
- ***Lucky Devil*** (2010): Local old-time jazz band **Meschiya Lake and the Little Big Horns** plays in various venues throughout the city. While Meschiya's incredibly soulful voice may be the main draw, the band itself is equally talented. Their live sets consist mostly of old jazz and blues favorites,

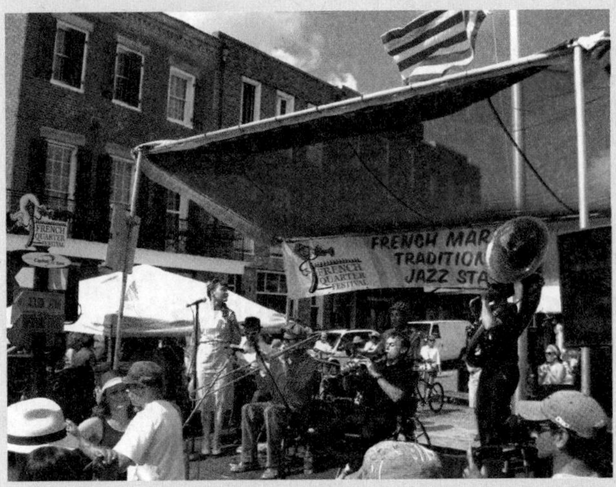

Meschiya Lake and the Little Big Horns perform at the annual French Quarter Festival.

such as "I Ain't Got Nuthin but the Blues" and "Backwater Blues," both of which you'll find on this debut album.

- ***The New Orleans Hit Story*** (1993): This two-disc compilation of Big Easy hits from 1950 to 1970 includes such winners as **Fats Domino**'s "Walking to New Orleans," **Ernie K-Doe**'s "Mother-in-Law," and **The Dixie Cups**'s "Iko Iko."
- ***New Orleans Jazz Preservation*** (1995): This album offers the experience of standing on a New Orleans street corner and watching a brass band parade by. Here, the boisterous **Olympia Brass Band** plays such selections as "Muskrat Ramble" and "This Train Is Bound for Glory."
- ***Rum and Coke*** (1993): Born in 1918 in the nearby town of Bogalusa, **Professor Longhair** performed as a street tap dancer long before he began playing the guitar and the piano. This lively album highlights not only his skills as a singing pianist but also his three principal musical styles: calypso, rhumba boogie, and slow blues. Some of my favorite renditions include "Whole Lotta Lovin,'" and "Jambalaya (On the Bayou)."
- ***The 12 Yats of Christmas*** (1998): The appeal of this seasonal album is less about the music and more about the laughs. But with locally influenced songs like "O Little Town of Destrehan" and "Norris the Nocturnal Nutria"—sung in the accent-thick voices of **Benny Grunch & the Bunch**—it's easy to see why this particular Christmas album makes me a wee bit homesick.

GIFTS AND SOUVENIRS

ISLAND OF SALVATION BOTANICA

Run by longtime voodoo practitioner Sallie Ann Glassman, this spiritual supply shop is a good place to find herbs, oils, specialty candles, Haitian artwork, decorated spirit boxes, and dashboard statues. You can even purchase custom-made gris-gris bags, made with various herbs, stones, and other materials—including a clipping of your own hair or nails. Housed within a ramshackle building along the edge of the Faubourg Marigny (admittedly, not the best part of town), the Island of Salvation Botanica also provides readings and healings.

MAP 2: 2372 St. Claude Ave., Ste. 100, 504/948-9961, http://islandofsalvationbotanica.com; Tues.-Sat. 10am-5pm

JEWELRY AND ACCESSORIES

ELECTRIC LADYLAND TATTOO

A top pick among locals, this popular tattoo parlor is nestled among some of the city's best live music joints in the Marigny. Besides state-certified tattoo artists, who are capable of inking everything from vampires to Celtic crosses to New Orleans-style fleurs-de-lis, you'll find a resident piercer on-site. Bear in mind that this is a cash-only shop.

MAP 2: 610 Frenchmen St., 504/947-8286, http://electricladylandtattoo.com; Mon.-Sat. noon-midnight, Sun. noon-10pm

Central Business and Arts Districts

Map 3

CLOTHING AND SHOES

RUBENSTEINS

If you need a men's jacket for your dinner at Galatoire's, consider Rubensteins, a classic, family-owned outfitter carrying such exclusive lines as Hugo Boss, Ralph Lauren, and Brioni. Situated in the CBD since 1924, this well-respected emporium is considered one of the finest men's specialty stores in the country, featuring suits, sweaters, jeans, and fine footwear. Special services include complimentary valet parking, expert alterations, and personal shoppers.

MAP 3: 102 St. Charles Ave., 504/581-6666, http://rubensteinsneworleans.com; Mon.-Thurs. 10am-5:45pm, Fri.-Sat. 10am-6pm

HEALTH AND BEAUTY

AIDAN GILL FOR MEN

Quirky Aidan Gill entices its loyal male customers—as well as tentative first-timers—with old-fashioned shaving instruments, upscale bath products, and well-made neckties and cuff links. Many come to experience "The Shave at the End of the Galaxy," a luxurious, hot-towel shave in the back room. There's also a location in the Uptown area (2026 Magazine St.).

MAP 3: 550 Fulton St., 504/566-4903, www.aidangillformen.com; Mon.-Wed. 10am-6pm, Thurs. 10am-7pm, Fri.-Sat. 10am-6pm, Sun. noon-6pm

JEWELRY AND ACCESSORIES

ADLER'S

Among New Orleans's many enticing jewelry shops, Adler's has the most loyal following—it's been serving the Crescent City since 1898. Fine watches and bracelets, engagement rings and wedding bands, and crystal stemware are among the offerings. Another branch is located in the Lakeside Shopping Center (504/523-1952), and Adler's is also affiliated with the longstanding Waldhorn & Adler antiques shop (343 Royal St., 504/581-6379).

MAP 3: 722 Canal St., 504/523-5292 or 800/925-7912, www.adlersjewelry.com; Mon.-Sat. 10am-5:30pm

MEYER THE HATTER

Established by Sam H. Meyer in 1894 as Meyer's Hat Box, this family-run business has since moved into a much bigger space. It now boasts the South's largest collection of headwear, from stylish Stetsons and satin top hats to jazz band caps and black-and-gold Saints visors.

MAP 3: 120 St. Charles Ave., 504/525-1048 or 800/882-4287, www.meyerthehatter.com; Mon.-Sat. 10am-5:45pm

SHOPPING CENTERS AND MALLS

THE OUTLET COLLECTION AT RIVERWALK

While The Outlet Collection at Riverwalk resembles many other midsize shopping malls, it's notable for its sweeping views of the adjacent Mississippi River. This lengthy, serpentine building has nearly 75 shops, some of which proffer local goods, souvenirs, and crafts, such as a Cajun-themed apparel store, a mask shop, and a hot sauce emporium. Discounted chain shops include Gap, American Eagle Outfitters, and Famous Footwear. You'll also find a small food court, several sit-down restaurants, and concierge desks for booking area tours.

MAP 3: 500 Port of New Orleans Pl., 504/522-1555, www.riverwalkneworleans.com; daily 10am-9pm

ANTIQUES AND VINTAGE

DUNN & SONNIER ANTIQUES

Situated in the Lower Garden District, Dunn & Sonnier specializes in flower bulbs, iron garden furniture, and eclectic European antiques, from buffets to barometers. Owned and operated by Roy Dunn and Stephen Sonnier—both of whom have been collectors for more than 25 years—this pleasant, old-world shop is ideal for those hoping to stumble upon a rare find, such as Venetian mirrors and painted toleware.

MAP 4: 2138 Magazine St., 504/524-3235, www.dunnandsonnierantiques.com; Mon.-Sat. 9am-5pm

FUNKY MONKEY

Favored by local fashionistas for more than 15 years, the offbeat Funky Monkey boutique offers new, used, and vintage clothing for men and women. Here, you'll find trendy cocktail dresses, handmade costumes, and colorful accessories, much of which is affordably priced. It's a popular stop prior to Halloween and Mardi Gras, so if you don't favor crowds, be sure to plan ahead.

MAP 4: 3127 Magazine St., 504/899-5587; Mon.-Sat. 11am-7pm, Sun. noon-6pm

LILI VINTAGE BOUTIQUE

As the name indicates, the lovely Lili Vintage Boutique invites shoppers to peruse an enviable, ever-changing collection of vintage jewelry and cocktail dresses, plus unique hats, shoes, and purses. Casual tops, dresses, and jackets are also available. Unlike ordinary thrift stores, the boutique cleans, repairs, and restores all items before displaying them in the shop. The store also ships items around the world.

MAP 4: 3329 Magazine St., 504/931-6848, www.lilivintage.com; Mon.-Sat. 11:30am-5:30pm

BOOKS AND MUSIC

GARDEN DISTRICT BOOK SHOP

Nestled in the residential Garden District, just a block south of St. Charles Avenue, this popular bookshop features both new and used titles. The selection includes regional books, art and design books, and limited editions by well-respected authors from around the country. You can also attend book signings and readings, and new members are always welcome to join the store's book group, which meets at 6pm on the second Wednesday of every month.

MAP 4: 2727 Prytania St., 504/895-2266, www.gardendistrictbookshop.com; Mon.-Sat. 10am-6pm, Sun. 10am-5pm

JIM RUSSELL'S RARE RECORDS

Founded in 1969, this spacious local institution is known for its more than half million LPs, 45s, and 78s in all musical genres. Jim Russell's Rare Records is in fact where ardent record collectors go to find the rarest and most obscure vinyl—not just because they'll usually find it, but if what you're seeking isn't here, the knowledgeable staff will try to track it down for you. Though records are the shop's mainstay, cassettes and CDs are also available.

MAP 4: 1837 Magazine St., 504/522-2602; Mon.-Sat. 11am-5pm

NEW ORLEANS MUSIC EXCHANGE

Local bands, DJs, club owners, and others flock to the New Orleans Music Exchange (NOME) for audio equipment, video cameras, and musical instruments—from Fender guitars to Yamaha keyboards to Jupiter trumpets and trombones. You have the choice of buying, selling, renting, or trading equipment and instruments, and the shop's experienced technicians can handle installations as well as repairs. If you're interested in playing the guitar, bass, piano, mandolin, trumpet, or drums, musical lessons are available through NOME.

MAP 4: 3342 Magazine St., 504/891-7670, www.neworleansmusicexchange.net; Mon.-Sat. 10:30am-6pm, Sun. 1pm-5pm

CLOTHING AND SHOES

PRIMA DONNA'S CLOSET

If you're looking for designer clothes at bargain prices, head to Prima Donna's Closet, a consignment shop in the Lower Garden District that offers gently worn, top-of-the-line designer apparel. Labels include everything from Prada and Chanel to Ralph Lauren and Calvin Klein. There's also a branch of Prima Donna's in the French Quarter (927 Royal St.).

MAP 4: 1206 St. Charles Ave., 504/525-3327, www.primadonnascloset.com; Mon.-Sat. 10am-6pm

FURNITURE AND HOME DECOR

AS YOU LIKE IT SILVER SHOP

At this well-regarded shop, you can choose from a large selection of silver holloware, flatware, and collectibles. On any given day, you might see a striking silver necklace fashioned with garnets and pearls, a pair of heavy sterling candlesticks adorned with chrysanthemums, and a small sauce ladle fashioned by silversmith and American revolutionary Paul Revere around 1770. Be prepared for steep prices.

MAP 4: 3033 Magazine St., 504/897-6915 or 800/828-2311, www.asyoulikeitsilvershop.com; Mon.-Fri. 11am-5pm, Sat. 10am-5pm

Louisiana Food Finds

Some of your most memorable—and distinctive—purchases may be edible. Here's a roundup of the best Louisiana-made products, most of which you'll find in local grocery stores:

- **Abita Beer:** Located on the Northshore about an hour from New Orleans, Abita Springs first became famous for its crystalline artesian wells. It's this perfectly pure water that's used by the **Abita Brewing Company** (166 Barbee Rd., Abita Springs, 985/893-3143, https://abita.com) to craft such classic Louisiana elixirs as Turbodog, Purple Haze, Jockamo IPA, Restoration Pale Ale, and the seasonally popular Mardi Gras Bock. Tours of the brewery are available at 2pm Wednesday-Friday and at 11am, noon, 1pm, and 2pm on Saturday; no reservations are required.
- **Blue Plate Mayonnaise:** Produced by Reily Foods Company (www.reily-products.com), Blue Plate mayo is made with local cottonseed oil and has been a favorite condiment in these parts since the late 1920s. Reily, which is based on Magazine Street in the CBD, also oversees the production of Luzianne coffee and tea.
- **Camellia Beans:** Since 1923, Harahan-based L. H. Hayward & Co., LLC, has been manufacturing dried kidney beans, the magic ingredient in New Orleans's famous red beans and rice, under the Camellia Brand (www.camelliabrand.com). Although red kidney beans are the big seller, Camellia also sells black beans, navy beans, pinto beans, pink beans, great northern beans, lima beans, garbanzo beans, and a varied selection of peas.
- **Community Coffee and Tea:** Better known nowadays for its string of festive coffeehouses, the Baton Rouge-based Community Coffee Company (www.communitycoffee.com) is, first and foremost, a coffee and tea producer. Its packaged ground coffee and bagged teas have a deeply loyal following. You can purchase these products at any Community Coffee (a.k.a. "CC's") café or at most specialty food and gift shops.
- **Crystal Hot Sauce:** TABASCO isn't the only game in town when it comes to pepper sauces. The slightly milder Crystal brand hot sauce has its diehard fans. It's made in the upriver town of Reserve by Baumer Foods (www.baumerfoods.com), which also produces sauces for steak, chicken wings, and Asian dishes.
- **Dixie Beer:** This rich, tasty beer is one of the most popular beers of the Deep South. Currently produced by other breweries, Dixie's most popular brews include Jazz Amber Light, Blackened Voodoo Lager, and Crimson Voodoo Ale. Sipping a Dixie Beer while slurping down raw oysters is a classic Louisiana tradition.
- **French Market Coffee:** Chicory, a faintly bitter herb root grown mostly in northern Europe, is dried, ground-roasted, and then blended with French Market coffee beans to create the inimitable flavor that so many java drinkers cherish. Founded in 1890 and now produced by the Reily Foods Company, French Market Coffee (www.frenchmarketcoffee.com) varieties are sold in shops and restaurants all around town.

Tony Chachere's spicy local products

- **Pralines:** These melt-in-your-mouth candies are made with cream, butter, caramelized brown sugar, and pecans. They're sold at virtually every food-related gift shop in southern Louisiana, but one of the best sources of authentic pralines is Aunt Sally's Creole Pralines in the French Quarter.

- **Steen's Pure Cane Syrup:** C. S. Steen's Syrup Mill, Inc. (www.steensyrup.com), a sugarcane syrup-processing plant in the small town of Abbeville, has been going strong since 1910. Buy a bottle of this thick sweetener to pour over pancakes or bake into cakes and cookies.

- **TABASCO Sauce:** The mother of all U.S. hot sauces, TABASCO hardly needs a description. Louisiana families are known to go through a large bottle of the stuff every month. The McIlhenny Company—based on Avery Island in the heart of the Cajun wetlands—also makes a number of related sauces, mustards, and snacks. Free tours of the TABASCO Pepper Sauce Factory (337/365-8173, www.tabasco.com; daily 9am-4pm) are available.

- **Tony Chachere's:** One of the leading Cajun and Creole prepared-foods companies in Louisiana, Tony Chachere's (www.tonychachere.com) is based in the Cajun town of Opelousas and is known for a vast array of sauces and boxed products. While the blended food mixes, such as Creole jambalaya, are especially good, be sure to check out the tasty seasoning blends, too.

- **Zapp's Potato Chips:** There's nothing that complements a muffuletta sandwich and a can of Barq's root beer better than a bag of Zapp's Potato Chips (www.zapps.com). Made in Gramercy, these super-crunchy chips truly zip with flavor. Popular selections include Spicy Cajun Crawtators, Hotter 'n Hot Jalapeño, and Mesquite BBQ.

- **Zatarain's:** A notable spice producer based in the West Bank suburb of Gretna, Zatarain's has been turning out tasty food mixes and spices since 1889, though it's now overseen by McCormick & Company, Inc. (www.mccormick.com/Zatarains). The dirty rice mix is particularly good, as are the crawfish, shrimp, and crab boils, but don't overlook such notable delicacies as the root beer extract, Creole mustard, and sausage and chicken gumbo.

GIFTS AND SOUVENIRS

BOOTSY'S FUNROCK'N

Perhaps the best, or at least the silliest, of the quirky gift and novelty shops throughout the city, Funrock'n carries bizarre and tacky knickknacks you probably never knew you needed: LSU Tiger capes, funny ice trays, Beatles' yellow submarine lunchboxes, inflatable turkeys, and face paint. There's also a branch in the French Quarter (1125 Decatur St.).

MAP 4: 3109 Magazine St., 504/895-4102; Sun.-Thurs. 11am-6pm, Fri.-Sat. 11am-7pm

GOURMET TREATS

SUCRÉ

While shopping along Magazine Street, treat yourself to something yummy from this sinful store. Brimming with candied pecans, dark chocolate bark, and signature macaroons, Sucré is sure to satisfy any sweet tooth. During Mardi Gras season, the shop offers its own unique king cakes, enhanced by a Creole cream-cheese filling. There's a new branch of Sucré in the French Quarter (622 Conti St.), and those in the suburbs are in luck, too, as there's also a branch at the Lakeside Shopping Center (504/834-2277).

MAP 4: 3025 Magazine St., 504/520-8311, www.shopsucre.com; Sun.-Thurs. 8am-10pm, Fri.-Sat. 8am-midnight

HEALTH AND BEAUTY

★ BELLADONNA DAY SPA

Hip celebs often call at Belladonna Day Spa, an airy, modern bath-and-body shop that's also a top-notch unisex spa. Set inside a Victorian house, the interior treatment rooms are soothing and minimalist, with a Japanese ambience. Detoxifying seaweed body treatments, therapeutic massages, and replenishing facials are among the most popular services, though you'll also have the option of various manicures, pedicures, and body buffs. This tranquil spa also offers an assortment of spa products and fine linens. And don't forget about the **Belladoggie Resort Spa** (815 Washington Ave., 504/309-9510, www.belladoggie.com), where your beloved pets can be pampered, too.

MAP 4: 2900 Magazine St., 504/891-4393, www.belladonnadayspa.com; Mon.-Tues. and Fri.-Sat. 9am-6pm, Wed.-Thurs. 9am-8pm, Sun. noon-5pm

KIDS' STUFF

PIPPEN LANE

Among the trendy boutiques and emporiums along Magazine Street is this whimsical shop, which, for more than a decade, has specialized in all sorts of cute, imaginative kids' apparel. Besides pajamas, outfits, and bathing suits for babies, girls, and boys, Pippen Lane offers shoes, linens, and backpacks. Kids may also appreciate the decent selection of books, stuffed animals, and classic toys, such as jumbo jacks, yo-yos, and puzzles.

MAP 4: 2930 Magazine St., 504/269-0106, www.pippenlane.com; Mon.-Sat. 10am-5pm

ANTIQUES AND VINTAGE

RETRO ACTIVE

Whether you're looking for a Mardi Gras costume or simply hoping to take a walk down memory lane, you'll do well to browse the vintage apparel and accessories at this friendly store. Opened in 1982, Retro Active offers both women's and men's fashions—from skirts, dresses, and evening gowns to ties, suits, and uniforms. The shop also boasts jewelry, vintage toys and games, and home furnishings.

MAP 5: 8123 Oak St., 504/864-8154, http://retroactivevintage.com; Mon.-Sat. 11am-6pm

TOP DRAWER ANTIQUES

With more than 7,000 square feet of showroom space, Top Drawer is one of the largest antiques shops in the Uptown area. You can peruse American and French antique furniture, from beds and bookcases to cabinets and card tables, plus chandeliers, paintings, and collectibles. Most items have been procured from Garden District homes, local country estates, and houses in rural France.

MAP 5: 4310 Magazine St., 504/897-1004, www.topdrawerantiques.net; Tues.-Sat. 10am-5pm

ARTS AND CRAFTS

SHADYSIDE POTTERY

Established in 1988 by Charlie Bohn, a former ceramics student at both Tulane and Loyola Universities, Shadyside Pottery features a veritable cornucopia of practical pottery. Pieces include microwaveable stoneware platters and mixing bowls, colorful fleur-de-lis trays and coasters, and traditional Raku vases, bowls, and urns—the latter of which were influenced by Bohn's apprenticeship in Japan. You'll even find carved, ceramic, and bronze sinks in the shop.

MAP 5: 8838 Plum St., 504/259-9179 or 504/570-6589, www.shadysidepottery.com; Mon.-Fri. 10am-3pm

BOOKS AND MUSIC

MAPLE STREET BOOK SHOP

Not far from Tulane's campus, you'll find this quaint bookstore, which two sisters, Mary Kellogg and Rhoda Norman, opened in 1965. Once a hotbed of avant-garde thinkers and book lovers, this independent shop now offers a wide array of new books, many by regional authors like Stephen Ambrose and James Lee Burke. It's a wonderful place to find used, rare, and children's books.

MAP 5: 7529 Maple St., 504/866-4916 or 504/861-2105, www.maplestreetbookshop.com; Mon.-Sat. 10am-6pm, Sun. 11am-5pm

Above: The Outlet Collection at Riverwalk. **Below:** Octavia Books.

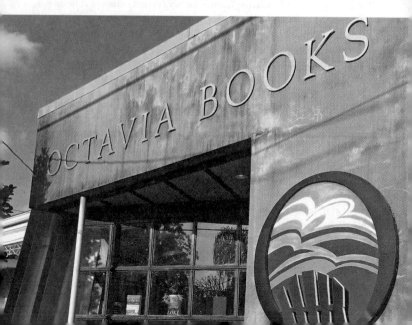

★ OCTAVIA BOOKS

Within easy driving distance of Audubon Park and Tulane University, and only a couple blocks south of Magazine Street, Octavia Books is especially popular among local residents and college students. Besides offering biographies, memoirs, and fiction, the store features plenty of local travel guides and cookbooks, as well as books about New Orleans's unique history, art, and celebrations. Stop by for regular in-store events like readings, signings, and book club meetings; there's a regular book club as well as one for science-fiction fans.

MAP 5: 513 Octavia St., 504/899-7323, www.octaviabooks.com; Mon.-Sat. 10am-6pm, Sun. noon-5pm

CLOTHING AND SHOES

DIRTY COAST

Appealing to New Orleanians with fierce local pride—as well as curious tourists—the lovingly named Dirty Coast T-shirt shop offers options for kids and adults. Designs honor such iconic images as jazz musicians, aboveground cemeteries, and other unique aspects of the Big Easy, including historic moments like the Louisiana Purchase. You can also pick up po-boy posters, Saints' hoodies and side-view mirror covers, as well as coasters, mouse pads, and doormats emblazoned with the Crescent City's unique water-meter covers.

MAP 5: 5631 Magazine St., 504/324-3745, www.dirtycoast.com; Mon.-Sat. 11am-6pm, Sun. 11am-4pm

MIMI

Encompassing 5,000 square feet in Uptown New Orleans, this high-end clothing boutique houses a remarkable collection of some of the world's best designers, including Donna Karan, Michael Kors, and Devi Kroll. You'll also find a slew of complimentary accessories. With its exclusive in-store salon, Mimi is also the Gulf South's largest retailer of Vera Wang bridal fashions.

MAP 5: 5500 Magazine St., 504/269-6464, www.miminola.com; Mon.-Sat. 10am-6pm

PERLIS CLOTHING

For more than seven decades, Perlis has stood on the corner of Webster and Magazine Streets. At this local institution, you can shop for men's, women's, and boys' clothing, from fancy styles to sportswear, plus gifts and accessories. At the branch inside the Quarter's Jackson Brewery (600 Decatur St., 504/523-6681), browsers can peruse Perlis's signature Cajun clothing, including polo shirts with the store's iconic crawfish logo—extremely popular souvenirs for tourists.

MAP 5: 6070 Magazine St., 504/895-8661 or 800/725-6055, www.perlis.com; Mon.-Sat. 9am-6pm

FURNITURE AND HOME DECOR

AUX BELLES CHOSES NEW ORLEANS

Established in 1991 by two sisters, Bettye Barrios and Anne Barrios Gauthier, this popular shop contains exactly what its name indicates: *belles choses*, which means "beautiful things" in French. After years of traveling and shopping around Europe, Bettye and Anne decided to share their love of European furnishings by selling handpicked home and garden items from the French and English countryside. Browse among lavender soaps and sachet bags, pastel kitchen towels, and vintage jugs and canisters.

MAP 5: 3912 Magazine St., 504/891-1009, www.abcneworleans.com; Wed.-Sat. 10am-5pm

HAZELNUT NEW ORLEANS

Whether you're a full-time resident or a first-time visitor, you're sure to spot something you like at Hazelnut, an elegant, eclectic Uptown shop that presents exquisite gifts and home accessories, such as towels, linens, and trays emblazoned with the St. Louis Cathedral, Steamboat *Natchez*, and other iconic local images. Other items include, but are certainly not limited to, clever salt-and-pepper shakers, eye-catching barware, and delicate chandeliers.

MAP 5: 5515 Magazine St., 504/891-2424, www.hazelnutneworleans.com; Mon.-Sat. 10am-6pm

GOURMET TREATS

BLUE FROG CHOCOLATES

Situated in a dainty, blue, wood-frame house in Uptown's Magazine Street shopping district, Blue Frog Chocolates specializes in sinful European candies and truffles. Frequent shoppers especially favor the whimsical, vibrant floral candy that's imported from Sulmona, Italy; typically filled with dark chocolate, nuts, or licorice, this graceful wedding tradition dates to the 15th century.

MAP 5: 5707 Magazine St., 504/269-5707, http://bluefrogchocolates.com; Mon.-Fri. 10am-6pm, Sat. 10am-5pm, Sun. noon-5pm

ST. JAMES CHEESE COMPANY

This well-loved Uptown store is definitely worth a stop—whether you're a dairy novice or aficionado. Established in 2006, the family-run St. James Cheese Company stocks a wide, well-selected assortment of artisanal cheeses and gourmet foods, from Oregon blue cheese to Italian salami. This delightful shop offers an array of well-attended classes focusing on chocolate, cheese, and wine pairings, and a new shop has recently opened in the Warehouse Arts District (637 Tchoupitoulas St.).

MAP 5: 5004 Prytania St., 504/899-4737, www.stjamescheese.com; Mon.-Wed. 11am-6pm, Thurs.-Sat. 11am-8pm, Sun. 11am-4pm

HEALTH AND BEAUTY

EARTHSAVERS

The environmentally sensitive EarthSavers has earned a loyal following for its essential oils, all-natural exfoliants, and skin moisturizers. The shop offers a wide array of spa services, including Dead Sea mud treatments, aromatherapy massages, and anti-aging foot and hand peels. If you find yourself in the suburbs, you'll happily find another branch in the Lakeside Shopping Center (504/835-0225).

MAP 5: 5501 Magazine St., 504/899-8555, http://secure.earthsaversonline.com; Mon.-Sat. 9am-6pm, Sun. 11am-5pm

GIFTS AND SOUVENIRS

RED ARROW WORKSHOP

The Red Arrow Workshop's Uptown location offers an ever-evolving, well-curated selection of apparel, accessories, toys, books, and prints crafted by Louisiana artists. Whether you're searching for a locally made souvenir or an unusual birthday gift, you're likely to find something incredibly unique (or at least whimsical), from baguette-shaped rolling pins and teakwood water bottles to inspiring "Not All Who Wander Are Lost" patches.

MAP 5: 3926 Magazine St., 504/309-5304, http://redarrowworkshop.com; Mon.-Sat. 10am-6pm, Sun. 11am-4pm

SCRIPTURA

Those who prefer the old-fashioned art of letter-writing will love this well-organized Uptown store, with lovely writing instruments, New Orleans-style holiday cards, and Italian, leather-bound albums and journals. You can even order customized invitations for weddings and parties. There's also a branch in the Lakeside Shopping Center (504/219-1113).

MAP 5: 5423 Magazine St., 504/897-1555, www.scriptura.com; Mon.-Sat. 10am-5pm

JEWELRY AND ACCESSORIES

★ MIGNON FAGET

Mignon Faget has an almost cult following among New Orleans's devotees of fine jewelry. Not surprisingly, Faget has won countless awards for her creations, many of which incorporate icons and images familiar to Louisianians, such as oyster earrings, red-bean charm necklaces, and fleur-de-lis cuff links. You'll find other locations inside The Shops at Canal Place (504/524-2973) and the Lakeside Shopping Center (504/835-2244).

MAP 5: 3801 Magazine St., 509/891-2005 or 800/375-7557, www.mignonfaget.com; Mon.-Sat. 10am-6pm

SYMMETRY JEWELERS AND DESIGNERS

Situated in Uptown's hip Riverbend area, just a half block from Carrollton Avenue, Symmetry Jewelers has been serving local jewelry lovers since 1975.

A variety of artists, including an in-house designer, are responsible for the lovely items you'll see, from Tom Mathis's gorgeous engagement rings to Nina Nguyen's whimsical necklaces. Interested in taking home a unique souvenir? Choose from the wide array of fleur-de-lis pins, earrings, and belt buckles. This full-service jewelry store and graphic-design studio handles repairs, restorations, and custom creations.

MAP 5: 8138 Hampson St., 504/861-9925 or 800/628-3711, www.symmetryjewelers.com; Tues.-Sat. 10am-5pm

KIDS' STUFF

ORIENT EXPRESSED

Started by two art teachers, Bee Fitzpatrick and Dabney Jacob, this quaint gift shop features an eclectic collection of antiques, amusing tchotchkes, and fine porcelain. Most notably, Orient Expressed offers high-quality, hand-smocked children's clothing, which Bee and Dabney started selling in the early 1980s, around the time that their children were born. Ranging from traditional to modern, these clothes are crafted in family-run sewing factories, utilizing fabrics from all around the world, from Vietnam to France to Peru.

MAP 5: 3905 Magazine St., 504/899-3060 or 888/856-3948, www.orientexpressed.com; Mon.-Sat. 10am-5pm

Tremé and Mid-City

Map 6

FURNITURE AND HOME DECOR

★ RICCA'S DEMOLISHING CORP.

Just south of City Park, Ricca's Demolishing Corp. is one of several wrecking companies in New Orleans that have seen a huge boom in business as a result of Hurricane Katrina. Since Peter A. Ricca opened it in 1956, this 50,000-square-foot emporium has been an amazing source of new and used building materials, including mahogany doors, fountains and hitching posts, and all sorts of vintage brackets and hardware. Some materials have been salvaged from historic New Orleans homes. Ricca's provides custom woodwork fashioned from reclaimed cypress and pine.

MAP 6: 511 N. Solomon St., 504/488-5524 or 504/482-7337, www.riccasarchitectural.com; Tues.-Fri. 9am-5pm, Sat. 9am-4pm

GIFTS AND SOUVENIRS

F & F BOTANICA SPIRITUAL SUPPLY

Curiously situated across from the Zulu Social Aid & Pleasure Club—the folks behind the Mardi Gras krewe of Zulu—this small shop has been selling spiritual candles and supplies for more than three decades. Owned by Felix Figueroa, F & F Botanica was completely remodeled after incurring damage from Hurricane Katrina. Today, you'll find an incredible selection of herbs, candles, charms, essential oils, Mardi Gras beads, and spiritual books.

MAP 6: 801 N. Broad St., 504/482-9142 or 504/482-5400, www.orleanscandleco.com; Mon.-Tues. and Thurs.-Sat. 8am-5pm

Greater New Orleans Map 7

FURNITURE AND HOME DECOR

HURWITZ MINTZ

The sleek showrooms of Hurwitz Mintz, a local fixture since 1923, are something to behold. Owned and operated by the Mintz family for three generations, this impressive store contains more than 126,000 square feet of well-arranged traditional and contemporary furniture. Though Hurwitz Mintz, which boasts one of the South's largest selections of bedroom, dining room, living room, and office furniture, isn't an antiques shop, it's a terrific place to find reproduction antiques, plus striking postmodern sofas, tables, and entertainment consoles that just might complement the antiques you already own. Even better, the prices are often surprisingly reasonable.

MAP 7: 1751 Airline Dr., Metairie, 504/378-1000 or 888/957-9555, www.hurwitzmintz.com; Mon.-Sat. 10am-9pm, Sun. noon-7pm

GOURMET TREATS

MARTIN WINE CELLAR

Although Martin Wine Cellar deserves ample praise for being the city's best wine and liquor shop and one of its top gourmet grocery stores, it also offers massive deli sandwiches. The food at the on-site bistro and deli (504/896-7350) is more typical of Sonoma's wine country than New Orleans. Step up to the bustling counter, order such toothsome sandwiches as the Steamboat (corned beef, ham, hickory-smoked bacon, Swiss cheese, onions, and Creole mustard served hot on an onion roll), and take a seat in the glass-brick dining room amid other epicureans. There are other branches in Uptown (3827 Baronne St.), Mandeville (2895 Hwy. 190), and Baton Rouge (7248 Perkins Rd.).

MAP 7: 714 Elmeer Ave., Metairie, 504/896-7300 or 888/407-7496, www.martinwine.com; Mon.-Fri. 9am-8pm, Sat. 9am-7pm, Sun. 10am-4pm

It's King Cake Season!

a traditional king cake

For a New Orleanian, one of the most anticipated times of the year is Mardi Gras season. Even if you're not a fan of the parades, the marching bands, and the drunken tourist hordes, you probably still have a taste for king cake, the season's most famous treat.

A king cake is essentially a large cinnamon roll-style cake, usually shaped like a ring or an oval, often covered with white icing, and almost always decorated with purple, green, and gold sprinkles. Nowadays, you'll also find filled king cakes, with flavors like cream cheese, lemon, and pecan praline. Typically, there's a small plastic baby—supposedly meant to represent the baby Jesus—embedded somewhere in each cake (or, for safety's sake, left outside the cake). Per tradition, if you accept a piece containing the baby, you must bring a king cake to the next gathering.

Although Christmas-style versions often appear in local grocery stores after Thanksgiving, traditional king cakes (which take their name from the three famed kings of the Bible) usually emerge by early January in celebration of the pre-Lenten period between the Feast of Epiphany and Ash Wednesday. You'll find such delicacies in groceries throughout the region, including **Rouses Market** (701 Royal St., 504/523-1353, http://shop.rouses.com; daily 6am-1am), the main grocery store for French Quarter denizens. Besides Rouses's skilled bakery, there are several local institutions known for their delicious king cakes, including **Gambino's Bakery** (4821 Veterans Memorial Blvd., Metairie, 504/885-7500 or 800/426-2466, www.gambinos.com; Mon.-Fri. 8am-8pm, Sat. 9am-8pm, Sun. 9am-5pm), **Haydel's Bakery** (4037 Jefferson Hwy., 504/837-0190 or 800/442-1342, www.haydelbakery.com; Tues.-Fri. 7:30am-5pm, Sat. 8:30am-4pm), and the seasonal **Manny Randazzo King Cakes** (3515 N. Hullen St., Metairie, 504/456-1476 or 866/456-1476, www.randazzokingcake.com), all of which provide overnight delivery anywhere in the country. Another option is **Maurice French Pastries** (3501 Hessmer, Metairie, 504/885-1526, www.mauricefrenchpastries.com; Mon.-Sat. 7am-6pm), which prepares ultra-decadent specialty king cakes like the Ponchatoula (filled with Bavarian and Chantilly creams, fresh strawberries, and toasted almonds).

SHOPPING CENTERS AND MALLS

LAKESIDE SHOPPING CENTER

If you're a fan of shopping malls, consider a trek to Metairie, which has one of the region's best options. The Lakeside Shopping Center contains more than 120 stores and boutiques, among them Victoria's Secret, Pottery Barn, and an Apple Store. Featuring several parking garages and parking lots, the mall is anchored by three major department stores: Dillard's, JCPenney, and Macy's. You'll find several dining choices on the premises, including Café Du Monde, Dat Dog, and a food court, and you can take advantage of on-site ATMs and gift-wrap services.

MAP 7: 3301 Veterans Memorial Blvd., Metairie, 504/835-8000, www.lakesideshopping.com; Mon.-Sat. 10am-9pm, Sun. noon-6pm

Hotels

PRICE KEY

$ Less than $125 per night
$$ $125–250 per night
$$$ More than $250 per night

At once classic and Bohemian, New Orleans contains a wide array of unique lodging options. (Although, given the Big Easy's reputation as a late-night party town, you probably won't be spending much time in your hotel room anyway.)

Historic hotels dot the French Quarter, like the literary Hotel Monteleone and the elegant Royal Sonesta New Orleans, not to mention smaller, more affordable guesthouses. The nearby Faubourg Marigny nurtures several funky hideaways and intimate mansions. Beyond high-end chain establishments, such as the pet-friendly Loews New Orleans Hotel, the Central Business District (CBD) houses boutique-style options like the International House New Orleans. The Garden District and Uptown areas feature elegant inns, such as the traditional Terrell House Bed and Breakfast. The Tremé and Mid-City areas encompass laid-back hostels and guesthouses, such as the 1896 O'Malley House.

If you're more comfortable with chain hotels, you'll find plenty here, especially in the convention-catering CBD, in the suburbs of Metairie and New Orleans East, and near Kenner's Louis Armstrong New Orleans International Airport. Besides standard room amenities, these often spacious hotels typically offer swimming pools, business centers, meeting rooms, and off-street parking.

Where you choose to stay will greatly depend on whether you have a car. Fortunately, staying in the main neighborhoods of the French Quarter, the Faubourg Marigny, the CBD, the Garden District, and Mid-City will ensure convenient access to public transportation, namely the streetcar lines. Note that some neighborhoods are safer than others and that not all hotels

Previous: the entrance of the CBD's Windsor Court Hotel; Hotel Monteleone.

Look for ★ to find recommended hotels.

Highlights

★ **Most Literary Landmark:** Distinctive for the enormous red neon sign on its roof, the handsome **Hotel Monteleone** has long been a favored address among American writers. Former guests have included Eudora Welty, Truman Capote, William Faulkner, Sherwood Anderson, Ernest Hemingway, Tennessee Williams, and Anne Rice (page 282).

★ **Best Hotel Service:** Situated amid the art galleries and antiques shops of Royal Street, the **Omni Royal Orleans** stands out not only for its stately historical architecture but also for its friendly and knowledgeable service. It's ideal if you're hoping to be pampered (page 283).

★ **Hottest Spot on Bourbon Street:** While most visitors favor the **Royal Sonesta New Orleans** for its hospitable staff, stylish decor, and on-site jazz club, it's also a suitable choice for those hoping to oversee the late-night revelry of Bourbon Street. From the balconies, you can even toss Mardi Gras beads to the eager throngs below (page 284).

★ **Best Music Lover's Retreat:** Just steps from the funky restaurants and music clubs along Frenchmen Street, **The Lanaux Mansion** offers four gracious lodging options in and around an exquisitely furnished Victorian mansion (page 286).

★ **Coolest Boutique Hotel:** Whimsically and creatively decorated, the 117-room **International House New Orleans** draws a hip crowd to its artful confines, which include a swanky cocktail lounge and a top-notch fitness center and spa (page 289).

★ **Most Inviting Pad for Pets:** Upon first seeing its glossy lobby, you might not realize how pet-friendly the **Loews New Orleans Hotel** really is. At this upscale spot in the CBD, pet lovers will find everything from dog beds and water bowls to pet-specific room service menus (page 289).

★ **Most Offbeat Retreat:** A departure from the many traditional, antiques-filled B&Bs in the Garden District, **The Green House Inn** delights visitors with its funky, tropical decor, flower-named rooms, and modern amenities, including a clothing-optional pool (page 293).

★ **Finest Bed-and-Breakfast:** Situated among the historic homes of the Lower Garden District, the **Terrell House Bed and Breakfast** provides luxurious accommodations in a grand, Italianate-style mansion built in the mid-1800s. The delicious breakfasts are especially memorable (page 294).

★ **Best Hidden Gem:** Many tourists miss out on one of the best B&Bs in the city, the **1896 O'Malley House,** simply because it's a bit off the beaten path in the less-touristy Mid-City neighborhood. This handsome inn is worth seeking out for its delightful owners and beautiful furnishings (page 298).

★ **Best Option for Lake Lovers:** If you'd prefer staying outside the main tourist areas, the elegant **Rose Manor Bed & Breakfast Inn** is an ideal choice, given that it lies a bit closer to Lake Pontchartrain than the Mississippi River (page 301).

welcome pets and children. Due to the 2015 citywide smoking ban, accommodations are completely smoke-free, and most of the privately owned inns have minimum stay requirements, particularly during the peak winter and spring seasons. At such times—especially during events like New Year's Eve, the Sugar Bowl, Mardi Gras, French Quarter Fest, and Jazz Fest—expect higher rates as well as the need for advance bookings. Even in the slower summer season, certain annual events—such as the Essence Festival and Southern Decadence—might necessitate a reservation.

CHOOSING A HOTEL

Given the sheer number of motels, hotels, inns, and cottages available in the Big Easy, choosing an accommodation can be daunting. Luckily, there are many websites and organizations willing to help. If you're looking for a bed-and-breakfast, consult the **Professional Innkeepers Association of New Orleans** (PIANO, www.bbnola.com) or the **Louisiana Bed & Breakfast Association** (LBBA, www.louisianabandb.com). You might also benefit from local reservation services like **New Orleans Bed & Breakfasts** (www.neworleansbandbs.com) and the **Inn the Quarter Reservation Service** (800/570-3085, www.innthequarter.com). For more specific accommodations, consider **Historic Hotels of America** (800/678-8946, www.historichotels.org) and **Bluegreen Resorts** (800/456-0009, www.bluegreenrentals.com).

Whether or not you decide to consult such organizations, it's important to keep a few pointers in mind when selecting your accommodations. If, for example, you're a business traveler, you'll likely want to stay in the centrally located CBD, which still offers easy access to the French Quarter; just bear in mind that many of the high-end chain hotels here charge exorbitant fees for parking and Internet access. If you've come for pleasure, you'll probably want to book a room in the French Quarter, Faubourg Marigny, or Garden District. New Orleans is manageable enough in size that any of these neighborhoods, in addition to Mid-City, will guarantee easy access to major attractions, stellar restaurants, and seasonal events. If you're backpacking across America, you might crave the eccentric vibe of an inexpensive Mid-City hostel, while those visiting their children on Tulane's campus or hoping for a relaxing romantic weekend might prefer an intimate Uptown B&B.

Another consideration is whether or not you expect to get a full night's sleep. Visitors with late-night intentions will probably welcome a room on or near Bourbon Street, while privacy-seeking couples and antiques shoppers will prefer a quieter place, like many of the inns in the Lower Quarter or Marigny. The rates listed are based on double occupancy during high season, so if you want to save a little money, consider visiting during the summer or fall. You also might want to take advantage of the special packages that many hotels and inns offer; depending on the deal, these can appeal to families, gourmands, romance-minded couples, and those in town for special events. Finally, most accommodations listed include standard amenities like air-conditioning.

French Quarter

AUDUBON COTTAGES $$$

If money is no object, then stay at this charming complex of 18th-century cottages. Guests appreciate the seclusion of this aging property, part of the New Orleans Hotel Collection. The clean, comfortable one- and two-bedroom cottages offer features like private courtyards, antique furnishings, and whirlpool tubs. Besides a daily continental breakfast, guests have access to the on-site swimming pool plus the Dauphine Orleans Hotel's fitness center and secured valet parking. History buffs may relish the Audubon Cottages, named after the famous naturalist, who occupied Cottage 1 in 1820 while completing his *Birds of America* paintings.

MAP 1: 509 Dauphine St., 504/561-5858 or 504/586-1516, www.auduboncottages.com

BIENVILLE HOUSE HOTEL $$$

Featuring hand-painted murals and wrought-iron balconies, this intimate, renovated hotel sits along Decatur, close to the river as well as several good bars and eateries with a more mellow ambience than those on Bourbon. (In fact, it's right across the street from one of my favorites, The Kerry Irish Pub.) By French Quarter standards, the 83 rooms are large and airy with stylish furnishings, attractive bathrooms, and upscale amenities, such as luxurious robes, 300-thread-count linens, and designer toiletries. The best rooms have an inviting sun deck; there's also a heated saltwater pool with a surrounding courtyard.

MAP 1: 320 Decatur St., 504/529-2345 or 800/535-9603, www.bienvillehouse.com

BISCUIT PALACE GUEST HOUSE $

Budget-conscious travelers favor the Biscuit Palace, a classic Creole mansion on a quiet stretch of Dumaine. Built in 1820, this no-frills inn features four mini-suites, three full suites, and one rooftop apartment, all individually decorated and equipped with tiny bathrooms. Curiously, most are named after key streets in the Vieux Carré, the city's oldest neighborhood. Though the staff is accommodating, be prepared for a funky, old-world building, in need of some renovations and safety updates.

MAP 1: 730 Dumaine St., 504/525-9949, www.biscuitpalace.com

BOURBON ORLEANS HOTEL $$$

This enormous, aptly named hotel occupies most of a block at Bourbon and Orleans Streets. It also lies within a heartbeat of Bourbon's all-night craziness, so if you plan to sleep, book a room facing one of the side streets. Even so, this historic, European-style hotel is one of the Quarter's finest properties. The rooms and suites are large and elegant, with tall windows, luxurious beds, and, in some cases, balconies. Amenities include concierge and in-room spa services, a heated outdoor pool, and valet parking. The on-site contemporary Creole restaurant, **Roux on Orleans** (504/571-4604), serves breakfast daily and dinner Tuesday-Saturday.

MAP 1: 717 Orleans St., 504/523-2222 or 866/513-9744, www.bourbonorleans.com

CHATEAU LEMOYNE–FRENCH QUARTER $$$

The hospitable Chateau LeMoyne occupies four mid-19th-century townhouses on Dauphine, one block from noisy Bourbon Street. Managed by Holiday Inn, the 171 nicely furnished rooms include period reproductions with the usual chain amenities. Some rooms are built in the classic Creole style, while others are richly architectural with cypress wood beams and exposed-brick walls. Depending on the room, balcony access may also be available. Facilities include a 24-hour business center, tree-shaded redbrick patios anchored by a heated pool, and the on-site **Richard Fiske's Martini Bar & Restaurant** (504/586-0972, www.richardfiskes.com), which offers classic Louisiana cuisine and live nightly music.

MAP 1: 301 Dauphine St., 504/581-1303 or 877/834-3613, www.chateaulemoynefrenchquarter.com

THE CORNSTALK HOTEL $$

With its distinctive, cornstalk-inspired, cast-iron fence, this gorgeous, Victorian-style hotel is a frequent stop for camera-wielding tourists. Built in 1816 and fronted by lush gardens, the historic, yellow-hued Cornstalk offers 14 sumptuous guest rooms, all of which feature high ceilings and antique furnishings. Besides the amicable staff, another advantage is the location, which offers guests an ideal spot for people-watching and easy access to art galleries, carriage tours, seafood restaurants, and late-night bars. No wonder it's lured such celebrities as Elvis Presley and Hillary Clinton and now serves as a popular spot for honeymoons.

MAP 1: 915 Royal St., 504/523-1515, www.thecornstalkhotel.com

COURTYARD NEW ORLEANS DOWNTOWN/IBERVILLE $$

This lovely, pet-friendly hotel features clean, spacious suites with separate sleeping and sitting areas, wet bars and refrigerators, and Bath & Body Works toiletries. It's ideal for families, business travelers, and small groups. Laundry service, pricey valet parking ($38 daily), and simple continental breakfasts are available. As a bonus, guests can access the pampering services offered by its elegant neighbor, The Ritz-Carlton New Orleans, whose spa (504/524-1331) features a fitness center, a resistance pool, a retail store, and an assortment of spa treatments.

MAP 1: 910 Iberville St., 504/523-2400 or 877/703-7072, www.marriott.com

DAUPHINE ORLEANS HOTEL $$

Opened in 1969, this elegantly simple hotel provides tranquility only a block from boisterous Bourbon. Inside the magnificent main building, you'll find 111 comfortable, contemporary guest rooms. The Dauphine Orleans

Legal and Illegal Guesthouses

Some of the most charming rooms in the city are found in unlicensed, illegal B&Bs, guesthouses, or vacation rentals. Many of these "underground" establishments advertise heavily online, especially during major annual events, such as Mardi Gras and French Quarter Fest. Likely no harm will come to you for staying at one, and plenty of travelers do it, so why think twice before booking a room at such a property?

First, the city of New Orleans requires all short-term rentals to be licensed, and yet it seems to make little effort to enforce this rule, despite growing pressure from community advocates like the French Quarter Citizens. Consequently, upstanding innkeepers who have gotten the approval (and paid the various fees) to open an inn are at a competitive disadvantage compared to those who run properties illegally.

Second, the main risk that you, as a consumer, face by staying at an illegal B&B is that you have little or no recourse for remedying any disputes that arise with the owners, and you have no legal protection should you be injured. Illegal short-term rentals often fail to comply with fire and safety regulations, as nobody inspects them. They also rarely carry the proper commercial insurance that is required of licensed inns, which poses a liability risk to visitors.

Finally, choosing to patronize only licensed, legal establishments actually helps the city of New Orleans. Illegal vacation rentals don't contribute taxes to the city—and worse, in a city with a high crime rate and other urban problems, they do little to foster community cooperation and neighborhood pride. Think of it this way: Every illegal vacation rental is a building that should, per zoning laws, be resident-occupied, and when neighborhoods such as the Lower French Quarter and Faubourg Marigny are filled with transient vacation rentals, neighborhood stability is lost. It's in the best interest of these areas for most buildings to be occupied by residents, or by legitimate inns where the owners live on premises or have regular on-site staff.

The easiest way to ensure that the B&B in which you're interested is licensed, legal, and adhering to proper standards is to choose one of the more than 50 properties that are members of **PIANO, the Professional Innkeepers Association of New Orleans** (www.bbnola.com), an organization that's been going strong since 2000.

also manages the 14-unit Hermann House, which features whirlpool tubs, and the 9-unit Carriage House, with period antiques and courtyard views. Other in-room amenities include bathrobes, free bottled water, and spa services. At the main property, guests can take a dip in the saltwater pool, enjoy the fitness room, and imbibe in **May Baily's Place,** the hotel bar. Concierge services, secured valet parking ($36-39 daily), and free continental breakfasts and afternoon teas are available.

MAP 1: 415 Dauphine St., 504/586-1800 or 800/521-7111, www.dauphineorleans.com

FOUR POINTS BY SHERATON FRENCH QUARTER $$

Occupying the site of the 19th-century French Opera House, this renovated hotel contains sumptuous rooms, many of which offer views of active Bourbon Street, quieter Toulouse, or the picturesque courtyard. In-room

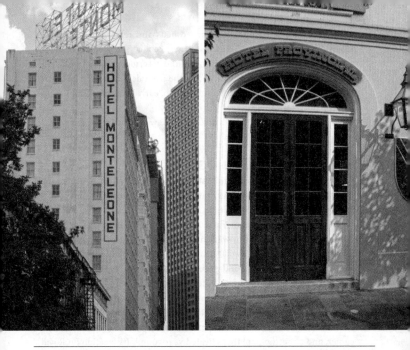

Clockwise from top left: Hotel Monteleone; Hôtel Provincial; The Cornstalk Hotel.

amenities include impressively carved beds and refreshment centers. Elsewhere in the hotel, you'll find a business center, fitness room, outdoor pool, and cocktail bar. Valet parking, laundry services, and a free continental breakfast are also available, and the front desk is staffed 24 hours daily. Given the hotel's location on Bourbon, early birds may find it hard to sleep in certain rooms.

MAP 1: 541 Bourbon St., 504/524-7611 or 866/716-8133, www.fourpointsfrenchquarter.com

★ HOTEL MONTELEONE $$$

Topped by a large red neon sign that seems to tower over the Quarter, the marvelous Hotel Monteleone is a favorite because of its rich history. This 1886 property hosted Tennessee Williams many times, as well as Ernest Hemingway, Truman Capote, and Anne Rice. You can sense the hotel's distinguished past simply by walking through the gorgeous marble lobby. This enormous hotel offers 600 luxurious rooms and 55 suites, equipped with in-room safes, marble-and-granite bathrooms, and comfortable robes. Additionally, the sumptuous suites feature Jacuzzi tubs and, in some cases, wet bars and sofa beds. On-site amenities include the stylish **Carousel Bar & Lounge,** the renovated **Criollo Restaurant** (http://criollonola.com), a full-service business center, the pampering **Spa Aria,** a modern fitness center, and a rooftop pool that's heated year-round. Its location on Royal Street is another huge bonus.

MAP 1: 214 Royal St., 504/523-3341 or 866/338-4684, www.hotelmonteleone.com

HÔTEL PROVINCIAL $$

Essentially a complex of historic buildings that includes a former 1830s military hospital, the Hôtel Provincial has been owned by the Dupepe family since 1961. The cheery guest rooms are decorated with Southern antiques and reproduction French period furnishings; some feature balconies, views of the river, or access to sunny, private courtyards. Amenities include a free continental breakfast, two swimming pools, an on-site bar, and secured valet parking ($27 daily). The staff is efficient and friendly, reason enough to stay at this upscale, family-run inn.

MAP 1: 1024 Chartres St., 504/581-4995 or 800/535-7922, www.hotelprovincial.com

LE RICHELIEU IN THE FRENCH QUARTER $$

One of the Quarter's most popular mid-priced hotels, Le Richelieu books up quickly. Contained within two historic buildings, the 69 guest rooms are clean and simple, but with reproduction antiques, varying color schemes, and, in some cases, pleasant views. There are also 17 suites with spacious sitting areas. This European-style property lies along a quiet stretch in the Lower Quarter, not far from the French Market and the Marigny. An on-site café serves breakfast all day, and there's also a lounge, an unheated swimming pool, and 24-hour concierge services. The hotel offers satellite TV, laundry and babysitting services, and secured self-parking ($25 daily).

MAP 1: 1234 Chartres St., 504/529-2492 or 800/535-9653, www.lerichelieuhotel.com

THE OLIVIER HOUSE HOTEL $$

Quirky, low-key, and affordable, this family-run hotel isn't far from the hubbub of Bourbon Street. Set within a towering 1839 Greek Revival-style townhouse and other nearby buildings, the rooms and suites boast a mixture of antique and modern furnishings. Each space has a different layout, from small, single-bed rooms to two-bedroom suites with a kitchenette and courtyard access. Three specialty options include the Honeymoon Suite, with a four-poster bed, working fireplace, and stunning balcony; the Garden Suite, a split-level space with tropical decor; and Miss Anna's Creole Cottage, featuring brick floors, a convenient kitchen, and a private courtyard. Other amenities include a swimming pool, off-street parking, and 24-hour concierge services. Children and pets are welcome.

MAP 1: 828 Toulouse St., 504/525-8456, www.olivierhousehotel.com

★ OMNI ROYAL ORLEANS $$$

With a prime spot in the Quarter—steps from dozens of great shops, galleries, and restaurants—and a wonderfully hospitable staff, this magnificent hotel obviously has a devoted following. The lavish, rambling property contains 346 smartly furnished rooms with 19th-century decor, marble bathrooms, and individual climate control. Premier rooms and certain suites feature balconies, and just about all options afford an impressive view of the Quarter. On the roof, you'll find a state-of-the-art fitness center, a heated pool, and a year-round observation deck. Other on-site amenities include a beauty salon, a full-service barber shop, a 24-hour business center, concierge and babysitting services, the cozy **Touché Bar,** and the hallowed **Rib Room** restaurant, a retro favorite of carnivores. An airport shuttle ($20 one-way, $38 round-trip) and pricey valet parking ($39 daily) are available.

MAP 1: 621 St. Louis St., 504/529-5333 or 888/444-6664, www.omnihotels.com

PLACE D'ARMES HOTEL $$

Part of the Valentino French Quarter Hotels family, the Place d'Armes stands only a few steps from Jackson Square. It's also just a short walk from those heavenly beignets at Café Du Monde. This charming hotel consists of eight restored 18th- and 19th-century townhouses, containing a total of 84 snazzy rooms and surrounding a delightful courtyard shaded by crape myrtle and magnolia trees and filled with lush plants and old-fashioned fountains. Some rooms have balconies, and all have exquisite furnishings and standard appliances. Other amenities include a daily continental breakfast, 24-hour concierge services, and a lovely swimming pool.

MAP 1: 625 St. Ann St., 504/524-4531 or 888/626-5917, www.placedarmes.com

PRINCE CONTI HOTEL $$

Housed within a regal three-story, 19th-century structure, this affordable hotel offers 76 basic guest rooms and suites, which vary greatly in features. For instance, some rooms don't have windows! The Prince Conti provides 24-hour concierge services. Given its location near Bourbon Street, this can be a particularly loud place to spend the night, so select your room carefully. Perhaps the hotel's best features are the on-site **Café Conti,** open for breakfast, and **The Bombay Club** (504/577-2237, www.bombayclubneworleans.com), a sophisticated restaurant, martini bar, and live music venue.

MAP 1: 830 Conti St., 504/561-8951 or 888/626-4812, www.princecontihotel.com

THE RITZ-CARLTON NEW ORLEANS $$$

This is the perfect choice for the ultimate pampering vacation: The Ritz has a state-of-the-art day spa and fitness center; the **Davenport Lounge,** which presents live jazz and afternoon tea service; and **M Bistro,** serving fresh, local cuisine. The well-trained staff tends to guests' every need, from valet parking to babysitting services to a free overnight shoeshine. Richly furnished rooms feature 400-thread-count sheets, goose-down pillows, and Italian marble baths. For extra-special attention, consider staying at the hotel's club-level **Maison Orleans** (904 Iberville St.).

MAP 1: 921 Canal St., 504/524-1331 or 800/542-8680, www.ritzcarlton.com

★ ROYAL SONESTA NEW ORLEANS $$$

Many out-of-towners choose the Royal Sonesta for its prime location on Bourbon Street, especially if they're able to snag a balcony room. From this perspective, you can oversee and participate in the late-night revelry, as many partygoers expect you to toss down a Mardi Gras-bead necklace or two. An even better enticement is the on-site jazz club, not to mention the hotel's hospitable staff, stylish decor, and pet-friendly policy. The 483 well-appointed guest rooms and suites feature standard amenities plus king-size pillows. Guests also appreciate the fitness center, outdoor swimming pool, spa services, and on-site eateries: **PJ's Coffee Café,** the **Desire Oyster Bar,** and **Restaurant R'evolution.**

MAP 1: 300 Bourbon St., 504/586-0300 or 800/766-3782, www.sonesta.com/royalneworleans

W NEW ORLEANS–FRENCH QUARTER $$$

The W Hotel combines the alluring pizzazz and old-world charm of the French Quarter with the modern elegance and high-tech sophistication associated with this pet-friendly chain. The 98 rooms, which include two deluxe suites and four carriage houses, are decorated in cool earth tones with pillow-top mattresses, 350-thread-count linens, wireless high-speed Internet access ($15 daily), Bliss bath products, and fully stocked minibars. Sip cocktails in the W Living Room or take a dip in the courtyard pool. The helpful staff will do just about anything to make your stay memorable.

MAP 1: 316 Chartres St., 504/581-1200, www.starwoodhotels.com/whotels

Faubourg Marigny and Bywater

Map 2

BALCONY GUESTHOUSE $

Situated above the **Silk Road Restaurant** (504/944-6666, www.silkroad-nola.com)—a popular hangout for artists, musicians, and other Bohemian types—this airy inn offers four guest rooms and one suite, all of which have hardwood floors, simple furnishings, microwaves, and mini-fridges. Two of the rooms also feature French doors and direct balcony access. The guesthouse lies only four blocks from Washington Square Park and the music clubs along Frenchmen Street. Be prepared for tight bathrooms and the possibility of noisy revelers on the sidewalk below.

MAP 2: 2483 Royal St., 504/810-8667, www.balconyguesthouse.com

B & W COURTYARDS BED AND BREAKFAST $$

To experience life in one of New Orleans's most charming and historic neighborhoods, stay at this romantic B&B set inside three mid-19th-century Creole cottages with connecting courtyards. This peaceful hideaway is a favorite with guests seeking privacy, and consequently is not suitable for children. The four rooms and two suites are decorated with fine antiques and linens; most rooms open onto one of the courtyards. In the rear patio, you can soak in a whirlpool tub under the stars. Other amenities include a small business center, unlimited local calls, and a continental breakfast.

MAP 2: 2425 Chartres St., 504/322-0474 or 800/585-5731, www.bandwcourtyards.com

THE BURGUNDY BED AND BREAKFAST $

Nestled within the residential Faubourg Marigny, this whimsical, red-white-and-blue cottage epitomizes the 19th-century, Eastlake-style shotgun doubles prevalent throughout New Orleans. Boasting original hardwood floors, 12-foot ceilings, and louvered shutters, this lovingly restored inn houses four cozy guest rooms, each of which has distinctive decor. Guests can utilize the communal kitchen, relax in the parlor, and enjoy the clothing-optional spa and sunbathing area. Smoking is allowed on the back porch or in the courtyard.

MAP 2: 2513 Burgundy St., 504/261-9477, www.theburgundy.com

FRENCHMEN HOTEL $$

The Frenchmen is an ideal lodging option for those hoping to explore the Marigny and the Quarter, as it's literally steps from the border between these two distinctive neighborhoods. This hospitable, though somewhat aging, hotel offers cozy guest rooms and spacious suites, some of which contain canopy beds, decorative fireplaces, and private balconies. Additional amenities include a free continental breakfast, affordable on-site parking, and a romantic brick courtyard with lush plants, wrought-iron tables, and a small pool and Jacuzzi. You're also close to the popular clubs of Frenchmen Street, so music can be heard into the wee hours.

MAP 2: 417 Frenchmen St., 504/945-5453, www.frenchmenhotel.com

HOTEL DE LA MONNAIE $$

The Hotel de la Monnaie promises convenience for travelers hoping to explore the Faubourg Marigny, the French Quarter, and the Mississippi riverfront. It's also a good place for families and small groups of friends, since it only offers clean, affordable suites with one or two bedrooms, dining and living areas, and kitchenettes. Built in 1984, the year that the World's Fair came to New Orleans, this spacious hotel blends traditional elements, such as balustrades, period furnishings, and outdoor courtyards, with modern amenities, such as whirlpool tubs. Other on-site features include a fitness center, a wading pool, and free parking.

MAP 2: 405 Esplanade Ave., 504/947-0009, http://hoteldelamonnaie.com

★ THE LANAUX MANSION $$

Conveniently situated on tree-lined Esplanade Avenue, the Lanaux Mansion lies within easy walking distance of laid-back eateries, famous jazz clubs, and the French Market. Built in 1879 by prominent attorney Charles Andrew Johnson, and featured in the film *The Curious Case of Benjamin Button* (2008), this exquisite Victorian hideaway offers four gracious lodging options: two spacious rooms in the former kitchen and servants' quarters, a suite in the main house, and a private cottage with its own patio. All possess sitting areas, antique furniture, and hardwood floors. Other possible amenities include kitchenettes and shared balcony access. You can relax in the enchanting garden, enjoy a daily continental breakfast in privacy, and consult the hospitable owner about the city's highlights.

MAP 2: 547 Esplanade Ave., 504/330-2826, www.lanauxmansion.com

LIONS INN BED & BREAKFAST $

Those seeking an authentic New Orleans ambience—and a bit more peace and quiet than most French Quarter hotels—will appreciate this accommodating B&B in the heart of the Faubourg Marigny. The two-story home contains 10 simply furnished rooms, and on-site amenities include a daily continental breakfast, a wine-and-cheese gathering each afternoon, and a fabulous pool and hot tub in a garden setting. Unfortunately, you'll have to rely on street parking, but once parked, you're welcome to use the available bikes to tour the city. The Lions Inn also manages a few off-site properties, including a Marigny cottage and a French Quarter condo.

MAP 2: 2517 Chartres St., 504/945-2339 or 800/485-6846, www.lionsinn.com

MAISON DUBOIS $$

Located on the Marigny side of Esplanade Avenue, this elegant yet unpretentious B&B provides easy access to jazz clubs, funky eateries, and major French Quarter attractions. The five clean, comfortable suites can accommodate up to 16 guests, making the inn ideal for reunions. All of the suites have antique furnishings. On-site amenities include a palm-shaded saltwater pool and hot tub, a well-appointed parlor and dining room, and a free continental breakfast served daily in the kitchen or sun room. The charming hosts do their best to accommodate special requests.

MAP 2: 1419 Dauphine St., 866/948-1619, www.maisondubois.net

MARIGNY MANOR HOUSE $$

Near the northern edge of this funky neighborhood, the Marigny Manor House sits along a quiet stretch that offers a wonderful sampling of vintage 19th-century residential architecture typical of New Orleans. Built in 1848, this lovingly restored Greek Revival-style house presents four color-themed, high-ceiling rooms, neatly furnished with designer fabrics, antique furnishings, and, in some cases, crystal chandeliers, four-poster beds, and Oriental rugs over hardwood floors. One room has a balcony overlooking the brick fern-and-flower-bedecked courtyard. Amenities include delicious Southern breakfasts. The offbeat bars and restaurants of Frenchmen Street are only a short walk away.

MAP 2: 2125 N. Rampart St., 504/943-7826, www.marignymanorhouse.com

OLD HISTORIC CREOLE INN $

This charming inn lies just a few blocks downriver from Washington Square Park and about eight blocks from the Quarter. A mix of single and two-bedroom suites, the inn features high ceilings, hardwood floors, and antique beds. Guests can relax on the outdoor patio, use the computer station in the parlor, and take advantage of amenities like free parking. This friendly, easygoing guesthouse is indeed one of the better values within walking distance of the Quarter.

MAP 2: 2471 Dauphine St., 504/941-0243, www.creoleinn.com

ROYAL STREET COURTYARD BED & BREAKFAST $$

Situated in the Faubourg Marigny, just a few blocks east of Washington Square Park, this moderately priced B&B with five cozy guest rooms occupies a rambling 1850s Greek Revival-style home with a wrought-iron balcony and towering 14-foot ceilings. The tropical courtyard is punctuated with fishponds, blooming flower gardens, and a secluded hot tub. A free continental breakfast is served. Children are not allowed.

MAP 2: 2438 Royal St., 504/943-6818 or 888/846-4004, www.royalstcourtyard.com

ROYAL STREET INN & BAR $$

If you're adventurous and don't mind noisy places, then you'll likely love the Royal Street Inn, a funky guesthouse situated above a popular neighborhood bar. You'll find five unique, unpretentious suites, from the cozy Marigny to the spacious Royal. All feature queen-size beds and couches;

three suites offer balcony access. This so-called "bed and beverage" even divvies out drink tickets to its overnight guests in an attempt to entice you downstairs, where the boisterous **R Bar** has a pool table, a decent jukebox, and endless opportunities to mingle with eccentric locals and wide-eyed fellow travelers.

MAP 2: 1431 Royal St., 504/948-7499, www.royalstreetinn.com

Central Business and Arts Districts

Map 3

COUNTRY INN & SUITES BY CARLSON–NEW ORLEANS FRENCH QUARTER $$

For a clean, comfortable room at a relatively affordable price, consider the Country Inn & Suites, which promises quiet accommodations within easy walking distance of Harrah's New Orleans, the riverfront aquarium, and, of course, French Quarter diversions. Encompassing seven 19th-century buildings, this historic hotel combines old-world charm with modern amenities, such as in-room microwaves and refrigerators, an outdoor pool, a 24-hour fitness center, a lending library, laundry facilities, concierge services, and valet parking, plus free hot breakfasts.

MAP 3: 315 Magazine St., 504/324-5400 or 800/830-5222, www.countryinns.com

DRURY INN & SUITES–NEW ORLEANS $$

This Midwest-based chain offers one of the best values in the CBD. Occupying a handsome eight-story building, this 156-unit, pet-friendly hotel lies five blocks from both the French Quarter and the Superdome. The standard rooms and suites feature contemporary—if generic—furnishings, high ceilings, tall windows, and microwaves. Many of the building's original details, such as the ornamental lobby staircase and Waterford crystal chandeliers, have been carefully preserved. Other amenities include a rooftop pool and hot tub, 24-hour fitness and business centers, off-site valet parking ($25 daily), a hot continental breakfast, and evening refreshments.

MAP 3: 820 Poydras St., 504/529-7800 or 800/378-7946, www.druryhotels.com

HAMPTON INN & SUITES NEW ORLEANS CONVENTION CENTER $$

This Hampton Inn differs a bit from the usual modern chain properties—it's set inside a five-story, redbrick, early-20th-century building where burlap sacks were once manufactured. Though completely renovated, the 288-unit hotel still contains original hardwood floors, exposed brick walls, tall windows, and high ceilings. Airy, spacious guest rooms, studios, and suites—some with kitchens—are available. An outdoor pool, business and fitness centers, a lobby bar, concierge services, and a free hot breakfast round out the amenities. The convention center, The National WWII

Museum, the Arts District, the Riverwalk shops, and Harrah's New Orleans all lie within walking distance.

MAP 3: 1201 Convention Center Blvd., 504/566-9990 or 800/292-0653, www.neworleanshamptoninns.com

★ INTERNATIONAL HOUSE NEW ORLEANS $$$

This stunning hotel occupies a 1906 Beaux-Arts building that once served as a bank and is now one of the coolest addresses in town. The 117 rooms, suites, and penthouses are decorated in stylish, muted tones with stereo systems, down comforters, and Aveda bath products. A 24-hour concierge and pricey valet parking are available. There's no pool, but you can work out in the fitness center and relax in the top-notch spa afterward. Given the fashionable clientele it courts, it's no surprise that the hotel's **Loa** bar is a favorite spot for the well-heeled to rub elbows. Several times each year, the ornate lobby is reborn to celebrate a particular festival or holiday that's dear to New Orleanians, from All Saints' Day in early November to the voodoo-based St. John's Eve in late June.

MAP 3: 221 Camp St., 504/553-9550 or 800/633-5770, www.ihhotel.com

LE MÉRIDIEN NEW ORLEANS $$$

Contemporary yet urbane, this pet-friendly hotel, which recently underwent a $29 million renovation, occupies a 23-story downtown skyscraper, not far from the aquarium, Harrah's New Orleans, the Riverwalk shops, and the galleries of the Arts District. Rooms on the upper floors have exceptional river and city views. Large LED televisions, 350-thread-count sheets, and monochromatic color schemes complete the oh-so-cool look and feel of the varied rooms and suites. The hotel's coffee-shop-and-cocktail-bar **Hub,** sleek **LMNO** restaurant (www.lmnonola.com), on-site business and fitness centers, and rooftop pool make this a favorite spot for young business execs.

MAP 3: 333 Poydras St., 504/525-9444, www.lemeridienneworleanshotel.com

LE PAVILLON HOTEL $$$

Constructed in 1907, this world-renowned hotel offers some of the most elegant rooms and suites in the CBD. Besides tall ceilings, mahogany armoires, and handmade drapes, you can expect terry-cloth robes, designer bath products, and minibars. There are also seven exquisite suites; each has a unique theme, from art deco to presidential. While here, relax in the stunning lobby, burn some calories in the fitness center, or take a dip in the heated rooftop pool, which affords incredible views. Also on-site is the well-regarded **Crystal Room,** an opulent, cavernous restaurant serving classic New Orleans fare and French-inspired cuisine.

MAP 3: 833 Poydras St., 504/581-3111 or 800/535-9095, www.lepavillon.com

★ LOEWS NEW ORLEANS HOTEL $$$

Part of the widespread Loews hotel chain, this towering downtown hot spot contains 285 spacious rooms and suites, featuring 300-thread-count

Welcome, Pets!

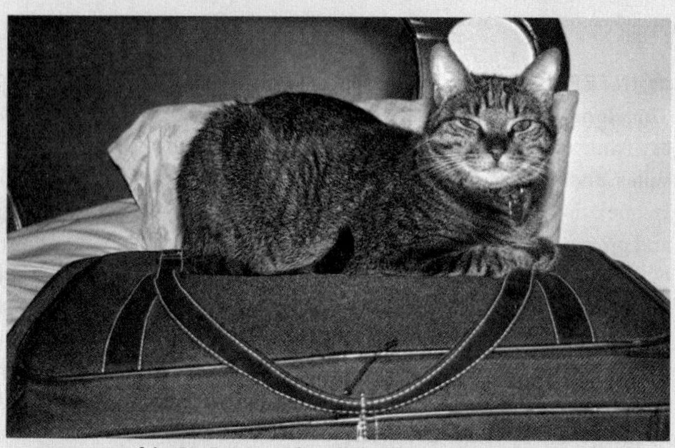

a guest at one of the Big Easy's pet-friendly hotels

In New Orleans, surprisingly few hotels allow pets. If you're traveling with your animal companion, consider one of these pet-friendly options:

Royal Sonesta New Orleans (page 284), in the French Quarter, allows pets under 30 pounds for a nonrefundable fee of $75 per animal.

W New Orleans—French Quarter (page 284) provides comfy pet beds, pet treats, and dog-walking services; however, the hotel only allows one pet per room and charges a daily cleaning fee of $25 as well as a nonrefundable deposit of $100.

Loews New Orleans Hotel (page 289), in the CBD, offers rooms specifically intended for pets, a "Loews Loves Pets" room service menu, pet-walking and pet-sitting services, and gifts such as placemats, water bowls, and special treats, plus maps of local dog-walking routes. Guests can take advantage of items like dog and cat beds, assorted leashes and collars, rawhide bones, scratch poles and catnip, litter boxes and litter, and, yes, pooper-scoopers. Loews limits the number of pets to two per room (and in the hotel overall) and charges both a $100 nonrefundable cleaning deposit and a daily $25 pet fee.

Given the city's relatively small size, you'll also find that most pet-friendly hotels are conveniently close to pet-related establishments. While downtown, you can seek emergency medical services at **The French Quarter Vet** (922 Royal St., 504/322-7030, www.thefrenchquartervet.com). If you're a small-dog owner, look for toys, costumes, and accessories at **Chi-wa-wa Ga-ga** (511 Dumaine St., 504/581-4242, www.chiwawagaga.com) or the adjacent **French Quarter Pet Asylum** (513 Dumaine St., 504/302-9845), which offers supplies for both dogs and cats. You and your leashed dogs might also appreciate **Cabrini Park** (at Dauphine and Barracks Sts.).

If you're staying in the Uptown area, venture to **Petcetera New Orleans** (3205 Magazine St., 504/269-8711, www.petceteraneworleans.com), which provides a wide array of products for cats and dogs, plus pet portraits, grooming and spa services, and a gourmet bakery. Meanwhile, visitors to the Bywater appreciate the **NOLA Bark Market** (3041 N. Rampart St., 504/949-1525, http://nolabarkmarket.com), which features a well-stocked pet shop, plus professional pet grooming, doggie daycare, and a small Barkey Park (daily 7am-dusk).

linens, all-natural bath products, luxurious robes, Keurig coffeemakers, and, in some cases, spectacular views. Other draws include the convenient business center, the on-site **Café Adelaide and Swizzle Stick Bar,** the full-service fitness center and indoor swimming pool, and the popular **Balance Spa.** Guests may also appreciate the babysitting and laundry services, complimentary shoeshine, valet parking ($39 daily), and live weekend entertainment in the lobby lounge. Pets ($25 daily) are both welcome and pampered here.

MAP 3: 300 Poydras St., 504/595-3300 or 866/211-6411, www.loewshotels.com

OMNI ROYAL CRESCENT HOTEL $$$

Intimate and nearly hidden away on a narrow CBD street, this classy hotel offers a low-key, boutique-style ambience. The 97 renovated rooms and suites of this eight-story property are decorated in earthy tones with custom-made mattresses, imported bath amenities, plush robes, and honor bars; some of the suites have whirlpool tubs, and many rooms boast floor-to-ceiling windows. The pet-friendly Omni Royal Crescent also features a rooftop sun deck and hot tub, a 24-hour fitness center, and a gourmet burger restaurant. Guests can take advantage of daily continental breakfasts, business and laundry services, and currency exchange.

MAP 3: 535 Gravier St., 504/527-0006 or 888/444-6664, www.omnihotels.com

QUALITY INN & SUITES NEW ORLEANS $$

Only a few blocks from Bourbon Street lies this retro-style building, with its hard-to-miss gray and blue outer panels. This Quality Inn offers comfortable accommodations, a welcoming staff, and a terrific location—all at a much better price than other options in the area. Amenities include microwaves, mini-fridges, and a free continental breakfast. Guests can take advantage of the on-site business center, fitness room, and indoor parking (for a daily fee).

MAP 3: 210 O'Keefe Ave., 504/525-6800 or 877/424-6423, www.qualityinn.com

RENAISSANCE NEW ORLEANS ARTS HOTEL $$

This upscale Marriott hotel occupies a five-story former warehouse dating from 1910. Its boutique-like ambience is distinctly urban—the 210 rooms and seven suites are modern, airy, and spacious with tall windows, luxurious bedding, marble bathrooms, and Aveda bath products. Guests can also enjoy the heated rooftop pool, an on-site fitness center, and the in-house restaurant, **Legacy Kitchen,** a neighborhood favorite for its creative American cuisine. Pricey amenities include high-speed Internet access ($11-15 daily) and valet parking ($43 daily).

MAP 3: 700 Tchoupitoulas St., 504/613-2330 or 800/431-8634, www.marriott.com

RENAISSANCE NEW ORLEANS PERE MARQUETTE HOTEL $$

Part of the Marriott chain, the Renaissance rises 18 stories over the CBD, with 272 spacious, smartly furnished rooms and suites. Each room features the work of local photographers, and every floor commemorates a jazz luminary. Amenities include deluxe bedding and stereos. The huge bathrooms are done in sleek marble and equipped with lighted makeup mirrors. This hotel offers an outdoor heated pool, a fitness center, high-speed Internet access ($11-15 daily), and valet parking ($43 daily). There's also a lobby bar, a Starbucks coffeehouse, and an on-site French restaurant, **MiLa,** which serves breakfast, lunch, and dinner.

MAP 3: 817 Common St., 504/525-1111 or 800/372-0482, www.marriott.com

THE ROOSEVELT NEW ORLEANS $$$

Extensively renovated and operated by the Waldorf Astoria hotel chain, the magnificent Roosevelt has exuded old-world charm since 1893. Fringing the French Quarter, this historic landmark features 369 stunning guest rooms and 135 sumptuous suites with 300 thread-count sheets, down-filled comforters, and Ferragamo bath products. This pet-friendly hotel also offers pricey extras like high-speed Internet access ($13 daily) and valet parking ($40-48 daily). **The Sazerac Bar** is another highlight of this property, as is **Teddy's Café,** a coffee lounge and sweets shop. The well-regarded **Domenica** restaurant, a rooftop pool, a 24-hour fitness center, a gift shop, concierge services, and the **Waldorf Astoria Spa** round out the amenities.

MAP 3: 130 Roosevelt Way, 504/648-1200 or 800/925-3673, www.therooseveltneworleans.com

WINDSOR COURT HOTEL $$$

Established in 1984 and recently refurbished, this art-filled structure has been ranked among the top hotels in the world. The large rooms, most of them full suites, contain elegant furnishings and Italian-marble baths, giving them the air of a posh English country home. Amenities include valet parking, 24-hour concierge services, in-room spa sessions, and authentic afternoon teas. Guests can take advantage of the 24-hour business center, the pool and health club, a stylish boutique, a rejuvenating spa, the upscale **Polo Club Lounge**, and **The Grill Room,** one of the most lavish, formal restaurants in the city.

MAP 3: 300 Gravier St., 504/523-6000 or 800/928-7898, www.windsorcourthotel.com

Garden District

Map 4

CLARION HOTEL GRAND BOUTIQUE $$

This art deco-style hotel offers fair rates, a business center, valet parking, and a convenient location on St. Charles Avenue, just a few steps from the streetcar line. The clean, modern rooms boast large windows that let in plenty of light, and all have refrigerators, microwaves, and bold, attractive furnishings; just bear in mind that, depending on your room, traffic noise can be an issue. Rates include a continental breakfast, though the adjacent Cheesecake Bistro by Copeland's also provides room service.

MAP 4: 2001 St. Charles Ave., 504/558-9966 or 877/424-6423, www.choicehotels.com

FAIRCHILD HOUSE BED & BREAKFAST $

Constructed in 1841, this Greek Revival-style home has served as an elegant B&B for more than two decades. All nine well-appointed rooms and suites feature hardwood floors and high ceilings. Guests can take advantage of free off-street parking and enjoy a complimentary continental breakfast in the lush courtyard. Situated in the Lower Garden District, the inn ensures convenient access to dog-friendly Coliseum Square, the St. Charles streetcar line, the CBD's well-regarded museums, and the antiques shops of Magazine Street.

MAP 4: 1518 Prytania St., 504/524-0154 or 800/256-8096, www.fairchildhouse.com

GARDEN DISTRICT BED & BREAKFAST $

Built in the late 1860s, this lovingly restored Victorian-style home now boasts four suites, all featuring hardwood floors, tall ceilings, queen-size beds, microwaves, and mini-fridges; each room promises either balcony or courtyard access. Guests are welcome to use the formal dining and living rooms. From the B&B, you can tour the historic houses of the Garden District, explore the shops and eateries along Magazine Street, and hop aboard the St. Charles streetcar, which runs around the clock.

MAP 4: 2418 Magazine St., 504/895-4302, www.gardendistrictbedandbreakfast.com

GRAND VICTORIAN BED & BREAKFAST $$

Get a sense of the famed River Road plantations by staying at this sumptuous inn, built in 1893 by celebrated local architect Thomas Sully. The rooms in this lovingly restored Victorian mansion are filled with antique period furnishings and named for Louisiana plantation homes, from Destrehan to Oak Alley. Whichever room you choose, expect an impressive antique bed and a comfortable feather mattress. Tall windows in the parlor overlook the clanging St. Charles Avenue streetcar, and a continental breakfast is served in the sunny dining room. Other amenities include whirlpool tubs, concierge services, and free parking.

MAP 4: 2727 St. Charles Ave., 504/895-1104 or 800/977-0008, www.gvbb.com

★ THE GREEN HOUSE INN $$

This unusual inn, set in the Lower Garden District, offers a pleasant change of pace from many of New Orleans's richly urbane B&Bs. Constructed in 1840, the Greek Revival-style townhouse has a tropical, whimsical vibe, from the palm tree-shaped, clothing-optional pool to the verdant landscaping. The flower-named rooms are well outfitted with the kind of amenities you'd expect at a much pricier hotel: king-size beds, deluxe sheets and towels, mini-fridges, all-natural bath products, guest robes, and individual climate control. Additionally, the pet-friendly inn offers gated off-street parking, an oversized hot tub near the pool, and easy access to area attractions, like Coliseum Square and The National WWII Museum.

MAP 4: 1212 Magazine St., 504/525-1333, www.thegreenhouseinn.com

THE QUEEN ANNE $$

Built in 1890, this stunning, carefully restored Victorian mansion contains a dozen elegantly furnished rooms, some of which boast 12-foot ceilings, hardwood floors, mahogany furniture, four-poster beds, and marble bathrooms. There are no elevators, and guests must be at least 25 years old. Like other inns in the Lower Garden District, the Queen Anne ensures easy access to historic homes, lovely parks, and the St. Charles streetcar line.

MAP 4: 1625 Prytania St., 504/524-0427 or 800/862-1984, www.thequeenanne.com

SULLY MANSION BED & BREAKFAST $$

The breezy, wraparound porch isn't the only inviting aspect of this historic mansion. Built in 1890 by celebrated architect Thomas Sully—the same man who crafted the Avenue Inn and Grand Victorian B&Bs—this well-regarded inn offers eight airy, distinctive rooms and suites, each named after a famous New Orleans street. All chambers feature 14-foot ceilings, hardwood floors, graceful antiques, and fine linens. Guests can enjoy continental breakfasts on weekdays and gourmet dishes on the weekends.

MAP 4: 2631 Prytania St., 504/891-0457 or 800/364-2414, www.sullymansion.com

★ TERRELL HOUSE BED AND BREAKFAST $$

Set amid the historic homes of Uptown's Lower Garden District, the hospitable Terrell House has a special connection to my family—it's where my great-grandmother spent much of her childhood. Today, this magnificent, Italianate-style mansion, built in the mid-19th century, offers luxurious accommodations, plus delicious Southern-style breakfasts. Only a block from restful Coliseum Square, this beloved B&B ensures convenient access to the shops and eateries along Magazine Street, plus the St. Charles streetcar line.

MAP 4: 1441 Magazine St., 504/247-0560 or 866/261-9687, www.terrellhouse.com

Uptown

Map 5

AVENUE INN BED & BREAKFAST $$

One of the South's most well-favored B&Bs sits along the St. Charles streetcar line, making it both an intimate resting place and a convenient home base for exploring the city's major attractions. Built in 1891 by Thomas Sully—the same architect who fashioned the equally lovely Grand Victorian Bed & Breakfast—this stunning Victorian mansion features 17 inviting, uniquely decorated guest rooms and suites, all of which have tall ceilings, hardwood floors, and antique furnishings. A complimentary continental breakfast is served daily in the elegant dining room or on the sunny veranda.

MAP 5: 4125 St. Charles Ave., 504/269-2640 or 800/490-8542, www.avenueinnbb.com

THE CHIMES BED AND BREAKFAST $$

A longtime favorite in the Uptown area, this delightful inn has just five lovingly furnished rooms facing a lush courtyard. Each has an elegant queen-size bed, fine linens, French doors, high ceilings, and hardwood or slate floors; two rooms have fireplaces, and two others have daybeds that can accommodate an additional guest. An expansive continental breakfast, a stocked refrigerator, and laundry room access are included. This is a great base for exploring Uptown.

MAP 5: 1146 Constantinople St., 504/899-2621 or 504/453-2183, www.chimesneworleans.com

HAMPTON INN NEW ORLEANS GARDEN DISTRICT $$

This particular Hampton Inn successfully combines old-world grace with contemporary amenities. While the lovely lobby and peaceful courtyard exude a classic New Orleans vibe, the spacious guest rooms and suites are decidedly modern and include microwaves. Freebies include parking and a hot breakfast. Sofa beds and whirlpool tubs are available in some rooms, and guests can enjoy the small on-site swimming pool. Situated on the St. Charles streetcar line, this hotel is ideal for a variety of visitors, from business-minded travelers to the parents of Tulane and Loyola students.

MAP 5: 3626 St. Charles Ave., 504/899-9990 or 800/292-0653, www.neworleanshamptoninns.com

MAISON PERRIER $$

Three blocks south of the St. Charles streetcar line, you'll encounter this whimsical yet elegant Victorian mansion. Built in 1892, Maison Perrier was the supposed site of a turn-of-the-20th-century gentlemen's club. In fact, the 16 spacious, distinctive rooms and suites are named after the ladies who might have entertained clients here, such as Jasmine, Claudette, and Desiree. Besides tall ceilings and antique furnishings, you can expect honor bars, blackout shades, and plush robes. Some rooms offer king-size beds, whirlpool tubs, and intimate balconies. Other amenities include a tranquil courtyard, inviting communal rooms, concierge services, free on-site parking, and complimentary Southern-style breakfasts, afternoon teas, and wine-and-cheese evenings.

MAP 5: 4117 Perrier St., 504/897-1807 or 888/610-1807, www.maisonperrier.com

PARK VIEW GUEST HOUSE $$

Literally situated beside Audubon Park, the aptly named Park View Guest House is ideal for travelers hoping to explore Audubon Zoo, the nearby

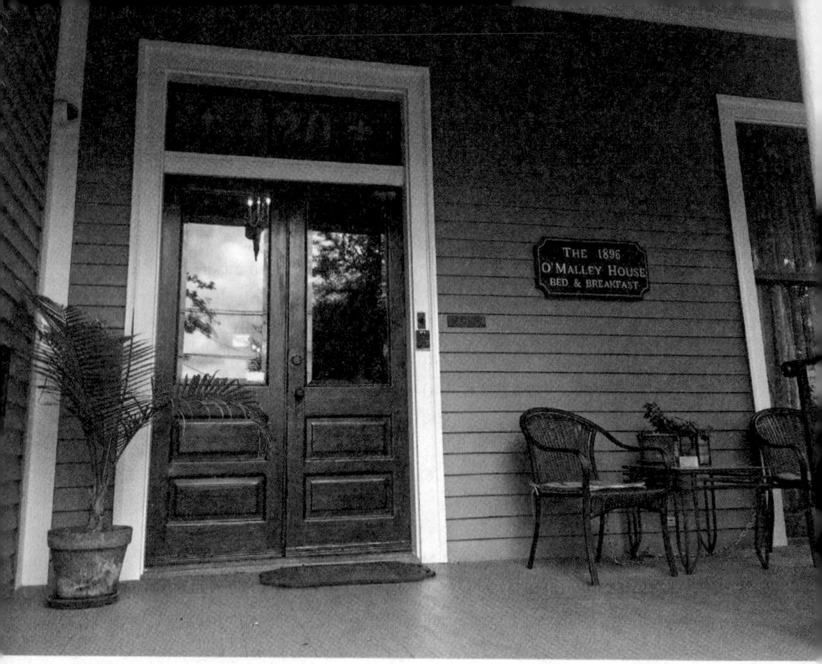

Above: the 1896 O'Malley House. **Below:** the historic Degas House.

campuses of Tulane and Loyola, and the rest of Uptown. The convenient St. Charles streetcar line is just a stroll away. Erected in 1884—just in time for the World's Industrial and Cotton Centennial Exposition—this magnificent, recently restored inn lures guests with its antique furnishings, luxurious beds, complimentary breakfasts and afternoon refreshments, and amicable staff. Relax on the inviting porch or, if you're lucky, on the upper balconies, which afford pleasant views of the oak-filled park.

MAP 5: 7004 St. Charles Ave., 504/861-7564 or 888/533-0746, www.parkviewguesthouse.com

SOUTHERN COMFORT BED & BREAKFAST $$

A couple of blocks north of the St. Charles streetcar line, this gorgeous B&B offers convenient access to the city's major attractions yet with all the ambience of an intimate hideaway. Built in 1910, this delightful cottage provides three unique guest rooms, each tastefully decorated and furnished with antique pieces as well as period reproductions. Every room features honor bars and Sonoma bath products. Guests can take advantage of the full gourmet breakfasts, concierge services, communal refrigerator, complimentary bikes, and day passes for a neighborhood gym. You might also appreciate the personalized airport pickup or free parking.

MAP 5: 1739 Marengo St., 504/895-3680 or 888/769-3868, www.southerncomfort-bnb.com

Tremé and Mid-City

Map 6

ASHTON'S BED & BREAKFAST $$

One of the city's most elegant inns sits in a laid-back Mid-City neighborhood, far from touristy hot spots. Built in 1861, this Greek Revival-style, antebellum mansion features an inviting veranda, lush gardens, a shady rear yard, and, within the main house and patio wing, eight spacious, uniquely decorated, and impeccably furnished rooms. Aptly, each room is named after events, landmarks, or other iconic images unique to New Orleans, such as Bourbon Street, Mardi Gras, and the *Creole Queen*. All have tall ceilings, luxurious linens, and individual thermostats. Secured parking and a full gourmet breakfast are included.

MAP 6: 2023 Esplanade Ave., 504/942-7048 or 800/725-4131, www.ashtonsbb.com

DEGAS HOUSE $$$

Relatively close to the New Orleans Museum of Art, the Degas House is both an inn *and* a museum. French Impressionist painter Edgar Degas lived here for about six months in 1872-1873 while visiting his maternal relatives, the Musson family; in fact, he painted several works while in residence. Built in 1852, the B&B contains six rooms and three suites that vary considerably in size and luxury. All have soaring ceilings, hardwood

RV Resources

New Orleans is a challenging destination for RV travelers. Besides the pothole-riddled streets, tight corners, and numerous blind spots—all of which are difficult for lengthy motorhomes to navigate—there simply aren't many RV parks in the Greater New Orleans area. Below are five options that might be able to accommodate you. Each of these campgrounds offers cable television, Internet access, 50-amp electric service, full hookups, and a swimming pool. In most cases, lengthy rigs are welcome. Weekly and monthly rates are often available, too.

- **French Quarter RV Resort** (565 Crozat St., 504/586-3000, www.fqrv.com; $96-250 daily): Though located in a rather sketchy part of town, between I-10 and Louis Armstrong Park, this gated, pet-friendly resort is the most convenient choice for those interested in exploring the nearby French Quarter. Besides the 52 paved sites, amenities include showers, a hot tub, a recreation room, fitness and laundry facilities, and 24-hour on-site management and security.

- **Jude Travel Park of New Orleans** (7400 Chef Menteur Hwy., 504/241-0632 or 800/523-2196, www.judetravelparkofneworleans.com; $30 daily): Situated in New Orleans East, this park is relatively far from the city's major attractions. So, if you plan to visit places like the French Quarter and Garden District, it will help to secure a bus pass or a separate vehicle. While in this gated, pet-friendly community, take advantage of the laundry area, hot tub, heated showers, and shuttle service.

floors, and well-chosen antiques; the two larger suites also have private balconies and whirlpool tubs. Other amenities include secured parking, a guided house tour, and a Creole breakfast.

MAP 6: 2306 Esplanade Ave., 504/821-5009, www.degashouse.com

★ 1896 O'MALLEY HOUSE $$

Not far from the busy intersection of Canal Street and North Carrollton Avenue, the O'Malley House is one of the more hidden, less-touristy inns in the city. It is named for one of New Orleans's most prominent Irish citizens of the late 19th century, Dominick O'Malley—a newspaper publisher credited with exposing the corruption of local politicos. This gracious, Colonial Revival-style mansion features original cypress-wood mantels, pocket doors, and other artful details. The eight sumptuous suites are filled with exceptional antiques, handsome Oriental rugs, plush four-poster beds, and elegant tables. Most rooms have whirlpool tubs. Run by exceedingly hospitable hosts, the house lies within walking distance of several restaurants and just steps from the Canal streetcar line, which links City Park to the French Quarter. An especially bounteous continental breakfast is included.

MAP 6: 120 S. Pierce St., 504/488-5896 or 866/226-1896, www.1896omalleyhouse.com

- **Mardi Gras RV Park & Campground** (6050 Chef Menteur Hwy., 504/243-0433 or 800/290-0085, www.mardigrasrvparkandmotel.com; $20-25 daily): Adjacent to a Red Carpet Inn & Suites in New Orleans East, this gated, pet-friendly campground lies within easy driving distance of the French Quarter. Offering 100 grassy and paved lots (including tent and pull-through sites), the park also provides a convenience store, meeting and exercise rooms, laundry and dining areas, gas and dump stations, barbecue facilities, phone access, and 24-hour surveillance and patrol.

- **New Orleans West KOA** (11129 Jefferson Hwy., River Ridge, 504/467-1792 or 800/562-5110, www.koa.com; $43-53 daily): This family-friendly park is an ideal option for those hoping to explore the suburbs west of the city as well as the plantations along River Road. Whether you bring an RV or a tent, you'll have access to on-site activities, propane gas, a tour shuttle bus, and nearby golf courses and fishing opportunities.

- **Pontchartrain Landing** (6001 France Rd., 504/286-8157 or 877/376-7850, www.pontchartrainlanding.com; $57-153 daily): As the name implies, this waterfront campground offers easy access to Lake Pontchartrain, which should appeal to boaters, anglers, and other water enthusiasts. This well-lit, gated community offers 125 sites (some of which have pull-through capabilities), 24-hour camera surveillance, 24-hour laundry access, a convenience store, a bar and seafood restaurant, a playground, a boat launch ramp, a dumping station, showers, propane gas, shuttle service to the French Quarter, furnished villas and campers, and proximity to a full-service marina.

FIVE CONTINENTS BED AND BREAKFAST $$

Admittedly not in the best part of town, the Five Continents B&B is nevertheless one of New Orleans's more well-respected inns. The name derives from the fact that the former and current owners have all traveled to at least five continents. Housed within a two-story, Greek Revival-style home built in the late 1880s, the inn features tall ceilings, crystal chandeliers, hardwood floors, and Oriental rugs. The four uniquely decorated two-room suites, situated in the main house or the pet-friendly garden cottage, boast continent-specific artwork, antique furnishings, ecofriendly toiletries, and luxurious linens. A gourmet breakfast is included.

MAP 6: 1731 Esplanade Ave., 504/324-8594, www.fivecontinentsbnb.com

HH WHITNEY HOUSE $$

Roughly eight blocks from the French Quarter, this Italianate-style home is adorned with ceiling medallions, elegant archways, antique Victorian furnishings, and numerous fireplaces. There are two suites and three well-appointed rooms, one of which is dedicated to Scarlett O'Hara. Besides standard amenities, this handsome inn offers private balconies, off-street parking, complimentary refreshments, and a full breakfast. Guests particularly relish the relaxing courtyard, swimming pool, and hot tub. Despite the inn's relative proximity to the Quarter, it's not advisable to walk through or alongside the Tremé at night.

MAP 6: 1923 Esplanade Ave., 504/948-9448 or 877/944-9448, www.hhwhitneyhouse.com

INDIA HOUSE HOSTEL $

In a city with few hostel options, budget-conscious travelers will find a lot to love about India House. Just off Canal Street, this lively Mid-City hostel offers a fully equipped kitchen, a relaxing rear courtyard and swimming pool, spacious common areas, both dorms and private rooms, plus discounted tour tickets. The hostel has no curfew, and all facilities are available 24 hours daily. Band nights, movie screenings, crawfish boils, and barbecues occur often, so it can definitely be noisy. Happily, though, you're sure to meet lots of kooky characters, and the streetcar line is just a short stroll away.

MAP 6: 124 S. Lopez St., 504/821-1904 or 504/324-4365, http://indiahousehostel.com

MONROSE ROW BED & BREAKFAST $$

The Greek Revival-style building that now houses the intimate Monrose Row Bed & Breakfast was originally constructed in 1839 for local baker Charles Monrose. Today, the carefully restored inn offers three individually decorated two-room suites with antique furnishings. Two of the rooms overlook the charming courtyard, while the third occupies the entire third floor of the main house. A continental breakfast is included.

MAP 6: 1303 Gov. Nicholls St., 504/524-4950, www.monroserow.com

NEW ORLEANS GUESTHOUSE $

With its lush, peaceful courtyard, the somewhat aging New Orleans Guesthouse serves as a popular, yet intimate, hideaway for budget travelers. The 14 guest rooms have high ceilings, antique furnishings, and, in many cases, vibrant color schemes. Although the privately owned inn lies within walking distance of the French Quarter, its dicey Tremé location means it's better to rely on taxis or bring your own car—which you can park in the small but secured on-site lot.

MAP 6: 1118 Ursulines Ave., 504/566-1179 or 800/562-1177, http://neworleansguest.house

COMFORT SUITES AIRPORT $$

In general, lodging options near the Louis Armstrong New Orleans International Airport constitute a variety of chain hotels, including this affordable property just off the interstate. The 95 spacious guest rooms have mini-fridges and satellite TV. You'll also find an indoor/outdoor pool, a hot tub, and an exercise room. Free airport transportation, on-site parking, and a continental breakfast are included.

MAP 7: 2710 Idaho Ave., Kenner, 504/466-6066 or 877/424-6423, www.choicehotels.com

HOUSE OF THE RISING SUN BED AND BREAKFAST $

Erected in 1896 and named after the fictitious brothel immortalized by the Animals' 1964 recording, this renovated hideaway features two unique lodging options: the Asian-style "Red" Allen room, honoring the local jazz trumpeter, and the smaller "Memphis Minnie" room, inspired by the Algiers-born blues singer. Both options include access to relaxing porches and a continental breakfast. Guests can easily walk to the free ferry that makes frequent trips across the Mississippi River to downtown New Orleans.

MAP 7: 335 Pelican Ave., Algiers Point, 504/231-6498, www.risingsunbnb.com

★ ROSE MANOR BED & BREAKFAST INN $

Nestled in the Lakeview neighborhood that was so famously flooded by Hurricane Katrina, this B&B is an ideal choice for those interested in exploring City Park, Lake Pontchartrain, and the nearby town of Metairie. Offering 10 spacious, uniquely decorated rooms and suites, the intimate Rose Manor epitomizes a medley of old and new, with its old-fashioned dining room and antique furnishings. The free, on-site parking is another big plus.

MAP 7: 7214 Pontchartrain Blvd., 504/282-8200, www.rosemanor.com

Excursions

Southern Louisiana encompasses the Northshore, the Great River Road, Baton Rouge, Cajun Country, and the swamps and bayous south of New Orleans.

This region extends about 200 miles east to west along the Interstate 10 (I-10) corridor, and only about 75 miles north to south. While it's fairly large, the most-visited areas are easily accessible from New Orleans, especially if you have your own vehicle. Most towns lie less than 90 minutes from the Big Easy, via I-10, US-90, or the 24-mile-long Causeway bridge.

Separated from New Orleans by enormous Lake Pontchartrain, the Northshore comprises a string of middle-class and upscale suburbs, north of which lies a patchwork of rural, wooded towns extending about 40 miles to the Mississippi border. This is one of Louisiana's top areas for golfing, bird-watching, biking, canoeing, kayaking, and fishing. Hidden gems here include the Global Wildlife Center and Pontchartrain Vineyards.

In southern Louisiana, the Great River Road actually refers to a series of byways running along both sides of the Mississippi River, from New Orleans through the rural plantation country northwest of the city, then on to Baton Rouge and up to charming St. Francisville, the quintessential antebellum Southern town. This region is rife with plantation homes, from relatively modest raised cottages to enormous Greek Revival-style wedding cakes amid 300-year-old, moss-draped live oak trees.

As the city's state capital, Baton Rouge makes a great base for exploring the entire length of Louisiana's Great River Road, but it also has a number of worthwhile attractions of its own, plus a wide range of affordable restaurants and chain hotels. Beyond Baton Rouge, Louisiana's Cajun Country is one of the most visited and most intriguing parts of the state. Although

Previous: Shadows-on-the-Teche, in Cajun Country; Bayou Teche.

Excursions

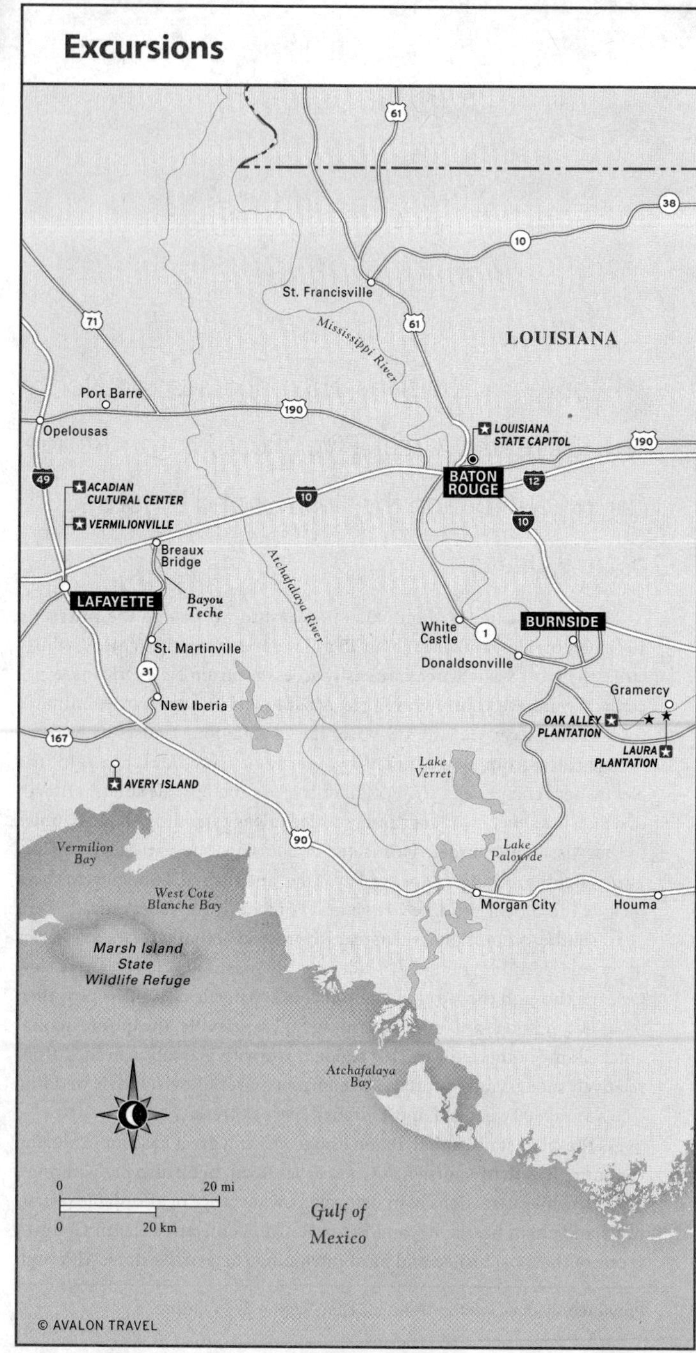

61
38
10
St. Francisville
71
61
Mississippi River
LOUISIANA
Port Barre
190
Opelousas
LOUISIANA STATE CAPITOL
190
49
ACADIAN CULTURAL CENTER
BATON ROUGE
12
10
VERMILIONVILLE
10
Breaux Bridge
Atchafalaya River
LAFAYETTE
Bayou Teche
White Castle
BURNSIDE
1
St. Martinville
Donaldsonville
31
Gramercy
New Iberia
OAK ALLEY PLANTATION
167
LAURA PLANTATION
Lake Verret
AVERY ISLAND
90
Lake Palourde
Vermilion Bay
West Cote Blanche Bay
Morgan City
Houma
Marsh Island State Wildlife Refuge
Atchafalaya Bay
0
20 mi
0
20 km
Gulf of Mexico
© AVALON TRAVEL

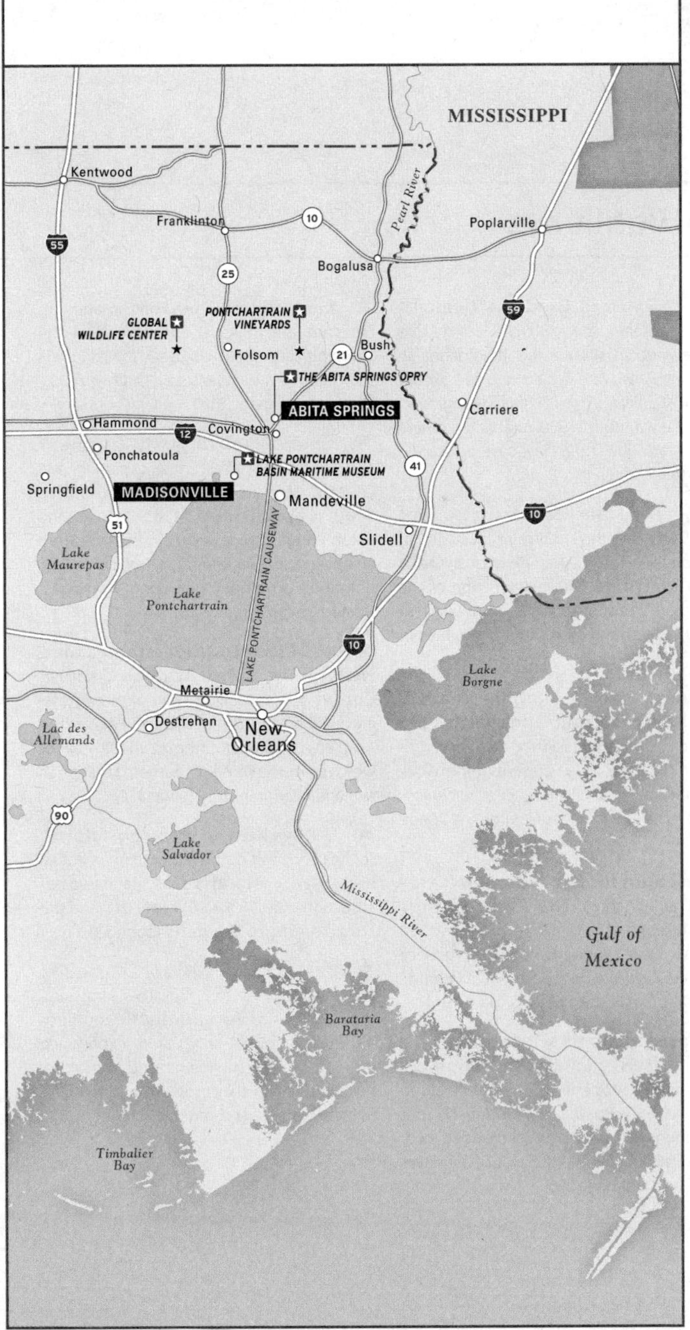
MISSISSIPPI
Kentwood
Franklinton
10
Poplarville
Pearl River
55
Bogalusa
25
59
PONTCHARTRAIN VINEYARDS
GLOBAL WILDLIFE CENTER
Folsom
21
Bush
THE ABITA SPRINGS OPRY
ABITA SPRINGS
Carriere
Hammond
12
Covington
Ponchatoula
LAKE PONTCHARTRAIN BASIN MARITIME MUSEUM
41
Springfield
MADISONVILLE
Mandeville
10
51
Slidell
Lake Maurepas
Lake Pontchartrain
LAKE PONTCHARTRAIN CAUSEWAY
10
Lake Borgne
Metairie
Destrehan
New Orleans
Lac des Allemands
90
Lake Salvador
Mississippi River
Gulf of Mexico
Barataria Bay
Timbalier Bay

Look for ★ to find recommended sights and activities.

Highlights

★ **Best Place to Feed the Animals:** Don't mistake the **Global Wildlife Center,** which sits on the Tangipahoa-St. Tammany Parish line, for a mere zoo. About 3,000 wild animals, from zebras to kangaroos, roam freely amid the 900 rural acres, where visitors can view them via covered-wagon safaris (page 308).

★ **Best Locale to Learn About the Sea:** In the charming village of Madisonville, the **Lake Pontchartrain Basin Maritime Museum** is one of the Northshore's best attractions, with excellent exhibits on the region's maritime history (page 308).

★ **Finest Place to Imbibe:** Not only does **Pontchartrain Vineyards,** just north of Covington, produce the finest vintages in the state, it also presents informative classes, popular concerts, and other enjoyable events on its bucolic grounds (page 309).

★ **Best Spot for Boot-Stompin':** A rollicking variety show, **The Abita Springs Opry** takes place once a month in the spring and fall. Hear wonderful country, gospel, bluegrass, Cajun, zydeco, Irish, and folk music in a quaint, small-town setting (page 310).

★ **Most Fascinating Plantation:** The engaging tours of **Laura Plantation** distinguish this property from others along the Great River Road. Learn about the four generations of women who presided over the plantation as well as the lives of the slaves who lived here (page 316).

★ **Best Photo-Op:** Few images in Louisiana are more recognizable than the stunning alley of live oak trees that brackets the Greek Revival-style home at **Oak Alley Plantation** (page 318).

★ **Coolest-Looking Government Building:** The tallest state capitol in the country, the art deco-style **Louisiana State Capitol** soars 34 stories over the Baton Rouge skyline. View the scenery from an observation deck—and see exactly where notorious Governor Huey Long was assassinated (page 325).

★ **Best Place to Understand Cajun History:** The modern **Acadian Cultural Center** tells the Cajun story with engrossing exhibits and an excellent movie on the Acadian banishment from Canada—all of which provide a sense of southern Louisiana's rich and moving history (page 330).

★ **Loveliest Pseudo-Island:** Technically a salt dome rather than an actual island, **Avery Island** is is the site of two key attractions: the **TABASCO factory** and the 170-acre **Jungle Gardens** (page 331).

★ **Best Living History Museum:** Louisiana's answer to Colonial Williamsburg, the fascinating **Vermilionville** outdoor museum recounts the Cajun experience through historic buildings and reproductions, music-and-dance presentations, crafts demonstrations, and regional cuisine (page 334).

several inland and coastal towns compose this lively region, its geographical and cultural center is the city of Lafayette, an ideal place to begin your explorations, as it has several excellent museums that interpret and introduce the heritage of the Cajun people.

PLANNING YOUR TIME

As with New Orleans, spring and fall are the most popular seasons for visiting southern Louisiana. If you only have a little time to spare, head to the **Northshore.** Though you could spend an entire weekend exploring the parks, communities, and other diversions north of Lake Pontchartrain, you can easily hit the highlights, such as the Abita Brewery, in less than a day.

From the Big Easy, you can also spend an entire day—if not a long weekend—touring the plantations along the **Great River Road,** from Destrehan to St. Francisville, about two hours from New Orleans. A day trip to **Baton Rouge** is more than feasible, especially if you focus on key attractions like the Louisiana State Capitol building and the USS *Kidd* Veterans Museum.

Cajun Country, which extends from Houma to Lafayette and beyond, is a more complicated endeavor. To get the most out of this region, plan at least two days. Most visitors head first to Lafayette, which lies about 2.5 hours northwest of New Orleans via I-10. As an alternative, you can take US-90 to Lafayette through the towns of Morgan City and New Iberia—a route that may require about three hours.

The Northshore

Mainly divided into St. Tammany and Tangipahoa Parishes, the Northshore might be less famous than New Orleans, but while its most prominent communities—Slidell, Mandeville, Covington, Madisonville, Ponchatoula, and Hammond—all contain their share of gated communities and strip shopping malls, they're also a treasure trove of nature preserves, tranquil forests, and funky historical districts. Diversions here include touring a brewery, shopping for antiques, and visiting assorted museums and wildlife attractions. The architecture, topography, and even climate are distinct from the rest of southern Louisiana, bearing a closer resemblance to the charming vintage towns of Mississippi, Alabama, and Georgia. Like New Orleans, the Northshore took a hard hit from Hurricane Katrina in August 2005, but in the decade since, most of its attractions, restaurants, and hotels have reopened.

SIGHTS

Abita Brewery

The Abita Brewing Company opened in 1986, taking full advantage of Abita Springs' famed water. Today, the **Abita Brewery** (166 Barbee Rd. off LA-36, Abita Springs, 985/893-3143, https://abita.com) offers free tours and tastings at 2pm on Wednesday, Thursday, and Friday and at 11am, noon,

1pm, and 2pm on Saturday. These tours are fun and low-key, offering the opportunity to learn about the brewing process from friendly staff members. Abita produces several kinds of beer, including seasonal varieties as well as standard ones that vary from the dark and rich Turbo Dog to the pleasantly fruity Purple Haze to the light and bubbly Abita Amber. All visitors to the brewery must wear closed-toe shoes and be at least 21 years of age. The gift shop is open 10am-3pm on tour days.

★ Global Wildlife Center

Though less visited than other attractions in southern Louisiana, the remarkable **Global Wildlife Center** (26389 LA-40, Folsom, 985/796-3585, www.globalwildlife.com; tours vary daily; $17 adult, $15 senior over 62, $11 child 2-11, free under 2) is well worth venturing off the beaten path. Once you're within the 900-acre grounds, it's hard to imagine that you're still in Louisiana. Giraffes, zebras, and three dozen other species of mostly African wildlife (nearly 3,000 animals all together) roam freely across the property. Visitors board covered wagons, which are pulled across the grounds by tractors, in tours that last 90 minutes.

The safari guides simply go where the animals are, and in many cases, you're allowed to come extremely close to the wildlife—an excellent opportunity for photographers. Reservations are not required (except for groups), but visitors should call for the schedule of guided tours, which changes weekly. The center has a huge gift shop, selling all manner of wildlife toys, books, and stuffed animals (the proceeds benefit the care of the animals), and there's a small concession stand. You can also buy sacks of feed to tempt some of the tamer animals.

Kliebert's Turtle & Alligator Farm

Southwest of Hammond, accessible via I-55, lies **Kliebert's Turtle & Alligator Farm** (41083 W. Yellow Water Rd., Hammond, 985/345-3617 or 800/854-9164, www.kliebertgatortours.com; tours Mar.-Oct. daily 11am-sunset, Nov.-Feb. Thurs.-Sun. 11am-sunset; $15 adult, $10 child 4-12, free under 4), one of the few alligator farms in southern Louisiana open to the public. Louisiana limits the hunting of American alligators in the wild, so these farms raise and harvest the animals, helping to protect the wild species. All farms, including Kliebert's (pronounced KLEE-BAIRS), are required to return to the wild a significant percentage of the alligators born in captivity. Here, you can get a firsthand look at more than 300 gators and 47,000 turtles; there's also a gift shop that offers alligator heads, turtle shells, and handcrafted novelties. Call ahead and confirm the hours, which often depend on the weather. Wintertime tours cost a bit less ($5 adult and child, free under 4).

★ Lake Pontchartrain Basin Maritime Museum

On the banks of the Tchefuncte River, you'll encounter the **Lake Pontchartrain Basin Maritime Museum** (133 Mabel Dr., Madisonville,

985/845-9200, www.lpbmm.org; Tues.-Sat. 10am-4pm, Sun. noon-4pm; $5 adult, $3 senior and child, free under 6), which contains several excellent exhibits documenting the region's seafaring heritage, including the canals of New Orleans and the lighthouses of Louisiana. Especially worth a look is the Port Century exhibit, which chronicles how steamboats played a vital role in the growth of the region. The museum offers boat-building classes, in which you learn to construct an authentic Cajun-style pirogue or a lake skiff. The museum also hosts a wide range of lectures, classes, and events, including the annual Wooden Boat Festival.

★ Pontchartrain Vineyards

In the rural, northern end of St. Tammany Parish lies the beautiful **Pontchartrain Vineyards** (81250 Old Military Rd., Bush, 985/892-9742, http://pontchartrainvineyards.com; tours and tastings Wed.-Sun. noon-4pm), set amid the horse farms of Bush and western Folsom. Begun in 1996, this award-winning winery is the only serious one in the state, and its food-friendly wines are served at some of the area's major restaurants. Depending on when you go, you might end up participating in the harvest or catching one of the many concerts held there during the spring, summer, and fall, including the Jazz'n the Vines series, which features jazz performances ($10 adult, free under 18) every two or three weeks. The inexpensive tastings are held in a French Provincial-style brick building, which overlooks the gentle hillside planted with grapes. The tours are short but informative and personable.

RESTAURANTS

While many people consider New Orleans to be the region's hub of exceptional cuisine, the Northshore boasts its own wealth of culinary options, including **The Dakota Restaurant** (629 N. US-190, Covington, 985/892-3712, www.thedakotarestaurant.com; Mon. 5:30pm-9pm, Tues.-Thurs. 11:30am-1:30pm and 5:30pm-9pm, Fri. 11:30am-1:30pm and 5:30pm-10pm, Sat. 5:30pm-10pm; $28-36). Here, the contemporary American cooking is anything but ordinary. Signature dishes include the jumbo lump crabmeat and French Brie soup, crispy soft-shell crab with lemon-parmesan risotto, and pan-sautéed tilapia with artichokes and wilted spinach.

Famed chef John Besh oversees **La Provence** (25020 US-190, Lacombe, 985/626-7662, www.laprovencerestaurant.com; Wed.-Sat. 5pm-9pm, Sun. 11am-9pm; $33-56), a welcoming temple of gastronomy. With its rustic facade, red-tiled roof, and authentic furnishings, this place looks as though it's been airlifted to the Northshore from the south of France. The constantly evolving menu might feature sweet potato ravioli, quail gumbo, or seared venison loin.

For a more casual meal, head to the **Abita Brew Pub** (72011 Holly St., Abita Springs, 985/892-5837, www.abitabrewpub.com; Tues.-Thurs. 11am-9pm, Fri.-Sat. 11am-10pm, Sun. 11am-9pm; $9-20), an offshoot of the famous Abita Brewery. The pub serves tasty comfort food that complements, and even incorporates, the locally crafted beers; crab claws are served with a rosemary, barbecue, and Abita Amber dipping sauce. Other good bets include pecan-crusted catfish, muffulettas, and barbecued ribs marinated in Abita's Purple Haze. The pub features scenic views of the Tammany Trace biking path, which plenty of patrons use to reach this down-home hangout. With several outdoor tables and a sports-bar atmosphere, it's no wonder that the crowd tends toward the young and hip.

NIGHTLIFE

Though it might seem more sedate than New Orleans, the Northshore has a handful of popular bars and music clubs, including the **Columbia Street Tap Room and Grill** (434 N. Columbia St., Covington, 985/898-0899, http://covingtontaproom.com; Mon. 11am-10pm, Tues.-Thurs. 11am-midnight, Fri. 11am-1:30am, Sat. noon-1:30am), a cool, smoke-free corner bar that presents first-rate rock, folk, funk, soul, and blues bands Thursday-Saturday. For a more down-home ambience, head to **Ruby's Roadhouse** (840 Lamarque St., Mandeville, 985/626-9748, www.rubysroadhouse.com; Mon.-Fri. 10am-close, Sat.-Sun. 9am-close), which presents everything from rock to Cajun.

ARTS AND EVENTS

Southeastern Louisiana University is home to the beautifully restored 850-seat **Columbia Theatre for the Performing Arts** (220 E. Thomas St., Hammond, 985/543-4371, www.columbiatheatre.org), an elegant 1928 building that now serves as the city's premier performing arts center. Events here include pop and classical concerts, plays, and dance performances.

Usually occurring in mid-April, the **Ponchatoula Strawberry Festival** (Memorial Park, 6th St. and Willow St., Ponchatoula, 800/917-7045, www.lastrawberryfestival.com) has lured oodles of visitors to Hammond for more than four decades. Considered one of the nation's largest three-day festivals, it features a wide array of family-friendly diversions, including live concerts, strawberry-eating contests, and, of course, a parade. You'll also find a slew of food booths offering strawberry lemonade, strawberry beignets, and chocolate-covered strawberries.

Boating enthusiasts should not miss the **Wooden Boat Festival** (985/845-9200, www.woodenboatfest.org) in mid-October. Hundreds of beautiful, mostly handcrafted wooden boats sail, motor, or row along Madisonville's Tchefuncte River. Beyond the boats themselves, you'll be treated to live concerts, a boatbuilding contest, and a model boatbuilding workshop for kids.

★ The Abita Springs Opry

The Northshore's most acclaimed musical event is the **Abita Springs Opry** (985/892-0711, www.abitaopry.org; $18 per concert). Essentially a series of six concerts, the Opry is held on every third Saturday March-May and September-November at the Abita Springs Town Hall (22161 Level St., Abita

Springs). The two-hour concerts begin at 7pm. Founded to preserve and celebrate Louisiana's "roots" music, the Opry features rollicking country, bluegrass, Southern gospel, Cajun, zydeco, and other traditional folk music. Given the intimate seating, homemade vittles on sale, and small-town ambience, the Opry feels like a welcome return to a simpler time.

RECREATION

Enjoying the great outdoors is the key draw for many visitors to St. Tammany and Tangipahoa Parishes, which are noted for swamps and wildlife preserves, several popular state parks, an exceptional bike trail, a few fine golf courses, and excellent fishing and boating opportunities.

Biking

St. Tammany Parish has one of the best biking resources in the South, the **Tammany Trace** (985/867-9490, www.tammanytrace.org), a 28-mile rails-to-trails bikeway that runs from Slidell west to Mandeville and then north to Abita Springs before curving west again into downtown Covington. The paved path also services joggers, strollers, inline skaters, wheelchair users, and horseback riders. This was the first rails-to-trails conversion in Louisiana; Tammany Trace follows the path of the old Illinois Central Railroad, winding beneath boughs of pine, oak, and magnolia trees, across 31 bridges, and through some of the state's verdant wetlands. The trail cuts right through or near all of the downtown retail and dining districts in the area.

Fishing and Boating

In addition to several charter-fishing operations, anglers will find plenty of great freshwater fishing in the muddy bayous of St. Tammany Parish, especially in lush 99-acre **Fairview-Riverside State Park** (119 Fairview Dr., Madisonville, 985/845-3318 or 888/677-3247, www.crt.state.la.us; Sun.-Thurs. 6am-9pm, Fri.-Sat. 6am-10pm; $2 pp, free over 62 and under 4). Shaded by dozens of massive live oak trees, the park includes campsites for tent and RV camping, picnic tables, and terrific fishing and crabbing opportunities along the Tchefuncte River. You can also put in a boat at the Madisonville public boat launch; besides fishing, waterskiing and tubing are popular on the Tchefuncte. Here, you're likely to encounter bass, white perch, bluegill, and bream, while down where the river joins Lake Pontchartrain, you can catch channel catfish, redfish, and speckled trout.

Golf

St. Tammany Parish has some of the best golf courses in the whole state, including the **Oak Harbor Golf Club** (201 Oak Harbor Blvd., Slidell, 985/646-0110, www.oakharborgolf.com), one of the best semi-private golf courses in the South. Originally opened in 1992 and extensively renovated in 2006 following Hurricane Katrina's destruction, the 18-hole championship course also offers private lessons, a nine-acre practice facility, and a well-appointed clubhouse.

Parks

At 2,800 acres, **Fontainebleau State Park** (62883 LA-1089, Mandeville, 985/624-4443 or 888/677-3668, www.crt.state.la.us; Sun.-Thurs. 6am-9pm, Fri.-Sat. 6am-10pm; $2 pp, free over 62 and under 4) is the region's largest recreation area, with camping facilities, a sandy beach, and direct access to Lake Pontchartrain. It's a great park for bird-watchers and hikers. Trails meander through the pine-shaded forest, passing through an ancient grove of live oaks and the crumbling brick ruins of an 1829 sugar mill opened by Mandeville's founder, Bernard de Marigny de Mandeville. The Tammany Trace trail runs through the park, drawing bikers, hikers, and inline skaters. Visitors can often observe turkeys, woodpeckers, and hundreds of other bird species, all of which are listed in the park's official bird-watching guide.

In Tangipahoa Parish, **Tickfaw State Park** (27225 Patterson Rd., Springfield, 225/294-5020 or 888/981-2020, www.crt.state.la.us; Sun.-Thurs. 7am-9pm, Fri.-Sat. 7am-10pm; $2 pp, free over 62 and under 4) lies in the middle of what seems like nowhere, about 15 miles west of Ponchatoula. This 1,200-acre park sits astride the Tickfaw River and features camping facilities, a water playground, and a mile of boardwalks through the lush wetlands, encompassing four different ecosystems: cypress/tupelo swamp, bottomland hardwood forest, mixed pine/hardwood forest, and the river itself. You might see herons and egrets swoop into the swamp to grab a crawfish snack. Other wildlife includes turtles, snakes, and opossums; on rare occasions, you might spot a coyote, deer, fox, or beaver. Rent a canoe for the best chance to see wildlife, and be sure to stop by the **nature center** (daily 9am-4:30pm), which contains excellent exhibits on the park's flora and fauna.

HOTELS

The Northshore features a decent selection of modern chain hotels just off the interstate in Slidell and Covington, plus a slew of enchanting inns, from Mandeville to Tickfaw. Just steps from Covington's historical district, the **Camellia House Bed & Breakfast** (426 E. Rutland St., Covington, 985/893-2442 or 985/264-4973, www.camelliahouse.net; $95-185) offers gorgeously furnished suites with plush linens and private entrances. The lovely, early-20th-century house is filled with stylish antiques, and guests can enjoy the home's wide veranda, courtyard garden, swimming pool, and hot tub, plus complimentary bikes. As a bonus, hosts Linda and Don Chambless know a great deal about the area.

Another unique option is **The Historic Michabelle Inn and Restaurant** (1106 S. Holly St., Hammond, 985/419-0550, www.michabelle.com; $90-132), a wonderfully decadent B&B on the south side of Hammond's historic downtown. This imposing white Greek Revival mansion adroitly blends classic French style with Old South charm. The four well-appointed rooms and four luxurious suites are rife with late-Victorian antiques, Oriental rugs, and gilt-framed paintings. In addition to relaxing amid the lush grounds, guests might also relish the excellent on-site restaurant and relatively new spa and fitness center.

For more seclusion, opt for **Little River Bluffs** (11030 Garden Ln., Folsom, 985/796-5257, www.littleriverbluffs.com; $150-300), which anchors a 50-acre wooded property on the artesian-fed Little Tchefuncte River. This is a naturalist's dream, offering the chance to kayak on the river, hike through the woods, and sunbathe on a sugary-white sandbar. Great blue herons, egrets, and otters inhabit this lush woodland, which feels light-years away from New Orleans. There are four accommodations here: the luxurious, light-filled Lodge House, which overlooks the river; the A-frame River Chalet, which sits on a forested bend in the river; the shaded Meadow Cabin, tucked near a stocked pond and a wildflower meadow; and the Tree House, perched high amid the pines and magnolias. All of these cabins are romantic, relaxing, and equipped with screened porches, complete kitchens, and other modern conveniences. Note that there's a two-night minimum.

PRACTICALITIES

Information

For more information about Slidell, Covington, Mandeville, and Abita Springs in St. Tammany Parish, contact the **St. Tammany Parish Tourist & Convention Commission** (68099 LA-59, Mandeville, 985/892-0520 or 800/634-9443, www.louisiananorthshore.com). The **Tangipahoa Parish Convention & Visitors Bureau** (13143 Wardline Rd., Hammond, 985/542-7520 or 800/542-7520, www.tangi-cvb.org) is a helpful resource if you plan to visit Hammond and Ponchatoula in Tangipahoa Parish.

Although most people in this region rely on New Orleans's *Times-Picayune* (www.nola.com), Hammond also has a daily newspaper, *The Daily Star* (www.hammondstar.com). Nondaily papers on the Northshore include the *St. Tammany News Banner* (www.thesttammanynews.com), the *Slidell Sentry* (www.thesttammanynews.com), and *The Ponchatoula Times* (www.ponchatoula.com/ptimes).

Getting There and Around

The Northshore lies at the junction of four interstates: I-10, I-12, I-59, and I-55. This makes driving here from New Orleans or Baton Rouge easy and direct. From New Orleans, you can come via I-10, a 40-minute route that deposits you in Slidell; the Lake Pontchartrain Causeway Bridge (www.thecauseway.us), a 45-minute drive that places you in Mandeville; or I-55, which skirts the western edge of Lake Pontchartrain, toward Hammond. There's no toll for crossing the Causeway from south to north, but you will be charged a toll of $3-15 for crossing north to south. Driving here is your best bet; you really need a car to explore this region. Rush-hour traffic jams are common along all of these routes, so figure an extra 20-30 minutes depending on when you make these drives.

Unfortunately, traffic can be rather slow throughout the region, especially US-190 in Slidell and LA-59 between Mandeville and Abita Springs. As a plus, some of the highways are quite scenic. For speed, I-12 can be a lifesaver, and it's usually free from major traffic jams. I-12 runs east to west across St. Tammany and Tangipahoa Parishes, connecting the junction of I-59 and I-10 in Slidell with Mandeville and Covington before continuing to Tangipahoa Parish, which sits at the crossroads of I-12 and I-55.

Great River Road

A leisurely drive along the Great River Road, which snakes along both banks of the Mississippi River, reveals some of the most striking contrasts between past and present that you'll find anywhere in the country. Less than 30 minutes after leaving New Orleans, you can find yourself standing on a plantation with fields of sugarcane and more acreage than the French Quarter. But the Great River Road, even in the sparsely populated areas, is not exactly quaint. Along considerable stretches, you'll also see oil refineries, chemical plants, and other fortresses of mining and manufacturing, sometimes within a stone's throw of old plantations. Another reminder that the days of paddlewheel riverboats and quiet agrarian living have long since passed is the high grassy levee that runs virtually uninterrupted along the Mississippi River. In most places, a path extends along the top, where you can jog, walk, or ride a bike, and it's often so peaceful that it's hard to believe the Mississippi River was the main thoroughfare between New Orleans and Baton Rouge well into the 19th century. The eventual construction of I-10 diverted traffic from many of the towns along the Great River Road, resulting in what you see today: a rural, Depression-era byway, pockmarked with refineries and factories, fringed by massive levees, and peppered with lovely plantation homes.

SIGHTS

Audubon State Historic Site

Good hiking trails wind through the magnolia and poplar trees at the 100-acre **Audubon State Historic Site** (11788 LA-965, St. Francisville, 225/635-3739 or 888/677-2838, www.crt.state.la.us; Tues.-Sat. 9am-5pm; $8 adult, $6 senior 62 and over, $4 child 6-17, free under 6). The on-site 1806 **Oakley House,** a distinctive West Indies-style colonial home, is where famed wildlife painter John James Audubon lived briefly in 1821; records indicate that he worked on at least 32 of his bird paintings while living in this house. Other facilities include a picnic shelter and several outbuildings from the original plantation. Guided tours of the house are given throughout the day.

Destrehan Plantation

One of the oldest house-museums on the Great River Road, and also one of the nearest to New Orleans, **Destrehan Plantation** (13034 River Rd., Destrehan, 985/764-9315 or 877/453-2095, www.destrehanplantation.org; tours daily 9am-4pm; $18 adult, $16 active military, $15 senior, $7 child 7-17, free under 7) was built in 1787, although the sweeping Greek Revival mansion you see today, with its eight front columns and double galleries, is the result of a major renovation and expansion in the 1830s. Robin de Logny originally commissioned the construction of the house, hiring a freed mulatto named Charles (whose last name isn't known) to build it. Years later, Jean Noel Destrehan, a French aristocrat, bought the house and added the twin wings on either side of the facade in 1810. Details still visible in this rambling structure include hand-hewn cypress timbers and the distinctive hipped roof typical of West Indies architecture. The house is less than 25 miles west of New Orleans and a mere 10-minute drive from the New Orleans airport, making it popular with visitors who don't have time to explore the entire River Road but would still like to see a grand Louisiana plantation before heading home.

Houmas House Plantation and Gardens

Once the setting of the Bette Davis film *Hush...Hush, Sweet Charlotte* (1964), the stunning **Houmas House Plantation and Gardens** (40136 LA-942, Darrow, 225/473-9380, www.houmashouse.com; daily 9am-8pm; tours $24 pp for mansion and gardens, $15 pp for gardens and grounds) encompasses a dramatic 1840 Greek Revival mansion, situated on an extensive property of oak-shaded grounds. At the plantation's peak, it encompassed 300,000 acres, much of which were devoted to sugarcane crops. An Irishman named John Burnside bought it for the princely sum of $1 million in 1857 and promptly declared his immunity during the Civil War, on the grounds that he was a British subject. Union forces honored the declaration and left Burnside and his house alone during their march up the Mississippi River from New Orleans to Baton Rouge.

By the end of the century, a new owner, Colonel William Porcher Miles, increased sugarcane production to 20 million pounds per year, more than any other operation in the state. Houmas House fell gradually upon hard times during the early 20th century, but in 1940, the house and remaining grounds were bought by Dr. George B. Crozat, who set about restoring the place. Hollywood came calling in the early 1960s, and a new owner took over in 2003, furthering the restoration efforts and helping to turn this into one of the most appealing plantation museums in the region.

Houmas House employs excellent guides who offer detailed tours of the plantation house, which is filled with antiques and artwork and decorated much as it might have looked during its prime in the mid-19th century. The last tour of each day occurs at 7pm, which is unusual for Louisiana plantations. Even if you don't tour the house, though, it's worth checking out the dramatic grounds and beautifully kept gardens.

Plantation Tours

Official bus tours of the plantations along the Mississippi River between New Orleans and St. Francisville provide a convenient way to see one or more plantations, particularly if you're visiting New Orleans for only a short time. Many of these companies also offer money-saving combination packages that include swamp tours, city tours, and the like.

Via small, air-conditioned buses, the **Cajun Encounters Tour Co.** (504/834-1770 or 866/928-6877, www.cajunencounters.com) leads guided excursions (daily 8:30am-2:30pm and noon-5:45pm; $80 adult, $59 child under 12) of the scenic Great River Road, which feature walking tours of two of the region's most notable structures: Laura Plantation and Oak Alley Plantation.

For a guided excursion of the national historic landmarks along the Great River Road, consider **Celebration Tours** (504/587-7115 or 888/587-7115, www.celebrationtoursllc.com), which offers a plantation tour (daily 8:30am-2pm; $85 pp) that, depending on your group's selections, may stop at Destrehan Plantation, Laura Plantation, Oak Alley Plantation, or Houmas House.

One of the best general tour companies in New Orleans, the ubiquitous **Gray Line Tours** (504/569-1401 or 800/233-2628, www.graylineneworleans.com) provides an assortment of excursions, including a cemetery tour, a walking cocktail tour, and a boat ride through Barataria Preserve. Luckily, Gray Line also features tours of Laura Plantation (daily noon-5pm; $62 adult, $31 child 6-12) and Oak Alley Plantation (daily noon-5pm; $62 adult, $31 child 6-12).

Through the **Louisiana Tour Company** (504/689-3599 or 888/307-9267, http://louisianaswamp.com), you can take a guided plantation tour of Oak Alley (daily 8:30am-2pm; $65 adult, $40 child), Laura Plantation (daily 8:30am-2pm; $65 adult, $40 child), or, if you have time, both plantations (daily 10:30am-6pm; $90 adult, $65 child).

Since 1979, the family-operated **Tours by Isabelle** (504/398-0365 or

★ Laura Plantation

You can embark on one of the most unusual plantation-tour experiences in the country at the **Laura Plantation** (2247 LA-18, Vacherie, 225/265-7690 or 888/799-7690, www.lauraplantation.com; tours daily 10am-4pm; $20 adult, $18 active military, $6 child 6-17, free under 6), which differs from most of the others along River Road in a couple of ways. First, it has a fascinating legacy, as its slave cabins were where the folktales known as *Br'er Rabbit* were recorded in the late 1870s. But maybe the most interesting thing about a visit to Laura is that tour guides base their one-hour talk on the memoirs—which total about 5,000 pages—of the four generations of women who oversaw the compound's inner workings; it's a condensation of the fascinating lives of the Creole women who ran the plantation, along with intimate and telling details about their children and extended family, and their slaves. The memoirs were compiled in the 1930s by Laura Locoul Gore, who grew up on the plantation and represents the final generation of women at Laura. The tour of Laura offers a provocative and colorful look into the high and low points of Creole life in the early 19th century, and its discussion of the lives of the slaves and the day-to-day, firsthand

Laura Plantation in Vacherie

877/665-8687, www.toursbyisabelle.com) has been providing personalized trips throughout the region, including tours of the city, area plantations, and nearby swamps. If you're curious about the Great River Road, you can choose from five options, including the Oak Alley and Laura Plantation Tour (daily 8:30am-2pm and 12:30pm-6pm; $105 pp), which entails guided tours of the two featured properties as well as narrated glimpses of Whitney, St. Joseph, and Evergreen Plantations, and the All Day Plantation Tour (daily 8am-5pm; $140 pp), which provides guided tours of Destrehan Plantation, St. Joseph Plantation (or, on Wednesday, San Francisco Plantation), and Houmas House.

observations of the plantation's occupants makes it stand out among plantation tours in the region.

Another difference at Laura is the plantation house itself, which is not one of the typical glowing white Greek Revival mansions found in this region, but rather a relatively modest, infinitely colorful, raised Creole house that has been, intentionally, only partly restored in order to give guests a more realistic sense of what the house looked and felt like when it was occupied by Laura and her ancestors. The house suffered a major fire in 2004, but staff still managed to give tours the very next day, and restoration work continued unabated. As good as this museum is, the quality of your tour varies from guide to guide, but most of the interpreters do a very nice job. French tours are offered daily at 11am, 1pm, and 3pm.

The Myrtles Plantation

One of the more colorful attractions in St. Francisville is the **Myrtles Plantation** (7747 US-61, St. Francisville, 225/635-6277 or 800/809-0565, www.myrtlesplantation.com; daily 9am-5pm; $10 adult, $7 under 13), which bills itself as being among the most haunted houses in the United

States. Apart from this considerable lure, the 1796 house is notable for its hand-painted stained glass and crystal chandeliers. Little expense seems to have been spared in its construction. Engaging historical tours touch on the house and its grounds, but the considerably more colorful Mystery tours (Fri.-Sat., reservations required) are the real draw. The home also operates as a bed-and-breakfast and there is an on-site restaurant.

Nottoway Plantation

The 64-room **Nottoway Plantation** (31025 LA-1, White Castle, 225/545-2730 or 866/527-6884, www.nottoway.com; daily 9am-4pm; tours $20 adult, $6 child 6-12, free under 6) is an immense Greek Revival mansion, with an interior of about 53,000 square feet. John H. Randolph built this "white castle" in 1859, where it served as the centerpiece of his sugarcane plantation. An on-site museum details the history of the Randolphs, up to and including the Civil War. Nottoway also functions as a small hotel and has a popular restaurant. Nottoway lies about 12 miles upriver from Donaldsonville, on the same side of the river.

★ Oak Alley Plantation

One of the best photo ops in the South, **Oak Alley Plantation** (3645 LA-18, Vacherie, 225/265-2151 or 800/442-5539, www.oakalleyplantation.com; Mar.-Oct. daily 9am-5pm, Nov.-Feb. Mon.-Fri. 9am-4:30pm, Sat.-Sun. 9am-5pm; $20 adult, $7.50 youth 13-18, $4.50 child 6-12) features an incredible alley of 28 live oak trees, planted in two rows bordering the front walk. Dating from about 300 years ago, these trees have been here much longer than the present mansion, which, though beautiful, certainly wouldn't stand out as it does today without the graceful, arching trees framing it. An early French settler planted the oaks in the early 1700s to lead from the river down a path to his rather modest house. More than 100 years later, the property's owner, Jacques Telesphore Roman, used his considerable sugarcane fortune to construct the present Oak Alley mansion. The entire property comprises about 25 acres; much of the original plantation, which had encompassed more than 1,000 acres, is now undeveloped forest, but about 600 acres are still leased to sugarcane farmers.

As you approach the property, you'll pass the rather modest front gate that marks the beginning of the alley of oaks; you can't enter the property here, as the actual driveway for automobiles lies a short distance farther down the road. But you can park your car along the dirt driveway leading up and over the Mississippi River levee and walk up to the gate to snap a picture and admire the trees and the house in the distance. If you walk up the short dirt drive to the top of the levee, you can glimpse a very nice view of the river—there's often a tanker or freighter chugging along, contributing to that peculiar contrast between modern industry and 19th-century plantation living that characterizes the region.

Once you drive onto the grounds, buy your tickets at a booth and proceed to the Big House, as the mansion is called, for a guided tour. The tours of the Big House are straightforward and not overly exciting, unless you happen to get an especially colorful guide, but after the tour, you can spend as much time as you'd like exploring the grounds, which include the "Slavery at Oak Alley" exhibit, the Civil War encampment, and the blacksmith shop. Relax amid the oaks, crape myrtles, and azaleas, admiring the peacocks and friendly bobtail cats that wander about the property.

San Francisco Plantation

The opulent **San Francisco Plantation** (2646 LA-44, Garyville, 888/322-1756, www.sanfranciscoplantation.org; Apr.-Oct. daily 9:30am-4:40pm, Nov.-Mar. daily 9:30am-4pm; $17 adult, $16 active military, $10 child, free under 7) sits on the east bank of the Mississippi River, about 23 miles upriver from Destrehan. The house was constructed by Edmond Bozonier Marmillion in 1855, shortly before he died; in the 1970s, it was authentically restored to its original, antebellum appearance. The exquisite hand-painted ceilings are an important detail, as are the fine antiques and extensive faux marbling.

RESTAURANTS

If you know where to look, you're likely to find several worthy eateries along the Great River Road, between New Orleans and St. Francisville. One such place is the **Grapevine Café & Gallery** (211 Railroad Ave., Donaldsonville, 225/473-8463, www.grapevinecafeandgallery.com; Tues.-Thurs. 11am-2pm and 5pm-9pm, Fri. 11am-2pm and 5pm-9:30pm, Sat. 11am-9pm, Sun. 11am-2pm; $8-28), a delightful restaurant housed within a 1920s art deco-style building in Donaldsonville's historical district. Award-winning Cajun and Creole cuisine is served in a cozy dining room filled with local artwork. Crawfish pie is a specialty here. If you have room for dessert, consider the white-chocolate bread pudding or lemon ice-box pie.

For a more casual option, head to **The Cabin Restaurant** (Hwy. 22 and Hwy. 44, Burnside, 225/473-3007, www.thecabinrestaurant.com; Mon. 11am-3pm, Tues.-Thurs. 11am-9pm, Fri.-Sat. 11am-10pm, Sun. 11am-6pm; $10-20), which is as much a museum of the area's Cajun culture as it is a restaurant. The walls of this former slave cabin (circa 1850), with its original cypress roof, are papered with old newspapers, a traditional insulation in the 19th century. The rustic dining room is packed with interesting memorabilia, including vintage farming tools, old paintings, and furniture. Dining is also available in an inviting courtyard out back. This is a terrific place to try classic Louisiana dishes, from crawfish pies to jambalaya.

Another casual choice in the region is the **Magnolia Café** (5689 Commerce St., St. Francisville, 225/635-6528; Sun.-Wed. 10am-4pm, Thurs. 10am-9pm, Fri. 10am-10pm, Sat. 10am-9pm; $6-24), which serves a nice mix of salads, sandwiches, pizzas, Mexican fare, and specialties like an eggplant pirogue, fried eggplant with seafood stuffing. Seafood enchiladas, French dip po-boys, and burgers are popular items, and there's live music on Friday nights.

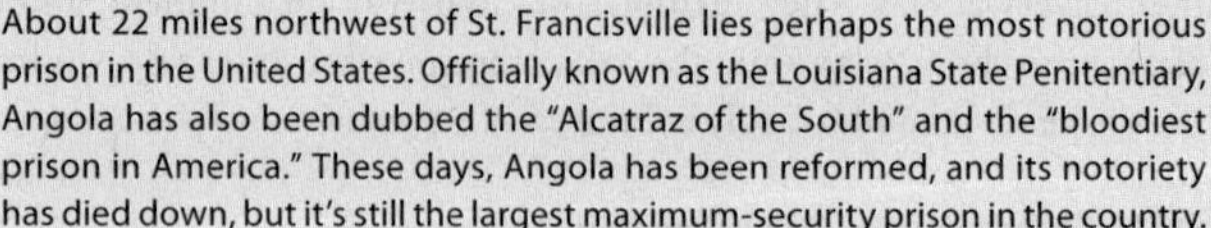

The Louisiana State Penitentiary

About 22 miles northwest of St. Francisville lies perhaps the most notorious prison in the United States. Officially known as the Louisiana State Penitentiary, Angola has also been dubbed the "Alcatraz of the South" and the "bloodiest prison in America." These days, Angola has been reformed, and its notoriety has died down, but it's still the largest maximum-security prison in the country.

The 18,000-acre prison sits in a bend of the Mississippi River, just a few miles south of the Mississippi border. Much of Angola is farmland, and inmates are required to work the fields five days a week, eight hours a day. Crops produced here include corn, cotton, and okra; in addition, there's a herd of cattle numbering about 2,000.

Angola's legacy is a grim one. The prison was run privately when it was founded in 1844, then occupied by Union troops during the Civil War, and then run privately again by a Confederate general from 1869 until 1900. Brutality was rampant in those years, when the reported average lifespan of inmates at Angola was just five years. The state took over Angola in 1901, but medical treatment and living conditions remained poor for many years.

Music played a vital role for many Angola inmates, the most famous being the blues pioneer Huddie William Ledbetter, known as Lead Belly, who served time here for brandishing a knife during a fight. Lead Belly's blues music caught the attention of record producers, who recorded his hit "Good Night, Irene" here while the promising talent served his time. Lead Belly was soon freed from prison, and in the late 1930s, he developed a tremendous musical reputation in New York City and, later, Paris.

Amazingly, for about 50 years, Angola operated with no paid guards. Instead, it was staffed with so-called "trusty guards," favored inmates who were furnished with weapons and were notorious for ignoring or perpetuating prison violence. In the 1960s and early '70s, stabbings, beatings, and deadly fights occurred once a day on average.

FESTIVALS AND EVENTS

The **Audubon Pilgrimage** (225/635-6330, www.audubonpilgrimage.info) is a mid-March festival in St. Francisville. Since 1972, the event has celebrated the life of painter John James Audubon by welcoming visitors to various historic gardens and homes where docents in authentic 1820s-period costumes offer guided tours.

Some of the plantations have annual events, such as the Destrehan Plantation's annual **spring and fall festivals** (www.destrehanplantation.org), which feature live music, regional foods, and a wide assortment of local arts, crafts, and antiques. You can often tour the historic mansion and witness living-history demonstrations, such as blacksmithing.

Christmas is one of the best times to explore the Great River Road, particularly during the **Festival of the Bonfires** (Lutcher Recreation Park, Lutcher, www.festivalofthebonfires.org; mid-Dec.), a three-day event of local food and crafts, carnival rides, live entertainment, and bonfire lightings. Ultimately, it's a precursor to the **Christmas Eve Bonfires,** when many riverside towns light bonfires of their own. Some claim that this longtime

In 1973, Angola eliminated the "trusty guard" system and began changing many of its policies. It finally obtained accreditation from the American Correctional Association (ACA) in 1993, though, in 2009, the prison cut costs by installing bunk beds, decreasing overtime, and replacing officers with security cameras. Perhaps Angola's most recent claim to fame, however, is the 1978 incarceration of Elmo Patrick Sonnier, whose presence on death row inspired Sister Helen Prejean's best-selling book *Dead Man Walking: The Eyewitness Account of the Death Penalty That Sparked a National Debate*. The book was eventually adapted into the Oscar-winning 1995 film *Dead Man Walking*, starring Sean Penn and Susan Sarandon. Angola has also appeared in such films as *Out of Sight* (1998) and *Monster's Ball* (2001).

In an effort to clean up its image, Angola has created the engaging and surprisingly forthcoming **LA State Penitentiary Museum** (225/655-2592, www.angolamuseum.org; Mon.-Fri. 8am-4:30pm, Sat. 8am-4pm, Sun. 11am-4pm; donation suggested), which examines the facility's history and historic reputation. To reach the museum, follow US-61 from St. Francisville, veer northwest onto Highway 66, and continue to the road's terminus.

A great time to visit is October, when from 2pm to 5pm on each Sunday, the prison hosts the **Angola Rodeo** (225/655-2030 or 225/655-2607, www.angolarodeo.com;$15pp), which was begun in 1965 and is the longest-running prison rodeo in the country. The event, which is indeed no amateur show, features professional judges and takes place in a 7,500-seat stadium. An arts-and-crafts show typically runs 9am-5pm on each day of the rodeo. This, like the rodeo itself, has become a phenomenally popular event. While here, you can also listen to live inmate bands and partake in a carnival fare and Louisiana favorites, from candy apples to jambalaya.

Louisiana tradition was begun as a way to welcome the Cajun version of Santa Claus, PaPa Noel, while others suggest that the fires were lit to help riverbound travelers make their way to midnight Mass.

HOTELS

Lodging options vary along the Great River Road, ranging from modern hotels in Gonzales to quaint inns in St. Francisville. You can even stay on the premises of some of the plantations, including the **Nottoway Plantation** (31025 LA-1, White Castle, 225/545-2730 or 866/527-6884, www.nottoway.com; $160-190), the largest plantation house remaining in the South. This renovated gem encompasses 40 rooms and two honeymoon suites, spread throughout the main house and various cottages. Overnight guests can enjoy a guided tour of the house, explore the oak-shaded grounds, and have a meal in the Mansion Restaurant, which serves Creole-inspired cuisine. This gorgeous property also features an outdoor pool, tennis courts, and a game and fitness center.

For the chance to stay in what many believe to be the most haunted

Above: the Madewood Plantation House, now a bed-and-breakfast. **Below:** live oak trees at Oak Alley Plantation.

house in Louisiana, book a room at **The Myrtles Plantation** (7747 US-61, St. Francisville, 225/635-6277 or 800/809-0565, www.myrtlesplantation.com; $115-250), one of the most popular touring plantations in the St. Francisville area. Situated on 70 lush acres, the ornately furnished 1796 French Mediterranean-style main house contains six handsome, expansive rooms and suites, including the luxurious General David Bradford Suite, which has two adjoining verandas and a huge four-poster bed. There are also six options in outbuildings near the main house: the old caretaker's cottage, which has its own porch; the four garden rooms, each with an antique Chippendale claw-foot tub; and the two-bedroom Coco House. The Myrtles Plantation also has a fine full-service restaurant, the Carriage House.

A less touristy plantation, the **Madewood Plantation House** (4250 Hwy. 308, Napoleonville, 985/369-7151, www.madewood.com; $229-298) is a Greek Revival-style mansion situated amid several outbuildings and 20 well-tended acres that were once part of a large, 19th-century sugar plantation. Built around 1846, the Madewood Plantation House had survived the American Civil War and passed through the hands of several families before the current owner's mother claimed it in 1964. Today, guests at this bed-and-breakfast can sleep in old-fashioned canopy beds, browse antiques and artifacts throughout the lower rooms, and relish classic Southern-style breakfasts. There are no phones or televisions in the rooms and suites, but modern amenities abound, such as whirlpool tubs and individual thermostats. Room prices include breakfast for two, a wine-and-cheese reception, a candlelit dinner of regional favorites, and coffee and brandy in the parlor.

If you want a more intimate experience, consider the **Cabahanosse Bed & Breakfast** (602 Railroad Ave., Donaldsonville, 225/474-5050, www.cabahanosse.com; $160), a handsome 1890s inn in downtown Donaldsonville. You'll find four sumptuously outfitted suites with high ceilings, separate sitting rooms, and wide-plank pine floors that date to the house's original construction. Each suite is uniquely decorated; the room with mallard duck decor has a relaxing balcony. All of these spacious suites are ideal for a romantic retrea. At night, you'll even find brandy and chocolates at your bedside.

PRACTICALITIES

Information

If you're curious about Destrehan and Luling, contact the **St. Charles Parish Tourist Information Center** (13825 River Rd., Luling, 985/783-5145, www.stcharlesgov.net). For information on Gramercy, Lutcher, Vacherie, and Convent, consult the **St. James Parish Welcome Center** (5800 LA-44, Convent, www.stjamesla.com). The **Ascension Parish Tourism Commission** (6967 LA-22, Sorrento, 225/675-6550 or 888/775-7990, www.ascensiontourism.com) handles tourism in the towns of Gonzales, Sorrento, Darrow, and Donaldsonville. Check in with the **Iberville Parish**

Tourist Commission (17525 LA-77, Grosse Tete, 225/687-5198, www.ibervilleparish.com) for information on White Castle and Plaquemine.

Information about New Roads and St. Francisville can be obtained from the **Pointe Coupee Parish Office of Tourism** (727 Hospital Rd., Ste. B, New Roads, 225/638-3998, www.pctourism.org) and **West Feliciana Parish Tourist Commission** (800/789-4221, www.stfrancisville.us), respectively. Jackson's tourism is handled by the **East Feliciana Tourist Commission** (225/634-7155, www.felicianatourism.org). There's also information about the entire River Road region available online (www.neworleansplantationcountry.com) or by phone (866/204-7782).

Getting There and Around

This part of the state has little or no public transportation, but it does have a very good network of roads, so plan to visit the area via car. If you're staying in New Orleans, check with your hotel concierge or bed-and-breakfast for information on companies that offer half- or full-day tours to some of the plantations.

To reach the lower towns along the Great River Road from New Orleans, follow I-10 west to I-310, and exit onto LA-48, which puts you right by Destrehan. From here, you can follow LA-48 northwest along the east bank of the Mississippi River, or you can cross the I-310 bridge and follow LA-18 along the west bank. Keep in mind that River Road is not just one road—it's a combination of numbered highways that run alongside both banks of the river. So, while traveling, it's best to have a map with you and to stick with the roads that hug the river, not just to a particular route number.

Along the west bank, LA-18 is River Road for many miles, as far as Donaldsonville. North of that, the river's west bank is traced by LA-405 and LA-988 up to Port Allen, opposite Baton Rouge. Along the east bank from Destrehan, the river is traced by LA-48, then Spillway Road across the Bonnet Carré Spillway (which can be closed because of high water and flooding, in which case traffic is detoured along the interior to US-61), and then along LA-628, LA-44, LA-942, LA-75, LA-141, LA-75 again, LA-991, and LA-327 clear to Baton Rouge. Several bridges and ferries connect roads on either bank of the river between New Orleans and Baton Rouge, making it very easy to get back and forth.

The highlights of River Road are mostly in St. James and Ascension Parishes, about midway between New Orleans and Baton Rouge. If you're planning to spend most of your time in this area, near Donaldsonville and Vacherie, it's quickest to drive up I-10 for 50 miles to Sorrento, and then follow LA-22 and LA-70 over the Sunshine Bridge to LA-18, which leads to Donaldsonville to the north and Vacherie to the south. To reach St. Francisville, it's roughly a 30-mile drive up US-61 from Baton Rouge. As with the rest of the Great River Road, a car is your best way to get around.

Baton Rouge

Ever since Hurricane Katrina, when many evacuees of New Orleans relocated to Baton Rouge, the city has witnessed a remarkable population surge, as evidenced by the enhanced number of new restaurants, shops, and hotels—not to mention the increased traffic. Even without Katrina's effects, however, Baton Rouge seems more like a typical new Southern city than New Orleans does. Sprawling in virtually every direction with charming residential neighborhoods, Baton Rouge feels clean and prosperous, but perhaps lacking a distinct identity of its own. At once the state capital and home to Louisiana State University, Baton Rouge is the sort of town where government and education provide its personality more than the streets, buildings, and topography. Nevertheless, you'll find several of Louisiana's most engaging attractions here.

SIGHTS

Louisiana's Old State Capitol

Once the seat of the state government, the **Old State Capitol** (100 North Blvd., Baton Rouge, 225/342-0500 or 800/488-2968, www.louisianaoldstatecapitol.org; Tues.-Sat. 9am-4pm; free) was constructed between 1847 and 1852; it's one of the state's few prominent examples of large-scale Gothic architecture. Inside, you'll find a vast and wonderfully presented collection of interactive and multimedia exhibits on a wide variety of topics, including the history of Baton Rouge and the legacy of controversial governor Huey P. Long. There's also a governors' portrait gallery, plus rotating exhibits. It's the sort of museum that's enjoyable for kids as well as adults, and the breadth of documents, artifacts, and collectibles displayed here is impressive.

★ Louisiana State Capitol

The **Louisiana State Capitol** (State Capitol Dr. and N. 3rd St., Baton Rouge, 225/342-7317, www.crt.state.la.us; daily 8am-4:30pm; free) was completed in March 1932. A nifty 34-story art deco wonder, it took 14 months to build with a resulting price tag of about $5 million. It is, at 450 feet, the tallest U.S. capitol building. One of the highlights of a visit here is touring the 27 acres of spectacularly landscaped gardens. In addition, you can look around the grand entrance and Memorial Hall; peek inside the chambers (when the state legislature is not in session); ride the elevator to the 27th-floor observation deck, which affords spectacular views of the city; and see exactly where the flamboyant governor Huey P. Long was assassinated.

LSU Rural Life Museum

Only a short drive southeast of downtown, the **LSU Rural Life Museum** (4560 Essen Ln., Baton Rouge, 225/765-2437, http://rurallife.lsu.edu; daily 8:30am-5pm; $7 adult, $6 senior and child 5-11, free under 5) is a living-history museum situated on the 450-acre **Burden Research Plantation.**

Dedicated to preserving and interpreting the lifestyles and cultures of preindustrial Louisiana, the museum comprises numerous buildings and exhibits, which show different aspects of early Louisiana living. The plantation quarters constitute a complex of authentically furnished 19th-century structures, including a kitchen, a schoolhouse, and slave cabins. Inside a large barn, you can examine tools and vehicles spanning more than 300 years. You'll also spy several historic houses that reveal Louisiana's rich tradition of folk architecture, from a country church to an Acadian house to a shotgun home. You can also tour the extensive Windrush Gardens, a 25-acre plot of semiformal gardens abundant with winding paths, ponds, and flora typically found in 19th-century plantation gardens.

USS *Kidd* Veterans Museum

The **USS *Kidd*** (305 S. River Rd., Baton Rouge, 225/342-1942, www.usskidd.com; daily 9am-5pm; $8 adult, $7 senior, $5 child 5-12, free under 5) is the only ship of its kind that's still in its wartime camouflage paint. This World War II-era Fletcher-class destroyer was awarded 12 battle stars for serving during World War II and the Korean War; it was struck by a Japanese kamikaze plane during the World War II Battle of Okinawa, an attack that killed 38 members of the *Kidd*'s crew. It has been carefully restored and can now be toured, along with the nearby Veterans Memorial Museum, which features a nuclear-powered submarine, a World War II-era fighter plane and a Vietnam-era bomber, and the South's largest model ship collection.

RESTAURANTS

Where there are politicians, there are almost always good restaurants, and Baton Rouge confirms this rule with its wide variety of well-favored eateries. It's also a student town, which means you can find several decent, relatively affordable joints around LSU's campus. Perhaps the most stylish restaurant in Baton Rouge is **Juban's** (3739 Perkins Rd., Baton Rouge, 225/346-8422, www.jubans.com; Mon. 5:30pm-10pm, Tues.-Fri. 11am-10pm, Sat. 5:30pm-10pm, Sun. 10:30am-3pm; $10-60). Juban's has been serving innovative Louisiana-influenced fare since the early 1980s, when owner-chef John Mariani's temple of fine cuisine was named one of America's "Best New Restaurants" in *Esquire*. The restaurant is known for such signature dishes as Louisiana crawfish pasta with shiitake mushrooms and white truffle Madeira cream, seafood-stuffed soft-shell crab topped with Creolaise sauce, and a pork rib chop with honey-bourbon glaze.

For local flavors that won't blow your budget, head to **Jasmines on the Bayou** (6010 Jones Creek Rd., Baton Rouge, 225/753-3668, www.jasminesonthebayou.com; Mon.-Thurs. 10:30am-8:30pm, Fri. 10:30am-9:30pm, Sat. 11am-9:30pm; $11-17). Essentially a Cajun seafood restaurant, Jasmines offers such tasty regional fare as corn and crab bisque, grilled shrimp rémoulade, and pasta jambalaya. Be sure to start with an order of rocket shrimp, which are lightly battered and tossed in a spicy chili aioli sauce.

Above: the Louisiana State Capitol. Below: the USS *Kidd*.

NIGHTLIFE

Between bars, music clubs, and casinos, Baton Rouge provides a decent share of nightlife options. The low-key **Phil Brady's Bar & Grill** (4848 Government St., Baton Rouge, 225/927-3786; Mon.-Fri. 11am-2am, Sat. 5pm-2am) is a fun place to drink with pals, play a round of pool, or enjoy some live music, particularly the well-attended Thursday night blues jams. College students and other music fans have been packing into **The Cadillac** (5454 Bluebonnet Blvd., Baton Rouge, 225/296-0288, www.cadillaccafe.net; Mon. 4pm-11pm, Tues.-Fri. 4pm-2am, Sat. 7pm-2am) since 1989 for hard-driving rock and blues; karaoke and DJ dance parties are also big draws at this cutting-edge joint.

The city's favorite gay and lesbian dance club is **Splash Nightclub** (2183 Highland Rd., Baton Rouge, 225/242-9491, www.splashbr.com; Thurs.-Sat. 9pm-2am), situated in a slightly dodgy neighborhood near LSU's campus. Featuring multiple rooms and several bars, Splash presents a variety of music, from country to techno, plus one of Baton Rouge's best drag shows. If you're in more of a gambling mood, head to the **Belle of Baton Rouge Casino** (103 France St., Baton Rouge, 225/242-2600 or 800/676-4847, www.belleofbatonrouge.com; daily 24 hours), which is housed inside a three-deck riverboat that's docked permanently on the Mississippi River.

ARTS AND EVENTS

For a bit of culture, head to the **Theatre Baton Rouge** (7155 Florida Blvd., Baton Rouge, 225/924-6496, www.brlt.org), which has been presenting live theater since the late 1940s. Each season's lineup typically includes several well-known plays and musicals, such as *A Streetcar Named Desire* and *Hairspray*. Another cultural option is the **Varsity Theatre** (3353 Highland Rd., Baton Rouge, 225/383-7018, www.varsitytheatre.com), a legendary concert venue that features salsa, alternative rock, and everything in between.

From balloon festivals to Fourth of July fireworks displays, Baton Rouge presents a slew of crowd-pleasing events throughout the year. One of the most popular is the **Baton Rouge Blues Festival** (www.batonrougebluesfestival.org), a free, one-day event that usually takes place in mid-April in the city's Town Square. Founded in 1980, it's one of America's oldest blues festivals, featuring a lineup of well-respected blues guitarists, pianists, and bands. In late October, literary fans will appreciate the **Louisiana Book Festival** (www.louisianabookfestival.org), a free, one-day event that typically occurs at various locations in downtown Baton Rouge, such as the Louisiana State Capitol and the State Library of Louisiana. Activities include readings, workshops, and a book discussion group.

HOTELS

While the Baton Rouge area has its share of quaint inns and B&Bs, most of the city's lodging options comprise major chain hotels and motels, primarily set just off I-12 and I-10, on the southeast side of town. Perhaps Baton Rouge's most impressive property is the **Hilton Baton Rouge Capitol**

Center (201 Lafayette St., Baton Rouge, 225/344-5866 or 877/862-9800, www.hiltoncapitolcenter.com; $159-209), which opened in 2006 in the historic buildings that once housed the Heidelberg and Capitol House Hotels. Developers spent about $70 million creating this elegant property with 290 smartly furnished rooms, a full-service spa and fitness center, a pool deck overlooking the Mississippi River, and a lavish restaurant, Kingfish. Other amenities include complimentary newspapers and 24-hour room service.

PRACTICALITIES

Information

For more information about the state's capital city, consult **Visit Baton Rouge** (359 3rd St., Baton Rouge, 225/383-1825 or 800/527-6843, www.visitbatonrouge.com). In addition, the city's daily newspaper, *The Advocate* (www.theadvocate.com), offers a plethora of helpful tidbits, including details about local sports and entertainment.

Getting There and Around

Unfortunately, there aren't too many back ways to drive from New Orleans to Baton Rouge. You could take the commercially robust Airline Highway (US-61), which has numerous traffic lights and little character, or slip along the Great River Road, a time-consuming route that only makes sense if you allow yourself an overnight stop and explore some of the plantations en route. Most visitors opt for the speedier if less interesting I-10, a straight 80-mile shot that, without traffic, usually takes less than 90 minutes. Although you can also reach Baton Rouge directly via the **Baton Rouge Metropolitan Airport** (9430 Jackie Cochran Dr., Baton Rouge, 225/355-0333, www.flybtr.com), it's easiest to explore the area by car. Even in Baton Rouge, which has a semi-compact downtown, many attractions, restaurants, and hotels lie beyond this pedestrian-friendly area, making a car handy and public transportation impractical.

Cajun Country

Cajun Country, also known as Acadiana, extends from just southwest of New Orleans, around the town of Houma, to the Texas border, out near the city of Lake Charles. It's in this down-home, hospitable region that you'll discover the rich and distinctive heritage of the Cajun people, who were expelled from Canada in the mid-1700s before eventually relocating to this terrain of swampland, rivers, and fertile prairies. Beyond Lafayette, however, and the region's other urban anchor, Lake Charles, Cajun Country is largely a collection of small to midsize towns, many of them rural and quite historic in character. Wetlands communities like New Iberia, St. Martinville, and Breaux Bridge are excellent destinations for dining on Cajun food (such as crawfish pie and blackened redfish), exploring historic sites, and venturing into the swamps on guided boat excursions. Prairie

Swamp Tours

Guided excursions into the swamps around New Orleans can be an ideal way to explore such vast, ravishingly beautiful areas. Although the top destinations for swamp tours are Slidell, Houma, and towns along the Atchafalaya Basin east and south of Lafayette, you can also find operators south of Baton Rouge and throughout metro New Orleans. Some operators offer hotel pickups (for an additional fee) and, depending on the season, extra tour times in the late afternoon, around sunset, and at night. As with many attractions in southern Louisiana, the best seasons are spring and fall, but no matter when you opt for a swamp tour, be sure to call ahead for reservations and precise directions.

Situated on the West Bank, near Barataria Preserve, **Airboat Adventures** (5145 Fleming Park Rd., Lafitte, 504/689-2005 or 888/467-9267, www.airboatadventures.com; daily 9:45am, noon, and 2pm; $30-65 pp) leads guided two-hour excursions into a private, 20,000-acre swamp. Via high-speed airboats of varying sizes, you'll have the chance to observe native swamp creatures amid vibrant wildflowers and haunting cypress trees.

A favorite near Houma is **A Cajun Man's Swamp Cruise** (251 Marina Dr., Gibson, 985/991-0141 or 985/868-4625, www.cajunman.com; times vary; $25 adult, $15 child under 13), an entertaining, two-hour tour conducted by Captain Ron "Black" Guidry, a former U.S. Army Green Beret and Louisiana State Trooper. Guidry, who is fluent in French and English, plays guitar and accordion and sings Cajun ditties while maneuvering his covered boat through the cypress swamps of southeastern Louisiana.

In the heart of Cajun Country, **Champagne's Cajun Swamp Tours** (1151 Rookery Rd., Breaux Bridge, 337/230-4068, http://champagnesswamptours.com; daily 6:30am-8pm; $20-25 adult, $10-15 child under 13) takes passengers out in relatively quiet, 20-foot aluminum crawfish skiffs. The narrated, two-hour tour leaves from the banks of Lake Martin and passes through a dramatic flooded cypress and tupelo forest, as well as one of the state's largest nesting areas of wading birds.

One of the most respected operators in the state, **Dr. Wagner's Honey Island Swamp Tours** (41490 Crawford Landing Rd., Slidell, 985/641-1769 or

towns such as Eunice and Opelousas are best known for their Cajun and zydeco musical heritage. You'll also find rustic bed-and-breakfasts, quaint house-museums, and relatively affordable antiques shops and art galleries.

SIGHTS

★ Acadian Cultural Center

The National Park Service's superb **Acadian Cultural Center** (501 Fisher Rd., Lafayette, 337/232-0789, www.nps.gov/jela; daily 8am-5pm; free) offers an excellent overview of Cajun history and culture. Housed within a contemporary building designed to resemble a Cajun cottage, the museum space contains well-labeled, often large-scale exhibits, artifacts, and photos. You can easily spend an hour in here absorbing the lore of Cajun music, family life, cooking, language, and fishing, and exploring the serpentine route that Acadians journeyed from Nova Scotia to southern Louisiana.

504/242-5877, www.honeyislandswamp.com; daily 9am, 11:30am, and 2pm; $23 adult, $15 child) offers two-hour excursions through Honey Island Swamp, a lush overflow river swamp and the second-largest swamp in Louisiana. Using small boats, the knowledgeable guides can access shallow backwater areas, home to feral hogs, alligators, and otters.

For a more intimate experience, try **The Last Wilderness** (33195 Hwy. 75, Plaquemine, 225/659-2499 or 225/692-4114, www.lastwildernesstours.com; times vary; $40 adult, $35 child under 10), which uses a small, six-person Cajun fishing boat for two-hour tours of the Atchafalaya Basin. In an effort to educate people about this fragile paradise, guide Dean A. Wilson takes passengers well off the beaten path, even by swamp standards, and into tight, shallow bodies of water that larger vessels can't reach.

A highly recommended company, **McGee's Landing** (1337 Henderson Levee Rd., Henderson, 337/228-2384, www.mcgeeslanding.com; daily 10am, 1pm, and 3pm; $20 adult, $18 senior, $15 child under 12) also operates narrated tours through the Atchafalaya Basin; other offerings include live entertainment, guest cabins, a campground, and a homestyle café.

To explore the relatively untouched Honey Island Swamp in a midsize boat, you can hitch a ride with **Pearl River Eco-Tours** (55050 Hwy. 90, Slidell, 985/649-4200 or 866/597-9267, www.pearlriverecotours.com; daily 10am and 2:30pm; $25 adult, $23 military personnel and senior 65 and over, $15 child under 12), which provides two-hour tours led by Coast Guard-certified guides who are all native to the area and experts on the swamp ecosystem and history. If you'd prefer a more intimate experience in a six-person skiff, expect to pay considerably more ($70 pp).

Southwest of New Orleans, **Torres Cajun Swamp Tours** (105 Torres Rd., Thibodaux, 985/633-7739, www.torresswamptours.net; times vary; $11-20 adult and student, $10-20 child under 12) operates tours in the scenic Bayou Boeuf area. Led by Coast Guard-certified guides, these educational 1.5-hour excursions provide guests with the opportunity to observe and photograph a wide array of native inhabitants.

Through such exhibits as well as varied films, you'll have a gut-wrenching but inspirational look at the plight of Cajuns and their astounding resolve, balanced with their love of celebration and tradition that has kept them a distinct cultural group to this day. Check for interpretive programs, videos, and performances scheduled regularly throughout the year.

The Acadian Cultural Center is a short drive southeast of downtown Lafayette, just off US-90 by Lafayette Regional Airport.

★ Avery Island

Perhaps the most visited section of New Iberia, the community of Avery Island is home to a pair of seminal Cajun Country attractions: Jungle Gardens and the TABASCO Factory. Avery Island is not, in fact, an island—it is not surrounded by water. Rather it is a salt dome, which rises rather gently above the surrounding wetlands and has been a source of commercial salt since the 1860s. The earliest salt works on the island were short-lived but important for Confederate troops during the Civil War. It was in 1862 that a significant cache of rock salt was discovered here—the first such deposit in all of North America. Union troops, upon securing the area, immediately destroyed the salt mines, which were not reopened until 1880.

MCILHENNY COMPANY

Though Avery Island continues to be a source of commercial salt, its actual claim to fame is another savory condiment, TABASCO Sauce, which Edward McIlhenny first bottled on Avery Island in 1868. The regular tour of the McIlhenny Company's **TABASCO factory** (337/365-8173 or 800/634-9599, www.tabasco.com; daily 9am-4pm; free) is underwhelming, beginning with a shamelessly promotional video expounding on the virtues of TABASCO Sauce. You're then given a small souvenir bottle of the vaunted condiment before proceeding along a wall of windows through which you can observe the inner workings of the factory, where a jumble of machines and conveyor belts bottle, cap, and label the sauces. At the end of your tour, you'll walk through a small museum of TABASCO memorabilia, after which you can wander across the parking lot to the old-fashioned Country Store. It's all good, clean fun, and the experience is especially nice for kids who might be getting a little tired of touring historic house-museums.

JUNGLE GARDENS AND BIRD CITY

Slightly less famous on Avery Island is the McIlhenny family's 170-acre **Jungle Gardens and Bird City** (337/369-6243, http://junglegardens.org, daily 9am-5pm; $8 adult, $5 under 13). A narrow four-mile country lane winds through this garden complex, which you can tour in less than an hour by car or in the course of a few hours if you decide to hoof it. (You can also park in several spots along the drive.) Thousands of subtropical plants and trees, including massive moss-draped live oaks, grow throughout these wild gardens, which are home to deer, turtles, nutria, raccoons, black bears, and alligators. The gardens also include the most complete collection of camellias in the world and a Buddhist temple containing a statue that dates to the 12th century. Although the gardens are open year-round, they're less thrilling in winter (Nov.-Feb.), when much of the plant life is dormant and the alligators hibernate.

No matter when you visit, take a few minutes to observe Bird City, a massive nesting ground for graceful great white egrets. Long stilted platforms rise out of a large marshy pond, and the egrets build nests here. The egrets are most prolific from December through July, when you may see hundreds of these creatures gathering branches, mating and courting, and putting on a spectacular show. A three-story observation deck sits opposite

Bayou Teche

Bayou Teche (pronounced "BYE-oo TESH"), a 125-mile-long waterway in southern Louisiana, runs through the Cajun towns of Breaux Bridge, St. Martinville, and New Iberia. Its name, *teche,* is an old Attakapas Indian term for "snake." Native American legends offer different origins for the name, including one that suggests that a snake actually created the river: Chitimacha warriors destroyed a massive venomous serpent many miles in length, and as the beast died from its wounds, it writhed and deepened a twisting track in the mud that became the riverbed of Bayou Teche.

The Teche begins just east of Opelousas in the town of Port Barre, where it flows from Bayou Courtableau. Roughly paralleling I-49, it meanders through the towns of Arnaudville and Cecilia before cutting beneath I-10 and entering Breaux Bridge. It's along this stretch, from Arnaudville to Breaux Bridge, that the banks of the river are shaded by tall oak trees, dramatically draped with moss. A couple of miles downstream from St. Martinville, the Teche passes through the Keystone Locks and Control Structure, constructed by the U.S. Army Corps of Engineers to increase the bayou's water level, making it navigable for boats heading upstream to Port Barre.

You can drive alongside much of the Teche via several state highways, especially from New Iberia south through Jeanerette and Franklin. From here, it passes through yet another flood-control structure before finally emptying into the Lower Atchafalaya River.

the nesting platforms, close enough to snap some wonderful pictures. You can reach Bird City by parking at the designated spot, as indicated on the souvenir trail map.

PRACTICALITIES

To reach Avery Island, follow LA-329 about six miles southwest from US-90 in New Iberia. You'll come to a small guardhouse where you'll have to pay a nominal toll of $1. From here, proceed to the driveways for the TABASCO factory and, beyond that, Jungle Gardens.

Shadows-on-the-Teche

To experience one of the true must-see museums of Acadiana, head to **Shadows-on-the-Teche** (317 E. Main St., New Iberia, 337/369-6446 or 877/200-4924, www.shadowsontheteche.org; Mon.-Sat. 9am-4:30pm; $10 adult, $8 senior, $6.50 student 6-17), a dignified white-columned brick house built by sugarcane farmer David Weeks in 1834. Unfortunately, Weeks died before ever living in the house. His wife, Mary Weeks, ran the house and oversaw the plantation for years afterward. The house is much smaller than some of the leviathan plantation houses along the Great River Road, and that's one reason it makes for a better tour—you aren't treated to an endless march through rooms and outbuildings. But the best thing about Shadows is that the National Trust for Historic Preservation, which owns the house, also has a collection of about 17,000 documents relevant to the lives of the plantation's inhabitants and its day-to-day inner workings. Guides at Shadows draw on these records to paint a vivid picture of life here, and often the most fascinating bits of information to modern visitors revolve around seeming minutiae, such as inventories of the kitchen pantry. Some of the volunteer guides are descendants of David and Mary Weeks. In addition to having a well-documented history, Shadows-on-the-Teche is one of the better-furnished plantation homes around. Other details inside the Classical Revival house include a lavish Italian marble floor in the formal dining room and the wide galleries at the exterior facade. Across the street from the plantation in a former bank building, a visitors center presents a brief film on the Weeks family and the plantation's history, and rotating exhibits offer further insights into the property.

Center Street in New Iberia is so named because it was the center of the vast Weeks plantation, which once extended many miles south from this building, clear out to Weeks Island (a.k.a. Grand Cote), the actual sugarcane-farming operation that so enriched the Weeks family. Like many others in Louisiana, the plantation was occupied by Union troops during the Civil War. Soldiers camped on the grounds, and officers lived on the ground floor.

The house's verdant grounds sweep right back to the muddy Bayou Teche, and you can stroll through the beautiful, somewhat formal gardens, which feature about 25 varieties of trees.

★ Vermilionville

Within view of the Acadian Cultural Center, **Vermilionville** (300 Fisher Rd., Lafayette, 337/233-4077, www.bayouvermilion.org; Tues.-Sun. 10am-4pm; $10 adult, $8 senior, $6 student 6-18, free under 6) is another must-see for understanding Cajun culture. This 23-acre, living-history compound comprises five restored historic houses, 12 reproduction period buildings, and exhibits about the indigenous people, the area's wetlands, and Cajun and zydeco music (which is performed live here regularly). You can attend cooking demonstrations, eat in the casual La Cuisine de Maman restaurant, and walk along a nature trail identifying Louisiana plant life. Vermilionville is, rather oddly, set near the airport and several modern warehouses, but once you enter the re-created village, it feels quite authentic; there's even a lazy bayou running through the property. The buildings here include a chapel and *presbytère,* where a clergyman would have lived; an Acadian barn where volunteers engage in boat-building and net- and trap-making; and several residences, the oldest dating from 1790. Every element of Vermilionville sheds light onto the culture of the area's original Cajuns, from homestyle cooking to live music-and-dance programs. As a bonus, the guides are knowledgeable and enthusiastic.

RESTAURANTS

Not surprisingly, Acadiana is widely celebrated for its Cajun cuisine. Cajun restaurants in Lafayette, New Iberia, Opelousas, and other Cajun towns feature staples like gumbo, jambalaya, red beans and rice, fresh seafood, and bread pudding with rum sauce. One ideal option is **Prejean's** (3480 NE Evangeline Trwy., Lafayette, 337/896-3247, www.prejeans.com; daily 7am-9:30pm; $9-25), which is as popular for its live Cajun music as for its delicious cuisine. The rambling dining room is presided over by a friendly and efficient staff; of the big Cajun dance hall-dining rooms in the region, Prejean's serves the best, most inventive Cajun and Creole food, including such specialties as catfish Catahoula (stuffed with shrimp, crawfish, and crab and served with a decadent crawfish and tasso cream sauce). While you're savoring dinner, you can also enjoy live music; once your food settles, you can even venture onto the dance floor. Lunch is also served, and the breakfasts at Prejean's are legendary.

For a more casual option, head to **Boudreau & Thibodeau's Cajun Cookin'** (5602 W. Main St., Houma, 985/872-4711, www.bntcajuncookin.com; Sun.-Thurs. 10am-10pm, Fri.-Sat. 10am-11pm; $5-24), which serves some of the tastiest home-style local fare in the area, from seafood gumbo to po-boys to redfish courtbouillon. You won't go home hungry after a platter of country-fried steak, soft-shell crab, or fried seafood. As the name indicates, the place is silly and festive, with goofy Cajun jokes printed on both the walls and the menu.

Cajun food isn't the only option in Acadiana. You'll also find creative, contemporary cuisine at places like **The French Press** (214 E. Vermilion St., Lafayette, 337/233-9449, www.thefrenchpresslafayette.com; Tues.-Thurs. 7am-2pm, Fri. 7am-2pm and 5:30pm-9pm, Sat. 9am-2pm and 5:30pm-9pm, Sun. 9am-2pm; $6-39). With high ceilings, weathered walls, and tall windows, this well-lit eatery is ideal for both casual lunches and romantic dinners. The constantly evolving menu features classic dishes such as grits and grillades, plus innovative options like smoked duck breast with sweet potato spaetzle, roasted brussels sprouts, and dried cranberry glacé. The wine, beer, and cocktail lists are worth considering, too.

Between Lafayette and Houma, the town of New Iberia nurtures its share of scrumptious eating options. After touring Shadows-on-the-Teche, head a couple blocks down Main Street to **Victor's Cafeteria** (109 W. Main St., New Iberia, 337/369-9924; daily 6am-2pm; $8-10), a spacious, no-frills

Above: Clementine Dining & Spirits in New Iberia. Below: The Fairfax House in Franklin.

eatery that has been serving large, inexpensive portions of fried chicken, grilled catfish, and other Cajun, Creole, and Southern staples since 1969. The offerings at this lunch counter, including heaping breakfast dishes, change daily, but you can always expect friendly service and filling comfort food, including classic sides and desserts. Fans of James Lee Burke's Dave Robicheaux detective novels, which are often set in New Iberia and frequently mention Victor's, especially favor this popular joint and its small shrine to Dave's bait shop. For a slightly fancier and infinitely more romantic meal, head across the street to **Clementine Dining & Spirits** (113 E. Main St., New Iberia, 337/560-1007, http://clementinedowntown.com; Tues.-Thurs. 11am-2pm and 5pm-9pm, Fri. 11am-2pm and 5pm-10pm, Sat. 6pm-10pm, $17-48), which has been preparing a wide array of eclectic dishes, from blackened shrimp pasta to jerk pork tenderloin, since the late 1990s.

NIGHTLIFE

In this part of the world, it's the restaurant that *doesn't* have live music that's the exception. You can catch Cajun and zydeco bands at a number of places all through the area, but Lafayette and the neighboring towns seem to support any kind of music that you can tap your toes to. Popular **Blue Moon Saloon & Guesthouse** (215 E. Convent St., Lafayette, 337/234-2422 or 877/766-2583, www.bluemoonpresents.com; show times vary) has a large, outdoor deck where musicians of all types perform Wednesday-Sunday to an eclectic crowd of all ages. The place, which also offers affordable overnight accommodations, is usually packed with locals and visitors alike.

The Cajun Prairie also boasts its share of swamp pop, zydeco, and other live music; in fact, it's one of the country's premier live-music regions. **Slim's Y-Ki-Ki** (8410 LA-182, Opelousas, 337/942-6242, www.slimsykiki.com) has been one of the area's favorite zydeco dance halls since shortly after World War II; it's open mostly on weekend evenings and brings in some of the top bands in Louisiana. The big, low-slung building is sparse on decor (except for a few palm trees painted on the walls), but there's a huge, wide-open dance floor where enthusiasts cut loose to the music and you're welcome to dance yourself. This is one of the best places in the region to hear zydeco.

ARTS AND CULTURE

Lafayette is home to the stately **Heymann Center** (1373 S. College Rd., Lafayette, 337/291-5555 or 337/291-5540, www.heymann-center.com; show times vary), which hosts a variety of entertainment, including pop concerts, dance troupes, and theater. Another good option for cultural events is the famous **Liberty Center for the Performing Arts** (S. 2nd St. and Park Ave., Eunice, 337/457-7389, www.eunice-la.com), an old movie house and vaudeville theater built in 1924. Back in the day, such illustrious performers as Tex Ritter, Fatty Arbuckle, and Roy Rogers performed here. After falling into a state of neglect, it was restored in 1986 when local citizens banded together to revive it. Today, it's the site of *Rendezvous des Cajuns* (Sat. 6pm; $5), a two-hour live radio and TV variety show with Cajun and zydeco music, along with storytelling, recipes, and other tidbits of Cajun lore. This legendary show is a memorable way to become acquainted with the region and its rich musical history. Tickets are available at the theater beginning at 4pm on the day of the performance.

FESTIVALS AND EVENTS

Outside New Orleans, no part of the state enjoys a good festival more than Acadiana. Scores of engaging events are held in towns throughout the region, virtually year-round. Besides staging the second-largest Mardi Gras celebration in the state, Lafayette hosts the annual **Festival International de Louisiane** (Lafayette, 337/232-8086, www.festivalinternational.com), a massive five-day party in late April that showcases all kinds of local and French music, French-language plays, and other Francophone fun, plus oodles of regional food.

In early May, fans of mudbugs gather at the **Breaux Bridge Crawfish Festival** (Breaux Bridge, 337/332-6655, www.bbcrawfest.com) to sample tasty treats and listen to live Cajun and zydeco music; it's one of the most popular events in the region. Fun-lovers also favor the family-oriented **Cajun Heartland State Fair** (Cajundome, 444 Cajundome Blvd., Lafayette, 337/265-2100, www.cajundome.com), a lively, 11-day indoor celebration that features carnival rides, regional cuisine, and live entertainment; it usually takes place in late May and early June. Over Labor Day weekend, music lovers flock to the **Southwest Louisiana Zydeco Music Festival** (Opelousas, 337/942-2392, www.zydeco.org), which has, for three decades, presented great concerts, varied foods, and lots of arts and crafts in Opelousas.

In mid-October, just as the hot weather generally begins to break, Lafayette holds its rollicking **Festivals Acadiens et Créoles** (Lafayette, www.festivalsacadiens.com), a chance for visitors to learn about Cajun culture through its rich musical traditions. You can learn the Cajun waltz or two-step, and how accordions and fiddles figure into the sounds of Cajun song and dance. Outside Mardi Gras, this is one of the region's most popular, well-attended festivals, comprising several smaller events, including the Festival de Musique, the Bayou Food Festival, the Louisiana Craft Fair, and Louisiana Folk Roots. Events are held at lovely Girard Park near the University of Louisiana at Lafayette.

SPORTS AND ACTIVITIES

The 6,000-acre **Lake Fausse Pointe State Park** (5400 Levee Rd., St. Martinville, 337/229-4764 or 888/677-7200, www.crt.state.la.us; Sun.-Thurs. 6am-9pm, Fri.-Sat. 6am-10pm; $1 pp, free over 62 and under 4) sits on the eastern side of Lake Fausse, fringing the Atchafalaya Swamp; it may take a little effort to get here, but the scenic drive through beautiful wetlands is well worth it. Although Lake Fausse is popular for boating and fishing, it's generally a tranquil place that is a favorite haunt of wildlife photographers and bird-watchers. Facilities include a boat dock with rentals, campsites, hiking trails, and 18 overnight camping cabins with screened-in porches, air-conditioning, and piers over the water.

SHOPS

Stores selling Cajun-related music, books, gifts, arts and crafts, and gourmet treats are easy to find throughout Acadiana. New Iberia is one of the region's best towns for shopping, as it's home to a handful of pleasant boutiques that deal in antiques. Be sure to check out **Books Along the Teche** (106 E. Main St., New Iberia, 337/367-7621 or 877/754-0849, www.booksalongtheteche.com; Mon.-Fri. 9:30am-5:30pm, Sat. 9:30am-5pm), a small, first-rate independent bookstore that offers both new and used books. It specializes in regional books and music, with signed copies of all the books written by James Lee Burke, author of the popular Dave Robicheaux detective novels and longtime resident of New Iberia.

For local treats, head to **Champagne's Breaux Bridge Bakery** (105 S. Poydras St., Breaux Bridge, 337/332-1117, www.champagnesbakery.com; Mon.-Fri. 7am-5:30pm, Sat. 7am-1pm), which has been a snacking institution in Breaux Bridge since 1888. The wonderful cakes, breads, and bite-size cookies make a wonderful picnic before an outing or a dessert en route to your hotel.

In downtown Lafayette, art lovers should stop by the **Sans Souci Fine Crafts Gallery** (219 E. Vermilion St., Lafayette, 337/266-7999, www.louisianacrafts.org; Tues.-Fri. 11am-5pm, Sat. 10am-4pm), featuring the traditional and contemporary works of members of the Louisiana Crafts Guild. Housed within a 19th-century structure, this well-regarded gallery features textiles, jewelry, pottery, glass, and wood.

HOTELS

Louisiana's Cajun Country boasts a wide selection of chain hotels, historic inns, and intimate cabins. If you're more comfortable with familiar names, then consider the **Hilton Lafayette** (1521 W. Pinhook Rd., Lafayette, 337/235-6111 or 800/445-8667, www.hilton.com; $119-159), perhaps the region's fanciest chain property. Situated on the banks of Bayou Vermilion, the Hilton houses 335 warmly furnished rooms and suites with French Provincial-inspired furnishings. The 15-floor, pet-friendly hotel offers scenic views of the countryside and proximity to the airport and downtown. Other amenities include a an outdoor pool and sundeck, a full-service restaurant, and a hotel bar that's popular with locals.

With rates lower than most of the cookie-cutter motels around the area, the **Bayou Cabins Bed & Breakfast** (100 W. Mills Ave., Breaux Bridge, 337/332-6158, www.bayoucabins.com; $60-135) is a fun and funky alternative. There are 13 cozy cabins right by Bayou Teche, close to downtown

The Atchafalaya Basin

The Atchafalaya (pronounced "UH-cha-fuh-lye-uh") is the main distributary of the Mississippi River and an active, living delta through which flows the 137-mile-long Atchafalaya River. At about 20 miles in width and 150 miles in length, the basin is the largest overflow swamp in the United States (as well as the country's largest existing wetland) and covers roughly 1.4 million acres, including the surrounding swamps beyond the levees.

A swamp is any low ground overrun with water but punctuated by trees; marshes are similar but have few or no trees. This swamp began forming around AD 900, when the Mississippi River started to change its course, which had previously favored a westerly shift once it reached southern Louisiana. For many centuries, the river then flowed through present-day Bayou Lafourche, which passes through the city of Houma and eventually empties into the Gulf.

Annual flooding forced heavy waters into the low-lying and dense forest on either side of the Mississippi River. Eventually, natural levees formed and contained the water permanently. In recent centuries, the Mississippi River has shifted still farther back toward the southeastern section of the state.

Historically, this swamp cultivated some of the richest and most fertile soil in the South, not to mention prolific fishing grounds, making it the perfect place for the exiled Acadian refugees who arrived in the mid- to late 18th century and established roots all through the basin. The geography of the swamp effectively cut the early Cajun settlements off from the rest of the state, helping them to preserve their distinct heritage and language. To this day, they remain a remarkably close-knit society.

The Atchafalaya Basin's appearance and character both changed dramatically throughout the 20th century. Discoveries in the 1920s of vast oil and natural-gas reserves brought prosperity to the region, as well as large numbers of newcomers. Major floods, most notably in 1927, have, at different times, forced small communities within the basin to abandon their homes and settle on higher land, and in 1973, the federal government constructed an 18-mile-long bridge through the swamp, extending I-10 from New Orleans and Baton Rouge to Lafayette. The work of the U.S. Army Corps of Engineers, which involved erecting massive floodgates at the intersection of the Mississippi and Atchafalaya Rivers, is what prevented the Mississippi from seeking a permanent shortcut through the swamp to the Gulf.

Breaux Bridge. The cabins are rustic but endearingly furnished: one has old newspaper for wallpaper, another contains a pencil-post, queen-size bed, some have screened porches, and one is decked in 1950s-style furnishings. There's also a home-style café right on the premises, serving pork boudin, cracklings, and beignets. A full breakfast is included.

If you'd prefer to stay amid the Cajun wetlands, head to **The Gouguenheim** (101 W. Main St., New Iberia, 337/364-3949, www.gouguenheim.com; $225-325), an impressive, elegant 1894 building originally constructed as the Washington Ballroom, where it hosted many wedding receptions and important social functions. In 2001, it was beautifully restored and converted into a B&B. There's a large veranda that wraps around the second floor, and four large guest apartments: a one-bedroom, a two-bedroom, and two with three bedrooms. Hardwood floors, detailed

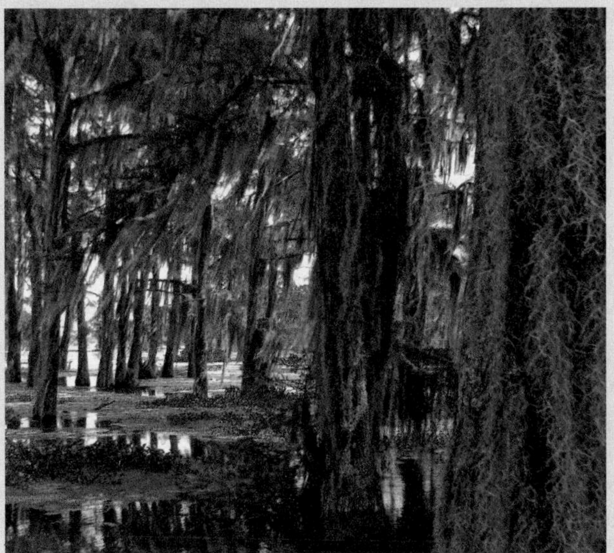

cypress trees in the Atchafalaya Basin

The construction of these flood-control systems and levees, as well as oil pipelines, access canals, and other man-made structures, has not only forever altered the swamp but has also, at times, threatened its well-being. As the largest bottomland hardwood forest in the United States, with the country's largest remaining contiguous tract of coastal cypress, the Atchafalaya is still home to fertile, productive fish and wildlife habitats. Nearly 400 bird species nest in the region, including egrets, ibises, and bald eagles. The basin also claims roughly 65 reptile species, including turtles, snakes, and alligators, and 90 types of fish; other inhabitants include white-tailed deer, black bears, and river otters.

woodwork, exposed brick, and posh furnishings give this the feel of a small luxury hotel; some units have spiral staircases leading up to sleeping lofts. Amenities include designer kitchens with granite counters and stainless-steel appliances, and private balconies overlooking downtown New Iberia's historic district.

Less than 40 miles southeast of New Iberia lies the even smaller town of Franklin, whose historic district boasts nearly 420 noteworthy 19th-century houses and structures and was listed on the National Register of Historic Places in 1982. Over the years, several of these buildings have become pampering inns. One such place is **The Fairfax House** (99 Main St., Franklin, 337/828-1195, www.thefairfaxhouse.net; $149-189), a sumptuous white mansion that stands amid moss-draped oak trees and well-tended grounds. With six comfortable rooms and suites on the upper and lower levels, it skillfully marries authentic furnishings with modern amenities, such as luxurious linens and whirlpool tubs. In addition to treating guests to a delicious, Southern-style breakfast every morning, this welcoming B&B also provides 24-hour access to elegant dining and living areas, a screened patio, and an upper gallery, complete with rocking chairs and a roomy porch swing.

Closer to New Orleans, you'll find the **Grand Bayou Noir Bed & Breakfast** (1143 Bayou Black Dr., Houma, 985/873-5849, www.grandbayounoir.com; $120-160), which sits on four acres studded with gracious oak and fruit trees, fronting the peaceful Bayou Black. The three guest rooms in this imposing 1930s Colonial Revival house have queen-size beds and elegant antiques; one suite has a private balcony, hot tub, and sitting area. You can relax on the large screened porch or the varied swings, rocking chairs, and hammocks that pepper the grounds, all of which make this B&B truly ideal for a quiet retreat or a romantic getaway.

PRACTICALITIES

Information

For more information about Louisiana's Cajun Country, consult the **Lafayette Convention & Visitors Commission** (LCVC, 1400 NW Evangeline Trwy., Lafayette, 337/232-3737 or 800/346-1958, www.lafayettetravel.com), which serves as an umbrella tourism organization for most of the Acadiana towns between Opelousas and Morgan City, and between Jennings and Henderson. Most of the nearby parishes also have tourism organizations, such as the **Iberia Parish Convention & Visitors Bureau** (2513 LA-14, New Iberia, 337/365-1540 or 888/942-3742, www.iberiatravel.com), the **St. Martin Parish Tourist Commission** (St. Martinville, 337/298-3556 or 888/565-5939, www.cajuncountry.org), and the **St. Landry Parish Tourist Commission** (978 Kennerson Rd., Opelousas, 337/442-1597 or 877/948-8004, www.cajuntravel.com). For more detailed information about the Cajun wetlands, contact the **Cajun Coast Visitors & Convention Bureau** (112 Main St., Patterson, 985/395-4905 or 800/256-2931, www.cajuncoast.com) or the **Houma Area Convention & Visitors Bureau** (114 Tourist Dr., Gray, 985/868-2732 or 800/688-2732, www.houmatravel.com).

The Times (www.timesofacadiana.com) provides Lafayette and its environs with tons of listings and entertainment coverage. Another great freebie is *The Independent Weekly* (www.theind.com), which is strong on arts, dining, and entertainment. Houma's free *Gumbo Entertainment Guide* (www.tri-parishtimes.com/gumbo) is a monthly paper filled with event and nightlife listings and other lively goings-on.

Getting There and Around

Roughly shaped like a scythe, Acadiana follows US-90 west to southeast, from Lake Charles to Houma. The long, rectangular handle of the scythe extends from Lake Charles to Lafayette along both US-90 and the parallel US-190 corridor, from Kinder to Eunice to Opelousas. This part of Acadiana is considered the Cajun prairie, where early settlers earned their livelihood by farming. The curving blade of the scythe extends southeast along the US-90 corridor from Lafayette down through New Iberia, Morgan City, and Houma. This region is considered the Cajun wetlands, where the settlers derived their livelihood chiefly from fishing and trapping. From Houma, it's just a 60-mile drive via US-90 to New Orleans.

In order to maximize your flexibility, the entire region is best explored by car. The **Lafayette Transit System** (LTS, 337/291-8570, www.ridelts.com) does provide bus service around Lafayette, but since many of the area's main attractions are in outlying towns not served by LTS, this is an impractical option.

From New Orleans, there are two main routes to Lafayette and its environs. You can either take the straight, easy 135-mile shot across I-10 through Baton Rouge, which takes a little more than two hours, or opt for the more circuitous 153-mile route via US-90, which requires a little less than three hours. I-10, which leads from Lafayette to Lake Charles, is a wide interstate highway with a 70-mph speed limit, as is I-49, which leads north from Lafayette to Opelousas. While US-190 is a much slower route, especially where it passes through the downtown areas of Eunice, Basile, and several other towns in the region, it definitely offers a more scenic view of Cajun Country.

Background

The Landscape

GEOGRAPHY

Louisiana, especially the southern end of the state, is—in ecological terms—brand spanking new. It's largely made up of sediment deposited by the Mississippi River or left in the wake of the continuously shifting Gulf of Mexico shoreline. It's tied with Florida for having the second-lowest mean elevation of any state (about 100 feet). Its highest point, "Mount" Driskill up north near Grambling and Minden, is only 535 feet in elevation. New Orleans itself lies eight feet below sea level, a point made abundantly clear during the flooding aftermath of Hurricane Katrina. The city rises to perhaps 300 feet in a few slightly elevated areas north of Lake Pontchartrain.

Rivers

The Mississippi River plays a vital role in the appearance, development, and economy of New Orleans. The river forms the border between Mississippi and Louisiana, cutting directly through Baton Rouge and New Orleans before emptying into the Gulf of Mexico. At its end, the mighty river and its many tributaries form a fan-shaped delta. The Mississippi River is the definitive drain for about 40 percent of the United States.

The Mississippi River Delta, which extends across the southern Louisiana shoreline, took about 6,000 years to form. Its largest tributary, the Atchafalaya River, flows into the western end of the delta, southeast of Lafayette. The Atchafalaya's delta will eventually fill in much of northern Atchafalaya Bay, and will come to resemble the fully formed Mississippi River Delta.

Louisiana's jagged shoreline comprises 3 million wetland acres, roughly 40 percent of the entire nation's marsh ecosystem. Unlike the considerably more stable Gulf shorelines, Louisiana's coast is continuously shifting, the result of the evolving play between the Gulf currents and the flow of the Mississippi and other tributaries.

Bayous

Rivers aren't the only major waterways found in southern Louisiana. Bayous are also an important part of the regional culture. The word "bayou" derives from the Choctaw term for a river, *bayuk*. These sluggish bodies of water are large enough here that they'd be called rivers elsewhere in the country. Some of the larger bayous include Teche (which flows through the Cajun Country through St. Martinville and Breaux Bridge), Vermilion (which flows through Lafayette), LaFourche (which runs through Houma), and Boeuf (which passes near Opelousas in St. Landry Parish).

Previous: the shadow of the statue of Christ on the St. Louis Cathedral; street sign in the French Quarter.

New Orleans Climate

Month	Average High	Average Low	Average Rainfall
January	62	43	4.7
February	65	46	5.6
March	71	52	5.2
April	78	59	4.7
May	85	66	4.4
June	89	71	5.4
July	91	73	6.4
August	90	73	5.9
September	87	70	5.5
October	80	59	2.8
November	71	51	4.4
December	64	45	5.5

Note: Temperatures are expressed in degrees Fahrenheit, while rainfall is calculated in inches.

Lakes and Lagoons

In the southern part of the state, many "lakes" are really salt- or brackish-water lagoons that were once bays or inlets of the Gulf but were eventually sealed off by the formation of barrier beaches or delta ridges. The largest and most famous of these is Lake Pontchartrain, which is traversed by one of the longest bridges in the world, the 24-mile Lake Pontchartrain Causeway Bridge (known colloquially as the Causeway). Other examples include Barataria Bay, south of New Orleans; Lake Maurepas, west of Lake Pontchartrain and connected to it by Bayou Manchac; and Lake Salvador, just southwest of New Orleans and fringed by Jean Lafitte National Historical Park and Preserve.

CLIMATE

Southern Louisiana is jokingly called the northernmost coast of Central America, and not just because of its banana-republic politics—it also has a climate that's more similar to Costa Rica's than to that of most of the United States. It is considered a semihumid, subtropical zone, and it almost never receives snow; in New Orleans, when the temperature occasionally dips to freezing on the coldest winter evenings, locals bundle up as though they're about to run the Iditarod. The average rainfall is about 58 inches per year, but some of the southern parishes average closer to 65 inches of rain annually. It's rainy all year, with the highest totals in the summer and the lowest in October, but there are no bone-dry months here.

With a low atmospheric ceiling and high humidity, nighttime-to-daytime low and high temperatures don't usually span a great range. The mean temperature for the year is about 68°F, but New Orleans usually feels warmer; there's less breeze and the concrete roads and buildings tend to absorb and retain heat. Average high temperatures in New Orleans in summer are about 90°F, with nighttime lows averaging a still warm 73°F. In winter (December, January, and February), highs average a pleasant 65°F, with lows a manageable 45°F. Winter is a wonderful time to visit. Summer can be simply unbearable on the most humid days even with air-conditioning. The touristy French Quarter, which can be littered with garbage along Bourbon and outside bars on weekend mornings, can feel and smell positively foul on a summer day. Spring and fall are fairly genial times to visit. Temperatures can easily reach into the 90s during warm spells, but

Muddy Waters

the Mississippi River

Contrary to popular belief, the muddiness of the Mississippi River, and many of the other rivers and bayous in the state, is not a sign of pollution. The rivers become muddy because the fast-moving current is constantly transporting natural and easily eroded bottom sediments. But this doesn't mean that the muddy Mississippi—the lifeblood of the Crescent City—is free from pollution. In fact, according to studies submitted to the Environmental Protection Agency (EPA), the Mississippi is one of the most contaminated rivers in the country, mainly due to cancer-causing toxic discharges from industrial facilities. Other Louisiana-based waterways, such as the Red, Pearl, and Calcasieu Rivers, are also suffering from chemical contamination.

Another potentially dangerous thing about the state's rivers is that many of them flow at a higher elevation than the floodplains that surround them. The sediment brought downriver and deposited in Louisiana has built up the riverbanks, forming natural levees. When the river runs higher than usual (as it did in the spring of 2011), as much as one-third of the state—including all of metropolitan New Orleans—would be one massive pool of water were it not for the intricate system of man-made levees and spillways constructed all along the river and its tributaries.

more typically average in the upper 70s in September and October and in April and May.

New Orleans itself averages 110 days a year with completely sunny skies, and about the same number of days with rain. Otherwise, it's partly sunny or partly cloudy, depending on whether you're an optimist or a pessimist.

Hurricane Season

The weather has been a hot topic in southern Louisiana for as long as people have lived here—long before Hurricanes Katrina and Rita barreled through the state in 2005. Hurricane season begins in June each year and lasts through November. Hurricanes have always been a threat to the Louisiana shoreline, and given the increasing numbers and magnitude of these storms in recent years, it is likely Louisiana will have plenty of brushes with violent storms in the future.

History

EARLY CIVILIZATION

In northeastern Louisiana, not too far from the city of Monroe, archaeologists have identified a series of ancient ceremonial mounds that some in the scientific community believe are the earliest physical evidence of human settlement on the entire continent. More recent but still prehistoric mounds dot the landscape of the state, especially in the northern and eastern regions. These mounds were a fixture in the early Native American farming communities that proliferated in these parts for the 2-3 millennia before European settlement.

Louisiana's Hopewell indigenous tribes thrived in the Gulf South from about 200 BC until nearly AD 900, with Mississippian tribes succeeding them in the 1500s. Native Americans of the 1600s and 1700s, when Europeans first began exploring the region, comprised three distinct branches, each with its own culture and language: Caddoan, Muskogean, and Tunican. It was this last branch, which included the Chitimacha and Attakapa, that mostly inhabited what is now southern Louisiana, with Muskogean and Caddoan Indians living in the central and northwestern parts of the state, respectively.

The effect of French and then Spanish settlement on indigenous people living in Louisiana was devastating. Many tribes were annihilated by disease, others squarely routed out, enslaved, or massacred by settlers. Still, some Native Americans managed to hang on and thrive in Louisiana, many of their members intermarrying with African Americans. Today, there are Chitimacha, Houma, Tunica-Biloxi, Coushatta, and Choctaw settlements in the state. Many geographical names in Louisiana have indigenous origins, among them Bogalusa (which means "black water"), Opelousas ("black leg"), and Ponchatoula ("hanging hair").

Most people think of the French explorer René-Robert Cavelier, Sieur de La Salle, as the earliest European settler in the region, and he was the first to establish a permanent stronghold in the name of his own country, in 1682. But 140 years earlier, Spaniards led by explorer Hernando de Soto first visited what is now Louisiana. They didn't stay, but they did leave behind diseases that proved fatal to many of the indigenous people they encountered.

La Salle entered Louisiana down the Mississippi River from the north and claimed for France all the land drained by not only this massive river but also its vast network of tributaries. This parcel covered about 830,000 square miles and ran from the Gulf of Mexico to Canada, and from the Rocky Mountains to Mississippi. He first termed the region Louisiana (well, technically, Louisiane, which is its name in French) after France's reigning monarch of that period, Louis XIV.

THE FOUNDING OF NEW ORLEANS

Louisiana's period of French rule was barely more than three generations—France would cede the territory to the Spanish in 1762 before occupying it again for a short period preceding the Louisiana Purchase. Neither the first nor second period of French rule proved to be profitable for France, and from a colonial perspective, one could say that the entire episode was a failure. On the flip side, the French occupation planted the seeds for the emergence of New Orleans as one of young America's most fascinating cities.

New Orleans was not the first settlement in Louisiana by the French, although explorer Pierre Le Moyne, Sieur d'Iberville, did establish a toehold near the city on March 3, 1699, which was coincidentally Mardi Gras. That same year, the French built a permanent fort about 90 miles east in Biloxi (now Mississippi) and, three years later, another 60 miles east in Mobile (now Alabama). The first permanent French settlement to go up in what is now Louisiana, in 1714, was Natchitoches, a still-charming small city in northwestern Louisiana, about 300 miles northwest of New Orleans. By the late 1710s, however, France had already failed to invest substantially in its new settlement, and unable to fund a full-fledged colony, the monarchy transferred control of Louisiana to Antoine Crozat, a French financier of considerable acclaim.

Crozat was able to make little headway with Louisiana, and just five years later, control of Louisiana was shifted to Compagnie d'Occident, led by a wealthy Scotsman named John Law. It became quickly apparent to Law and other authorities, however, that the southern Mississippi was vulnerable to plays for control by the two key competing European powers in colonial America, Great Britain and Spain. To protect their interests, the French built a new fort in 1718 along the lower Mississippi, christening the settlement La Nouvelle-Orléans, after Philippe, Duc d'Orléans. A handful of settlements were added along the Mississippi River to the north, and in 1722, France named young New Orleans the territorial capital of Louisiana.

The beginnings of Nouvelle Orléans were almost pathetically modest. The site, at a sharp bend of the Mississippi River more than five feet *below* sea level, was little more than bug- and alligator-infested swampland, which the city's earliest residents shored up with landfill and dams. Part of the settlement covered one of the few bumps of higher ground along the river's banks. The site was chosen in part because a bayou (now known as Bayou St. John) connected the Mississippi River at this point to Lake Pontchartrain, which itself emptied into the Gulf. For eons, the area's Native Americans had used the bayou as a shortcut for getting from the river to the Gulf without having to paddle all the way south, nearly another 100 miles, to where the Mississippi entered the Gulf.

Today's French Quarter, also known as the Vieux Carré (literally, Old Square), encompassed all of New Orleans for the first several decades. It was anchored by the Place d'Armes, which would later be renamed Jackson Square. The river's course in relation to the city has changed slightly since the city's founding; in the early days, Jackson Square faced the riverfront directly, whereas today a significant strip of land and levee acts as a barrier between it and the river.

Law can be credited with making the earliest effort to attract European settlers to Louisiana. His first successful campaign brought not Frenchmen but Germans to the new territory. Law would convince Germans to move to Louisiana as indentured workers, meaning they were bound to work for an established period, and once their service commitment was complete, they were granted freedom. Law's Occidental Company used all the usual trickery and false advertising common throughout Europe in those days to attract immigrants and investors: It promised vast riches, huge mining reserves, and easy agricultural opportunities, virtually none of which was accurate.

During Law's first few years of controlling Louisiana, his company managed to convince about 7,000 mostly German and French residents to migrate to Louisiana. A significant percentage of these migrants died from disease or starvation, as the colonial authorities were in no position at all to feed, clothe, and house the arrivals. In all likelihood, if you stayed in Louisiana during these early days, you did so only because you hadn't the means to return to Europe. Word of the false promise of Louisiana spread quickly back to France, but authorities allowed Law and his company to administer the territory until 1731, when the French monarchy finally stepped in to resume control.

Law was responsible for first importing West African slaves to Louisiana. His Compagnie d'Occident also owned the French Compagnie du Senegal, which controlled all French slave trade. During roughly a 10-year period, about 3,000 slaves, mostly Senegalese, were taken from their homeland to Louisiana. Slaves worked on the handful of early plantations and also on the countless smaller subsistence farms that developed around southern Louisiana, most engaged in the production and export of indigo and tobacco.

Back in control of the colony from 1731 through 1762, France failed to turn Louisiana into a profitable venture. Furthermore, its strategic importance diminished sharply as England developed an upper hand during the French and Indian War, which had begun in 1754, toward controlling Canada. In 1762, France hatched a diplomatic scheme to help impel Spain to join it and rout the British: It secretly handed over the Louisiana Territory to Spain in the Treaty of Fontainebleau. In fact, the territory stayed in the family, as France's King Louis XV simply transferred the land to his own cousin, Spain's King Charles III.

The move ended badly for both France and Spain. France lost the war with Britain in 1763 and lost control of Canada. And Spain ended up with a lemon. One might argue that France really didn't lose a colony so much as rid itself of what had become an enormous and depressing financial burden. Furthermore, as part of the peace treaty between the joint powers of Spain and France with their victor, Great Britain was awarded all of Louisiana east of the Mississippi River, which became known as West Florida. Spain kept a much larger tract, which included all of Louisiana west of the river, along with a critical little area along the lower Mississippi River called Île d'Orléans, which included the city of New Orleans. France was free of any part of Louisiana.

SPANISH RULE

The actual physical transfer of Louisiana, and especially New Orleans, to Spain was an unmitigated disaster fraught with rebellion, virtual martial law, and ugly acts of violence. It didn't help that the residents of New Orleans had no idea that they had become subjects of Spain until 1766, when the first Spanish governor, Antonio de Ulloa, arrived that March and, like a wicked stepmother, immediately instituted a strict rule upon the city's inhabitants.

Almost as immediately, there were insurgencies, and in 1768, the situation became particularly dire when locals actually drove Ulloa and his cronies clear out of town. Spain hired a tyrannical military man, General Alejandro O'Reilly, to beat down the rebellion, which he did in August 1769. He managed to get Spain in firm control of New Orleans, a rule that would last until the United States orchestrated the Louisiana Purchase in 1803, for although France technically owned Louisiana at that time, Spaniards continued to govern the city's day-to-day affairs right through to the end.

The Spanish, like the French, made every possible effort to boost the colony's population, sending plenty of Spaniards to Louisiana. From a cultural standpoint, Louisiana remained squarely French, as the colonists from France far outnumbered any newcomers. The only reason the appearance of the French Quarter today more closely resembles Spanish colonial than French colonial architecture is that two huge fires burned much of the city during the Spanish occupation, and many of the new buildings that went up were constructed by Spanish authorities. It's Spain's influence that resulted in the wrought-iron balconies, shaded courtyards, and other features that typify French Quarter architecture.

Ironically, the majority of the newcomers to Louisiana during the

Spanish period were actually French, or French-speaking, refugees. The most famous were the Acadians, who had been cruelly expelled from the Maritime Provinces of Canada after the British victory. The French immigrants living in Acadian Canada were typically rounded up and forced onto ships—some were sent back to France, and others were reluctantly taken in by certain British colonies in what is now the United States. Many died in passage or of poverty that they encountered where they landed. Spain, looking to boost the population of the Louisiana colony, enthusiastically welcomed the Acadians, who arrived in two major waves, the first in 1764 and an even larger one in 1785. Most of them settled in the marshes and swamplands of south-central and southwestern Louisiana. In Louisiana, the name Acadian gradually morphed into Cajun, as we all know it today, and Lafayette, Louisiana, became the hub of Cajun settlements.

A lesser-known group of refugees that came to New Orleans and Louisiana in great numbers from 1791 through 1803 were white French settlers and some free people of color from the French colony of Saint-Domingue (now Haiti), who fled the island during the violent revolution of the 1790s.

Louisiana's makeup changed a bit during the American Revolution, as Spain worked in concert with the American colonists to undermine their rivals, the British. They sent supplies and munitions to the colonists, and in 1779, after formally declaring war on Britain, their Louisiana militia captured all of the British settlements of West Florida. This included all of the Gulf Coast region between the Mississippi River and the Perdido River, which today forms the east-west state border between Alabama and Florida. Per the terms of the Treaty of Paris in 1783, Spain's assistance was, at the war's conclusion, rewarded with a chunk of land that included all of both East Florida (today's Florida) and West Florida (which today includes Alabama, Mississippi, and the nine Louisiana parishes east and north of the Mississippi River, now sometimes referred to as the Florida parishes).

With the young United States now in control of all the land east of the Mississippi River (except for East and West Florida), New Orleans and the entire Louisiana Territory grew dramatically in strategic importance. New Orleans became the seaport serving America's interior, as important rivers throughout Ohio, Kentucky, and Tennessee all fed into the Mississippi.

In yet another secret treaty, however, Spain in 1800 decided to transfer all of the Louisiana Territory, including New Orleans, back to France. The actual residents of New Orleans never even knew they were residents of a French colony for the three years they were back under the country's rule. In 1803, the United States bought Louisiana from France for a mere $15 million. Even by the standards of that day, $15 million was a paltry sum for such an enormous parcel of land—approximately one-third of the land that now makes up the present-day continental United States. Because Spain still possessed East and West Florida, the nine Louisiana parishes east and north of the Mississippi River remained in Spanish hands until 1810, when

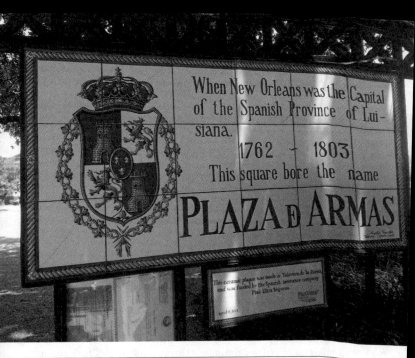

Above: Place d'Armes, called Plaza d'Armas during Spanish rule, is now known as Jackson Square. **Below:** the Andrew Jackson statue in Jackson Square.

the American residents of West Florida declared their independence and asked to be annexed by the United States.

LIFE IN THE 19TH CENTURY

Upon buying Louisiana from France, the United States immediately split the territory in two at the 33rd parallel, which today forms the northern border of Louisiana. All land south of that point became known as the Territory of Orleans, and, confusingly, all land to the north became known as the Territory of Louisiana.

In 1790, about 10,000 new refugees from Saint-Domingue moved into New Orleans, doubling the population and adding further chaos to the city. In many respects, it's this final wave of French-speaking people from Haiti—white colonists of French descent and free people of color *(gens de couleur libres)*—that ultimately established the French-Caribbean character that exists to this day in New Orleans.

For a time, New Orleans deviated from rural Louisiana in its relative tolerance of racial diversity. The *gens de couleur libres* were, in many cases, well educated and quite able to forge good livings as builders, designers, artisans, and chefs. These early Creole immigrants were in a large way responsible for the intricate and fanciful Creole cottages and other buildings still found throughout the city and southern Louisiana, and these same immigrants helped to develop New Orleans's inimitable Creole cuisine, which blended the traditions of France, Spain, the Caribbean, Africa, and even the American frontier and Native Americans.

Intermingling was considerable in this early New Orleans society, as wealthy Europeans and Creoles commonly had mistresses, some who were *gens de couleur libres*, quadroons (one-fourth black), octoroons (one-eighth black), or some other mix of Anglo, Latin, African, and Native American descent. It's largely for this reason that the term Creole, when applied to people, is rather confusing. The name was first applied to upper-crust French settlers born in Louisiana but descended from mostly wealthy European families, as the very word derives from the Spanish *criollo,* a term that described people born in the colonies rather than born in Europe or, for that matter, Africa. These days, just about any New Orleanian or Louisianian who can claim some direct combination of French, Spanish, Caribbean, and African blood can justly consider him- or herself a Creole, the exception being the descendants of the original French-Canadian refugees from Acadia, known as Cajuns.

The United States accepted the Territory of Orleans as the state of Louisiana on April 30, 1812. It thereby became the 18th state of the union. The political system, with William C. C. Claiborne as governor and New Orleans the capital, continued largely as it had from the time of the Louisiana Purchase.

America wasted no time in exploiting its new purchase, as thousands of entrepreneurial-minded settlers flocked to the busy port city during the first decade after the Louisiana Purchase. They were not welcomed in the

French Quarter at all, and in fact, the original Creoles would have nothing to do with American settlers for many decades. Some of these upstarts immediately began amassing great riches in shipping and trade enterprises, building lavish homes in the American Sector, which is now the Central Business District (CBD). Canal Street divided the two enclaves, and the median down this street came to be considered New Orleans's "neutral ground." Today, the city's residents refer to any street median as a neutral ground.

By the early 1800s, a century's worth of immigrants from all walks of life had contributed to one of the most racially, culturally, and economically diverse populations in the nation. Freed prisoners from France, Haitian refugees, slaves, European indentured servants, American frontiersmen, Spanish Canary Islanders, nuns, military men, and others now formed New Orleans's population.

The War of 1812

Britain and the United States had remained hostile to one another since the Revolution, and shortly after Louisiana became a state, the two nations entered into the War of 1812, which would last three years. By 1814, New Orleans figured heavily in the campaign, as the faltering British decided to go after several key ports along the Gulf Coast and the Mississippi River in an effort to cut off the supply-and-trade system serving the interior United States. New Orleans, defended by Major General Andrew Jackson, was attacked by the British on January 8, 1815—several days after British and American leaders had signed a peace treaty ending the War of 1812. Still, many believe that the British would not have formally ratified the treaty had they been able to pull off that final battle. Andrew Jackson's victory in the Battle of New Orleans helped to propel his political career, and in 1828, he was elected the seventh president of the United States.

The year 1812 was significant in New Orleans for another reason—it received the first steamboat, aptly called the *New Orleans,* ever to navigate the Mississippi River system; the boat steamed all the way from Pittsburgh via the Ohio River. Steamboats would greatly alter the nature of commerce in New Orleans, as, up until 1812, trade had been conducted by small vessels propelled chiefly by the river current, meaning that they could not return upstream once they arrived in New Orleans. In many cases, the boats were simply scrapped once they arrived.

By the mid-1840s, more than 1,000 different steamboats were calling on New Orleans each year. Steamboats left New Orleans for the Midwest and the East Coast carrying tobacco, cotton, sugarcane, and many other goods. New Orleans also became a major trade port with the Caribbean Islands, from which it imported fruit, tobacco, rum, and—illegally, after their importation was banned in 1808—slaves.

The Civil War Era

Louisiana's population stood at about 150,000 by 1820, having increased

The History of Fat Tuesday

It's appropriate that New Orleans should have the most famous Mardi Gras—or Carnival—celebration in the United States. After all, it was on Mardi Gras (French for "Fat Tuesday") of 1699 that explorer Pierre Le Moyne, Sieur d'Iberville, first encamped here along the Mississippi River. Well, to be exact, Le Moyne chose a spot about 60 miles downriver from today's New Orleans, but his visit marked the city's beginning.

Records suggest that the city's early French inhabitants began holding parties and dances coinciding with Fat Tuesday as early as the 1720s; such pre-Lenten festivities continued until the late 1700s, when New Orleans fell under Spanish rule. Even after New Orleans became part of the United States, street masking wasn't legalized again until 1827. In fact, the first documented Mardi Gras parade was held in 1837, though the krewes (private clubs that sponsor parades and gala balls) were not formed until 1857, when the krewe of **Comus** illuminated the city with its fiery torches. Comus started the traditions of having secret Carnival societies named after mythological characters, presenting thematic, pageant-style parades—with dancers and entertainers frolicking alongside the floats and marchers—and holding post-parade balls.

Amid the kaleidoscopic costumes and floats, you'll see three principal colors while experiencing Mardi Gras: purple, green, and gold. These hues represent justice, faith, and power, respectively, and were introduced to Mardi Gras in 1872 by the first parade of **Rex,** which also gave the event an official anthem, "If Ever I Cease to Love," from a burlesque play of that period.

One of the most notable 20th-century developments for New Orleans's Mardi Gras was the formation of the **Zulu** krewe in 1909. Its African American

greatly since statehood with the arrival of settlers from other parts of the United States, who moved here to pursue new land and to farm. The population grew to 350,000 by 1840, and to 700,000 by 1860, the start of the Civil War. During this period, the state became a U.S. superpower owing to its phenomenal agricultural growth, chiefly in cotton and sugarcane. Both small farms and massive plantations grew these crops, using largely slave labor. Cotton was grown just about everywhere in the state, but somewhat less in the swampy southern regions, where sugarcane thrived in the warmer and wetter climate. In fact, sugarcane was always a more lucrative crop than cotton. The state also became a major rice grower—the crop was first planted in the southern and Mississippi River areas to feed slaves, but it proved profitable and was developed into a valuable commercial crop by the end of the 19th century.

With the outlying areas seeing huge growth in agriculture, the region's key port and gateway, New Orleans, grew dramatically. By 1820, it had already become the largest city in the South, with a population of about 27,500, surpassing Charleston. After New York City, it was America's leading immigrant port of entry from 1830 until the Civil War. By the 1850s, New Orleans had grown to become the fourth-largest city in the United members joined together to make fun of the exclusive Rex krewe; its king, for instance, "ruled" with a scepter made of a banana stalk and a crown fashioned from a can of lard. Zulu continues to be one of the most-watched parades of Mardi Gras.

The celebration has seen both low and high points throughout the past century. It was canceled for a couple of years during both World War I and World War II. It enjoyed somewhat limited success during the Depression. By the 1950s, however, Mardi Gras was back in full swing, beginning to enjoy international acclaim, expanding to the suburbs beyond New Orleans, and utilizing tractors in lieu of mules to pull the floats. It was in the late 1960s that the krewe of **Bacchus** altered tradition by using gigantic floats in its parade, inviting a Hollywood celebrity to serve as its king (Danny Kaye was the first, in 1969), and replacing its private ball with a dinner dance to which both members and outsiders were invited via ticket purchase.

Since that time, Mardi Gras has grown tremendously. Many new krewes and parades have come and gone since the 1970s, and many more events and parties have opened to the public. In 1991, the New Orleans City Council passed an antidiscrimination ordinance that made it illegal for parading krewes to maintain a private membership. A few of the long-running krewes protested by canceling their parades, but Rex complied and, for the first time, opened its membership to persons of all colors. The number of visitors, foreign and domestic, who descend upon New Orleans during Mardi Gras has skyrocketed, and although attendance was down in 2006, the first Mardi Gras following Hurricane Katrina, the event has since become hugely popular and highly successful once again.

States and a leading cultural hub. Visitors from other parts of the country were struck by the city's distinctly Spanish architecture and Parisian ambience—it was a city of high fashion, opera and theater, lavish dining, and sophisticated parties. Already by this time, the city was beginning to celebrate Mardi Gras with parties and simple parades.

The hot and humid summers proved to be breeding grounds for yellow fever and other subtropical maladies, and although many residents died from the disease during these years, the city's population still grew to a staggering 170,000 by 1860.

The dynamic changed in the middle of the 19th century with the construction of railroads and canals, which made it possible for Midwestern states to move their products to the eastern United States more quickly and cheaply than by way of New Orleans and the Gulf. The city continued to prosper as a shipper of cotton and sugarcane. Louisiana relied heavily on slave labor to ensure the profitability of its agricultural markets, and New Orleans prospered hugely in this ignominious trade.

As the state capital, New Orleans enjoyed significant economic and political advantages that alienated it from the rest of Louisiana. After years of debate about this issue, the legislature finally resolved, in 1849, to move the capital to Baton Rouge, about 60 miles upriver, where it has remained to this day the state political seat, excepting a 20-year period during and after the Civil War.

When South Carolina seceded from the Union in December 1860 after the election of Republican Abraham Lincoln, who sought to curb the spread of slavery, it set off a flurry of similar withdrawals among other southern states, with Louisiana seceding on January 26, 1861, the sixth to do so. It then joined in the effort toward war in becoming a member of the Confederate States of America.

Although much of the fighting took place in the coastal and mid-Atlantic states, New Orleans and Louisiana were vulnerable to Union attack for exactly the same reason they were attacked by the British during the War of 1812. If the Union army could capture and control the Mississippi River, it could cut off supply lines between the Confederacy and any states west of the river, and it could enjoy a continuous supply line to the interior Midwest. Anticipating just such an attack, the Confederates built fortifications along the river south of New Orleans.

In April 1862, Captain David G. Farragut led a flotilla of Union Navy ships to the mouth of the Mississippi, where it proceeded north toward New Orleans. He made it with little trouble, shelling and ultimately disabling the Confederate fortification and sailing rather easily to capture the South's largest city. Immediately, New Orleans was named the Union capital of all the territory held by the Federal army in Louisiana. The Confederate state government moved west about 60 miles to Opelousas and then scrambled nearly another 200 miles northwest to Shreveport, where it remained until the war's end.

A corrupt northern fat cat, Union Major General Benjamin F. Butler, assumed control of New Orleans and Union-occupied Louisiana, running things a bit like the Spanish had—he was hated by all, including more than a few Union troops, and eventually was removed from office. By the war's end, the state itself stood politically divided, with the Mississippi River valley (including New Orleans and Baton Rouge) in Union control and the western and northern regions still under Confederate control.

THE RECONSTRUCTION PERIOD

The period immediately after the Civil War, known as Reconstruction, was a grim one, and its policies, which attempted to create an integrated society of whites and free blacks, backfired.

President Lincoln signed the Proclamation of Amnesty and Reconstruction into law in December 1863, and so, even before the war had ended, a civil government was established in those parts of Louisiana held by Union troops. When the war ended, this civil government assumed control of the state. Early on, it seemed as though little had changed for blacks, even though slavery had been formally abolished by this civil government.

A number of the former Confederate leaders of prewar Louisiana held office in this new civil government, which immediately passed the infamous Black Codes. These edicts placed enormous restrictions on the rights and freedoms of the state's African Americans, who were also denied the right to vote.

These conditions led to an extreme seesaw of power between the Republican and (largely ex-Confederate) Democratic sides of the government, which would bitterly divide Louisianians and precipitate tragic violence for the rest of the 19th century and well into the 20th. Blacks struck back against the government in New Orleans, first by rioting violently in 1866 until finally the federal government stepped in to impose order. These same issues, revolts, and riots flared up in other Southern states, and Congress responded by drafting the Reconstruction Acts in 1867 and 1868, which President Andrew Johnson vetoed, but which passed with a two-thirds' majority nonetheless. And so, formally, began the period of Reconstruction in the American South.

Reconstruction dictated that the 10 ex-Confederate states that had been returned to the Union would lose their rights to self-govern, and the federal military would instead step in to govern until these states rewrote their constitutions with laws and language that Congress deemed acceptable. In effect, Louisiana was no longer a state until it submitted to the wishes of the federal government. The federally controlled state government then drafted a new constitution in March 1868, which wholly deferred to the sentiments of Congress: Adult males of all races were granted the right to vote—excepting fully declared ex-Confederates, who actually had their voting rights revoked—and blacks were assured full civil rights. Interestingly, when the new constitution was presented to Louisiana citizens, voters approved it overwhelmingly. The majority of those who registered to vote that year were black; whites, discouraged and disgusted by the process, largely stayed away from the polls.

Pro-Union white Southerners (called "scalawags" by their detractors), opportunity-seeking whites from the North (called "carpetbaggers" and hated even more by their detractors), and former slaves held the clear majority of political seats in Louisiana (and many other Southern states) during the eight years of Reconstruction. Among these Republican officeholders were Louisiana's first elected black governor, P. B. S. Pinchback; the first black U.S. senator, Blanche K. Bruce; as well as black members of the U.S. Congress and black holders of just about every state political post.

In the meantime, the most ardent opponents of Reconstruction, including quite a few prominent ex-Confederate leaders, went to extreme lengths to sabotage, tear down, and otherwise render ineffective the state's Republican leadership. From this effort came the development of such anti-black groups as the Ku Klux Klan (in northern Louisiana), the Knights of the White Camellia (in southern Louisiana), and the especially terror-driven White League. These and other groups, sometimes systematically and sometimes randomly, intimidated, beat, and often lynched blacks and white sympathizers. The White League took credit for the assassination of several Republican-elected officials. About 3,500 members of the White League attempted to overthrow the state government during what came to be known as the Battle of Liberty Place in New Orleans in 1874. During a fierce riot, they took over the city hall, statehouse, and state arsenal until federal troops arrived to restore order. For the next four years, the troops remained in New Orleans, overseeing the city's—and the state's—order.

During the course of Reconstruction, the voting situation in Louisiana grew increasingly volatile, as whites intimidated or threatened blacks to keep them from voting and rallied voter support among anti-Republican whites. More and more officials and congressmen sympathetic to the South gained office, and they in turn pardoned and restored voting rights to many of the ex-Confederates.

White Democrats were swift in removing from blacks any rights they had gained during Reconstruction, and then some. In 1898, the state constitution was rewritten. Without expressly denying suffrage to blacks, it required poll taxes, literacy, and property ownership in order to vote, which disqualified most of the state's black voters.

While Reconstruction had a profoundly negative effect on the plight of blacks, a few strides were made during the 19th century. Many blacks ended up returning to work at a subsistence level on the farms where they once had been slaves, but some headway was made in education and social relief. The federal government established the Freedmen's Bureau, which helped to fund public schools for blacks throughout the South and issued other forms of assistance and economic relief.

The economy of the rural South faltered greatly after the Civil War, and various depressions, labor problems, and episodes of social unrest conspired to put many large and small farm owners out of business. For much of the 19th century, a large proportion of southern farms were run by sharecroppers, whereby the owners of the land—many of them northerners who had bought failed farms—gave tenants equipment and materials to farm the land and live on a fairly basic level. The workers were also entitled to a small cut of the crop yield. Farm production in Louisiana began to increase under this system, but it was still far lower than before the Civil War, and even with bounteous crops, many farmers could not make ends meet.

New Orleans, whose economy had been devastated by the war, gradually staged an economic comeback during the course of the next half century. The renewed growth in cotton and sugarcane trafficking helped to jump-start the city's shipping and trade economy, and the mouth of the Mississippi River was deepened and made accessible to much larger ships, many of which sailed from ports much farther away than in earlier times. Railroads were built across much of Louisiana, and in 1914, the opening of the Panama Canal brought new trade to New Orleans by way of Latin

America. The city's population stood at 290,000 by 1900, with the state population up to about 1.4 million.

THE 20TH CENTURY

Louisiana's economy began to diversify throughout the early 20th century, much more so than in most other agrarian southern states. Significant sources of oil were discovered in the northwestern part of the state, and natural gas sources were developed all over Louisiana. In 1938, huge oil deposits were discovered off the coast, and a massive oil-drilling industry grew up in southern Louisiana, especially in the towns southeast of Lafayette and southwest of Houma. Salt and sulfur mining also grew into a big contributor to the economy, chiefly in the southern belt extending from Lake Charles to southeast of Lafayette.

The farming economy continued to suffer through the early 1900s, and a severe recession took hold throughout the 1920s. The growing anguish and desperation among rural farmers helped to promote the ascendancy of one of the most notorious and controversial political figures in American history, Huey P. Long, a colorful, no-nonsense straight talker whose fervently populist manner played well with poor farmers and laborers. Long declared war on big corporations, especially Standard Oil, and took up the cause of small businesses and the common people. His actions early in his political career squarely favored those he claimed to want to help. Long was elected governor in 1928 and then U.S. senator in 1930, although he kept the governor's seat until 1932, when a handpicked successor took office. Still, he pretty much called the shots in state politics right up until his death. Long was assassinated in 1935 by Dr. Carl Weiss, the son-in-law of one of his political archenemies.

Long was instrumental in developing state public assistance and public works programs across Louisiana during the Great Depression, but he was also infamous for his nepotism and corruption, routinely buying off colleagues and tampering with the political process. The "Kingfish" ran the state like a fiefdom, and he actually ended up preventing federal funds from reaching the state during his last few years in office as a U.S. senator. Long may have died in 1935, but his brother, Earl K. Long, succeeded him as governor, as did his son, Russell Long. Until the early 1960s, anti- and pro-Long factions continued to dominate Democratic party politics and therefore, because Democrats controlled just about everything in Louisiana, state politics.

World War II boosted the Louisiana economy with its need for mineral and oil resources. It was during this period that Louisiana developed the massive refineries and chemical plants still found along much of the Mississippi River and all through the lower third of the state (especially Lake Charles and Baton Rouge), and it was also during the 1940s that the state's population demographic changed so that more Louisianians lived in cities than in rural areas.

At the same time, many rural citizens, especially blacks fed up with the state's segregation and racial mistreatment, left the South to seek factory jobs in Chicago, Oakland, and other northern and western cities. Other Louisianians moved to southeastern Texas, where jobs at refineries, factories, and shipyards in Beaumont, Orange, and Port Arthur abounded.

CONTEMPORARY TIMES

During the second half of the 20th century, New Orleans steadily blossomed into one of the nation's—and the world's—most popular vacation destinations. Mardi Gras evolved, especially during the 1960s, from a largely regional celebration into an international festival, and Jazz Fest became similarly popular. The economy came increasingly to depend on tourists, and then, throughout the 1970s and 1980s, convention business. Though Hurricane Katrina dampened both tourism and convention business for a while, the city has worked hard to regain its stature as a leading leisure and business destination.

Hurricane Katrina and Recovery

On August 29, 2005, Hurricane Katrina's storm surge caused the breach of 53 levees in New Orleans, flooding 80 percent of the city and resulting in the deaths of more than 1,500 people.

The French Quarter, CBD, Garden District, and Uptown were largely spared the worst flooding and, with significant exceptions, rebounded fairly quickly. Within two months of New Orleans's horrifying brush with the storm, most restaurants, hotels, and shops had reopened, and many residents had returned. In 2006, New Orleans enjoyed well-attended and lively Mardi Gras and Jazz Fest celebrations.

A year after Katrina, parts of the city that experienced extensive damage, such as Mid-City and City Park, had come back significantly. However, the population of New Orleans stood at about half that prior to the hurricane. Crowds, both in terms of residents and visitors, hadn't returned anywhere near pre-Katrina numbers.

The hardest-hit neighborhoods were residential areas north and east of the French Quarter and CBD, where the destruction affected residents of all income brackets, ages, races, and creeds. Visitors saw little of these neighborhoods in the past, and weren't keenly affected by their demise. Although some of these neighborhoods have been slow to recover—with blocks that are still lined with empty, decimated homes and businesses—some, such as Lakeview, are thriving once again. Arguably, nothing in the past five decades has had more impact on the city than Hurricane Katrina, but though parts of New Orleans will take years to rebuild, the city as a whole is as vibrant as ever. While many residents vacated New Orleans never to return, an entirely new crop of residents (including many young, Bohemian types) has helped to inject some much-needed vitality back into one of the country's unique cities.

Above: one of many houses damaged by Hurricane Katrina. **Below:** tourists near Jackson Square.

Government and Economy

GOVERNMENT

New Orleans is a predominantly Democratic, politically left-of-center city, and is generally quite progressive on social issues. Louisiana, however, tends to be more conservative regarding social issues, and the proportion of Democrats to Republicans is closer statewide.

ECONOMY

New Orleans has several important industries going for it. Even before Katrina, the city had experienced quite a few booms and busts since World War II. Today, it is the largest port in the United States, and it's second in the world only to Rotterdam in its value of foreign commerce and water-borne commerce. The state continues to rely heavily on the seafood industry as well as natural resources like salt, agricultural products, sulfur, petroleum, and natural gas, and many of the ships transporting these goods leave by way of New Orleans.

The intense trade presence has spawned an important commercial by-product: banking. The CBD remains one of the nation's leading centers of finance, with dozens of commercial banks. During the strongest oil years of the early 1970s through the early 1980s, the city's banks and other industries raked in plenty of money financing offshore oil production. Although Katrina's devastation and BP's Gulf oil spill have put a damper on the industry's growth, oil and natural gas industries remain vital to both the city and state economies.

Agriculture (namely sugar) remains an important aspect of Louisana's economy, and plantations along River Road and throughout Cajun Country were once sugarcane plantations. Finally, tourism, which has been an important source of revenue for New Orleans for centuries, has grown dramatically during the past five decades.

Local Culture

The strongest influence on New Orleans may arguably be French, but no one nationality represents a decisive majority here. The city's distinctive cuisine and music, the pervasive infatuation with things carnal and pleasurable, the Gothic literary traditions, and the longstanding practice of voodoo-tinged Catholicism are legacies contributed not only by the French and Spanish settlers, but by the vast numbers of Acadian refugees ("Cajuns"), slaves brought from West Africa, American frontier settlers and traders, German farmers, Irish and Italian laborers, Slavs, Creole refugees from Haiti, and Vietnamese. These people haven't just left their mark on a particular neighborhood during a specific period; they've migrated to New Orleans in significant enough numbers to have a pervasive and lasting influence. The cultural gumbo has resulted in some rather odd traditions that last to this day. Many street and neighborhood names are pronounced differently in New Orleans than anywhere else in the world, from Conti (KON-tie) and Cadiz (KAY-diz) Streets to the Michoud (MEE-shoh) neighborhood. Sometimes, French and Spanish names are pronounced roughly as the French and Spanish would pronounce them; sometimes, they're pronounced as virtually nobody else on the planet would say them.

Given the ethnic diversity of southern Louisiana, it's no surprise that residents tend to practice a variety of religions, or none at all. New Orleans was founded by Catholics, as evidenced by historic landmarks like the St. Louis Cathedral, and influenced by cultural traditions such as Mardi Gras. Nevertheless, you'll spot a wide array of religious institutions here, from Touro Synagogue to the First Unitarian Universalist Church of New Orleans.

The cuisine unique to New Orleans also borrows widely from myriad cultures. Ingredients and dishes like filé (a powder of dried sassafras leaves popularized by the Choctaw), jambalaya (a rice casserole very similar to Spanish paella), okra (a podlike vegetable introduced by African slaves), and crawfish (a small freshwater crustacean that's prevalent in local waters) are as common in New Orleans's restaurants as hamburgers and apple pie.

SOUTHERN ETIQUETTE

New Orleans has always been a big city with small-town sensibilities, and many New Orleanians adhere to the same temperament and traditions of other Southern states; you'll often hear "please," "thank you," "yes, ma'am," and "no, sir" while visiting New Orleans. It's also common for restaurant staff to call patrons "sweetie" or "darling." Residents appreciate qualities like modesty, chivalry, patience, and friendliness, and while having a good time is encouraged in the Big Easy, being loud and disrespectful is rarely tolerated. Although some old-fashioned manners have gone by the wayside in modern-day New Orleans, others are still common: always open doors for others, smile at and make eye contact with strangers, use proper table manners, apologize when you're at fault, and say "excuse me" when having to walk in front of someone.

By the same token, it's easy to misinterpret the friendliness that you'll surely encounter. When walking through the French Quarter, many a tourist has been stopped by a seemingly friendly local with a scam up his or her sleeve. One such scam entails what seems like a harmless wager: A man might approach you and say, "I bet I can guess where you got those shoes," and if you choose to accept his challenge, he'll inevitably win with a simple reply, "On your feet." So, as in any major U.S. city, it pays to be both courteous and cautious.

Because of the region's multiethnic history and reliance on tourism, foreigners and tourists are generally welcome here. Overall, the residents are helpful, hospitable, and gregarious, so while in New Orleans, do as the natives do. Be kind and considerate, ask for help when you need it, thank others for their time, and, as a courtesy, seek permission before taking a photo.

LANGUAGE

Many visitors often wonder how to pronounce "New Orleans." Though it's sometimes heard as "N'AW-luhns" in movies and TV commercials, native New Orleanians definitely don't pronounce it this way. The more conventional incorrect pronunciation is "NOO or-LEENS." Say it this way, and you'll be marked as an outsider (probably a Northerner), but at least, you won't be accused of being disrespectful. Locals pronounce the

Say It Like a Local

New Orleanians have their own special way of saying things, including local street names, neighborhoods, and suburbs. In many cases, there are two or more commonly accepted (though often hotly debated) ways to pronounce the same word. If you hope to sound like a local, here's a guide to the more puzzling pronunciations.

Streets and Neighborhoods

Burgundy (street): bur-GUN-dee
Cadiz (street): KAY-diz
Calliope (street): KAIL-ee-ohp
Carondelet (street): kair-OHN-deh-LET
Chalmette (suburb): SHALL-mett
Chartres (street): CHAR-ters
Clio (street): KLYE-o
Conti (street): KON-tie
Decatur (street): de-KAY-dur
Iberville (street): IBB-bur-vill
Loyola (street/school): lye-O-luh
Marigny (street/neighborhood): MAH-rah-nee
Melpomene (street): MEL-po-MEEN
Metairie (suburb): MED-uh-ree
Michoud (street/neighborhood): MEE-shoh
Milan (street): MYE-lan
Pontchartrain (street/lake): PON-chuh-train
Prytania (street/theater): prih-TAN-ya
Socrates (street): SO-kraits
Tchoupitoulas (street): chop-ah-TOO-lehs
Terpsichore (street): TERP-sih-kore
Toulouse (street): tuh-LOOS
Tulane (street/school): TOO-lain
Vieux Carré (neighborhood): VOO kah-RAY

Greater New Orleans

New Orleans (noo OHR-lins or noo OHR-lee-ahns) isn't the only place in Louisiana (luh-WEE-zee-ann-ah or LOO-zee-ann-ah) with some oddly sounding locales. If you're planning to explore other parts of the state, it might help to be able to pronounce where you're going.

Towns and Parishes

Amite: AYE-meet

city's name in a handful of relatively similar ways, the simplest and most common being "noo OHR-lins." You don't have to say it with a big, silly drawl or with delicious emphasis, as if you're a damsel in a Tennessee Williams play. Just say it quickly and casually, though you might hear some locals, especially those with aristocratic tendencies, pronounce it "noo OHR-lee-ahns."

As for the name of the state, that is a bit more straightforward. Here,

Basile: bah-ZEEL
Baton Rouge: BAT-ten ROOZH
Bossier City: BOH-zher SIT-ee
Breaux Bridge: BROH BRIDGE
Calcasieu: KAL-kuh-shoo
Carencro: KAIR-en-krow
Cloutierville: KLOO-chee-vill
Erath: EEH-rath
Grand Coteau: GRAND kuh-TOE
Houma: HOAM-uh
Iowa: EEH-o-way
Jeanerette: JENN-urh-ett
Lafayette: LAFF-ee-ett
Lafourche: la-FOOSH
Mamou: MAH-moo
Monroe: MUN-roe
Natchitoches: NACK-ih-tish
Opelousas: AH-puh-loo-suss
Plaquemines: PLACK-ih-mens
Ponchatoula: PON-chuh-tool-uh
Port Barre: PORT BAR-eeh
Shreveport: SHREEV-port
Tangipahoa: TAN-jah-puh-ho
Thibodaux: TIB-uh-doe
Vacherie: VASH-er-ee

Parks and Waterways

Atchafalaya (river/swamp): UH-cha-fuh-lye-uh
Bayou Teche (bayou): BYE-oo TESH
Bogue Chitto (river): boe-guh CHEE-tuh
Bonnet Carré (spillway): BON-ee KAIR-ee
Borgne (lake): BORN
Fontainebleau (park): FOWN-ten-bloo
Manchac (bayou): MAN-shack
Maurepas (lake): MOOR-uh-paw
Ouchita (river): WAW-shuh-taw
Sabine (river): suh-BEAN
Tchefuncte (river): chuh-FUNK-tuh

you have two options: "LOO-zee-ann-ah" or "le-WEE-zee-ann-ah." Both pronunciations are common and considered acceptable.

Pronouncing the rest of the rivers, lakes, towns, and streets of New Orleans and Louisiana can be extremely tricky for outsiders. "Correct" pronunciation isn't really the point here. After all, according to your French teacher, Chartres Street, in New Orleans's French Quarter, would be pronounced "SHART," but the correct local pronunciation is "CHAR-ters" or "CHART-uz."

If you'd rather not sound like an outsider, do your best to learn the major place-name pronunciations. Granted, locals won't generally torment you for mispronouncing words, especially since, depending on one's regional accent, there are often two or more commonly accepted (though hotly debated) ways to pronounce the same word.

While the pronunciation keys listed in this guide are approximate and imperfect—owing to the many regional nuances among locals, who sometimes have grown up on the same block but still favor one pronunciation over another—they will surely assist you in your travels. Syllables set in capital letters are stressed (as in "CHAR-ters"). If a common street or place-name isn't listed, assume that it's generally pronounced as it is elsewhere in the United States. For example, St. Louis Street in the French Quarter is said here as the Missouri city is—"saynt LOO-iss"—and not the way that the French would pronounce it.

THE ARTS

While New Orleans is known for its fine art galleries and historical architecture, and has inspired countless writers, artists, actors, and filmmakers over the decades, its biggest artistic claim to fame is indeed its music. This city is one of the world's most dynamic live-music scenes. Jazz was invented here, a conglomeration of mostly African-American traditions that has rural counterparts elsewhere in southern Louisiana in the form of zydeco and Cajun music. There are only a handful of large-scale venues for formal concerts; in fact, many big-name musicians favor comparatively smaller stages when in town. New Orleanians are loyal, knowledgeable, and excited about music, and performers appreciate the enthusiasm, relishing the chance to play a club that's small enough to encourage a close connection between the musicians and the fans. It takes almost no planning and very little effort to find a place to catch a jamming live show in New Orleans, even on a Monday or Tuesday night. Just check the listings in the *Gambit* or *The Times-Picayune,* or simply stroll through the French Quarter or Faubourg Marigny. Dozens of clubs bellow music from their doors every night of the week, and many of these places rarely charge a cover (or at least a terribly high one), though they will typically have a one- or two-drink minimum.

Jazz and Blues

Jazz wasn't invented in one definitive instant—it evolved over 20 or 30 years during the early part of the 20th century and in several parts of New Orleans's African American community. The state has produced several jazz luminaries, among them Jelly Roll Morton, Sidney Bechet, and crooner Harry Connick Jr.

Jazz music typically uses both individual and collective improvisation, syncopation, and distinctive vocal effects, and it has its origins in European, African, and Caribbean traditional music. Commonly, you'll hear blues vocalizing sung to jazz instrumental accompaniment. Many people trace jazz to a popular cornet player named Buddy Bolden, who performed regularly in New Orleans from the mid-1890s until about 1910. Through the 1910s and '20s, ragtime-style jazz and other music forms, with a spontaneous, upbeat tempo, began to attract a following, albeit an underground one, in New Orleans.

This thoroughly modern and iconoclastic style of music was not, initially, well received by the mainstream. In fact, it was shunned by organizers of Mardi Gras parades for years. During the early years, many people considered this musical style to be scandalous and impudent—they criticized it at least as harshly as early critics of rock-and-roll denounced that music. Jazz was seen as a crude bastardization of more acceptable musical styles. But through time, jazz would win the hearts of even the harshest naysayers, and today, there's really no style of music for which the city is better regarded.

Blues music has its origins upriver a bit from New Orleans, about 300 miles north in the fruitful delta farming regions of northwestern Mississippi, especially the towns near Clarkdale. It's said that blues derives from the field hollers of cane and cotton workers in these parts. Eventually, the soulful vocals were joined with guitars, drums, and horns to become the modern form of blues celebrated today all through the South and especially in Louisiana. Huddie "Lead Belly" Ledbetter, who wrote such classics as "Good Night, Irene" and "Midnight Special," grew up in Shreveport, in the northwestern corner of the state, and is often credited as the father of blues music.

Blues, along with New Orleans jazz, melded together in the 1950s to influence a new genre: rhythm and blues, or R&B. It is a distinctly commercial genre that was begun with the express intent of getting airplay on the radio and acclaim for its stars through record sales, and to that end, it has always incorporated the catchiest and most accessible elements of the genres from which it borrows.

All around the state—though especially in Baton Rouge and New Orleans—clubs present live blues performers, and this often sorrowful, sometimes joyous, style of music also influences much of the jazz, rock, country-western, and gospel music heard elsewhere in the state.

Cajun and Zydeco

Cajun and zydeco are terms often confused with one another or used to describe the same music, but they have distinct origins and subtle but important differences. Both have their origins in southwestern Louisiana's Cajun Country, and they have each enjoyed a huge surge in worldwide popularity since the 1980s. They're also sometimes credited with being the progenitors of modern country-and-western music, which is a relatively new phenomenon when compared with Cajun and zydeco.

Cajun music derives, as one would guess, from the French culture of Cajun settlers who came to southwestern Louisiana primarily during the 18th and early 19th centuries—it's nearly always sung in French—but this upbeat, danceable musical form also has German, Anglo American, and African influences. Originally, Cajun tunes revolved around fiddles, but the influence of German settlers led to the use of push-button accordions during the late 1800s, and now both these instruments are the keystones of any good Cajun band. Nowadays, Cajun bands typically include a bass and drums. A *tit fer* is another instrument common to the genre—this iron triangle struck with a spike is used to add rhythm.

When live Cajun is performed, you'll generally see folks dancing either waltzes or two-steps. Like many of the country tunes that have been inspired by it, Cajun music often tells the tale of something tragic or unhappy, such as failed romances, early deaths, or other hardships common to life among the Acadian immigrants of early southern Louisiana.

But many songs are funny and self-effacing, playing on an often unfortunate circumstance for laughs. Many of today's Cajun tunes have their origins in the Acadian folk music of Canada and also in the traditional fiddling tunes of France. It is truly folk music, and the early traditions were never written down but passed along from generation to generation, just as many old Cajun tales were. The earliest recordings of Cajun music date to the late 1920s. Top venues for Cajun tunes today include Prejean's Restaurant in Lafayette and Mulate's in New Orleans.

One of the most famous and distinguished Cajun-western bands was the Hackberry Ramblers, whose albums were nominated for Grammies. Back in 1933, fiddler Luderin Darbone and accordionist Edwin Duhon formed the band, mixing the toe-tapping sounds of traditional Cajun music with western swing and folky hillbilly influences. They used to power the electric sound system at local dance halls by hooking up to Darbone's Model-T Ford. They released their first album with RCA Bluebird in 1935, and they continued to perform and record for decades. In the early 1980s, a renewed interest in Cajun music was born, and the Ramblers, based in Lake Charles, enjoyed a popular resurgence. The music now tends toward a faster-paced, rollicking honky-tonk vibe.

While Cajun is a predominantly Anglo musical form, its cousin zydeco has its roots with the African American sharecroppers and farmers of the same region. The two musical styles clearly influenced each other, with zydeco evolving from a tradition called "La La," a term for an early style of music played among African Americans in homes and at some clubs that used only an accordion and a washboard for instruments. Zydeco is much more closely linked to blues and R&B music. It's a younger musical genre than Cajun; it uses either an accordion or push-button piano and also incorporates a *frottoir* (literally "rub board," or washboard), as opposed to the *tit fer* (triangle) used in Cajun music.

Many of the Creole African Americans in southern Louisiana came from the Caribbean, which also helped to shape this musical style. In Afro-Caribbean culture, there's a syncopated style of a cappella music called *juré* that is sometimes cited as zydeco's true predecessor.

In the middle of the 20th century, zydeco came to be influenced by the burgeoning R&B and blues music of the South, and it continues to evolve and change as zydeco musicians borrow from rock, jazz, soul, and even rap and hip-hop. Clifton Chenier, of Opelousas, is often considered the father of modern zydeco—he toured throughout the United States and Europe in the 1960s, helping to spread the popularity of this inimitable style.

The name zydeco is said to derive from the French phrase, *les haricots sont pas salés,* meaning "the snapbeans are not salty." The first two words, *les haricots,* are pronounced lay-ZAH-ree-coh, which has been shortened through the years to zydeco, pronounced ZAHY-di-koh. The phrase in question referred to a period of such financial hardship that one could not afford to so much as season basic foods—and so, as with Cajun music, zydeco often touches on themes of struggling to persevere and make do during difficult times.

Both zydeco and Cajun music are best appreciated live, ideally someplace where you can get out on the dance floor and cut loose, or at the very least tap your toes a bit. Both forms go hand-and-hand with eating, and you'll find that many of the best Cajun and soul restaurants of southern Louisiana, especially near Lafayette, have live zydeco and Cajun music many nights of the week. The little town of Eunice, about 45 miles northwest of Lafayette, is one of the best places to catch live performances—here the Liberty Center for the Performing Arts hosts live Cajun and zydeco music on Saturday evenings.

Rock and Soul

Rock music was a natural outgrowth of blues, gospel, and country-western traditions, and some say it was born in New Orleans, where, in the late 1940s, a singer named Roy Brown sang a tune called "Good Rockin' Tonight," the first song that used "rock" as a term for this faster-paced, danceable variation on the blues. A book by music historian Robert Palmer called *Tale of Two Cities: Memphis Rock and New Orleans Roll* traces the development of rock music to these two cities along the Mississippi.

New Orleans's jazz traditions contributed the sassy roll to rock music, while Memphis contributed the harder-edged blues born in the Mississippi Delta towns south of the city. The area between the two cities was rich with Pentecostal gospel sounds, which also influenced the development, ironically, of that devil music, rock-and-roll. New Orleans's brand of rock music is especially influenced by piano playing, keyboards, and even accordions, which suggests a link between rock and zydeco.

Maybe the most famous Louisiana rock legend is Fats Domino, who emerged from the New Orleans club scene and made famous the song "Walkin' to New Orleans." Local session musicians have long attracted the attention of big-city record producers, who sent stars such as Little Richard to the Big Easy to make albums. Other rock, pop, and soul greats from the New Orleans area include Allen Toussaint, Percy Mayfield, the Dixie Cups, Ernie K-Doe, Irma Thomas, the Neville Brothers, Professor Longhair, Frankie Ford, Lee Dorsey, and Dr. John, many of whom recorded at the Cosimo Matassa music studio. More recently, New Orleans's music scene spawned the alternative pop-rock band Better Than Ezra, as well as the gangsta sounds of Master P and his empire of rappers, including his young son, Lil' Romeo.

Rock has been shaken up a bit with Louisiana influences, such as country and bluegrass, to form rockabilly music, made famous by the likes of Jimmy Clanton, Joe Clay, Floyd Kramer, Jerry Lee Lewis, Jim Reeves, Farron Young, Slim Whitman, and Hank Williams Sr. The term bandied about today for Cajun- and zydeco-tinged rock music is "swamp pop," and you'll hear it in the more current clubs all throughout Cajun Country.

Country and Bluegrass

Country music, and its close cousin bluegrass (or perhaps child is a better term, since this style was born out of old-time country music traditions), share certain similarities with Cajun and even zydeco, but their routes are distinctly Anglo American (specifically Scots-Irish) rather than French, German, or African American. Many of the first Anglo settlers in Louisiana, who began arriving in the early 1800s, hailed from Kentucky and neighboring states and brought with them traditions of fiddling and ballad-singing.

Early barn dances and jamborees gave country music a widespread following, and the *Louisiana Hayride*, broadcast out of Shreveport's Municipal Auditorium on KWKH, popularized the genre in the 1940s and '50s, introducing Americans to Hank Williams, Johnny Horton, Johnny Cash, and Elvis Presley. The rocking honky-tonk style of country music, though not unique to Louisiana, thrives throughout the state. Western swing, which bands like the Hackberry Ramblers once performed, mixes country music with Cajun, blues, jazz, and other genres in a distinctly Louisiana way.

Northern Louisiana has especially strong country and bluegrass traditions, but you can find live performances at venues in New Orleans, as well as in the Florida Parishes. Jerry Lee Lewis was born in Ferriday, and in Abita Springs, *The Abita Springs Opry* is an annual, six-concert series of bluegrass, country, and other "roots" music. Former governor Jimmie Davis was one of the state's earliest country recording stars; his most famous song was "You Are My Sunshine," which became the official state song of Louisiana in 1977. Current country stars with Louisiana roots include Sammy Kershaw, Tim McGraw, and Michael Rhodes.

Gospel

Gospel has deep roots in Louisiana, although it tends to be more often performed in the northern half of the state. Black gospel music, which has been celebrated in the state for many years, has its origins with the African slaves who first sang biblical songs and hymns known as "spirituals." Generally, these songs, which are performed in churches today, are performed a cappella, but other gospel music is accompanied by instruments and often has jazz, bluegrass, soul, and blues overtones. You can find performances not only at churches but at festivals and conventions. Some of the bigger music clubs in New Orleans, notably the House of Blues, feature gospel choirs from time to time.

Classical and Opera

Classical music and opera have been little influenced by Louisiana's other more homegrown musical forms, but they've been appreciated in this region since the late 18th century, when the first opera ever performed in the United States made its debut in New Orleans. An early American classical composer, Louis Moreau Gottschalk, was born in New Orleans, and he incorporated African and Caribbean themes in his music. Classical concerts are held in just about every city in the state, and the Louisiana Sinfonietta, based in Baton Rouge and led by acclaimed composer Dinos Constantinides, is especially well regarded. Notable Louisianians who have earned acclaim in this genre include Shirley Verrett, a New Orleans-born opera singer, and Van Cliburn, a virtuoso pianist from Shreveport.

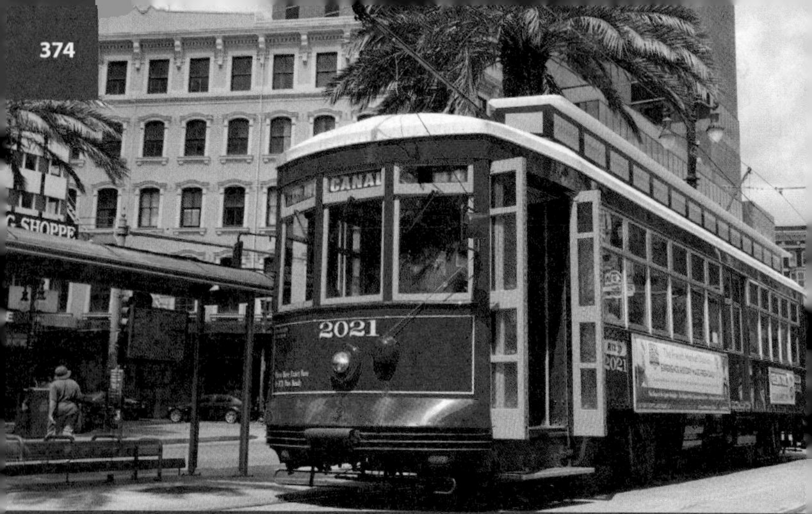
CANAL
2021
G SHOPPE

Essentials

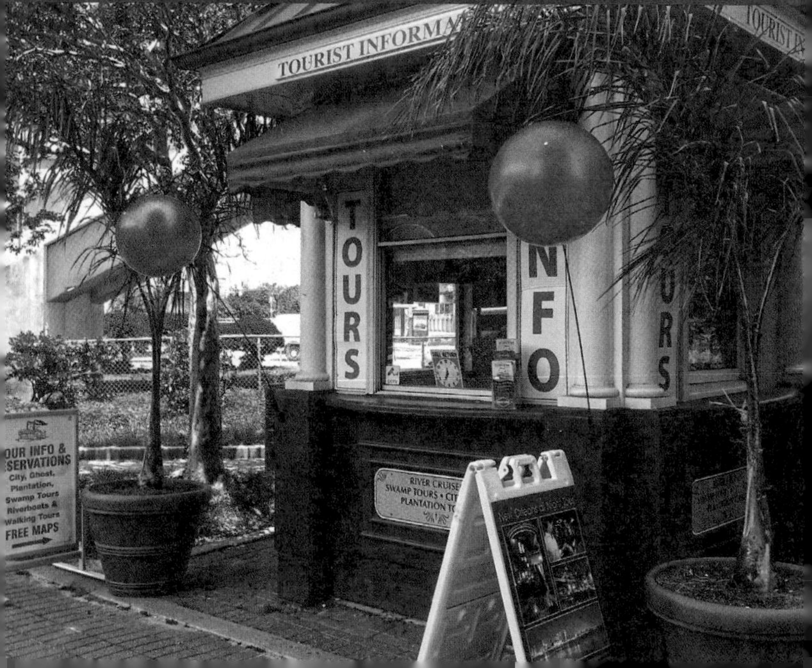
TOURIST INFORMA
TOURS
INFO
RIVER CRUISE
SWAMP TOURS • CIT
PLANTATION TO
OUR INFO &
ESERVATIONS
City, Ghost,
Plantation,
Swamp Tours
Riverboats &
Walking Tours
FREE MAPS

Transportation

GETTING THERE

New Orleans's airport is well served by most major airlines and has direct flights to many of the nation's largest cities. It's conveniently located in a nearby suburb and is pleasant to fly into and out of. The city also has direct Amtrak train service and Greyhound bus service from many big cities, but these modes of transport are often quite time-consuming and, especially in the case of trains, not always less expensive than flying. Some travelers arrive here via cruise ship and many come by car—the major east-west I-10 runs directly through New Orleans, less than a half mile from the French Quarter.

Air

Louis Armstrong New Orleans International Airport (900 Airline Dr., Kenner, 504/303-7500, www.flymsy.com), 15 miles west of downtown New Orleans via I-10, is a massive facility that accommodates the entire Gulf South with service on several airlines. Despite the decreased capacity immediately following Hurricane Katrina, it's easy to find direct flights from most major U.S. cities: Dallas, Houston, Atlanta, Orlando, Miami, Charlotte, Newark, New York, Chicago, Minneapolis, Denver, Las Vegas, Reno, and San Francisco.

Commercial air service is also available to Baton Rouge, Lafayette, and Lake Charles. Generally, it's more expensive to fly to one of the smaller regional airports than to New Orleans, especially when factoring in the cost of driving. Situated roughly eight miles north of downtown Baton Rouge via I-110, **Baton Rouge Metropolitan Airport** (9430 Jackie Cochran Dr., 225/355-0333, www.flybtr.com) is served by American Airlines, Continental Airlines, Delta Air Lines, and US Airways, with frequent direct flights to and from Atlanta, Dallas, Houston, and Memphis. **Lafayette Regional Airport** (200 Terminal Dr., 337/266-4400, www.lftairport.com) is three miles southeast of downtown Lafayette via US-90. It is served by American Eagle, the Delta Connection, and Continental Express, with direct flights to and from Atlanta, Dallas, Houston, and Memphis. **Lake Charles Regional Airport** (500 Airport Blvd., 337/477-6051, www.flylakecharles.com) is nine miles south of downtown Lake Charles via LA-385. You can take direct flights to and from Houston, courtesy of Continental Airlines, and Dallas, courtesy of American Airlines. If you choose to fly into one of these three regional airports, you'll have to rent a car to reach New Orleans; Avis, Budget, Hertz, National, and Enterprise serve all three locales.

Previous: a streetcar on Canal Street; a helpful tourism kiosk.

Depending on traffic, the 15-mile trip from the airport to the French Quarter can take 25-35 minutes by car. A **taxi** from the airport to the Central Business District (CBD) usually costs $33 for one or two passengers and $14 per person for three or more passengers. Pickup occurs on the airport's lower level, just outside the baggage claim area. Extra baggage might require an additional charge; credit cards are typically accepted.

If you'd prefer to travel in style, consider **Airport Limousine** (504/305-2450 or 866/739-5466, www.airportlimousineneworleans.com), the airport's official limo service, which has handy kiosks in the baggage claim area. The number of passengers will determine the type of vehicle selected: sedans for up to three passengers, SUVs for up to five, and limos for six or more. For one-way trips to the French Quarter and CBD, rates start at $58 for one or two passengers; a nominal fuel charge is generally applied to all rides.

To save a little money, opt for the **Airport Shuttle** (504/522-3500 or 866/596-2699, www.airportshuttleneworleans.com; $20 adult one-way, $38 adult round-trip, children under 6 free), which offers shared-ride service to hotels in the French Quarter, the CBD, and Uptown as well as the Ernest N. Morial Convention Center (www.mccno.com). From the upper level of the airport, you can also hop aboard the **E-2 Airport Bus** (504/818-1077 or 504/364-3450, www.jeffersontransit.org; $2 pp). On weekdays, the bus takes about 35 minutes to reach the CBD; on weekends, it only travels to Mid-City and you'll have to rely on an RTA bus route to reach destinations in Uptown or downtown New Orleans.

If you're headed north of New Orleans, there are two helpful services at the airport. The **Northshore Airport Express** (985/386-3861, www.nsairportexpress.com) offers shuttle service to and from Slidell, Covington, Hammond, and other communities on the Northshore; advance reservations are required. The **Tiger Airport Shuttle** (225/333-8167, www.tigerairportshuttle.com) provides transportation to and from Baton Rouge. Though fares vary for both, it's often more economical to share such lengthy rides with other passengers.

Train

Amtrak (800/872-7245, www.amtrak.com) operates three rail routes across southern Louisiana, all of which include stops at the New Orleans Amtrak Station (1001 Loyola Ave.; daily 5am-10pm). Amtrak offers a number of promotions and special rail passes (which allow you to overnight in U.S. cities served by Amtrak), making this a practical way to visit several places on one pass. The USA Rail Passes are available in three travel durations: 15 days/8 rail segments ($460 adult, $230 child 2-12), 30 days/12 rail segments ($670 adult, $345 child 2-12), and 45 days/18 rail segments ($900 adult, $450 child 2-12). All passes allow you to hop between routes

Mileage Matters

To help plan your trip, consider these estimated driving distances between the Big Easy and other destinations:

- **Atlanta, Georgia:** 469 miles
- **Baton Rouge, Louisiana:** 80 miles
- **Chicago, Illinois:** 926 miles
- **Dallas, Texas:** 514 miles
- **Gulfport, Mississippi:** 78 miles
- **Houma, Louisiana:** 58 miles
- **Houston, Texas:** 348 miles
- **Jackson, Mississippi:** 186 miles
- **Lake Charles, Louisiana:** 206 miles
- **Little Rock, Arkansas:** 427 miles
- **Memphis, Tennessee:** 395 miles
- **Miami, Florida:** 863 miles
- **Mobile, Alabama:** 144 miles
- **Nashville, Tennessee:** 532 miles
- **St. Louis, Missouri:** 677 miles
- **San Antonio, Texas:** 543 miles
- **Shreveport, Louisiana:** 327 miles

during your trip. Even with a pass, you'll still need to reserve a ticket for each train you plan to board. There are rental car agencies at Amtrak stations in most big cities.

These rail routes serve New Orleans:

- **City of New Orleans** runs daily from Chicago to New Orleans, with major stops in Memphis, Jackson, and Hammond (19 hours).
- **Crescent** runs daily between New York City and New Orleans, with major stops in Philadelphia, Baltimore, Washington D.C., Charlotte, Atlanta, Birmingham, and Slidell (30 hours).
- **Sunset Limited,** an east-west train, runs from Los Angeles to New Orleans three times weekly, with major stops in Tucson, El Paso, San Antonio, Houston, Lake Charles, and Lafayette (48 hours).

Bus

Greyhound (800/231-2222, www.greyhound.com) is the definitive bus provider for New Orleans, with frequent and flexible service throughout the country. Buses depart daily from the New Orleans Greyhound Station (1001 Loyola Ave., 504/525-6075, daily 5:15am-10:30am, 11:30am-1pm, 2:30pm-9:30pm) with multiple stops throughout Louisiana to many neighboring states. Travel times can be significantly longer than by train (although not always), but fares are generally much cheaper.

If you're planning a lengthy trip, consider Greyhound's **Discovery Pass,** which you can buy in increments of 7-60 days, allowing unlimited stopovers throughout the duration of the pass. Different types and prices of passes are available to U.S., Canadian, and international travelers. As with

Amtrak's USA Rail Passes, a ticket is required for each bus trip taken with the Discovery Pass.

Car

The New Orleans metro area is about 20 miles from west to east and 10 miles from north to south. The I-10 runs directly through New Orleans and provides the closest access to the French Quarter. West of the Quarter, the I-10 connects with the Pontchartrain Expressway (US-90) in the CBD. The Pontchartrain Expressway splits west through Uptown; south alongside the Garden District, crossing the Mississippi River; and north to Mid-City and I-610. Though traffic can be difficult in this city, you can usually get from one end of New Orleans to the other in about 30-40 minutes.

If you plan to stay in New Orleans the entire time you're visiting this region, then you won't need a car. If, however, you're planning one or two days outside the city, rent a car downtown for a short term. A car may also be handier than public transportation for exploring Uptown and Mid-City. Consult the **Louisiana Department of Transportation & Development** (225/379-1100, wwwsp.dotd.la.gov) for maps, publications, and extensive information about public transportation, highway safety, traveler resources, road conditions, and upcoming projects.

CAR RENTAL

Just about all the major car-rental agencies are represented at Louis Armstrong New Orleans International Airport (900 Airline Dr., Kenner, 504/303-7500, www.flymsy.com): **Advantage** (800/777-5500, www.advantage.com), **Alamo** (800/462-5266, www.alamo.com), **Avis** (800/331-1212, www.avis.com), **Budget** (800/527-0700, www.budget.com), **Dollar** (800/800-4000, www.dollar.com), **Enterprise** (800/736-8222, www.enterprise.com), **Hertz** (800/654-3131, www.hertz.com), **National** (800/227-7368, www.nationalcar.com), and **Thrifty** (800/847-4389, www.thrifty.com). In New Orleans, rates for car rentals typically start at $30 daily for economy cars but can easily rise at busy times, such as during Mardi Gras or when conventions are in town. Weekly rates begin at $180 for an economy car and $200 for a midsize car. While most car-rental agencies will only rent to properly licensed drivers who are at least 25 years old, some will rent to customers between the ages of 21 and 24, as long as they have a valid credit card and driver's license and are willing to pay a daily surcharge of $27.

GETTING AROUND

New Orleanians rarely refer to compass directions when discussing how to navigate the city. The city is bound on one side by the highly irregular Mississippi River, which forms the western, southern, or eastern border; main roads tend to run parallel or perpendicular to the river. Since the river's direction changes, this means that New Orleans's street grid also changes its axis in different places. As a result, most residents employ the terms "lakeside" (meaning north toward Lake Pontchartrain) and "riverside" (meaning south toward the Mississippi) when referring to streets perpendicular to the river. The terms "upriver" or "uptown" refer to westerly directions; the terms "downriver" or "downtown" are used for easterly directions. For example, Canal Street, which tourists generally consider a north-south thoroughfare, actually runs in a southeasterly direction toward the river. If you're still confused, be sure to have a city map with you at all times, as this is one place where it is absolutely indispensable—whether you're walking, driving, taking public transportation, or even using cabs. New Orleans is very much a collection of neighborhoods, and residents refer to neighborhood names almost as much as specific streets.

Public Transportation

New Orleans is served by an extensive network of buses and streetcars, operated by the **New Orleans Regional Transit Authority** (RTA, 504/248-3900, www.norta.com). The standard fare is $1.25 per person ($0.40 senior, free under 3) plus $0.25 per transfer; express buses cost $1.50 per person. You must pay with exact change by depositing coins or inserting $1 bills into the fare box at the front of the bus or streetcar. Food, beverages, smoking, and stereos are not permitted on buses and streetcars.

The handy **Jazzy Pass,** a magnetized card presented upon boarding the bus or streetcar, allows unlimited rides during the active period; it's available in 1-day ($3), 3-day ($9), or 31-day ($55) increments. The 1-day pass can be purchased on the bus or streetcar, though only cash is accepted. Other passes are available from various hotels, banks, and retailers, such as Walgreens.

BUS

Bus service is available throughout the city, and all RTA buses can accommodate people with disabilities. The one-way fare is $1.25 (plus $0.25 per transfer) and passengers must pay with either exact change (coins or $1 bills) or the Jazzy Pass.

Tourists often utilize the **Magazine line** (11), which runs from Canal Street in the CBD through the Garden District and Uptown, along a six-mile stretch of galleries, shops, and restaurants, before ending at Audubon Park. Another important route is the **Jackson-Esplanade line** (91), which runs from Rousseau Street in the Garden District, through the CBD, along the north edge of the French Quarter, up Esplanade Avenue, and past City Park, ending at the Greenwood Cemetery. For a complete map of all bus lines, plus individual maps and schedules, visit the RTA website (www.norta.com).

STREETCAR

The RTA also operates New Orleans's iconic streetcars. The one-way fare is $1.25 per person (plus $0.25 per transfer), and passengers must pay with either exact change (coins or $1 bills) or the Jazzy Pass.

The famous **St. Charles streetcar** line, which operates 24 hours daily, runs along St. Charles and South Carrollton Avenues, from Canal Street to Claiborne Avenue; a one-way trip lasts about 45 minutes. Given their historic status, the St. Charles streetcars are exempt from ADA (the Americans with Disabilities Act) compliance, so unfortunately passengers with disabilities may have trouble boarding them. The St. Charles line has been in operation since 1835, when it began as the main railroad line connecting the city of New Orleans with the resort community of Carrollton, now part of the city; the olive-green cars date to the 1920s, when they were built by the Perley Thomas Company. Today, the line is a wonderful, scenic, and atmospheric way to travel between the CBD and Uptown.

The **Canal Street streetcar** line extends from Canal Street to Mid-City before splitting into two branches. The "Cemeteries" branch (daily 5am-3am) runs from the foot of Canal Street, not far from the ferry terminal for Algiers Point, all the way up to the historic cemeteries along City Park Avenue. The "City Park/Museum" branch (daily 7am-2am) takes North Carrollton Avenue to Esplanade Avenue, right beside City Park and the New Orleans Museum of Art. A one-way trip along either branch lasts about 30 minutes.

The **Riverfront streetcar** line (daily 7am-10:30pm) uses newer streetcars and runs a short but scenic 1.8-mile route along the Mississippi River, from the French Quarter to the CBD. These modern red streetcars were built by New Orleans metal- and woodworkers; a one-way ride lasts about 15 minutes.

Lastly, the relatively short **Loyola-UPT** line (daily 6am-midnight) travels between the downtown Amtrak station, the intersection of Canal and Rampart Streets, and Harrah's New Orleans before linking with the Riverfront route. For maps and schedules of all five streetcar lines, visit the RTA website (www.norta.com).

FERRY

The **Algiers Point/Canal Street ferry** (504/309-9789, http://nolaferries.com or www.friendsoftheferry.org; Mon.-Fri. 6am-9:45pm, Sat. 10:45am-8pm, Sun. 10:45am-6pm; $2 pp, $1 senior, free under 3) provides ferry service across the Mississippi River, from the foot of Canal Street in the CBD to Algiers Point. The five-minute service no longer transports vehicles; the boat departs every 30 minutes on either shore. The **Lower Algiers/Chalmette ferry** (daily 6am-8:45pm; $2 per pedestrian or vehicle driver, $1 senior pedestrian or vehicle passenger, free under 3) offers hourly service between Lower Algiers and the East Bank community of Chalmette; the trip usually lasts 15-20 minutes. Contact the **Crescent City Connection Police** (504/376-8180) for up-to-the-minute information regarding breakdowns.

Taxi and Pedicab

Taxis are *highly* recommended over public transportation at night, especially when traveling solo. This is the sort of city where it's easy to lose track of time, particularly if you're bar-hopping, so it's always a smart idea to have the name and number of at least a couple of cab companies with you at all times. Taxi rates within the city typically start at $3.50 per ride, plus $2 per mile thereafter; there's also a charge of $1 for each additional passenger. You will often find taxis waiting at major intersections near Bourbon Street and other nighttime hot spots in the Quarter. Be sure to use taxis operated by licensed and established cab companies, such as **Checker Yellow Cabs** (504/943-2411), **New Orleans Carriage Cab** (504/207-7777, www.neworleanscarriagecab.com), **United Cabs** (504/522-9771 or 504/524-9606, www.unitedcabs.com), and **White Fleet Cab and Elk's Elite Taxi** (504/822-3800). Taxi rates are often higher during peak times, such as Mardi Gras and Jazz Fest; expect to pay $5 per person or the meter rate, whichever is greater.

As an alternative to taxis, hop aboard one of the relatively new pedicabs often seen trolling the streets of the French Quarter. Operated by knowledgeable guides and equipped with safety belts, headlights, and flashing taillights, these ecofriendly, person-powered vehicles can accommodate up to three or four passengers, making them ideal for getting you and a couple friends back to your home or hotel after a long night of partying in the Quarter. Currently, there are two pedicab companies in the city: **Bike Taxi Unlimited** (504/891-3441, www.neworleansbiketaxi.com), which serves the French Quarter, the Faubourg Marigny, the CBD, the Arts District, and Uptown; and **NOLA Pedicabs** (504/274-1300, www.nolapedicabs.com), which mainly serves the Quarter, the CBD, and the Arts District. Standard fares are $5 per passenger for the first six blocks, after which each passenger will be charged $1 per city block. During special events, such as Mardi Gras, expect to pay $50 per half hour and $100 hourly.

Driving

When driving in New Orleans, be forewarned that many streets are one-way and riddled with potholes, street parking is scarce, and garage and hotel parking is expensive. On the other hand, the main neighborhoods are easily walkable, taxis are easy to find, and public transportation is decent, especially from the French Quarter to Uptown and Mid-City, so having a car isn't necessary. Given the city's compact size, many travelers rely on motorcycles and bikes, which are often much easier to park on the street. If you do bring or rent a car to explore the Greater New Orleans area, note that most city roads have speed limits of 25-35 mph; two-lane state and U.S. highways generally have speed limits of 55 mph along narrow rural stretches and 70 mph in wider spots. Roads in rural areas are sometimes very heavily patrolled by police. They are also highly unsafe to speed on—they're bumpy and narrow, with virtually no shoulders. As in other parts of the country, it's illegal to drive without a seatbelt or while intoxicated.

PARKING

Given New Orleans's high crime rate, parking here is a gamble—if parking on the street or in an unattended lot, keep as few of your belongings in your car as possible. For a bit more security, you can pay $15-50 nightly to park your car at a hotel or commercial lot. Relying on hourly rates can be considerably more expensive, though many downtown businesses and stores offer free or discounted parking with minimum purchase and validated parking tickets. Even with secured parking areas, refrain from leaving valuables in plain sight.

Even beyond security concerns, finding street parking in the French Quarter, the CBD, and other tourist areas can be extremely difficult. The Quarter is especially tough because most blocks are restricted for residents with permits. In such cases, you can usually park for no more than two hours during the restricted time period. Many hotel properties in the Quarter have no dedicated parking facilities. You'll find parking meters throughout the French Quarter and CBD—both the old-fashioned, coin-operated meters as well as new-fangled ones that accept dollar bills and credit cards and offer a printed receipt to place on your dashboard. The meters are typically enforced Monday-Saturday 8am-6pm; while they're not usually enforced on Sundays or holidays, always read the meters before parking. If you're staying beyond the downtown area, it might be better to park in the Uptown or Mid-City neighborhoods and use public transportation to visit the French Quarter and CBD.

If you do decide to park on the street, be sure to read the parking signs carefully; the rules can differ from neighborhood to neighborhood, and some violations can be extremely costly—from $20 for an expired meter to $200 for parking on a French Quarter sidewalk. In general, avoid parking:

- over 18 inches from the curb
- at bagged or broken meters
- across a driveway or fire lane
- on sidewalks or neutral grounds
- on a narrow street without allowing 10 feet of unobstructed roadway
- on the street for more than 24 consecutive hours
- in handicapped spaces
- in loading, service, bus, and taxi zones
- within 15 feet of fire hydrants
- within 20 feet of corners and crosswalks
- within 50 feet of railroad crossings
- during rush hours (Mon.-Fri. 7am-9am and 4pm-6pm) on major streets
- on street-cleaning days (usually Tues. and Thurs. 8am-noon)
- on a parade route within two hours of a parade

Additionally, avoid parking vehicles longer than 22 feet overnight in the CBD and having three or more unpaid parking violations. If your car is towed away, contact the **Claiborne Auto Pound** (504/565-7450 or

504/565-7451). For general questions about parking in New Orleans, consult the city's **Parking Division** (504/658-8200).

Travel Tips

FOREIGN TRAVELERS

While international travelers are required to show a valid passport upon entering the United States, most citizens from Canada and the 36 countries that are part of the **Visa Waiver Program (VWP)**—including France, Italy, Germany, Spain, Australia, New Zealand, Japan, and the United Kingdom—are allowed to travel to New Orleans and its environs without a visa. However, they still need to apply to the **Electronic System for Travel Authorization (ESTA).** All other temporary international travelers are required to secure a nonimmigrant visa before entering Louisiana. For more information, consult the **U.S. Department of State's Bureau of Consular Affairs** (202/663-1225, www.travel.state.gov).

Upon entering Louisiana, international travelers must declare any dollar amount over $10,000 as well as the value of any articles that will remain in the country, including gifts. A duty will be assessed for all imported goods, though visitors are usually granted a $100 exemption. Illegal drugs, Cuban cigars, obscene items, toxic substances, and prescription drugs (without a prescription) are generally prohibited. In order to protect American agriculture, customs officials will also confiscate certain produce, plants, seeds, nuts, meat, and other potentially dangerous biological products. For more information, consult the **U.S. Customs and Border Protection** (703/526-4200, www.cbp.gov).

While the embassies for most countries are located in Washington, D.C., some nations have consular offices and honorary consuls in New Orleans. Though you should research such matters before leaving your home country, you can also contact the **World Trade Center of New Orleans** (WTCNO, 365 Canal St., Ste. 1120, 504/529-1601, www.wtcno.org) for assistance.

VOLUNTEER VACATIONS

Sometimes, being a tourist isn't enough. If you want to explore southeastern Louisiana *and* lend a helping hand, then perhaps "voluntourism" is right up your alley. National and state parks can especially use some extra assistance, and working in such diverse environments can be a truly rewarding experience. Hurricane Katrina left behind a great need for volunteers. Even today, organizations like the **New Orleans Area Habitat for Humanity** (504/861-2077 or 504/861-4121, www.habitat-nola.org) and the **Preservation Resource Center of New Orleans** (504/581-7032, www.prcno.org) welcome the assistance of dedicated volunteers. Both have been

Louisiana Tax Free Shopping

If visiting from another country, you're entitled to a refund of the state sales tax and, in certain cases, the local sales tax on certain goods bought in Louisiana. This policy, first among the 50 states, was introduced as a way to help promote visitation by foreign travelers, and depending on how much shopping you do, you really can save a bit of money.

The refund is available to visitors who have a valid foreign passport *and* an airline or other international round-trip ticket of up to 90 days' duration. Canadians are the one exception to the passport rule; they may provide proof of residency by showing a driver's license or birth certificate. If you are a resident of any other country, however, you must supply a passport. Resident aliens, foreign students, U.S. citizens living in other countries, citizens with dual citizenship in the United States and another country, and visitors staying in the United States for more than 90 days are not eligible. The refund does not apply to entertainment, services, hotel charges, car rentals, food and beverages, or personal goods bought for use while in Louisiana, and only purchases made at participating shops qualify.

To take advantage of the Louisiana Tax Free Shopping (LTFS) program, ask for a refund voucher at the shop where you make your purchase—any participating merchant will be able to provide you with this, once you show your passport (or other ID, if Canadian). Remember that you will not be given the refund at the time of purchase—this happens at the **Louisiana Tax Free Shopping Refund Center** (900 Airline Dr., Terminal C, Kenner, 504/467-0723, www.louisianataxfree.com; Mon.-Fri. 8am-5pm, Sat.-Sun. 9am-3pm) at the Louis Armstrong New Orleans International Airport or at four other locations in southern Louisiana: the **New Orleans Refund Center** (The Outlet Collection at Riverwalk, 500 Port of New Orleans Pl., Level B, 504/568-3605; Mon.-Sat. 10am-6pm, Sun. 11am-6pm), **Macy's Refund Center—Lakeside Shopping Center** (3301 Veterans Memorial Blvd., 3rd Fl., Metairie, 504/484-4665; Mon.-Sat. 10am-5pm, Sun. 11am-6pm), **Macy's Refund Center—Mall of Louisiana** (6401 Bluebonnet Blvd., 2nd Fl., Baton Rouge, 225/757-7394; daily 11am-6pm), and **Dillard's Refund Center—Acadiana Mall** (5725 Johnston Rd., Lafayette, 337/989-8139; Mon.-Sat. 10am-5pm, Sun. 11am-5pm). At the actual shop, you'll pay the full price, including tax, for your purchase, and you'll be issued a voucher in the amount of the refund that you're due. You must present the voucher and all original sales receipts for every purchase to qualify for the refund.

Refunds under $500 are issued in cash; refunds over $500 are issued by check and mailed to your home. You can also mail in your vouchers and receipts to receive a refund. In this case, you must mail the original vouchers and sales receipts, copies of your travel ticket and passport, and a statement explaining two things—why you didn't redeem the vouchers at any of the refund centers and where the merchandise is currently located—to the Louisiana Tax Free Shopping Refund Center (P.O. Box 20125, New Orleans, LA 70141).

instrumental in helping to restore the city's most damaged historic areas since Hurricane Katrina.

TRAVELING WITH CHILDREN

Although New Orleans tends to be geared more toward adults than children, there are nevertheless some outstanding attractions for kids, such as the Audubon Aquarium of the Americas, the Audubon Butterfly Garden and Insectarium, Blaine Kern's Mardi Gras World, the Audubon Zoo, Storyland at City Park, and the Louisiana Children's Museum, right in the CBD. Many of the excursions offered throughout the city, such as swamp tours, riverboat rides, and haunted strolls, are a big hit with kids, especially teenagers. For more ideas, consult www.neworleanskids.com, which offers a slew of tips regarding family-friendly hotels, restaurants, attractions, and activities.

While plenty of inns and hotels welcome children—such as the Quarter's Ritz-Carlton New Orleans and the CBD's Loews New Orleans Hotel, both of which offer babysitting services—some lodging options are adults-only establishments.

WOMEN TRAVELERS

It's important to take precautions when traveling in New Orleans. Although much of the French Quarter is relatively safe, there are still too many things that can go wrong—even in a crowd—and other neighborhoods, such as the Tremé and Bywater, can be downright perilous for women.

If you venture out alone, tell someone back home about your intended travel plans, stick to daytime driving, and stay close to busy attractions and streets. Stow your money, credit cards, and identification close to your person, as big purses make easy targets. If you feel that someone is stalking you, find a public place (such as a store or late-night restaurant), and don't hesitate to alert the police. Keep the doors to your hotel room and vehicle locked at all times.

Before heading out on your trip, invest in a canister of pepper spray as well as a cell phone, which can be useful in an emergency (however, cellular reception is limited in the more remote areas of southeastern Louisiana).

SENIOR TRAVELERS

Although the wild nightlife scene around the French Quarter can be off-putting to some, New Orleans is overall quite appealing to senior travelers, particularly those who appreciate historical architecture and one-of-a-kind attractions, such as The National WWII Museum. For those who'd prefer a quieter place to sleep, the good news is that the Quarter isn't the only neighborhood that offers unique hotels. For a more relaxed local experience, consider staying in the Garden District or farther Uptown, especially at one of the hotels and inns along St. Charles Avenue.

Even better, seniors often qualify for age-related discounts at restaurants, attractions, and other establishments throughout New Orleans. The **American Association of Retired Persons** (AARP, 888/687-2277, www.aarp.org) offers members a myriad of travel discounts as well as a newsletter that often touches on travel issues. **Road Scholar** (800/454-5768, www.roadscholar.org) also organizes a wide variety of educationally oriented tours and vacations that are geared toward seniors; some even highlight the distinct cultures of New Orleans and Lafayette.

In general, New Orleans and southeastern Louisiana are exceptionally helpful places, so senior travelers should have little trouble finding assistance here.

GAY AND LESBIAN TRAVELERS

New Orleans is a bastion of gay-friendliness, with gay newspapers, numerous gay and lesbian organizations and gay-owned businesses, and several gay-dominated bars and nightclubs, many of which are in the midst of the nightlife district in the French Quarter. Locals tend to be rather blasé about the sight of two women or two men walking hand in hand in the Big Easy, especially in the Quarter, the Faubourg Marigny, and Uptown, which tend to have the highest lesbian and gay populations. Some tourists, however, come from less tolerant places, and sadly, drunken disagreements occasionally occur along Bourbon Street, where the city's straight and gay nightclub rows collide.

Three annual events—Mardi Gras in the late winter, the Southern Decadence celebration over Labor Day weekend, and Halloween in the fall—draw the greatest numbers of gay and lesbian visitors to New Orleans, but the city is always popular with gay and lesbian travelers. Many inns and B&Bs, especially in the Faubourg Marigny, are gay-owned.

For more information about gay and lesbian activities, consult the free bimonthly ***Ambush Mag*** (www.ambushmag.com). The same publication also has a website just for gay goings-on during Mardi Gras (www.gaymardigras.com). Another helpful website is www.gayneworleans.com.

TRAVELERS WITH DISABILITIES

Within new hotels, some large restaurants, and most major attractions, you can expect to find wheelchair-accessible restrooms, entrance ramps, and other helpful fixtures; RTA buses are wheelchair-accessible. But New Orleans has many hole-in-the-wall cafés, tiny B&Bs, historic house-museums with narrow staircases or uneven thresholds, and other buildings that are not easily accessible to people using wheelchairs. Unfortunately, the city's historic streetcars are also not wheelchair-accessible. If you're traveling with a guide animal, be sure to contact every hotel or restaurant in question to confirm access and accommodation. A useful resource is the **Society for Accessible Travel & Hospitality** (212/447-7284, www.sath.org).

TRAVELING WITH PETS

Although pets aren't allowed within many of New Orleans's hotels, restaurants, and stores, several places do welcome them, including state park campgrounds and some downtown hotels. Typically, guests will be asked to keep pets on a leash at all times, walk animals in designated areas, control their behavior so as not to disturb or endanger others, and always pick up their droppings. Barking or aggressive dogs are usually forbidden everywhere. When in doubt, call ahead to verify the pet policies of a particular hotel, park, attraction, or establishment.

BUSINESS HOURS

New Orleans and Louisiana fall within the central standard time (CST) zone. The region observes central daylight time (CDT). Standard business hours for banks tend to be Monday-Friday 9am-4pm, with limited hours on Saturday.

Smaller attractions are frequently staffed by volunteers and tend to have limited hours; call ahead to ensure that the place will be open or to set up an appointment to visit. In many cases, hours for popular attractions are reduced on Sunday and may fluctuate during the summer months. Given New Orleans's laid-back vibe, posted hours and other policies aren't always observed, especially in the case of small or privately owned businesses.

In the French Quarter, many bars stay open 24 hours daily; you may see folks with plastic "to go" cups wandering around, especially during Mardi Gras. Elsewhere in the city, bars more commonly close between 2am and 4am.

COSTS AND TIPPING

As a town that relies heavily on tourism, New Orleans has its share of pricey hotels, restaurants, boutiques, and parking lots. Luckily, it's easy to find deals here. Staying outside the Quarter and CBD can often save you quite a bit of money, especially since public transportation is very inexpensive. There are also plenty of affordable eateries, vintage shops, and close-to-free attractions throughout the city; at many attractions, children, college students, senior citizens, military personnel, and holders of AAA cards will receive substantial discounts. However, most retail items and services cost more than their listed price due to sales taxes. The state sales tax is 4 percent, while the sales tax for Orleans Parish is 5 percent; this means that in New Orleans, most goods and services will incur a rather high sales tax of 9 percent. In Metairie, Kenner, and other cities in Jefferson Parish, goods and services will incur an 8.75 percent sales tax. The hotel tax in New Orleans is a whopping 13 percent.

Given the city's reliance on tourism, tipping is critical here. Although the amount of a gratuity depends on the level of service received, there are general tipping guidelines. Restaurant servers should receive 15-20 percent of the entire bill, while pizza delivery drivers should receive at least

10 percent. Taxi and limousine drivers should receive at least 15 percent of the entire fare, while valets, porters, and skycaps should expect around $2 per vehicle or piece of luggage. The housekeeping staff of your inn or hotel also deserves a tip; a generally accepted amount is $2 per night.

Tour guides, fishing guides, and other excursion operators should be tipped as well. No matter how much such experiences cost, the gratuity is never included in the quoted price. How much you choose to tip is entirely up to you. While the exact amount of a tip will depend on the cost, length, and nature of the trip in question—not to mention your satisfaction—it's generally accepted to tip 10-20 percent of the overall cost. If a guide or operator makes an exceptional effort, then it's highly recommended to increase the size of the tip accordingly.

PUBLIC RESTROOMS

In the French Quarter, you'll find public restrooms at the Shops at Canal Place, the Shops at Jax Brewery, and the French Market. Plenty of bars and restaurants also have reliable facilities, which you're welcome to use as long as you're willing to purchase something. Public urination is a frequent occurrence in New Orleans and can result in being ticketed or getting arrested.

Health and Safety

HOSPITALS

There are several well-regarded hospitals and clinics in New Orleans and its environs, including the **Tulane Medical Center** (1415 Tulane Ave., 504/988-5263, www.tulanehealthcare.com), the closest general hospital to the French Quarter and the CBD; the **Interim LSU Public Hospital** (2021 Perdido St., 504/903-3000, www.mclno.org), the active part of a major medical center still in progress; and the **Ochsner Baptist Medical Center** (2700 Napoleon Ave., 504/899-9311, www.ochsner.org), an Uptown hospital with a 24-hour emergency room.

If you're in need of emergency dental care, consider the **Louisiana Dental Center** (4232 St. Claude Ave., 504/947-2958, www.ladentalcenter.com; Mon.-Thurs. 7:30am-4pm, Fri. 7:30am-3pm, Sat. 9am-3pm), which offers several locations in southeastern Louisiana, from Metairie to Gonzales. Most medical and dental facilities will require insurance or a partial payment before admitting patients for treatment or dispensing medication.

PHARMACIES

Some pharmacies in New Orleans and southeastern Louisiana include **Walgreens** (619 Decatur St., 504/525-7263 or 800/925-4733, www.walgreens.com; daily 8am-10pm) in the French Quarter; **CVS/pharmacy** (4901

Prytania St., 504/891-6307 or 800/746-7287, www.cvs.com; daily 24 hours) in the Uptown area; and **Rite Aid Pharmacy** (760 Harrison Ave., 504/483-2383 or 800/748-3243, www.riteaid.com; Mon.-Sat. 7am-9pm, Sun. 8am-8pm) in Lakeview. In all cases, the in-house pharmacy has shorter hours than the rest of the store, so be sure to call ahead.

EMERGENCY SERVICES

All of Louisiana is tied into the **911** emergency system. Dial 911 free from any telephone (including pay phones) to reach an operator who can quickly dispatch local police, fire, or ambulance services. While this service also works from cell phones, you may find it difficult to make calls from rural areas or offshore waters, where reliable cellular service isn't always guaranteed. For non-emergencies, contact the **Louisiana State Police** (504/471-2775, www.lsp.org) or the **New Orleans Police Department** (www.nola.gov/government/nopd)—including the First District (501 N. Rampart St., 504/658-6010) in the Tremé, the Second District (4317 Magazine St., 504/658-6020) in Uptown, the Fifth District (4015 Burgundy St., 504/658-6050) in the Bywater, and the Eighth District (334 Royal St., 504/658-6080) in the French Quarter. In the event of a hurricane or other natural disaster, contact the **New Orleans Office of Homeland Security and Emergency Preparedness** (504/658-8700) for instructions and evacuation assistance.

CRIME AND HARASSMENT

New Orleans has a reputation for crime—partially deserved, partially exaggerated. While crime is prevalent in sketchy neighborhoods, such as the Tremé and Bywater, a lot of crime is also centered in or near tourist areas, and muggings or carjackings, while infrequent, do occur. To minimize any threat to your safety and your belongings, follow these commonsense precautions:

- Never leave valuables in plain view on a car seat; secure them in the trunk, where they're less tempting to thieves.
- In case of an accident on the highway, do not abandon your vehicle, as this might also invite thieves.
- Don't display money, valuables, or jewelry conspicuously.
- Keep your money, credit cards, identification, and other important items hidden on your person; purses and backpacks are much easier to steal.
- Leave all but the most necessary items at home or at your hotel.
- Store laptop computers, cameras, jewelry, or any other expensive or irreplaceable item in the hotel safe.
- Secure your bike whenever it's left unattended.
- Lock your hotel and car doors at all times.
- Pay attention to your surroundings and walk along well-lit, well-traveled streets.

- Avoid dark and mostly residential areas.
- Never go into cemeteries after dark.
- Travel in groups of at least two whenever possible.
- Take cabs to parts of town with which you're unfamiliar.
- If you're traveling via RV, do not boondock alone in an isolated place; try to stay in an RV park, a campground, or, at the very least, a well-lit parking lot.

The most frequent targets of crime in New Orleans are inebriated tourists, and these, unfortunately, are easy to find in the French Quarter late at night. The simplest way to keep safe is to avoid drinking yourself into a stupor. If anticipating a night of revelry, keep the name and address of your hotel written down someplace safe—but never write your hotel room number down somewhere that a thief or pickpocket could get it. Also be sure to carry the name and number of at least one or two cab companies, and keep your cell phone handy.

If you require assistance while in downtown New Orleans, contact **SafeWalk** (504/415-1730; daily 10am-10pm), a free service provided in the CBD and Arts District. With at least 20 minutes' advance notice, Public Safety Rangers will escort residents and visitors to their cars or other areas within the designated zone. If you do find yourself in trouble, whether in the CBD or another area of New Orleans, don't hesitate to find a phone and dial **911.** Remember that the time it takes police and emergency vehicles to reach you will depend upon your location.

If you witness a crime of any kind while in New Orleans, contact the **Greater New Orleans Crimestoppers** (504/822-1111, www.crimestoppers-gno.org) to offer an anonymous tip. Likewise, you can consult the **Orleans Parish Sheriff's Office** (504/822-8000 or 504/826-7045, www.opcso.org).

HEATSTROKE

Hot, sunny days are common in southeastern Louisiana, and it's crucial to prepare for them. Apply sunscreen frequently and liberally. Prolonged sun exposure, high temperatures, and little water consumption can cause dehydration, which can lead to heat exhaustion—a harmful condition whereby your internal cooling system begins to shut down. Symptoms may include clammy skin, weakness, vomiting, and abnormal body temperature. In such instances, you must lie down in the shade, remove restrictive clothing, and drink some water.

If you do not treat heat exhaustion promptly, your condition can worsen quickly, leading to heatstroke (or sunstroke), a dangerous condition whereby your internal body temperature starts to rise to a potentially fatal level. Symptoms can include dizziness, vomiting, diarrhea, abnormal breathing and blood pressure, cessation of sweating, headache, and confusion. If any of these occur, head to a hospital as soon as possible.

HURRICANE PREPARATION

Since Hurricane Katrina, some out-of-towners have become apprehensive about visiting southern Louisiana during the Atlantic hurricane season, which usually runs June-November (though hurricanes have certainly occurred beyond this time frame). The truth is, however, that hurricanes are infrequent in this region. Nevertheless, it's always a good idea to be prepared for the worst.

If you do plan to visit New Orleans during hurricane season, the best advice is to stock up on extra water, flashlights, batteries, and other supplies, as you'll surely face long lines and depleted supplies once a storm threatens. For a list of some suggested items that will come in handy whether you're forced to stay through the storm or you find yourself stuck in an evacuation route, see the **National Oceanic and Atmospheric Administration** (NOAA) website (www.noaa.gov). Be sure to set aside items such as cash, cell phones and adapters, identification and credit/debit cards, house and car keys, important papers, pet supplies, asthma inhalers, and other necessities. You might want to keep your valuables, such as jewelry or family heirlooms, in an easy-to-reach place, too.

You should also develop a possible exit strategy, and keep apprised of the weather at all times. Although most radio and TV stations provide weather updates, the **National Weather Service** (62300 Airport Rd., Slidell, 504/522-7330 or 985/649-0357, www.srh.noaa.gov) is a good source of information for tropical storms and hurricanes.

INSURANCE

Insurance is highly recommended while traveling in southeastern Louisiana. Whether you're a U.S. citizen driving your own car or an international traveler in a rented RV, you should invest in medical, travel, and automotive insurance before embarking upon your trip in order to protect yourself as well as your assets. Research your insurance options and choose the policies that best suit your needs and budget. For travel insurance (which should include medical coverage), consider a company like **Travel Guard** (800/826-4919, www.travelguard.com).

WATER SAFETY

Given New Orleans's location at the southern end of the Mississippi River, it's not surprising that some people would question the safety of its water supply. In general, the tap water here is relatively safe. It's tested daily by the **Sewerage & Water Board of New Orleans** (www.swbno.org) for microbial, organic, chemical, and metallic contaminants.

While visiting New Orleans, you might venture into the countryside, bayous, and lakes beyond the city. If so, you'll encounter a lot of brackish water, which you should never drink, due to the high probability of dehydration. In various places, you may also find fresh water, and while the water may look inviting, don't take a chance. Many of Louisiana's inland bodies of water may be tainted with *Giardia lamblia,* a nasty little parasite that is most commonly transmitted through mammal feces. The resulting illness, **giardiasis,** can result in severe stomach cramps, vomiting, and diarrhea. While Halizone tablets, bleach, and other chemical purifiers may be effective against such organisms, your best bet is to use an adequate water filter (which filters down to 0.4 micron or less) or boil the water for at least five minutes.

SMOKING

All restaurants in New Orleans are nonsmoking, and, as of April 2015, a citywide ban has made smoking illegal inside taverns, lounges, concert halls, hotels, and other establishments throughout New Orleans. You can, however, still smoke outside, such as on balconies and in courtyards, depending on the place in question.

WILDLIFE ENCOUNTERS

With its humid, subtropical climate and prevalence of marshes, southeastern Louisiana is home to a wide array of insects, from harmless dragonflies to more bothersome critters. Perhaps the biggest concern is **mosquitoes,** whose stings can cause itchy red welts or worse. Mosquitoes are typically more prevalent June-September, when the humidity is at its worst. To protect against these relentless creatures, use a combination of defenses, including light-colored clothing, long-sleeved shirts, long pants, closed shoes, scent-free deodorant, and insect repellents containing DEET. Avoid grassy areas and shady places and instead seek open, breezy locales (especially out on the water) and avoid peak hours for mosquito activity, namely sunrise and sunset. Try to open and close your car doors quickly and keep your car windows rolled up, as there's little worse than being stuck in a vehicle with a roving mosquito.

If you are stung you should be fine, unless you have an unforeseen allergy or the mosquito is a carrier for a disease like the West Nile virus. Beyond cleaning the affected area and treating it with calamine lotion, hydrocortisone cream, or aloe vera gel, all you can do is take some anti-inflammatory or antihistamine medication for the pain and swelling and wait for the skin to heal.

Insects aren't the only perils in the wild. While hiking amid southeastern Louisiana's forests, marshes, and beaches, be careful where you step; it's easier than you think to trip on a root or other obstruction. Refrain from digesting any tempting berries, flowers, and plants without first consulting local residents or expert field guides.

Since much of southeastern Louisiana comprises undeveloped marshes and forests, not to mention surrounding waters, you're bound to encounter wild animals. While many of these, such as lizards and shorebirds, are fairly harmless, more dangerous creatures, such as alligators, live here, too. To avoid perilous encounters with such animals, don't venture into places like

Barataria Preserve or the Atchafalaya Basin by yourself, and try to observe all wildlife from a distance. Although it should go without saying, never taunt, disturb, or feed any of the wildlife.

Information and Services

MAPS AND TOURIST INFORMATION

For general information about traveling in southeastern Louisiana, your best source is the state-run **Louisiana Office of Tourism** (800/994-8626, www.louisianatravel.com), which offers a tour guidebook, interactive maps, travel tips, and oodles of information about the state's accommodations, restaurants, attractions, events, live entertainment, and outdoor activities, plus live operators willing to assist with your tourism needs. Visitors to the Big Easy should also consult the **New Orleans Convention & Visitors Bureau** (2020 St. Charles Ave., 504/566-5011 or 800/672-6124, www.neworleanscvb.com; Mon.-Fri. 8:30am-5pm) or the **New Orleans Tourism Marketing Corporation** (2020 St. Charles Ave., 504/524-4784, www.neworleansonline.com), both of which provide a slew of information about the city's myriad lodging, dining, and activity options. The **New Orleans Welcome Center** (529 St. Ann St., 504/568-5661, www.crt.state.la.us; daily 9am-5pm) also provides maps and brochures and arranges tours. For information about the Greater New Orleans area, consult the **Jefferson Convention & Visitors Bureau** (1221 Elmwood Park Blvd., Ste. 411, 504/731-7083 or 877/572-7474, www.experiencejefferson.com). The Northshore, Tangipahoa Parish, Baton Rouge, Houma, Lafayette, and Lake Charles all have helpful CVBs as well.

In a state known for its tourism industry, you'll find no shortage of helpful maps, including those produced by **AAA** (800/564-6222, www.aaa.com), which offers both a *Louisiana/Mississippi* state map ($5 nonmember, free for members) as well as a *New Orleans* map ($5 nonmember, free for members) that features smaller maps of the city's airport and streetcar system. **Rand McNally** (800/333-0136, www.randmcnally.com) publishes several helpful maps, including an easy-to-fold *Louisiana* map ($8), a folded *New Orleans, Hammond, Ponchatoula, Slidell* map ($6), a folded *Baton Rouge, Shreveport, Bossier City* map ($6), a laminated *Streetwise New Orleans* map ($7), and a comprehensive *New Orleans Street Guide* ($20). If exploring the backcountry, you may also want to order an official topographical (topo) map produced by the **U.S. Geological Survey** (888/275-8747, www.usgs.gov).

MONEY

Bank debit cards and major credit cards (like Visa and MasterCard) are accepted throughout southeastern Louisiana, especially in major cities like New Orleans and Baton Rouge. Automated teller machines (ATMs) are prevalent, and most banks—such as **Chase** (800/935-9935, www.chase.com), **Regions** (800/734-4667, www.regions.com), **Iberia Bank** (800/682-3231, www.iberiabank.com), **First NBC Bank** (866/441-5552, www.firstnbcbank.com), **First Bank and Trust** (888/287-9621, www.fbtonline.com), and **Bank of Louisiana** (800/288-9811, www.bankoflouisiana.com)—provide access to ATMs inside and/or outside their branches. (Be prepared to pay $2-3 per ATM transaction if the machine isn't operated by your bank.)

Many bars, eateries, stores, and tour operators will accept only cash or travelers checks, so you should never rely exclusively on plastic. Foreign currency can be exchanged at the **Whitney Bank** branch (900 Airline Dr., Kenner, 504/838-6491 or 800/844-4450, www.whitneybank.com; Mon.-Fri. 8:30am-4pm) in the ticket lobby of the Louis Armstrong New Orleans International Airport; cash advances and travelers checks are also available here. For up-to-date exchange rates, consult www.xe.com.

COMMUNICATIONS AND MEDIA

Newspapers and Periodicals

The major newspaper for New Orleans is ***The Times-Picayune*** (www.nola.com), which provides up-to-date information about restaurants, sporting events, and live entertainment. For nightlife and live music listings, pick up a copy of the monthly ***OffBeat Magazine*** (www.offbeat.com); the website includes a monthly electronic newsletter, for which you can sign up online, and a free iPhone app keeps club listings in your pocket. An excellent resource for arts, dining, shopping, clubbing, and similar diversions in metro New Orleans is the decidedly left-of-center ***Gambit*** alternative newsweekly (www.bestofneworleans.com). The monthly ***Where Y'at*** magazine (www.whereyat.com) also offers information about the city's dining and nightlife scenes.

New Orleans Magazine (www.myneworleans.com) is a useful, well-produced monthly, with excellent dining, shopping, arts, and events coverage. Its glossy offshoot, ***Louisiana Life*** (www.myneworleans.com/Louisiana-Life), comes out six times yearly and has a wide variety of features on what to see and do across the state, with a focus on food, history, art, and music. Two other offshoots are the quarterly ***New Orleans Homes & Lifestyles*** (www.myneworleans.com/New-Orleans-Homes-Lifestyles) and the monthly ***St. Charles Avenue*** (www.myneworleans.com/St-Charles-Avenue), both glossy lifestyle magazines. Other helpful publications include ***The Louisiana Weekly*** (www.louisianaweekly.com) and ***Louisiana Cookin'*** (www.louisianacookin.com).

Radio and Television

Local radio and TV stations can be useful sources of information for everything from upcoming concerts and festivals to weather updates during hurricane season. For excellent local music, tune your radio to **WWOZ**

(90.7 FM, www.wwoz.org), which typically plays jazz, blues, and R&B, plus healthy doses of swing, Cajun and zydeco, country and bluegrass, and gospel. Other popular radio stations in the Big Easy include **WWNO** (89.9 FM, www.wwno.org), which is broadcast from the University of New Orleans and offers classical music, cultural programming, and NPR news; **WTUL** (91.5 FM, www.wtulneworleans.com), Tulane University's progressive radio station; and **WRNO** (99.5 FM, www.wrno.com), which offers an all-news format featuring the likes of Rush Limbaugh, Glenn Beck, and other conservative personalities. The city's four main TV stations include **WWL-TV** (www.wwltv.com), the CBS affiliate; **WDSU** (www.wdsu.com), the NBC affiliate; **WGNO** (www.abc26.com), the ABC affiliate; and **FOX8** (www.fox8live.com).

Resources

Glossary

andouille: (an-DOO-ee) a spicy, smoked pork sausage prepared with garlic and Cajun seasonings and used in dishes like red beans and rice, gumbo, and jambalaya

bananas Foster: a rich dessert consisting of bananas, butter, brown sugar, cinnamon, and rum over vanilla ice cream, invented at Brennan's in the French Quarter

bayou: (BAHY-oo) a sluggish body of water within a marsh, prevalent throughout southern Louisiana

beignet: (ben-YAY) a squarish, fried pastry made from doughnut batter and sprinkled with powdered sugar

blackened: a Cajun preparation that involves coating fish or meat with a spicy seasoning blend and flash-frying it in a hot, cast-iron pan

bobo: (BOH-boh) a small injury, similar to a "boo boo"

boil: a quintessential, often seasonal Cajun seafood dish in which shrimp, crabs, or crawfish are boiled in a spicy broth

boudin: (boo-DAN) a hot, spicy pork sausage typically mixed with onions, herbs, cayenne pepper, and cooked rice

brackish water: a mixture of freshwater and saltwater

brake tag: an annual vehicle inspection sticker

bread pudding: a traditional dessert made with soaked French bread and often served with rum sauce

buggy: a shopping cart

café au lait: (KAFF-ay oh LAY) a hot drink made equally of coffee (usually coffee with chicory) and steamed milk

Cajun: a term referring to the French Acadians that relocated from Canada to southern Louisiana

calas: (KAH-luhs) Creole rice fritters usually covered with cane syrup or powdered sugar

cher: (SHA) a Cajun French term of endearment

cochon de lait: (koh-SHON duh LAY) a French term that literally means "pig in milk" and regionally refers to a Cajun pig roast

Coke: a term used locally to describe any soda; also known as a "soft drink"

courtbouillon: (KOO-boo-YAWN) a Creole-style, tomato-based bouillabaisse, or seafood stew, the most popular version being redfish courtbouillon

Creole: a term referring to the descendants of French, Spanish, and Caribbean slaves and natives

Crescent City: a nickname for New Orleans, referring to how the Mississippi River curves around the city

Crescent City Connection: (CCC) the twin cantilever bridges that span the Mississippi River and connect the East Bank of New Orleans with the West Bank; formerly known as the Greater New Orleans Bridge (GNO)

dirty rice: pan-fried rice cooked with onions, green peppers, celery, stock, and giblets

dressed: an expression used when ordering a sandwich, meant to indicate that everything (e.g., lettuce, tomato, and mayonnaise) be included

epiphyte: a plant, such as an orchid, fern, or moss, that grows on the branches, trunks, and leaves of trees and derives its water and nutrients from the air

étouffée: (ay-too-FAY) a dark roux of seasoned vegetables, usually poured over rice and served with shrimp or crawfish

fais do-do: (FAY doh-doh) a Cajun dance party

filé: (FEE-lay) ground sassafras leaves used to season gumbo and other dishes

fixin' to: a Southern expression used when one is preparing to do something

gallery: a second-floor balcony that covers the sidewalk, especially common in the French Quarter

grillades: (gree-YAHDZ) a dish of diced meat marinated in vinegar to produce a rich gravy, usually served with grits

gris-gris: (GREE-gree) a voodoo good-luck charm

grits: ground corn kernels, typically boiled and served with a Southern-style breakfast

gumbo: a thick filé soup made from a roux, served with rice, and filled with ingredients like chicken, andouille, okra, shrimp, and crab meat

haint blue: a specific shade of pale blue paint visible on many porch ceilings throughout New Orleans, used to symbolize water and prevent evil "haints," or ghosts, from entering the premises

hoodoo: the ancient West African practice of "folk magic," which, in New Orleans, incorporates European and Native American influences and involves the use of herbs, incense, candles, talismans, and Biblical psalms

hurricane: a multi-use term referring to a destructive tropical storm and a popular drink made of rum and fruit punch

hush puppy: a crunchy, cornmeal fritter popular in the South and typically served with fried seafood

jambalaya: (juhm-buh-LAHY-uh) a Cajun or Creole rice dish containing celery, onions, tomatoes, spices, and meats like chicken, sausage, and seafood

j'eat: a local expression used in place of "Have you eaten yet?"

lagniappe: (LAN-yap) a French expression meant to indicate a bonus

laissez les bons temps rouler: (lay-ZAY lay BAWN tawn ROO-lay) a French expression meaning "let the good times roll"

make dodo: a local expression meaning "to sleep"

make groceries: a local expression meaning "to buy groceries"

maque choux: (MOCK SHOO) a popular side dish of sautéed corn, tomatoes, bell peppers, onions, and various spices

mirliton: (MER-li-tawn) a pear-shaped squash commonly stuffed with seasoned meat or seafood; also called "chayote"

mosquito hawk: a colloquial term for a dragonfly

mudbug: a slang expression for crawfish, the freshwater shellfish that other states refer to as "crayfish"

muffuletta: (muff-uh-LET-uh) a round, oversized sandwich made from Italian bread, ham, salami, mortadella, provolone, and olive salad; also spelled "muffaletta"

neutral ground: the grassy part between the paved areas of a boulevard; also known as a "median"

nutria: a large, beaver-like rodent commonly seen in the canals and swamps of southern Louisiana, often considered a nuisance due to its destructive tendencies

parish: the official term for a county in Louisiana

picayune: (pick-uh-YOON) a historical Spanish coin worth a little over six cents, which inspired the name of the city's newspaper, *The Times-Picayune*

pirogue: (PEE-rohg) a small, flat-bottomed canoe, prevalent throughout southern Louisiana

po-boy: the quintessential New Orleans sandwich, made on French bread, with fillings like roast beef or fried shrimp; also spelled "po' boy," "po boy," or "poor boy"

praline: (prah-LEEN or PRAY-leen) a sweet confection made from pecans, cream, butter, and carmelized brown sugar

red beans and rice: a traditional New Orleans dish consisting of kidney beans and a spicy gravy, often served with ham hocks, tasso, or andouille

rémoulade: (rey-moo-LAHD) a spicy, mustard-based sauce, typically served with boiled shrimp

Romeo spikes: 19th-century, cast-iron protrusions at the top of ground-floor gallery polls in the French Quarter, meant to deter male suitors from shimmying upward for unauthorized, nighttime visits to young women

roux: (ROO) a slowly cooked mixture of butter (or water) and flour used to thicken gumbo, sauces, and soups

Sazerac: a popular cocktail made with bitters, Pernod, sugar, lemon oil, and rye whiskey or bourbon

shotgun: a one-level architectural style whereby all rooms are positioned consecutively, interconnected by doors in lieu of a hallway

slave quarters: a smaller house situated behind a mansion or large plantation home, common in the French Quarter

sno-ball: a cup of shaved ice served with flavored syrups; usually called a "snowcone" in other states

Spanish moss: a specific epiphyte that resembles a grayish, lacy cluster and typically hangs from live oak trees

tasso: smoked beef or pork sausage, specially seasoned and often used in regional stews and pastas

Twinspan: the two parallel bridges that cross Lake Pontchartrain, from New Orleans to the Northshore

Vieux Carré: (VOO kah-RAY) a reference to the French Quarter, meaning "old square" in French

voodoo: an ancient West African religious faith that, in New Orleans, blends African, Haitian, Native American, European, and Catholic traditions; also known as the "dancing religion"

wetland: a lowland area saturated by surface or ground water, with vegetation adapted to such conditions, prevalent throughout southern Louisiana

where y'at?: a local expression used in place of "Where are you?"

Who dat?: a local idiom meaning "who is that?" that was originally used in poetry, minstrel shows, and movies and now serves as a chant of team support for the New Orleans Saints, fans of which are known as "Who Dats"

y'all: a commonly used contraction for "you all"

Yat: an English dialect spoken throughout the Greater New Orleans area, heavily influenced by European, Southern American, and Louisiana French accents; also referring to a native New Orleanian who speaks with this Brooklyn-style accent, commonly heard in communities like Chalmette

zydeco: (ZAHY-di-koh) a blues-influenced, Cajun-style type of dance music popular in southern Louisiana and typically featuring the sounds of guitars, violins, and accordions

Suggested Reading

CUISINE

Besh, John. *My New Orleans: The Cookbook*. Kansas City, MO: Andrews McMeel Publishing, LLC, 2009. Written by the celebrated chef-owner of Restaurant August, Lüke, and several other New Orleans-area restaurants, this collection contains roughly 200 of Besh's favorite local recipes and stories about his hometown.

Fitzmorris, Tom. *Tom Fitzmorris's Hungry Town: A Culinary History of New Orleans, the City Where Food Is Almost Everything*. New York, NY: Stewart, Tabori & Chang, 2010. Penned by a native New Orleanian, this fascinating history of the New Orleans dining scene, before and after Hurricane Katrina, also includes key recipes related to the text.

Lagasse, Emeril, and Marcelle Bienvenu. *Louisiana Real & Rustic*. New York, NY: William Morrow & Company, Inc., 2009. Compiled by the city's most boisterous celebrity chef, this collection features 150 classic Louisiana recipes, from gumbo to jambalaya to meat pies.

Link, Donald, and Paula Disbrowe. *Real Cajun: Rustic Home Cooking from Donald Link's Louisiana*. New York, NY: Clarkson Potter/Publishers, 2009. A culinary expedition through Cajun Country, the childhood home of Chef Donald Link, the owner of New Orleans-based restaurants Cochon and Herbsaint.

Murphy, Michael. *Eat Dat New Orleans: A Guide to the Unique Food Culture of the Crescent City.* Woodstock, VT: The Countryman Press, 2014. Sandwiched between a "mostly" bona fide history of New Orleans cuisine and an appendix filled with lists of eateries, culinary tours, and cooking classes, this mouth-watering book offers a neighborhood-by-neighborhood breakdown of the city's best eating spots, from food carts to famous restaurants.

Prudhomme, Paul. *Chef Paul Prudhomme's Louisiana Kitchen.* New York, NY: William Morrow & Company, Inc., 1984. A compendium of classic recipes by the New Orleans master of Cajun cooking.

St. Pierre, Todd-Michael. *Taste of Tremé: Creole, Cajun, and Soul Food from New Orleans's Famous Neighborhood of Jazz.* Berkeley, CA: Ulysses Press, 2012. An exploration of the soulful music and cuisine, from crawfish and corn beignets to chargrilled oysters, that define this gritty neighborhood.

FICTION AND PROSE

Burke, James Lee. *The Tin Roof Blowdown.* New York, NY: Simon & Schuster, 2007. Set in the wake of Hurricane Katrina, this gripping mystery is one of 20 novels in a popular crime series featuring Dave Robicheaux, a homicide detective living in southern Louisiana. Other titles include *The Neon Rain* (1987), *Purple Cane Road* (2000), and *Creole Belle* (2012).

Cable, George Washington. *Old Creole Days: A Story of Creole Life.* Gretna, LA: Pelican Publishing Company, Inc., 1991. In this reprint of his 1879 story collection, Victorian novelist and essayist Cable, who wrote many popular books about the city, captures life in old Creole New Orleans during the 19th century.

Chopin, Kate. *The Awakening and Selected Stories.* New York, NY: Penguin Putnam, Inc., 2002. One of the great literary classics of the South, Chopin's 1899 novella, which focuses on a woman who flouts New Orleans Creole society by leaving her husband and children, caused a huge scandal when it was first published. Though the circumstances may seem tame today, this remains an emotionally powerful work.

Clark, Joshua, ed. *French Quarter Fiction: The Newest Stories of America's Oldest Bohemia.* New Orleans, LA: Light of New Orleans Publishing, LLC, 2003. This riveting anthology explores "America's oldest Bohemia" through the eyes of local writers like John Biguenet, Andrei Codrescu, and Tennessee Williams.

Grisham, John. *The Pelican Brief.* New York, NY: Dell, 1992. In this thriller, a New Orleans law student seeks the help of an investigative reporter after her legal brief about a deadly conspiracy between a local tycoon, the U.S. President, and two murdered Supreme Court Justices results in the deaths of her law professor and an FBI agent.

Keyes, Frances Parkinson. *Dinner at Antoine's.* New Orleans, LA: Second Line Press, 2013. Originally published in 1948, this classic New Orleans novel revolves around the apparent suicide of a young woman and the subsequent efforts to prove that she was murdered. Keyes, who once lived in the French Quarter, penned several other Louisiana-based novels, including *Crescent Carnival* (1942), *The River Road* (1945), and *Steamboat Gothic* (1952).

Leonard, Elmore. *Bandits.* New York, NY: Arbor House Publishing Company, 1987. After uncovering a private fundraising scheme to aid the Contras in Nicaragua, three very unlikely partners—an ex-con, an ex-cop, and an ex-nun—decide that the several million dollars in question shouldn't leave New Orleans.

Long, Judy, ed. *Literary New Orleans.* Athens, GA: Hill Street Press, 1999. A delightful anthology of fiction, poetry, memoirs, and essays by some of the city's most notable authors, including James Lee Burke, William Faulkner, and Tennessee Williams.

Percy, Walker. *The Moviegoer.* New York, NY: Vintage Books, 1998. Percy was one of Louisiana's most talented writers, and this existential story about a New Orleans stockbroker, originally published in 1961, is one of his finest.

Rice, Anne. *Interview with the Vampire.* New York, NY: Alfred A. Knopf, Inc., 1976. Perhaps the Garden District's most famous former resident, Anne Rice has set several vampire and witchcraft tales throughout the New Orleans area, including the first of her acclaimed *Vampire Chronicles* series.

Saxon, Lyle, and Robert Tallant. *Gumbo Ya-Ya: Folk Tales of Louisiana.* Gretna, LA: Pelican Publishing Company, Inc., 1987. This reprint, originally sponsored by the Works Progress Administration (WPA) in 1945, offers an enthralling look at the state's legends and practices.

Smith, Julie. *New Orleans Mourning.* New York, NY: St. Martin's Press, 1990. An award-winning entry in the series of popular mystery books revolving around New Orleans policeman Skip Langdon. Other engrossing books in the collection include *Jazz Funeral* (1993), *Crescent City Connection* (1997), and *Mean Woman Blues* (2003).

Toole, John Kennedy. *A Confederacy of Dunces.* Baton Rouge, LA: Louisiana State University Press, 1980. A critically acclaimed tragicomic novel published more than a decade after the suicide of its young author, this peculiar tale presents a bizarre yet entertaining cast of New Orleans characters.

Warren, Robert Penn. *All the King's Men.* Orlando, FL: Harcourt Brace & Company, 1990. A thinly veiled fictional look at the life of Governor Huey Long, Warren's Pulitzer Prize-winning work, which was originally published in 1946, goes beyond mere political rehashing to become a gripping and compelling study of one of 20th-century America's most controversial figures.

Williams, Tennessee. *A Streetcar Named Desire.* New York, NY: New Directions Publishing Corporation, 2004. Originally published in 1947, this is the seminal Williams play set in New Orleans. Less famous but more directly about life in the French Quarter is *Vieux Carré,* which was inspired by journals that Williams kept while living in New Orleans.

HISTORY AND GEOGRAPHY

Asbury, Herbert. *The French Quarter: An Informal History of the New Orleans Underworld.* New York, NY: Thunder's Mouth Press, 2003. In an unconventional look at the city's seedy side, Asbury's colorful account, originally published in 1936, surveys the city's infamous red-light districts, illegal gaming, and other not-so-legitimate activities.

Brinkley, Douglas. *The Great Deluge: Hurricane Katrina, New Orleans, and the Mississippi Gulf Coast.* New York, NY: William Morrow & Company, Inc., 2006. This is one of the most comprehensive and insightful accounts of Hurricane Katrina, written by a noted historian and Tulane professor who experienced the storm's devastating aftermath firsthand.

Chase, John Churchill. *Frenchmen, Desire, Good Children...and Other Streets of New Orleans!* Gretna, LA: Pelican Publishing Company, Inc., 2001. Originally published in 1949, this humorous book reveals the origin of the Big Easy's fascinating, often hard-to-pronounce street names.

Duncan, Jeff. *From Bags to Riches: How the New Orleans Saints and the People of Their Hometown Rose from the Depths Together.* Lafayette, LA: Acadian House Publishing, 2010. Focusing on the 2009-2010 football season that culminated in the New Orleans Saints's first Super Bowl win, a sports columnist for *The Times-Picayune* demonstrates how the struggling NFL team and the people of New Orleans and the Gulf Coast bolstered one another in the years following Hurricane Katrina.

Garvey, Joan B., and Mary Lou Widmer. *Beautiful Crescent: A History of New Orleans*. Gretna, LA: Pelican Publishing Company, Inc., 2013. Originally published in 1982, recently updated by Kathy Chappetta Spiess and Karen Chappetta, and considered a definitive text for tourists, historians, and tour guides alike, this concise history offers details about the city's founding, changing European rule, African American community, jazz heritage, and notable figures and events.

Johnson, Walter. *Soul by Soul: Life Inside the Antebellum Slave Market*. Cambridge, MA: Harvard University Press, 1999. Using narratives, court records, bills of sale, and other documents to trace the harrowing legacy of slavery, this book offers a gripping and raw account of North America's largest and most notorious slave market, which was centered in New Orleans.

Piazza, Tom. *Why New Orleans Matters*. New York, NY: HarperCollins Publishers, 2005. This heartfelt, firsthand celebration of the Big Easy after Hurricane Katrina makes a case for why it's so important that the city rebuild and flourish.

Sublette, Ned. *The World That Made New Orleans: From Spanish Silver to Congo Square*. Chicago, IL: Lawrence Hill Books, 2008. A well-researched study of the Crescent City's economic and cultural roots prior to the 20th century.

Williams, T. Harry. *Huey Long*. New York, NY: Vintage Books, 1981. Originally published in 1969, this gripping biography explores the infamous "Kingfish," the man who shaped Louisiana politics for many years after his death.

MUSIC AND CULTURE

Alvarado, Denise. *The Voodoo Hoodoo Spellbook*. San Francisco, CA: Red Wheel/Weiser, LLC, 2011. Written by a New Orleans-born native Creole who has spent a lifetime studying indigenous healing traditions, this folk magic compilation offers serious practitioners a slew of authentic prayers, spells, rituals, and instructions.

Armstrong, Louis. *Satchmo: My Life in New Orleans*. Cambridge, MA: Da Capo Press, Inc., 1986. Originally published in 1954, this is the definitive autobiography by the definitive New Orleans jazz icon.

Berry, Jason, Jonathan Foose, and Tad Jones. *Up from the Cradle of Jazz: New Orleans Music Since World War II*. Lafayette, LA: University of Louisiana at Lafayette Press, 2009. A terrific survey tracing the history of music in the Big Easy, from the 1940s to the post-Katrina era.

Florence, Robert. *New Orleans Cemeteries: Life in the Cities of the Dead.* New Orleans, LA: Batture Press, Inc., 1997. An insider's history and tour of the city's famous aboveground cemeteries.

Gessler, Diana Hollingsworth. *Very New Orleans: A Celebration of History, Culture, and Cajun Country Charm.* Chapel Hill, NC: Algonquin Books of Chapel Hill, 2006. Filled with the author's detailed sketches and watercolors, this charming book celebrates all that makes southern Louisiana unique, from Jackson Square and the Garden District to Creole cuisine and Cajun music.

Huber, Leonard V. *Mardi Gras: A Pictorial History of Carnival in New Orleans.* Gretna, LA: Pelican Publishing Company, Inc., 2003. A decent overview of the city's most famous celebration, originally published in 1977.

Lomax, Alan. *Mister Jelly Roll: The Fortunes of Jelly Roll Morton, New Orleans Creole and "Inventor of Jazz."* Los Angeles, CA: University of California Press, 2001. Originally published in 1950, this fascinating examination of a New Orleans jazz luminary also explores the development of the city's music scene.

Ondaatje, Michael. *Coming Through Slaughter.* New York, NY: Vintage Books, 1996. Penned by the author of *The English Patient* and originally published in 1976, this colorful tale illustrates the life of Buddy Bolden, one of the earliest New Orleans jazz greats.

Tallant, Robert. *Voodoo in New Orleans.* Gretna, LA: Pelican Publishing Company, Inc., 2003. Written by the author of *The Voodoo Queen* and originally published in 1946, this classic compendium covers one of New Orleans's most fascinating topics.

RECREATION AND TRAVEL

Bronston, Barri. *Walking New Orleans: 30 Tours Exploring Historic Neighborhoods, Waterfront Districts, Culinary and Music Corridors, and Recreational Wonderlands.* Birmingham, AL: Wilderness Press, 2015. Written by a lifelong resident of New Orleans, this guide offers a wide array of self-guided tours, each of which includes dining and recreational tips.

Douglas, Lake, and Jeannette Hardy. *Gardens of New Orleans: Exquisite Excess.* San Francisco, CA: Chronicle Books LLC, 2001. This sumptuous tome, filled with photographs by Richard Sexton, takes readers into the many secret and sensuous gardens of the Big Easy.

Fry, Macon, and Julie Posner. *Cajun Country Guide.* Gretna, LA: Pelican Publishing Company, Inc., 1999. Originally published in 1992, this in-depth tour guide of Cajun Country offers extensive anecdotes and histories on just about every town in the region, large or small.

Sternberg, Mary Ann. *Along the River Road: Past and Present on Louisiana's Historic Byway.* Baton Rouge, LA: Louisiana State University Press, 2013. Originally published in 1996, this revised and expanded edition provides an amazingly thorough history and description, mile by mile, of the towns and plantation homes strung along the Great River Road.

Welch, Michael Patrick. *New Orleans: The Underground Guide.* Baton Rouge, LA: Louisiana State University Press, 2014. Beyond the traditional jazz, dishes, and carriage rides that visitors expect, New Orleans is home to Bohemian locals, genre-defying music, transnational cuisine, lesser-known bars and events, and a slew of obscure activities favored by the author, his friends, and other locals—as described in this unconventional guide.

Suggested Viewing

The lush landscape, antebellum plantation homes, lively music clubs, and well-preserved historic districts of southern Louisiana have long been favored by filmmakers and television producers. The classic, Oscar-winning films *Jezebel* (1938) and *A Streetcar Named Desire* (1951) were both partially shot in this region, and more recent productions have included the Nicholas Sparks adaptations *The Best of Me* (2014) and *The Lucky One* (2012), the novel-inspired film *A Love Song for Bobby Long* (2004), the television spin-offs *NCIS: New Orleans* (2014-present) and *The Originals* (2013-present), the "Coven" season of *American Horror Story* (2011-present), and HBO's much-acclaimed series *Treme* (2010-2013), which authentically chronicles the lives of various Big Easy residents and musicians in the wake of Hurricane Katrina. Before your trip, take the time to view some of the following selections.

Angel Heart (1987). Written and directed by Alan Parker, starring Mickey Rourke, Robert De Niro, and Lisa Bonet. In this sultry thriller, based on a novel by William Hjortsberg and partially shot in New Orleans, New York-based gumshoe Harry Angel follows a voodoo trail to the Big Easy in search of a missing singer.

The Big Easy (1986). Written by Daniel Petrie Jr., directed by Jim McBride, and starring Dennis Quaid, Ellen Barkin, Ned Beatty, and John Goodman. Set in New Orleans, this film focuses on a local homicide detective facing three concurrent dilemmas: bribery charges, a series of gang killings, and a sexy lawyer from the District Attorney's police corruption task force.

Cat People (1982). Written by Alan Ormsby, directed by Paul Schrader, and starring Nastassja Kinski, Malcolm McDowell, John Heard, and Annette O'Toole. Featuring New Orleans landmarks like the Audubon Zoo and the Gallier House, this erotic, Golden Globe-nominated remake of the 1942 horror classic follows two unusual siblings, whose sexual urges transform them into deadly black leopards.

The Curious Case of Benjamin Button (2008). Written by Eric Roth, directed by David Fincher, and starring Brad Pitt, Cate Blanchett, and Taraji P. Henson. Based on a short story by F. Scott Fitzgerald and filmed throughout southern Louisiana, this Oscar-winning drama tells the fantastical story of a man who ages backwards.

Dead Man Walking (1995). Written and directed by Tim Robbins, starring Susan Sarandon and Sean Penn. Based on a biographical account by Sister Helen Prejean and partially filmed at the Angola state prison, this Oscar-winning drama follows the story of a nun who, while comforting a convicted killer on death row, comes to empathize with both the killer and his victims' families.

Eve's Bayou (1997). Written and directed by Kasi Lemmons, starring Samuel L. Jackson, Lynn Whitfield, Jurnee Smollett, and Debbi Morgan. Filmed amid the marshes north of Lake Pontchartrain, this atmospheric saga follows the ill-fated Batiste family, torn apart by adultery, obsession, and murder in 1962 Louisiana.

Heaven's Prisoners (1996). Written by Harley Peyton and Scott Frank, directed by Phil Joanou, and starring Alec Baldwin, Kelly Lynch, Mary Stuart Masterson, Eric Roberts, and Teri Hatcher. In this adaptation of a James Lee Burke novel, ex-detective Dave Robicheaux and his wife, Annie, rescue a young girl from a plane crash in the outskirts of New Orleans—an act that forever alters their lives.

Interview with the Vampire: The Vampire Chronicles (1994). Written by Anne Rice, directed by Neil Jordan, and starring Tom Cruise, Brad Pitt, Antonio Banderas, Kirsten Dunst, and Christian Slater. In this award-winning adaptation of Anne Rice's acclaimed novel, a brooding vampire records his epic history, beginning with a life-altering encounter with the flamboyant vampire Lestat in 18th-century New Orleans. Partially filmed in Louisiana, the movie showcases famous landmarks like Vacherie's Oak Alley Plantation and the Big Easy's Lafayette Cemetery No. 1.

JFK (1991). Written by Oliver Stone and Zachary Sklar, directed by Oliver Stone, and starring Kevin Costner, Gary Oldman, Jack Lemmon, and Sissy Spacek. In this Oscar-winning film, based on real-life events as well as historical interpretations by Jim Garrison and Jim Marrs, a New

Orleans district attorney tries to uncover the truth behind the Kennedy assassination.

Panic in the Streets (1950). Written by Richard Murphy and Daniel Fuchs, directed by Elia Kazan, and starring Richard Widmark, Paul Douglas, Barbara Bel Geddes, Jack Palance, and Zero Mostel. Set in New Orleans, this Oscar-winning crime thriller tells the action-packed story of a policeman and a doctor who have less than 48 hours to locate a killer infected with pneumonic plague.

Pretty Baby (1978). Written by Polly Platt, directed by Louis Malle, and starring Brooke Shields, Susan Sarandon, and Keith Carradine. In this sobering, Oscar-nominated drama, a young girl grows up in a house of prostitution in the Storyville section of 1917 New Orleans.

The Princess and the Frog (2009). Written by Ron Clements, John Musker, and Rob Edwards, directed by Ron Clements and John Musker, and featuring the voices of Anika Noni Rose, Bruno Campos, Keith David, Jennifer Cody, Jenifer Lewis, Oprah Winfrey, Terrence Howard, and John Goodman. Inspired by the classic story "The Frog Prince," this animated, Oscar-nominated fantasy tells the story of a New Orleans waitress who, while trying to fulfill her dream of restaurant ownership, embarks on a journey to turn a cursed frog back into a human prince. This family-friendly musical incorporates many local attributes, including jazz, voodoo, streetcars, swamps, and landmarks like Jackson Square.

Runaway Jury (2003). Written by Brian Koppelman, David Levien, Rick Cleveland, and Matthew Chapman, directed by Gary Fleder, and starring John Cusack, Rachel Weisz, Gene Hackman, and Dustin Hoffman. Based on a John Grisham novel and featuring iconic New Orleans settings like Café Du Monde and St. Charles Avenue, this riveting thriller pits a mysterious juror and his girlfriend against a man who manipulates court trials involving gun manufacturers.

The Skeleton Key (2005). Written by Ehren Kruger, directed by Iain Softley, and starring Kate Hudson, Gena Rowlands, Peter Sarsgaard, John Hurt, and Joy Bryant. When a young hospice nurse takes a position at a creepy plantation home outside New Orleans, she becomes ensnared in a mystery involving hoodoo folk magic and the property's dark past.

When the Levees Broke: A Requiem in Four Acts (2006). Directed by Spike Lee. Originally televised as an HBO mini-series, this Emmy-winning documentary examines the disastrous effects of Hurricane Katrina on New Orleans, including the government incompetence that led to the tragic flooding and the subsequent abandonment of the city's more underprivileged citizens.

CUISINE AND TRAVEL

Cajun Coast Visitors & Convention Bureau
www.cajuncoast.com
Through this website, visitors to St. Mary Parish can learn about swamp tours, Cajun restaurants, and day trips in the coastal area west of New Orleans.

Gambit
www.bestofneworleans.com
The official website of this free alternative weekly contains plenty of information about the city's bars, restaurants, shops, film screenings, music and arts scenes, and current events.

GayNewOrleans.com
www.gayneworleans.com
Here, gay and lesbian travelers will find advice about tours, attractions, bars, restaurants, and accommodations, plus gay-friendly organizations and events, such as PFLAG and Southern Decadence.

Lafayette Louisiana
www.lafayettetravel.com
Hosted by the Lafayette Convention & Visitors Commission, this comprehensive website features a wealth of information for visitors to Cajun Country, including dining and lodging options, event and attraction listings, shopping and nightlife suggestions, and Cajun recipes.

Louisiana's Bayou Country
www.houmatravel.com
Here, travelers can search for information about swamp tours, fishing camps, and Cajun cuisine in and around Houma.

Louisiana's Northshore
www.louisiananorthshore.com
The official website of the St. Tammany Parish Tourist & Convention Commission features plenty of shopping, dining, lodging, and activity suggestions for travelers to Slidell, Covington, Madisonville, Abita Springs, and other Northshore towns.

LouisianaTravel.com
www.louisianatravel.com
The state's official online travel source provides a variety of links related to events, attractions, hotels, restaurants, and entertainment options throughout Louisiana.

New Orleans Convention & Visitors Bureau
www.neworleanscvb.com
This comprehensive website offers a ton of resources for travelers to the Big Easy, including maps, current temperatures, and information about the city's music, dining, shopping, lodging, nightlife, tours, festivals, attractions, and outdoor recreation.

New Orleans Official Guide
www.neworleansonline.com
Operated by the New Orleans Tourism Marketing Corporation, the city's official tourism website provides comprehensive information about area accommodations, attractions, and activities, plus maps, itineraries, coupons, and a neighborhood guide.

NewOrleansRestaurants.com
www.neworleansrestaurants.com
In addition to featuring a New Orleans restaurant guide, this food-focused website invites gourmands to peruse local recipes, learn key culinary terms, and make dining reservations.

St. Landry Parish
www.cajuntravel.com
Visitors can use this website, operated by the St. Landry Parish Tourist Commission, to learn more about the tours, festivals, attractions, accommodations, and other diversions in the region between Lafayette and Baton Rouge.

Tangipahoa Tourism
www.tangi-cvb.org
Through the official website of the Tangipahoa Parish Convention & Visitors Bureau, travelers will find plenty of useful dining, shopping, lodging, and activity information about Hammond, Ponchatoula, Kentwood, and other communities in Tangipahoa Parish.

The Times-Picayune
www.nola.com
Produced by the state's most widely read newspaper, this website ranks among the most informative online resources related to New Orleans.

Visit Baton Rouge
www.visitbatonrouge.com
Visitors will find a wealth of information about the events, tours, shops, attractions, restaurants, accommodations, recreational opportunities, and nightlife options in Louisiana's capital city.

Visit Louisiana Coast
www.visitlouisianacoast.com
With help from the Louisiana Tourism Coastal Coalition, visitors will find extensive information about accommodations, restaurants, and outdoor activities related to the areas along Louisiana's southern coast.

GENERAL INFORMATION

City of New Orleans
www.nola.gov
The city's official website allows you to pay for parking tickets, receive up-to-date emergency information, and find resources for area attractions, shopping locations, sporting events, and transportation facilities.

Louisiana Department of Transportation & Development
wwwsp.dotd.la.gov
This website provides extensive information about area bridges and ferries, public transit, road and traffic conditions, and upcoming construction projects, plus useful state, parish, and tourist maps.

State of Louisiana
http://louisiana.gov
The official state website comes in handy when you're looking for detailed information about regional demographics, state and local politics, the state library system, various state departments, weather and road conditions, and fishing licenses.

U.S. Department of State/Bureau of Consular Affairs
www.travel.state.gov
International travelers will find guidelines for flying into and out of southern Louisiana.

HISTORY AND CULTURE

The Gumbo Pages
www.gumbopages.com
This no-frills website offers travelers plenty of information and helpful links about the Big Easy's history, music, and culture, including recipes and local lingo.

LSU Press
www.lsupress.org
Since 1935, the official press of Louisiana State University has been publishing books about Louisiana history, culture, music, and architecture, most of which you can find through this website.

MardiGrasDay.com
www.mardigrasday.com
Curiosity seekers can learn all about the Big Easy's most famous holiday, from parade routes and related lingo to the history of king cakes. Note that the website contains some outdated information regarding annual festivities.

PARKS AND RECREATION

Louisiana Department of Culture, Recreation & Tourism
www.crt.state.la.us
This state government-run website provides information regarding state museums, cultural districts, historical preservation, the Audubon Golf Trail, and the state park system, including details about pets, trails, and wireless Internet access.

Louisiana Department of Wildlife & Fisheries
www.wlf.louisiana.gov
Among Louisiana's top Internet resources for outdoor enthusiasts, this website provides information and policies pertaining to boating, fishing, and hunting.

Louisiana Golf Association
www.lgagolf.org
Here, golfers can learn about the state's many public golf courses, including those in the New Orleans area.

Orleans Audubon Society
www.jjaudubon.net
Bird-watchers will appreciate this website, which offers specifics on the National Audubon Society's chapter in southern Louisiana, an organization that encompasses 11 parishes, from Orleans to St. Tammany.

Index

DE

F

G

H

IJ

KL

M

N

O

P

QR

S

T

UV

INDEX

Restaurants Index

Nightlife Index

Shops Index

Hotels Index

Photo Credits

Title page photo: entrance to the Balcony Music Club © Daniel Martone; page 2 (top left) © Daniel Martone, (top right) © Daniel Martone, (bottom) © Walleyelj | Dreamstime.com; page 3 (top) © Cafebeanzphoto | Dreamstime.com, (bottom) © Daniel Martone; page 20 (top left) © Daniel Martone, (top right) © Daniel Martone; page 21 © Matthew Knoblauch/123rf.com; page 22 © Daniel Martone; page 23 © Laura Martone; page 24 © Henryk Sadura/123rf.com; page 25 © Nicola Gordon/123rf.com; page 26 © Daniel Martone; page 27 © Daniel Martone; page 28 © Daniel Martone; page 30 © Laura Martone; page 31 © Laura Martone; page 32 © Laura Martone; page 33 © Laura Martone; page 34 © Daniel Martone; page 35 (top) © Daniel Martone, (bottom) © Courtesy Louisiana Travel; page 39 © arinahabich/123rf.com; page 41 (top) © Laura Martone, (bottom) © Sean Motola/123rf.com; page 44 (top) © Daniel Martone, (bottom) © Laura Martone; page 46 (top) © courtesy Louisiana Travel, (bottom) © Courtesy Louisiana Travel; page 50 (top) © Daniel Martone, (bottom) photo by Matthew Hinton, courtesy *The New Orleans Advocate*; page 54 © Becky Plexco/Enigma Arts Photography for the ARVLFC; page 56 (top) © Laura Martone, (bottom) © Laura Martone; page 59 © Daniel Martone; page 60 (top) © Mora Mahoney, (bottom) © Daniel Martone; page 62 (top) © Laura Martone, (bottom) © Laura Martone; page 67 © Laura Martone; page 70 (top) © Daniel Martone, (bottom) © Daniel Martone; page 71 © Daniel Martone; page 77 (top left) © Daniel Martone, (top right) © Daniel Martone, (bottom) © Daniel Martone; page 80 (top left) © Daniel Martone, (top right) © Daniel Martone, (bottom) © Daniel Martone; page 84 (top left) © Daniel Martone, (top right) © Laura Martone, (bottom) © Peter Titmuss/123rf.com; page 86 © Laura Martone; page 88 (top left) © Laura Martone, (top right) © Laura Martone, (bottom) © Daniel Martone; page 92 (top) © Daniel Martone, (bottom) © Daniel Martone; page 96 (top left) © Daniel Martone, (top right) © fotoluminate/123rf.com, (bottom) © Creativeworks64 | Dreamstime.com; page 101 (top) © Laura Martone, (bottom) © Daniel Martone; page 106 (top left) © Laura Martone, (top right) © Daniel Martone, (bottom) © Laura Martone; page 110 (top) © Daniel Martone, (bottom) © Laura Martone; page 114 (top) © Daniel Martone, (bottom) © Laura Martone; page 118 (top left) © Daniel Martone, (top right) © Daniel Martone, (bottom) © Daniel Martone; page 122 (top left) © Daniel Martone, (top right) © Daniel Martone, (bottom) © Daniel Martone; page 127 © Daniel Martone; page 129 (top) © Daniel Martone, (bottom) © Laura Martone; page 131 (top) © Daniel Martone, (bottom) © Daniel Martone; page 134 (top left) © Daniel Martone, (top right) © Laura Martone, (bottom) © Daniel Martone; page 137 (top) © Daniel Martone, (bottom) © Daniel Martone; page 140 (top) © Daniel Martone, (bottom) © Daniel Martone; page 143 (top left) © Laura Martone, (top right) © Daniel Martone, (bottom) © Laura Martone; page 147 © Daniel Martone; page 151 (top left) © Laura Martone, (top right) © Laura Martone, (bottom left) © Laura Martone, (bottom right) © Daniel Martone; page 156 (top left) © Laura Martone, (top right) © Daniel Martone, (bottom) © Laura Martone; page 166 (top left) © Laura Martone, (top right) © Daniel Martone, (bottom) © Laura Martone; page 169 (top) © Laura Martone, (bottom) © Daniel Martone; page 171 (top) © Walleyelj | Dreamstime.com, (bottom) © Meinzahn | Dreamstime.com; page 177 (top left) © Laura Martone, (top right) © Laura Martone, (bottom) © Daniel Martone; page 183 (top) © Walleyelj | Dreamstime.com, (bottom) © Daniel Martone; page 194 (top) © Daniel Martone, (bottom) © Daniel Martone; page 198 (top left) © Laura Martone, (top right) © Laura Martone, (bottom) © Laura Martone; page 200 (top) © Aneese | Dreamstime.com, (bottom) © www.kentwang.com; page 207 (top left) © Daniel Martone, (top right) © Laura Martone, (bottom) © Daniel Martone; page 212 (top left) © courtesy Louisiana Travel, (top right) © Laura Martone, (bottom) © Laura Martone; page 217 (top) © Laura Martone, (bottom) © Daniel Martone; page 220 (top) © Starryvoyage | Dreamstime.com, © Daniel Martone; page 225 (top left) © Starryvoyage | Dreamstime.com, (top right) © Visions of America LLC/123rf.com, (bottom) © Daniel Martone; page 228 © Adpower99 | Dreamstime.com; page 231 (top) © Fotoluminate | Dreamstime.com, (bottom) © Laura Martone; page 232 © Daniel Martone; page 239 (top) © designpics/123rf.com, (bottom) © Patricia | Dreamstime.com; page 244 (top) © Daniel Martone, (bottom) © Daniel Martone; page 248 (top) © Daniel Martone, (bottom) © Daniel Martone; page 253 © Daniel Martone; page 255 (top) © Unfetteredmind | Dreamstime.com, (bottom) © Daniel Martone; page 257 © Daniel Martone; page 263 © Daniel Martone; page 266 (top) © Daniel Martone, (bottom) © Daniel Martone; page 272 © Adpower99 | Dreamstime.com; page 274 (top) © Daniel Martone, (bottom) © Daniel Martone; page 281 (top left) © Daniel Martone, (top right) © Daniel Martone, (bottom) © Daniel Martone; page 290 © Laura Martone; page 296 (top) © Daniel Martone, (bottom) © Laura Martone; page 302 (top) © Laura Martone, (bottom) © Daniel Martone; page 317 © Zinchik | Dreamstime.com; page 322 (top) © Laura Martone, (bottom) © Laura Martone; page 327 (top) © Auntpittypat | Dreamstime.com, (bottom) © Laura Martone; page 333 © Laura Martone; page 336 (top) © Daniel Martone, (bottom) © Daniel Martone; page 341 © Laura Martone; page 344 (top) © Filedimage | Dreamstime.com, (bottom) © Fotoluminate | Dreamstime.com; page 347 © Daniel Martone; page 353 (top) © Daniel Martone, (bottom) © Maciejbledowski | Dreamstime.com; page 363 (top) © Daniel Martone, (bottom) © Laura Martone; page 374 (top) © Pjworldtour | Dreamstime.com, (bottom) © Daniel Martone

Acknowledgments

Having grown up in New Orleans and spent much of my adulthood there, I find it difficult to thank each and every person who's helped me, often unknowingly, to write this guide. Naturally, there are several people to whom I'm particularly grateful. First, I offer a special thanks to the ultra-patient editors of Avalon Travel who offered invaluable assistance during the preparation of *Moon New Orleans;* in particular, I couldn't have finished this guide without the support of Nikki Ioakimedes, Elizabeth Jang, and Albert Angulo. Thanks also to Grace Fujimoto and Elizabeth Hansen, who each gave me the chance to write about my favorite U.S. city, and Andrew Collins, who wrote the first two editions of this book.

In addition, I'd like to thank my friends and family, all of whom have supported me during each of my frenzied writing projects. Most of all, I'm grateful to my beloved kitty, Ruby Azazel, who encouraged me to take breaks whenever possible, and to my husband, Daniel, who even provided many of the images in this guide.

Moreover, I thank the city of New Orleans, for despite tragic events like Hurricane Katrina and the much-publicized Gulf oil spill, this continues to be one of the most vibrant, resilient, and extraordinary cities I've ever encountered. Lastly, I thank you, the reader. May your next trip to the Big Easy be safe, thrilling, and memorable!